Venice & the Veneto

written and researched by

Jonathan Buckley

with additional contributions from

Charles Hebbert

ROUGH
GUIDES

www.roughguides.com

1

Contents

Festivals colour section following p.144

Venetian palaces colour section following p.240

Colour maps following p.440

3

Introduction to
Venice
& the Veneto

Nobody arriving in Venice for the first time is seeing the city for the first time. Depicted and described so often that its image has become part of the world's collective consciousness, Venice can initially create the slightly anticlimactic feeling that everything looks exactly as it should. The water-lapped palaces along the Canal Grande are just as the brochure photographs made them out to be, Piazza San Marco does indeed look as perfect as a film set, and the panorama across the water from the Palazzo Ducale is still more or less as Canaletto painted it. The sense of familiarity quickly fades, however, as you start to look at the city closely – and the longer you look, the stranger and more intriguing Venice becomes.

Founded fifteen hundred years ago on a cluster of mudflats in the centre of the lagoon, Venice rose to become Europe's main trading post between the West and the East, and at its height controlled an empire that spread north to the Dolomites and over the sea as far as Cyprus. As its wealth increased and its population grew, the fabric of the city grew ever more dense. Cohabiting with the ocean, Venice has a closer relationship to nature than most cities, but at the same time it's one of the most artificial places on earth – there's hardly any undeveloped space on the hundred or so islets that compose the historic centre. And very few of its closely knit streets and squares bear no sign of the city's long lineage. Even in the most insignificant alleyway you might find fragments of a medieval building embedded in the wall of a house like fossil remains lodged in a cliff face.

The famously melancholic air of Venice is in part a product of the discrepancy between the grandeur of its history and what the city has become. In the heyday of the Venetian Republic, some 200,000 people lived in Venice – more than three times its present population. Merchants from Germany, Greece, Turkey and a host of other countries maintained warehouses here; transactions in the banks and bazaars of the **Rialto** dictated the value of commodities all over the continent; in the dockyards of the **Arsenale** the workforce was so vast that a warship could be built and fitted out in a single day; and the **Piazza San Marco** was perpetually thronged with people here to set up business deals or

▶ Piazza dei Signori, Padua

Fact file

• The Veneto is **mountainous** in the north, where the Dolomites extend towards the Austrian border, and flat in the more extensive southern part of the region, where the Po river forms the boundary with Emilia-Romagna. This **fertile plain** is one of Italy's major agricultural zones, with wine production being especially important: 20 percent of all Italian DOC (Denominazione di origine controllata) wine is bottled in the Veneto.

• A little under 4.5 million **people** live in the Veneto, which is divided into seven **regions**, centred on the cities of Venice (capital of the Veneto), Belluno, Padua (Padova), Rovigo, Treviso, Verona and Vicenza. The historic core of Venice, a major industrial centre as recently as the start of the twentieth century, is now home to around 60,000 people – more than 100,000 fewer than in 1945. The neighbouring conurbation of Mestre-Marghera today has a population more than three times that of Venice.

• **Engineering** is the most important manufacturing sector of the Veneto economy, but there are numerous other large-scale industries here: Vicenza is one of Europe's largest leather-processing areas, and is also a major centre for goldsmithing; 80 percent of Italian eyewear and 70 percent of Italian sports shoes are made in the Veneto; and local firms such as Benetton, Diesel and Stefanel are mainstays of the Italian clothing industry. And then there's **tourism**. Attracting one in six of all visitors to the country, the Veneto is the most popular of all Italy's regions, and Venice is its single most popular city.

The acqua alta

Floods – **acque alte** – have been an element of the Venetian winter for hundreds of years, but since the middle of the twentieth century there's been a relentless increase in their frequency (see p.395 for more). It's now very rare indeed, between October and late February, for a week to pass without a significant **flooding** – in the notoriously wet winter of 2000 there was an *acqua alta* on thirty consecutive days. Winter is the peak period, but *acqua alte* nowadays occur as often as 200 times per year.

An *acqua alta* begins with water seeping up through the pavement of the Piazza and other low-lying areas, forming puddles that quickly merge into a shallow pool. Soon after, wavelets start spilling over the quayside in front of the Palazzo Ducale. If you hear **sirens** wailing it means that there's about four hours to go before the peak of an *acqua alta*, which is defined as a flood that rises in excess of 90cm above the mean lagoon level at the Salute. A single siren tone, repeated, signifies a minor *acqua alta*; floods of greater seriousness are signalled by repeated rising patterns of two, three or four notes – four notes means they're expecting 140cm or more, enough to make many areas impassable. Instruments on the side of the Campanile di San Marco display a continuous measurement of the water level and a prediction of the day's high tide – if the red light is on, a big flood is on its way.

Having lived with *acque alte* for so long, the city is well geared to dealing with the nuisance. Shopkeepers insert steel shutters into their doorways, while teams of council workers construct walkways of **duckboards** (*passerelle*) along the major thoroughfares and between the chief vaporetto stops and dry land. In extreme instances the *passerelle* get washed away from the Piazza, but usually the city keeps functioning, and even on severe days there are some sectors that remain above the waves – maps at most ACTV stops show walkway routes and where the high ground lies. On a serious *acqua alta* day almost every Venetian wears rubber boots, and you'd be well advised to follow suit – plenty of shops sell them. And one other tip: if the water is high and *passerelle* are in place, use them. If you try to improvise a route down the back alleys, the odds are that sooner or later you'll end up beating an ignominious retreat in the face of an unruly canal.

report to the Republic's government. Nowadays it's no longer a living metropolis but rather the embodiment of a fabulous past, dependent for its survival largely on the people who come to marvel at its relics.

Where to go

The monuments which draw the largest crowds are the **Basilica di San Marco** – the mausoleum of the city's patron saint – and the **Palazzo Ducale** – the home of the doge and all the governing councils. Certainly these are the most dramatic structures in the city: the first a mosaic-clad emblem of Venice's Byzantine origins, the second perhaps the finest of all secular Gothic buildings. Every parish rewards exploration, though – a roll call of the churches worth visiting would feature over fifty names, and a list of the important paintings and sculptures they contain would be twice as long. Two of the distinctively Venetian institutions known as the *scuole* retain some of the outstanding examples of Italian Renaissance art – the **Scuola di San Rocco**, with its dozens of pictures by Tintoretto, and the **Scuola di San Giorgio degli Schiavoni**, decorated with a gorgeous sequence by Carpaccio.

Although many of the city's treasures remain in the buildings for which they were created, a sizeable number have been removed to one or other of Venice's **museums.** The one that should not be missed is the **Accademia**, an assembly of Venetian painting that consists of virtually nothing but

masterpieces; other prominent collections include the museum of eighteenth-century art in the **Ca' Rezzonico** and the **Museo Correr**, the civic museum of Venice – but again, a comprehensive list would fill a page.

Then, of course, there's the inexhaustible spectacle of the streets themselves, of the majestic and sometimes decrepit palaces, of the hemmed-in squares where much of the social life of the city is conducted, of the sunlit courtyards that suddenly open up at the end of an unpromising passageway. The cultural heritage preserved in the museums and churches is a source of endless fascination, but you should discard your itineraries for a day and just wander – the anonymous parts of Venice reveal as much of the city's essence as the highlighted attractions. Equally indispensable for a full understanding of Venice's way of life and development are expeditions to the **northern and southern islands** of the lagoon, where the incursions of the tourist industry are on the whole less obtrusive.

Taking its name – as does Venice itself – from the pre-Roman people known as the Veneti, the present-day region of the **Veneto** essentially covers the area that became the core of the Republic's mainland empire. Everywhere in the Veneto you'll find the imprint of Venetian rule. In **Belluno**, right under the crags of the Dolomites, the style of the buildings declares the town's former allegiance. A few kilometres away, the Lion of Saint Mark looks over the central square of the hill town of **Feltre**, as it does over the market square of **Verona**, on the Veneto's western edge. On the flatlands of the Po basin (the southern border of the region) and on farming estates all over the Veneto, the elegant villas of the Venetian nobility are still standing.

Yet the Veneto is as diverse culturally as it is geographically. The aspects of Verona's urban landscape that make the city so attractive were created

Venetian names and dialect

Venice has an array of idiosyncratic names for features of the cityscape. A canal is a **rio**, and an alleyway that cuts through a building is a **sottoportico** or **sottoportego**, to give its dialect version. A street in Venice is generally a **calle**, but a parish's major thoroughfare might be a **ruga** or a **salizzada**, a small street may be a **ramo**, a street alongside a body of water is a **fondamenta** (or a **riva** if it's really big), and a street formed by filling in a canal is customarily a **rio terrà** (or *terà*). A square is usually a **campo** (there's only one Piazza), but it might be a **campiello** if it's tiny, a **piscina** if it was formed by filling in a place where boats used to turn, or a **corte** if it's more a courtyard than a square.

Among the chief characteristics of the Venetian vernacular are its tendencies to slur or drop consonants and to swallow vowels. For example, the Italian name Giuseppe here becomes Isepo, Luigi becomes Alvise, Giuliano becomes Zulian, Eustachio becomes Stae, Biagio becomes Biasio (or Blasio), Agostino shrinks to Stin, and Giovanni is Zuan or Zan – as in San Zan Degolà, for San Giovanni Decollato. You'll see *dose* instead of *doge*, *crose* instead of *croce*, *do* for *due* (two), *nove* instead of *nuove*, *fontego* for *fondaco* and *sestier* for *sestiere*. In Venetian dialect a shop isn't *aperto* (open), it's *verto*, while a vaporetto is a *batèo* and an ice cream is a *geato*, not a *gelato*. You'll also notice that the letter "x" occasionally replaces "z" (as in *venexiana*), and that the final vowel is habitually lopped off Venetian surnames, as in Giustinian, Loredan, Vendramin and Corner, to cite just four of the most conspicuous instances.

long before the expansion of Venice's terra-firma empire, and nearby **Padua** – for centuries a place of pilgrimage and a university city – similarly has a character that is quite distinct from that of Venice. Even in **Vicenza**, which reached its present form mainly during its long period of

▶ Off-duty gondolas

subservience, the very appearance of the streets is proof of a fundamental independence.

This is Italy's wealthiest region, and there's plenty of support here for the sharp-suited mediacrats of Silvio Berlusconi's Forza Italia party, and for the xenophobic separatists of the Lega Nord, who like to depict the north as a sort of overburdened life-support system for the parasitic south. But the economics of the Veneto have undergone a reversal over the last century or so. Venice, formerly the great power, is now the region's biggest headache, tourist-choked and physically fragile. The one-time provinces are now dominant: Verona, Padua, Vicenza and **Treviso** are all major industrial and commercial centres, while intensive dairies, fruit farms and vineyards (around **Conegliano** and Verona especially) have made the Veneto a leading agricultural producer as well. The Veneto's income is boosted by the industrial complex of **Mestre** and **Marghera**, the grim conurbation through which all road and rail lines from Venice pass before spreading out over the mainland. It's less a city than an economic support system for Venice, and the negative impression you get on your way through is entirely justified.

When to go

Venice's tourist season is very nearly an all-year affair. **Peak season** is from **Easter** to **early October**, when hotel rooms are virtually impossible to come by at short notice; if possible, try to avoid July and August, when the crowds are at their fullest, the climate can be oppressively hot and clammy, and many of the restaurants and bars take their annual break. The other two popular spells are the **Carnevale** (leading

▼ The view from the Campanile

up to Lent) and the weeks on each side of **Christmas**; again, hotels tend to be heavily booked, but at least the authentic life of the city isn't submerged during the December festive period, as it is by the summer inundation.

For the ideal combination of comparative peace and pleasant climate, the two or three weeks **immediately preceding Easter** are perhaps the best time of year. The days should be mostly mild – though the weather can be capricious – and finding accommodation won't present insuperable problems, as long as you plan a few months ahead. Climatically the months at the end of the high season are somewhat less reliable: some **November and December** days are so clear that the Dolomites seem to start on the edge of the mainland, but others bring torrential rain or fog so dense you can't see across the Canal Grande. However, the desertion of the streets in winter is magical, and the sight of the Piazza under floodwater is unforgettable. This **acqua alta**, as Venice's seasonal flooding is called (see p.6), is an increasingly common occurrence between October and March, and you should anticipate a few inconvenient days in the course of a two-week visit in winter. If you want to see the city at its quietest, **January** is the month to go – take plenty of warm clothes, though, as the winds of the Adriatic can be savage, and you should be prepared for some rain.

Average monthly temperatures and rainfall

	Jan	Feb	Mar	Apr	May	Jun	Jul	Aug	Sep	Oct	Nov	Dec
Venice												
Max/min °C	6/-1	8/1	12/4	16/8	21/12	25/16	28/18	27/17	24/14	18/9	12/4	7/0
Rainfall (mm)	58	54	57	64	69	76	63	83	66	69	87	54

things not to miss

It's not possible to see everything that Venice and the Veneto have to offer in one trip – and we don't suggest you try. What follows is a selective taste of the city's highlights and the best of the Veneto arranged in three colour-coded categories, so that you can browse through to find the very best things to see, do and experience. All highlights have a page reference to take you straight into the Guide, where you can find out more.

01 Santi Giovanni e Paolo Page **156** • The huge church of Santi Giovanni e Paolo (or Zanipolo, as it's known locally) is the doges' mausoleum.

02 Rialto market Page **116** • In business for around a thousand years, the Rialto market is still buzzing.

04 The Miracoli Page **153** • Clad inside and out with panels of marble, the Miracoli is one of the most photogenic edifices in Venice.

03 The Frari Page **129** • Titian's glorious Assumption presides over the nave of the mighty Gothic church of Santa Maria dei Frari.

05 Basilica di San Marco Page **46** • The mosaic-encrusted cathedral of Saint Mark is the most lavish of Europe's cathedrals.

06 **Torcello** Page **210** • Take a trip out to the northern reaches of the lagoon, to the almost deserted island of Torcello, Venice's ancient ancestor.

07 **Possagno** Page **351** • Birthplace of Antonio Canova, the quiet upland town of Possagno has a magnificent museum devoted to his sculpture.

08 **Scuola Grande di San Rocco** Page **132** • A stupendous cycle of paintings by Jacopo Tintoretto fills both floors of the Scuola Grande di San Rocco.

09 **Padua** Page **287** • The Veneto's liveliest city, thanks largely to its famous university, Padua also offers some amazing sights, such as the Basilica di Sant' Antonio.

10 **San Giorgio Maggiore**
Page **213** • A handsome building in itself, San Giorgio Maggiore also offers amazing views from its bell tower.

11 **Verona** Page **322** • Piazza delle Erbe is the social hub of the magnificent city of Verona.

12 **Palazzo Ducale** Page **57** • Home to the doge and seat of the government and law courts, the Palazzo Ducale was the hub of the Venetian Republic.

13 **Scuola di San Giorgio degli Schiavoni** Page **178** • Carpaccio's beguiling pictures make this tiny building an essential sight.

14 **Regata Storica** See *Festivals* colour section • A spectacular procession along the Canal Grande marks the start of Venice's historic boat race.

15 **The Accademia** Page **96** • The city's top museum is home to a superb collection of Venetian art.

16 **Wine bars** Page **253** • There are plenty of places in Venice where you can sample the wines of the Veneto – *Al Volto* is one of the best.

17 **Palladian villas** Page **285** • Palladio created many influential houses in the Veneto, and with the Villa Fóscari he produced one of the most beautiful residences of its time.

Basics

Basics

Getting there

Obviously the easiest way to get to Venice from the UK and Ireland is to fly, and the lowest priced air tickets are generally cheaper than those for the long train or bus journey. From New York there are some direct flights to Venice, but for most American and Canadian visitors it will be easier to fly to Milan or Rome, both of which have frequent air and rail connections to Venice. There are no direct flights to Italy from Australia or New Zealand, but there is plenty of choice when travelling via an Asian or European city.

Airfares always depend on the season, with the highest being around June to August; fares drop during the "shoulder" seasons – September to October and April to May – and you'll get the best prices during the low season, November to March (excluding Christmas and New Year when prices are hiked up and seats are at a premium). Note also that it is generally more expensive to fly at weekends; price ranges quoted below assume midweek travel.

You can, of course, book online with airlines and discount travel websites. Good deals can often be found through discount or auction sites, as well as through the airlines' own websites.

From the UK and Ireland

Direct flights take around two hours from London. Most services go to Marco Polo airport, 13km from the centre of Venice, on the edge of the lagoon, but Ryanair's flights and a few charters arrive at Treviso, 30km to the north of Venice (see p.33 for details of arrival at both airports). EasyJet flies twice daily from Gatwick to Venice Marco Polo, and also flies daily from East Midlands and Bristol; its chief low-cost rival, Ryanair, flies up to three times a day from Stansted to Treviso. In addition, flights to Marco Polo are offered by Jet2, who fly there weekly in high season from Edinburgh and Leeds–Bradford and Bradford, and by Thomsonfly, who operate once- or twice-weekly services from Gatwick and Manchester – but again, with no flights in winter. Of the "full-service"

airlines, British Airways (BA) operates direct flights from London Gatwick (2–3 daily) throughout the year, while bmi flies daily from Heathrow. As a broad generalization, the "low-cost" carriers, as you'd expect, are somewhat cheaper than the "full-service" airlines, costing from around £50 return in low season, to about £150 in high season, provided you book well in advance, whereas "full-service" returns tend to cost in the region of £120–160 in low season, and more like £250–300 in high season. However, prices can rise so much for last-minute bookings on no-frills airlines (ie within two weeks of departure date) that they become more expensive than their full-service rivals, while the latter often offer huge midweek discounts if you book a long time in advance. In high season, there's a remote chance of **charter flight** bargains: it's worth checking with a specialist agent or scouring the classified section of the weekend newspapers for last-minute deals.

The only direct service **from Dublin** to Venice is provided by Aer Lingus, who fly the route up to five times per week. Aer Lingus special offers go as low as €30 in low season; in summer you'll probably pay in the region of €150–200. Alternatively, you can take a Ryanair flight (from Dublin, Cork, Derry, Kerry or Shannon) to London and catch a link to Venice from there. **From Belfast**, bmi fly to Venice via Heathrow, but the cheapest option is to fly easyJet to Gatwick and then on to Venice.

Airlines in the UK and Ireland

Aer Lingus ⓦ www.aerlingus.com
bmi ⓦ www.flybmi.com
British Airways ⓦ www.ba.com
EasyJet ⓦ www.easyjet.com
Jet2 ⓦ www.jet2.com
Ryanair ⓦ www.ryanair.com
Thomsonfly ⓦ www.thomsonfly.com

Flight and travel agents in the UK and Ireland

ebookers UK ⓣ 0800/082 3000, Republic of
Ireland ⓣ 01/488 3507; ⓦ www.ebookers.com.
Low fares on an extensive selection of scheduled
flights and package deals.
North South Travel UK ⓣ 01245/608 291,
ⓦ www.northsouthtravel.co.uk. Friendly,
competitive travel agency, offering discounted fares
worldwide. Profits are used to support projects in
the developing world, especially the promotion of
sustainable tourism.
STA Travel UK ⓣ 0870/1630 026, ⓦ www
.statravel.com. Worldwide specialists in independent
travel; also student IDs, travel insurance, car rental,
rail passes and more. Good discounts for students
and under-26s.
Trailfinders UK ⓣ 0845/058 5858, Republic of
Ireland ⓣ 01/677 7888; ⓦ www.trailfinders.com.
One of the best-informed and most efficient agents
for independent travellers.
Usit Dublin ⓣ 01/602 1904, ⓦ www.usit.ie. Student
and youth specialists for flights and trains.

Packages from the UK and Ireland

Venice's ludicrous accommodation costs
can make a flight-plus-hotel **package** an
attractive proposition, as the preferential
hotel rates given to the holiday firms can
offset the slightly higher price of the flight.

Six steps to a better kind of travel

At Rough Guides we are passionately committed to travel. We feel strongly that only
through travelling do we truly come to understand the world we live in and the
people we share it with – plus tourism has brought a great deal of **benefit** to
developing economies around the world over the last few decades. But the
extraordinary growth in tourism has also damaged some places irreparably, and of
course **climate change** is exacerbated by most forms of transport, especially flying.
This means that now more than ever it's important to **travel thoughtfully** and
responsibly, with respect for the cultures you're visiting – not only to derive the
most benefit from your trip but also to preserve the best bits of the planet for
everyone to enjoy. At Rough Guides we feel there are six main areas in which you
can make a difference:

- Consider what you're contributing to the **local economy**, and how much the
  services you use do the same, whether it's through employing local workers and
  guides or sourcing locally grown produce and local services.
- Consider the **environment** on holiday as well as at home. Water is scarce in
  many developing destinations, and the biodiversity of local flora and fauna can
  be adversely affected by tourism. Try to patronize businesses that take account
  of this.
- Travel with a purpose, not just to tick off experiences. Consider **spending longer**
  in a place, and getting to know it and its people.
- Give thought to how often you **fly**. Try to avoid short hops by air and more harmful
  night flights.
- Consider **alternatives to flying**, travelling instead by bus, train, boat and even by
  bike or on foot where possible.
- Make your trips "**climate neutral**" via a reputable carbon offset scheme. All Rough
  Guide flights are offset, and every year we donate money to a variety of charities
  devoted to combating the effects of climate change.

The brochures are dominated by three- and four-star hotels, sometimes offering rooms at discounts as high as 30 percent, and there's occasionally a limited choice of one- and two-star rooms as well. You can expect to pay from around £400 per person for 3 nights for a three-star double room in low season; the same deal in peak season will cost anywhere between £100 and £200 more. At the upper end of the market, packages offering four nights at a top-notch establishment might cost you around £1000–2000 per person for similar periods.

If you can find a particularly conscientious travel agent, they might contact the package company for you to find out if any of the hotels have rooms cheaper than advertised – something they're more likely to do in the winter months. Special offers do crop up from time to time, but very rarely between April and October.

Package tour operators

Abercrombie & Kent ⓦ www.abercrombiekent .co.uk. Classy operator with a strong reputation.
Citalia ⓦ www.citalia.co.uk. Hotel and villa packages plus tailor-made itineraries, city breaks and self-catering holidays.
Martin Randall Travel ⓦ www.martinrandall.com. Small-group (and expensive) cultural tours led by genuine experts on art, archeology or music.
Sunvil ⓦ www.sunvil.co.uk. Wide-ranging holiday options, focused on small-group tours for a more independent-minded traveller, as well as tailor-made trips.
Thomas Cook ⓦ www.thomascook.co.uk. Long-established one-stop travel agency for package holidays, city breaks or flights.

Trains from the UK

The most direct rail route from London to Venice is to take the **Eurostar** from London to Paris, then pick up the overnight service from Paris to Venice, via Milan (ⓦ www .artesia.eu), or take the high-speed TGV from Paris to Milan, and change there for Florence; total journey time is around 14–18hr, and with some online research you can put together a one-way ticket for a little over £100 in low season, though peak prices can go as high as £250. Discounts

for under-26s are sometimes available and advance booking is essential. Bear in mind also that if you travel via Paris you'll have to change both trains and stations which means lugging your bags on the metro from the Gare du Nord to the Gare de Bercy – for a stress-free transfer, allow yourself at least 90 minutes between arrival in Paris and departure.

If a trip to Venice and the Veneto is only part of a longer exploration of the continent, you might consider investing in an Interrail pass. The Interrail Global pass, which enables you to roam all over Europe (but isn't valid in your home country), comes in two forms: Flexi, which gives 5 days' travel in a 10-day period (£146 for 12- to 25-year-olds; £229 for over-25s) or 10 days' travel in 22 days (£220/330); and Continuous, valid for 22 days (£284/431) or one month (£367/550). The pass also gives discounts on Eurostar and cross-Channel ferry services. InterRail passes are available from all main British Rail stations and youth/ student travel agencies, and you need to have been resident in Europe for at least six months to qualify for one.

Rail contacts

European Rail ⓦ www.europeanrail.com. Independent specialist in European rail travel.
Eurostar ⓦ www.eurostar.com.
Rail Europe ⓦ www.raileurope.co.uk. Information on international train travel, including tickets and passes.
The Man in Seat 61 ⓦ www.seat61.com. An excellent site, packed with useful tips.
Trainseurope ⓦ www.trainseurope.co.uk. Another good agency for European rail tickets.

By bus from the UK

Travelling to Venice and back by **bus** will appeal only to those with phobias about planes and trains. Eurolines (ⓦ www .eurolines.co.uk) has three services a week **from London** to Venice, with a change in Paris, which takes around 30 hours. Summer fares are in the region of £130 for a return ticket.

Getting to Venice from the US and Canada

The best return fares to **Venice from the US** are with Delta/Alitalia, who jointly fly direct from New York to Venice five times a week, and offer connecting flights via Milan or Rome from several other North American cities. Between them, British Airways, Lufthansa, Delta, Northwest/KLM and United offer daily flights from all the major US cities via a variety of European hubs. The cheapest **return fares** from New York in low season (roughly Nov–March, outside Christmas and Carnival) are around $500, rising to about $1500 during the summer. From Miami or Chicago fares are roughly US$100 higher, while from Los Angeles you'll pay more like US$200 extra. Wherever you're flying from, be on the lookout for special promotional offers, which can bring fares down as much as US$300 in high season. The prices quoted above are for midweek travel (add about US$50 for weekend travel), exclusive of taxes.

From **Canada**, Air Canada and Alitalia have flights from Toronto to Milan and Rome (often via Frankfurt) for a low-season fare of around Can$500 midweek, increasing to around Can$1300 in high season without taxes. With other carriers and from other Canadian cities you'll have to change planes at a North American airport as well as in Europe.

Airlines in North America

Air Canada ⓦ www.aircanada.com.
Alitalia ⓦ www.alitalia.com.
Delta ⓦ www.delta.com.
Lufthansa US ☎ 1-800/645-3880, Canada ☎ 1-800/563-5954; ⓦ www.lufthansa.com. Daily fights via Frankfurt from a large number of North American cities.
Northwest/KLM US ☎ 1-800/225-2525, ⓦ www.nwa .com, ⓦ www.klm.com. Daily flights via Amsterdam from more than twenty North American cities.
United Airlines US ☎ 1-800/UNITED-1, ⓦ www .united.com. Daily flights via Frankfurt from several US cities.

Packages and organized tours from North America

While there's no shortage of multi-city packages with a couple of days in Venice as part of a more extensive Italian itinerary, there's not much out there that offers Venice exclusively, apart from basic city breaks from the major airlines' vacation subsidiaries. So your best bet may be just to get a travel agent to customize one for you.

Getting to Venice from Australia and New Zealand

There are no direct flights to Italy **from Australia or New Zealand**, but plenty of airlines fly to Rome and Milan via Asian hubs. Round-trip fares from Sydney with the major airlines (Alitalia, Qantas, Japan, Singapore or Malaysian) start at around A$2000 in low season, rising to upwards of A$3500 in high season. From New Zealand you can expect to pay from around NZ$2200 in low season to NZ$3500 in high season.

Airlines in Australia and New Zealand

Cathay Pacific ⓦ www.cathaypacific.com.
Garuda ⓦ www.garuda-indonesia.com.
JAL ⓦ www.jal.com.
Malaysia Airlines ⓦ www.malaysia-airlines.com.
Qantas ⓦ www.qantas.com.
Singapore Airlines ⓦ www.slngaporeair.com.
Sri Lankan Airlines ⓦ www.srilankan.aero.
Thai Airways ⓦ www.thaiair.com.

Travel essentials

Costs

There is no getting round the fact that Venice is a fantastically **expensive city**. Even in the dead of winter there are very few double rooms in Venice costing less than €60, and in high season some one-star hotels charge more than €100. For a three-star hotel, you'll be paying more than twice that amount. A strict diet of coffee and croissant (*cornetto*) in the mornings, a picnic at lunchtime and pizza in the evening will account for another €30 at least – and if you go to a proper restaurant you're unlikely to spend less than €35 per person. Then you have to add the cost of the odd entrance fee and boat ticket – Venice's water-buses are exorbitantly expensive – see p.36. In total, you need to budget for a basic outlay of **around €50** per person per day for a summer trip to Venice, **not counting accommodation costs**. There are, though, various museum and transport passes that will save you a fair amount of cash – see p.34 for more. If you are thinking of splashing out on a designer outfit or some other expensive item, bear in mind that visitors from outside the EU are entitled to an IVA (**purchase tax**) rebate on single items valued at over €155. The procedure is to get a full receipt from the shop, describing the purchase in detail. This receipt must be presented to customs on your return home, and then sent back to the shop within ninety days of the date of the receipt; the shop will then refund the IVA component of the price, a saving of eighteen percent.

Note that in almost every restaurant you'll pay a **cover charge** (*coperto*) on top of the cost of your food and drink; in most places the *coperto* is €1–3, but in Venice an inexcusable €5 isn't unknown. As well as the *coperto*, **service** (*servizio*) will often be added, generally about ten percent; if it isn't, you should **tip** this amount.

Crime and personal safety

Venice is a very sedate city, and attacks on tourists are virtually unknown; **pickpockets** on crowded vaporetti are the chief threat to the visitor. On the mainland, Treviso, Padua, Verona and Vicenza – like any sizeable European town, have their dodgier quarters, but as a tourist you're very unlikely to be straying out of the city centre, where the odd bag-snatching is as dangerous as things get.

In Italy there are several different branches of the **police**, ostensibly to prevent any single branch seizing power. You're not likely to have much contact with the Guardia di Finanza, who investigate smuggling, tax evasion and other finance-related felonies. Drivers may well come up against the **Polizia Urbana**, or town police, who are mainly concerned with traffic and parking offences, and also the **Polizia Stradale**, who patrol motorways.

The **Carabinieri** – the ones Italians are most rude about – are dressed in military-style uniforms and white shoulder belts (they're part of the army), and deal with general crime, public order and drugs control. The **Polizia Statale**, the other general crime-fighting branch, enjoy a fierce rivalry with the Carabinieri, and are the ones to whom you should **report a theft** at their base, the **Questura** (police station). They'll issue you with a *denuncia*, a form which you'll need for any insurance claims after you get home. The Questura is also where you should to go to obtain a visa extension or a *permesso di soggiorno* (permit to stay).

If your passport goes astray, you'll also need to report to your nearest embassy or consulate – these are listed on p.275.

Although the streets of Venice are safer than those of any other major city in the country, **sexual harassment** can occasionally be a

Emergencies

In an emergency, dial the following national emergency telephone numbers.
⊤ 112 for the police (*Carabinieri*).
⊤ 113 for any emergency service (*Soccorso Pubblico di Emergenza*).
⊤ 115 for the fire brigade (*Vigili del Fuoco*).
⊤ 116 for road assistance (*Soccorso Stradale*).
⊤ 118 for an ambulance (*Ambulanza*).

problem for a woman travelling on her own. The Venetian male might not be as aggressive in his attentions as some of his more southerly compatriots, but he can still be a pain in the neck. Complete indifference is generally the most effective policy, but you may find it difficult to emulate the glacial brush-off that comes as second nature to many Italian women. A mouthful of Anglo-Saxon will often do the trick, but if he persists, *lasciátemi in pace* ("leave me alone") should see him off.

Electricity

The supply in Italy is 220V, though anything requiring 240V will work. Most plugs are two round pins: UK equipment will need an adaptor, US equipment a 220-to-110 transformer as well.

Entry requirements

All EU citizens can enter Italy, and stay as long as they like, simply on production of a valid passport. Citizens of the United States, Canada, Australia and New Zealand need only a valid passport, but are limited to stays of ninety days. All other nationals should consult the relevant embassies about visa requirements. Legally, you're required to **register** with the police within three days of entering Italy. This will be done for you if you're staying in a hotel (this is why you have to surrender your passport on arrival), but if you're on a self-catering trip you should register at the Questura (HQ of the state police). It used to be the case that nobody bothered too much about this formality, but in recent years the police have begun to be more pedantic with backpacking types in Venice. So if you think you look like the sort of person a Venetian policeman might deem undesirable, get registered (see p.276 for the address of the Venice Questura).

Italian embassies and consulates abroad

Australia Embassy: 12 Grey St, Deakin, Canberra, ACT 2600 ⊤ 02/6273 3333, Ⓦ www.ambcanberra .esteri.it. Consulates in Melbourne ⊤ 03/9867 5744 and Sydney ⊤ 02/9392 7900.
Canada Embassy: 275 Slater St, Ottawa, ON K1P 5H9 ⊤ 613/232-2401, Ⓦ www.ambottawa.esteri.it. Consulates in Montréal ⊤ 514/849-8351 and Toronto ⊤ 416/977-1566.
Ireland Embassy: 63–65 Northumberland Rd, Dublin 4 ⊤ 01/660 1744, Ⓦ www.ambdublino.esteri.it.
New Zealand Embassy: 34–38 Grant Rd, PO Box 463, Thorndon, Wellington ⊤ 04/473 5339, Ⓦ www .ambwellington.esteri.it.
South Africa Embassy: 96 George Ave, Arcadia 0083, Pretoria ⊤ 12/423 0000, Ⓦ www .ambpretoria.esteri.it.
UK Embassy: 14 Three King's Yard, London W1Y 2EH ⊤ 020/7312 2200, Ⓦ www.amblondra.esteri.it. Consulates in Edinburgh ⊤ 0131/226 3695 and Manchester ⊤ 0161/236 9024.
US Embassy: 3000 Whitehaven St NW, Washington D.C. 20008 ⊤ 202/612-4400, Ⓦ www .ambwashingtondc.esteri.it. Consulates in Chicago ⊤ 312/467-1550, New York ⊤ 212/737-9100 and San Francisco ⊤ 415/292-9210.

Gay and lesbian travellers

Attitudes to gay men and women in northern Italy are on the whole tolerant, but public displays of affection that extend much beyond hand-holding might raise a few eyebrows, especially outside the bigger towns. The national gay organization ARCI-Gay (Ⓦ www.arcigay.it) has branches in most big towns; Ⓦ www.gay.it has a wealth of information on the scene in Italy. The age of consent in Italy is 18.

Health

If you're arriving in Italy from elsewhere in Europe, North America or Australasia, you don't need any jabs. Citizens of all EU countries are entitled to emergency medical care under the same terms as the residents of the country. As proof of entitlement, British citizens will need a **European Health Insurance Card (EHIC)**, which is free of charge and valid for five years – application forms are issued at UK post offices, or you can apply online at ⓦwww .dh.gov.uk. Note, however, that the EHIC won't cover the full cost of major treatment, and the high medical charges make travel insurance essential. You normally have to pay the full cost of emergency treatment upfront, and claim it back when you get home (minus a small excess); make very sure you hang onto full doctors' reports, signed prescription details and all receipts to back up your claim.

Italian **pharmacists** (*farmacie*) are well qualified to give advice on minor ailments and to dispense prescriptions; there's one open all night in bigger towns and cities. They work on a rota system, and the address of the one currently open is posted on any *farmacia* door. If you require a **doctor** (*médico*), ask for help in the first instance at your hotel or the tourist office. Follow a similar procedure if you have dental problems. Again, keep all receipts for later insurance claims.

In an emergency go to the *Pronto Soccorso* (Casualty/A&E) section of the nearest hospital or phone ☎113 and ask for *ospedale* or *ambulanza*. Major train stations and airports often have first-aid facilities with qualified doctors on hand.

Insurance

Even though EU health care privileges apply in Italy, you'd do well to take out an **insurance policy** before travelling to cover against theft, loss, illness or injury. Before paying for a new policy, however, it's worth checking whether you're already covered: some all-risks home insurance policies may cover your possessions when overseas, and many private medical schemes include cover when abroad. In Canada, provincial health plans usually provide partial cover for medical mishaps overseas, while holders of official student/teacher/youth cards in Canada and the US are entitled to meagre accident coverage and hospital in-patient benefits. Students will often find that their student health coverage extends during the vacations and for one term beyond the date of last enrolment.

After checking the possibilities above, you might want to contact a specialist **travel insurance** company. A typical travel insurance policy usually provides cover for the loss of baggage, tickets and – up to a certain limit – cash or cheques, as well as cancellation or curtailment of your journey. Most exclude so-called dangerous sports unless an extra premium is paid: in Italy this can mean scuba diving, windsurfing, trekking or skiing. If you do take medical coverage, ascertain whether benefits will be paid as treatment proceeds or only after you return home, and whether there is a 24-hour medical emergency number. When securing baggage cover, make sure that the per-article limit will cover your most valuable possession. If you need to make a claim, you should keep receipts for medicines and medical treatment, and in the event you have anything stolen, you must obtain an official statement from the police (see p.276).

Internet access

Internet points are now widespread in the larger towns of the Veneto (see p.275 for Venice listings), though many of them are short-lived ventures. The company with the widest network in Italy is Internet Train, whose franchises are listed at ⓦwww .internettrain.it. Reckon on paying around €5 for an hour online. It's increasingly common for hotels and even hostels to provide Internet access, usually for free; in the more sizeable towns, you'll also come across cafés and bars offering free wi-fi.

Mail

Post offices are generally **open** Monday to Saturday from around 8.30am until 5pm (until around 7.30pm at the largest offices), but smaller towns won't have a service on a Saturday, or it will be restricted to the morning only. **Stamps** can also be bought in *tabacchi*, as well as in some gift shops. The Italian postal service is one of the tardiest in Europe – if your letter is urgent, consider spending the extra few cents for the "posta prioritaria" service. Letters can be sent poste restante to any Italian town, by addressing them "Fermo Posta" followed by the name of the town. **Mail** will be sent to the central post office; when picking something up take your passport, and make sure they check under middle names and initials – and every other letter when all else fails – as filing is often diabolical.

Maps

The **maps** provided in this guide will be more than adequate for general navigation, but such is the intricacy of Venice's alleyways and courtyards that absolute accuracy requires a larger scale than book-format can easily provide. Rough Guides publishes a waterproof and rip-proof fold-out **Venice map** which details sights, accommodation, restaurants, bars and shops. Even more detail is provided by the *Touring Club Italiano* (TCI) 1:5000 fold-out map of the city, but if you feel you're going to need the most precise street-plan in existence, go for the *TCI* map that comes packaged with an even larger-scale mini-atlas of the city, plus a directory of street names. It's hard to find outside Italy, but it's widely on sale in Venice. *TCI* publish the best road map of the Veneto as well as excellent maps of other cities of the province, though in the case of the latter you're very unlikely to need anything more than the maps in this book and the free plans handed out at the tourist offices.

Media

Local and national newspapers form an essential accompaniment to bar culture: in small towns, folk are drawn to a bar for a read as much as for a drink. However, television plays a central role in Italian life: it's a rare household that doesn't have the TV switched on from morning to night, regardless of the poor quality of Italy's numerous local and heavily censored national channels.

Newspapers

The Veneto's major **newspaper** is *Il Gazzettino* (ⓦ www.gazzettino.it), which runs national and international stories on the front pages, with local news further in;

each city has its own edition so the local coverage in Verona, for example, will differ from coverage in Treviso. Venice's own local paper, *La Nuova Venezia* (ⓦ www .nuovavenezia.it), also sells well in the city, and is a good source of information on events. Of the nationals, the centre-left *La Repubblica* (ⓦ www.repubblica.it) and right-slanted *Corriere della Sera* (ⓦ www.corriere .it) are the two most widely read and available. The most avidly read papers of all, however, are the pink *Gazzetta dello Sport* and *Corriere dello Sport*; essential reading for the serious Italian sports fan, they devote as much attention to players' ankle problems as most papers would give to the resignation of a government. News magazines are also widely read in Italy, from the similar *L'Espresso* and *Panorama* to the lighter and celeb-obsessed offerings of *Gente* and *Oggi*.

English and **US newspapers** can be found for around twice the normal price in all the larger towns and established resorts, usually on the day of issue in bigger cities like Florence and Siena. Pan-European editions of Britain's *Guardian* and *Financial Times* and the Rome editions of the *International Herald Tribune* and *USA Today* are also usually available on the day of publication.

TV and radio

Italy's three main national **TV** channels are RAI 1, 2 and 3. Silvio Berlusconi's Mediaset runs three additional nationwide channels: Canale 5, Rete 4 and Italia 1. Although all six are blatantly pro-Berlusconi, the degree of sycophancy displayed on the TG4 news has reached such ludicrous heights (newscaster Emilio Fede is variously overcome by tears of joy or despair, depending on the fortunes of Berlusconi) that most Italians now tune in solely for a giggle. Although the stories of Italian TV's stripping housewives are overplayed, the output is pretty bland across the board, with the accent on quiz shows, soaps and plenty of American imports. The RAI channels carry less advertising and try to mix the dross with above-average documentaries and news coverage. Numerous other channels concentrate on sport; if you want to see the weekend's

Italian League football action, settle into a bar from 5pm on a Sunday.

Radio is highly deregulated in Italy, with FM so crowded that you continually pick up new stations whether you want to or not. There are some good small-scale stations if you search hard enough, but on the whole the RAI stations are the most professional – though even with them daytime listening is virtually undiluted dance music. The **BBC World Service** (⊕www.bbc.co.uk) is in English on 648kHz medium wave most of the day; they also broadcast continuously online, as do Voice of America (⊕www.voa.gov) and Radio Canada (⊕www.rcinet.ca) among others.

Money

The Italian currency is the euro (€), which is composed of 100 cents. Although it's an idea to have at least some euros for when you arrive, it is safer to bring the bulk of your money in the form of traveller's cheque. The usual fee for traveller's cheque sales is 1 or 2 percent and you'll usually pay a small commission when they're cashed. Make sure to keep the purchase agreement and a record of cheque serial numbers safe and separate from the cheques themselves. In the event that cheques are lost or stolen, the issuing company will expect you to report the loss forthwith to their office in Italy; most companies claim to replace lost or stolen cheques within 24 hours. As an alternative to traveller's cheque, you could take a **pre-paid card**, which you load with cash that can then be withdrawn from an ATM (*bancomat*) abroad. Various companies (eg Travelex, Virgin, Tesco) offer these cards; British travellers can compare them at ⊕www.what-prepaid-card.co.uk .

Credit cards are a very handy backup source of funds and can be used in ATMs (*bancomat*) provided you have a PIN that's designed to work overseas. Remember that all cash advances on a credit card are treated as loans, with interest accruing daily from the date of withdrawal. You can also make withdrawals from ATMs using your **debit card**, which is not liable to interest payments, but nearly all banks make charges for cash withdrawals from ATMs abroad – you could find yourself paying a fee as high as 5.5 percent of the amount taken out. Note that payment by credit card is not yet as prevalent in Italy as in the UK and US; many budget hotels won't accept payment by card, and it's not unusual for restaurants to insist on cash.

You'll usually get the best rate of exchange (*cambio*) from a **bank**. Banking hours vary slightly, but generally are Monday to Friday from 8.30am to 1.30pm and from 3 to 4.30pm, with major branches often opening for a couple of hours on Saturday morning. American Express and Travelex offices are open longer hours, and in the larger towns you'll find an **exchange bureau** at the train station that stays open late. As a rule, though, the kiosks offer pretty bad rates – the only places where you'll get less for your money are the exchange desks of the biggest hotels.

Opening hours and holidays

Basic hours for small **shops and businesses** in the Veneto are Monday to Saturday from 8 or 9am to around 1pm, and from around 3pm to 7 or 8pm, though an increasing number of places (especially in Venice) stay open continuously from around 10am to 7/8pm, with shorter hours on Sunday. Many of Venice's churches now function as museums; others tend to open for Mass in the early morning, around 7 or 8am, and close around noon, then open again at 4 or 5pm, closing at 7pm; more obscure ones will only open for early morning and evening services; some only open on Sunday and on religious holidays. Wherever possible, the opening hours of churches are given in the Guide. It's impossible to generalize about the opening hours of **museums and historic sites** except to say that the largest ones tend to be open every day, most of the others are open six days a week, with Monday and Tuesday the favoured days of closure, and that winter hours are a lot shorter than summer ones; we've given opening hours of every museum covered in the Guide. The museum **entry charges** quoted in the Guide are the full adult charge – bear in mind that some museums give student discounts, and all state museums give free admission to visitors from EU countries who can prove they are aged **under 18 or over 65**, and half-price admission to young people **under 26**.

National holidays

Nearly all fee-charging sights (but not bars and restaurants) will be closed on the following dates:

January 1 (New Year's day)
January 6 (Epiphany)
Easter Monday (variable)
April 25 (Liberation Day and St Mark's Day)
May 1 (Labour Day)
June 2 (Day of the Republic)
August 15 (Assumption of the Blessed Virgin Mary)
November 1 (Ogni Santi, "All Saints")
December 8 (Immaculate Conception of the Blessed Virgin Mary)
December 25 (Christmas)
December 26 (St Stephen's Day)

In addition, many Venetian shops and businesses close or work shorter hours for the local festival of the Salute on November 21 (see *Festivals* colour section).

One problem you'll face is that many churches and monuments are either completely or partly **closed for restoration** (*chiuso per restauro*): at any one time dozens of projects are in progress all over Venice (see Contexts), and it's impossible to predict which buildings will be under wraps in the near future – all that can be said with any degree of certainty is that you'll find restorers at work in parts of the Basilica di San Marco and the Palazzo Ducale.

Telephones

Nearly all public **phones**, run by Telecom Italia, will accept coins, but they have a tendency to swallow the cash before announcing that they are out of order, so if you need to use a phone box you'd best buy a **phonecard** (*carta* or *scheda telefonica*), available from *tabacchi* and newsstands. There are two types of *carta telefonica*: one is a rigid plastic card which has a microchip in it (on some of these you have to snap off a corner of the card before inserting it into the phone box); the other is a more fragile piece of plastic that functions as a sort of credit card. With the latter type it's necessary to call a free operator number (given on the back of the card) when you use it for the first time, and to key in a PIN number for subsequent calls – a complicated process that has a high failure rate. **Tariffs** are among the most expensive in Europe; for national calls, the off-peak period runs Mon–Fri 6.30pm–8am, then Sat 1pm until Mon 8am. Note that many Internet points offer international calls at lower rates than phone boxes. **Telephone area codes** are now an integral part of the number and must always be dialled, regardless of where you're calling from. Numbers beginning ☎800 are free, an English-speaking operator is on ☎170, and international directory enquiries is on ☎176.

To use your **mobile phone**, check with your provider whether it will work in Italy and what the charges will be. Technology in Italy is GSM (ⓦwww.gsmworld.com). Unless you have a triband phone, it's unlikely that a mobile bought for use in North America will work elsewhere.

To call Italy from abroad dial your **international access code** (00 from the UK, Ireland and New Zealand; 011 from the US and Canada; 0011 from Australia), followed by **39** for Italy, followed by the full Italian number. For direct international calls from Italy, dial the country code, the area code (minus its first 0), and finally the subscriber number. Country codes are as follows: UK 0044; Ireland 00353; US & Canada 001; Australia 0061; New Zealand 0064; South Africa 0027.

To make international **reversed charge** or **collect** calls from Italy (*cárico al destinatario*), dial 170 or 172, followed by the country code, which will connect you to an operator in your home country.

Time

Italy is on Central European Time (CET): one hour ahead of Britain, six hours ahead of Eastern Standard Time and nine hours ahead of Pacific Standard Time.

Tourist information

Virtually every Veneto town has a **tourist office**, and we've given their addresses and opening hours throughout this guide. Their usefulness is variable: some will hand out maps, hotel lists and additional leaflets on special events, whereas others will offer next to nothing in the way of printed material. As a general rule, the bigger the better, though the service in Venice itself can be somewhat cursory at busy times. Before you leave home, it's worth dropping in at the nearest **Italian State Tourist Office** (ENIT) to pick up some maps and brochures – a full list of all Italian State Tourist Offices, in Italy and abroad, can be found at Ⓦwww .enit.it. Don't overload yourself, though. Not only can most of the material be picked up in Venice, but the practical information is often out of date in the offices outside Italy.

Useful websites

Ⓦ**www.govenice.com**
A Venice information portal, with loads of good links.
Ⓦ**www.hellovenezia.it**
This site gives information on transport and events.
Ⓦ**www2.comune.venezia.it/mappacomune**
The city council's superb online map – type in any address, and it'll give you the precise location.
Ⓦ**www.turismovenezia.it**
The official Venice tourist office site – packed with practical stuff, and the best source of info on opening hours.
Ⓦ**www.veneto.to**
The official Veneto tourist office site with information on places to visit, hotels, weather, festivals and exhibitions.
Ⓦ**www.venicexplorer.net**
A terrific site, featuring hundreds of images, a calendar of daily events, a superb map search facility and a vast range of information, covering everything from Venetian cuisine to conservation issues.

Travellers with disablities

Although a few key bridges are now fitted with wheelchair lifts, and an increasing number of bridges have ramps as well as steps, Venice presents significant problems for anyone who is not able-bodied. The islands that make up the city are joined by bridges that are usually steeply stepped, and getting in and out of the water-buses can be hazardous if the water level is low or the canals are choppy, despite the helpfulness of most conductors. **Wheelchair** users should try to avoid the smaller boats – principally the #41, #42, #51 and #52 lines (see p.36) – as they have just a small platform around the pilot's cabin, with the main passenger area being below deck level, down steep steps. The captains of these boats, moreover, are not obliged to let wheelchairs on board. The #1 down the Canal Grande, however, is accessible and spacious. It's also important to note that many Venetian hotels, especially in the lower price ranges, occupy the upper storeys of their addresses, and that in many instances staircases provide the only access. So if mobility is at all problematic, check the layout of your hotel before making a booking.

The **tourist office** provides a map of accessible Venice, making it possible, with careful route planning, to get around the main sights in the San Maroo district; it also keeps keys to the wheelchair lifts. "Venezia-pertutti" ("Venice for All") produces another map grading the accessibility of different islands of the city – it's on display at some of the major vaporetto stops (train station, Rialto, Accademia and San Marco) and at the information office at Piazzale Roma. The website of Venice's local council has a section devoted to the disabled – Ⓦwww .comune.venezia.lt/handlcap. It gives details of wheelchair-accessible accommodation, an accessibility map of the city and news on the latest initiatives, such as the installation of wheelchair ramps.

Travelling with children

It's hard to imagine any child not enjoying Venice hugely, for a few days at least. The experience of travelling around a city by **boat** is a thrill in itself, as is the freedom from road-going traffic. The whole city is a labyrinth, and kids can explore it with no risk of colliding with anything more dangerous than a pedestrian. There are church towers to climb, stray cats to follow, weird carvings and pictures to spot. In winter there are some spectacular puddles to negotiate, and as in any Italian city you're only a few minutes away from a delicious ice cream. In summer you can nip over to the Lido for a paddle and a bout of sandcastling. With younger children, however, you might find that their patience begins to wear thin quite quickly: it's easy for them to get the feeling that Venice is just one damned church after another. The stone pavements can be tiring, and Venice has very few green spaces, with just one **playground** of any size, over on the eastern edge of the city, in the Giardini Pubblici. The city's **museums** aren't especially kid-friendly either: you'll find some moderately diverting objects in the Correr (such as stilt-like shoes), plenty of model boats in the Museo Storico Navale, and a few prehistoric skeletons in the Museo Storico Naturale (only part of which is currently open), but otherwise it's mostly paintings. Diet might also be an issue in seafood-centric Venice – some **restaurants** offer kids' favourites such as lasagne and spaghetti Bolognese, but many do not. And if you're going to be pushing a buggy around all day, the endless bridges can become wearying. On the other hand, anyone equipped with a baby is very likely to be warmly received in child-mad Italy, and restaurants won't treat the small ones as an occupational hazard – quite the opposite. As for **accommodation**, nearly all hotels will gladly put a cot or an extra bed in your room, usually for a surcharge of around ten percent.

The City

The City

Venice: practicalities

The historic centre of Venice is made up of 118 islands, most of which began life as a micro-community, each with a parish church or two, and a square for public meetings. Though many Venetians maintain a strong attachment to their particular part of the city, the autonomy of these parishes has been eroded since the days when traffic between them moved by water. Some 400 bridges now tie the islands together, forming an amalgamation that's divided into six large administrative districts known as sestieri, three on each side of the Canal Grande.

The *sestiere* of **San Marco** is the hub of Venice and the zone in which the most visited sights are clustered – and is accordingly the most expensive district of the city. On the east it's bordered by **Castello**, and on the north by **Cannaregio** – both of which become more residential, and quieter, the further you go from San Marco. On the other bank the largest of the *sestieri* is **Dorsoduro**, which stretches from the fashionable quarter at the tip of the Canal Grande, south of the Accademia gallery, to the docks in the west. **Santa Croce**, named after a now demolished church, roughly follows the curve of the Canal Grande from Piazzale Roma to a point just short of the Rialto, where it joins the commercially most active of the districts on this bank – **San Polo**.

Points of arrival

More than twenty million visitors pour into Venice each year, many of them funnelled through Venice's small Marco Polo airport, on the outskirts of Venice itself, or through Treviso, 30km inland. Arriving by train and coach is painless – but driving into Venice is hellish in summer.

By air

Most **scheduled** flights and some charters arrive at the recently enlarged and redesigned **Marco Polo**, a little over 7km north of Venice, on the edge of the lagoon. If you're on a package holiday the cost of transport to the city centre, either by land or by water, might already be covered. If it's not, the most inexpensive alternative is to take one of the two road-going **bus services** to the terminal at Piazzale Roma: the ATVO (*Azienda Trasporti Veneto Orientale*) coach, which departs every half-hour and takes around twenty minutes (€3), or the ACTV (*Azienda del Consorzio Trasporti Veneziano*; Ⓦ www.actv.it) bus #5/5D, which is equally frequent, usually takes a few minutes longer (it's a local bus service, so it picks up and puts down passengers

Addresses in Venice

Within each **sestiere** the buildings are numbered in a sequence that makes sense solely to the functionaries of the post office – it's possible to find houses facing each other which have numbers separated by hundreds. This is because, in essence, the numbering system tends to follow walls rather than streets: thus if a small alleyway intersects with a major one the numbering on the major alley may well continue round the corner and down the minor alleyway before turning around to flow back towards the main drag. For this reason Venetian **addresses** are conventionally written as the street name followed by the *sestiere* followed by the number – eg Calle Vallaresso, San Marco 1312. Sometimes, though, the *sestiere* is placed before the street, and sometimes the street is omitted altogether, which makes the place impossible to find unless you're in the know.

between the airport and Piazzale Roma), and costs €2.50.

If you'd prefer to approach the city by water, you could take one of the Alilaguna **water-buses**, which operate on four routes from the airport: Murano – Fondamente Nove – Lido – San Zaccaria – San Marco – Záttere (6.10am–midnight); Murano – Fondamente Nove – Rialto – Sant'Angelo (9.55am–4pm); Murano – Lido – Arsenale – San Marco – Záttere (9.15am–9.15pm); and directly to San Zaccaria and then San Marco (9.30am–3.30pm). The Alilaguna fare is €6.50 to Murano and €13 to central Venice. All services are hourly, and the journey time to San Marco is about 70 minutes. Ticket offices for Alilaguna, ATVO and ACTV buses are in the arrivals hall; in addition to single tickets, you can also get ACTV passes and Venice Cards here (see below) – a wise investment for most visitors. Note that ACTV passes are not valid on the Alilaguna service nor on the ATVO bus, but a version of the Venice Card can be used on Alilaguna's boats.

Water-taxi drivers tout for business in and around the arrivals hall. This is the most luxurious means of getting into the city, but it's a ruinously expensive option: you'll pay in the region of €100 to San Marco, for up to six people. Ordinary **car-taxis** cost about €35 to Piazzale Roma.

Treviso is a very small airport used chiefly by **charter** companies, some of which provide a bus link from the airport into Venice. An ATVO bus service to Venice meets the twice-daily Ryanair flights as well; the fare is €6 single and the journey takes 1 hour 10 minutes. (On the way back to the airport the bus departs from rank D2 at Piazzale Roma – you have to buy tickets in the ATVO office beforehand.) Otherwise, take the #6 bus from right outside the arrivals building into Treviso train station (20min), from where there are very frequent bus and train connections to Venice; tickets are sold at the bar across the road.

The Venice and Rolling Venice cards

Aimed at tourists who are doing some intensive sightseeing, the **Venice Card** comes in two forms and is valid for either three or seven days, with a meagre discount for under-30s. The "Transport" version (3-day €48/47; 7-day €68/67) gives unlimited use of ACTV public transport, reduced admission to some one-off exhibitions and free access to the city's supervised public toilets; the ACTV travel passes (see p.36) are a better investment than this. The "Transport & Culture" version (3-day €73/66; 7-day €96/87), however, also gives you one free visit to all the museums and churches covered by the Museum Pass and Chorus Pass (see p.39), plus the Querini-Stampalia and Jewish museums. For a €23 supplement you can buy a version of the blue and orange cards that's valid on Alilaguna services to and from the airport. Note that kids under 6 get free museum entrance anyway, but only under-4s get free travel on public transport. You can buy Venice Cards from the tourist offices and at some of the larger vaporetto stops, notably Piazzale Roma, the train station, Accademia, Rialto and San Marco Vallaresso (outlets are identified by the Hellovenezia sign); alternatively, you can order the card a minimum of 48 hours in advance online at Ⓦwww.hellovenezia.com, which gives a discount of at least ten percent. You will be given a code number which you will need to present when you turn up to collect your ticket from one of the offices listed above.

If you're aged between 14 and 29, you are eligible for a **Rolling Venice** card, which entitles you to discounts at some shops, restaurants, hostels, campsites, museums, concerts and exhibitions, plus a discount on the 72-hour ACTV travel pass; details are given in a leaflet that comes with the card. The card costs €4, is valid until the end of the year in which it's bought, and is worth buying if you're in town for at least a week and aim to make the most of every minute. The Rolling Venice card is available from all outlets for the Venice Card, on production of a passport or similar ID.

By road and rail

People arriving **by car** must leave their vehicle either on the mainland or try for the car parks of Venice itself – either at **Piazzale Roma** or at the adjacent and ever-expanding **Tronchetto**, Europe's largest car park. Piazzale Roma is well connected with the main water-bus services, Tronchetto rather less so, though you won't have to wait more than thirty minutes for transport to the San Marco area. Neither is a cheap option (from about €20 per day), and in summer the tailbacks can be horrendous. Rates are at least fifty percent lower at the Mestre train station car park, which is connected to central Venice by regular ACTV buses (10min).

Arriving by **train, coach or bus**, you simply get off at the end of the line. The **Piazzale Roma** bus station and **Santa Lucia** train station (not to be confused with Venezia Mestre, the last stop on the mainland) are just five minutes' walk from each other at the top of the Canal Grande, and both are well served by vaporetto services to the core of the city.

Information

The main **tourist office** – known as the Venice Pavilion – occupies the Palazzina del Santi, the waterfront building on the west side of the Giardinetti Reali, within a minute of the Piazza (daily 10am–6pm; ☎041.529.8711, ⊛www.turismovenezia.it); other offices operate at Calle dell'Ascensione 71/f, in the corner of the Piazza's arcades (daily 9am–3.30pm; ☎041.520.8740), the train station (daily 8am–6.30pm; ☎041.529.8727), in the airport arrivals area (Mon–Sat 9.30am–7.30pm; ☎041.541.5887), at the multistorey car park at Piazzale Roma (daily 9.30am–4.30pm; ☎041.529.8746), and on the Lido at Gran Viale S.M. Elisabetta 6 (June–Sept daily 9.30am–12.30pm & 3–6pm; ☎041.526. 5721). The Calle dell'Ascensione office is also the city's main outlet for information on the whole Veneto.

These offices distribute copies of *Eventi & Manifestazioni*, a free, quarterly publication that lists the latest museum and gallery opening hours and prices, plus details of exhibitions, concerts and other one-off events; some of the information is in Italian only, but the essentials are in English too. Also useful is the English–Italian magazine *Un Ospite di Venezia* (⊛www .unospitedivenezia.it); produced fortnightly in summer and monthly in winter, it gives slightly fuller information on some events, plus extras such as vaporetto timetables; it's free from the reception desks of many four- and five-star hotels. The fullest source of information, though, is *VENews* (€2.50; ⊛www.venezianews.it), published on the first day of each month and sold at newsstands all over the city; it has good coverage of exhibitions, cultural events, bars and restaurants, with a fair amount of text in English as well as Italian.

City transport

Venice has two interlocking street systems – the canals and the pavements – and, contrary to what you might expect, you'll be using the latter for most of the time. With the exceptions of the #1, #2 and the night service, the water-buses skirt the city centre, connecting points on the periphery and the outer islands. **Taking a water-bus** is usually the quickest way of getting between far-flung points, but in many cases the speediest way of getting from A to B is **on foot** – you don't have to run, for instance, to cover the distance from the Piazza to the Rialto Bridge quicker than the #1 boat. You walk from one side of the city to the other in an hour, and once you've got your general bearings you'll find that navigation is not as daunting as it

---

Venice connected

In 2009 Venice's tourism authorities launched ⊛www.veniceconnected .com, a website through which tourists can buy museum tickets, Venice Cards and transport passes at **discounts** that vary according to the time of year. As we went to press the system was still experiencing teething problems, but it should soon be functioning smoothly.

Water-bus services

What follows is a run-through of the **water-bus routes** that visitors are most likely to find useful; a full timetable can be downloaded from the ACTV website (Ⓦwww.actv .it). Be warned that so many services call at San Marco, San Zaccaria, Rialto and the train station that the stops at these points are spread out over a long stretch of waterfront, so you might have to walk past several stops before finding the one you need. Note that the main San Marco stop is also known as San Marco Vallaresso, or plain Vallaresso, and that the San Zaccaria stop is as close to the Basilica as is the Vallaresso stop.

#1: The #1 is the slowest of the waterbuses, and the one you're likely to use most often. It starts at Piazzale Roma, calls at every stop on the Canal Grande except San Samuele, works its way along the San Marco waterfront to Sant'Elena, then goes over to the Lido. The #1 runs every 20min between 5 and 6.30am, every 10min between 6.30am and 10pm, and every 20min between 10 and 11.40pm.

#2: The #2 is in effect a speeded-up version of the #1, as it makes far fewer stops on the Canal Grande. Its clockwise route takes it from San Zaccaria to San Giorgio Maggiore, Giudecca (Zitelle, Redentore and Palanca), Zàttere, San Basilio, Sacca Fisola, Tronchetto, Piazzale Roma, the train station, then down the Canal Grande (calling at Rialto, San Tomà, San Samuele and Accademia; from around 4–8pm it also calls at San Marcuola) to San Marco (Vallaresso); the anti clockwise version calls at the same stops. From Monday to Friday the #2 runs along most of the route (in both directions) every 10min from 5am to 8.30pm, then every 20min until about 11pm, but for the section between Rialto and San Marco it runs only from around 9am to 5pm, every 20min; at weekends the #2 runs every 20min for the whole route. In summer the #2 is extended from San Zaccaria to the Lido.

#41/42: The circular service, running right round the core of Venice, with a short detour at the northern end to San Michele and Murano. The #41 travels anticlock-wise, the #42 clockwise and both run every 20min from about 7am to 8pm; before and after that, the #41/42 together act as a shuttle service between Murano and Fondamente Nove, running every 20min from 4am and until around 11.30pm.

seems at first. Helpful yellow signs posted high up on street corners all over central Venice indicate the main routes to San Marco, Ferrovia (train station) and Rialto.

Water-buses

The ACTV map of the lagoon transport system seems at first glance to resemble the wiring diagram of a telephone exchange, but in fact the routes are pretty straightforward. There are two basic types of boat: the **vaporetti**, which are the workhorses used on the Canal Grande (#1 & #2) and other heavily used routes, and the **motoscafi**, which are smaller vessels employed on routes where the volume of traffic isn't as great (notably the two "circular routes" – #41/42 & #51/52).

The standard **fare** is an exorbitant €6.50 for a single journey; the ticket is valid for sixty minutes, and for any number of changes of water-bus, as long as you're travelling from point A to point B – it cannot, in other words, be used as a return ticket. There's a €2 ticket for one-stop trips such as a crossing of the Canal Grande, or a hop between San Zaccaria and San Giorgio Maggiore, or Zàttere to Giudecca. Should you have more than one piece of large luggage, you're supposed to pay €6.50 per additional item. Children under 4 travel free on all public transport. Unless you intend to walk all day, you'll almost certainly save money by buying some sort of **travel card** as soon as you arrive. ACTV produces tickets valid for **12 hours** (€16), **24 hours** (€18), **36 hours** (€23), **48 hours** (€28),

#51/52: Similar to the #41/42, this route also circles Venice, but heads out to the Lido (rather than Murano) at the easternmost end of the loop. The #51 runs anticlockwise, the #52 clockwise, and both run fast through the Giudecca canal, stopping only at Záttere and Santa Marta between San Zaccaria and Piazzale Roma. Both run every 20min for most of the day. In the early morning and late evening (4.30–6.20am & 8.30–11.20pm) the #51 doesn't do a complete lap of the city – instead it departs every 20min from Fondamenta Nove and proceeds via the train station and Záttere to the Lido, where it terminates; similarly, from about 8–11pm the #52 (which starts operating at 6am) shuttles between the Lido and Fondamente Nove in the opposite direction, and from 11pm to around 12.20am goes no farther than the train station.

#LN: For most of the day, from 4.30am, the "Laguna Nord" runs every half-hour from Fondamente Nove (approximately hourly from 7.40pm to 11pm), calling first at Murano-Faro before heading on to Mazzorbo, Burano (from where there is a connecting half-hourly #T shuttle to Torcello), Treporti, Punta Sabbioni, the Lido, Sant'Elena and San Zaccaria; it runs with the same frequency in the opposite direction.

#DM: From around 6am to 6pm the "Diretto Murano" runs from Tronchetto via Piazzale Roma and Ferrovia to Murano, where it always calls at Colonna and Museo, and often at other Murano stops too.

#N: This night service (11.30pm–4.15am) is a selective fusion of the #1 and #2 routes, running from the Lido to Giardini, San Zaccaria, San Marco (Vallaresso), Accademia, San Samuele, San Tomà, Rialto, Ca' d'Oro, San Stae, San Marcuola, train station, Piazzale Roma, Tronchetto, Sacca Fisola, San Basilio, Záttere, Giudecca (Palanca, Redentore and Zitelle), San Giorgio and San Zaccaria – and vice versa. It runs along the whole of the route in both directions every 40min, and along the Rialto to Tronchetto part every 20min. Another night service connects Venice with Murano and Burano, running to and from Fondamente Nove every hour between 11.30pm and 3am.

72 hours (€33), and **seven days** (€50), which can be used on all ACTV services within Venice (including ACTV land buses from the airport).

Tickets are available from most landing stages, shops displaying the ACTV sign, and all the tourist offices; the travel passes are available from the tourist offices and at the Piazzale Roma, train station, Ca' d'Oro, Rialto, Accademia, San Marco Vallaresso, San Zaccaria, Arsenale, Záttere, Fondamente Nove and Tronchetto vaporetto stops. The ticket offices at these larger stops are generally open 8am–9pm daily, whereas smaller ones tend to close between 3 and 5pm. If you can't find anywhere to buy a ticket before you get on board, ask the conductor for one immediately – if you delay, you could be liable for a €30 spot-fine on top of the fare. Conductors cannot issue travel passes.

If you're staying a long time, or are a frequent visitor, it could be worth buying a **Cartavenezia**: valid for three years, it costs €40 for non-residents, is valid for three years (renewal is €10) and entitles you to a hugely reduced fare of €1.10 for a single ticket (valid for 75min). It's available, on presentation of ID and a passport photo, from the ACTV office by the Tronchetto vaporetto stop.

If you buy an ordinary single ticket at the train station, Piazzale Roma, San Zaccaria or San Marco it will in all likelihood be automatically **validated**. Most tickets, however, must be validated before embarking, at one of the orange-coloured punching machines at the vaporetto stops.

Travel cards have to be swiped at the meter-like machines which are also at every stop, and must be swiped **before each journey**.

Traghetti

There are just four bridges spanning the Canal Grande – the Ponte Calatrava (at Piazzale Roma), Ponte dei Scalzi (at the train station), Ponte di Rialto and Ponte dell'Accademia – so the **traghetti** (gondola ferries) that cross it can be useful time-savers. Costing just 50 cents, they are also the only cheap way of getting a ride on a gondola, albeit a stripped-down version, with none of the trimmings and no padded seats: most of the locals stand rather than sit. The gondola traghetti across the Canal Grande are as follows (proceeding from the San Marco end to the station end): San Marco (Vallaresso)–Dogana di Mare (daily 9am–2pm; Santa Maria del Giglio–Salute (daily 9am–6pm); Ca' Rezzonico–San Samuele (Mon–Sat 8.30am–1.30pm); San Tomà–Santo Stefano (Mon–Sat 7.30am–8pm, Sun 8.30am–7.30pm); Riva del Carbon–Riva del Vin (near Rialto; Mon–Sat 8am–1pm); Santa Sofia–Rialto (Mon–Sat 7.30am–8pm, Sun 8.45am–7pm); San Marcuola–Fondaco dei Turchi (Mon–Sat 9am–1pm). In the winter months it's common for traghetti to cease operating considerably earlier than the times indicated above, or even to be suspended altogether.

Gondolas

The **gondola**, once Venice's chief form of transport, is now purely an adjunct of the tourist industry. But however much the gondola's image has become tarnished, it is an astonishingly graceful craft, perfectly designed for negotiating the tortuous and shallow waterways: a gondola displaces so little water, and the gondoliers are so dexterous, that there's hardly a canal in the city they can't negotiate. Until very recently, gondoliers inherited their jobs from their fathers; nowadays the profession is open to anyone who can get through four hundred

hours of tough training, which involves acquiring not just the requisite manual skills and a perfect grasp of the city's waterways, but also a deep knowledge of the history of the profession. In June 2009 Giorgia Boscolo successfully completed the course, and thus became Venice's first female gondolier. To hire one costs €80 per forty minutes for up to six passengers, rising to €100 between 7pm and 8am; you pay an extra €40 for every additional twenty minutes, or €50 from 8pm to 8am. Further hefty surcharges will be levied should you require the services of an on-board accordionist or tenor – and a surprising number of people do. (There have been moves to outlaw the singing of the perennial tourist favourite, *O Sole Mio*, on the grounds that performances of this Neapolitan ditty merely reinforce the prejudices of visitors who demand nothing more than a generic "Italian" experience.) Even though the tariff is set by the local authorities, it's been known for gondoliers to try to extort even higher rates than these – if you do decide to go for a ride, establish the charge before setting off. To minimize the chances of being ripped off by a private individual making a few dozen euros on the side (and there are plenty of those in Venice), take a boat only from one of the following **official gondola stands**: west of the Piazza at Calle Vallaresso, Campo San Moisè or Campo Santa Maria del Giglio; immediately north of the Piazza at Bacino Orseolo; on the Molo, in front of the Palazzo Ducale; outside the *Danieli* hotel on Riva degli Schiavoni; at the train station; at Piazzale Roma; at Campo Santa Sofia, near Ca' d'Oro; at San Tomà, to the east of the Frari; or by the Rialto Bridge on Riva Carbon. Your gondolier will assume that you'll want to be taken along the Canal Grande or across the Bacino di San Marco, but you'll probably not be making the best use of the opportunity if you opt for one of these: for one thing, these major waterways look much the same from a vaporetto as from a gondola; and for another, the gondola will tend to get bashed around by the wash from the bigger boats. Better to choose a quarter of the city that has struck you as being particularly alluring, head for the gondola stand that's nearest to it, and ask to be taken there. (For more on gondolas, see p.104.)

Taxis

Venice's **water-taxis** are sleek and speedy vehicles that can penetrate most of the city's canals. Unfortunately their use is confined to all but the owners of the deepest pockets, for they are possibly the most expensive form of taxi in western Europe: the clock starts at €13 and goes up €1.80 every minute. All sorts of surcharges are levied as well: €5 for each extra person if there are more than two people in the party; €3 for each piece of luggage other than the first item; €8 for a ride between 10pm and 6am. There are three ways of getting a taxi: go to one of the main stands (at Piazzale Roma, the train station, Rialto and San Marco Vallaresso), find one in the process of disgorging its passengers, or call one by phone (☎041.522.2303). If you phone for one, you'll pay a surcharge, of course.

Museums and monuments

In an attempt to make sure that tourists go to see more than just the big central monuments, a couple of **Museum Cards** have been introduced for the city's **civic museums** (🌐www.museicivicivenezlani.it). The card for the museums of the Piazza comes in two forms: the **Musei di Piazza San Marco** card is available from November 2 to March 31, costs €12 (€6.50 for ages 6–14, students under 30, EU citizens over 65 & Rolling Venice Card holders), and gets you into the Palazzo Ducale, Museo Correr, Museo Archeologico and the Biblioteca Marciana; the **San Marco Plus** card, issued from April 1 to November 1, costs €1 more, and additionally gives you one visit to one other civic museum of your choice. The **Museum Pass**, costing €18/12, covers the museums listed above, plus all the other civic museums: Ca' Rezzonico, Casa Goldoni,

Palazzo Mocenigo, Museo Fortuny, Ca' Pésaro (the modern art and oriental museums), the Museo del Merletto (Burano) and the Museo del Vetro (Murano). Passes allow one visit to each attraction, are valid for six months and are available from any of the participating museums. The Palazzo Ducale and Museo Correr can be visited only with a museum card; at the other places you have the option of paying an entry charge just for that attraction. Note also that the more expensive version of the Venice Card (see p.34) covers all of the museums covered by the Museum Pass, and that accompanied disabled people have free access to all of the civic museums. There is also a combined ticket for the city's **state museums** (the Accademia, Ca' d'Oro and Museo Orientale), costing €11/5.50.

Sixteen churches are now part of the ever-expanding **Chorus Pass** scheme (🌐www.chorusvenezla.org), whereby a €9 ticket allows one visit to each of the churches over a one-year period. All of the proceeds from the scheme are ploughed back into the maintenance of the buildings. The individual entrance fee at each of the participating churches is €3, and all the churches (except for the Frari) observe the same opening hours: Monday to Saturday 10am to 5pm. The churches involved are: the Frari (Mon–Sat 9am–6pm, Sun 1–6pm); the Gesuati; Madonna dell'Orto; the Redentore; San Giacomo dell'Orio; San Giobbe; San Giovanni Elemosinario; San Pietro di Castello; San Polo; San Sebastiano; San Stae; Sant'Alvise; Santa Maria dei Miracoli; Santa Maria del Giglio; Santa Maria Formosa; and Santo Stefano. The Chorus Pass is available at each of these churches and the Venice Pavilion tourist office; the pricier version of the Venice Card gives admission to all of them.

Opening hours are listed throughout this guide, but bear in mind that these times are prone to sudden alterations, especially in winter, when afternoon opening hours are frequently truncated if business is slack. Last admission for the major museums is one hour before closing time; for smaller sights, tickets are generally sold up to half an hour before closing. Children under 6 are exempt from entrance charges, while 6–12s are entitled to reductions at nearly all attractions, provided they are accompanied by an adult. Visitors from EU countries who can prove they are aged under 18 or over 65 are entitled to free admission at the Accademia, Ca' d'Oro, Museo Archeo-logico and Museo Orientale.

San Marco

Enclosed by the lower loop of the Canal Grande, the *sestiere* of San Marco – a rectangle smaller than 1000m by 500m – has been the nucleus of Venice for more than a millennium. When, in the early years of the ninth century, the lagoon settlers decamped from the coastal town of Malamocco to settle on the safer islands of the inner lagoon, the area now known as the **Piazza San Marco** was where their rulers built the citadel that evolved into the **Palazzo Ducale**, and it was here that they established their most important church – the **Basilica di San Marco**. Over the succeeding centuries the Basilica became the most ostentatiously rich church in Christendom, and the Palazzo Ducale grew to accommodate and celebrate a system of government that endured for longer than any other republican regime in Europe. Meanwhile, the setting for these two great edifices developed into a public space so grandiose that no other square in the city was thought fit to bear the name "piazza" – all other Venetian squares are campi or campielli.

Nowadays the Piazza is what keeps the city solvent. Fifty percent of Venice's visitors make a beeline for this spot, spend a few hours and a pocketful of euros here, then head for home without staying for even one night. For those who do hang around, San Marco has multitudinous ways of easing the cash from the pockets: the plushest hotels are concentrated in this *sestiere*; the most elegant and exorbitant cafés spill out onto the pavement from the Piazza's arcades; the most extravagantly priced seafood is served in this area's restaurants; and the swankiest shops in Venice line the Piazza and the streets radiating from it – interspersed with dozens of hugely profitable souvenir suppliers.

And yet, small though this *sestiere* is, it harbours plenty of refuges from the crush. Even within the Piazza you can escape the throng, as the **Museo Correr** and the adjoining **archeological museum** are rarely crowded. The Renaissance church of **San Salvador** – only a few minutes' walk from the Piazza – and the Gothic **Santo Stefano** are both magnificent and comparatively neglected buildings, while **San Moisè**, **Santa Maria del Giglio** and the **Scala del Bovolo** rank among the city's most engaging oddities.

On the fringes of the *sestiere* you'll find two of Venice's major exhibition spaces: the immense **Palazzo Grassi**, where the city's most prestigious art exhibitions are held, and the **Museo Fortuny**, which as well as staging special events also contains a permanent collection of work by the designer Mariano Fortuny.

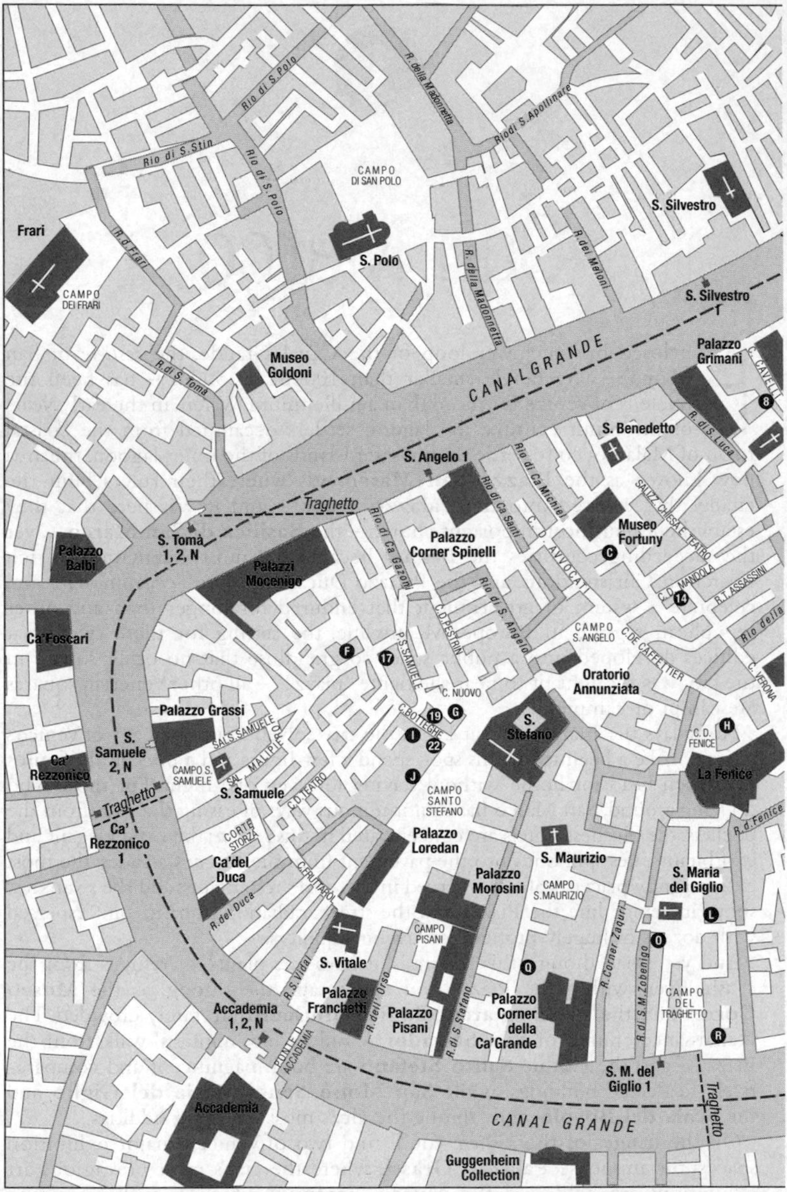

HOTELS

Ai Do Mori	B	Fiorita	G	Orseolo	E
Ala	O	Flora	N	San Giorgio	C
Al Gambero	A	Gritti Palace	R	San Samuele	F
Art Deco	I	Kette	K	Santo Stefano	J
Bel Sito & Berlino	L	La Fenice et des Artistes	H		
Casa Petrarca	D	Monaco and Grand Canal	M		
Europa e Regina	P	Novecento	Q		

RESTAURANTS

Al Bacareto
Da Carla
Da Fiore
Harry's Bar
Le Bistrot de Venise
Osteria-Enoteca San Marco
Rosticceria Gislon

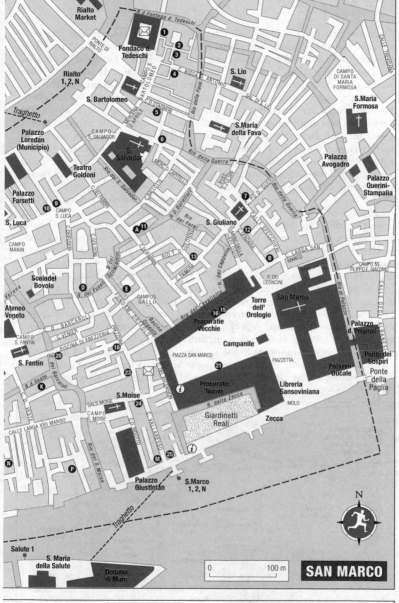

Rialto Market

R.d Fontego d. Tedeschi

PONTE DI RIALTO

Fondaco d. Tedeschi

Rialto 1, 2, N

C. BISSA S. ANTONIO

S. Lio

CAMPO DI SANTA MARIA FORMOSA

S. Maria Formosa

Traghetto

S. Bartolomeo

CAMPO S. BARTOLOMEO

SAL DI S. LIO

Palazzo Loredan (Municipio)

CAMPO S. SALVADOR

RIO della FAVA

C.D. STAGNERI

S. Maria della Fava

Palazzo Avogadro

S. Salvador

MERC. D. CAPITELLO

Rio della Guerra

Palazzo Querini-Stampalia

Teatro Goldoni

RUGA d. S. Salvador

C. DEI FABBRI

Palazzo Farsetti

CAMPO S. LUCA

R. D. Baratteri

RIO D. BARETTERI

S. Giuliano

C. LARGA SAN MARCO

S. Luca

C. GOLDON

RIO T. O.

R. d. FUMER

CAMPO SS. FILIPPO E. GIACOMO

CAMPO MANIN

RIO DEL CAPPELLER

CALLE D. SPECCHIERI

SPADARIA

MERCERIA

Scala del Bovolo

R. dei FUSERI

CAMPO S. GALLO

R. del Cavalletto

P. DEI LEONCINI

Ateneo Veneto

D. BARCAROLI

RIO del Fontego di Orseolo

Torre dell'Orologio

San Marco

Palazzo d. Prigioni

CAMPO S. FANTIN

C. VENIER

PISCINA DI FREZZERIA

Procuratie Vecchie

Campanile

Palazzo Ducale

Ponte dei Sospiri

S. Fantin

F. dei BARCAROLI

PIAZZA SAN MARCO

PIAZZETTA

Ponte della Paglia

R. d. VESTE

CALLE XXXIII MARZO

Procuratie Nuove

Libreria Sansoviniana

S. Moisè

SAL S. MOISE

R. della Zecca

MOLO

CALLE LARGA XXII MARZO

CAMPO S. MOISE

LCA BISSON

Giardinetti Reali

Zecca

RIO dei S. Moise

Palazzo Giustinian

S. Marco 1, 2, N

Traghetto

N

Salute 1

S. Maria della Salute

Dogana di Mare

| 0 | 100 m |

SAN MARCO

	BARS & SNACKS				**CAFÉS & GELATERIE**			
17	Alla Botte			3	Florian	21	Rosa Salva	6 & 13
23	Al Volto	Devil's Forest	5	Igloo	14	
19	Bácaro Jazz	I Rusteghi	2	Lavena	15	
25	Bácaro Lounge	Torino	10	Marchini	12	
11	Cavatappi		24	Marchini Time	9	
18	Centrale Restaurant			Paolin	22	
4	Lounge		20	Quadri	16	

The Piazza

When the first Palazzo Ducale was built, in the ninth century, the area now occupied by the **Piazza San Marco** was an islet known as Morso. Two churches stood here – San Teodoro and San Geminiano – but most of the land was covered by the orchard of the nuns of San Zaccaria. It was in the late twelfth century, under the direction of **Doge Sebastiano Ziani**, that the land was transformed into a public space – the canal connecting the waterways to the north with the Bacino di San Marco was filled in, the canalside San Geminiano was demolished (a plaque close to the Campanile marks where it stood) and a replacement built at the far end. The general shape of the Piazza hasn't changed much since Ziani's scheme, but most of the buildings you see today, excluding the Basilica and the Campanile, date from the great period of urban renewal which began at the end of the fifteenth century and went on for much of the following hundred years.

"The finest drawing room in Europe" was how Napoleon described the Piazza, but less genteel epithets might seem appropriate on a summer afternoon, as your sightlines are repeatedly blocked by tour groups and the café orchestras try to drown each other out with selections from the oeuvre of Andrew Lloyd-Webber. You can take some consolation from the knowledge that the throngs and the racket are maintaining a long tradition, even if the discarded burger wrappers are a thoroughly modern blight. (The locals fought hard to keep the golden arches off the Piazza itself, but *McDonald*'s have a toehold in a nearby alley, and *Hard Rock Café* have pitched camp within a few metres of the square.) The Piazza has always been overcrowded, and foreigners have always made up a sizeable proportion of the crowds – long before the tourist industry got into its stride, the swarms of foreign merchants and travellers in the Piazza were being cursed as "the monsters of the sea", to quote one disgruntled native.

If anything, life on the Piazza is less diverse nowadays than it used to be. From the foundation of the city, this area was used by traders (the slave market was

PIAZZA SAN MARCO

Piazza festivities

The Piazza's brightest splash of colour comes from the **Carnevale**. Though gangs of masked and wildly costumed revellers turn every quarter of the city into a week-long open-air party, all the action tends to drift towards the Piazza, and the grand finale of the whole proceedings is a huge Shrove Tuesday ball in the square, with fireworks over the Bacino di San Marco.

Mass entertainments used to be far more frequent, taking over the Piazza on feast days and whenever a plausible excuse could be found. From the twelfth century onwards **pig hunts** and **bullfights** were frequent spectacles, but around the beginning of the seventeenth century the authorities became increasingly embarrassed by these sanguinary pursuits, and they were relegated to other squares in the city. The blood sports were succeeded by gymnastic performances known as **Labours of Hercules**, in which teams of young men formed human pyramids and towers on platforms that were often no more than a couple of planks resting on a pair of barrels. Military victories, ducal elections and visits from heads of state were commonly celebrated with tournaments and pageants: a three-day tournament was held in the Piazza in 1364 after the recapture of Crete, with guest appearances by a gang of English knights on their way to create bedlam in the Holy Land, and in 1413 the election of Doge Tommaso Mocenigo was marked by a tournament that was watched by 70,000 people.

The **coronation of Doge Ziani** in 1172 was celebrated with a procession around the Piazza, with the new head of state scattering coins to the populace; this ritual, adapted from Byzantine custom, was observed by all subsequent doges. Major religious festivals were also the occasion for lavish celebrations, the most spectacular of which was the **Procession of Corpus Domini**, a performance meticulously recorded in a painting by Gentile Bellini in the Accademia. Regrettably, not all of Venice's holy processions achieved the solemn dignity captured in Bellini's picture – in 1513 one stately progress went wrong when a row broke out over which group had the right to enter the Piazza first, a disagreement that rapidly escalated into an almighty punch-up.

But no festivities were more extravagant than those of **Ascension Day**, and it was in the wake of Ascension that the Piazza most closely resembled the modern tourist enclave. From the twelfth century until the fall of the Republic, the day itself was marked in Venice by the ceremony of **The Marriage of Venice to the Sea**, a ritual which inaugurated a short season of feasts and sideshows in the Piazza, culminating in a trade fair called the Fiera della Sensa (Sensa being dialect for Ascension). The Fiera began in 1180, when, as a result of Pope Alexander III's proclamation that an indulgence would be granted to anyone who prayed in San Marco during the year, the city was flooded with pilgrims. Before long it became a cornucopia of luxury commodities, and by the last century of the Republic's existence it had grown into a fifteen-day fair that filled the Piazza with temporary wooden shops and arcades.

here until the end of the ninth century), and as the city grew, so the range of activities taking place on the Piazza multiplied; by the end of the fifteenth century butchers and grocers had established their pitches, moneylenders and notaries had set up kiosks nearby, and makeshift stages for freak shows and masques were regular additions to the scene.

By the eighteenth century the Piazza might have become a touch more decorous, but it was certainly no quieter. One English visitor characterized the throng as "a mixed multitude of Jews, Turks, and Christians; lawyers, knaves, and pick-pockets; mountebanks, old women, and physicians; women of quality, with masks; strumpets barefaced…a jumble of senators, citizens,

The pigeons of the Piazza

Until recently the Piazza was perpetually swarming with **pigeons**, whose presence was held to be so crucial to the identity of the square that they were fed daily by a council official – though it was also rumoured that the council-sponsored bird-seed was laced with **contraceptive**, in an attempt to control the pigeon population. In 2008 it was decided that the droppings of the disease-ridden birds were presenting too great a hazard to the citizens of Venice and the stonework of the Piazza's buildings, and so feeding the birds was **banned**, which very quickly led to the dispersal of the flocks. You can choose between three improbable stories about the origins of the pigeons: either they came here with the refugees from Attila's army; or they're the descendants of caged birds given to a doge's wife in an attempt to cheer her up; or they're the distant relatives of pigeons released by successive doges during Holy Week, in a ceremony commemorating the return of Noah's dove.

gondoliers, and people of every character and condition". Jugglers, puppet-eers, sweet-sellers, fortune-tellers and a host of other stallholders seem to have been almost perennial features of the landscape, while Venetian high society passed much of the day in one or other of the Piazza's dozen **coffee shops** – Europe's first *bottega del caffè* opened here in 1683, and within a few decades Goldoni had created a play in which the hero, a café owner, declared "My profession is necessary to the glory of the city." During the Austrian occupation of 1814–66 the coffee houses were drawn into the social warfare between the city's two hostile camps. Establishments used by the occupying troops were shunned by all patriotic Venetians – *Quadri* became an Austrian coffee house, whereas *Florian* remained Venetian. Certain prominent Venetians even went to the length of shunning the Piazza whenever the Austrian band was playing, a policy that entailed a thrice-weekly withdrawal from the centre of the city.

The Piazza remains a pivot of social life in Venice. Contrary to first appearances, the tables of *Florian* and *Quadri* – the only eighteenth-century survivors – or at the equally high-toned *Lavena*, the favourite haunt of Richard Wagner, are not exclusively the preserve of tourists. Wander through at midday and there'll be clusters of Venetians taking the air and chatting away their lunch-hour; the evening *passeggiata* often involves a circuit of the Piazza; and even at midnight you'll almost certainly see a few groups rounding off the day with a stroll across the flagstones.

The Basilica di San Marco

San Marco is the most exotic of Europe's cathedrals, and it has always provoked strong reactions. To Herman Melville it was beautiful and insubstantial – as though "the Grand Turk had pitched his pavilion here for a summer's day"; Mark Twain adored it for its "entrancing, tranquilizing, soul-satisfying ugliness"; Herbert Spencer found it "a fine sample of barbaric architecture"; and to John Ruskin it was the most gorgeous of holy places, a "treasure-heap…a confusion of delight". The Basilica is certainly confusing, increasingly so as you come nearer and the details emerge, but some knowledge of the building's background helps bring a little order out of the chaos.

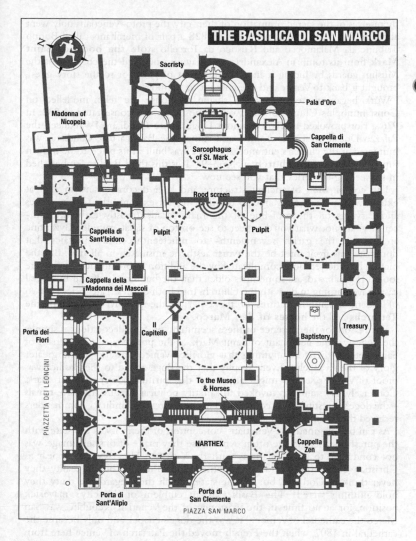

Sacristy

Pala d'Oro

Madonna of Nicopeia

Cappella di San Clemente

Sarcophagus of St. Mark

Rood screen

Cappella di Sant'Isidoro

Pulpit

Pulpit

Treasury

Cappella della Madonna dei Mascoli

Il Capitello

Baptistery

Porta dei Flori

PIAZZETTA DEI LEONCINI

To the Museo & Horses

NARTHEX

Cappella Zen

Porta di Sant'Alipio

Porta di San Clemente

PIAZZA SAN MARCO

The history of the Basilica

All over Venice you see images of the lion of Saint Mark holding a book on which is carved the text "Pax tibi, Marce evangelista meus. Hic requiescet corpus tuum" ("Peace be with you Mark, my Evangelist. Here shall your body rest"). These supposedly are the words with which Saint Mark was greeted by an angel who appeared to him on the night he took shelter in the lagoon on his way back to Rome. This **legend of Saint Mark's annunciation** was adopted as fact in order to overcome the discrepancy between the first Venetians' notion of their spiritual pedigree – as successors of the shattered Roman Empire and as the first state to be founded as a Christian community – and the inglorious fact that the settlement of the lagoon islands had begun as a scramble to get out of the way of Attila the Hun. Having thus assured themselves of the sacred ordination of their city, the proto-Venetians duly went about fulfilling the angelic prophecy. In **828** a pair of merchants called Buono Tribuno da Malamocco and Rustico da Torcello **stole the body of Saint Mark** from its tomb in Alexandria and, having smuggled the corpse past the Muslim guards by hiding it in a consignment of pork (or so the story goes), brought it back to Venice and presented it to the doge.

Work began immediately on a shrine to house the relic; modelled on Constantinople's Church of the Twelve Apostles, it was consecrated in **832**. In 976 a riot provoked by the tyrannous Doge Pietro Candiano IV reduced the Palazzo Ducale to a pile of ashes and ruined the Basilica too; Candiano was murdered at the church's entrance. A replica was built in its place, to be in turn superseded by a **third church** in 1063–94. It is this third Basilica, embellished in succeeding centuries, that you see now.

The combination of ancient structure and later decorations is, to a great extent, what makes San Marco so bewildering: for example, the Gothic arches and carvings on the roof-line of the main facade (mostly early fifteenth-century) are not what you'd expect to see on top of squat, rounded Byzantine arches, and the garish seventeenth- to nineteenth-century mosaics that dominate this front must be the worst aesthetic mismatch in all Italy. But the picture is made yet more complicated by the addition of ornaments which were looted from abroad, are sometimes older than the building itself and in several cases have nothing to do with the Church. Into both of these categories fall two of the most famous features of the exterior: the porphyry figures of the **Tetrarchs** and the **horses of San Marco**.

The reason for the presence of these seemingly profane decorations is simple: the doge was the lieutenant of Saint Mark, as the pope was the lieutenant of Saint Peter – therefore anything that glorified Venice was also to the greater glory of the Evangelist. Every trophy that the doge added to the Basilica was proof of Venice's secular might and so of the spiritual power of Saint Mark. Conversely, the saint was invoked to sanctify political actions and state rituals – the doge's investiture was consecrated in the church, and military commanders received their commissions at its altar.

As can be imagined, the Venetians' conception of their city as the state with the purest lineage, and the often cynical use they made of this self-image, was not conducive to good relations with the Vatican. "They want to appear as Christian before the world," commented Pope Pius II, "but in reality they never think of God and, but for the state, which they regard as a deity, they hold nothing sacred." The Basilica is an emblem of the city's maverick position, for at no time in the existence of the Venetian Republic was San Marco the cathedral of Venice – it was the doge's chapel, and only became the cathedral in 1807, when the French moved the Patriarch of Venice here from San Pietro di Castello. Until the eighteenth century it was common practice

---

Visiting San Marco

San Marco is open to tourists Monday to Saturday 9.45am–5pm, and Sunday 2–5pm (4pm from Nov to Easter); one part of the church, the Loggia dei Cavalli, is open on Sunday morning. Entrance to the main body of the church is free, but admission fees totalling €9.50 are charged for certain parts. You cannot take large bags inside – they have to be left, free of charge, at nearby Calle San Basso 315a. If you're visiting San Marco in summer, get there early – by midday the queues are enormous.

▲ The Basilica di San Marco

for the doge to advertise his proprietorship by hanging his coat of arms on the front of the building.

In effect, the Venetians ran a semi-autonomous branch of the Roman Church: the Patriarch of Venice could convene a synod only with the doge's permission, bishops were nominated by the Senate, priests were appointed by a ballot of the parish and had to be of Venetian birth, and the Inquisition was supervised by the Republic's own, less draconian, doctrinal office. Inevitably, there were direct clashes with the papacy; for the story of the most serious, the interdict of 1606, see p.149.

The exterior of the Basilica

Shortly after becoming the architectural custodian (*Proto Magister*) of San Marco in 1529, Jacopo Sansovino set about strengthening the building and replacing some of its deteriorating decoration, a procedure that resulted in the removal of around thirty percent of the church's mosaics. On the main facade, the only mosaic to survive this and subsequent restorations is the scene above the **Porta di Sant'Alipio** (far left) – *The Arrival of the Body of St Mark*. Made around 1260, it features the earliest known image of the Basilica. In the lunette below the mosaic are fourteenth-century bas-reliefs of the symbols of the Evangelists; the panels comprising the door's architrave are fifth century; and the door itself dates from 1300. The next door is from the same period, and the reliefs on the arch are thirteenth century; the mosaic of *Venice Worshipping St Mark*, however, is an eighteenth-century effort.

The worst and the best aspects of the facade are to be found above the **central entrance**: the former being the nineteenth-century mosaic of the *Last Judgement*, the latter the **Romanesque carvings** of the arches. Begun with the innermost arch in the 1220s and completed about a century later, these are among the outstanding sculptural works of their time, but about one visitor in a thousand spares them a glance, despite their recently restored sparkle.

The **inner arch** depicts animals, the Earth and the Ocean on its underside, with fighting figures (perhaps intended as the savage antithesis of Venetian civilization) on the outer face; the **middle arch** shows the labours of the months and the signs of the zodiac, with the Virtues and Beatitudes on the outer side; and the **outer arch** depicts the trades of Venice, and Christ and the prophets. The carved panel in the lunette, *The Dream of St Mark*, is also thirteenth century, but the door – known as the **Porta di San Clemente** – is 700 years older, and is thought to have been a gift from the Byzantine emperor Alexius Comnenus.

The fourth portal follows closely the model of the second; the mosaic of the fifth is similarly an eighteenth-century job, but the marble decoration is a mixture of eleventh- to thirteenth-century carvings, except for the architrave panel of *Christ Blessing*, a remnant of the second Basilica, built after the 976 fire.

Of the six marble panels between the entrance arches, only the Roman bas-relief of *Hercules and the Erymanthean Boar* isn't a twelfth- or thirteenth-century piece. The terrace running across the facade above them was the spot from which the doge and his guests watched the festivities in the Piazza; the mosaics on this level all date from the early seventeenth century, and the huge blank window was occupied by a Byzantine screen until a fire in 1419 destroyed everything except the four half-columns. The roof-line's encrustation of Gothic pinnacles, kiosks, figures and ornamental motifs was begun in 1385 under the direction of the **Dalle Masegne** family, the leading sculptors in Venice during that period, and was continued through the early part of the following century by various Tuscan and Lombard artists, of whom **Niccolò Lamberti** and his son **Pietro** were the most proficient.

To see the real **horses of San Marco** you have to go into the church – these are modern replicas.

The north and south facades

In the 1860s and 1870s an extensive and controversial **restoration** of the Basilica was begun, a scheme which would probably have finished with the rearrangement of the main facade. An international protest campaign, supported by Ruskin, forced the abandonment of the project soon after it had reached the Piazzetta corner of the west front, and the damage caused to that section was largely reversed in later years. The **north and south facades**, though, were altered irrevocably by the restorers, who replaced the old polychromatic marble panels with badly fitted sheets of grey stone, creating an effect described by an English stonemason in 1880 as resembling "a dirty lime wash on a white plastered wall".

The **north side** of San Marco, the last to be completed (in the first half of the thirteenth century), is studded with panels from a variety of sources – they include a seventh- or eighth-century relief showing the Apostles as twelve lambs, and a tenth-century piece illustrating Alexander the Great's mythical attempt to reach heaven by harnessing a pair of griffons to his chariot. The entrance on this side, the **Porta dei Fiori**, is thirteenth century (the tomb of **Daniele Manin** is a bit further on), and most of the sculpture on the upper part is by the **Lambertis**.

Jutting out between the **south facade** and the entrance to the Palazzo Ducale is the wall of the treasury, thought by some to be a remnant of the **first palace of the doges** and the chamber in which the body of St Mark was first placed after its arrival in Venice. The screen fragments (*plutei*) set into the walls date from the ninth to the eleventh centuries.

Sometimes the heads of freshly dispatched villains were mounted on the **Pietra del Bando**, the stump of porphyry against the corner of the Basilica; a more benign service was done on the day the Campanile collapsed, when it stopped the avalanche of bricks from hitting the church. Its routine use was as one of the two stones from which the laws of the Republic were proclaimed (the other is at the Rialto). The stone was brought back from Acre in 1258, following Venice's victory over the Genoese there; the two square pillars near to it – Syrian works dating from the fifth century – were filched from Constantinople's church of St Polyeuktos after the Fourth Crusade. High on the Basilica's facade, above the two pillars, a thirteenth-century mosaic of the Madonna is flanked by two lanterns that are kept perpetually lit, in observance of the vow of a mariner who was led to safety across the stormy waters of the lagoon by a light burning on the Piazzetta.

A number of tales centre on the group of porphyry figures set into the angle of the treasury. Thomas Coryat tells a version in which four Albanian brothers plotted against each other for possession of the cargo their ship was carrying, and ended up poisoning each other. But the most popular version turns them into a gang of Saracens who raided the treasury and then contrived to murder each other in a squabble over the spoils – hence they're often nicknamed "The Moors". More properly they're known as the **Tetrarchs**, as in all likelihood they depict Diocletian and the three colleagues with whom he ruled the unravelling Roman Empire – peculiar adornments for a church, bearing in mind Diocletian's notoriety as a persecutor of Christians. What's certain is that, like so much of the Basilica's stonework, they were taken from Constantinople.

The narthex

From the Piazza you pass into a vestibule called the **narthex**, which once, before the partitioning of the baptistery and the Cappella Zen, bracketed the entire west end of the church. The intricately patterned stonework of the narthex **floor** is mostly eleventh and twelfth century, and one fragment of it is especially significant: the small white lozenge set into the floor in front of the main entrance is said to mark the spot on which Emperor Frederick Barbarossa knelt before Pope Alexander III on August 23, 1177. Prior to this, the empire and the papacy had been at each other's throats, and this symbolic reconciliation in the portal of San Marco clinched one of Venice's greatest diplomatic triumphs.

Most of the **mosaics** (see plan, p.54) on the domes and arches constitute a series of **Old Testament scenes** which complements the New Testament iconography in the main body of the church. Predominantly thirteenth century, the mosaics were begun in the dome on the far right, with scenes from Genesis (c.1230 but much restored, as indicated by the inset red lines), and executed in a continuous series right round the narthex. The Genesis dome is followed by: **first arch** – *Noah and the Flood* (note the preferential treatment handed out to the lion); in the **bay in front of main door** – double tier of niches containing the **oldest mosaics in San Marco**, a group showing *The Madonna with Apostles and Evangelists* (c.1065); **second arch** – end of *Life of Noah*, and the *Tower of Babel*; **second dome** – *Story of Abraham* and four tondi of *Prophets*; **third arch** – *SS. Alipio and Simon Stylites* and tondo of *Justice*; **third, fourth and fifth domes** – *Story of Joseph*; **sixth dome** – *Story of Moses*.

Three doges and one dogaressa have tombs in the narthex. That of **Vitale Falier**, the doge who consecrated the Basilica in 1094, two years before his death, is the **oldest funerary monument in Venice** – it's at the base of the first arch. The others are of Felicità, wife of Doge Vitale Michiel I (1101; second arch), Doge Bartolomeo Gradenigo (1342; northwest corner of narthex, beyond third dome) and Doge Marin Morosini (1253; under fourth dome). Two other doges besides these are buried in the narthex, but nobody has a clue where.

The Museo Marciano, the Loggia and the horses

On the right of the main door from the narthex into the body of the church (made in 1113–18 and based on the Basilica's main door) is a steep staircase up to the **Museo Marciano** and the **Loggia dei Cavalli** (daily 9.45am–4.45pm; €4). The Loggia offers a wonderful view of the Piazza, the Gothic carvings of the facade, and the ceiling mosaics inside, but the reason most people haul themselves up the steps is to see the famed **horses of San Marco**.

Thieved from the hippodrome of Constantinople in 1204, the horses spent a few years in front of the Arsenale before being installed on the terrace of the Basilica. So close did the association become between them and the people who had stolen them, that the Genoese in 1378 didn't boast that they would tame the lion of Saint Mark, but rather that they would "bridle those unbridled horses". The statues are almost certainly Roman works of the second century, and are the only *quadriga* (group of four horses harnessed to a chariot) to have survived from the classical world. Made from a bronze that contains an unprecedentedly high percentage of copper, they were cast in two parts, the junction being masked by their collars; medallions used to hang round their necks, but they had gone missing by the time the horses returned to Venice in 1815 after an eighteen-year sojourn on the Champs Élysées. The marks on the horses' skins are not the result of mistreatment – it's thought that the scratches and the partial gilding were added at the time of their creation in order to catch the sun.

The small **Museo Marciano** is a miscellany of mosaic fragments, manuscripts, vestments and so forth from the church. The most interesting exhibits are the wooden cover for the Pala d'Oro, painted in 1345 by **Paolo Veneziano** and his sons, and the cycle of ten tapestries of *The Life of Christ* made around 1420 to designs by **Nicolò di Pietro** – but as likely as not they'll be under lock and key.

▲ The horses of San Marco

The interior of the Basilica

With its undulating floor of patterned marble, its plates of eastern stone on the lower walls, and its 4000 square metres of mosaic covering every other inch of wall and vaulting, the golden **interior** of San Marco achieves a hypnotic effect. Whether you look down or up, some decorative detail will catch your eye, drawing you into the narratives of its mosaics, or the geometric complexities of its pavements. One visit is not enough: there's too much to take in at one go, and the shifting light reveals some parts and hides others as the day progresses. The only way to do it justice is to call in for at least half an hour at the beginning and end of a couple of days. Be warned, however, that a system of barriers is used to channel visitors in one direction round the interior of the Basilica, that there is nowhere to sit down inside the church, and that at peak times – which is almost the entire day between May and September – the congestion makes it impossible to stop for a decent look at anything.

The mosaics

The majority of the **mosaics** were in position by the middle of the thirteenth century, but scenes were added right down to the eighteenth century, most of the later work being carried out to replace damaged early sections. An adequate guide to them would take volumes: the following account is only a key to the highlights. The mosaics in the nave, transepts and presbytery are dealt with first; the mosaics in the chapels come into the entries on those chapels. The complex shape of the Basilica makes it most convenient to locate the various features by points of the compass, with the high altar marking the east.

On the **west wall**, **above the door** – *Christ between the Virgin and St Mark* (thirteenth century, restored). **West dome** – *Pentecost* (early twelfth century); the paired figures between the windows represent the diverse nations in whose languages the Apostles spread the Word after Pentecost. **Arch between west and central domes** – *Betrayal of Christ, Crucifixion, Marys at the Tomb, Descent into Limbo, Incredulity of Thomas* (all late twelfth century except the *Marys*, which is a fifteenth-century copy); these are among the most inventive of all the ancient mosaics, both in terms of their richness of colour and their presentation of the intense drama of the events.

The **central dome**, a dynamic composition of concentric circles, depicts the *Ascension, Virgin with Angels and Apostles, Virtues and Beatitudes, Evangelists, Four Allegories of the Holy Rivers* (late twelfth century except *Sant Mark* and *Sant Matthew*, which are mid-nineteenth century); the four allegorical figures shown watering the earth are almost certainly a coded reference to the Christian destiny of the city built on water.

East dome (the *Dome of Emanuel*) – *Religion of Christ Foretold by the Prophets* (early to mid-twelfth century; tondo of Christ restored c.1500). A *Christ Pantocrator* (1506, based on twelfth-century figure) blesses the congregation from the position in the **east apse** traditionally occupied by such figures in Byzantine churches; between the windows below stand the *Four Patron Saints of Venice*, created around 1100 and thus among the earliest works in San Marco. **Arches above north and south singing galleries** (ie linking chancel to side chapels) – *Acts from the Lives of St Peter and St Mark* (early twelfth century, altered in the nineteenth century); this sequence, mingled with *Scenes from the Life of St Clement*, is continued on the end walls, but is obscured by the organs.

North transept: **dome** – *Acts of St John the Evangelist* (early to mid-twelfth century); **arch to west of dome** (continued on upper part of adjacent wall) – *Life of the Virgin, Life of the Infant Christ* (late twelfth- to early thirteenth century);

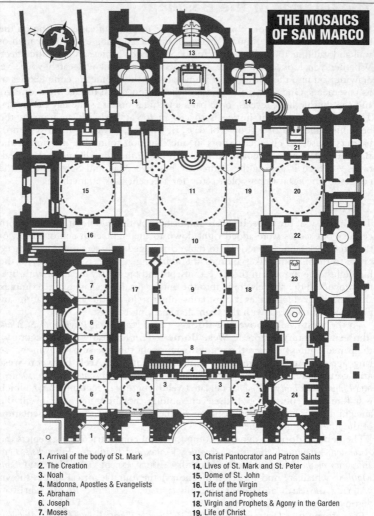

THE MOSAICS OF SAN MARCO

1. Arrival of the body of St. Mark
2. The Creation
3. Noah
4. Madonna, Apostles & Evangelists
5. Abraham
6. Joseph
7. Moses
8. Christ, the Virgin and St. Mark
9. Dome of Pentecost
10. From the Betrayal to the Resurrection
11. Dome of the Ascension
12. Dome of Emmanuel
13. Christ Pantocrator and Patron Saints
14. Lives of St. Mark and St. Peter
15. Dome of St. John
16. Life of the Virgin
17. Christ and Prophets
18. Virgin and Prophets & Agony in the Garden
19. Life of Christ
20. Dome of St. Leonard
21. Parables and Miracles
22. The 'Inventio'
23. The Lives of Christ & John the Baptist
24. Life of St. Mark

arch at north end of transept (above Cappella di Sant'Isidoro) – *Miracles of Christ* (late twelfth to early thirteenth century). On **wall of north aisle** – five mosaic tablets of *Christ with the Prophets Hosea, Joel, Micah and Jeremiah* (c.1210–30). This series is continued on the **wall of the south aisle** with figures of *The Virgin, Isaiah, David, Solomon* and *Ezekiel*; above these five is the large and complex *Agony in the Garden* (early thirteenth century); Mark's Gospel tells us that Christ fell on the ground in the Garden of Gethsemane, Matthew describes him falling on his face, and Luke writes that he simply knelt down – the mosaic thus shows Christ in three different positions. On the wall above and on the arch overhead are *Scenes from the Lives of the Apostles* (late twelfth to early thirteenth century).

South transept: **dome** (the *Dome of St Leonard*) – *SS. Nicholas, Clement, Blaise and Leonard* (early thirteenth-century), with *St Dorothea* (thirteenth century), *St Erasma* (fifteenth century), *St Euphamia* (fifteenth century) and *St Thecla* (1512) in the **spandrels**. The formality of the mosaics in the **arch between dome and nave** – *Scenes from the Life of Christ* (early twelfth century) – makes a striking contrast with the slightly later scenes on the church's central arch; the depiction of Christ's temptation is especially beautiful, showing the protagonists suspended in a field of pure gold. **Arch above Altar of the Sacrament** – *Parables and Miracles of Christ* (late twelfth or early thirteenth century); **arch in front of Gothic window** – *SS. Anthony Abbot, Bernardino of Siena, Vincent Ferrer and Paul the Hermit* (1458); **west wall of transept** – the *Rediscovery of the Body of St Mark* (second half of thirteenth century).

This last picture refers to a miraculous incident known as the *Inventio* (or "Rediscovery"). In 1094 the body of Saint Mark, having been so well hidden during the rebuilding of the Basilica in 1063 that nobody could find it again, interrupted the service of consecration by breaking through the pillar in which it had been buried. The actual pillar is to your right as you enter the sanctuary, and the very place at which the Evangelist's arm appeared is marked by a marble and mosaic panel.

The sanctuary and the Pala d'Oro

Steps lead from the south transept up to the **sanctuary** (€2.50), via the **Cappella di San Clemente**, where most of the sculpture is by the **Dalle Masegne** family.

On the fronts of the singing galleries next to the rood screen are eight **bronze panels** of *Scenes from the Life of St Mark* by **Sansovino** (1537), who also executed the figures of *The Evangelists* on the balustrade of the high altar. The other four figures, *The Doctors of the Church*, are seventeenth-century pieces.

Officially the remains of Saint Mark lie in the sarcophagus underneath the altar, but it's quite likely that the body was actually destroyed in the fire of 976. The altar **baldachin** is supported by four creamy **alabaster columns** carved with mostly indecipherable scenes from the lives of Christ and His Mother; the date of the columns is a matter of intense argument – estimates fluctuate between the fifth and the thirteenth centuries.

Behind the altar, and usually enveloped by a scrum, is the most precious of San Marco's treasures, the astonishing **Pala d'Oro** – the "golden altar screen". Commissioned in 976 in Constantinople, the *Pala* was enlarged, enriched and rearranged by Byzantine goldsmiths in 1105, then by Venetians in 1209 to incorporate some of the less cumbersome loot from the Fourth Crusade, and again (finally) in 1345. The completed screen, teeming with jewels and minuscule figures, holds 83 enamel plaques, 74 enamelled roundels, 38 chiselled figures, 15 rubies, 300 sapphires, 300 emeralds, 400 garnets, 1300 pearls and a couple of hundred other stones. Such is the delicacy of the work that most of the subjects depicted on the screen are impossible to make out if you don't have 40/20 vision, and you'd need an encyclopedic knowledge of medieval iconography to decipher every episode and figure, but the rough scheme is easy enough to follow.

In the top section there's the Archangel Michael surrounded by medallions of saints, with *The Entry into Jerusalem, The Crucifixion, The Resurrection,*

Ascension, Pentecost and *The Death of the Virgin* to the sides. Below, *Christ Pantocrator* is enclosed by the four Evangelists, to the side of whom are ranked a host of angels, prophets and saints; these ranks are framed on three sides by scenes from the life of Christ (the horizontal band) and the life of Saint Mark (the vertical bands). The outer frame of the entire *Pala d'Oro* is adorned with small circular enamels, some of which (in the lower part of the frame) represent hunting scenes; most of these enamels survive from the first *Pala* and are thus its oldest components.

Before leaving the sanctuary, take a look at **Sansovino**'s door to the sacristy (invariably shut) – it incorporates portraits of Titian (top left) and Sansovino himself (under Titian's head).

The treasury

Tucked into the corner of the south transept is the door of the **treasury** (€3), installed in a thick-walled chamber which is perhaps a vestige of the first Palazzo Ducale. This dazzling warehouse of chalices, icons, reliquaries, candelabra and other ecclesiastical appurtenances is an unsurpassed collection of Byzantine work in silver, gold and semi precious stones. Particularly splendid are a twelfth-century Byzantine incense burner in the shape of a domed church, and a gilded silver Gospel cover from Aquileia, also made in the twelfth century.

Much of the treasury's stock owes its presence here to the great Constantinople robbery of 1204, and there'd be a lot more of the same on display if the French occupation force of 1797 hadn't given Venice a taste of its own medicine by helping itself to a few cartloads. To be fair to the Venetians, they at least gave the stuff a good home – the French melted down their haul, to produce a yield of 55 gold and silver ingots.

The sanctuary attached to the treasury, in which are stored more than a hundred reliquaries, is hardly ever open to the public.

The baptistery and the Cappella Zen

The **baptistery**, entered from the south aisle (usually reserved for prayer), was altered to its present form by **Doge Andrea Dandolo** (d.1354), whose tomb (facing the door) was Ruskin's favourite monumental sculpture in the city. It was Dandolo who ordered the creation of the baptistery **mosaics** of *Scenes from the Lives of Christ and John the Baptist*, works in which the formality of Byzantine art is blended with the anecdotal observation of the Gothic. "The most beautiful symbolic design of the Baptist's death that I know in Italy," wrote Ruskin. The tomb of Dandolo's predecessor, Doge Giovanni Soranzo (d.1328), is on the right as you come in, and **Jacopo Sansovino** – who designed the enormous font – lies beneath a slab at the eastern end. The huge granite block at the altar is said to have been brought back from Tyre in 1126; more imaginatively, it's also claimed as the stone from which Christ delivered the Sermon on the Mount.

In the **Cappella Zen** (also reserved for prayer), adjoining the baptistery, there's an object of similar mythical potency – a bas-relief of the Virgin that is supposed to have been carved from the rock from which Moses struck water. As its rich decoration indicates, the portal from the chapel into the narthex used to be the entrance from the Piazzetta; this portico was closed in 1504, when work began on the tomb of Cardinal Giambattista Zen, whose estate was left to the city on condition that he was buried within San Marco. The two **mosaic angels** alongside the Virgin on top of the doorway are twelfth century; the mosaics below are early fourteenth century and the small statues between them date from the thirteenth. The mosaics on the **vault** show *Scenes from the Life of*

St Mark (late thirteenth century, but restored). The Cappella Zen is sometimes known as the Chapel of the Madonna of the Shoe, taking its name from the gold shoe that adorns the *Virgin and Child* by **Antonio Lombardo** (1506) on the high altar.

Stonework, carvings and icons

Back in the main body of the Basilica, make sure you give the **pavement** a good look – laid out in the twelfth and thirteenth centuries, it's a constantly intriguing patchwork of abstract shapes and religious symbols. Of the church's other marvels, the next three paragraphs are but a partial list.

The **rood screen** is surmounted by a silver and bronze **cross** (1394) and marble figures of *The Virgin, St Mark and the Apostles* (also 1394) by **Jacobello and Pietro Paolo Dalle Masegne**. The **pulpits** on each side of the screen were assembled in the early fourteenth century from assorted panels, some of them taken from Constantinople; the new doge was presented to the people of Venice from the right-hand one.

Venice's most revered religious image is the tenth-century **Icon of the Madonna of Nicopeia**, in the chapel on the east side of the north transept; until 1204 it was one of the most revered in Constantinople, where it used to be ceremonially carried at the head of the emperor's army. At the north end of this transept is the **Cappella di Sant'Isidoro**: the mosaics, which have scarcely been touched since their creation in the mid-fourteenth century, depict scenes from the life of the saint, whose remains were grabbed from Chios by Doge Domenico Michiel in 1125. A beautiful mid-fifteenth-century mosaic cycle of *Scenes from the Life of the Virgin*, one of the earliest Renaissance works in Venice, is to be seen in the adjacent **Cappella della Madonna dei Mascoli**, which takes its name from the male confraternity that took it over in the seventeenth century. (The Sant'Isidoro chapel is nearly always closed or reserved for prayer, and you may find the entire north transept roped off to prevent incursions from sightseers.)

Against the west face of the end pillar on the north side of the nave stands **Il Capitello**, a tiny chapel fabricated from a variety of rare marbles to house the *Crucifix* on the altar; the painting arrived in Venice the year after the Nicopeia icon (and came from the same source), and in 1290 achieved its exalted status by spouting blood after an assault on it. Finally, the **galleries** merit a perusal from below (visitors are very rarely allowed to walk round them): the parapets facing the aisle consist of reliefs dating from between the sixth and the eleventh centuries, some of them Venetian, some Byzantine. They weren't designed as catwalks, as they now appear: this is what was left when the women's galleries over the aisles were demolished in the late twelfth century to let more light into the building, after some windows had been bricked over to make more surfaces for mosaics. Apart from this, no major structural change has been made to the interior of San Marco since its consecration in 1094.

The Palazzo Ducale

Architecturally, the **Palazzo Ducale** is a unique mixture: the style of its exterior, with its geometrically patterned stonework and continuous tracery walls, can only be called Islamicized Gothic, whereas the courtyards and much of the interior are based on Classical forms – a blending of influences that led

1. Porta della Carta
2. Porta del Frumento
3. Ticket office
4. Museo dell'Opera
5. Arco Fóscari
6. Scala dei Giganti
7. Cafeteria
8. Cloakroom
9. Pozzi
10. Scala dei Censori
11. Scala d'Oro
12. Ponte dei Sospiri
13. Prigioni Nuove
14. Censori
15. Avogaria
16. Sala dello Scrigno
17. Milizia da Mar
18. Bookshop
19. Administration offices
20. Sala degli Scarlatti

Ground Floor

First Floor

Ruskin to declare it "the central building of the world". Unquestionably, it is the finest secular building of its era in Europe, and the central building of Venice. The Palazzo Ducale was far more than the residence of the doge – it was the home of all of Venice's governing councils, its law courts, a sizeable number of its civil servants and even its prisons. All power in the Venetian Republic and its domains was controlled within this one building.

The exterior of the Palazzo Ducale

Like San Marco, the Palazzo Ducale has been rebuilt many times. The original fortress, founded at the start of the ninth century, was razed by the fire of 976,

21. Sala dello Scudo
22. Sala Grimani
23. Sala Erizzo
24. Sala dei Filosofi
25. Sala degli Scudieri
26. Liagò del Maggior Consiglio
27. Sala della Quarantia Civil Vecchia
28. Sala dell'Armamento or del Guariento
29. Sala del Maggior Consiglio
30. Sala della Quarantia Civil Nuova
31. Sala dello Scrutinio
32. Quarantia Criminale

33. Magistrato alle Legge
34. Scala d'Oro
35. Atrio Quadrato
36. Sala delle Quattro Porte
37. Sala dell'Anticollegio
38. Sala del Collegio
39. Sala del Senato
40. Sala del Consiglio dei Dieci
41. Sala della Bussola
42. Armoury

[Itinerari Segreti]
A Sala dei Tre Capi
B Sala degli Inquisitori
C Passage to the Piombi and Torture Chamber

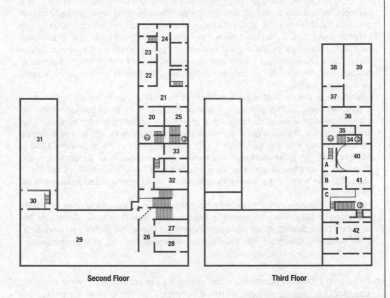

Second Floor **Third Floor**

PALAZZO DUCALE

and fire destroyed much of its replacement in 1106. The third palace was habitable within ten years, and was extended and altered frequently over the next couple of centuries. But it was with the construction of a new hall, parallel to the waterfront, for the Maggior Consiglio, that the Palazzo began to take on its present shape. Work began in 1340, and the hall was inaugurated in 1419; then, three years later, it was decided to knock down the dilapidated remnant of the old Palazzo Ducale and extend the new building along the Piazzetta, adhering to the same style. One feature of the exterior gives away the fact that its apparent unity is the product of two distinct phases of building: if you look at the Piazzetta side, you'll notice that the seventh column is fatter than the rest and has a tondo of *Justice* above it – that's where the two stages meet. (Incidentally, folklore has it

The government of Venice

Virtually from the beginning, the **government of Venice** was dominated by the merchant class, despite the existence, in the early years, of nominally democratic assemblies in which the general male populace was represented. The principal governing council, the **Maggior Consiglio**, was established in 1172 by Doge Vitale Michiel II, and from the start was in effect a self-electing assembly of the upper class. In 1297 the exclusion of the public was institutionalized by an act known as the **Serrata del Maggior Consiglio** (Locking of the Great Council): any man not belonging to one of the patrician families on the list compiled for the Serrata was ineligible to participate in the running of the city. After a while, this list was succeeded by a register of patrician births and marriages called the **Libro d'Oro**, upon which every patrician's claim to membership of the elite was based. In times of economic emergency the Maggior Consiglio was "unlocked" and new families were enrolled in the Libro d'Oro in return for huge cash payments: after the plague of 1630, for example, the already dwindling ranks of the patriciate were so severely depleted that between 1647 and 1718 some 127 families (mainly a mix of *nouveaux riches* Venetians and long-established clans from the mainland) were allowed to buy their way in. Nonetheless, by the second decade of the fourteenth century, the constitution of Venice had reached a form that was to endure until the coming of Napoleon; its civil and criminal code, defined in the early thirteenth century, was equally resistant to change.

What made the political system stable was its web of counterbalancing councils and committees, and its exclusion of any youthful element. Most patricians entered the Maggior Consiglio at 25 (although a group of younger high-fliers was admitted annually) and could not expect a middle-ranking post before 45; from the middle ranks to the top was another long haul – the average age of the doge from 1400 to 1600 was 72. As promotion was dependent upon a network of supporters in the elderly and conservative upper ranks, a situation was created in which, as the diarist Marin Sanudo wrote in the sixteenth century, "Anyone who wishes to dissent must be mad."

However, although Venice's domestic history can seem placid to the point of tedium, backstage politics were as sordid a business as anywhere else. Cabals of the so-called **Case Grandi** (Great Houses) for centuries had a stranglehold on most influential positions, corruption in various guises was endemic, and voting conspiracies

that the two reddish columns on the upper arcade on this side were crimsoned by the blood of traitors, whose tortured corpses were hung here for public edification; certainly this is the spot where Filippo Calendario, one of the Palazzo Ducale's architects, was quartered for abetting the conspiracy of Marin Falier – see p.151 for more.)

A huge restoration project in the 1870s entailed the replacement or repair of every external column of the palace, the opening up of the arcade on the waterfront side (partly blocked up since the 1574 fire – see p.64) and the repositioning of some of the columns there, and the substitution of copies for fifteen of the fourteenth- and fifteenth-century **capitals** of the lower portico. (It's fairly obvious which are the copies; many of the originals have been restored, and are on display in the Palazzo's Museo dell'Opera.) In the eyes of John Ruskin, these carvings exemplified the transition from the purity of the Gothic (see the heads of children on the fourth capital from the *Drunkenness of Noah*) to the vulgar decadence of the Renaissance (compare the fifteenth-century children, second from the Porta della Carta – "capable of becoming nothing but perfumed coxcombs").

were constantly being hatched and thwarted. Even within the Case Grandi there were struggles for influence, the battle lines being drawn between the **Longhi**, the families who claimed descent from the city's founders, and the **Curti**, whose genealogical tables ran a bit short. An outside observer, exposed to the machinations of Venice's rulers, noted "They kill not with blood but with ballots."

The seeming compliance of the 98 percent of the population that was shut out from active politics is largely explained by the economic cohesion of the city: its governors were also its businessmen and its chief employers, so were unlikely to adopt policies damaging to the financial interests of themselves and their workforce. The paternalism of the Venetian system helped keep things quiet too – the public health measures and emergency plans for bad harvest years were admired throughout Europe. And when, on the odd occasion, the bosses did contemplate measures that would have been unpopular outside the council chambers, there is evidence that "the murmuring in the city" quickly put them right. In 1510, for example, a massive demonstration in the Piazza persuaded the government that they should imprison the defeated general whose arrest the people were demanding.

The doge
Regarding the **doge**, it's a common misunderstanding that he was a mere figurehead, confined to his palace under a sort of luxurious house arrest. It's true that there were numerous restrictions on his activities – all his letters were read by censors, for example, and he couldn't receive foreign delegations alone – but these were steps taken to reduce the possibility that an ambitious leader might exploit his office, and they didn't always succeed. Whereas his colleagues were elected for terms as brief as a month, the doge was **elected for life** and sat on all the major councils of state, which at the very least made him extremely influential in the formation of policy. The dogeship was the monopoly of old men not solely because of the celebrated Venetian respect for the wisdom of the aged, but also because a man in his seventies would have fewer opportunities to abuse the unrivalled powers of the dogeship. So it was that in 1618 a certain Agostino Nani, at 63 the youngest candidate for the dogeship, feigned a life-threatening decrepitude to enhance his chances of getting the job. A neat summary of the doge's position was made by **Girolamo Priuli**, an exact contemporary of Sanudo – "It is true that if a doge does anything against the Republic, he won't be tolerated; but in everything else, even in minor matters, he does as he pleases."

The interventions of restorers are less obtrusive on the late fourteenth-century to early fifteenth-century **corner sculptures**: by the Ponte della Paglia – *Archangel Raphael* and *Drunkenness of Noah*; Piazzetta corner – *Archangel Michael* and *Adam and Eve*; Basilica corner – *Archangel Gabriel* and *Judgement of Solomon*. Some see these pieces as a cogent sequence, illustrating justice (Solomon) and the counterbalancing qualities of severity (expulsion of Adam and Eve) and compassion (Noah's sons) needed for its administration; Ruskin, naturally, saw things slightly differently – whereas the pious Gothic mind dwells on the frailty of humanity (Noah's intemperance, Adam and Eve's disobedience), the vainglorious Renaissance celebrates Solomon's God-like wisdom. The **balconied window** on the lagoon side is another contribution from the **Dalle Masegne** family (1404); the corresponding window on the Piazzetta facade is a mid-sixteenth-century imitation.

The principal entrance to the Palazzo was the **Porta della Carta**, the name of which derives perhaps from the archives kept nearby, or from the clerks' stalls around it. Commissioned in 1438 by **Doge Francesco Fóscari** from **Bartolomeo and Giovanni Bon**, this is one of the most ornate Gothic works

▲ The lagoon facade of the Palazzo Ducale

in the city. Many of its carvings used to be painted and gilded, and the lack of colour isn't the only respect in which the Porta della Carta differs nowadays from its original state – the figures of Fóscari and his attendant lion are nineteenth-century replicas. (For more on Doge Fóscari, see p.192.) The fifteenth-century pieces were smashed to bits in 1797 by the head of the stone-masons' guild, who offered to do Napoleon a favour by removing from his sight all images of the lion of Saint Mark. Luckily, his iconoclastic career seems to have ended soon after it began. The solitary remnant of the original is on display inside the Palazzo Ducale.

The passageway into the Palazzo ends under the **Arco Fóscari** (see opposite), which you can see only after getting your ticket, as tourists are nowadays directed into the building through the Porta del Frumento, under the arcades on the lagoon side.

The interior

Several sections of the Palazzo Ducale (daily: April–Oct 9am–7pm; Nov–March 9am–5pm; entrance with Museum Card/Venice Card) can be dealt with fairly briskly. The building is clad with paintings by the hectare, but a lot of them are wearying exercises in civic self-aggrandizement (no city in Italy can match Venice for the narcissism of its art), and if you take away the paintings, there's not much left to some of the rooms. But it would be perverse not to visit so integral a part of the city, and there are parts you will not want to rush. For this reason a visit needs to be timed carefully. In high season scores of tour groups are being propelled round the place by multilingual guides for much of the day. If you want any control over what you get a look at, buy your ticket within half an hour of opening, or a couple of hours before closing.

A word of warning: as with San Marco, restoration work is always taking place somewhere in the Palazzo Ducale, and there is rarely any indication before you go in as to how much of the building is under wraps, so prepare to be disappointed – you are almost certain to come across scaffolding and barriers at some point.

The courtyard, Museo dell'Opera and Arco Fóscari

From the ticket office you're directed into the **Museo dell'Opera**, where the originals of more than forty of the capitals from the lower and upper loggias are well displayed and explicated. In the last room look out for the stone head of Doge Francesco Fóscari, the only item salvaged from the great sculpture on the Porta della Carta.

On the far side of the courtyard, opposite the entrance, stands the Arco Fóscari, which like the Porta della Carta was commissioned from the Bons by Doge Fóscari, but it was finished a few years after his death by **Antonio Rizzo** and **Antonio Bregno**. Rizzo's *Adam* and *Eve* (c.1470), the best of the Arco Fóscari sculptures, have been replaced by copies – the originals, along with the original of Bandini's late sixteenth-century statue of Francesco Maria I della Rovere (on the courtyard side), are on show inside. In 1483 yet another fire demolished most of the wing in front of you (the east), and led to more work for Rizzo – he designed the enormous, over-ornamented staircase called the **Scala dei Giganti**, and much of the new wing. Underneath the lion at the top of the staircase is the spot where the new doge was crowned with the jewel-encrusted cap called the *zogia*; the ungainly figures of *Neptune* and *Mars* were sculpted in 1566 by **Sansovino**. Reconstruction of the east wing continued under **Pietro Lombardo, Spavento** and **Scarpagnino** (who created the **Senators' Courtyard** to the left of the staircase), and finally (c.1600) **Bartolomeo Monopola**, who finished the façade overlooking the Rio di Palazzo and completed the main courtyard by extending the arcades along the other two sides.

The Scala d'Oro and the Doge's Apartments

From ground level the traffic is directed up the Scala dei Censori to the upper arcade and thence up Sansovino's gilded **Scala d'Oro**, the main internal staircase of the Palazzo Ducale, with its stuccoes by Vittoria (c.1558). A subsidiary staircase on the right leads to the **Doge's Apartments**, in which the head of the republic was obliged to live after his election (and which he was also obliged to furnish). All the furniture and much of the decoration have been stripped from this floor, but some of the rooms have ornate ceilings and fireplaces, several of which were installed when the Lombardo family were in charge of rebuilding this part of the palace. The first room, the **Sala degli Scarlatti**, is one of the finest. Probably named after the scarlet robes of the officers who attended the corpse of the doge as it lay in state in the adjacent Sala dello Scudo (they wore red rather than funereal black to signify that the death of an individual doge did not diminish the government), it has a fireplace by **Antonio and Tullio Lombardo**, a bas-relief by **Pietro Lombardo** over the door and a gilded ceiling from 1505. Also displayed here is a heavily restored *Madonna and Child with St John*, by Carpaccio. The **Sala dello Scudo**, the largest room of the apartments, is where the doge would receive those to whom he had granted a private audience. The fire of 1483 reduced to ashes the maps that had been painted on the walls, depicting the extent of Venice's domains and the lands visited by the Polo family. Replacements were soon created and were later augmented; the ones you see now date from 1762, and similarly celebrate the explorations of great Venetians and the wide reach of the city's control.

The **Sala Grimani**, which marks the beginning of the doge's private accommodation, now houses four large paintings of the Lion of St Mark, including the most famous such image, the one by Carpaccio, in which the heraldic lion stands on an imaginary wild island in the lagoon, with the Palazzo Ducale behind him. Next door, the **Sala Erizzo** has another vast fireplace and is decorated with gold and scarlet wall hangings of the sort that would once have adorned many of the building's rooms. Beyond here lies a stucco-laden room from which the doge could enter the patriarchal palace (the door remains but the connecting passageway has gone), which in turn connects with the **Sala dei Filosofi**, a corridor-like extension of the Sala dello Scudo. On one side of this long room a doorway opens onto a staircase; above the door, on the stair side, hides **Titian**'s *St Christopher*, a fresco in which the artist conflates the Venice cityscape with the mountains of his native Cadore. On the other side of the corridor, the final sequence of rooms contains a picture showing the mayhem of the annual Ponte dei Pugni brawls (see p.110) and a poor Giovanni Bellini (*Dead Christ*), and culminates with the **Sala dei Scudieri**, the room through which the doge's visitors would have entered his apartments.

The Atrio Quadrato and Sala delle Quattro Porte

The Scala d'Oro continues up to the **secondo piano nobile**, ending in the **Atrio Quadrato**, which has a ceiling painting of *Justice* by Tintoretto. This small anteroom opens into the first of the great public spaces, the **Sala delle Quattro Porte**. Before 1574 this room was the meeting place of the Collegio (see below), but in that year a fire gutted this portion of the building, necessitating a major programme of reorganization and decoration. (Three years later an even worse blaze destroyed the hall of the Maggior Consiglio and other rooms around it – this is why the Palazzo Ducale contains so few paintings that predate the 1570s.) After the repairs the Sala delle Quattro Porte was where ambassadors awaited their summons to address the doge and his councillors. **Tintoretto**'s ceiling frescoes, most of which are allegories of the Veneto cities subservient to the Republic, are in a generally dilapidated condition. The painting opposite the entrance is a reasonably accurate record of the show put on to welcome Henry III of France when he arrived in the city a few weeks before the fire of 1574 – by all accounts the young king never quite got over this week of overwhelming Venetian hospitality. The easel painting at the far end of the room – *Venus Receiving the Homage of Neptune* by **Giambattista Tiepolo** – can be seen at closer range when the itinerary doubles back through here.

The Sala dell'Anticollegio

As regards the quality of its decorations, the next room – the **Sala dell'Anticollegio** (the inner waiting room) – is one of the richest in the Palazzo Ducale. It has looked like this only since the early eighteenth century, though – after the 1574 fire it was decked out with tapestries and gilded leather, a Venetian speciality. Four pictures by **Tintoretto** hang on the door walls: *Vulcan's Forge*, *Mercury and the Graces*, *Bacchus and Ariadne* and *Minerva Dismissing Mars* (all c.1578); it almost goes without saying that these pictures were open to a propagandist reading – eg Ariadne = Venice, Bacchus = the Adriatic. Facing the window wall is **Veronese**'s characteristically benign *Rape of Europa* – "The brightest vision that ever descended upon the soul of a painter," sighed Henry James. The ensemble is completed by Jacopo Bassano's *Jacob's Return to Canaan*, and by Paolo Veronese's badly deteriorated ceiling fresco of *Venice Distributing Honours*.

The Sala del Collegio

Thoroughly humbled by now, the emissaries to Venice were ultimately admitted to the **Sala del Collegio**. Presiding over the Senate and deciding the agenda it would discuss, the full Collegio was the cabinet of Venetian politics, and consisted of the doge, six ducal councillors, the three heads of the judiciary, and sixteen *Savi* (senators with special responsibility for maritime, military and governmental affairs). The **Signoria**, Venice's highest executive body, was the inner council of this inner council, comprising the Collegio minus the *Savi*. In Ruskin's opinion, in no other part of the palace could you "enter so deeply into the heart of Venice" as in the Sala del Collegio – his observation referred not to the mechanics of Venetian power, however, but to the luscious cycle of ceiling paintings by **Veronese**.

Outstanding is *Venice Triumphant*, the central panel above the throne. Veronese also produced the picture on the wall over the throne – *Doge Sebastiano Venier Offering Thanks to Christ for the Victory of Lépanto*, in which, as is often the case in Venetian state-sponsored art, the Son of God is obliged to share top billing. Other doges get similarly immodest treatment in the adjoining paintings: *Doge Alvise Mocenigo Adoring Christ, Doge Niccolò da Ponte Invoking the Protection of the Virgin, The Mystic Marriage of St Catherine, with Doge Francesco Donato* (all by Tintoretto and his workshop) and, over the door to the Anticollegio, *Doge Andrea Gritti before the Virgin* (Tintoretto). For more on Doge Andrea Gritti, see p.175.

The Sala del Senato

The room next door – the **Sala del Senato** – was where most major policies, both domestic and foreign, were determined. It was also where the ambassadors of Venice delivered their reports on the countries in which they had served. These *relazioni* were essential to the formation of foreign policy, and a Venetian nobleman did his career prospects no harm by turning in a detailed document; few, however, equalled the conscientiousness of the sixteenth-century ambassador to France whose speech to the Senate kept them in their seats for two whole days. Originally comprising just sixty councillors (who were formally invited to take up office by the doge, hence the alternative name Sala dei Pregadi, from *pregati*, meaning "beseeched"), the Senate grew to contain almost three hundred officials under the doge's chairmanship, holding office for one year and elected by the Maggior Consiglio.

A motley collection of late sixteenth-century artists, Tintoretto and his pupils prominent among them, produced the mechanically bombastic decoration of the walls and ceiling. Tintoretto's personal touch is most evident in the picture above the throne: *Descent from the Cross, with doges Pietro Lando and Marcantonio Trevisan*. For sheer shamelessness, however, nothing can match the centrepiece of the ceiling, Tintoretto's *Venice Exalted Among the Gods*. (On rare occasions the doors to the side of the throne are open – they lead to the doge's chapel and its anteroom; only the marble *Virgin and Child* by Sansovino, in the former, is of interest.)

The Sala del Consiglio dei Dieci and Sala della Bussola

After recrossing the Sala delle Quattro Porte you enter the **Sala del Consiglio dei Dieci**, the room in which all matters relating to state security were discussed. The **Council of Ten** was established in 1310 in response to the revolt of disaffected nobles led by Bajamonte Tiepolo – and the secrecy and speed of its deliberations, and the fact that it allowed no defence counsel, soon made it the most feared of the Republic's institutions. Its members held office for one year and their number was supplemented by the doge and the ducal councillors – which meant, confusingly, that the Ten were never fewer than seventeen.

In the sixteenth century the Ten became even stronger, as an indirect result of the War of the League of Cambrai, when places on the Senate were given to an assortment of social climbers in reward for the loans they'd made for the war effort. The men of the *Case Grandi* (see p.60) retaliated by increasing the power of the bodies they could still control – the Collegio and the Ten. Only in the seventeenth century, when the power of the old families was fatally weakened by the sale of places on the Maggior Consiglio, did the Senate revert to being the nucleus of the Venetian state.

Of the paintings here, the finest are a couple of **Veronese** panels on the ceiling, painted at the age of 25 – *Juno Offering Gifts to Venice* and *Old Man in Oriental Costume with Young Woman*. The central panel is a copy of a Veronese original that was packed off to the Louvre by Napoleon's army and has never made it back.

The unfortunates who were summoned before the Ten had to await their grilling in the next room, the **Sala della Bussola**; in the wall is a *Bocca di Leone* (Lion's Mouth), one of the boxes into which citizens could drop denunciations for the attention of the Ten and other state bodies. Nobody could be convicted without corroborating evidence, and all anonymous accusations were rejected (or at least were technically illegal), but nonetheless the legend spread throughout Europe that one word to the Ten was tantamount to a death sentence. The door in the corner leads to the office of the Three Heads of the Council of Ten, which in turn leads to the State Inquisitors' room, then on to the torture chamber and finally the prisons – a doleful route that can be followed on the *Itinerari Segreti* (see p.68). As for the decoration, the last sentence of the previous paragraph applies.

The armoury and the Andito del Maggior Consiglio

From the landing, steps lead up to the **armoury**, consisting in part of weapons assembled for the defence of the Palazzo Ducale, and in part of specially commissioned pieces and gifts from foreign rulers. Amid the horrifying but sometimes exquisitely manufactured metalwork you'll find immense two-handed swords, an ancient twenty-barrelled gun, early sixteenth-century firearms that could also be used as swords, crossbows, maces or axes, and two outstanding pieces of armour: a unique sixteenth-century beaked helmet, and a suit of white armour given to Henry IV of France in 1603 (both in room 2). There's also a bust of Marcantonio Bragadin, whose gruesome demise has kept his name alive (for the story, see p.159), and one grotesque piece of non-military hardware – a pronged chastity-belt.

The **Scala dei Censori** takes you back to the second floor; here you go along the **Liagò** (or **Andito**) **del Maggior Consiglio** (Lobby of the Great Council), past the **Sala della Quarantia Civil Vecchia**, the seat of the civil court, and the **Sala del Guariento**, the old ammunition store, containing the remnants of a fourteenth-century fresco of *Paradise* by Guariento that used to be in Sala del Maggior Consiglio, where it was covered by Tintoretto's massive image of the same subject. The veranda at the end now houses the sculptures by **Rizzo** and Bandini from the Arco Fóscari; allegedly, the Duke of Mantua offered to buy Rizzo's *Eve* for her weight in gold, but for once the Venetians found it within themselves to resist the lure of huge sums of money.

The Sala del Maggior Consiglio

Now comes the stupendous **Sala del Maggior Consiglio**, the assembly hall of all the Venetian patricians eligible to participate in the running of the city.

By the mid-sixteenth century 2500 men were entitled to sit here, but frequently as few as half that number were present. This was the forum of the so-called *giovani*, the younger men on the bottom rung, and it was here that the voice of the populace filtered into the system. Technically, the Maggior Consiglio had little direct impact on government as it voted directly only on administrative legislation, and for much of the time the *giovani* kept fairly quiet in order to stay on the right side of the power-brokers. But if the bosses did something that alienated the majority of the underlings, the Maggior Consiglio was able to make things awkward, because the electoral process for nearly all state officials, including the doge, began here. Its last political act was on May 12, 1797, when it put an end to Venice's independence by voting to accept Napoleon's constitution.

The disastrous fire of December 1577 destroyed the paintings by Bellini, Titian, Carpaccio, Veronese and others that had lined this room; most of the replacements have the sole merit of covering a lot of space. There are, of course, notable exceptions. The immense *Paradiso*, begun by **Tintoretto** at the age of 77 and completed by his son Domenico, is an amazing feat of pictorial organization and a perfect work for its setting; the cast of five hundred figures is arrayed in the ranks ordained by Dante in Canto XXX of his *Paradiso*. Two of the **ceiling panels** are well worth a crick in the neck – *The Apotheosis of Venice*, a late work by Veronese (large oval above tribune), and *Venice Welcoming the Conquered Nations* by Palma il Giovane (large oval at opposite end).

Tintoretto was commissioned to replace the room's **frieze of portraits** of the first 76 doges (the series continues in the Sala dello Scrutinio), but in the event his son (with assistants) did the work. On the Piazzetta side the sequence is interrupted by a painted black veil, marking the place where **Marin Falier** (see p.151) would have been honoured had he not conspired against the state in 1355 and (as the inscription on the veil says) been beheaded for his crime. After two years spent in Venice, Byron wrote that Falier's black veil was for him the city's most memorable image.

Falier remains the most celebrated of Venice's errant leaders, but he is far from being alone in the ranks of the disgraced – by the end of the twelfth century about half the doges had been killed, exiled or simply run out of office. Nor is he the only eminent Venetian to be posthumously vilified in such a manner: for instance, under the arcade of the Palazzo Ducale you'll find a plaque perpetuating the dishonour of Girolamo Loredan and Giovanni Contarini, exiled for abandoning a fort to the Turks. In the Venetian Republic, where staunch service to the state was regarded as a duty, the backsliders were the ones singled out for special treatment, and the city is almost devoid of public monuments to its great statesmen.

The Sala della Quarantia Civil Nuova and Sala dello Scrutinio

The door at the far end (often closed) gives access to the **Sala della Quarantia Civil Nuova**, where civil cases involving Venetian citizens outside the city were heard; it retains some rare examples of Venetian gilt leatherwork (downstairs you'll see another room decorated with it), though nothing really grabs the attention. The adjacent **Sala dello Scrutinio** is where votes by the Maggior Consiglio were counted and certain electoral committees met. The system for **electing the doge** was the most complex of these procedures. In a nutshell: 30 men were selected by lot from the Maggior Consiglio; they reduced themselves by lot to 9 members; these 9 elected 40, who reduced themselves to 12, who elected 25, who reduced themselves to 9, who elected 45, who reduced themselves to 11, who elected 41, who finally elected the doge – 25 votes was

The Itinerari Segreti

If you want to see the rooms in which the day-to-day administration of Venice took place, take the **Itinerari Segreti del Palazzo Ducale**, a fascinating 75-minute guided tour through the warren of offices and passageways that interlocks with the public rooms of the building. (Tours in English daily at 9.55am, 10.45am [except July & Aug] & 11.35am; €16, or €10 with Venice Card/Museum Card; full-price ticket includes entry to rest of palace. Tickets can be booked up to 48hr in advance on ☎041.520.9070; for visits on the next or same day go in person to Palazzo Ducale ticket desk to check availability.)

The myriad councils and committees of Venice required a vast civil service, which was staffed by men drawn from the social class immediately below the patriciate – the *cittadini originarii*. (To be accepted into this class of full citizens one had to have lived in Venice for 25 years and never engaged in manual labour.) Roaming through the shadow-palace in which these functionaries carried out their duties, you begin to understand why, for all the Palazzo Ducale's extravagant show of democratic rectitude, the Venetian Republic aroused in many people the sort of dread a police state inspires.

The tour begins with the chambers of the **Chancellery**, the tiny rooms in which all acts of state were drafted and tabulated, then passes through the eighteenth-century Hall of the Chancellery, lined with cabinets for filing state documents. From here it's onward into the belly of the beast, through the judiciary's suites and into a high-ceilinged den where a rope hangs between two tiny wooden cells – the idea being that their two occupants, hearing the screams of the suspended victim, would need no further encouragement to talk. Paintings by Veronese and Tintoretto provide a civilizing gloss in the **Sala dei Tre Capi** – for the Heads of the Council of Ten – and the **Sala degli Inquisitori** – for the officers who investigated charges of treason.

After these, you're led up into the roof to see the timber-lined **Piombi**. By the standards of the day they are not too grim, but the climate up here could be unbearable, and there's a typically Venetian touch of refined malevolence – the doors have a superfluity of locks, just so that the noise of turning keys and slamming bolts would impress upon the inmate the finality of his incarceration. A few recalcitrant cases were not deterred – you're shown the cell from which Casanova escaped in 1775, with the assistance of a fellow prisoner called Father Balbi. (Displaying typical *sangfroid*, Casanova made his way to the Scala d'Oro, where the doors were unlocked for him by a guard who mistook him for a civil servant, then stopped on the Piazza for a coffee before heading for the border.) Under the rafters there's a museum of Venetian history that deserves more time than is allotted for it, but you do have time to be stunned by the views from the portholes in the roof. And if you wondered, when you were in the Sala del Maggior Consiglio, how that vast ceiling stays up with no visible means of support, all is revealed near the end.

the winning number. This rigmarole could last quite a while, you might think, and you'd be right – it took a minimum of five days, and in the record-breaking 1615 election the last stage alone went to 104 ballots and lasted 24 days. And what might appear to have been an intricately democratic machinery was in fact extremely undemocratic, because only those with a lot of friends and hangers-on could expect to be nominated to the decisive committees.

Perhaps to ensure that the electoral colleges kept their minds on the job, the decoration of the room is stunningly dreary; among the celebrations of great moments in Venetian military history there is just one decent picture – *The Conquest of Zara*, a late **Tintoretto** painting (first on right). The frieze of the last 42 doges was begun by assistants of Tintoretto and continued by contemporaries of each of the doges.

The prisons and beyond

Sometimes visits are directed down the staircase from the Sala dello Scrutinio, but more often the route backtracks through the Sala del Maggior Consiglio and then goes into the **Quarantia Criminale**, the office of the appeal court. This is followed by the **Magistrato alle Leggi**, in which three works by **Hieronymus Bosch** are displayed: *Heaven and Hell*, the *Triptych of the Hermits* and the *Martyrdom of St Liberata*. They were left to the Palazzo Ducale in the will of Cardinal Domenico Grimani, a connoisseur whose art collection also provided the foundations of the city's archeological museum.

The Scala dei Censori descends from here to the **Ponte dei Sospiri** (Bridge of Sighs) and the **Prigioni Nuove** (New Prisons). The bridge was built in 1600 by Antonio Contino, and takes its popular name from the sighs of the prisoners who shuffled through its corridor. In reality, though, anyone passing this way had been let off pretty lightly, and would soon be at liberty again. Before the construction of these cells in the early seventeenth century, prisoners were kept either in the sweltering **Piombi** (the Leads), under the roof of the Palazzo Ducale, or in the damp, stygian gloom of the **Pozzi** (the Wells) in the bottom two storeys. This new block, which was in use until 1919, was occupied mainly by petty criminals, whose graffiti still adorns the walls. Political prisoners were still incarcerated in the *Piombi*, and a few hard cases went to the *Pozzi*.

One room of the Prigioni Nuove contains a very miscellaneous display of pottery fragments, zoological debris unearthed in the Piazza, and objects relating to the prisons, such as old shoes and toilet-buckets. From here a staircase descends to the prison courtyard, overlooked by the heavily barred windows of the *Pozzi*. You now have to double back, and after recrossing the bridge you pass through the offices of the **Censori**, a two-man institution set up in 1517 to maintain standards of political behaviour at a time when corruption was getting out of hand. After this comes the **Avogaria**, which was occupied by the officers who prepared documents for the courts from the sixteenth century onwards, and maintained the records of patrician marriages. Marriage certificates were filed in the adjoining **Sala dello Scrigno**, which connects with the office of the **Milizia da Mar**, the functionaries who from 1541 were put in charge of naval recruitment. Leaving this room you emerge at the bookshop, from where you can either go on into the cafeteria, or step outside to the top of the Scala dei Giganti, from where the exit signs take you past the original statue of St Theodore and his dragon from the Piazzetta.

The Campanile and the Clock Tower

The **Campanile** (daily: Easter–June & Oct 9am–7pm; July–Sept 9am–9pm; Nov–Easter 9am–3.45pm; usually closed for 20 days after Christmas; €8) began life as a combined lighthouse and belltower in the early tenth century, when what's now the Piazzetta was the city's harbour. Modifications were made continually up to 1515, the year in which Bartolomeo Bon the Younger's rebuilding was rounded off with the positioning of a golden angel on the summit. Each of its five bells had a distinct function: the *Marangona*, the largest, tolled the beginning and end of the working day; the *Trottiera* was a signal for members of the Maggior Consiglio to hurry to the council chamber; the *Nona* rang midday; the *Mezza Terza* announced a session of the Senate; and the smallest, the *Renghiera* or *Maleficio*, gave notice of an execution.

▲ The Campanile di San Marco

The Campanile played another part in the Venetian penal system – "persons of scandalous behaviour" ran the risk of being subjected to the *Supplizio della Cheba* (Torture of the Cage), which involved being stuck in a crate which was then hoisted up the south face of the tower; if you were lucky you'd get away with a few days swinging in the breeze, but in some cases the view from the Campanile was the last thing the sinner ever saw. A more cheerful diversion was provided by the *Volo dell'Anzolo* or *del Turco* (Flight of the Angel or Turk), a stunt performed each year at the end of the Carnevale, in which an intrepid volunteer from the Arsenale would slide on a rope from the top of the Campanile to the first-floor loggia of the Palazzo Ducale, there to present a bouquet to the doge.

But the Campanile's most dramatic contribution to the history of the city was made on July 14, 1902, the day on which, at 9.52am, the tower succumbed to the weaknesses caused by recent structural changes, and fell down. (At some postcard stalls you can buy faked photos of the very instant of disaster.) The collapse was anticipated and the area cleared, so there were no human casualties; the only life lost was that of a cat named Mélampyge (after Casanova's dog). What's more, the bricks fell so neatly that San Marco was barely scratched and the Libreria lost just its end wall. The town councillors decided that evening that the Campanile should be rebuilt "dov'era e com'era" (where it was and how it was), and a decade later, on St Mark's Day 1912, the new tower was opened, in all but minor details a replica of the original.

At 99m, the Campanile is the tallest structure in the city, and from the top you can make out virtually every building, but not a single canal – which is almost as surprising as the view of the Dolomites, which on clear days seem to rise in Venice's back yard. Among the many who have marvelled at the panorama were Galileo, who demonstrated his telescope from here; Goethe, who had never before seen the sea; and the Emperor Frederick III, whose climb to the top was achieved with a certain panache – he rode his horse up the tower's internal ramp. The ready access granted to the tourist is a modern privilege: the Venetian state used to permit foreigners to ascend only at high tide, when they would be unable to see the elusive channels through the lagoon, which were crucial to the city's defences.

The collapse of the Campanile of course pulverized the **Loggetta** at its base, but somehow it was pieced together again, mainly using material retrieved from the wreckage. **Sansovino**'s design was for a building that would completely enclose the foot of the Campanile, but only one quarter of the plan was executed (in 1537–49). Intended as a meeting place for the city's nobility, it was soon converted into a guardhouse for the *Arsenalotti* (workers from the Arsenale) who patrolled the area when the Maggior Consiglio was sitting, and in the last years of the Republic served as the room in which the state lottery was drawn. The bronze figures in niches are also by Sansovino (*Pallas*, *Apollo*, *Mercury* and *Peace*), as is the terracotta group inside (although the figure of St John is a modern facsimile); the three marble reliefs on the attic are, as ever, allegories of the power and beneficence of the *Serenissima* (the Most Serene Republic): *Justice* = Venice, *Jupiter* = Crete, *Venus* = Cyprus.

The Torre dell'Orologio and Piazzetta dei Leoncini

The other tower in the Piazza, the **Torre dell'Orologio** (Clock Tower), was built between 1496 and 1506, the central portion being by **Mauro Codussi** and the wings possibly by Pietro Lombardo. (The three ornate **flagstaff bases** between the Campanile and the Torre were made at the same time by **Leopardi**, the sculptor who finished the Colleoni monument.) A gruesome popular tale relates that the makers of the clock's elaborate mechanism, Gian Paolo and his son Gian Carlo Rainieri, slaved away for three years at their project, only to have their eyes put out so that they couldn't repeat their engineering marvel for any other patrons. In fact the grateful Venetians gave the pair a generous pension and installed Gian Carlo in an apartment in the tower, so that he could keep the timepiece in perfect condition – presumably too dull an outcome for the city's folklorists.

The bell on the tower's roof terrace is struck by two bronze wild men known as "The Moors", because of their dark patina; they were cast in the Arsenale in 1497. If you're in Venice on Epiphany or during Ascension week, you'll witness the clock's star turn – on the hour the Magi, led by an angel, troop out and bow to the figure of the Madonna.

The Bicentenary Siege

Now Italy's wealthiest region, the Veneto is fertile territory for separatist ideologues. It is no coincidence that Umberto Bossi, leader of the virulently anti-immigrant **Lega Nord**, chose Venice as the place in which to announce the birth of the Republic of Padania, his notional independent nation of the north, whose citizens he will one day liberate from the iniquitous taxes they have to pay to support the backward south. In 1997 the rabble-rousing rhetoric of Bossi and his ilk was translated into action, in an incident that was both farcical and frightening.

Shortly after midnight on May 9, just three days short of the two-hundredth anniversary of the fall of the Venetian Republic, a camper van and an armour-plated lorry were driven onto the last ferry from Tronchetto to the Lido. Eight men piled out of the vehicles and **hijacked the boat**, forcing the pilot at gunpoint to take them to the quayside at San Marco. Once the ferry had docked, the gang drove across the Piazzetta, smashed the gates of the Campanile by ramming them with their customized armoured transport and ascended the tower, having barricaded the entrance with the camper van. At the summit they unfurled a flag bearing the Lion of St Mark and broadcast a message to the people of Venice, declaring themselves to be the soldiers of the Most Serene Venetian Government. Prepared for a lengthy siege, the guerrillas had brought with them a sub-machine-gun, a bottle of grappa, and a few sets of crisply laundered underwear. In the event, they were evicted at 8.30am, when a squad of *carabinieri* scaled the Campanile, using enormous extending ladders. Not a shot was fired, but a policeman did report that one of the self-styled soldiers swore at him in Venetian dialect.

The episode was widely ridiculed – Bossi's second-in-command, Roberto Maroni, described the gang as a group of nutcases who had turned up two months late for Carnevale. But nobody in Venice doubted that the Campanile siege was indicative of a deep and widespread feeling of discontent in the Veneto, and that more serious trouble might well arise in the region if the government fails to reform the country's constitution in a way that appeases the north's wealth creators. The Veneto remains a Lega Nord stronghold – in the 2008 general election it won almost thirty percent of the vote in this region.

Almost completely replaced in the 1750s, the clock's mechanism has been frequently overhauled since – most recently (and controversially) during a decade-long restoration of the whole tower, which was finished in 2006. You can now take an hour-long guided tour of the interior, which stops on each of the five floors to explicate the history and the workings of this complex machine (daily 9am–3.30pm; tours in English Mon–Wed 10am & 11am, Thurs–Sun 1, 2 & 3pm; €12 ticket includes admission to the Correr museum, and must be pre-booked, either on ☎041.520.9070 or at ⊛www.museiciviciveneziani.it).

To your right as you face the Torre is the **Piazzetta Giovanni XXIII**, familiarly known as **dei Leoncini**, after the two eighteenth-century marble lions – if you can't see them immediately, it's because they're smothered in children. Facing San Marco's flank is **San Basso**, a deconsecrated church now used for exhibitions, and at the far end is the **Palazzo Patriarcale**, which was rebuilt in the nineteenth century after it became the home of the Patriarch of Venice, who had previously been based over in San Pietro di Castello. The Palazzo retains the splendid banqueting hall in which the doge used to entertain official guests and, once a year, the Arsenalotti (it can be seen on a €10 guided tour of the palazzo, every Fri at 3, 4 and 5pm; reservations on ☎041.241.3817); a corridor, now demolished, ran from the hall, through San Marco and into the Palazzo Ducale.

The Procuratie

Away to the left, from the Torre dell'Orologio, stretches the **Procuratie Vecchie**, once the home of the **Procurators of San Marco**, whose responsibilities included the upkeep of San Marco and the administration of the other government-owned properties. Never numbering more than nine, the procurators were second in position only to the doge, who himself was generally drawn from their ranks. With the doge and the Grand Chancellor – the head of the civil service – they shared the distinction of being the only state officials elected for life.

From the time of Doge Ziani, the procurators and their attendant bureaucracies were installed on this side of the Piazza, but the present building was begun around 1500 by **Codussi**, continued after a fire in 1512 by **Bartolomeo Bon the Younger** and completed around 1532 by **Sansovino**. Much of the block earned rents for the city coffers, the upper floors housing some of the choicest apartments in town and the ground floor being leased to shopkeepers and craftsmen.

Within a century or so, the procurators were moved across the Piazza to new premises. Sansovino, who had only recently completed the old offices, proposed a development that involved knocking down a pilgrims' hospice, along with the unsightly shacks around it. The **Procuratie Nuove** were eventually built between 1582 and 1640, first to designs by **Scamozzi**, and then under Longhena's control. Napoleon's stepson Eugène Beauharnais, the Viceroy of Italy, appropriated the quarters for use as a royal palace, and then discovered that the accommodation lacked a ballroom. His solution had the true, gossamer-light Napoleonic touch to it: he demolished Sansovino's church of San Geminiano and used the vacated space to connect the Procuratie Nuove and Vecchie with a wing containing the essential facility. Generally known as the **Ala Napoleonica**, the building is topped by a gallery of Roman emperors – no prizes for guessing whose effigy was meant to fill the gap in the middle.

The Correr and archeological museums

Many of the rooms in the Ala Napoleonica and Procuratie Nuove have been occupied since 1923 by the **Museo Correr** (daily: April–Oct 9am–7pm; Nov–March 9am–5pm; entrance with Museum Card/Venice Card), the chief civic museum of Venice. In an attempt to siphon tourists into this neglected museum, the authorities have combined the Correr's entry ticket with that for the Palazzo Ducale, and have made the archeological museum and Sansovino's library accessible only through the Correr. The strategy has had only limited success, for the Correr is generally given the whistle-stop treatment by sightseers who just want to feel that they've got their money's worth. Nobody could make out that this immense collection is consistently fascinating, but it incorporates a picture gallery that more than makes up for the duller stretches, and its sections on Venetian society contain some eye-opening exhibits.

The first floor starts off with a gallery of Homeric reliefs by **Canova**, whose self-portrait stands nearby. In the small room at the end of the gallery, beyond the marble bowls of fruit that the young Canova made as a bravura exercise in stone carving, are displayed his model for the tomb of Titian (which became his own tomb – see p.131), and his figure of *Paris*. Sculpted in gypsum, the latter was in effect Canova's final draft before moving on to the marble: the pins that cover the hero's skin were placed there to enable his assistants to map the coordinates on the block of marble. (Canova's working methods are fully revealed at his birthplace museum in Possagno – see p.351.) The next room, the Throne Room, contains Canova's *Daedalus and Icarus*, the group that made his name at the age of 21; in the adjacent Dining Room you'll find his faux-modest *Venus Italica* and some of the rough clay models he created as first drafts for his classically poised sculptures. After that you're into the **historical collection**, which might be enlightening if your Italian is good and you already have a pretty wide knowledge of Venetian history. A beautiful reconstructed seventeenth-century library is followed by rooms devoted to ducal edicts, Venetian elections, coinage, ceremonials, bureaucracy and the Arsenale. After that you pass through an armoury (look out for a key that fired poisoned darts) and a celebration of Doge Francesco Morosini's exploits in the Morea, and then comes an exhibition of small bronze sculptures from Padua and Venice, featuring tabletop gods, nymphs and suchlike by Vittoria, Campagna and Roccatagliata.

The Museo Archeologico

From here you can pass into the **Museo Archeologico**, which – along with the **Libreria Sansoviniana** – can also be visited independently, via the entrance at no. 17 on the Piazzetta (daily 8.15–10am & 5–7pm; €4). The core of the museum is formed by Greek and Roman sculptures that were bequeathed by members of the Grimani family: Cardinal Domenico Grimani became the first major collector to endow a civic museum when he left his finest specimens to the city in 1523; his nephew Giovanni Grimani, who had inherited the rest of the cardinal's pieces and added to them over the years, left everything to the state in 1587, a donation so substantial that Scamozzi was commissioned to turn the vestibule of Sansovino's library into a public gallery for its display. Augmented by various other gifts over the intervening centuries, the Museo Archeologico is a somewhat scrappy museum, with cases of Roman coins and gems, fragments of sarcophagi and inscriptions, miscellaneous headless statues and bodiless heads interspersed with the odd Bronze Age, Egyptian or Assyrian relic, generally presented in a manner that isn't very inspiring. Yet the drearier exhibits are punctuated by some interesting pieces from the Grimani collections, with the bulk of the finest items being concentrated towards the end of the itinerary: look out for an assertive head of Athena from the fourth century BC, a trio of wounded Gallic warriors (Roman copies of Hellenistic originals) and busts of a phalanx of Roman emperors, including Domitian, Vitellius, Hadrian, Trajan, Tiberius, Marcus Aurelius, Septimius Severus and the demented Caracalla.

At the furthest point of the archeological museum a door opens into the hall of Sansovino's library, which is covered on p.77.

The Quadreria and the rest of the Correr

Back in the Correr, a staircase beyond the sculpture section leads to the **Quadreria**, which may be no rival for the Accademia's collection but nonetheless sets out clearly the evolution of painting in Venice from the thirteenth century to around 1500, and does contain some gems, as well as **Jacopo de'Barbari**'s astonishing aerial view of Venice, engraved in 1500. A print of de'Barbari's masterpiece is displayed alongside the original wooden blocks, a dumbfoundingly accurate mirror-image of the city.

In the early rooms the outstanding Venetian figure is **Paolo Veneziano**, who in the second half of the fourteenth century began to blend the city's Byzantine pictorial conventions with the more supple styles of Padua, Bologna and other mainland centres. The influence of other artistic schools – especially those of the Low Countries, a region with strong mercantile links to Venice – is a dominant theme in the succeeding rooms, where there are remarkable pieces by **Cosmè Tura** (an angular *Pietà*) and **Antonello da Messina** (a defaced but nonetheless powerful *Pietà*), the latter artist being a conduit through which the compositional techniques of the Tuscan Renaissance came to Venice. The delicate colouring and stillness of Flemish painting are central to the cultural genealogy of the **Bellini** family, to whom the Correr devotes a whole room, featuring a *Crucifixion* that's probably by Jacopo and a few pictures that are definitely by his sons: Gentile's touching portrait of Doge Giovanni Mocenigo, and Giovanni's *Transfiguration, Madonna and Child, Crucifixion* and *Christ Supported by Angels* (the last sporting a fake Dürer monogram, which once fooled the experts).

After the Bellini section you'll pass Alvise Vivarini's portrait of a fine-boned Saint Anthony of Padua, before coming to the museum's best-known possession, the **Carpaccio** painting once known as *The Courtesans*, but which in fact depicts a couple of late fifteenth-century bourgeois ladies at ease, dressed in a style at which none of their contemporaries would have raised an eyebrow. Originally it illustrated both men and women at leisure, but the top half of the picture – showing young men hunting – was at some point sawn off, and is now owned by the Getty museum. The younger woman's pearl necklace identifies her as a bride, while the plants that flank her – lilies and myrtle – are symbols of purity within marriage. The perilous platform shoes (*ciapine* or *pianelle*), placed beside the balustrade, served a twin function: they kept the silks and satins out of the mud, and they enabled the wearer to circumvent the sumptuary laws, which attempted to limit the volume of expensive materials used in dresses by forbidding trailing hems. (In 1514, about fifteen years after this picture was painted, a permanent government department – the Magistrato alle Pompe – was set up solely to enforce the numerous regulations against extravagant private display; most of the upper crust just paid the fines and went on spending.) It's also been argued that *ciapine* might be seen as proto-feminist footwear: one Luciano Bursati, writing in 1621, accused Venetian women of using *ciapine* "to make themselves equal and even superior in stature to men".

In the room beyond there's another much-reproduced image, the *Portrait of a Young Man in a Red Hat*, once attributed to Carpaccio, now given to an anonymous painter from Ferrara or Bologna. A roomful of fine ivory carvings comes next, then a cubicle of pictures from Venice's community of **Greek artists**, some of whom continued to paint in pre-Renaissance style well into the seventeenth century; this immensely conservative community was the nursery of the painter who later became known as El Greco – there's a picture by him here which you'd walk straight past if it weren't for the label. At room 42 the Quadreria turns into a display of Renaissance ceramics, most of them hideous to modern eyes; beyond it lies the last section on this floor, the library from the Palazzo Manin, which contains **Alessandro Vittoria**'s bust of Tomasso Rangone – his full-length portrait of the same subject is on the facade of the nearby church of San Zulian.

From the Quadreria you're directed to the **Museo del Risorgimento**, which resumes the history of the city with its fall to Napoleon, and takes it through to the career of Daniele Manin, the anti-Austrian revolt of 1848 and the eventual birth of a united Italy. Although there are some mildly amusing contemporary cartoons on display, and some strange memorabilia (a bottle in the form of Garibaldi's head; portraits of Risorgimento heroes painted on tiny buttons), extensive prior knowledge is again immensely helpful.

Back downstairs, the itinerary passes through a section on Venetian festivals and then a fascinating sequence devoted to Venetian crafts, trades and everyday life, where the frivolous items are what catch the eye, especially a pair of eighteen-inch *ciapine* (as worn by the women in the Carpaccio painting), and an eighteenth-century portable hair-care kit that's the size of a suitcase. After a miscellany of restored stonework you'll encounter various exhibits relating to Venetian games and sports, with some remarkable prints of the alarming displays of strength known as the Labours of Hercules (see p.45) and some early jigsaws. Finally you're steered down a corridor containing **Canova**'s reliefs of scenes from the life of Socrates and his immense bust of Pope Clement XIII (the Rezzonico pope – see p.111), and then into the beautiful mirrored ballroom, where again Canova takes pride of place: the floor is left to his *Orpheus and Eurydice*, created in 1777, when the sculptor was still in his teens.

The Piazzetta and the Molo

For much of the Republic's existence, the **Piazzetta** – the open space between San Marco and the waterfront – was the area where the councillors of Venice would gather to scheme and curry favour. Way back in the earliest days of the city, this patch of land was the garden – or *broglio* – of the San Zaccaria convent: this is the probable source of the English word "imbroglio". But as well as being a sort of open-air clubhouse for the city's movers and shakers, the Piazzetta played a crucial part in the penal system of Venice.

Those found guilty of serious crime by Venice's courts were often done away with in the privacy of their cells; for public executions the usual site was the pavement between the **two granite columns** on the **Molo**, as this stretch of the waterfront is called. Straightforward hanging or decapitation were the customary techniques, but refinements were available for certain offenders, such as the three traitors who, in 1405, were buried alive here, head down. The last person to be executed here was one Domenico Storti, condemned to death in 1752 for the murder of his brother. Superstitious Venetians avoid passing between the columns.

The columns should have a companion, but the third one fell off the barge on which they were being transported and has remained submerged somewhere off the Piazzetta since around 1170. The columns themselves were purloined from the Levant, whereas the figures perched on top are bizarre hybrids. The statue of **St Theodore** – the patron saint of Venice when it was dependent on Byzantium – is a modern copy; the original, now on show in a corner of one of the Palazzo Ducale's courtyards, was a compilation of a Roman torso, a head of Mithridates the Great (first century BC) and miscellaneous bits and pieces carved in Venice in the fourteenth century (the dragon included). The **winged lion** on the other column is an ancient 3000-kilo bronze beast that was converted into a lion of Saint Mark by jamming a Bible under its paws. When this was done is not clear, but the lion is documented as having been restored in Venice as far back as 1293. Of numerous later repairs the most drastic was in 1815, when its wings, paws, tail and back were recast, to rectify damage done by the French engineers who, in the course of arranging its return from Paris, broke it into twenty pieces. Scientific analysis for its most recent restoration revealed that the lion is composed of a patchwork of ancient metal plates, but its exact provenance

Monuments and Mammon – advertising on the Piazza

In 2009 the annual subsidy paid by central government for the **restoration** of Venice's crumbling buildings was cut by more than 25 percent. Shortly before this cut, a law was introduced that allowed the scaffolding on public structures under restoration to carry advertisements, as long as the superintendent (the council official in overall charge of such projects) considered that the adverts did not "detract from the appearance...or public enjoyment of the building". With most of the monuments of the Piazza in need of very expensive work, the consequence was inevitable: the Libreria Sansoviana and parts of the Palazzo Ducale have been turned into gigantic **billboards**, and the Correr museum will soon be going the same way. It's hard to see how anyone could argue that these colossal adverts don't detract from the appearance of the Piazza, but Mayor Massimo Cacciari says that the city has no other option. "It is neither ugly nor beautiful but simply necessary," he has said. "We need to take care of the buildings and monuments that make up the artistic beauty of Venice, but to do so we need a hand." Renata Codello, the Venice superintendent, makes the point that restoration is a matter of some urgency: "I have no choice: last year some of the marble facing of the Palazzo Ducale fell down; this year it was part of the cornice of the Correr museum. Under law I am personally responsible if a tourist is hurt." So, with exterior restoration projects scheduled to last until at least 2015, the mega-ads are going to be a feature of the Piazza for quite some time. And it could soon look a lot worse – there's talk of installing huge electronic billboards on the scaffolding.

remains a mystery – the currently favoured theory is that it was originally part of a Middle Eastern monument made around 300 BC.

The Libreria Sansoviniana

The Piazzetta is framed by two outstanding buildings – the Palazzo Ducale on one side and the **Libreria Sansoviniana** or **Biblioteca Marciana** on the other. **Sansovino**'s contemporaries regarded the Libreria as one of the supreme designs of the era: Palladio remarked that it was "perhaps the richest and most ornate building to be created since the times of ancient Greece and Rome". Venice had an opportunity to establish a state library in the fourteenth century, when Petrarch left his priceless collection to the city, but the beneficiaries somehow mislaid the legacy. In the end, the impetus to build the library came from the bequest of Cardinal Bessarion, who bequeathed his celebrated hoard of classical texts to the Republic in 1468. Bessarion's books and manuscripts were housed in San Marco and then the Palazzo Ducale, but finally it was decided that a special building was needed.

Sansovino got the job, and in 1537 the site was cleared of its hostels, slaughterhouse and bakery, thus turning the Campanile into a freestanding tower. Construction was well advanced when, in December 1545, the project suffered a major setback: frost got into the vaulted ceiling of the main hall and brought it crashing down. Charged with incompetence, Sansovino was thrown into prison, and it took some determined pleading by his cronies – Titian among them – to get him out. Upon being allowed back on the job he belatedly took notice of conventional wisdom, which argued that heavy stone vaults really weren't a terrific idea in a place where the land keeps shifting, and stuck a flat ceiling in its place, with a light wooden vault attached, to keep up appearances. The library was finished in 1591, two decades after Sansovino's death.

Entering the library from the archeological museum, you come straight into the **main hall**, one of the most beautiful rooms in the city. Paintings by **Veronese**, **Tintoretto**, **Andrea Schiavone** and others cover the walls and ceiling: five of the *Philosophers* are by Tintoretto, while the pair that flank the entrance door, and three of the ceiling medallions, are by Veronese, whose work in the library earned him a gold chain from the procurators in charge of the project, acting on Titian's recommendation. Special exhibitions of precious items from the library, such as the *Grimani Breviary* of 1500 or Fra' Mauro's 1459 map of the world, are sometimes held here; at other times, reproductions are on show. **Titian**'s *Allegory of Wisdom* occupies the central panel of the ceiling of the **anteroom**, which has been restored to the appearance it had from the end of the sixteenth century, when the Giovanni Grimani collection was first put on show here, until 1812, when Napoleon turned the library into an annexe to the viceroy's palace and shifted its contents over to the Palazzo Ducale. Beyond lies the intended approach to the library, a magnificent staircase encrusted with stuccowork by Vittoria.

The Zecca and the Giardinetti Reali

Attached to the Libreria, with its main facade to the lagoon, is Sansovino's first major building in Venice, the **Zecca** or Mint. Constructed in stone and iron to make it fireproof (most stonework in Venice is just skin-deep), it was built between 1537 and 1545 on the site occupied by the Mint since the thirteenth century, when it was moved from a factory near the Rialto bridge. Some of the finance for the project was raised on the Venetian colony of Cyprus, by selling the island's slaves their liberty. By the beginning of the fifteenth century the city's prosperity was such that the Venetian gold ducat was in use in every European exchange, and Doge Tommaso Mocenigo could look forward to the day when the city would be "the mistress of all the gold in Christendom". In later years the ducat became known as the *zecchino*, source of the word "sequin". The rooms of the Mint are now part of the library, but are not open to tourists.

Beyond the Zecca, and behind a barricade of postcard and toy gondola sellers, is a small public garden – the **Giardinetti Reali** – created by Eugène Beauharnais on the site of the state granaries as part of his improvement scheme for the Procuratie Nuove. It's the nearest place to the centre where you'll find a bench and the shade of a tree, but in summer it's about as peaceful as a school playground. The spruced-up building at the foot of the nearby bridge is the Casino da Caffè, another legacy of the Napoleonic era, now the city's main tourist office.

North of the Piazza

From the Piazza the bulk of the pedestrian traffic flows **north to the Rialto** along the **Mercerie**, the most aggressive shopping mall in Venice and the part of the city which comes closest to being devoid of magic. Apart from the church of **San Giuliano** – one of Venice's lesser eccentricities – only the stately **San Salvador** provides a diversion from the spotlights and price tags until you come to the **Campo San Bartolomeo**, the forecourt of the Rialto bridge and one of the locals' favoured spots for an after-work drink, along with the nearby **Campo San Luca**. Secreted in the folds of the alleyways are the old Armenian quarter and the spiralling **Scala del Bovolo** – featured on a thousand postcards, but actually seen by a minority of visitors. And slotted away in a tiny square

NORTH OF THE PIAZZA

0 100 m

N

S. Maria Formosa
CAMPO DI S. MARIA FORMOSA
Ospedale
Paradiso
Rio di S. Marina
Rio del Piombo
CAMPO DI S. MARINA
Rio del Remedio
Pal. Trevisan
Rio di Palazzo
Prigioni
Formosa
Rio di S. Maria
Rio della Guerra
Torre dell' Orologio
Basilica di San Marco
Campanile
PIAZZA SAN MARCO
S. Lio
S. Giuliano
SPADARIA
Fondaco di Tedeschi
S. Maria della Fava
Rio della Fava
S. Croce degli Armeni
Rio del Cappello
Bacino Orseolo
S. Bartolomeo
S. Salvador
Rio di San Salvador
CAMPO S. SALVADOR
R. d. Bacino Orseolo
Bacino Orseolo
MERCERIA
Rialto 1,2, N
Pal. d. Camerlenghi
Scuola di San Teodoro
CALLE DEL FABBRO
CALLE DEL FUSERI
Scala del Bovolo
S. Giacomo
RIALTO
Pal. Dieci Savi
Teatro Goldoni
CALLE DEI FUSERI
Rio del Barcaroli
Ateneo Veneto
CANAL GRANDE
Pal. Loredan (Municipio)
CAMPO S. LUCA
CALLE LOREDAN
Cassa d. Risparmio
CAMPO MANIN
S. Silvestro
S. Silvestro 1
Traghetto
Pal. Farsetti
S. Luca
Rio di S. Luca
Pal. Grimani
CALLE D. BALLOTTE
Museo Fortuny
Pal. Corner Contarini dei Cavalli
S. Benedetto
CAMPO S. ANGELO
Rio di S. Angelo
Rio di Cà Garzoni
Oratorio Annunziata

close to the Canal Grande you'll find the most delicate of Venice's museum buildings – the Palazzo Pésaro degli Orfei, home of the **Museo Fortuny**.

The Mercerie

The **Mercerie**, the chain of streets that starts under the Torre dell'Orologio and finishes at the Campo San Bartolomeo, is the most direct route between the Rialto and San Marco and thus, as the link between the city's political and commercial centres, was always a prime site for Venice's shopkeepers, a status it retains today. (Each of the five links in the chain is a *merceria*: Merceria dell'Orologio, di San Zulian, del Capitello, di San Salvador and 2 Aprile.) A wide-eyed inventory of the Mercerie in the sixteenth century noted "tapestry, brocades and hangings of every design, carpets of all sorts, camlets of every colour and texture, silks of every variety; and so many warehouses full of spices, groceries and drugs, and so much beautiful white wax!" Nowadays it's both slick and tacky: the empire of kitsch has a firm base here, sharing the territory with the likes of Prada, La Perla, Gucci, Furla, Cartier and Benetton (one of the Veneto's most successful companies). The mixture ensnares more window-shoppers and buyers than any other part of Venice, and even in the off-season a stroll along the Mercerie is akin to a slalom run. In summer things get so bad that the police often have to enforce a pedestrian one-way system.

For those immune to the charms of consumerism there are only a couple of things to stop for between the San Marco end of the Mercerie and the church of San Salvador. Over the Sottoportego del Cappello (first left after the Torre) is a relief known as **La Vecia del Morter** – the Old Woman of the Mortar. The event it commemorates happened on the night of June 15, 1310, when the occupant of this house, an old woman named Giustina Rossi, looked out of her window and saw a contingent of a rebel army, led by Bajamonte Tiepolo, passing below. Possibly by accident, she knocked a stone mortar from her sill, and the missile landed on the skull of the standard-bearer, killing him outright. Seeing their flag go down, Tiepolo's troops panicked and fled back towards the Rialto. (Scores of other rebels were killed in the Piazza; those ringleaders who survived the carnage were punished with execution or exile – Tiepolo, as a relative of the doge, was let off with banishment, but his house was razed to the ground.) Asked what she would like as her reward for her patriotic intervention, Giustina requested permission to hang the Venetian flag from her window on feast days, and a guarantee that her rent would never be raised; both requests were granted. From then on, until the fall of the Republic, June 15 was celebrated as a public holiday.

Further on is the church of **San Giuliano** or San Zulian (daily 8.30am–7pm), rebuilt in the mid-sixteenth century with the generous aid of the physician **Tommaso Rangone**. His munificence and intellectual brilliance (but not his Christian faith) are attested by the Greek and Hebrew inscriptions on the facade and by **Alessandro Vittoria**'s portrait statue above the door, for which Rangone paid almost as much as he paid for the church's stonework. (He originally wished to be commemorated by an effigy on the facade of his parish church, San Geminiano, which used to stand facing the Basilica, but the city's governors vetoed this excessively vainglorious proposal.) Inside, the central panel of the ceiling, *St Julian in Glory* by **Palma il Giovane** and assistants, is a cut above the usual slapdash standard of this over-prolific artist; over the first altar on the right is a late work by **Veronese** – *Pietà with SS. Roch, Jerome and Mark*; and in the chapel to the left of the chancel there are ceiling stuccoes by **Vittoria**, and three pieces by **Campagna** – terracotta figures of *The Virgin* and *The Magdalen*, and a marble altar panel (all from c.1583).

Obscure corners are to be discovered even in the vicinity of this main avenue. Very close to San Giuliano is the heart of the old **Armenian quarter**: take Merceria di San Zulian, which comes into the Campo San Zulian opposite the church, then cross the bridge into Calle Fiubera, and then take the first right – Calle degli Armeni. Under the sottoportego is the door to the best-hidden church in Venice, **Santa Croce degli Armeni**, which was founded as an oratory in 1496 and rebuilt as the community's church in 1688. Nowadays the congregation is small (the church has just one Mass each week, at 11am on Sunday) and the most visible Armenian community is the one on the island of San Lazzaro. For more on the Armenians in Venice, see p.226.

San Salvador and around

At its far end, the Mercerie veers right at the church of **San Salvador** or Salvatore (June–Aug Mon–Sat 9am–noon & 4–7pm, Sun 4–7pm; Sept–May Mon–Sat 9am–noon & 3–7.15pm, Sun 3–7.15pm) which was consecrated in 1177 by Pope Alexander III, on the occasion of his reconciliation with Emperor Barbarossa (see p.51). The facade, applied in 1663, is less interesting than the interior, which was begun around 1508 by Spavento and continued by Tullio Lombardo and Sansovino. It's cleverly designed in the form of three domed Greek crosses placed end to end, thus creating the longitudinal layout required by the religious orders while paying homage to the centrally planned churches of Byzantium and, of course, to the Basilica di San Marco. One major defect marred this elegant conceit, however – which was that it didn't let enough light into the church. Scamozzi rectified the situation in the 1560s by inserting a lantern into each of San Salvador's domes.

In the middle of the right-hand wall stands the **tomb of Doge Francesco Venier**, designed by Sansovino, who also sculpted the figures of *Charity* and *Hope*; these were possibly his last sculptures. To the left of it hangs **Titian's** *Annunciation* (1566), signed *"Fecit, fecit"*, supposedly to emphasize the wonder of his continued creativity in extreme old age; its cumbersome angel is often held to be the responsibility of assistants. A scrap of paper on the rail in front of the picture records the death of the artist on August 25, 1576. The end of the right transept is filled by the **tomb of Caterina Cornaro** (see p.354), one of the saddest figures in Venetian history. Born into one of Venice's pre-eminent families, she became Queen of Cyprus by marriage, and after her husband's death was forced to surrender the strategically crucial island to the doge. On her return to Venice she was led in triumph up the Canal Grande, as though her abdication had been entirely voluntary, and then was presented with possession of the town of Ásolo as a token of the city's gratitude. She died in 1510 and was given a heroine's funeral in the Apostoli church; her body was removed to San Salvador, and this tomb erected, at the end of the century.

The **altarpiece**, a *Transfiguration* by **Titian** (c.1560), covers a fourteenth-century silver reredos that is exposed to view at Easter. In front of the main altar, a glass disc set into the pavement allows you to see a recently unearthed merchant's tomb, with badly damaged decoration by Titian's brother Francesco, who also painted the doors of the church organ (on the left side of the church) and frescoed a delightful fantasy of bird-filled vegetation high on the walls of the sacristy (the sacristan will let you in, and probably expect a donation). The lustrous *Supper at Emmaus* to the left of the altar is probably from the workshop of Giovanni Bellini, and the third altar of the left aisle (the altar of the sausage-makers' guild) was designed by Vittoria, who sculpted its figures of *St Roch* and *St Sebastian*.

Next door to the church, the beautifully restored **cloisters** (attributed to Sansovino) now house the **Telecom Italia Future Centre** (Tues–Sun 10am–6pm; free), which is essentially a showcase for the cutting-edge technologies of the Italian phone company.

Overlooking the campo is the home of the last of the major scuole to be established (see p.132), the **Scuola di San Teodoro**, which was founded in 1530; the facade was designed in 1655 by Sardi, the architect responsible for the front of San Salvatore. It's now a general-purpose exhibition hall, but the shows hardly ever live up to their setting. The column in the centre of the campo is a memorial to the 1848–49 revolt against the Austrians, and was placed here on the fiftieth anniversary of the insurrection.

Campo San Bartolomeo

Campo San Bartolomeo, terminus of the Mercerie, is at its best in the evening, when it's as packed as any bar in town. To show off their new wardrobes the Venetians take themselves off to the Piazza, but Campo San Bartolomeo is one of the favoured spots to just meet friends and talk. Access to the **church of San Bartolomeo** (Tues, Thurs & Sat 10am–noon) is limited because it's in effect become the property of the musicians who use the building for their recitals, as is the case at the Pietà. For the foreseeable future, anyway, its best paintings – organ panels by Sebastiano del Piombo – will remain in the Accademia; its most famous picture, the altarpiece painted by Dürer in 1505 at the request of the German merchant Christopher Fugger, long ago migrated to Prague. In the sixteenth century this area would have been swarming with men like Dürer's patron, because the base for the German traders was the **Fondaco dei Tedeschi**, now the main post office, at the far end of the campo.

Campo San Luca and around

If the crush of San Bartolomeo is too much for you, you can retire to **Campo San Luca** (past the front of San Salvatore and straight on), another open-air social centre. From Campo San Luca, Calle Goldoni is a direct route back to the Piazza, via the Bacino Orseolo – the city's major gondola depot, and one of the few places where you can admire the streamlining and balance of the boats without being hassled by their owners. Calle dei Fuseri leads down to the smart **Frezzeria**, which takes you in one direction to La Fenice and in the other to the area just west of the Piazza.

Trading places

Frezzeria, which takes its name from the arrows – *frecce* – that were made and sold there, is just one of the many Venetian streets that bear witness to the traders who once operated in these localities. Roaming round the city, you'll encounter the following businesses, among others:

Barretteri = hatmakers	Pistor = baker
Beccaria = butcher	Remer = oar-maker
Botteri = barrel-makers	Saoneri = soap-makers
Cafettier = coffee shop	Spadaria = sword-maker
Frutariol – greengrocer	Spechieri = mirror-makers
Legnami = carpenters	Spezier = pharmacist
Magazen = pawnbroker	Tagiapiera = stonecutter
Pestrin = milk-seller	Tintor/Tentor = dyer

Unusually, the church of **San Luca** is not on the campo named after it, but on a campiello some way off, down Salizzada San Luca, then right and then left. Somewhere in the church is buried a writer whose name would have been known to all Venetians in the mid-sixteenth century – **Pietro Aretino**. Nicknamed "The Scourge of Princes", Aretino milked a hefty income from the rulers of a dozen states, who coughed up either in response to his flattery or out of terror at the damage his vicious tongue could do. So adept was he at juggling his various sponsors that he managed simultaneously to be on the payroll of Emperor Charles V and his enemy King Francis I of France. With Sansovino and Titian (who painted his portrait several times and used him as a model for Pontius Pilate) he formed a clique that dominated artistic circles in the city and made life intolerable for anyone they didn't like – both Lorenzo Lotto and Pordenone suffered at their hands. Aretino's notoriety rested as much on his dubious morals as on his scurrilous poetry and brilliant letters (which were a Venetian bestseller); some idea of the man is given by the story that his death was brought about by his uncontrollable laughter at a filthy story about his own sister. Today there's not even a tombstone left to mark his existence. The church itself is a drab nineteenth-century reconstruction, and its one picture of any importance – *The Virgin and St Luke* by **Veronese** (on the high altar) – is in a ruinous state.

Campo Manin and around

Unusually, the most conspicuous building on **Campo Manin** is a modern one – the clumsy **Cassa di Risparmio di Venezia** (designed in the 1960s by Angelo Scattolin and Pier Luigi Nervi), which stands on the spot once occupied by the famous printing press of Aldus Manutius (see p.127). The campo was enlarged in 1871 to make room for the monument to **Daniele Manin**, the lawyer who led the 1848–49 revolt against Austrian occupation; his statue looks towards his house, alongside the left-hand bridge (as you look west). Under Manin's management the provisional government of Venice was run with exemplary efficiency – a legislative assembly was set up, a new currency printed, and a newspaper was even circulated. In the course of the Austrian blockade Venice became the first city ever to be bombarded from the air, when explosives attached to balloons were floated over the city. The damage caused by this ploy was not too substantial, but inevitably the resistance was short-lived, and on August 23, 1849, weakened by hunger and disease, the Venetians surrendered. Manin and the other leaders of the uprising died in exile, but his native city honours his reputation not just here but also in the Basilica di San Marco (his tomb is there) and in Calle Large a XXII Marzo, which takes its name from the date on which the uprising started. (Incidentally, the other famous Manin – the unloved Lodovico, the feeble last doge – though not an ancestor, was quite closely associated with Daniele's family: when Daniele's parents converted from Judaism to Catholicism, they took the surname of their sponsor, who was one of Lodovico's brothers.)

On the wall of the alley on the south side of Campo Manin, a sign directs you to the staircase known as the **Scala del Bovolo** – *bovolo* is the word for snail shell in Venetian dialect. External staircases, developed originally as a way of saving space inside the building, were a common feature of Venetian houses into the sixteenth century, but this specimen, dating from around 1500, is the most flamboyant variation on the theme. At the moment it's under restoration; when the work is finished, it should be possible to go up the staircase (for a fee) – though it should be said that the view of the staircase is more impressive than the view from it.

▲ The Scala del Bovolo

The Museo Fortuny and San Benedetto

The fifteenth-century Palazzo Pésaro degli Orfei, now the **Museo Fortuny** (10am–6pm; closed Tues; €8), is close at hand, hidden away in a campo you'd never accidentally pass – take either of the bridges out of the Campo Manin, turn first right, and keep going.

Born in Catalonia, **Mariano Fortuny** (1871–1949) is famous chiefly for the body-clinging silk dresses he created, which were so finely pleated that they could be threaded through a wedding ring, it was claimed. However, Fortuny was also a painter, architect, engraver, photographer, theatre designer and sculptor, and the contents of this rickety and atmospheric palazzo reflect his versatility, with ranks of exotic landscapes, symbolist scenes (several of them derived from Wagner, for whose operas he had a lifelong passion), languorous nudes (including one painted when he was just seventeen), terracotta portrait busts, photographs, stage machinery and so forth – but none of the sexy frocks. The top floor houses a collection of paintings by Virgilio Guidi (1892–1983), about which the kindest comment would be that they are generally no worse than Fortuny's. Design and photography exhibitions are held regularly in the Museo Fortuny (the Venice Card is valid for these), and how much of the building you get to see depends on how extensive the show is – often only a couple of rooms are used. And in high season you'll have to queue, as the palazzo is so fragile that only 75 people are allowed in at a time.

The church of **San Benedetto** (San Beneto in dialect) – founded in the eleventh century, rebuilt in 1685 – gangs up with Fortuny's house to overwhelm the little square. It has a few good pictures: *St Sebastian* by Strozzi (second altar on right); two paintings of *St Benedict* by Mazzoni (over the doors to the side of the high altar); and *St Francis of Paola* by Giambattista Tiepolo (first altar on left). Finding this church open is a matter of pot luck – late afternoon is normally a good bet.

West of the Piazza

Leaving the Piazza **by the west side**, through the colonnade of the Ala Napoleonica, you enter another major shopping district, but one that presents a contrast to the frenetic Mercerie: here the clientele is drawn predominantly from the city's well-heeled or from the four-star tourists staying in the hotels that overlook the end of the Canal Grande – though in recent years it's also become a favourite pitch for African street-traders, whose presence has not been entirely welcomed by local shop-owners. To a high proportion of visitors, this part of the city is just **the route to the Accademia** – many pass through with their noses buried in their maps, and hardly break step before they reach the bridge over the Canal Grande. It's true that none of the first-division attractions is here and that much of the northern part of the area offers little but the pleasure of wandering through its alleyways, but there are things to see apart from the latest creations from Milan and Paris – the extraordinary Baroque facades of **San Moisè** and **Santa Maria del Giglio**, for instance, or the graceful **Santo Stefano**, which rises at the end of one of the largest and most attractive squares in Venice. Two of the city's great artistic venues lie within this district: **La Fenice**, one of the world's greatest opera houses; and the **Palazzo Grassi**, an exhibition centre with the highest production values in Italy.

San Moisè and Calle Larga XXII Marzo

Heading west from the Piazza, on the most direct road to the Accademia, you soon pass on the left the **Calle del Ridotto**, named after the most notorious of Venice's gambling dens, which operated from 1638 to 1774 in the Palazzo Dandolo (no. 1332). Gamblers of all social classes were welcome at the Ridotto's tables – as long as they wore masks – but most of the clients came from the nobility. The consequent damage to the financial resources of the Venetian upper class became so great that the government was finally forced to close the joint. There was, though, no shortage of alternative houses in which to squander the family fortune – in 1797 some 136 gambling establishments were operating in the city. The modern visitor to Venice can experience the frisson of self-induced financial crisis by dropping in at the insanely expensive *Harry's Bar*, right by the San Marco Vallaresso landing stage in nearby Calle Vallaresso.

The first church you come across on this route is **San Moisè** (Mon–Sat 9.30am–12.30pm), which was founded back in the eighth century but would nowadays be the runaway winner of any poll for the ugliest church in Venice. (Its neighbour, the modern extension of the *Hotel Bauer*, would garner several

WEST OF THE PIAZZA

N

0   100 m

PIAZZA SAN MARCO

CALLE DELL'ASCENSION

CALLE VALLARESSO

S. Marco Vallaresso 1, 2, N

CALLE DEL RIDOTTO

S. Moisè

Pal. Giustinian

Rio di S. Moise

CANAL GRANDE

R. Bacino Orseolo

FONDAM. ORSEOLO

CAMPO S. GALLO

FREZZERIA

Bacino Orseolo

C. GOLDONI

CALLE DEI FUSERI

Scala del Bovolo

Rio del Fuser

Barcaroli

Rio de' Barcaroli

PISCINA DI FREZZERIA

CALLE DEL TRAGHETTO

Pal. Contarini Fasan

San Luca

CAMPO MANIN

Ateneo Veneto

S. Fantin

C. D. VESTE

CALLE LARGA XXII MARZO

Rio di S. Luca

C.VERONA

CAMPO S. FANTIN

La Fenice

Rio delle Ostreghe

Pal. Pisani

S. Benedetto

C. D. MANDOLA

C. D. FENICE

CALLE D. OSTREGHE

Traghetto

Museo Fortuny

C. DEL PIOVAN

CAMPO S. MARIA DEL GIGLIO

S. Maria del Giglio

Rio di S. Maria Zobenigo

S. M. del Giglio 1

Oratorio dell' Annunziata

CAMPO S. ANGELO

ZAGURI

Rio Corner

FONDAMENTA CORNER

Rio di Ca' Michiel

Rio di Ca' Santi

Rio Malatin

S. Maurizio

CAMPO S. MAURIZIO

Pal. Zaguri

Pal. Corner Spinelli

Rio di S.Angelo

CALLE D. PESTRIN

CAMPO NOVO

S. Stefano

CALLE DEL DOSE

Pal. Corner della Ca' Grande

CANAL GRANDE

S. Angelo 1

Rio di Ca' Garzoni

PISC. S. SAMUELE

CALLE LE BOTTEGHE

CAMPO SANTO STEFANO

Pal. Morosini

Rio del Santissimo S. Stefano

Pal. Pisani

Palazzi Mocenigo

S. Tomà 1, 2, N

Traghetto

CALLE CROSERA

Pal. Loredan

CAMPO PISANI

Pal. Barbaro

Rio dell' Orso

S. Vitale

Pal. Franchetti

Pal. Contarini delle Figure

CALLE LEZZE

CALLE MOCENIGO

S. Samuele 2, N

Pal. Grassi

CAMPO SAN SAMUELE

S. Samuele

Traghetto SAMUELE

Pal. Malipiero

CALLE GIUSTINIAN

Accademia 1, 2, N

PONTE DELL'ACCADEMIA

Ca' del Duca

Accademia

▲ Ca' Rezzonico 1

votes for the nastiest building in all categories.) The church's name means "Saint Moses": the Venetians were following the Byzantine custom of canonizing Old Testament figures, while simultaneously honouring Moisè Venier, who paid for a rebuilding in the tenth century. Its facade, featuring a species of camel unknown to zoology, was designed in 1668 by Alessandro Tremignon and sculpted largely by **Heinrich Meyring** (aka Enrico or Arrigo Meyring), a follower of Bernini; it was funded by the Fini family, whose portraits occupy the positions in which one might expect to see saints or members of the Holy Family. And if you think this bloated display of fauna, flora and portraiture is in questionable taste, wait till you see the miniature mountain that Tremignon and Meyring created as the main altarpiece, representing *Mount Sinai with Moses Receiving the Tablets*. In the sacristy you'll find a fine example of comparatively restrained proto-Baroque – a bronze altar panel of the *Deposition* by Niccolò and Sebastiano Roccatagliata.

If you're looking for an escritoire for your drawing room, an oriental carpet for the reception area, a humble Dutch landscape or a new designer suit, then you'll probably find what you're after on or around the broad **Calle Larga XXII Marzo**, which begins over the canal from San Moisè. Many of the streets off the western side of the Piazza are dedicated to the beautification of the prosperous and their dwellings, with names such as Ferragamo, Gucci, Missoni and Vuitton lurking round every corner.

Campo San Fantin and La Fenice

Halfway along Calle Larga XXII Marzo, on the right, Calle del Sartor da Veste takes you over a canal and into **Campo San Fantin**. The church of **San Fantin**, begun in 1507 by Scarpagnino, is notable for its graceful domed apse, built in 1549–63 to plans by Sansovino. On the far side of the campo is the home of the **Ateneo Veneto**, a cultural institution which organizes some of Venice's more arcane exhibitions. The building was formerly occupied by a confraternity whose main service to the community was to comfort those sentenced to death – hence the name by which it was generally known: the Scuola della Buona Morte. Part of the scuola's collection of works of art has been dispersed, but pieces by Veronese and Alessandro Vittoria, among others, are still in the building, inaccessible to *hoi polloi*.

The square is dominated by the **Teatro la Fenice**, Venice's oldest and largest theatre. Meaning "The Phoenix", the name of La Fenice is wholly appropriate to a building that is inextricably associated with fire. Built as a replacement for the San Benedetto theatre, which burned to the ground in 1774, **Giannantonio Selva**'s gaunt Neoclassical design was not deemed a great success on its inauguration on December 26, 1792, but nonetheless very little of the exterior was changed when the opera house was rebuilt following a second conflagration in 1836. Rather more extensive changes were made to its interior, a luxuriant, late Empire confection of gilt, plush and stucco which has been fastidiously replicated in the re-reborn Fenice, albeit with the addition of a fireproof steel roof and an extra 150 seats squeezed in. (Forty-five-minute guided tours, conducted every weekday between 10am and 6pm and costing €7, give visitors a close-up view of the new structure – backstage as well as the auditorium.) La Fenice saw some major musical events in the twentieth century – Stravinsky's *The Rake's Progress* and Britten's *The Turn of the Screw* were both premiered here, as were works by Prokofiev, Nono (the one great Venetian composer of modern times), Maderna, Sciarrino and Rihm – but the music scene was more exciting in the nineteenth century, when, in addition to staging the premieres of several

The 1996 Fenice fire

Seating just 850 people, the old Fenice had an intimate atmosphere that brought out the best in performers, and its acoustics were superb, thanks largely to the fact that the interior structure was entirely wooden. It was this last characteristic that made the **fire** on the night of January 29, 1996, so disastrous – though the fire brigade was at the site within twenty minutes of the alarm being raised, it was all they could do to prevent the blaze spreading to the surrounding houses. Unable to get right up to the building because the flanking canals had been drained for dredging (in order eventually to allow the emergency services easier access), the firefighters had to pump water from the Canal Grande and scoop it out of the lagoon by helicopter to contain the damage. La Fenice itself was quickly reduced to its external walls.

A picture taken from a nearby apartment appeared to show that the fire sprang from two different places in the top storey – the only explanation for which would be that the fire was started deliberately. Suspicions of **foul play** were strengthened by the fact that, though by law a caretaker and two firefighters should have been on duty at La Fenice throughout the night, there was just one doorman inside the building to operate its fire extinguishers and the smoke detectors were turned off. When investigators realized that the fire could only have spread with such speed if someone had poured inflammable liquids onto the timbers, arson was incontrovertibly established as the cause. Inquiries soon focused on the contractors who were at work on the opera house at the time, and had fallen behind schedule on a major refurbishment project. Very quickly a conspiracy theory was in circulation and gaining wide acceptance: the contractors were controlled by organized crime, the argument ran, and their bosses had decided to torch the opera house either to avoid paying the penalties for failing to meet their deadlines, or because they fancied their chances of getting the lucrative contracts to rebuild the theatre. It was pointed out that the **mafia** had turned out to be behind the destruction by fire of the Bari opera house in 1991, and that the boss of the mafia in the Veneto was not only a friend of the man who had ordered the Bari fire, but had once stated in court that he had considered destroying La Fenice. Eventually **prosecutions** were brought against Enrico Carella – the owner of the electrical subcontractors who had been rewiring La Fenice – and his cousin Massimiliano Marchetti. Both were found guilty, but the judges described them as "surrogates" for unnamed third parties, the presumption being that Carella's uncle Renato – whose financial dealings looked irregular, to say the least – was the link-man between the mob and the arsonists. Renato Carella's death, soon after his nephew's conviction, left many Venetians convinced that the real instigators of the Fenice fire have escaped punishment. Enrico Carella was sentenced to seven years in prison and Marchetti to six. Released while awaiting an appeal hearing, Carella went on the run, and he remained at liberty until the eleventh anniversary of the fire, when he was tracked down to Cancún in Mexico, after Interpol had tapped the phones of his mother and friends. As *Corriere della Sera* put it: "He was betrayed in the end by homesickness and his love for his Mamma."

Straight after the disaster it was claimed that the new Fenice would open before the end of 1998, but no sooner had reconstruction begun than it ran into litigation. A Fiat-controlled company originally won the contract on the basis of a plan drawn up by Gae Aulenti, but the firm that came second in the competition for the work promptly objected that Aulenti's scheme failed to meet the specified brief. **Legal action** ensued, and in the end the former runners-up – a German-Italian construction consortium headed by **Aldo Rossi**, one of Europe's greatest modern architects (who was killed in a car crash the year after the fire) – were told they could start building their state-of-the-art replica of La Fenice, a process that was aided by the discovery of the plans that had been used to rebuild the opera house after the 1836 blaze. Even then, progress was so shamefully slow that the replacement builders were themselves dismissed and the work handed over to a Venetian company. Only at the end of 2003 was the new Fenice at last completed.

operas by Rossini, Bellini and Verdi (*Rigoletto* and *La Traviata* both opened here), La Fenice became the focal point for protests against the occupying Austrian army. Favourite forms of nationalist expression included bombarding the stage with bouquets in the colours of the Italian tricolour, and yelling "Viva Verdi!" at strategic points in the performance – the composer's name being the acronym for *Vittorio Emanuele, Re d'Italia* (Vittorio Emanuele, King of Italy).

The Fenice remains one of Italy's great cultural institutions, but its future is not secure: the government of Silvio Berlusconi has reduced its funding to such an extent that performances have had to be cancelled and fund-raising concerts organized. Insolvency is a real possibility.

Santa Maria del Giglio and San Maurizio

Back on the route to the Accademia, another vainglorious church facade awaits – **Santa Maria del Giglio** (Mon–Sat 10am–5pm; €3, or Chorus Pass), more commonly known as Santa Maria Zobenigo, an alternative title derived from the name of the Jubanico family, who founded it in the ninth century. You can stare at the front of this church for as long as you like, but you still won't find a single unequivocally Christian image. The main statues are of the five **Barbaro** brothers, who financed the rebuilding of the church in 1678; *Virtue, Honour*, Fame and *Wisdom* hover at a respectful distance; and relief maps at eye level depict the towns distinguished with the brothers' presence in the course of their military and diplomatic careers. Antonio Barbaro – the central figure and chief benefactor of the church – was not rated by his superiors quite as highly as he was by himself: he was in fact dismissed from Francesco Morosini's fleet for incompetence. The interior, full to bursting with devotional pictures and sculptures, overcompensates for the impiety of the exterior. In the main body of the church the major works are the *Stations of the Cross* by various eighteenth-century artists and the *Evangelists* by **Tintoretto** behind the altar. The sacristy – packed with reliquaries that house, among other sacred scraps, a lock of Saint Francis's hair and a scrap of the garb of Saint Catherine of Siena – has a *Madonna and Child* that's attributed to Rubens. Outside again, the detached one-storey shop right by the church occupies the stump of the campanile, pruned to its present dimensions in 1774.

The tilting campanile of Santo Stefano (see below) soon looms into view over the vapid and deconsecrated church of **San Maurizio**, a collaboration between Giannantonio Selva and Antonio Diedo, secretary of the Accademia. The inside of the church is used as an exhibition space (currently it houses a display of Baroque musical instruments; daily 9.30am–7.30pm; free), and the exterior is overshadowed by the fifteenth-century **Palazzo Zaguri**, on the campo's east side. This district is the antiques centre of Venice, and from time to time the Campo San Maurizio is taken over by an antiques and bric-a-brac fair. The antiques business has a permanent representative on the campo in the form of V. Trois, an outlet for genuine Fortuny fabrics.

If you wander off the campo down Calle del Dose you'll come to a short fondamenta on the Canal Grande, with fabulous views of its lower reach. Continuing along the Accademia route, at the beginning of Calle del Piovan stands a diminutive building that was once the **Scuola degli Albanesi**; it was established in 1497 and the reliefs on the facade date from shortly after that. In 1504 Carpaccio produced a cycle of *Scenes from the Life of the Virgin* for the scuola, and the pictures remained here even after the declining Albanian community led to the disbanding of the confraternity in the late eighteenth century. It wasn't until 1808, when the bakers' guild that had moved into the building was itself scrapped, that the series was broken up. The bits that remained in Venice are now in the Correr collection and the Ca' d'Oro.

Stop for a second on the bridge just after the Scuola, and look down the canal to your right – you'll see that it runs under the east end of Santo Stefano, the only church in Venice to have quite so intimate a relationship with the city's waterways.

The church of Santo Stefano and its campo

The church of Santo Stefano closes one end of the next square, **Campo Santo Stefano**. Large enough to hold several clusters of tourists, a few dozen café tables plus a kids' football match or two, the campo is one of the city's sunniest spots (it opens to the west), but is at its liveliest in the run-up to Christmas, when a small village of food and crafts stalls is set up here. Bullfights were held here regularly until 1802, when the collapse of a bank of seats killed a number of spectators and provoked a permanent ban on such events.

Founded in the thirteenth century, rebuilt in the fourteenth and altered again in the first half of the fifteenth, **Santo Stefano** (Mon–Sat 10am–5pm; €3, or Chorus Pass) is notable for its Gothic doorway and beautiful **ship's-keel roof**, both of which belong to the last phase of building. The airy and calm interior is one of the most pleasant places in Venice to just sit and think, but it also contains some major works of art. The **tomb of Giacomo Surian**, on the entrance wall, was designed and carved in the final decade of the fifteenth century by Pietro Lombardo and his sons. Less easily overlooked is the **tomb of Francesco Morosini**: it's the oversized bronze badge in the centre of the nave. The major **paintings** are in the sacristy: a *St Lawrence* and a *St Nicholas of Bari* by Bartolomeo Vivarini, a trio of late works by Tintoretto – *The Agony in the Garden*, *The Last Supper* and *The Washing of the Disciples' Feet*. The choir of the church (which has superb inlaid choirstalls) is connected to the sacristy by a corridor that houses a small assemblage of sculpture, including items by the Dalle Masegnes and Tullio Lombardo, and Canova's stele for his first patron, Giovanni Falier (1808).

▲ Campo Santo Stefano

The sacristan might let you into the **cloister** (far door in left aisle), to see the **tomb of Doge Andrea Contarini**, head of state when the Venetians took on the Genoese at Chioggia. The weather long ago wiped out the frescoes by Pordenone that used to cover much of the walls – a few scraps are preserved in the Ca' d'Oro. Pordenone was for a while Titian's main rival in the city, and such was his fear of the great man and his cronies that he invariably turned up to work here with daggers and swords hanging from his belt. No assault actually occurred, but there has been plenty of bloodshed within the church precincts – so much, in fact, that the place has had to be reconsecrated half a dozen times.

Premature death on a terrible scale accounts for the peculiar raised pavement of nearby **Campo Novo**, off Calle del Pestrin: formerly the churchyard of Santo Stefano, it was used as a burial pit during the catastrophic plague of 1630, and such was the volume of corpses interred here that for health reasons the site remained closed to the public from then until 1838.

Campo Santo Stefano

Nicolò Tommaseo, the Risorgimento ideologue who was Manin's right-hand man during the 1848 insurrection, is commemorated by the statue in the middle of Campo Santo Stefano; the unfortunate positioning of the pile of books (representing Tommaseo's voluminous literary output) has earned the statue the nickname *il Cagalibri* – the Book-shitter. The campo has an alias – Campo Francesco Morosini – that comes from a former inhabitant of the palazzo at no. 2802. The last doge to serve as military commander of the Republic (1688–94), **Francesco Morosini** became a Venetian hero with his victories in the Peloponnese, as is attested by the triumphal arch built in his honour in the Palazzo Ducale's Sala dello Scrutinio, and the exhaustive documentation of his career in the Museo Correr. But to those few non–Venetians to whom his name means anything at all, he's known as the man who lobbed a missile through the roof of the Parthenon, detonating the Turkish gunpowder barrels that had been stored there. He then made matters even worse by trying to prise some of the decoration off the half-wrecked temple, shattering great chunks of statuary in the process. Morosini and Venice didn't come back from that campaign empty-handed though – the Arsenale gate is guarded by two of his trophies.

Campiello Pisani, at the back of Morosini's house, is effectively a forecourt to the **Palazzo Pisani**, one of the biggest houses in the city, and now the Conservatory of Music. Work began on it in the early seventeenth century, continued for over a century, and was at last brought to a halt by the government, who decided that the Pisani, among the city's richest banking families, were getting ideas above their station. Had the Pisani got their way, they wouldn't have stopped building until they reached the Canal Grande.

The most prominent palazzo on the campo itself, the **Palazzo Loredan** (originally fifteenth-century but rebuilt around 1540, with the facade added in 1618), is being converted into a cultural centre by the Istituto Veneto di Scienze Lettere e Arte, an organization that also holds large-scale shows in the vast **Palazzo Franchetti**, which flanks the Accademia bridge. An instructive exhibition relating to the Venetian lagoon and its maintenance can be seen at **Puntolaguna**, virtually next door to the Loredan at no. 2949 (Mon–Fri 2.30–5.30pm; free; W www.salve.it).

Opposite the Franchetti palace stands the deconsecrated church of **San Vitale** (or Vidal). It's now used for concerts (second-rate renditions of Vivaldi favourites, ninety-nine percent of the time), but still possesses a fine painting by

Carpaccio (*San Vitale and other Saints*, above the high altar), and Piazzetta's *Archangel Raphael and Sts Anthony and Louis* (third altar on the right); unfortunately, you can rarely get closer to the pictures than the ticket desk at the entrance to the church. If the facade of the church seems strangely familiar, that's because it's a replica of San Giorgio Maggiore's.

Campo Sant'Angelo

A door leads from the cloister of Santo Stefano into the **Campo Sant'Angelo** (or Anzolo), a square almost as capacious as Campo Santo Stefano, but which feels more like a crossroads than a meeting place. It's bounded by some fine buildings, however, including two magnificent fifteenth-century palaces: the **Palazzo Gritti** and, facing it, the **Palazzo Duodo**, home of the composer Cimarosa, who died there in 1801. The minuscule **Oratorio dell'Annunziata** – founded in the tenth century, rebuilt in the twelfth and once the home of the Scuola dei Sotti ("of the Lame") – contains a sixteenth-century crucifix and an *Annunciation* by the omnipresent Palma il Giovane. Nothing remains of Sant'Angelo church, which was demolished in 1837 but is still remembered as a leading player in one of Venice's great architectural cock-ups. By 1445 the tilt of the church's campanile had become so severe that urgent measures were deemed necessary to right it. It was discovered that there was a builder in Bologna who had made such problems his speciality, and he was duly hired. The expert fixed it so the tower stood as straight as a pine tree; the scaffolding was taken down; a banquet was held to honour the engineering genius; and the next morning the whole edifice keeled over.

San Samuele and Palazzo Grassi

From opposite the entrance to Santo Stefano church, Calle delle Botteghe and Crosera lead up to Salizzada San Samuele, a route that's lined with private galleries, arty shops and a few good places to eat; a left turn along Salizzada San Samuele takes you past the house in which **Paolo Veronese** lived his final years, and on to **Campo San Samuele**. Built in the late twelfth century and not much altered since, the campanile of the church is one of the oldest in the city. The church itself was founded in the previous century but was largely reconstructed in the late seventeenth century; apart from some fifteenth-century frescoes by Paduan artists in the apse, the interior is of little interest.

San Samuele is dwarfed by the **Palazzo Grassi** (ⓦ www.palazzograssi.it), which in 1984 was bought by Fiat and converted into a cultural centre. No expense was spared in realizing the plans drawn up by Gae Aulenti (best known for Paris's Musée d'Orsay), and blockbuster overviews of entire cultures and epochs became the Grassi's speciality, with exhibitions on subjects such as the Phoenicians, the Celts, the Etruscans and the Pharoahs attracting thousands of visitors from all over the continent. But with Fiat's fortunes continuing to slide at the start of the new century, the Agnelli family – owners of the company – put the Grassi up for sale, and it seemed likely that it would become yet another swanky hotel. Into the breach stepped the phenomenally wealthy **François Pinault**, chairman of the company that owns, among many other big names, Gucci, Fnac, Le Printemps and Christie's auction house. He is also France's pre-eminent collector of modern art, having bought about 2500 pieces to date, ranging from Picasso, Miró, Brancusi and Mondrian to contemporaries such as Jeff Koons, Damien Hirst, Maurizio Cattelan and Mario Merz.

Abandoning long-held plans to establish a museum for his collection in Paris, Pinault paid €30 million in 2005 for an eighty percent share in the Grassi (the Venice casino holds the other twenty percent), and hired the Japanese architect **Tadao Ando** (who was to have designed the Paris museum) to restyle the interior in his customary bleached tones. A couple of years later, Pinault acquired the warehouses of the Dogana di Mare (see p.102), which has become the main showcase for his vast collection, while the Grassi stages immense and wide-ranging art shows that usually draw heavily on works owned by Pinault. As if that weren't enough, he has also undertaken to restore the small eighteenth-century theatre behind the Grassi, so that it can be used for concerts, lectures and so forth.

From San Samuele a fairly straightforward chain of alleys leads back to Campo Santo Stefano (follow the trail of "Palazzo Grassi" signs). On the corner of the first of these – Calle Malipiero – is a plaque marking the birthplace of one of the paltry band of world-famous native Venetians: **Giovanni Giacomo Casanova**. Both his parents were actors, and the family lived within a stone's throw of one of Venice's main theatres, the San Samuele, which until its demolition in the nineteenth century stood in the adjoining Calle del Teatro.

Dorsoduro

There were not many places among the lagoon's mudbanks where Venice's early settlers could be confident that their dwellings wouldn't slither down into the water, but with Dorsoduro they were on relatively solid ground: the *sestiere*'s name translates as "hard back", and its buildings occupy the largest area of firm silt in the centre of the city. Some of the finest

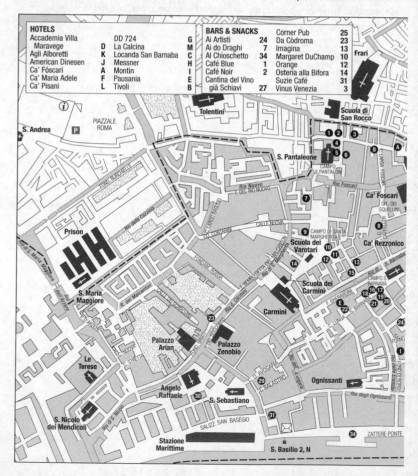

HOTELS

Accademia Villa		DD 724	G
Maravege	D	La Calcina	M
Agli Alboretti	K	Locanda San Barnaba	C
American Dinesen	J	Messner	H
Ca' Fóscari	A	Montin	I
Ca' Maria Adele	F	Pausania	E
Ca' Pisani	L	Tivoli	B

BARS & SNACKS

Ai Artisti	24	Corner Pub	25
Ai do Draghi	7	Da Còdroma	23
Al Chioschetto	34	Imagina	13
Café Blue	1	Margaret DuChamp	10
Café Noir	2	Orange	12
Cantina del Vino		Osteria alla Bifora	14
già Schiavi	27	Suzie Café	31
		Vinus Venezia	3

minor domestic architecture in Venice is concentrated here, and in recent years many of the area's best houses have been bought up by industrialists and financiers from elsewhere in northern Italy, investing in permanent homes or merely weekend havens from their places of work. The top-bracket colony is, however, pretty well confined to a triangle defined by the Accademia, the Punta della Dogana and the Gesuati. Stroll up to the area around Campo Santa Margherita and the atmosphere is quite different, in part because of the proximity of the main part of the university.

During the day at least, it's the paintings of Dorsoduro's art galleries and religious institutions that draw most visitors across the Ponte dell'Accademia. The **Gallerie dell'Accademia**, replete with masterpieces from each phase in the history of Venetian painting up to the eighteenth century, is the area's essential port of call, and figures on most itineraries as the place to make for when the Piazza's sights have been done. The huge church of **Santa Maria della Salute**, the grandest gesture of Venetian Baroque and a prime landmark when looking across the water from the Molo, is architecturally the major religious building of the district – but in terms of artistic contents it takes

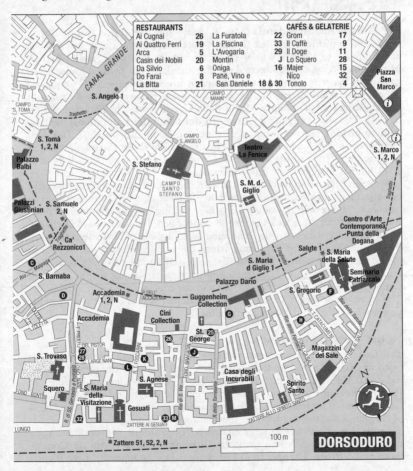

RESTAURANTS					
Ai Cugnai	26	La Furatola	22		
Ai Quattro Ferri	19	La Piscina	33		
Arca	5	L'Avogaria	29		
Casin dei Nobili	20	Montin	J		
Da Silvio	6	Oniga	16		
Do Farai	8	Pane, Vino e			
La Bitta	21	San Daniele	18 & 30		

CAFÉS & GELATERIE			
Grom	17		
Il Caffè	9		
Il Doge	11		
Lo Squero	28		
Majer	15		
Nico	32		
Tonolo	4		

DORSODURO

0   100 m

second place to **San Sebastiano**, the parish church of **Paolo Veronese**, whose paintings clad much of its interior. **Giambattista Tiepolo**, the master colourist of a later era, is well represented at the **Scuola Grande dei Carmini**, and for an overall view of Tiepolo's cultural milieu there's the **Ca' Rezzonico**, home of Venice's museum of eighteenth-century art and artefacts. Unusually for Venice, art of the twentieth century is also in evidence – at the **Guggenheim Collection**, which is small yet markedly superior to the city's public collection of modern art in the Ca' Pésaro. Art of the twenty-first century is amply represented at the new **Centro d'Arte Contemporanea Punta della Dogana**, Europe's largest centre of its kind. And yet despite all these attractions the district as a whole is remarkably quiet – most tourists step across the Accademia bridge, whirl through the gallery, then cross back over the Canal Grande again.

The Accademia

The **Gallerie dell'Accademia** (Mon 8.15am–2pm, Tues–Sun 8.15am–7.15pm; €6.50) – one of Europe's finest specialized art collections – began its existence as an annexe to Venice's school of art, the **Accademia di Belle Arti**. A Napoleonic decree of 1807 moved the Accademia to this site and instituted its galleries of Venetian paintings, a stock drawn largely from the city's suppressed churches and convents. Parts of the premises themselves were formerly religious buildings: the church of **Santa Maria della Carità** (rebuilt by Bartolomeo Bon in 1441–52) and the adjoining **Convento dei Canonici Lateranensi** (built by Palladio in 1561 but not completed) were both suppressed in 1807. The third component of the Accademia used to be the **Scuola della Carità**, founded in 1260 and the oldest of the six Scuole Grande; the Gothic building dates from 1343, but has an eighteenth-century facade.

With San Marco and the Palazzo Ducale, the Accademia completes the triad of obligatory tourist sights in Venice, but admissions are presently restricted to batches of 300 people at a time, so if you're visiting in high summer and don't want to wait, get there well before the doors open. This situation will change when the gallery takes over the renovated ground-floor and basement rooms of the convent buildings, an expansion which has entailed moving the art college to the nearby **Casa degli Incurabili** (see p.103). When this huge rebuilding project is completed, the Accademia will have space not just for the scores of paintings currently held in storage, but also for large-scale one-off exhibitions. The upper-floor galleries of the new Accademia will also have a somewhat different lay out than the one given below.

To the early Renaissance

The **first room** is the fifteenth-century former chapterhouse of the *scuola* (with its original gilded ceiling), now filled with pieces by the earliest-known individual Venetian painters. The icon-like Byzantine-influenced figures of **Paolo Veneziano** (first half of the fourteenth century) are succeeded by the Gothic forms of his follower **Lorenzo Veneziano** – look at the swaying stances of his figures and the emphasis on the sinuous lines of the drapery.

Room 2 is given over to large altarpieces from the late fifteenth and early sixteenth centuries, including works by **Giovanni Bellini**, **Cima da Conegliano** and **Vittore Carpaccio**. All of these paintings appear to have slightly warped perspectives: this is because they were intended to be placed above head height – a fact that the Accademia's picture-hangers have not taken into consideration. Carpaccio's strange *Crucifixion and Glorification of the Ten Thousand Martyrs of Mount Ararat* is the most gruesome painting in the room, and the most charming is by him too: *The Presentation of Jesus in the Temple*, with its pretty, wingless, lute-playing angel.

The beginnings of the Venetian obsession with the way in which forms are defined by light (as differentiated from the Florentines' more geometrical notions of form) and the emergence of the characteristically soft and rich Venetian palette are seen in **rooms 3, 4 and 5**, the last two of which are a high point of the Accademia. Almost all of the small paintings here would alone be worth a detour, but outstanding are an exquisite *St George* by **Mantegna** (c.1466), a series of *Madonna*s and a *Pietà* by **Giovanni Bellini**, and two pieces by the most mysterious of Italian painters, **Giorgione** – his *Portrait of an Old Woman* (c.1509) and the so-called *Tempest* (c.1500). The former is an urgent and compassionate study of mortality (the inscription means "with time"), while the latter resists all attempts to deduce its meaning – the first known painting to have no historical, religious, mythological or factual basis, it seems to have been as perplexing to Giorgione's contemporaries as it is to us.

Tintoretto, Titian and Veronese

Rooms 6 to 8 mark the entry of the heavyweights of the Venetian High Renaissance, the period in which the cult of the artist really took hold, with painters cultivating their reputations and writers boosting their favourites while damning their rivals. These works would be the prize of many other collections, but here they are just appetizers for what's to come. In **room 6**, Jacopo Robusti, alias **Tintoretto**, is represented by several paintings, including a *Creation of the Animals* that features a few species that must have followed the unicorn into extinction; a muscular *John the Baptist* by Tiziano Vecellio, alias **Titian**, presides over the room; and Paolo Caliari, better known as **Paolo Veronese** (he came to Venice from Verona), is represented by a series of ceiling panels, a genre at which he excelled. In the parallel suite, **rooms 7 and 8**, you'll find a beguiling *Tobias and the Angel* that has recently, after being cleaned, been identified as a Titian, but the most compelling picture is the *Young Man in His Study* by **Lorenzo Lotto** (c.1528), a portrait in which the subject's gaze manages to be simultaneously sharp and evasive.

Room 6 is in effect the anteroom to the large **room 10**, one whole wall of which is needed for *Christ in the House of Levi*, painted by **Paolo Veronese** in 1573. Originally called *The Last Supper* – being a replacement for a Titian painting of the same subject that was destroyed by a fire in the refectory of San Zanipolo – this picture brought down on Veronese the wrath of the Inquisition, who objected to the inclusion of "buffoons, drunkards, Germans, dwarfs, and similar indecencies" in the sacred scene. (What really raised their hackles was the German contingent, who were perceived by the Holy Office as the incarnation of the Reformation menace.) Veronese's response was simply to change the title and append an inscription identifying the subject (it's on the balustrade in the lower left portion), emendations that apparently satisfied his critics.

Among the works by **Tintoretto** is the painting that made his reputation: *St Mark Freeing a Slave* (1548), painted for the Scuola Grande di San Marco, it shows Saint Mark's intervention at the execution of a slave who had defied his master by travelling to the Evangelist's shrine. Comparison with Gentile

Bellini's unruffled depictions of miraculous events in rooms 20–21 makes it easy to understand the sensation caused by Tintoretto's whirling, brashly coloured scene. The legend of Venice's patron saint is further elaborated by three other pictures that were also commissioned by the scuola: the dreamlike *Translation of the Body of St Mark* (see p.48 for the story of the "translation"), *St Mark Saving a Saracen* (both from the 1560s), and *The Dream of St Mark* (1570), which is largely by his son **Domenico**. Tintoretto's love of physical and psychological drama, the energy of his brushstrokes, and the sometimes uncomfortable originality of his colours and poses, are all displayed in this group. Opposite hangs **Titian**'s highly charged *Pietà* (1576), painted for his own tomb in the Frari; the immediacy of death is expressed in the handling of the paint, here scratched, scraped and dolloped onto the canvas not just with brushes but with the artist's bare hands. It was completed after Titian's death by Palma il Giovane, as the inscription explains.

The eighteenth century

In **room 11** there's more from **Tintoretto**, including the sumptuous *Madonna dei Tesorieri* (1566), showing the city's treasurers hobnobbing with the Mother of Our Saviour. Pordenone and Leandro Bassano are also on show here, but a major shift into the eighteenth century occurs in this room, with some dazzling works by **Giambattista Tiepolo**. The fragments of the ceiling he created for the Scalzi church (1743–44) are all that's left after a bomb went through the roof in 1915; his *St Helena Discovering the Cross* was painted at around the same time, for a convent in Castello; and the long frieze of *The Miracle of the Bronze Serpent* (c.1735) was brought here from a now-defunct church over on La Giudecca and sustained some damage when it was rolled up for storage in the nineteenth century, at a time when the artist was out of fashion. The long corridor of **room 12** marks the beginning of a rather dull section of the gallery. Although some of the side rooms contain a few decent sixteenth- and seventeenth-century pieces, in particular works by **Jacopo Bassano**, and **Tintoretto**'s portraits of officials of the republic, the chief interest is provided by eighteenth-century painters. **Giambattista Piazzetta**'s extraordinary *The Fortune-Teller* (1740), in **room 16a**, is also known as *The Enigma*, although the woman is offering the least enigmatic sexual invitation you'll ever see on canvas; some interpreters see it as a satirical allegory, showing how once-glorious Venice now behaved towards the rest of the world. In **room 17** there is a trio of small Canalettos, accompanied by **Guardi**'s impressionistic views of Venice, **Pietro Longhi**'s documentary interiors and a series of portraits by **Rosalba Carriera**, one of the very few women shown in the collection. Carriera's work established the use of pastel as a medium in its own right, rather than as a preparation for oil paint, and her moving *Self-Portrait*, done at a time when her sight was beginning to fail, is a high point of her work.

To the Miracles of the Relic of the Cross

The top part of the Carità church now forms **room 23**, which houses works mainly from the fifteenth and early sixteenth centuries, the era of two of Venice's most significant artistic dynasties, the **Vivarini** and **Bellini** families. Of the pieces by the Vivarini – **Antonio**, his brother **Bartolomeo** and his son **Alvise** – the most striking is perhaps Alvise's *Madonna and Child with Saints Andrew, John the Baptist, Dominic and Peter*. **Giovanni Bellini** is represented by four workshop-assisted triptychs (painted for this church in the 1460s), and his brother **Gentile** by the intense portrait of *The Blessed Lorenzo Giustinian* (1445). One of the oldest surviving Venetian canvases and Gentile's earliest signed work, it was possibly used as a standard in processions, which would account for its tatty state.

There's more from Gentile over in **room 20**, which is entirely filled by the cycle of *The Miracles of the Relic of the Cross*. The work was produced by various artists between 1494 and 1501, and was commissioned by the Scuola Grande di San Giovanni Evangelista to extol the holy fragment it had held since 1369. Gentile's *Procession in Piazza San Marco* (1496), executed the year the Torre dell'Orologio was started, is perhaps the best-known image of the group; the devotional moment is easily missed – the bare-headed man in a red cloak kneeling as the relic passes him is one Jacopo de' Salis, praying for his son's recovery from a fractured skull. In *The Miracle of the True Cross at the Bridge of San Lorenzo* (1500) Gentile shows Andrea Vendramin, Grand Guardian of the Scuola, retrieving the relic from the spot where it had floated after being knocked into the water during a procession; the fourth figure from the left in the group of donors in the right foreground is alleged to be a self-portrait, and Caterina Cornaro (see p.354) is portrayed on the far left.

A wealth of anecdotal detail adds historical veracity to **Carpaccio**'s *Miracle of the True Cross at the Rialto Bridge* (1494). Set by the Rialto (and showing one of the wooden precursors of the present bridge), its cast of characters includes turbanned Turks and Arabs, Armenian (or Greek) gentlemen in tall brimmed hats, an African gondolier, a woman beating carpets on an *altana* and a man repairing a roof; the miracle – the cure of a lunatic – is happening on the first floor of the building on the left. **Giovanni Mansueti**'s *Miracle of the Relic in Campo San Lio* (1494) shows what happened at the funeral of a dissolute and impious member of the confraternity: the relic refused to allow itself to be carried into the church for his service. Each window has a woman or child in it, witnessing the shame of the old reprobate. The reason for all these anecdotal details and the marginalizing of the miracles was not a lack of piety but quite the reverse: the miracle was authenticated by being depicted in the documentary context of everyday life.

Carpaccio's St Ursula paintings – and Titian's Presentation

Another remarkable cycle fills **room 21** – **Carpaccio**'s *Story of St Ursula*, painted for the Scuola di Sant'Orsola at San Zanipolo in 1490–94. A superlative exercise in pictorial narrative, the paintings are especially fascinating to the modern viewer as a meticulous record of domestic architecture, costume, the decorative arts, and even ship design in Venice at the close of the fifteenth century. The legend is that a British prince named Hereus proposed marriage to Ursula, a Breton princess, who accepted on two conditions: that Hereus convert to Christianity, and that he should wait for three years, during which time he should escort Ursula and her company of 11,000 virgins on a pilgrimage to Rome. The conditions were accepted, and the eventual consequence was that Ursula and her troop were massacred by the Huns near Cologne – as she had been forewarned by an angel in a dream.

After this room, you leave the Accademia through the former *albergo* of the scuola; **Titian**'s *Presentation of the Virgin* (1539) occupies the wall over the door, the place for which it was painted – and the triptych by **Antonio Vivarini** and **Giovanni d'Alemagna** (1446) similarly hangs where it always has.

Eastern Dorsoduro

Along the east flank of the Accademia runs the wide Rio Terrà Foscarini, named after **Senator Antonio Foscarini**, victim of the Venetian judicial system's most notorious gaffe; he lived at no. 180–181, but the house was radically altered in the nineteenth century. (For the story of Antonio Foscarini, see p.198.) The street cuts down almost as far as the Záttere, but for the direct route to the mouth of the Canal Grande turn left along Calle Nuova a Sant'Agnese, one of the district's main shopping streets.

To the Guggenheim Collection

Just before the Rio San Vio you pass the Palazzo Cini (no. 864), once the home of the industrialist Vittorio Cini (founder of the Fondazione Cini on San Giorgio Maggiore) and now occupied by the **Galleria di Palazzo Cini**. Sadly, the Cini's private collection of Tuscan paintings, including pieces by Filippo Lippi, Piero di Cosimo and Pontormo, is no longer on permanent display, although special exhibitions are sometimes held here – keep an eye out for posters or check the Cini website (Ⓦ www.cini.it).

Over the water lies the **Campo San Vio**, a fine platform from which to watch the traffic on the Canal Grande. The reason this little square opens out onto the water is that the houses on that side were demolished in order to make it easier for the doge and his entourage to disembark for the annual thanksgiving service in the church of saints Vito and Modesto (contracted to Vio in Venetian); held on the saints' joint feast day, June 15, the service commemorated the defeat of the Bajamonte Tiepolo revolt (see p.80), which occurred on June 15, 1310. The church itself was demolished in 1813; the walls of the chapel that took its place (St George – the city's Anglican church) are encrusted with stone fragments taken from the Tiepolo palazzo, which was destroyed in punishment for their treason.

From here you just follow your nose for the **Peggy Guggenheim Collection** (10am–6pm; closed Tues; €12; Ⓦ www.guggenheim-venice.it), installed in the quarter-built Palazzo Venier dei Leoni, a bit further down the Canal Grande.

In the early years of the twentieth century the leading lights of the Futurist movement came here for the parties thrown by the dotty Marchesa Casati, who was fond of stunts like setting wild cats and apes loose in the palazzo garden, among plants sprayed lilac for the occasion. Peggy Guggenheim, a considerably more discerning patron of the arts, moved into the palace in 1949; since her death in 1979 the Guggenheim Foundation has looked after the administration of the place, and has turned her private collection into one of the city's glossiest museums – and the second most popular after the Accademia. It's a small but generally top-quality assembly of twentieth-century art, touching on most of the major modern movements, and the Guggenheim is also a prime venue for touring shows, which can help to make the entrance fee seem less extortionate. In the permanent collection the core pieces include Brancusi's *Bird in Space* and *Maestra*, De Chirico's *Red Tower* and *Nostalgia of the Poet*, Max Ernst's *Robing of the Bride* (Guggenheim was married to Ernst in the 1940s), some of Joseph Cornell's boxes, sculpture by Laurens and Lipchitz, and works by Malevich and Schwitters; other artists include Picasso, Braque, Chagall, Pollock, Duchamp, Giacometti, Picabia and Magritte. Marino Marini's *Angel of the Citadel*, out on the terrace, flaunts his erection at the passing canal traffic; more decorous pieces by Giacometti, Moore, Paolozzi and others are planted in the garden, surrounding Peggy Guggenheim's burial place.

The Salute and around

After the wrought iron and greenery of the tiny **Campo Barbaro** (from where you can see the Gothic back half of the Palazzo Dario – see p.194) you'll come to the Gothic church of San Gregorio (now a restoration centre). The flank of the Salute is visible at the other end, but this preview doesn't quite prepare you for the mountain of white stone that confronts you when you emerge from the tunnel.

In 1630–31 Venice was devastated by a plague that exterminated nearly 95,000 of the lagoon's population – one person in three. In October 1630 the Senate decreed that a new church would be dedicated to Mary if the city were saved, and the result was the **Salute** (daily 9am–noon & 3–5.30pm) – *salute* meaning "health" and "salvation" – or Santa Maria della Salute, to use its full title.

Resting on a platform of more than 100,000 wooden piles, the Salute took half a century to build; its architect, **Baldassare Longhena**, was only 26 years old when his proposal was accepted. He lived just long enough to see it finished – he died in 1682, one year after completion. Each year on November 21 (the feast of the Presentation of the Virgin) the Signoria processed from San Marco to the Salute for a service of thanksgiving, crossing the Canal Grande on a pontoon bridge laid from Santa Maria del Giglio. The Festa della Madonna della Salute is still a major event in the Venetian calendar, with thousands of people making their way over the water in the course of the day to pray for, or give thanks for, their health.

The form of the Salute owes much to the plan of Palladio's Redentore – the obvious model for a dramatically sited votive church – and to the repertoire of Marian symbolism. The octagonal shape of the building alludes to the eight-pointed Marian star, for example, while the huge dome (a perilous engineering project in a city of mudbanks) represents Mary's crown and the centralized plan is a conventional symbol of the Virgin's womb. Its decorative details are saturated with coded references: the inscription in the centre of the mosaic floor, "Unde Origo, Inde Salus" (From the Origins came Salvation), refers to the coincidence

▲ Santa Maria della Salute

of Mary's feast day and the legendary date of Venice's foundation – March 25, 421; the Marian rosary is evoked by the encircling roses.

Less arcane symbolism is at work on the **high altar**, where the Virgin and Child rescue Venice (kneeling woman) from the plague (old woman); in attendance are Saint Mark and Saint Lorenzo Giustiniani, first Patriarch of Venice. The Byzantine painting, a little uneasy in this Baroque opulence, was brought to Venice in 1672 by Francesco Morosini, never a man to resist the opportunity for a bit of state-sanctioned theft. (For more on Francesco Morosini, see p.91.)

The most notable paintings in the Salute are the **Titian** pieces brought from the suppressed church of Santo Spirito in Isola in 1656, and now displayed in the sacristy (€2): an early altarpiece of *St Mark Enthroned with SS. Cosmas, Damian, Sebastian and Roch* (the plague saints), three violent ceiling paintings of *David and Goliath*, *Abraham and Isaac* and *Cain and Abel* (1540s), and eight late tondi of the *Doctors of the Church* (Jerome, Augustine, Gregory and Ambrose) and the *Evangelists*. Tintoretto has included himself in the dramatis personae of his *Marriage at Cana* (1561) – he's the first Apostle on the left. Nearby is a fine *Madonna* by Palma il Vecchio, one of the sixteenth century's more placid souls.

The Manfrediana and the Dogana di Mare

Longhena was also the architect of the **Seminario Patriarcale**, within which lurks one of the city's more ramshackle museums. The collection of tombstones and sculptural pieces around the cloister, many of them trawled from suppressed religious foundations, was thrown together in the early years of the nineteenth century; it was augmented soon after by the **Pinacoteca Manfrediana**, a motley collection of artworks incorporating paintings by Antonio Vivarini and Paolo Veronese, and portrait busts by Vittoria, Bernini and Canova. It's many years since the museum was last opened to the public.

On the point where the Canal Grande and the Giudecca canal merge stands the huge **Dogana di Mare** (Customs House), another late seventeenth-century building, which was serving as a customs office as recently as the mid-1990s but in 2009 became the **Centro d'Arte Contemporanea Punta della Dogana** (Mon & Wed–Sun 10am–7pm; €15). Financed by François Pinault, the co-owner of Palazzo Grassi (see p.92), the Dogana arts centre – like the Grassi – has been renovated to designs drawn up by the ever-discreet Tadao Ando. The exterior has been restored in a way that gives no indication of the building's new function (the weathervane figure on top of the Dogana's gold ball is said by most to represent Fortune, though others identify it as Justice), and the shell of the interior has similarly been left unaltered, with massive wooden roof-beams spanning walls of beautiful raw red brick. Within this casing, Ando has inserted walls of pale gray concrete, to create two storeys of elegant exhibition space, centered on a single double-height room. Some 300 works are usually on show at any one time, and Pinault has invested in most of the really big names of the current art scene, so you can expect to see pieces by the likes of Cindy Sherman, Luc Tuymans, Cy Twombly, Thomas Schütte, Maurizio Cattelan, Jeff Koons and Marlene Dumas.

The Záttere and western Dorsoduro

Known collectively as the **Záttere**, the sequence of waterfront pavements between the Punta della Dogana and the Stazione Maríttima is now a popular place for a stroll or an alfresco pizza, but was formerly the place where most of the bulky goods coming into Venice were unloaded onto floating rafts called *záttere*. A fair quantity of cargo was carted into the state-run and highly lucrative **Magazzini del Sale** (Salt Warehouses), the vast low structure near the Punta della Dogana. In the tenth century the Venetians established a regional monopoly in salt production by destroying the rival town of Comacchio, near the Po delta; some 44,000 tons of salt, most of it made in salt pans near Chioggia, could be stored in this one building, a stockpile that represented at its peak nearly ten percent of the state's income. Part of it is now a boathouse, and part is used as exhibition space during the Biennale and occasionally at other times.

From the Gesuati to San Trovaso

There's an appealing mix of architectural exteriors on the eastern reaches of the Zàttere: the fifteenth-century facade of **Spirito Santo** church, the **Casa degli Incurabili** (once one of Venice's four main hospitals, now the HQ of the Accademia art college), and the Veneto-Byzantine church of **Sant'Agnese**, begun in the twelfth century but much remodelled since then. However, the first building to break your stride for is the church of the **Gesuati** or Santa Maria del Rosario (Mon–Sat 10am–5pm; € 3 or Chorus Pass).

Rebuilt in 1726–43, about half a century after the church was taken over from the order of the Gesuati by the Dominicans, this was the first church designed by **Giorgio Massari**, an architect whose work combines Rococo preciousness with a more robust classicism – here his creation forms a sort of counterpoint to the Redentore, over the water. He often worked with **Giambattista Tiepolo**, who painted the first altarpiece on the right, *The Virgin with SS. Catherine of Siena, Rose and Agnes* (c.1740), and the three magnificent ceiling panels of *Scenes from the Life of St Dominic* (1737–39), which are seen to best effect in the afternoon, when the natural light comes from the same direction as the artificial light in the paintings. The third altar on this side of the church is adorned with a painting of *SS. Vincent Ferrer, Giacinto and Luigi Beltran* by Tiepolo's principal forerunner, Giambattista Piazzetta; opposite, the first altar has Sebastiano Ricci's *Pius V with SS. Thomas Aquinas and Peter Martyr* (1739), completing the church's array of Rococo propaganda on behalf of the exalted figures of Dominican orthodoxy, followed by a tragically intense *Crucifixion* by Tintoretto (c.1555) on the third altar.

Santa Maria della Visitazione (daily 8am–noon & 3–7pm), a couple of doors down, has an attractive Lombardesque facade, but the only notable aspect of the interior is its sixteenth-century **ceiling**, with panels painted by Umbrian artists. The lion's-mouth letter box to the right of the facade was for the use of residents with complaints relating to health and sanitation; a complaint sent to the authorities in 1498 resulted in punishment for the tradesmen who had sold oil that was full of "immonditie e sporchezi" (filth and dirt) – syphilitic patients had been immersed in it as a cure.

The squero di San Trovaso

Ten thousand gondolas operated on the canals of sixteenth-century Venice, when they were the standard form of transport around the city; nowadays the tourist trade is pretty well all that sustains the city's fleet of around five hundred gondolas, which provide steady employment for a few **squeri**, as the gondola yards are called. A display in the Museo Storico Navale (see p.183) takes you through the construction of a gondola, but no abstract demonstration can equal the fascination of a working yard, and the most public one in

Gondolas

The earliest mention of a gondola is in a decree of 1094, but the vessel of that period bore little resemblance to today's streamlined thoroughbred. As late as the thirteenth century the gondola was a twelve-oared beast with an iron beak – an adornment that evolved into the saw-toothed projection called the **ferro**, which fronts the modern gondola. (The precise significance of the ferro's shape is unclear – tradition has it that the six main prongs symbolize the six *sestieri*, with the backward-facing prong representing La Giudecca.) Over the next two centuries the gondola shrank to something near its present dimensions, developed multicoloured coverings and sprouted the little chair on carved legs that it still carries. The gondola's distinctive oarlock, an elaborately convoluted lump of walnut or cherry wood known as a **forcola**, which permits the long oar to be used in eight different positions, reached its definitive form at this time too.

By the sixteenth century the gondola had become a mode of social ostentation, with gilded prows, fantastically upholstered **felzi** (cabins), cushions of satin and silk, and hulls decked out with a profusion of embroidery, carvings and flowers. Sumptuary laws were introduced to quash this aquatic one-upmanship, and though some of them had little effect, one of them changed the gondola's appearance for good – since an edict of 1562 gondolas have been uniformly black, a livery which prompted Shelley to liken them to "moths of which a coffin might have been the chrysalis".

There's been little alteration in the gondola's dimensions and construction since the end of the seventeenth century: the only significant changes have been adjustments of the gondola's asymmetric line to compensate for the weight of the gondolier – a characteristic that's particularly noticeable when you see the things out of water. All gondolas are 10.87m long and 1.42m wide at their broadest point, and are assembled from nearly three hundred pieces of seasoned mahogany, elm, oak, lime, walnut, fir, cherry and larch. Plenty of gondolas pass through, under repair, but each *squero* turns out only about four new gondolas a year.

Venice is the **squero di San Trovaso**, which you'll see when you turn off the Zàttere towards San Trovaso church. The San Trovaso *squero* is the oldest one still functioning – established in the seventeenth century, it looks rather like an alpine farmhouse, a reflection of the architecture of the Dolomite villages from which many of Venice's gondola-builders once came. Another *squero* is tucked away on the Rio dell'Avogaria, a short distance west of here, beyond the former Benedictine convent of Ognissanti (which is now a hospital); a third is to be found on the other side of the city, on Rio dei Mendicanti, beside the hospital.

San Trovaso

Don't bother consulting your dictionary of saints for the dedicatee of **San Trovaso** church (Mon–Sat 2.30–5.30pm) – the name's a baffling dialect version of Santi Gervasio e Protasio. Since its tenth-century foundation the church has had a chequered history, falling down once, and twice being destroyed by fire; this is the fourth incarnation, built in 1584–1657.

Venetian folklore has it that this church was the only neutral ground between the Nicolotti and the Castellani, the two factions into which the working-class citizens of the city were divided – the former, coming from the west and north of the city, were named after the church of San Nicolò dei Mendicoli (see p.106), the latter, from the *sestieri* of Dorsoduro, San Marco and Castello, took their name from San Pietro di Castello. The rivals celebrated inter marriages and other services here, but are said to have entered and departed by separate doors: the

Nicolotti by the door at the traditional "west" end, the Castellani by the door on the "south" side.

Inside, San Trovaso is spacious and somewhat characterless, but it does boast a pair of fine paintings by **Tintoretto**: *The Temptation of St Anthony* and *The Last Supper*. The former is in the chapel to the left of the high altar (put 50 cents in the slot to turn the lighting on), with *St Crysogonus on Horseback* by Michele Giambono (c.1450), Venice's main practitioner of the International Gothic style; the latter is in the chapel at ninety degrees to the first one. The two large pictures on each side of the choir, *The Adoration of the Magi* and *The Expulsion from the Temple*, were begun by Tintoretto at the very end of his life, but so much of the finished work is by his son and other assistants that they are now attributed to Domenico. Finally, in the chapel next to the south door you'll find a marble altar-front carved with angels – dated around 1470, it's one of the first Renaissance low-reliefs produced in Venice.

San Sebastiano and beyond

At the end of the Záttere the barred gates of the Stazione Maríttima deflect you away from the waterfront and towards the church of **San Sebastiano** (Mon–Sat 10am–5pm; €3, or Chorus Pass). The parish church of **Paolo Veronese**, it contains a group of resplendent paintings by him that gives it a place in his career comparable to that of San Rocco in the career of Tintoretto, but the church attracts nothing like the number of visitors that San Rocco gets. Perhaps the latest bout of large-scale restoration work, funded by Save Venice Inc, will rectify that situation.

Veronese was still in his twenties when, thanks largely to his contacts with the Verona-born prior of San Samuele, he was asked to paint the ceiling of the **sacristy** with a *Coronation of the Virgin* and the *Four Evangelists* (1555); once that commission had been carried out, he decorated the **nave ceiling** with *Scenes from the Life of St Esther*. His next project, the dome of the chancel, was later destroyed, but the sequence he and his brother Benedetto then painted on the walls of the church and the nun's choir at the end of the 1550s has survived in pretty good shape. In the following decade he executed the last of the pictures, those on the **organ shutters** and around the **high altar** – on the left, *St Sebastian Leads SS. Mark and Marcellian to Martyrdom*, and on the right *The Second Martyrdom of St Sebastian* (the customarily depicted torture by arrows didn't kill him). Other riches include a late **Titian** of *St Nicholas* (on the left wall of the first chapel on the right), and the early sixteenth-century majolica pavement in the Cappello Lando, to the left of the chancel – in front of which is Veronese's tomb slab.

Angelo Raffaele

Across the campo, the exterior of the seventeenth-century church of **Angelo Raffaele** (Mon–Sat 8am–noon & 3–5pm, Sun 9am–noon) is notable only for the two huge war memorials blazoned on the canal facade. Over the doorway, a sixteenth-century relief depicts the angel Raphael with Tobias, whose life is illustrated in the scene on the organ loft inside, which was painted by one or other of the **Guardi** brothers (nobody's sure which). Although small in scale, the free brushwork and imaginative composition make the panels among the most charming examples of Venetian Rococo, a fascinating counterpoint to the grander visions of Giambattista Tiepolo, the Guardis' brother-in-law.

In the campo behind the church is a wellhead built from the bequest of Marco Arian, who died of the Black Death in 1348, an outbreak which he blamed on contaminated water. The **Palazzo Arian**, on the opposite bank of the canal, was built in the second half of that century and is adorned by one of the finest and earliest Gothic windows in Venice. It's the only window in the city that replicates the distinctive pattern of the Palazzo Ducale's stonework.

San Nicolò dei Mendicoli

Although it's located on the edge of the city, the church of **San Nicolò dei Mendicoli** (Mon–Sat 10am–noon & 3–5.30pm, Sun 10am–noon) is one of Venice's oldest – said to have been founded in the seventh century, San Nicolò is traditionally predated only by San Giacomo di Rialto. Its long history was reflected in the fact that it gave its name to the **Nicolotti** faction, whose titular head, the so-called *Gastaldo* or the *Doge dei Nicolotti*, was elected by the parishioners and then honoured by a ceremonial greeting from the Republic's doge.

The church has been rebuilt and altered at various times, and was being restored by Venice in Peril in the 1970s when Nic Roeg used it as a setting for *Don't Look Now*. In essence, however, its shape is still that of the Veneto-Byzantine structure raised here in the twelfth century, the date of its rugged campanile. The other conspicuous feature of the exterior is the fifteenth-century porch, a type of construction once common in Venice, and often used here as makeshift accommodation for penurious nuns. (The only other example left standing is at San Giacomo di Rialto.) The interior is a miscellany of periods and styles. Parts of the apse and the columns of the nave go back to the twelfth century, but the capitals were replaced in the fourteenth – the penultimate one on the left side bears an inscription dating it January 25, 1366. Above, the darkened gilded woodwork that gives the interior its rather overcast appearance was installed late in the sixteenth century, as were most of the paintings, many of which were painted by Alvise dal Friso and other pupils of Paolo Veronese. Occupying the high altar is a large wooden statue of Saint Nicholas, a mid-fifteenth-century piece, possibly from the workshop of Bartolomeo Bon.

The convent and church of **Le Terese**, on the other side of the canal, have been restored as student accommodation and a university auditorium (the church has famously fine acoustics); there's no reason to set foot on the island on which it stands, as it's a zone of docks, new housing developments and warehouses, one of which has been converted into a home for the city's well-reputed University of Architecture.

Northern Dorsoduro

Campo di Santa Margherita is the social heart of Dorsoduro, and is one of the most appealing squares in the whole city. The Piazza San Marco nowadays is overrun with tourists, but Campo di Santa Margherita – the largest square on this side of the Canal Grande – belongs to the Venetians and retains a spirit of authenticity. Ringed by houses that date back as far as the fourteenth century, it's spacious and at the same time modest, taking its tone not from any grandiose architecture (it's one of very few squares with no palazzo), but from its cluster of market stalls and its plethora of bars and cafés, which draw a lot of their custom from the university.

The church that gives the campo its name was closed in 1810, for a while functioned as a cinema, and is now a university property; the dragons that feature so prominently in the decorative stonework on and around the church

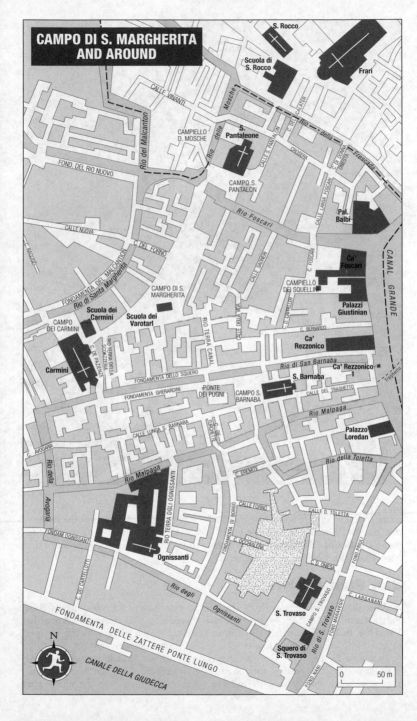

CAMPO DI S. MARGHERITA AND AROUND

S. Rocco

Scuola di S. Rocco

Frari

CALLE VINANTI

Rio del Malcanton

Rio delle Mosche

C. DEL CALATER

Rio — della — Frascada

CAMPIELLO D. MOSCHE

S. Pantaleone

CALLE S. PANTALON

CROSERA

C. DI DONNA ONESTA

FOND. DEL RIO NUOVO

CAMPO S. PANTALON

Rio Foscari

CALLE LARGA FOSCARI

Pal. Balbi

CALLE NUOVA

C. DEL FORNO

C. RAGUSEO

Ca' Foscari

CANAL GRANDE

FONDAMENTA DEL MALCANTION

CAMPO DI S. MARGHERITA

Rio di Santa Margherita

CALLE SAONERI

C. FOSCARI

CAMPIELLO DEI SQUELLINI

Palazzi Giustinian

Scuola dei Carmini

Scuola dei Varotarl

CALLE DELLA VIDA

CALLE DE CAPELLER

U. CAPPELLER

C. BERNARDO

Ca' Rezzonico

CAMPO DEI CARMINI

C. DE PAZIENZE

RIO TERRA DELLA SCAZZERIA

RIO TERRA CANAL

Rio di San Barnaba

Ca' Rezzonico 1

Carmini

FONDAMENTA DELLO SQUERO

S. Barnaba

Traghetto

FONDAMENTA GHERARDINI

PONTE DEI PUGNI

CAMPO S. BARNABA

CALLE DEL TRAGHETTO

Rio Malpaga

CALLE LUNGA S. BARNABA

C. DI TURCHETE

Palazzo Loredan

C. AVOGARIA

Rio della

Avogaria

Rio Malpaga

C. EREMITE

Rio della Toletta

RIO TERRA DEGLI OGNISSANTI

CALLE DI BORGO

CALLE FORNO

CALLE D. TOLETTA

FOND. PRIULI

FONDAM. OGNISSANTI

C. OCCHIALERA

C. D. ONIESA

Ognissanti

C. DEL CARTELLOTTI

Rio degli

Ognissanti

CAMPO S. TROVASO

Rio di S. TROVASO

FOND MARVEGIE

C. LARGANANI

S. Trovaso

FONDAMENTA DELLE ZATTERE PONTE LUNGO

Squero di S. Trovaso

N

CANALE DELLA GIUDECCA

FOND. NANI

0   50 m

▲ Il Caffè, Campo Santa Margherita

relate to the legend of Saint Margaret, who emerged unscathed after the dragon that had swallowed her exploded. Isolated at the fish-stall end of the campo stands the **Scuola dei Varotari** (Tanners' Guild), bearing an eroded relief of the Madonna with members of the scuola.

San Pantaleone

A short distance to the north of the campo rises the raw brick hulk of **San Pantaleone** (Mon–Sat 4–6pm), which possesses a picture by **Antonio Vivarini and Giovanni d'Alemagna** (*Coronation of the Virgin*, in the Chapel of the Holy Nail, to the left of the chancel) and **Veronese**'s last painting, *St Pantaleone Healing a Boy* (second chapel on right). San Pantaleone was credited with medicinal capabilities only slightly less awesome than San Rocco's, and Veronese's scene emphasizes the miraculous nature of his power (he spurns the offered box of potions) and the impotence of non-Christian treatment (symbolized by the limbless figure of Asclepius, the Classical god of medicine).

The church can also boast of having the most melodramatic **ceiling** in the city: *The Martyrdom and Apotheosis of St Pantaleone*. Painted on sixty panels, some of which actually jut out over the nave, it kept **Gian Antonio Fumiani** busy from 1680 to 1704. Sadly, he never got the chance to bask in the glory of his labours – he died in a fall from the scaffolding from which he'd been working.

Behind the church runs the teeming Crosera San Pantalon, where the atmosphere in the shops, cafés and bars has a lot to do with the proximity of the university. North of the Crosera, you're into the San Polo *sestiere*.

The Carmini scuola and church

Just off Campo di Santa Margherita's southwest tip is the **Scuola Grande dei Carmini** (daily 10am–5pm; €5), once the Venetian base of the Carmelite order. Originating in Palestine towards the close of the twelfth century, the Carmelites blossomed during the Counter-Reformation, when they became the shock-troops through whom the cult of the Virgin was disseminated, as a response to the inroads of Protestantism. As happened elsewhere in Europe, the Venetian Carmelites became immensely wealthy, and in the 1660s they called in an architect – probably Longhena – to redesign the property they had acquired. The core of this complex, which in 1767 was raised to the status of a *scuola grande*, is now effectively a showcase for the art of **Giambattista Tiepolo**, who in the 1740s painted the ceiling of the upstairs hall.

The central panel, framed by four *Virtues* in the corners of the ceiling, was recently restored after the cords that suspended it rotted away, causing it to crash from the ceiling. Depicting *Simon Stock Receiving the Scapular*, it is not the most immediately comprehensible image in Venetian art. The Carmelite order was in some disarray by the mid-thirteenth century, but it acquired a new edge when the English-born Simon Stock was elected prior general in 1247; under his control, the Carmelites were transformed into a well-organized mendicant order, with houses in the main university cities of Europe – Cambridge, Oxford, Paris and Bologna. Some time after his death the tradition grew that he had experienced a vision of the Virgin, who presented him with a scapular (two pieces of cloth joined by cords) bearing her image: as the scapular was the badge of the Carmelites, its gift was evidently a sign that Simon should undertake the development of the order. Tiepolo has translated this crucial episode from the place where it allegedly happened (Cambridge) to his customary floating world of blue skies and spiralling perspectives (a world seen at its most vertiginous in the painting of an angel rescuing a falling mason). The painting was such a hit with Tiepolo's clients that he was instantly granted membership of the scuola, a more generous reward than you might think – a papal bull had ordained that all those who wore the scapular would, through the intercession of the Virgin, be released from the pains of Purgatory on the first Saturday after the wearer's decease, "or as soon as possible" (sic). This edict was probably a forgery, but the Carmelites believed it, and it would seem that Tiepolo did too.

The adjacent **Carmini** church (or Santa Maria del Carmelo) – identifiable from a long way off, by the statue of the Virgin atop the campanile – is a collage of architectural styles, with a sixteenth-century facade, a Gothic side doorway which preserves several Byzantine fragments, and a fourteenth-century basilican interior (Mon–Sat 2.30–5.30pm). A dull series of Baroque paintings illustrating the history of the Carmelite order covers a lot of space inside (the same subject is covered by the gilded carvings of the nave), but the second altar on the right has a fine *Nativity* by Cima da Conegliano (before 1510), and Lorenzo Lotto's *SS. Nicholas of Bari, John the Baptist and Lucy* (1529) – featuring what Bernard Berenson ranked as one of the most beautiful landscapes in all Italian art – hangs on the opposite side of the nave.

The most imposing building on Fondamenta del Soccorso (leading from Campo dei Carmini towards Angelo Raffaele) is the **Palazzo Zenobio**, built in the late seventeenth century when the Zenobio family were among the richest in Venice. It's been an Armenian college since 1850, but visitors are sometimes allowed to see the ballroom: one of the city's richest eighteenth-century interiors, it was painted by Luca Carlevaris, whose trompe l'oeil decor provided a model for the decoration of the slightly later Ca' Rezzonico. In the late sixteenth century a home for prostitutes who wanted to get out of the business was set up at no. 2590 – the chapel of Santa Maria del Soccorso – by **Veronica Franco**, a renowned ex-courtesan who was as famous for her poetry and her artistic salon as she was for her sexual allure; both Michel de Montaigne and King Henry III of France were grateful recipients of samples of her literary output.

The parish of San Barnaba

Cutting down the side of the Carmini church takes you over the Rio di San Barnaba, along which a fondamenta runs to the church of San Barnaba. Just before the end of the fondamenta you pass the **Ponte dei Pugni**, the main link between San Barnaba and Santa Margherita, and one of several bridges with this name, which means "Bridge of the Fists". Originally built without parapets, these bridges were the sites of ritual battles between the Castellani and Nicolotti (see p.104); this one is inset with marble footprints marking the starting positions. These massed punch-ups took place between September and Christmas, and obeyed a well-defined etiquette, with prescribed ways of issuing challenges and deploying the antagonists prior to the outbreak of hostilities, the aim of which was to gain possession of the bridge. The fights themselves, however, were sheer bedlam, and fatalities were commonplace, as the armies slugged it out not just with bare knuckles but with steel-tipped lances made from hardened rushes. The lethal weaponry was outlawed in 1574, after a particularly bloody engagement that was arranged for the visit of Henry III of France, and in 1705 the brawls were finally banned, and less dangerous forms of competition, such as regattas, were encouraged instead. Pugilists have now been replaced by tourists taking shots of the photogenic San Barnaba grocery barge that's usually moored at the foot of the bridge.

The huge, damp-ridden **San Barnaba** church, built in 1749, has a trompe l'oeil ceiling-painting of *St Barnabas in Glory* by Constantino Cedini, a follower of Tiepolo. Despite recent restoration, the ceiling is being restored again because of moisture damage; while that's going on, the church has been turned over to a touristic exhibition on the "machines of Leonardo". At the time of the church's construction the parish was swarming with so-called *Barnabotti*, impoverished noble families who had moved into this area's cheap lodgings to eke out their meagre incomes. Forbidden as members of the aristocracy to practise a craft or run a shop, some of the *Barnabotti* supported themselves by selling their votes to the mightier families in the Maggior Consiglio, while others resigned themselves to subsistence on a paltry state dole. Visitors to the city often remarked on the incongruous sight of its silk-clad beggars – the nobility of Venice were obliged to wear silk, regardless of their ability to pay for such finery.

Ca' Rezzonico

The eighteenth century, the period of Venice's political senility and moral degeneration, was also the period of its last grand flourish in the visual and decorative arts. The main showcase for the art of that era, the **Museo del Settecento Veneziano** (April–Oct 10am–6pm; Nov–March 10am–5pm; closed Tues; €6.50) spreads through most of the enormous **Ca' Rezzonico**, which the city authorities bought in 1934 specifically as a home for the museum. Recently restored, it's a spectacular building, furnished and decorated mostly with genuine eighteenth-century items and fabrics: where originals weren't available, the eighteenth-century ambience has been preserved by using almost indistinguishable modern reproductions. Sumptuary laws in Venice restricted the quantities of silk, brocade and tapestry that could be draped around a house, so legions of painters, stuccoists, cabinet-makers and other such applied artists were employed to fanfare the wealth of their patrons to the world. The work they produced is certainly not to everyone's taste, but even if you find most of the museum's contents frivolous or grotesque, the frescoes by the Tiepolo family and Pietro Longhi's affectionate Venetian scenes should justify the entrance fee, and the informative sheets in each room allow you to get the most from the displays.

A man in constant demand in the early part of the century was the Belluno sculptor-cum-woodcarver **Andrea Brustolon**, much of whose output consisted of wildly elaborate pieces of furniture. A few of his pieces are displayed in the chandeliered ballroom at the top of the entrance staircase, and in the last room on this floor, the Brustolon Room, you'll find a whole lot more of them, including the *Allegory of Strength* console. Featuring Hercules underneath, two river gods holding four vases and a fifth vase held up by three black slaves in chains, this is a creation that makes you marvel at the craftsmanship and wince at the ends to which it was used.

The less fervid imaginations of **Giambattista Tiepolo** and his son **Giandomenico** are introduced in room 2 (off the far right-hand corner of the ballroom) with the ceiling fresco celebrating Ludovico Rezzonico's marriage into the hugely powerful Savorgnan family in 1758. This was quite a year for the Rezzonico clan, as it also brought the election of Carlo Rezzonico as **Pope Clement XIII**; the son of the man who bought the uncompleted palace and finished its construction, Carlo the pontiff was notorious both for his nepotism (a small painting in this room shows him with his nephews and niece) and for his prudery – he insisted that the Vatican's antique nude statuary be made more modest by the judicious application of fig leaves. Beyond room 4, with its array of pastels by **Rosalba Carriera**, you come to two other Giambattista Tiepolo ceilings, enlivening the rooms overlooking the Canal Grande on each side of the main portego: an *Allegory of Merit*, and *Nobility and Virtue Triumphing over Perfidy* (which was brought here in the 1930s). Below the latter you'll see some pictures by Giambattista's sons: Giandomenico, and the younger and far less famous Lorenzo. Giambattista's first teacher, Gregorio Lazzarini, is represented by a huge *Death of Orpheus* in Room 12, where the ceiling panels (and those of the adjoining Brustolon Room) are by the seventeenth-century artist Francesco Maffei, who painted them for a palazzo over in Cannaregio; should Ca' Rezzonico kindle a desire to see more work by him, you should take yourself off to his home city, Vicenza.

2

In the portego of the second floor hang the only two canal views by **Canaletto** on show in public galleries in Venice. An adjoining suite of rooms contains the museum's most engaging paintings – Giandomenico Tiepolo's sequence of **frescoes from the Villa Zianigo** near Mestre, the Tiepolo family home. Begun in 1759, the frescoes were completed towards the end of the century, by which time Giandomenico's decorative and virtuosic style was going out of fashion, which may be one reason for the undertone of wistful melancholy in pictures such as *The New World* (1791). Showing a crowd turned out in its best attire to watch a sideshow at a Sunday fair, this picture features a self-portrait – Giandomenico is on the right-hand side, standing behind his father. Another room is devoted to the antics of *Pulchinello*, the ancestor of our Mr Punch, including a marvellous ceiling depicting Punch on a swing; typically good-humoured centaurs and satyrs lark around on nearby walls. There then follows a succession of rooms with delightful portraits and depictions of everyday Venetian life by **Francesco Guardi** (including high-society recreation in the parlour of San Zaccaria's convent) and **Pietro Longhi**, whose artlessly candid work – such as a version of the famous *Rhinoceros* – has more than enough curiosity value to make up for its shortcomings in execution. Visitors at Carnevale time will recognize several of the festival's components in the Longhi room: the beak-like *volto* masks, for example, and the little doughnuts called *frittelle* or *fritole*. Room 19 boasts a full suite of green and gold lacquer pieces, one of the finest surviving examples of Venetian chinoiserie, and from there you come to the last rooms, a re-creation of an eighteenth-century bedroom suite, complete with wardrobe and boudoir.

The low-ceilinged rooms of the top floor house the reconstructed **Farmacia ai do San Marchi** (a sequence of wood-panelled rooms heavily stocked with old ceramic jars and glass bottles) and the **Pinacoteca Egidio Martini**, a huge private donation of Venetian art from the fifteenth to the twentieth centuries. Here you'll find a sprinkling of good pieces by Cima da Conegliano, Alvise Vivarini, Palma il Vecchio, Guercino, Sebastiano Ricci and Luca Giordano, but to find them you have to wade through an awful lot of mediocrity – and there cannot be a dafter painting in all of Venice than Pelagio Pelagi's *Birth of Venus*, which makes the arrival of the goddess of love look like the grand finale of an aquatic burlesque show. A far smaller private donation – the **Mestrovich** collection – occupies a couple of rooms reached via a staircase off the entrance hall; it contains no masterpieces, but Francesco Guardi's wacky *Madonna* might raise a smile.

From the Ca' Rezzonico, the quickest route up to the Rialto takes you across the herringbone-patterned pavement of the Campiello dei Squellini, past the entrance to the main university building and over the Rio Fóscari. Just to the right of the Ponte dei Fóscari, on the north side, is the central station of Venice's **fire brigade**. One of the few Fascist-era constructions in Venice, it's easily recognizable by the red launches moored under the arches.

San Polo and Santa Croce

The area covered by this chapter comprises the **San Polo** *sestiere*, which extends from the Rialto market to the Frari area, and the *sestiere* of **Santa Croce**, a far less sight-heavy district which lies to the north of San Polo and reaches right across to Piazzale Roma. Navigation through this sector of the city is not as baffling as it at first appears. There are two main routes through the district, each following approximately the curve of the Canal Grande – one runs between the Rialto and the Scalzi bridge, the other takes you in the opposite direction from the Rialto, down towards the Accademia. Virtually all the essential sights lie on, or just off, one of these two routes, and once you've become familiar with these the exploration of the streets and squares between them can be attempted with only a minimal risk of feeling that you'll never see friends and family again. Wherever you are in this area, you cannot be more than a couple of minutes' well-navigated walk from one of the two roads to the Rialto.

As far as the day-to-day life of Venice is concerned, the focal points of the district are the sociable open space of **Campo di San Polo** and the **Rialto** area, once the commercial heart of the Republic and still the home of a **market** that's famous far beyond the boundaries of the city. The bustle of the stalls and the unspoilt bars used by the porters are a good antidote to cultural overload. Nobody, however, should miss the extraordinary pair of buildings in the southern part of San Polo: the colossal Gothic church of the **Frari**, embellished with three of Venice's finest altarpieces, and the **Scuola Grande di San Rocco**, decorated with an unforgettable cycle of paintings by Tintoretto.

In the northern part of the district, Venice's **modern art**, **oriental and natural history museums** are clustered together on the bank of the Canal Grande; the first two collections occupy one of the city's most magnificent palaces, while the third is installed in the former headquarters of the Turkish merchants. As ever, numerous treasures are also scattered among the minor churches, most notably **San Cassiano** and **San Simeone Profeta**. Lastly, if you're in search of a spot in which to sit for an hour and just watch the world go by, head for the **Campo San Giacomo dell'Orio**, one of Venice's better-kept secrets.

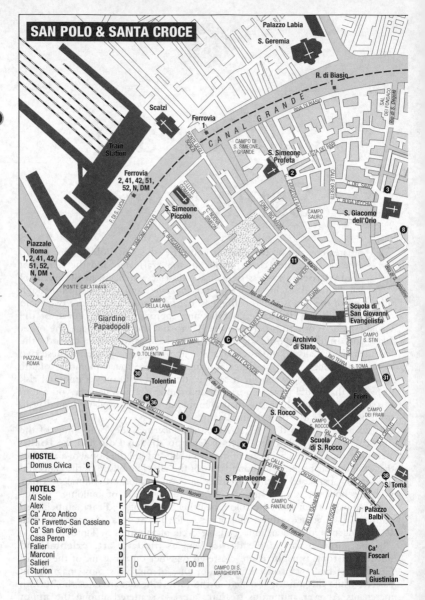

Map labels:

SAN POLO & SANTA CROCE

Palazzo Labia
S. Geremia
R. di Biasio
Scalzi
Ferrovia
Train Station
CANAL GRANDE
RIVA DI BIASIO
CAMPO DI S. SIMEONE GRANDE
S. Simeone Profeta
Ferrovia 2, 41, 42, 51, 52, N, DM
CALLE DI S. SAVIO
RUGA VECCHIA
S. Simeone Piccolo
CAMPO SAURO
S. Giacomo dell'Orio
Piazzale Roma 1, 2, 41, 42, 51, 52, N, DM
PONTE CALATRAVA
Giardino Papadopoli
CAMPO DELLA LANA
Rio di San Zuane
Scuola di San Giovanni Evangelista
CAMPO S. STIN
PIAZZALE ROMA
CORTE AMAI
CAMPO D.TOLENTINI
Archivio di Stato
S. TOMA
Tolentini
FOND. MINOTTO
S. Rocco
CAMPO S. ROCCO
Frari
CAMPO DEI FRARI
Scuola di S. Rocco
S. Pantaleone
CALLE DEI PRETI
CAMPO S. PANTALON
Rio Nuovo
Palazzo Balbi
S. Tomà
CALLE NUOVA
Rio Foscari
Ca' Foscari
Pal. Giustinian
CAMPO DI S. MARGHERITA

HOSTEL
Domus Civica — C

HOTELS
Al Sole	I
Alex	F
Ca' Arco Antico	G
Ca' Favretto-San Cassiano	B
Ca' San Giorgio	A
Casa Peron	K
Falier	J
Marconi	D
Salieri	H
Sturion	E

0   100 m

From the Rialto to San Simeone Piccolo

Relatively stable building land and a good defensive position drew some of the earliest lagoon settlers to the high bank (*rivo alto*) that was to develop into the **Rialto** district. By 810, when the capital of the lagoon confederation was moved – in the wake of Pepin's invasion – from Malamocco to the more secure

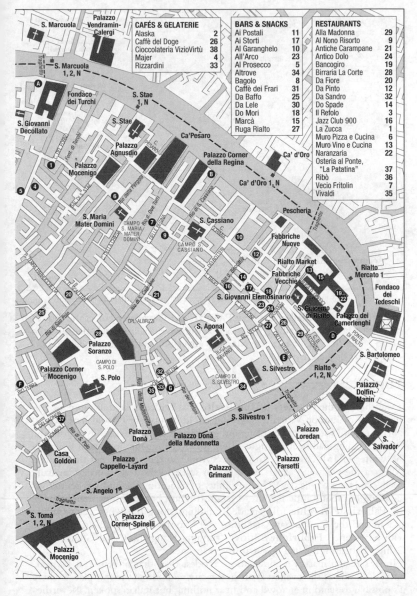

CAFÉS & GELATERIE	
Alaska	2
Caffè del Doge	26
Cioccolateria VizioVirtù	38
Majer	4
Rizzardini	33

BARS & SNACKS	
Ai Postali	11
Ai Storti	17
Al Garanghelo	10
All'Arco	23
Al Prosecco	5
Altrove	34
Bagolo	8
Caffè dei Frari	31
Da Baffo	25
Da Lele	30
Do Mori	18
Marcà	15
Ruga Rialto	27

RESTAURANTS	
Alla Madonna	29
Al Nono Risorto	9
Antiche Carampane	21
Antico Dolo	24
Bancogiro	19
Birraria La Corte	28
Da Fiore	20
Da Pinto	12
Da Sandro	32
Do Spade	14
Il Refolo	3
Jazz Club 900	16
La Zucca	1
Muro Pizza e Cucina	6
Muro Vino e Cucina	13
Naranzaria	22
Osteria al Ponte,	
"La Patatina"	37
Ribò	36
Vecio Fritolin	7
Vivaldi	35

islands around here, the inhabited zone had grown well beyond the Rialto itself. While the political centre of the new city was consolidated around San Marco, the Rialto became the commercial area. In the twelfth century Europe's first state bank was opened here, and the financiers of this quarter were to be the heavyweights of the international currency exchanges for the next three hundred years and more. The state departments that oversaw all maritime business were here as well, and in the early sixteenth century the offices of the

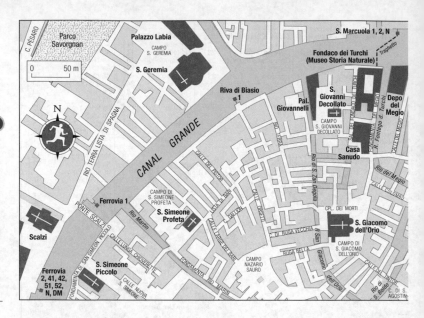

exchequer were installed in the new **Palazzo dei Camerlenghi**, at the foot of
the Rialto bridge. It's telling that, in this quintessentially mercantile city, the
Rialto rather than the Piazza San Marco is advertised as the "Cuore della Città"
– the Heart of the City.

The Market

It was through the **markets of the Rialto** that Venice earned its reputation as
the bazaar of Europe. Virtually anything could be bought or sold here: Italian
fabrics, precious stones, silver plate and gold jewellery, spices and dyes from the
Orient. Trading had been going on here for over four hundred years when, in
the winter of 1514, a fire destroyed everything in the area except the church.
(Most of the wells and canals were frozen solid, so the blaze burned virtually
unchecked for a whole day.) The possibility of relocating the business centre was
discussed but found little favour, so reconstruction began almost straight away:
the **Fabbriche Vecchie** (the arcaded buildings along the Ruga degli Orefici
and around the Campo San Giacomo) were finished eight years after the fire,
with Sansovino's **Fabbriche Nuove** (running along the Canal Grande from
Campo Battisti) following about thirty years later.

Today's Rialto market is much more modest than that of Venice at its peak,
but it's still one of the liveliest spots in the city, and one of the few places where
it's possible to stand in a crowd and hear nothing but Italian spoken. Nevertheless, the traders nowadays can't keep going without the revenue from tourists,
who account for some forty percent of their income, and in recent years several
stallholders have gone out of business, having found it impossible to turn a
profit in the winter months.

There's a shoal of trinket sellers by the church, gathered to catch the sightseers as they spill off the bridge, and a strong showing of glass junk, handbags
and "Venezia" sweatshirts further on, but the true Rialto market comprises

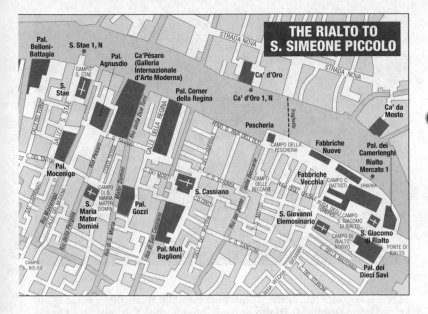

THE RIALTO TO
S. SIMEONE PICCOLO

Pal. Belloni-Battagia
S. Stae 1, N
Pal. Agnusdio
Ca'Pésaro (Galleria Internazionale d'Arte Moderna)
Ca' d'Oro
STRADA NOVA
CAMPO S. STAE
S. Stae
Pal. Corner della Regina
Ca' d'Oro 1, N
Ca' da Mosto
Rio della Due Torri
Pescheria
CALLE DEL FORNO
SALIZZ S. STAE
C.D RAVANO
CALLE DELLA REGINA
FOND DI RIVA DELL OCIO
CAMPO DELLA PESCHERIA
Fabbriche Nuove
Pal. dei Camerlenghi
DEL TINTOR
Pal. Mocenigo
CALLE TRON
CALLE DELLA REGINA
Rialto Mercato 1
CALLE DEL BAVANO
Rio Pésaro
CALLE DEI MORTI
Pal. Muti Baglioni
CALLE CAMPANILE
Calle Beccarie
CAMPO DELLE BECCARIE
RUGA DEGLI OREFICI
ERBARIA
CALLE CARMINATI
CAMPO DI S. MARIA MATER DOMINI
Mater Domini
Fabbriche Vecchia
CAMPO C. BATTISTI
CALLE DEL SCRIMIA
RUGA DEI
S. Cassiano
Rio della Pergola
Calle del Mocenigo
S. Maria Mater Domini
Pal. Gozzi
RUGA DEL PONTE
CALLE DEL BOTTERI
S. Giovanni Elemosinario
CAMPO DI RIALTO NUOVO
S. Giacomo di Rialto
Rio di S. Maria
Rio di San Cassiano
CA DEI CRISTI
C.D SANSONI
C. DELLA MADONNA
PONTE DI RIALTO
CAMPO S. BOLDO
Pal. Muti Baglioni
RUGA VECCHIA S. GIOVANNI
C. DEL STIVIONE
Pal. dei Dieci Savi

3

SAN POLO AND SANTA CROCE | From the Rialto to San Simeone Piccolo | www.roughguides.com

the fruit sellers around the **Campo San Giacomo**, the vegetable stalls and butcher's shops of **Campo Battisti**, and the **Pescheria** (fish market) beyond. The Pescheria and most of the larger wholesalers at the Rialto close down for the day at around 1pm, but many of the smaller fruit and vegetable stalls keep normal shop hours. Around the junction of **Ruga degli Orefici** and **Ruga Vecchia San Giovanni** you'll find wonderful cheese kiosks, and the bars and *osterie* of this district are among the best in the city. In short, if you can't find something to excite your taste buds around the Rialto, they must be in a sorry state.

San Giacomo and the Gobbo di Rialto

A popular Venetian legend asserts that the city was founded at noon on Friday, March 25, 421; from the same legend derives the claim that the church of **San Giacomo di Rialto** or San Giacometto (Mon–Sat 9.30am–noon & 4–6pm) was consecrated in that year, and is thus **the oldest church in Venice**. It might actually be the oldest, but all that's known for certain is that it was rebuilt in 1071, about the same time as San Marco's reconstruction.

Parts of the present structure date from this period – the interior's six columns of ancient Greek marble have eleventh-century Veneto-Byzantine capitals – and it seems likely that the reconstruction of the church prompted the establishment of the market here. On the outside of the apse a twelfth-century inscription addresses the merchants of the Rialto – "Around this temple let the merchant's law be just, his weights true, and his promises faithful." Early Venetian churches often had lean-to porticoes like that of San Giacomo, but this is one of only two examples left in the city (the other being San Nicolò dei Mendicoli). The inaccuracy of the clock above – a fifteenth-century addition, like the portico – has been a standing joke in Venice since the day it was installed. Like so many of Venice's under-used churches, San Giacometto is often pressed into service as a concert venue, with Vivaldi, as ever, featuring heavily.

117

▲ The Pescheria, Rialto market

On the opposite side of the campo from the church crouches a stone figure known as the **Gobbo di Rialto** or the Rialto hunchback. It was carved in the sixteenth century and supports a granite platform from which state proclamations were read simultaneously with their announcement from the Pietra del Bando, beside San Marco; it had another role as well – certain wrongdoers were sentenced to run the gauntlet, stark naked, from the Piazza to the Gobbo.

From the Pescheria to Santa Maria Mater Domini

Once past the Pescheria, you're into a district which quickly becomes labyrinthine even by Venetian standards. A stroll between the Rio delle Beccarie and the Rio di San Zan Degolà will satisfy any addict of the picturesque – you cannot walk for more than a couple of minutes without coming across a workshop crammed into a ground-floor room or a garden spilling over a canalside wall.

The barn-like church of **San Cassiano** (daily 9am–noon & 5–7pm) is a building you're bound to pass as you wander out of the Rialto. The thirteenth-century campanile is the only appealing aspect of the exterior, and the interest of the interior lies mainly with its three paintings by **Tintoretto**: *The Resurrection, The Descent into Limbo* and *The Crucifixion* (all 1565–68). The first two have been mauled by restorers, but the third is one of the most startling pictures in Venice – centred on the ladder on which the executioners stand, it's painted as though the observer were lying in the grass at the foot of the Cross. The obscure dedicatee of the church is depicted in the Tintoretto *Resurrection* and in a painting that can be seen in a small chapel off the left aisle (reached via the sacristy), where he's shown being stabbed to death by his pupils, a demise that earned him the status of patron saint of schoolteachers.

Campo San Cassiano was the site of the **first public opera house** in the world – it opened in 1636, at the peak of Monteverdi's career. Long into the following century Venice's opera houses were among the most active in Europe;

around five hundred works received their first performances here in the first half of the eighteenth century.

A sign directs you from the campo over the right-hand bridge towards the Ca' Pésaro, passing the back of the **Palazzo Corner della Regina** (see p.191). A few metres beyond this palazzo, a diversion down Corte Tiossi from Calle Tiossi brings you to the small **Campo Santa Maria Mater Domini**, which is a perfect Venetian miscellany, untouched by tourism – a thirteenth-century house (the Casa Zane), a few ramshackle Gothic houses, an assortment of stone reliefs of indeterminate age, a fourteenth-century wellhead in the centre, a workaday bar, a couple of shops and a hairdresser's.

Off the end of the campo stands **Santa Maria Mater Domini** (Tues–Fri 10am–noon), an early sixteenth-century church of disputed authorship – Mauro Codussi and Giovanni Buora are the leading candidates. The rescue of this building is one of Venice in Peril's proudest achievements; now protected by a totally reconstructed roof, the crisp white and grey interior boasts an endearing *Martyrdom of St Christina* by **Vincenzo Catena** (second altar on the right), showing a flight of angels plucking the saint from a carpet-like Lago di Bolsena, into which she had been hurled with a millstone for an anchor. Few works by the elusive Catena have survived, and it is not even certain what he

Sex on the Rialto

A sixteenth-century survey showed that there were about 3000 patrician women in Venice, but more than 11,000 **prostitutes and courtesans**, the majority of them based in the Rialto. (Courtesans were self-sufficient and costlier women who usually lived in their own homes or with a small number of similarly upmarket ladies.) Two Venetian **brothels** – the state-run *Casteletto*, which was especially esteemed for the literary and musical talents of its staff, and the privately operated *Carampane* – were officially sanctioned; both were in the Rialto and operated in the same manner, with curfews, armed guards, and a system for sharing the revenue equally among the staff. These establishments were founded in the fourteenth century, and efforts were then made to limit prostitution to the Rialto, but by the end of the following century there were brothels all over the city, prompting one writer to remark that "Venice seems to me to have been made a bordello." The *Catalogue of the Chief and Most Renowned Courtesans of Venice*, a directory that told you everything you needed to know (right down to prices), became a perennial bestseller, and if Thomas Coryat's report of 1608 is anything to go by, the courtesans were seen by some as the city's main attraction – "So infinite are the allurements of these amorous Calypsoes that the fame of them hath drawn many to Venice from some of the remotest parts of Christendome."

Coryat, like so many male observers and customers of the city's "Calypsoes", was happy to perpetuate the myth that these women were happy in their work. That so many Venetian courtesans were the well-educated offspring of "good" families seemed to indicate that their profession was a matter of free choice. But in a society in which sons were generally the major (and often the sole) beneficiaries of their parents' wills, and fathers were often reluctant to disperse the family fortune by lavishing dowries on their daughters, many young women could expect to be dispatched to a convent as adulthood approached, if no wealthy suitor were on the horizon. It's thus hardly surprising that a large number of **patrician women** should instead choose a way of life that at least offered the prospect of independence and a social life. But even the most celebrated of the city's courtesans, **Veronica Franco**, a woman whose beauty and intellectual distinction were praised by princes and writers, was adamant that the cost of selling herself was too great: "to subject one's body and industry to a servitude whose very thought is most frightful...What greater misery? What riches, what comforts, what delights can possibly outweigh all this?"

did for a living. He seems to have been a successful spice trader, and thus may have been a businessman who painted for recreation; alternatively, he may have been an artist who subsidized himself through commercial 'dealings – he is mentioned on the reverse of one of Giorgione's paintings as a "colleague". On the opposite side of the church you'll find yet another of the city's legion of Tintoretto paintings, a *Discovery of the Cross*, painted in the 1560s.

Ca' Pésaro

Back at the end of Calle Tiossi, in front of you on the other side of the bridge as you turn right for the Ca' Pésaro, is the late fourteenth-century **Palazzo Agnusdio**, which takes its name not from the family that lived there but from the *patera* of the mystic lamb over the watergate.

The immense **Ca' Pésaro** was bequeathed to the city at the end of the nineteenth century by the Duchessa Felicità Bevilacqua La Masa, an energetic patron of the arts who stipulated in her will that the palazzo should provide studio and exhibition space for impoverished young artists. Although enterprising exhibitions were later held at Ca' Pésaro, and the Bevilacqua La Masa foundation still promotes progressive art (see p.266), the Duchess's enlightened plans were never fully realized, and in place of the intended living arts centre the palazzo became home to the **Galleria Internazionale d'Arte Moderna** (Tues–Sun: April–Oct 10am–6pm; Nov–March 10am–5pm; €5.50, or Museum Pass/Venice Card). The Rodin *Thinker* outside the door creates a somewhat misleading impression: although the galleries contain a smattering of work by such heavyweights as Klimt, Kandinsky, Matisse, Klee, Nolde, Morandi, Ernst and Miró, all in all this is a rather parochial collection, with far too many pieces that are modern only in the chronological sense of the word. It starts with a display of Italian art from the late nineteenth century, a generally cosy array of landscapes and Venetian scenes that becomes considerably more interesting when you reach the sculptures of Medardo Rosso, in which figures emerge ambiguously from a matrix of wax. Pieces bought from the Biennale fill the main hall, but in its early years the Biennale was far from being a celebration of radicalism, and many of the paintings in this room are tedious examples of salon art. Another room is devoted to the portentously intense sculpture of Adolfo Wildt (*Mask of Pain – Self-Portrait* sets the tone), and the rooms dedicated to the exhibitions held here from 1908 to 1924, when Ca' Pésaro had a reputation for being a more daring venue than the Biennale, aren't likely to thrill – it's hard to imagine how anyone could have been excited by pictures such as Felice Casorati's "metaphysical" *Young Ladies*. In the later sections of the museum, covering the years in which the Biennale established its avant-garde credentials, the Venetian artist Emilio Vedova is the outstanding figure among a generally underpowered showing of Italian work.

In the creaky and poorly lit top-floor rooms of Ca' Pésaro you'll find the chronically neglected **Museo Orientale** (same hours & ticket), where, amid the cases of samurai ceremonial armour that line the entrance, you'll read a notice telling you that this is a temporary display, pending removal to a new museum – but the sign has been there for more than twenty years. Built round a hoard of artefacts amassed by the Conte di Bardi (a Bourbon prince) during a long Far Eastern voyage in the nineteenth century, it's a jumble of porcelain, musical instruments, clothing, paintings on silk, and enough swords, daggers and lances to equip a private army. Many of the pieces are exquisite (look out for an incredibly intricate ivory-and-coral chess set and a room packed with marvellous lacquerwork), but the labelling and general presentation are so woeful as to render the collection virtually incomprehensible to the uninitiated.

Before leaving Ca' Pésaro you might want to stop for a coffee at the café that's installed at the end of the ground-floor hall (where large-scale artworks are displayed) – its tables offer a superb view of the Canal Grande.

From San Stae to the Museo di Storia Naturale

Continuing along the line of the Canal Grande from the Ca' Pésaro, Calle Pésaro takes you over the Rio della Rioda, and so to the seventeenth-century church of **San Stae**, a contraction of San Eustachio (Mon–Sat 10am–5pm; €3, or Chorus Pass). Its Baroque facade, added around 1710, is enlivened by precarious statues, and the *marmorino* (pulverized marble) surfaces of the interior make San Stae as bright as an operating theatre on sunny days. In the chancel there's a series of paintings from the beginning of the eighteenth century, the pick of which are *The Martyrdom of St James the Great* by Piazzetta (low on the left), *The Liberation of St Peter* by Sebastiano Ricci (same row) and *The Martyrdom of St Bartholomew* by Giambattista Tiepolo (opposite). In the first chapel on the left side there's a bust of Antonio Foscarini (see p.198), wrongly executed for treason, as the inscription explains. Exhibitions and concerts are often held in San Stae, and exhibitions are also held from time to time in the diminutive building alongside, the early seventeenth-century **Scuola dei Battioro e Tiraoro** (Goldsmiths' Guild).

Halfway down the salizzada flanking San Stae is the early seventeenth-century **Palazzo Mocenigo** (Tues–Sun: April–Oct 10am–5pm; Nov–March 10am–4pm; €4, or Museum Pass/Venice Card), now the home of the Centro Studi di Storia del Tessuto e del Costume (Centre for the Study of the History of Textiles and Clothing). The library and archive of the study centre occupy part of the building, but a substantial portion of the *piano nobile* is open to the public, and there are few Venetian interiors of this date that have been so meticulously preserved. The main room is decorated with workaday portraits of various Mocenigo men, while the rooms to the side are full of miscellaneous pictures, antique furniture, Murano chandeliers and display cases of dandified clothing and cobweb-fine lacework. The curtains are kept closed to protect such delicate items as floral silk stockings, silvery padded waistcoats, and an extraordinarily embroidered outfit once worn by what must have been the best-dressed five-year-old in town.

The signposted route to the train station passes the deconsecrated and almost permanently shut church of **San Giovanni Decollato** (Mon–Sat 10am–noon), known as San Zan Degolà in dialect – it means "St John the Beheaded". Established in the opening years of the eleventh century, it has retained its basilican layout through several alterations; the columns and capitals of the nave date from the first century of its existence, and parts of its fragmentary frescoes (at the east end) could be of the same age. Some of the paintings are certainly thirteenth-century, and no other church in Venice has frescoes that predate them. The church also boasts one of the city's characteristic ship's-keel ceilings.

The **Museo di Storia Naturale** is right by the church, in the **Fondaco dei Turchi**. Top-billing exhibits are the remains of an eleven-metre-long ancestor of the crocodile and an Ouranosaurus, both dug up in the Sahara in 1973; of stricter relevance to Venetian life is the display relating to the lagoon's marine life, and a pre-Roman boat dredged from the silt. However, for many years the building has been undergoing a major restoration, and at the moment only the aquarium and dinosaur room are open (Tues–Fri 9am–1pm, Sat & Sun 10am–4pm; free); for information on the building itself, see p.190.

From San Giacomo dell'Orio to San Simeone Piccolo

Far more appealing than the natural history museum is **San Giacomo dell'Orio** (Mon–Sat 10am–5pm; €3, or Chorus Pass), a couple of minutes from the Fondaco dei Turchi. Standing in a shaded campo which, despite its size, you could easily miss if you weren't looking for it, the church perhaps takes its enigmatic name from a laurel (*lauro*) that once grew here, or might once have been called San Giacomo dal Rio (St James of the River), or once have stood on a *luprio*, the term for a tract of dried swampland.

The fascinating **interior** is an agglomeration of materials and styles from the thirteenth century to the sixteenth. Founded in the ninth century and rebuilt in 1225 – the approximate date of the campanile – San Giacomo was remodelled on numerous subsequent occasions. Its **ship's-keel roof** dates from the fourteenth century; the massive columns, made stockier by frequent raisings of the pavement, are a couple of hundred years older. Two of the columns – behind the pulpit and in the right transept – were brought to Venice by the fleet returning from the Fourth Crusade; the latter, an extraordinary chunk of *verde antico*, was compared by the excitable Gabriele d'Annunzio to "the fossilized compression of an immense verdant forest". The shape of the main apse betrays its Byzantine origins, but the inlaid marbles were placed there in the sixteenth century. The main altarpiece, *Madonna and Four Saints*, was painted by Lorenzo Lotto in 1546, shortly before he left the city complaining that the Venetians had not treated him fairly; the *Crucifix* that hangs in the air in front of it is attributed to Paolo Veneziano. In the left transept there's an altarpiece by Paolo Veronese, and there's a fine set of pictures from Veronese's workshop on the ceiling of the **new sacristy**: *Faith* and *The Doctors of the Church*. Also in the new sacristy you'll see Francesco Bassano's *Madonna in Glory* and *St John the Baptist Preaching* – Bassano's family provide the Baptist's audience, while the spectator on the far left, in the red hat, is Titian. The **old sacristy** is a showcase for the art of Palma il Giovane, whose cycle in celebration of the Eucharist covers the walls and part of the ceiling.

Originating in the tenth century, the nearby church of **San Simeone Profeta** or San Simeone Grande (Mon–Sat 8am–noon & 5–6.30pm) has often been rebuilt – most extensively in the eighteenth century, when the city sanitation experts, anxious about the condition of the plague victims who had been buried under the flagstones in the 1630 epidemic, ordered the relaying of the whole floor. An undistinguished building, it's remarkable for its reclining **effigy of Saint Simeon** (to the left of the chancel), a luxuriantly bearded, larger than lifesize figure, whose half-open mouth disturbingly creates the impression of the moment of death. According to its inscription, it was sculpted in 1317 by **Marco Romano**, but some experts doubt that the sculpture can be that old, as nothing else of that date bears comparison with it. On the left immediately inside the door, there's a run-of-the-mill *Last Supper* by **Tintoretto**.

Close by the church, the **Riva di Biasio** allows a short walk on the bank of the Canal Grande, with a view across the water of San Geremia. This stretch of paving allegedly takes its name from a butcher named Biasio who was decapitated between the columns of the Piazzetta after it was discovered that his prime pork cuts were in fact lumps of human flesh. San Simeone Profeta is the last stop before the Scalzi bridge. Immediately after the bridge rises the green dome of the early eighteenth-century **San Simeone Piccolo**, where for many years Venice's only Latin Mass has been conducted, despite the church's notorious state of dilapidation; it is now at last receiving a facelift.

From the Rialto to San Tomà

South of the Rialto, **Ruga Vecchia San Giovanni** constitutes the first leg of the right bank's nearest equivalent to the Mercerie of San Marco, a reasonably straight chain of alleyways that is interrupted by Campo di San Polo and then resumes with the chic Calle dei Saoneri. The Ruga Vecchia itself – its shops typifying the economic mix that is characteristic of many right-bank districts – has just one major monument, **San Giovanni Elemosinario** (Mon–Sat 10am–5pm; €3, or Chorus Pass), a church so solidly packed into the surrounding buildings that its fifteenth-century campanile is the only conspicuous indication of its presence. Founded in the eleventh century, it was wrecked in the huge Rialto fire of 1514 – only the campanile survived, and after the church was rebuilt in 1527–29 (to designs by Scarpagnino) a bell was rung here every evening, as a signal for all fires to be extinguished for the night. Most of the church's decoration dates from the decades immediately following the rebuild; several pictures by the ubiquitous Palma il Giovane are here, alongside work by Leonardo Corona, but the best are **Titian**'s high altarpiece (*St John the Almsgiver*), and **Pordenone**'s nearby *SS Catherine, Sebastian and Roch*. The frescoes in the cupola, featuring a gang of very chunky cherubs, are also by Pordenone.

The route to San Polo widens momentarily at **Sant'Aponal** (in full, Apollinare), which is now used as an archive for Venice's marriage registers. Its most interesting feature is on the outside, anyway – the *Crucifixion and Scenes from the Life of Christ* (1294), in the tabernacle over the door. Venetian legend has it that Pope Alexander III, on the run in 1177 from the troops of Emperor Frederick Barbarossa, found refuge close to Sant'Aponal; over the entrance to the Sottoportego della Madonna (to your left and slightly behind you as you face the church facade), a plaque records his plight and promises a perpetual plenary indulgence to anyone saying a Pater Noster and Ave Maria on the spot.

Slip down Calle Sbianchesini from Sant'Aponal (towards the Canal Grande), and you come to the nondescript church of **San Silvestro** (Mon–Sat 7.30–11.30am & 4–6pm), which deserves a visit for Tintoretto's *Baptism of Christ*. Across from the church, at no. 1022, is the Palazzo Valier, where Giorgione died in 1510.

If you wander in the opposite direction from Sant'Aponal you'll find yourself in one of the district's most seductive backwater townscapes. Leave Campo Sant'Aponal by Calle Ponte Storto, which leads to the crook-backed Ponte Storto; the gorgeous building on your right, as you cross the water, is the palace where Bianca Cappello was living when she met Pietro Bonaventuri (see p.169 for the story). At the foot of the bridge go left onto Fondamenta Banco Salviati, then halfway along the colonnade turn right into Calle Stretta, the narrowest alley in the whole city. Calle Stretta emerges on Campiello Albrizzi, which is dominated by the huge, late seventeenth-century **Palazzo Albrizzi**, the interior of which remains virtually unchanged since the time of its construction (but at the moment you can admire it only in picture books). Cross the

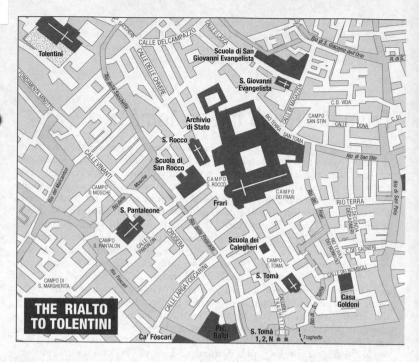

campiello and go down Calle Albrizzi; turn left at the end and you'll come to the water at Fondamenta delle Tette. Stand on the little bridge here – **Ponte delle Tette** – and to the north you have a terrific view of a ravine of palaces leading off towards the Canal Grande, while to the south you'll see the side of the Palazzo Albrizzi, with the foliage of a neighbouring garden spilling over towards it across the canal. If you're wondering about the name of the delle Tette bridge and canalside, it means exactly what you suspect it means: the bridge marks the edge of the zone within which the Rialto prostitutes were allowed to solicit, and one of their advertising ploys was to air their breasts on the balconies of their houses.

Campo San Polo

The largest square in Venice after the Piazza, **Campo San Polo** is the best place in the area to sit down and tuck into a bagful of supplies from the Rialto market. Once the site of weekly markets and occasional fairs, this square was also used as a parade ground and bullfighting arena – and on one notorious occasion it was the scene of a bloody act of political retribution. On February 26, 1548, Lorenzaccio de'Medici, having fled Florence after murdering the deranged Duke Alessandro (a distant relative and former friend), emerged from San Polo church to come face to face with the emissaries of Duke Cosimo I, Alessandro's successor. A contemporary account records that a struggle ensued, at the end of which Lorenzaccio's head was "split in two pieces" and his uncle, Alessandro Soderini, lay dead beside him. The assassins took refuge in the Spanish embassy, but the Venetian government, with customary pragmatism, decided that the internal squabbles of Florence were of no concern to Venice, and let the matter rest.

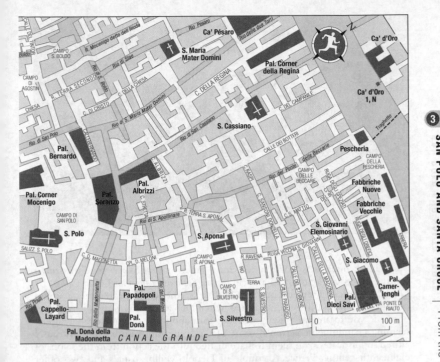

Several palaces overlook the campo, the most impressive of which is the double **Palazzo Soranzo**, across the square from the church. Built between the late fourteenth and mid-fifteenth centuries, this might seem an exception to the rule that the main palace facade should look onto the water, but in fact a canal used to run across the campo just in front of the Soranzo house. Casanova gained his introduction to the Venetian upper classes through a senator who lived in this palace; he was hired to work as a musician in the house and so impressed the old man that he was adopted as his son. On the same side of Campo San Polo as the church, but in the opposite corner, is the **Palazzo Corner Mocenigo**, designed around 1550 by Sanmicheli – the main facade is visible from the bridge beyond the church. In 1909 **Frederick Rolfe** (Baron Corvo) became a tenant here, an arrangement that came to an abrupt end the following year when his hosts discovered that the manuscript he was working on – *The Desire and Pursuit of the Whole* – was a vitriolic satire directed at them and their acquaintances. Rolfe was given the alternative of abandoning the libellous novel or moving out; he moved out, contracted pneumonia as a result of sleeping rough and became so ill he was given the last rites – but he managed to pull through, and lived for a further three disreputable years.

San Polo church

Restoration carried out in the early nineteenth century made a thorough mess of the fifteenth-century Gothic of **San Polo** church (Mon–Sat 10am–5pm; €3, or Chorus Pass), which was established as far back as the ninth century. The beautiful main **doorway**, possibly by Bartolomeo Bon, survives from the first church; the detached campanile, built in 1362, has a couple of twelfth-century lions at its base, one of which is playing with a snake, the other with a severed human head.

▲ Campo San Polo

The bleak interior is worth a visit for a superior *Last Supper* by **Tintoretto** (on the left as you enter) and a cycle of the *Stations of the Cross* (*Via Crucis*) by **Giandomenico Tiepolo** in the Oratory of the Crucifix (entrance under organ). This powerful series, painted when the artist was only twenty, may persuade you to amend a few preconceptions about the customarily frivolous-seeming Giandomenico, even if some of the scenes do feature some lustrously attired sophisticates who seem to have drifted into the action from the salons of eighteenth-century Venice. A couple of Tiepolo ceiling panels and two other easel paintings supplement the *Via Crucis*; back in the main part of the church, paintings by Giandomenico's father and Veronese are to be found on the second altar opposite the door and in the chapel on the left of the chancel respectively, but neither shows the artist at his best.

South from Campo San Polo

If you turn right halfway down Calle dei Saoneri, you're on your way to the Frari; carry on to the end and then turn left, and you'll soon come to the fifteenth-century **Palazzo Centani**, in Calle dei Nomboli. This was the birthplace of **Carlo Goldoni** (1707–93), who practised law until 1748, by which time he had accumulated some fourteen years' part-time experience in writing pieces for the indigenous *commedia dell'arte*. Like all *commedia* pieces, the scripts written during that period were essentially just vehicles for the semi-improvised clowning of the actors impersonating the genre's stock characters – tricky Harlequin, doddering Pantalon, capricious Colombine, and so on. Goldoni set about reforming the *commedia* from within, turning it eventually into a medium for sharp political observation – indeed, his arch-rival Carlo Gozzi accused Goldoni of creating an "instrument of social subversion". Despite his enormous success, in 1762 he left Venice to work for the Comédie Italienne in Paris, where he also taught Italian in the court of Louis XVI, and received a royal pension until the outbreak of the Revolution. Goldoni's plays are still the staple of theatrical life in Venice, and there's plenty of material to choose from – allegedly, he once bet a friend that he could produce one play a week for a whole year, and won. The Goldoni family home, the **Casa Goldoni** (Mon, Tues & Thurs–Sun 10am–5pm, Nov–March closes 4pm; €2.50, or Museum Pass/Venice Card), now houses the Istituto di Studi Teatrali and

Aldus Manutius

Except for the scurrilous hack Pietro Aretino and the altogether more proper Cardinal Bembo (whose Ciceronian prose spawned an imitative style known as Bembismo), Renaissance Venice produced virtually no writers of any importance – and yet it was the greatest printing centre in Italy. By the second half of the sixteenth century there were more than one hundred presses in Venice, and their output was more than three times greater than that of Rome, Florence and Milan combined. The doyen of **Venetian printers** was **Aldus Manutius** (Aldo Manuzio), creator of italic typeface and publisher of the first pocket editions of the classics, whose workshop stood close to Campo San Polo. Founded in 1490, the Aldine Press employed teams of printers, die-cutters, proof-readers and compositors, but was always on the lookout for casual labour, as the sign over the door made clear – "Whoever you are, Aldus earnestly begs you to state your business in the fewest words possible and begone, unless, like Hercules to weary Atlas, you would lend a helping hand. There will always be enough work for you and all who pass this way." Erasmus once grudgingly did a stint here, when the Aldine workshop was producing an edition of his *Proverbs*.

If you leave Campo San Polo at its northeast corner, walk along Calle Bernardo (past the florid Palazzo Bernardo), cross the canal to Calle del Scaleter and then follow that alley to its end, you'll come to Rio Terrà Seconda, where a plaque at no. 2311 identifies a small Gothic house as the site of the workshop of Manutius. However, documentary evidence makes it clear that the Manutius shop was located "by the Santo Agostino baker": off Campo San Agostin, which lies at the south end of Rio Terrà Seconda, you'll find a Calle del Pistor ("Baker's Alley"), where a bakery is still in operation. So in all likelihood it was here rather than at no. 2311 that Manutius was based until the last years of his life, when he moved over the Canal Grande to what is now Campo Manin.

the **Museo Goldoni**. Containing a very small collection of first editions, a few portraits of the playwright, some eighteenth-century marionettes, a miniature theatre (similar to the puppet theatre Goldoni's father made for him), and not a lot more, this is the most undernourished museum in the whole city. The Gothic courtyard is one of Venice's finest, however, and has a beautiful wellhead.

The parish of San Tomà, the base of many of Venice's best silver- and goldsmiths, is focused on **San Tomà** church, a few metres past Goldoni's house. For many years a sad, broken-backed structure encased in scaffolding, San Tomà has been gleamingly restored, but is hardly ever open. In the days when the Venetians were known as the sharpest religious relic-hunters around, San Tomà was the city's bumper depository, claiming to possess some 10,000 sacred bits and pieces, and a dozen intact holy corpses. At the other end of the campo stands the **Scuola dei Calegheri** – the shoemakers' guild, as advertised by the footwear carved into the lintel, below the relief by Pietro Lombardo (1478) that shows Saint Mark healing the cobbler Ananias. The building is now used as a library and exhibition space.

From the Frari to the Tolentini

For a rapid survey of the summit of Venetian painting in its golden age, your first stop after the Accademia should be the constellation of buildings a few alleys west of San Polo – the **Frari**, the **Scuola Grande di San Rocco** and **San Rocco** church. The genesis of Ruskin's obsession with Venice was a visit

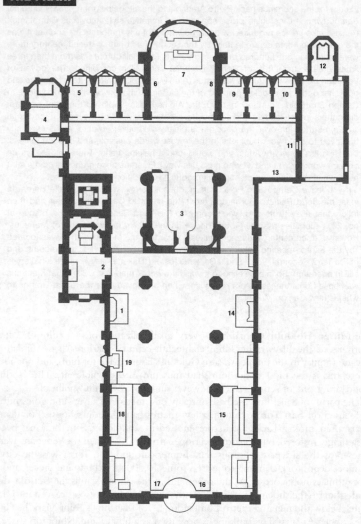

THE FRARI

1. 'Madonna di Ca'Pésaro'
2. Cappella Emiliani
3. Monks' Choir
4. Cappella Corner
5. Vivarini and Basaiti's 'St. Ambrose'
6. Tomb of Doge Niccolo Tron
7. Titian's 'Assumption'
8. Tomb of Doge Francesco Fóscari
9. Donatello's 'St. John'
10. Bartolomeo Vivarini Altarpiece
11. Tombs of Paolo Savelli, Benedetto Pésaro and Beato Pacifico
12. The Bellini Altarpiece
13. Tomb of Jacopo Marcello
14. Vittoria's 'St. Jerome'
15. Titian's Monument
16. Tomb of Alvise Pasqualino
17. Tomb of Pietro Bernardo
18. Mausoleum of Canova
19. Tomb of Doge Giovanni Pésaro

to the Scuola, where a pictorial interpretation of the life of Christ by **Tintoretto** flows through the entire building; and if you can take yet more after the intensity of the Scuola's cycle, the church next door contains further works by him. Paradoxically, Venice is under-endowed with paintings by **Titian**, one of its greatest artists: apart from the Accademia and the Salute, the Frari is the only building in Venice with more than a single first-rate work by him. It also boasts a magnificent altarpiece by **Bellini** and a remarkable assembly of monuments and other art works.

Santa Maria Gloriosa dei Frari

San Zanipolo and **Santa Maria Gloriosa dei Frari** (Mon–Sat 9am–6pm, Sun 1–6pm; €3, or Chorus Pass) – customarily abbreviated to the **Frari** – are the twin Gothic giants of Venice: from the campanile of San Marco they can be seen jutting above the rooftops on opposite sides of the Canal Grande, like a pair of destroyers amid a flotilla of yachts.

The Franciscans were granted a plot of land here around 1250, not long after the death of their founder, but almost no sooner was the first church completed (in 1338) than work began on a vast replacement – a project which took well over a hundred years. The campanile, one of the city's landmarks and the tallest after San Marco's, was finished in 1396; in recent years it's been showing signs of instability, and reinforcement work has been in progress for a considerable time.

You're unlikely to fall in love at first sight with this mountain of brick. Only a few pieces of sculpture relieve the monotony of the exterior: on the **west front**, there's a figure of *The Risen Christ* by **Vittoria**, and a *Virgin* and *St Francis* from the workshop of **Bartolomeo Bon**; an impressive early fifteenth-century Tuscan relief of the *Madonna and Child with Angels* is set into the side of the left transept. As is so often the case in Venice, though, the outside of the church is a misleadingly dull prelude to a remarkable interior.

Titian's altarpieces

Entry to the Frari is sometimes through the main door and sometimes through the Cappella Emiliani, on the left flank of the church, but whichever way you come in, you'll almost immediately be confronted by Titian's great **Assumption** as you look towards the high altar through the monks' choir. (The choir itself was built in the late fifteenth century, with a marble screen by Bartolomeo Bon and Pietro Lombardo; it's the only one left in Venice that occupies a site in the nave.) A piece of compositional and colouristic bravura for which there was no precedent in Venetian art – for one thing, no previous altarpiece had emphasized the vertical axis over the horizontal – the *Assumption* nevertheless fits its surroundings perfectly. The spiralling motion of the Apostles and the Virgin complements the vertical movement of the surrounding architecture, an integration that is strengthened by the coincidence between the division of the painting's two major groupings and the division of the windows in the chancel. It seems to have disconcerted the friars for whom it was painted, but nonetheless was instantly recognized as a major work. **Marin Sanudo**, whose *Diaries* are an essential source for historians of the Republic, somehow wrote 58 volumes containing scarcely a mention of any Venetian artist – yet even he refers to the ceremony on May 19, 1518, at which the picture was unveiled.

The other Titian masterpiece here, the **Madonna di Ca' Pésaro** (on the left wall, between the third and fourth columns), was completed eight years after the *Assumption* and was equally innovative in its displacement of the figure of the Virgin from the centre of the picture. The altarpiece was commissioned by Bishop Jacopo Pésaro, who managed to combine his episcopal duties with a military career; in 1502 he had led a successful naval campaign against the Turks – hence the prisoners being dragged in, behind the kneeling figure of Pésaro himself, to meet the Redeemer and His Mother. Pésaro's tomb (c.1547), with an effigy, is to the right of the picture.

The chapels, chancel and sacristy

Beyond the Pésaro monument you'll find the **Cappella Emiliani**, which has a fifteenth-century marble altarpiece by followers of Jacobello Dalle Masegne but has been closed to visitors since the huge task of reinforcing the church's campanile was started several years ago. The **Cappella Corner**, at the end of the left transept, contains a vibrant painting by Bartolomeo Vivarini, *St Mark Enthroned* (1474), and, on the font, a damaged figure of *St John the Baptist* by Sansovino (1554).

St Ambrose and other Saints, the last painting by **Alvise Vivarini**, the nephew of Bartolomeo, stands in the adjoining chapel; it was finished around 1503 by a pupil, Marco Basaiti. A plaque in the floor marks the **grave of Monteverdi**, who for thirty years was the choirmaster of San Marco. The chapel to the left of the chancel contains another striking altarpiece, a *Madonna and Saints* by Bernardino Licinio; one of the finest creations of this Titian-influenced artist, it was probably painted in 1535.

Two monuments illustrating the emergence in Venice of Renaissance sculptural style flank the Titian *Assumption*: on the left the proto-Renaissance **tomb of Doge Niccolò Tron** (1476), by Antonio Rizzo and assistants; on the right, the more archaic and chaotic **tomb of Doge Francesco Fóscari**, carved shortly after Fóscari's death in 1457 (after 34 years as doge) by **Antonio and Paolo Bregno**. The story of Fóscari's last days is one of the most poignant in Venice's history. Already in ill health and constantly harried by political enemies, Fóscari went into a rapid decline when his son, Jacopo, was found guilty of treason and exiled for life. Within half a year Jacopo was dead, and Doge Fóscari sank further into a depression which his opponents lost no time in exploiting. After several months of pressure, they forced him into resignation; a week later he died. It was reported that when the senators and new doge heard of his death, during Mass in the Basilica, they looked guiltily at each other, "knowing well that it was they who had shortened his life".

The wooden statue of *St John the Baptist*, in the next chapel, was commissioned from **Donatello** in 1438 by Florentine merchants in Padua; recent work has restored the luridly naturalistic appearance of what seems to be the sculptor's first work in the Veneto. In the last of the chapels stands a Bartolomeo Vivarini altarpiece, *Madonna and Child with Saints*; painted in 1482, it illustrates the conservatism of most Venetian *quattrocento* art in comparison to that being created at the same time in Donatello's native Tuscany.

Above the door to the sacristy most of the space is occupied by three very different tombs. The one on the left is the **tomb of Paolo Savelli** (c.1406), the first equestrian monument in Venice; next along is **Lorenzo Bregno**'s tomb of another Pésaro – Benedetto, head of the Venetian army, who died in Corfu in 1503. The flamboyant Gothic work on the other side of the door is the terracotta **tomb of Beato Pacifico**, who is traditionally credited with beginning the present church; he was placed here in 1437, nearly a century after his death.

Giovanni Bellini's *Madonna and Child with SS Nicholas of Bari, Peter, Mark and Benedict* was painted in 1488 for the altar of the **sacristy**. It's still there, in its original frame, and alone would justify a long visit to the Frari. Gazing at this picture is like looking into a room that's soaked in a warm dawn light; in the words of Henry James – "it is as solemn as it is gorgeous and as simple as it is deep". While you're here, take a look at the wooden frame carved by **Francesco Pianta** for the clock that hangs beside the sacristy door; it's an astounding piece of work, teeming with symbols of mortality and the passage of time. From the sacristy there's access to the **chapterhouse**, where you'll find the tomb of Doge Francesco Dandolo (c.1340); the painting above it by **Paolo Veneziano** contains what is probably the first portrait of a doge ever painted from life.

The rest of the church

Back in the right transept, on the west wall, there's the odd **tomb of Jacopo Marcello**, supported by small stooping figures (c.1485, probably by Giovanni Buora). High on the wall round the corner is something far less florid but equally strange – a plain black coffin which is said to have been meant for the body of the *condottiere* **Carmagnola**, who, having shown a suspicious reluctance to earn his money against the Milanese (his former employers), was executed after a dodgy treason trial in 1432. Carmagnola is now in Milan, and another tenant occupies the coffin.

Facing the Pésaro altarpiece stands one of **Alessandro Vittoria**'s best marble figures – *St Jerome*, for which Titian was reputedly the model. The house-sized tomb further along is the bombastic **monument to Titian**, built in the mid-nineteenth century on the supposed place of his burial. He died in 1576, in around his ninetieth year, a casualty of the plague; such was the esteem in which Titian was held, he was the only victim to be allowed a church burial in the course of the outbreak, one of the most terrible in the city's history.

The delicate statuettes on the water stoups against the last columns, facing each other across the nave, are *St Anthony of Padua* and *St Agnes* by Campagna (1609). The **tomb of Procurator Alvise Pasqualino**, to the left of the door, is attributed to Lorenzo Bregno, whose death in 1523 preceded his client's by five years. Ordering your tomb in advance was not an unusual practice: **Pietro Bernardo** (died 1538), whose tomb (possibly by Tullio Lombardo, who died in 1532) is on the other side of the door, did the same thing – although the finished article was rather more humble than he had intended. In his will he specified, among other provisions, that his epitaph should be cut in letters legible from 25 paces, and should be accompanied by an epic poem of eight hundred stanzas, extolling the Bernardo family. His executors seem to have wriggled out of these clauses, and out of another that ordered that a monastic choir should sing psalms in front of his tomb on the first Sunday of every month until Judgement Day.

The marble pyramid with the troop of mourners is the **Mausoleum of Canova**, erected in 1827 by pupils of the sculptor, following a design he himself had made for the tombs of Titian and Maria Christina of Austria. Only the artist's heart is actually entombed here – most of the body was interred at his birthplace, Possagno (see p.351), but his right hand is somewhere in the Accademia. Finally, moving along from the Canova monument, you'll be stopped in your tracks by what is surely the most grotesque monument in the city; this is the tomb of yet another Pésaro – **Doge Giovanni Pésaro** (1669). The architecture is usually attributed to Longhena; for the gigantic ragged-trousered Moors and decomposing corpses, a German sculptor called Melchiorre Barthel must take the blame.

The state archive

At the fall of the Republic the Franciscan monastery attached to the church was taken over for use as the **Archivio di Stato** (State Archive). Its documents, cramming more than three hundred rooms, relate to the Council of Ten, the courts, the embassies, the Arsenale, the scuole – to every aspect of Venetian public life – and go back as far as the ninth century. From time to time the archive puts on an exhibition of material dredged from the shelves; the shows habitually sound unenthralling, but if you're at all interested in the city's past you should get something from them.

The Scuola Grande di San Rocco

Venice may not tell you much about Titian's work that you didn't already know, but in the case of **Tintoretto** the situation is reversed – until you've been to Venice, and in particular the **Scuola Grande di San Rocco** (daily 9am–5.30pm; €7), you haven't really got to grips with him.

The scuole

The Venetian institutions known as the **scuole** seem to have originated in the early thirteenth century, with the formation of the flagellant orders, whose public scourgings were intended to purge the sins of the world. The interaction between these societies of flagellants and the lay brotherhoods established by the city's branches of the mendicant orders (the Franciscans and the Dominicans) gave rise in 1260 to the formation of the confraternity called **Scuola di Santa Maria della Carità**, the first of the so-called **Scuole Grande**. By the middle of the sixteenth century there were five more of these major confraternities – **San Giovanni Evangelista**, **San Marco**, **Santa Maria della Misericordia**, **San Rocco** and **San Teodoro** – plus scores of smaller bodies known as the *Scuole Minore*, of which at one time there were as many as four hundred.

The *Scuole Grande*, drawing much of their membership from the wealthiest professional and mercantile groups, and with rosters of up to six hundred men, received subscriptions that allowed them to fund lavish **architectural and artistic projects**, of which the Scuola Grande di San Rocco is the most spectacular example. The *Scuole Minore*, united by membership of certain guilds (eg goldsmiths at the Scuola dei Battioro e Tiraori, shoemakers at the Scuola dei Calerghi), or by common nationality (as with San Giorgo degli Schiavoni, the Slavs' scuola), generally operated from far more modest bases. Yet all scuole had the same basic functions – to provide assistance for their members (eg dowries and medical aid), to offer a place of communal worship, and to distribute alms and services in emergencies (anything from plague relief to the provision of troops). It was a frequently expressed complaint, however, that the *Scuole Grande* were prone to lose sight of their original aims in their rush to outdo each other.

To an extent, the scuole also acted as a kind of political safety-valve. The councils of state were the unique preserve of the city's self-designated patrician class, but the scuole were administered by traders, doctors, lawyers, artisans and civil servants. Technically they had no real power, but a wealthy private club like the Scuola Grande di San Rocco was capable of being an effective pressure group. Like all other Venetian institutions, the scuole came to an end with **Napoleon**, who disbanded them in 1806. Most of their possessions were scattered, and their headquarters were in time put to new uses – the Scuola Grande di San Marco became the city hospital, for example, and the Scuola Grande di Santa Maria della Carità became the galleries of the Accademia. The Scuola di San Giorgio degli Schiavoni and Scuola Grande di San Rocco, however, were revived in the middle of the nineteenth century and continue to function as charitable bodies in the magnificently decorated buildings that they commissioned centuries ago. A third scuola, San Giovanni Evangelista, was reinstituted in the twentieth century.

"As regards the pictures which it contains, it is one of the three most precious buildings in Italy," wrote Ruskin, and although the claim's open to argument, it's not difficult to understand why he resorted to such hyperbole. (His other votes were for the Sistine Chapel and the Campo Santo at Pisa – the latter was virtually ruined in World War II.) The unremitting concentration and restlessness of Tintoretto's paintings won't inspire unqualified enthusiasm in everyone: Henry James, though an admirer, found the atmosphere of San Rocco "difficult to breathe". But even those who prefer their art at a lower voltage will find this an overwhelming experience.

From its foundation in 1478, the special concern of this particular scuola was the relief of the sick – a continuation of the Christian mission of its patron saint, Saint Roch (Rocco) of Montpellier, who in 1315 left his home town to work among plague victims in Italy, then returned home only to be spurned by his wealthy family and die in prison, aged just 32. The Scuola had been going for seven years when the body of the saint was brought to Venice from Germany, and the consequent boom in donations was so great that in 1489 it acquired the status of *scuola grande*.

The intervention of Saint Roch was held to be especially efficacious in cases of bubonic plague, an illness from which he himself had been saved by the ministrations of a divinely inspired dog, which brought him bread and licked his wounds clean (which is why the churches of Venice are littered with paintings of the saint pointing to a sore on his thigh, usually with a dog in attendance). When, in 1527, the city was hit by an outbreak of plague, the Scuola's revenue rocketed to record levels as gifts poured in from people hoping to secure Saint Roch's protection against the disease. In 1515 the Scuola, previously based in a room within the Frari, had commissioned a prestigious new headquarters from **Bartolomeo Bon the Younger**, but for various reasons the work had ground to a halt within a decade; the fattened coffers prompted another phase of building, and from 1527 to 1549 the scheme was taken over by **Scarpagnino**.

When the scaffolding came down in 1560, the end product was somewhat incoherent and lopsided. Not that the members of the Scuola would have been bothered for long; within a few years the decoration of the interior was under way, and it was this decoration – **Tintoretto**'s cycle of more than fifty major paintings – that secured the confraternity's social standing. An opportunistic little trick won the first contract for Tintoretto. In 1564 the Scuola held a competition to decide who should paint the inaugural picture for the recently completed building. The subject was to be *The Glorification of St Roch*, and four artists were approached for proposals: Salviati, Zuccari, Veronese and Tintoretto, who had already painted a number of pictures for the neighbouring church of San Rocco. On the day for submissions the first three duly presented their sketches; Tintoretto, though, had painted a finished panel and persuaded a sidekick to rig it up, hidden by a veil, in the very place in which the winning picture was to be installed – the centre of the ceiling in the Sala dell'Albergo. A rope was pulled, the picture revealed, and Tintoretto promptly offered the picture as a gift to the Scuola. Despite his rivals' fury, the crucial first commission was his.

The paintings

The narrative sequence of the cycle begins with the first picture in the lower room – the *Annunciation*. But to appreciate Tintoretto's development you have to begin in the smaller room on the upper storey – the **Sala dell'Albergo**. This is dominated by the stupendous *Crucifixion* (1565), the most compendious image of the event ever painted. Henry James made even greater claims for it: "Surely no single picture in the world contains more of human life; there is everything in it." Ruskin was reduced to a state of dumbfounded wonder – his loquacious commentary on the San Rocco cycle concludes with the entry: "I must leave this picture to work its will on the spectator; for it is beyond all analysis, and above all praise." Tintoretto's other works in this room – aside from the contract-winning *Glorification of St Roch* in the middle of the ceiling – are on the entrance wall: *The Way to Calvary*, *Christ Crowned with Thorns* and *Christ before Pilate*.

Tintoretto finished his contribution to the Sala dell'Albergo in 1567. Eight years later, when the Scuola decided to proceed with the embellishment of the main upper hall – the **chapterhouse** – he undertook to do the work in return for nothing more than his expenses. In the event he was awarded a lifetime annuity, and then commenced the three large panels of the **ceiling**, beginning with *The Miracle of the Bronze Serpent*. With their references to the alleviation of physical suffering, this colossal picture and its companions – *Moses Striking Water from the Rock* and *The Miraculous Fall of Manna* – constitute a coded declaration of the Scuola's charitable programme, and the Scuola's governors were so satisfied with Tintoretto's conception that he was given the task of completing the decoration of the entire interior. It was a project to which he would give precedence over all his other commissions in the city; thereafter, on every Saint Roch's day until 1581, Tintoretto presented the Scuola with three new pictures, a sequence that extended at a slower rate of production until 1588, when he painted the altarpiece of the chapterhouse, with the help of his son, Domenico.

The New Testament scenes around the **walls** defy every convention of perspective, lighting, colour and even anatomy, an amazing feat of sustained inventiveness from a mind that was never content with inherited ideas. On the **left wall** (as you face the altar) – *The Nativity*, *The Baptism*, *The Resurrection*, *The Agony in the Garden*, *The Last Supper*; on the **right wall** – *The Temptation of Christ*, *The Miracle at the Pool of Bethesda*, *The Ascension*, *The Raising of Lazarus*, *The Miracle of the Loaves and Fishes*; on the **end wall** by the Sala dell'Albergo – *St Roch* and *St Sebastian*; on the **altar** – *The Vision of St Roch*. On easels to the side of the altar are displayed an *Annunciation* by **Titian**, a *Visitation* and a portrait by **Tintoretto** that's often wrongly called a self-portrait, and *Christ Carrying the Cross*, an early Titian (though it's attributed to Giorgione by some) that from about 1510 until 1955 was displayed in the church of San Rocco, where it was revered as a miraculous image. At the other end of the hall, beside the door into the Sala dell'Albergo, you'll find *Hagar, Ishmael and an Angel* and *Abraham and an Angel*, both by **Giambattista Tiepolo**.

The **carvings** underneath the paintings – a gallery of vices, virtues and other allegorical figures, plus an amazing trompe l'oeil library – were created in the late seventeenth century by **Francesco Pianta**. Not far from the altar, opposite the stairs, you'll find the allegory of painting: a caricature of the irascible Tintoretto, with a jarful of brushes. The painter's short temper was notorious; for instance, when a group of senators, seeing him at work on the *Paradiso* in the Palazzo Ducale, observed that some of his rivals painted more slowly and more carefully, he's said to have replied that this was possibly because they didn't have to contend with such stupid interruptions.

The **lower hall** – connected to the chapterhouse by a stairway that's lined with pictures recording the plague that struck Venice in the 1630s – was painted between 1583 and 1587, when Tintoretto was in his late sixties. The tempestuous *Annunciation*, with the Archangel crashing into the room through Joseph's shambolic workshop, trailing a tornado of cherubim, is followed by *The Adoration of the Magi*, *The Flight into Egypt*, *The Massacre of the Innocents*, *St Mary*

Magdalen, St Mary of Egypt, The Circumcision and *The Assumption.* The landscapes in the *Flight into Egypt* and the meditative depictions of the two saints are among the finest Tintoretto ever painted.

The church of San Rocco

Yet more Tintorettos are to be found in the neighbouring **church of San Rocco** (same hours as the scuola), built in 1489–1508 to designs by **Bartolomeo Bon the Younger**, but altered extensively in the eighteenth century. On the right wall of the nave you'll find *St Roch Taken to Prison*, and below it *The Pool of Bethesda*; only the latter is definitely by Tintoretto. Between the altars on the other side are a couple of good pictures by **Pordenone** – *St Christopher* and *St Martin*. Four large paintings by Tintoretto hang in the chancel, often either lost in the gloom or glazed with sunlight; the best (both painted in 1549) are *St Roch Curing the Plague Victims* (lower right) and *St Roch in Prison* (lower left). The two higher pictures are *St Roch in Solitude* and *St Roch Healing the Animals* – the second is a doubtful attribution.

(Before you leave the San Rocco area, you might want to nip behind the Scuola, taking the alleyway that cuts south from the front of the church; this will bring you to one of the city's most attractive waterscapes, with a broad pavement jutting out into an unusually wide confluence of canals.)

The Scuola di San Giovanni Evangelista

Another of the *Scuole Grande* nestles in a line of drab buildings very near to the Frari – the **Scuola di San Giovanni Evangelista**, founded in 1261 by one of the many flagellant confraternities that sprang up at that time. Suppressed by Napoleon, it was reborn as the HQ of the Società delle Arti Edificatorie (Society of Building Arts) in the 1850s and was re-established as a charitable foundation in 1929. The quickest way to get to it is to take the bridge facing the Frari's facade, turn left and then left again, then second right into Calle del Magazzen – the Scuola is halfway down on the left.

▲ Scuola di San Giovanni Evangelista

This institution's finest hour came in 1369, when it was presented with a **relic of the True Cross**, an item that can be seen to this day in the first-floor **Oratorio della Croce**. The miracles effected by the relic were commemorated in the Oratory by a series of paintings by Carpaccio, Gentile Bellini and others, now transplanted to the Accademia.

Nowadays the delights of the Scuola are architectural. The **courtyards** are something of a composite; the mid-fifteenth-century facade of the Scuola incorporates two mid-fourteenth-century reliefs, and the **screen** of the outer courtyard was built in 1481 by **Pietro Lombardo**. Approached from the train station direction, this screen just looks like any old brick wall, but round the other side it reveals itself to be as delicate a piece of marble carving as any church interior could show. Inside (entry by reservation on ☎041.718.234; donation of €5 required), a grand **double staircase**, built by Codussi in 1498, rises to the main hall and the Oratorio; the ceiling of the hall is covered with rather refined scenes of the Apocalypse, painted by a variety of eighteenth-century artists after Giambattista Tiepolo defaulted on his contract (two of the panels were painted by his son). Around the walls are scenes from the life of Saint John, most of them by Domenico Tintoretto. As for the church of San Giovanni Evangelista, it's one of the select company of religious buildings in Venice that are of no interest whatsoever.

The Tolentini, the Giardino Papadopoli and beyond

Calle della Lacca–Fondamenta Sacchere–Corte Amai is a dullish but uncomplicated route from San Giovanni Evangelista to the portentous church of San Nicolò da Tolentino – alias the **Tolentini** (daily 8am–noon & 4–7pm). Venetian home of the Theatine Order, which found refuge in Venice after the Sack of Rome by the army of Charles V in 1527, it was begun in 1590 by Palladio's follower Scamozzi, and finished in 1714 by the addition of a freestanding portico – the first in Venice – designed by Andrea Tirali. Among the scores of seventeenth-century paintings, just two stand out. The first is a *St Jerome* by Johann Lys, at the foot of the chancel steps, on the left; it was painted in 1628, just two years before German-born Lys died of the plague, aged 33. The other is *St Lawrence Giving Alms* by Bernardo Strozzi, round the corner from the Lys painting, to the left. Up the left wall of the chancel swirls the best Baroque monument in Venice: the **monument to Francesco Morosini**, created in 1678 by a Genoese sculptor, Filippo Parodi. That's Francesco Morosini, the Patriarch of Venice, who is on no account to be confused with Francesco Morosini, Doge of Venice (1688–94), buried in Santo Stefano – though the latter Francesco Morosini did present the Tolentini with the banner of the Turkish general whom he had trounced in the Morea in 1685.

If fatigue is setting in and you need a pit stop, the **Giardino Papadopoli**, formerly one of Venice's biggest private gardens but now owned by the city, is just over the Rio dei Tolentini.

Much of the westernmost reaches of the Santa Croce *sestiere* have been taken over by the **Piazzale Roma** bus terminal and multistorey car park. The fifteenth-century church of **Sant'Andrea della Zirada**, in the lee of the car park, is rarely open and only has its Baroque altar to recommend it anyway; the diminutive Neoclassical **Nome di Gesù**, cringing in the lee of the road to the mainland, has absolutely nothing going for it. Immediately to the south of Piazzale Roma lies a predominantly residential area; its major church, Santa Maria Maggiore, is now part of the city **prison**.

Cannaregio

Within the northernmost section of Venice, Cannaregio, you pass from one urban extreme to another in a matter of minutes, the time it takes to escape the hubbub of the train station and the hustle of the Lista di Spagna – the tawdriest street in Venice – and into the backwaters away from the Canal Grande. There may no longer be any signs of the bamboo clumps that were probably the source of the *sestiere*'s name (*canna* means "reed"), but in all of Venice you won't find as many village-like parishes as you'll see in Cannaregio, and in few parts of the city are you more likely to get well away from the tourist crowds.

Imprisoned in the heart of Cannaregio is the **Ghetto**, the first area in the world to bear that name, and one of Venice's most evocative areas. Within a short walk of the Ghetto you'll find **Madonna dell'Orto**, with its astonishing Tintoretto paintings, as well as **Sant'Alvise** and **Palazzo Labia**, the first remarkable for canvases by Giambattista Tiepolo, the second for the same artist's frescoes. The chief museum of Cannaregio is the **Ca' d'Oro**, a gorgeous Canal Grande palace housing a decent collection of paintings and carving. Over in the eastern part of the *sestiere* lie three outstanding churches: the exquisite little church of **Santa Maria dei Miracoli**; the often overlooked **San Giovanni Crisostomo**; and the **Gesuiti**, a Baroque creation which boasts perhaps the weirdest interior in the city.

From the train station to San Giobbe

The area around Venice's train station is one in which nearly every visitor sets foot but very few actually investigate. Nobody could pretend that it's one of the city's enticing spots (for one thing, it's the city's main red-light district), but it does repay a saunter. The station building itself is a gracefully functional 1950s effort, but the rail link to the mainland was opened in 1846; within a few years the expansion of traffic had made it necessary to demolish Palladio's church of Santa Lucia, the building from which the station's name is taken.

The Scalzi

Right by the station stands the **Scalzi**, formally **Santa Maria di Nazaretta** (daily 7–11.50am & 4–6.50pm). Begun in 1672 for the barefoot ("scalzi") order of Carmelites, it is anything but barefoot itself. Giuseppe Sardi's facade – now restored after years of being fenced off to protect mortals from falling angels – is fairly undemonstrative compared with **Baldassare Longhena**'s opulent interior, where the walls are plated with dark, multicoloured marble and overgrown with Baroque statuary. Ruskin condemned it as "a perfect type of the vulgar abuse of marble in every possible way, by men who had no eye for colour, and no understanding of any merit in a work of art but that which rises from costliness of material, and such powers of imitation as are devoted in England to the manufacture of peaches and eggs out of Derbyshire spar".

Before 1915, when an Austrian bomb that was aimed at the train station instead plummeted through the roof of the Scalzi, the church had a splendid **Giambattista Tiepolo** ceiling; a few scraps are preserved in the Accademia, and some wan frescoes by the man survive in the first chapel on the left and the second on the right. The second chapel on the left is the resting place of **Lodovico Manin** (d.1802), Venice's last doge. The bare inscription set into the floor – "Manini Cineres" (the ashes of Manin) – is a fair reflection of the low esteem in which he was held. His chief rival for the dogeship wailed "A Friulian as doge! The Republic is dead!" when Manin was elected, and although Lodovico can't take the blame for the death of independent Venice, he did display a certain lack of backbone when the final crisis loomed. In response to French demands he meekly surrendered his insignia of office to be burned on a bonfire in the Piazza, and when later called upon to swear an oath of allegiance to Austria, he fell down in a dead faint.

The Lista di Spagna, San Geremia and Palazzo Labia

Foreign embassies used to be corralled into this area to make life a little easier for the Republic's spies, and the **Lista di Spagna** takes its name from the Spanish embassy which used to be at no. 168. (*Lista* indicates a street leading to an embassy.) It's now completely given over to tourism, with a plethora of shops, restaurants and hotels making most of their money from people who are too tired or lazy to look any further.

If you turn left up Calle della Misericordia you'll eventually come to the entrance to the small **Parco Savorgnan** (open 8am–dusk), one of Venice's immensely rare public green spaces. It's not much of a park, but the benches and the shade of the trees make it a good picnic spot. Carrying on along the Lista you'll reach the church of **San Geremia** (Mon–Sat 8am–noon & 3.30–6.30pm, Sun 9.15am–12.15pm & 5.30–6.30pm), where the travels of **Saint Lucy** eventually terminated – martyred in Syracuse in 304, she was stolen from Constantinople by Venetian Crusaders in 1204, then ousted from her own church in Venice by the railway board in the mid-nineteenth century. (She was also stolen from this church in 1994, but was soon returned.) Lucy's response to an unwanted suitor who praised her beautiful eyes was to pluck out the offending organs, a display of otherworldliness which led to her adoption as the patron saint of eyesight and artists. Her desiccated body, wearing a lustrous silver mask, lies behind the altar, reclining above a donations box that bears the prayer "Saint Lucy, protect my eyes". Nothing else about the church is of interest, except the twelfth-century **campanile**, one of the oldest left in the city.

The **Palazzo Labia**, next door to San Geremia, was built in 1720–50 for a famously extravagant Catalan family by the name of Lasbias, who had bought their way into the *Libro d'Oro* (the register of the nobility) for the obligatory 100,000 ducats in the middle of the previous century. Their taste for conspicuous expenditure wasn't lessened by the cost of the house – a party here once finished with a member of the Labia family hurling the gold dinner service from the window into the canal and declaiming the memorable Venetian pun:

"L'abia o non l'abia, sarò sempre Labia" (Whether I have it or whether I have it not, I will always be a Labia). The impact of the gesture is somewhat lessened by the rumour that fishing nets had been placed in the canal so that the service could be retrieved under cover of darkness.

No cost was spared on decoration either, and no sooner was the interior completed than **Giambattista Tiepolo** was hired to cover the walls of the ballroom with **frescoes** depicting the story of Antony and Cleopatra. (The architectural trompe l'oeil work is by another artist – Gerolamo Mengozzi Colonna.) This is the only sequence of Tiepolo paintings in Venice that is comparable to his narrative masterpieces in such mainland villas as the Villa Valmarana near Vicenza (see p.318), and RAI, the Italian state broadcasting company, which now owns the palace, usually allows visitors inside for a few hours each week. At the moment, however, the palazzo is undergoing restoration – the tourist office will have the latest details on admission.

The San Giobbe district

The Palazzo Labia's longest facade overlooks the **Canale di Cannaregio**, the main entrance to Venice before the rail and road links were constructed; if you turn left along its fondamenta rather than going with the flow over the Ponte delle Guglie, you'll be virtually alone by the time you're past the late seventeenth-century **Palazzo Savorgnan**. This was the home of one of Venice's richest families – indeed, so great was the Savorgnans' social clout that the Rezzonico family marked their intermarriage by getting Tiepolo to paint a fresco celebrating the event in the Ca' Rezzonico. Beyond the palazzo, swing left at the Ponte dei Tre Archi (Venice's only multiple-span bridge) and you're at the church of **San Giobbe** (Mon–Sat 10am–5pm; €3, or Chorus Pass), like San Moisè an example of Venice's habit of canonizing Old Testament figures.

"So went Satan forth from the presence of the Lord and smote Job with sore boils from the sole of his foot unto his crown," records the Bible. Job's physical sufferings – sanctioned by the Almighty in order to test his faith – greatly endeared him to the Venetians, who were regularly afflicted with malaria, plague and a plethora of water-related diseases, and in the fourteenth century an oratory and hospice dedicated to him were founded here. In 1428 the complex was taken over by the Observant Franciscans, and in 1443 the order's greatest preacher, Bernardine of Siena, was a guest here, in what turned out to be the last year of his life. Bernardine's canonization followed in 1450, an event commemorated here by the construction of a new church, a Gothic structure commenced by Antonio Gambello soon after the canonization. However, the specially interesting parts of the building are its exquisitely carved, early Renaissance doorway and chancel – begun in 1471, they were the first Venetian projects of **Pietro Lombardo**.

After the Lombardo carvings, the most appealing elements of the interior are the roundels and tiles from the Florentine **della Robbia** workshop, in the Cappella Martini (second chapel on left); the presence of these Tuscan features is explained by the fact that the chapel was funded by a family of Lucca-born silk weavers. The tomb slab in the centre of the chancel floor is that of **Doge Cristoforo Moro**, the donor of the new building; a satirical leaflet about Moro may have been a source for Shakespeare's *Othello*, even though – as the portrait in the sacristy shows – Moro bore no racial similarity to the Moor of Venice. San Giobbe's great altarpieces by Bellini and Carpaccio have been removed to the damp-free environment of the Accademia (the original marble frame for the Bellini now encloses a dull *Vision of Job*); in the main part of the church the most notable features are the ludicrous marble beasts that prop up the tomb of

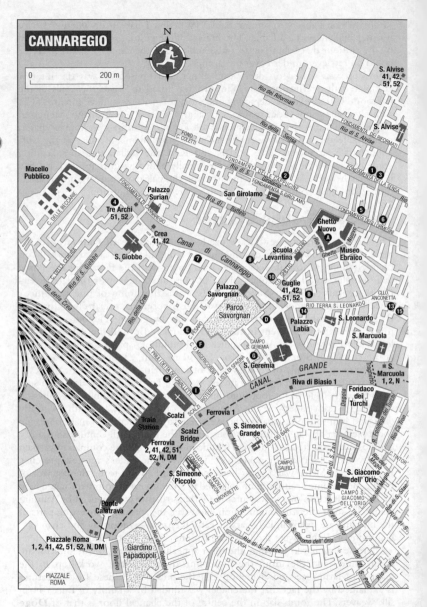

the magnificently named **Renato de Voyer de Palmy Signore d'Argeson**, who served as the French ambassador to Venice and died here in 1651. At the end of the nave, beyond Paris Bordone's altarpiece of *SS Andrew, Peter and Nicholas*, a doorway leads into a room that was once part of the original oratory, which in turn connects with the **sacristy**, where there's a fine triptych by Antonio Vivarini, a fifteenth-century terracotta bust of Saint Bernardine and a *Marriage of St Catherine* attributed to Andrea Previtali.

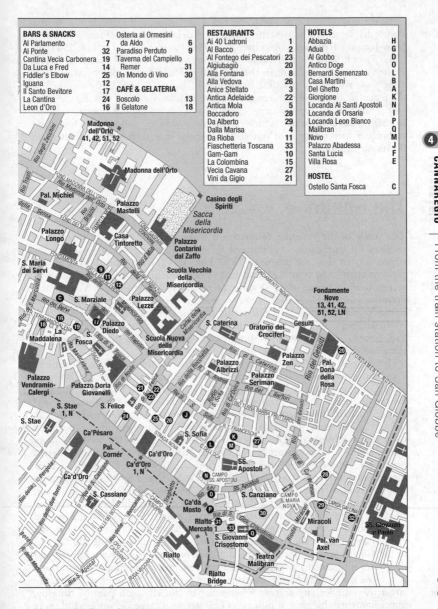

BARS & SNACKS

Al Parlamento	7
Al Ponte	32
Cantina Vecia Carbonera	19
Da Luca e Fred	14
Fiddler's Elbow	25
Iguana	12
Il Santo Bevitore	17
La Cantina	24
Leon d'Oro	16
Osteria ai Ormesini da Aldo	6
Paradiso Perduto	9
Taverna del Campiello Remer	31
Un Mondo di Vino	30

CAFÉ & GELATERIA

Boscolo	13
Il Gelatone	18

RESTAURANTS

Ai 40 Ladroni	1
Al Bacco	2
Al Fontego dei Pescatori	23
Algiubagiò	20
Alla Fontana	8
Alla Vedova	26
Anice Stellato	3
Antica Adelaide	22
Antica Mola	5
Boccadoro	28
Da Alberto	29
Dalla Marisa	4
Da Rioba	11
Fiaschetteria Toscana	33
Gam-Gam	10
La Colombina	15
Vecia Cavana	27
Vini da Gigio	21

HOTELS

Abbazia	H
Adua	G
Al Gobbo	D
Antico Doge	O
Bernardi Semenzato	L
Casa Martini	B
Del Ghetto	A
Giorgione	K
Locanda Ai Santi Apostoli	N
Locanda di Orsaria	I
Locanda Leon Bianco	P
Malibran	Q
Novo	M
Palazzo Abadessa	J
Santa Lucia	F
Villa Rosa	E

HOSTEL

Ostello Santa Fosca	C

North of San Giobbe

At the top of the fondamenta to the north of San Giobbe, looking over the lagoon to the mainland, is the **Macello Pubblico** (municipal slaughterhouse), built by the hygiene-conscious Austrians in 1843 and adorned with ox skulls. It is now used by the university, following many years of discussion – Le Corbusier designed a hospital for the site, but the plan was shelved in the face of local opposition to the demolition of the building.

On the opposite side of the Canale di Cannaregio, immediately east of the Ponte dei Tre Archi, stands the **Palazzo Surian**, once the French embassy. **Jean-Jacques Rousseau** lived here in 1743–44 as secretary to an indolent boss: "The French who lived in Venice would never have known that there was a French ambassador resident in the city, had it not been for me," he wrote. His *Confessions* record the political bickerings of his time here, and a number of discreditable sexual adventures. At the far northern end of this fondamenta you'll find one of the few new building projects in central Venice – a new **housing development** which elegantly combines modern architectural techniques with elements of Venetian vernacular style, such as the characteristic flowerpot chimneys.

The Ghetto

The name of the Venetian **Ghetto** – a name bequeathed to all other such enclaves of deprivation – is derived from the Venetian dialect *geto*, foundry, which is what this area was until 1390. The city's **Jewish population** at that time was small and dispersed, and had only just achieved any degree of legal recognition: a decree of 1381 gave them the right to settle in Venice, and permitted them to lend money and to trade in second hand items. Before the decade's end the Jews of Venice had become subject to legislation which restricted their residency to periods of no more than fifteen consecutive days, and forced them to wear distinguishing badges. Such punitive measures remained their lot for much of the succeeding century.

The creation of the Ghetto was a consequence of the War of the League of Cambrai, when hundreds of Jews fled the mainland in fear of the Imperial army. Gaining safe haven in Venice, many of the terra firma Jews donated funds for the defence of the city, and were rewarded with permanent protection – at a price. In 1516 the **Ghetto Nuovo** became Venice's Jewish quarter, when all the city's Jews were forced to move onto this small island in the north of Cannaregio. At night the Ghetto was sealed by gates (marks left by their hinges can still be seen in the Sottoportego Ghetto Nuovo) and guarded by Christian watchmen, whose wages were levied from the Jews. In the daytime their movement wasn't restricted, but they were still obliged to wear distinctively coloured badges or caps. Regarded warily because of their mercantile and financial astuteness, yet exploited for these very qualities, the Jews were barred from certain professions but allowed to pursue others: they could trade in used cloth, lend money (you'll find the inscription *Banco Rosso* on no. 2911 in the campo) and also practise medicine – doctors were the only people allowed out of the Ghetto at night. In addition, the Jews' property rights were limited and they were subjected to a range of financial penalties. Changing faith was not a way to escape the shackles, as converts were forbidden "to enter or to practise any activity under any pretext whatsoever in this city…on pain of hanging, imprisonment, whipping or pillory". (This statute is carved in stone a little way down Calle di Ghetto Vecchio.)

Yet the fact remains that Venice was one of the few states to tolerate the Jewish religion, and the Ghetto's population was often swelled by refugees from more oppressive societies. Jews expelled from Spain and Portugal in the 1490s came here, as did Jews later displaced from the Veneto by the Habsburg army during the War of the League of Cambrai, and from the eastern Mediterranean by the

▲ The Ghetto Nuovo

Ottoman Turks. Venice's burdensome protection was entirely pragmatic, however, as is shown by two conflicting responses to Church interference: when criticized by the Inquisition for not burning enough Jews as heretics, Venetian leaders replied that non-Christians logically could not commit heresy; yet when Pope Julius II ordered the destruction of the Talmud in 1553, the Signoria obligingly arranged a bonfire of Jewish books in the Piazza.

Parts of the Ghetto look quite different from the rest of Venice, as a result of the overcrowding that remained a problem even after the Jewish population was allowed to spread into the **Ghetto Vecchio** (1541) and the **Ghetto Nuovissimo** (1633), where all accommodation was rented, as in the Ghetto Nuovo – Jews were not allowed to own their accommodation. (The adjectives attached to the three parts of the ghetto can be confusing. The Ghetto Nuovo is *nuovo* – new – because the foundries spread here from the Ghetto Vecchio – the old foundry. The Ghetto Nuovissimo, on the other hand, is "most new" because it was the last part to be settled by the city's Jews.) As buildings in the Ghetto were not allowed to be more than one-third higher than in the rest of Venice, storeys were made as low as possible in order to fit in the maximum number of floors; seven is the usual number. The gates of the Ghetto were finally torn down by Napoleon in 1797, but it wasn't until the city's unification with the Kingdom of Italy in 1866 that Jews achieved equal status with their fellow citizens.

At its peak, in the middle of the seventeenth century, the Ghetto was home to a little over five thousand people. Today Venice's Jewish population of around six hundred (which includes a recent influx of young Italians and North Americans belonging to the Lubavitch sect) is spread all over the city, but the Ghetto remains the centre of the community, with a library in Calle Ghetto Vecchio, a nursery, an old people's home, a kosher restaurant, and a baker of unleavened bread. There are currently around thirty students at the small school on the campo, and on Saturdays the normally serene atmosphere of the Ghetto gives way to something of a party spirit.

The scole and the campo

Each wave of Jewish immigrants, while enriching the overall cultural environment of the city (Venetians of all religions frequented the Ghetto's salons), also maintained their own synagogues with their distinctive rites: the **Scola Tedesca** (for German Jews) was founded in 1528, the **Scola al Canton** (probably Jews from Provence) in 1531–32, the **Scola Levantina** (eastern Mediterranean) in 1538, the **Scola Spagnola** (Spanish) at an uncertain date in the later sixteenth century, and the **Scola Italiana** in 1575. Since the Jews were disqualified from the profession of architect and forbidden to use marble in their buildings, the *scole* tend to have oddly church-like interiors, thickly adorned with gilt and stucco. Funded by particularly prosperous trading communities, the Scola Levantina and the Scola Spagnola are the most lavish of the synagogues (the latter, redesigned by Longhena, greatly influenced the look of the others), and are the only two still used on a daily basis – the Levantina in summer and the Spagnola in winter, as there is only one rabbi. Depending on the season, one of the above can be viewed, along with the Scola al Canton and the Scola Italiana, in an informative guided tour that begins in the **Museo Ebraico**, above the Scola Tedesca in Campo del Ghetto Nuovo (daily except Sat & Jewish hols: June–Sept 10am–7pm; Oct–May 10am–5.30pm; €3, or €8.50 with tour; tours in English on the half-hour; last tour June–Sept 5.30pm; Oct–May 4.30pm). The museum's collection consists mainly of silverware, sacred objects, textiles and furniture.

In a corner of the campo is a reminder of the ultimate suffering of the Jewish people: a series of reliefs by **Arbit Blatas**, with a poem by André Tranc, commemorating the two hundred Venetian Jews deported to the death camps in 1943 and 1944; the names and ages of all the victims are inscribed on a separate memorial entitled *The Last Train*, on your left as you walk towards the wide iron bridge on the north side of the ghetto.

Northern Cannaregio

Land reclamation and the consolidation of the lagoon's mudbanks has been a continuous process in Venice since the time of the first settlers, but the contours of the city have been modified with particular rapidity in the last hundred years or so. As its long, straight canals and right-angled alleyways suggest, much of northern Cannaregio has come into existence comparatively recently: the Sacca (inlet) di San Girolamo, for example, was reclaimed in the first half of the

Festivals

Venice celebrates enthusiastically a number of special days either not observed elsewhere in Italy, or, like the Carnevale, generally celebrated to a lesser extent. Although they have gone through various degrees of decline and revival, most of them are still strongly traditional in form. The film festival, the Biennale and music festivals are covered in Chapter 12, along with a handful of smaller events.

Carnevale ▲

Fancy-dress pup at the Carnevale ▼

Vogalonga ▼

Carnevale

John Evelyn wrote of the 1646 Carnevale: "All the world was in Venice to see the folly and madness…the women, men and persons of all conditions disguising themselves in antique dresses, & extravagant Musique & a thousand gambols." Today's Carnevale is not quite so riotous, but it's nonetheless become the city's main tourist jamboree.

The origins of the Carnevale can be traced in the word itself: *carne vale*, a "farewell to meat" before the rigours of Lent. The medieval European carnival developed into a period of liberation from the constraints of social rank, and a means of quelling discontent by a ritualized relinquishing of power. Venice's Carnevale – which became so famous that the city's mask-makers had their own guild (the *mascarei*) – had its heyday in the eighteenth century, when it began on December 26 and lasted until Shrove Tuesday. Today's Carnevale is limited to the ten days leading up to **Lent**, finishing on Shrove Tuesday with a masked ball for the glitterati, and dancing in the Piazza for the plebs. Having ceased with the collapse of the Republic, Carnevale was revived in 1979 by a group of non-Venetians, prompted by the Carnival-themed theatre performances at that year's Biennale. The city authorities, sensing a way of attracting tourists in the dead months of the year, soon gave their support, and nowadays the town hall organizes various pageants and performances during the festival. Apart from these events, Carnevale is very much a case of see and be seen: you'll spot the most extravagant costumes on the Piazza in the evenings, but even at lunchtime you'll see businesspeople doing their shopping in the classic white mask, black cloak and tricorne hat, an ensemble known as a *baùtta*.

Masks are on sale throughout the year (see p.272), and during Carnevale there's a mask-making marquee on Campo San Maurizio. If you want to hire a full outfit, the places to try are Pietro Longhi (ⓦ www.pietrolonghi.com), Nicolao (ⓦ www.nicolao.com) and Flavia (ⓦ www .veniceatelier.com).

La Sensa and Vogalonga

The feast of **La Sensa** happens in May on the **Sunday after Ascension Day** – the latter being the day on which the doge enacted the wedding of Venice to the sea (see p.221). A feeble modern version of that ritual is followed by a gondola regatta, but far more spectacular is the **Vogalonga** or "long row", held a week later. Established in 1974, the Vogalonga is open to any crew in any class of rowing boat, and covers a 32-kilometre course from the Bacino di San Marco out to Burano and back, with the competitors setting off from in front of the Palazzo Ducale around 9am.

Festa del Redentore

The **Festa del Redentore**, which marks the end of the plague epidemic of 1576, is celebrated on the **third Sunday in July**, and is centred on Palladio's church of the Redentore, which was built in thanksgiving for the city's deliverance. It's marked by a procession over a bridge of boats that's strung across the Giudecca canal, and on the preceding Saturday night hundreds of people row out for a picnic on the water. The night ends with a grand fireworks display, after which it's traditional to row to the Lido for the sunrise.

▲ Rowers at the Vogalonga

▼ Fireworks at the Festa del Redentore

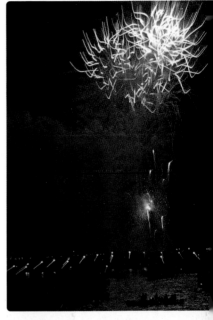

▼ Festa del Redentore

The Regata Storica

Held on the **first Sunday in September**, the **Regata Storica** is the annual trial of strength and skill for the city's gondoliers and other expert rowers. It starts with a procession of historic craft along the Canal Grande course, their crews all decked out in period dress, followed by a series of races right up the canal. Re-enacting the return of Caterina Cornaro to her native city in 1489 (see p.354), the opening parade is a spectacular affair, and is followed by a race for young rowers in two-oared *pupparini*; the women come next (in boats called *mascarete*), followed by a race for canoe-like *caorline*; and then it's the men's race, in specialized two-man racing gondolas called *gondolini*.

The Regata Storica has been increasingly marketed as a touristic spectacle, but there's nothing artificial about the smaller regate that are held throughout the year: the **Regata di San Zanipolo** (late June); the **Regata di Murano** (early July); the **Regata di Malamocco** (mid-July); the **Regata del Redentore** (during the Festa del Redentore); the **Regata di Pellestrina** (early Aug); and the **Regata di Burano** (late Sept).

Regata Storica ▲

Historic craft at the Regata Storica ▼

La Salute

Named after the church of the Salute, the **Festa della Salute** is a reminder of the plague of 1630–31, which killed one third of the city's population. The church was built after the outbreak, and every **November 21** people process to it over a pontoon bridge across the Canal Grande, to give thanks for their good health or to pray for sick friends and relatives.

twentieth century to provide working-class housing of a higher standard than in much of the rest of the city.

In the area **northwest from the Ghetto**, inland from the Sacca, there's nothing to ferret out: the tiny seventeenth-century church of the Cappuccine (open for services only) faces the equally dull but bigger and uglier (and closed) San Girolamo, a church once used by the Austrians as a steam-powered flour mill, with the campanile converted to a chimney. **Northeast of the Ghetto**, though, is one of the most attractive domestic quarters of Venice, and some of the city's best restaurants and bars are dotted along its lengthy fondamente.

Sant'Alvise to Campo dei Mori

For all the apparent rationality of the city's layout in this district, the church of **Sant'Alvise** (Mon–Sat 10am–5pm; €3, or Chorus Pass) is fairly tricky to get to, standing as it does on an island with no eastward land connection with the rest of the city. Dedicated to Saint Louis of Toulouse (Alvise being the Venetian version of Louis/Luigi), the church was commissioned in the 1380s by Antonia Venier, daughter of Doge Antonio Venier, after the saint appeared to her in a vision. Despite having undergone major restoration work, Sant'Alvise is still suffering from severe damp, and more restoration is now under way – paintings may be moved around as work progresses. Still in its original position is the chancel's immense *Road to Calvary* by **Giambattista Tiepolo**, which was restored last time round. His *Crowning with Thorns* and *Flagellation*, slightly earlier works, hang on the right-hand wall of the nave. Under the nuns' choir you'll find eight small tempera paintings, familiarly known as "The Baby Carpaccios" since Ruskin assigned them to the painter's precocious childhood; they're not actually by Carpaccio, but were produced around 1470, when he would indeed have been just an infant. The likeliest candidate for their authorship is an unknown pupil of Lazzaro Bastiani, Carpaccio's master. The extraordinary seventeenth-century trompe l'oeil **ceiling** is a collaboration between Antonio Torri (the architectural work) and Paolo Ricchi (the religious scenes).

To get from Sant'Alvise to Madonna dell'Orto you can either take a one-stop vaporetto trip, or cross over the canal to the Fondamenta della Sensa, the main street immediately to the south. One bridge after the early fifteenth-century **Palazzo Michiel** (the French embassy at the time of Henry III's visit), the fondamenta opens out at the **Campo dei Mori**, a square whose name possibly comes from the proximity of the now extinct Fondaco degli Arabi (Arabs' warehouse). There is another explanation: the four thirteenth-century **statues** around the campo are popularly associated with a family of twelfth-century merchants called the Mastelli brothers, who used to live in the palace into which two of the figures are embedded – they hailed from the Morea (the Peloponnese), and hence were known as *Mori*. Aggrieved citizens used to leave denunciations at the feet of "Sior Antonio Rioba" (the statue with the rusty nose), and circulate vindictive verses signed with his name. For more on the Mastelli brothers' house, see p.147.

Just beyond the campo is the elegant fifteenth-century house where **Tintoretto** lived for the last two decades of his life (1574–94), accompanied by one of his daughters, **Marietta**. Skilled as a painter, and a fine musician and singer too, Marietta was married off to a man who preferred his wife to produce portraits of his colleagues and friends instead of painting more ambitious works. She died aged 34, four years before her father, her career having epitomized the restriction of women's talents to genres compatible with a life of domesticity. None of her paintings is on public show in Venice, though scholars have detected her touch in some of her father's large-scale works.

Madonna dell'Orto

Marietta, her father, and her brother Domenico are all buried in **Madonna dell'Orto** (Mon–Sat 10am–5pm; €3, or Chorus Pass), the family's parish church and one of Venice's superlative pieces of ecclesiastical Gothic. The church was founded in the name of Saint Christopher some time around 1350; ferrymen for the northern islands used to operate from the quays near here, and it's popularly believed that the church received its dedication because Christopher was their patron saint, though there's a stronger connection with the merchants' guild, who funded much of the building and who also regarded Christopher as their patron.

It was popularly renamed after a large stone *Madonna* by **Giovanni de'Santi**, who put it on display in his nearby garden (*orto*), where it supposedly began working miracles; under pressure from the city's ecclesiastical authorities, he sold the statue to this church in 1377, in a deal that was mutually beneficial – the sculptor received a hefty sum of money plus a promise that a mass would be said for him every day after his death, while the donations attracted by the *Madonna* enabled the monks to finance further building work. The heavily restored figure now sits in the Cappella di San Mauro, which is through the door at the end of the right aisle, next to the chapel containing Tintoretto's tomb; it's set aside for prayer, but access is often allowed if no one's using it.

▲ Madonna dell'Orto

The main figure on the **facade** is a *St Christopher* by the Florentine **Nicolò di Giovanni**; commissioned by the merchants' guild in the mid-fifteenth century, it became the first major sculptural project in the restoration programmes that began after the 1966 flood. **Bartolomeo Bon the Elder** designed the portal in 1460, shortly before his death. The **campanile**, finished in 1503, is one of the most notable landmarks when approaching Venice from the northern lagoon.

Restoration work in the 1860s made a mess of the **interior**, ripping up memorial stones from the floor, for instance, and destroying the organ, once described as the best in Europe. Partial reversal of the damage was achieved in the 1930s, when some over-painting was removed from the Greek marble columns, the fresco work and elsewhere, and in 1968–69 the whole building was given a massive overhaul.

An amusing if implausible tale explains the large number of **Tintoretto** paintings here. Having added cuckold's horns to a portrait of a doge that had been rejected by its subject, Tintoretto allegedly took refuge from his furious ex-client in Madonna dell'Orto; the doge then offered to forget the insult if Tintoretto agreed to decorate the church, figuring it would keep him quiet for a few years. Famously rapid even under normal circumstances, the painter finished the job within six months, most of which time must have been spent on the epic images on each side of the choir: *The Last Judgement*, described by Ruskin as the only painting ever to grasp the event "in its Verity…as they may see it who shall not sleep, but be changed"; and *The Making of the Golden Calf*, in which the carriers of the calf have been speculatively identified as portraits of Giorgione, Titian, Veronese and the artist himself (fourth from the left), with Aaron (pointing on the right) identified as Sansovino.

There could hardly be a sharper shift of mood than that from the apocalyptic temper of *The Last Judgement* to the reverential tenderness of *The Presentation of the Virgin*, at the end of the right aisle. It's by a long way the best of the smaller Tintorettos, but most of the others are interesting: *The Vision of the Cross to St Peter* and *The Beheading of St Paul* flank an *Annunciation* by Palma il Giovane in the chancel; four *Virtues* (the central one is ascribed to Sebastiano Ricci) are installed in the vault above; and *St Agnes Reviving Licinius* stands in the fourth chapel on the left. A major figure of the early Venetian Renaissance – **Cima da Conegliano** – is represented by a *St John the Baptist and Other Saints*, on the first altar on the right; a *Madonna and Child* by Cima's great contemporary, Giovanni Bellini, used to occupy the first chapel on the left, but thieves made off with it in 1993. Finally, in the second chapel off the left aisle you'll find a small *Tobias and the Angel* by Titian.

To the Scuole della Misericordia

Diagonally opposite the church, on the other side of the canal, stands the **Palazzo Mastelli**, former home of the mercantile family of the same name. The facade of the much-altered palazzo is a sort of architectural scrap-album, featuring a Gothic top-floor balcony, thirteenth-century Byzantine fragments set into sixteenth-century work below, a bit of a Roman altar set into a column by the corner, and a quaint little relief of a man leading a laden camel – hence its alternative title, Palazzo del Cammello.

On the canal's north side, at its eastern end, stand the seventeenth-century **Palazzo Minelli Spada** and the sixteenth-century **Palazzo Contarini dal Zaffo**, the latter being one of the many palaces owned by the vast Contarini clan. Numerous though they once were, the last male of the Contarini line died in 1836, thus adding their name to the roll call of patrician dynasties that vanished in the nineteenth century. Lack of money almost certainly accounts for their extinction – already impoverished by loans made to the dying Republic and by the endless round of parties, many of the Venetian aristocracy were bankrupted during the Napoleonic and Austrian occupations, and so, no longer having money for dowries and other related expenses, they simply chose not to marry.

In the garden of the Palazzo Contarini dal Zaffo stands the sixteenth-century house known as the **Casinò degli Spiriti**. (It can be seen from the Fondamente Nuove.) A *casinò* (little house) – a suite set aside for private entertainments – was a feature of many Venetian palaces, and a few were set up in separate pavilions in the grounds. This is one of only two surviving examples of the latter, yet it's best known not for its architectural rarity but for the ghost story that's sometimes said to be the source of its name. A certain noblewoman took her husband's best friend as a lover, and this is where they would meet. At her paramour's sudden death she began to pine away, and shut herself in the *casinò* to die. No sooner had she exhaled her last breath than the ghost of her lover came in, raised her from the bed and, pushing the nursemaid to one side, made off with her. It's likelier, though, that *spiriti* refers to the exalted "spirits" who met here to discuss poetry, philosophy and so forth.

Crossing the canal in front of the Palazzo Contarini dal Zaffo, you quickly come to the fondamenta leading to the defunct **Abbazia della Misericordia** and the **Scuola Vecchia della Misericordia**; neither is particularly lovely, and the latter's proudest adornment – Bartolomeo Bon's relief of the *Madonna della Misericordia* – is exiled in London's Victoria and Albert Museum. The complex is now used as a restoration centre. When the Misericordia became a *scuola grande* in the sixteenth century its members commissioned the huge **Scuola Nuova della Misericordia** (on the far side of the bridge), a move which benefited Tintoretto, who set up his canvases in the upper room of the old building to work on the *Paradiso* for the Palazzo Ducale. Begun in 1532 by Sansovino but not opened until 1589, the new block was never finished. It's been used as a sports centre in recent years, and there are now plans to restore it for use as a concert hall and museum of music. Its neighbour is the **Palazzo Lezze**, another project by Longhena.

Southern and eastern Cannaregio

If you follow the main route east from the station, crossing the Canale di Cannaregio by the Guglie bridge, you come onto the shopping street of **Rio Terrà San Leonardo**. Like the Lista di Spagna, this thoroughfare follows the line of a former canal, filled in during the 1870s by the Austrians as part of a scheme to rationalize movement round the north bend of the Canal Grande. The continuation of the route to the Rialto bridge – the Strada Nova – was by contrast created by simply ploughing a line straight through the houses that used to stand there.

Rio Terrà Cristo, on the south of Rio Terrà San Leonardo, just before the market stalls of the Campiello dell'Anconetta, runs down to Giorgio Massari's church of **San Marcuola** (daily 8am–noon & 4–6.30pm), whose unfinished brick front is as clear a landmark on the Canal Grande as the facade of the Palazzo Vendramin-Calergi, which stands a little to the east of it. The tiered ledges and sockets of the exterior, intended for marble cladding but now crammed with pigeons, are a more diverting sight than the inside, where statues of the church's two patron saints by Gian Maria Morleiter, and an early *Last Supper* by Tintoretto (left wall of the chancel) are the only things to seek out. Those apart, the church's main interest is in a story about one of its priests. He was once foolish enough to announce from the pulpit that he didn't believe in ghosts, and that "where the dead are, there they stay"; that night all the corpses buried in the church rose from their graves, dragged him from his bed and beat him up. Incidentally, the church's name is perhaps the most baffling of all Venetian diminutives – it's somehow derived from Santi Ermagora e Fortunato.

The Maddalena district

Take the angled bridge that's visible from the northern flank of San Marcuola and you'll come to the land entrance of the **Palazzo Vendramin-Calergi**, where a plaque records the death of Richard Wagner here in 1883; the surprisingly tatty entrance is as far as you'll get unless your wallet's full and your attire smart, because it's now the home of the casino (see p.265). Cut straight up from here and you're back on the main route between the train station and the centre of town, a street here named Rio Terrà della Maddalena, after the little Neoclassical church of **La Maddalena** (1760), which is set back on its own small campo. Its designer, the unprolific **Tomasso Temanza**, was more noted as a

---

Paolo Sarpi and the excommunication of Venice

Unswerving moral rectitude and fierce intellectual rigour made Servite priest **Fra' Paolo Sarpi** one of the heroes of Venetian history. Author of a magisterial history of the Council of Trent, discoverer of the mechanics of the iris of the eye and a partner in Galileo's optical researches, Sarpi was described by Sir Henry Wotton, the English ambassador to Venice, as "the most deep and general scholar of the world". Sarpi is best known, however, as the adviser to the Venetian state in its row with the Vatican at the start of the seventeenth century.

Although Venice's toleration of non-Christians was a cause of recurrent friction with the Vatican, the area of greatest discord was the Republic's insistence on separating the sovereignty of the Church and that of the State – "The Church must obey the State in things temporal and the latter in things spiritual, each maintaining its proper rights," to quote Sarpi himself. Matters came to a head when Venice restricted the amount of money that monasteries on the mainland could return to Rome from their rents and commerce, and then imprisoned two priests found guilty in secular courts of secular crimes. Pope Paul V's demand for the return of the priests and the repeal of the monastic legislation was firmly rebuffed, and the upshot was a **papal interdict** in April 1606, forbidding all religious services in Venice. Excommunication for the entire city then followed. In retaliation, Venice booted out the Jesuits and threatened with exile or death any priests who didn't ignore the interdict – a priest in Padua who insisted that the Holy Spirit had moved him to obey the pope was informed by the Council of Ten that the Holy Spirit had already moved them to hang any who disagreed with them. Sarpi and Doge Leonardo Donà maintained their closely argued defiance of Rome until French mediation brought about a resolution which in fact required no compromises from the Venetians. The moral authority of Rome was diminished forever.

Six months later, Sarpi was walking home past Santa Fosca when he was set upon by three men and left for dead with a dagger in his face. "I recognize the style of the Holy See," the dauntless Sarpi quipped, punning on the word "stiletto". He eventually died of natural causes on January 15, 1623.

theoretician than as an architect, and his *Lives of the Most Famous Venetian Architects and Sculptors* (modelled on Vasari's *Lives of the Artists*) remains the classic text for those interested in the subject.

If you follow the main drag eastward, the next sight is the nineteenth-century monument of **Paolo Sarpi** (see box, p.149) that fronts the church of **Santa Fosca**, an architecturally unmemorable building, containing nothing of interest to the casual visitor apart from a Byzantine *Pietà* at the facade end of the north aisle. Across the Strada Nova, the Farmacia Ponci has the oldest surviving shop interior in Venice, a wonderful display of seventeenth-century heavy-duty woodwork in walnut, kitted out with eighteenth-century majolica vases.

The western part of the island immediately north of Santa Fosca is occupied by the **Palazzo Diedo**, scene of a peculiar incident in 1606. An astrologer named Benedetto Altavilla rushed in to tell its owner that the stars had revealed to him that a quantity of gun powder had been stacked feloniously under the Sala del Maggior Consiglio. The Council of Ten duly found the explosives, but suspected, not unreasonably, that Altavilla had put them there. Shaved and shorn, in case his hair gave him occult strength, the astrologer was tortured to unconsciousness and then hanged, protesting throughout his ordeal that the stars had told him everything. On the little island to the north of Palazzo Diedo stands **San Marziale**, where, if you nip inside just before or after Mass (Mon–Sat 10am & 6.30pm), you'll see **Sebastiano Ricci**'s ceiling paintings, a set of works that made his reputation in the city. Those who haven't acquired the taste will get more of a buzz from the dotty Baroque high altar, depicting Saint Jerome at lunch with a couple of associates – Faith and Charity.

Most of the island to the west of San Marziale is occupied by the remnants of the church and ex-convent of **Santa Maria dei Servi**. When the church was demolished in 1812, some of its monuments were thrown away and others were shuffled around Venice – such as Doge Andrea Vendramin's tomb, now in Santi Giovanni e Paolo; the ruins themselves were offered to Ruskin, who turned down the deal.

Along the Strada Nova

Continuing east from Santa Fosca, you're on the **Strada Nova**, a brisk, broad and basic shopping street where you can buy anything from delicious home-made cakes to surgical trusses. Cross the first bridge after Santa Fosca and you come to the church of **San Felice** (daily 9am–noon & 4–7pm) – rebuilt in the 1530s and savagely renovated in the last century, it's a workaday place of worship rather than a major monument, though it does have a painting by Tintoretto – *St Demetrius with Donor*, on the third altar on the right. One local curiosity: at the far end of the fondamenta going up the east side of the church is the only parapet-less bridge left in the main part of Venice; it leads to someone's front door.

Ca' d'Oro

Nearly halfway along the Strada an inconspicuous calle leads down to the **Ca' d'Oro**, or House of Gold (Mon 8.15am–2pm, Tues–Sat 8.15am–7.15pm; €5), a masterpiece of domestic Gothic architecture and now home to a somewhat patchy art collection, the **Galleria Giorgio Franchetti**. Built for procurator Marino Contarini between 1425 and 1440, the palace takes its name from its Canal Grande **facade**: incorporating parts of the thirteenth-century palace that used to stand here, it was highlighted in gold leaf, ultramarine and vermilion – materials which, as the three most expensive pigments of the day, spectacularly publicized the wealth of its owner. The house's cosmetics have now worn off, but the facade has at least survived unaltered, whereas the rest of the Ca' d'Oro was badly abused by later owners.

After the dancer Maria Taglioni had finished her home improvements, Ruskin lamented that it was "now destroyed by restorations", and today, despite the subsequent structural repairs, the interior of the Ca' d'Oro is no longer recognizable as that of a Gothic building. The staircase in the beautiful **courtyard** is an original feature, though – ripped out by Taglioni, it was reacquired and reconstructed by Franchetti, who likewise put back the wellhead by Bartolomeo Bon (1427). He also imported the mosaic pavement, which is certainly magnificent but not at all authentic – no house would have had a floor like this.

The gallery's main attraction is undoubtedly the *St Sebastian* painted by **Mantegna** shortly before his death in 1506, now installed in a chapel-like alcove on the first floor. Many of the big names of Venetian art are found on the second floor, but the canvases by Titian and Tintoretto are not among their best, and Pordenone's fragmentary frescoes from Santo Stefano require a considerable feat of imaginative reconstruction, as do the remains of Giorgione's and Titian's work from the exterior of the Fondaco dei Tedeschi. The Ca' d'Oro's collection of sculpture, though far less extensive than the array of paintings, has more outstanding items, notably **Tullio Lombardo**'s beautifully carved *Young Couple*, and superb portrait busts by Bernini and Alessandro Vittoria. Also arresting are a sixteenth-century English alabaster polyptych of *Scenes from the Life of St Catherine* and a case of Renaissance medals that includes fine specimens by **Gentile Bellini** and **Pisanello**.

Santi Apostoli

At the eastern end of the Strada Nova, past the negligible little church of Santa Sofia, you come to the Campo dei Santi Apostoli, an elbow on the road from the Rialto to the train station, with the church of **Santi Apostoli** (daily 7.30–11.30am & 5–7pm), a frequently renovated building last altered substantially in the eighteenth century. The **campanile** was finished in 1672 – and soon afterwards, according to James (Jan) Morris, "an old and simple-minded sacristan" fell from it, "but was miraculously caught by the minute hand of the clock, which, slowly revolving to six o'clock, deposited him safely on a parapet".

The **Cappella Corner**, stuck onto the right side of the hall-like interior, is the most interesting part of the church. It's attributed to Mauro Codussi, and its altarpiece is a beautiful *Communion of St Lucy* by Giambattista Tiepolo (1748). One of the inscriptions in the chapel is to Caterina Cornaro, who was buried here before being moved to San Salvatore; the tomb of her father Marco (on the right) is probably by Tullio Lombardo, who also carved the plaque of Saint Sebastian's head in the chapel to the right of the chancel.

Palazzo Falier to San Giovanni Crisostomo

Two of the oldest houses in Venice are to be found on the small patch between the Rio dei Santi Apostoli and San Giovanni Crisostomo. At the foot of the bridge arching over to Campo Santi Apostoli there's the **Palazzo Falier**, parts of which date back to the second half of the thirteenth century. Traditionally this was the home of the ill-fated **Doge Marin Falier**, a branch of whose family was certainly in possession at the time of his dogeship (1354–55). A man noted for his unswerving rectitude, Falier was greatly offended by the licence routinely allowed to the unruly nobles of Venice; when a lenient punishment was given to a young nobleman who had insulted Falier, his wife and her ladies, he finally went right off the rails and hatched a conspiracy to install himself as the city's benevolent despot – a plot into which he conscripted the overseer of the Arsenale and Filippo Calendario, one of the architects of the Palazzo Ducale. Their plan was discovered and Falier, having admitted the conspiracy, was beheaded on the very spot on which he had earlier been invested as doge. See p.67 for an unusual memorial to Marin Falier.

Interlocking with the Falier house is the equally ancient **Ca' da Mosto**, reached through the passage going towards the Canal Grande – though the best view of it is from the deck of a vaporetto. This was the birthplace of **Alvise da Mosto** (1432–88), a Venetian merchant-explorer who threw in his lot with Portugal's Henry the Navigator and went on to discover the Cape Verde Islands. The ruinous state of the building, and the trash littering the grand staircase makes it hard to imagine the days when it housed the popular *Albergo del Leon Bianco*; among its guests were J.M.W. Turner, who had himself rowed up and down the Canal Grande while he sketched the city, and two German officers who in 1716 fought a duel in the courtyard and contrived to skewer each other to death.

San Giovanni Crisostomo and the Teatro Malibran

Tucked into the southernmost corner of Cannaregio stands **San Giovanni Crisostomo** (John the Golden-Mouthed), named after the famously eloquent Archbishop of Constantinople (Mon–Sat 8.30am–noon & 3.30–7pm, Sun 3.30–7pm). An intimate church with a compact Greek-cross plan, it was possibly the last project of Mauro Codussi, and was built between 1497 and 1504. It possesses two outstanding altarpieces: in the chapel to the right hangs one of the last works by **Giovanni Bellini**, *SS Jerome, Christopher and Louis of Toulouse*, painted in 1513 when the artist was in his eighties; and on the high altar, **Sebastiano del Piombo**'s gracefully heavy *St John Chrysostom with SS John the Baptist, Liberale, Mary Magdalen, Agnes and Catherine*, painted in 1509–11. On the left side is a marble panel of the *Coronation of the Virgin* by Tullio Lombardo, a severe contrast with his more playful stuff in the nearby Miracoli (see below).

Calle del Scaletter, virtually opposite the church, leads to a secluded campiello flanked by the partly thirteenth-century **Palazzo Lion-Morosini**, whose external staircase is guarded by a little lion apparently suffering from indigestion; the campiello opens onto the Canal Grande, and if you're lucky you'll be able to enjoy the view on your own. Behind the church is the **Teatro Malibran**, which opened in the seventeenth century, was rebuilt in the 1790s, and soon after renamed in honour of the great soprano Maria Malibran (1808–36), who saved the theatre from bankruptcy by giving a fund-raising recital here, then topping the proceeds by donating the fee she had just been paid for singing at the Fenice. Rebuilt again in 1920, the Malibran has now emerged from a very protracted restoration to resume its place as the city's major venue for classical music concerts. The Byzantine arches on the facade of the theatre are said to have once been part of the house of **Marco Polo**'s family, who probably lived in the heavily restored palace overlooking the canal at the back of the Malibran, visible from the Ponte Marco Polo.

Polo's tales of his experiences in the empire of Kublai Khan were treated with incredulity when he returned to Venice in 1295, after seventeen years of trading with his father and uncle in the Far East. His habit of talking in terms of superlatives and vast numbers earned him the nickname *Il Milione* (The Million), the title he gave to the memoir he dictated in 1298 while he was a prisoner of the Genoese. It was the first account of Asian life to appear in the West, and for centuries was the most reliable description available in Europe – and yet on his deathbed Polo was implored by his friends to recant at least some of his tales, for "there are many strange things in that book which are reckoned past all credence". Polo's nickname is preserved by the adjoining **Corte Prima del Milion** and **Corte Seconda del Milion** – the latter is an interesting architectural mix of Veneto–Byzantine and Gothic elements, with a magnificently carved twelfth-century arch.

Santa Maria dei Miracoli

Inland from these palaces, beyond the dull San Canziano, stands the church which Ruskin paired with the Scuola di San Marco as "the two most refined buildings in Venice" – the jewelbox-like **Santa Maria dei Miracoli**, usually known simply by the last word of its name (Mon–Sat 10am–5pm; €3, or Chorus Pass).

It was built in 1481–89 to house an image of the Madonna that was painted in 1409 then began working miracles seventy years later – it was credited with the revival of a man who'd spent half an hour at the bottom of the Giudecca canal and of a woman left for dead after being stabbed. Financed by gifts left at the painting's nearby shrine, the church was most likely designed by **Pietro Lombardo**; certainly he and his two sons **Tullio** and **Antonio** oversaw the construction, and the three of them executed much of the carving. Richness of effect takes precedence over classical correctness on the **exterior**; pilasters are positioned close together along the sides to create the illusion of longer walls, for example, and Corinthian pilasters are placed below Ionic (in defiance of classical rules) so that the viewer can better appreciate the former's more elaborate detailing. Venetian folklore has it that the materials for the multicoloured marble cladding and inlays, typical of the Lombardi, were the surplus from the decoration of the Basilica di San Marco.

The marble-lined **interior** contains some of the most intricate decorative sculpture to be seen in Venice. The *Annunciation* and half-length figures of two saints on the balustrade at the altar end are thought to be by Tullio; nobody is sure which members of the family created the rest of the carvings in this part of the church, though it's likely that Antonio was responsible for the children's heads at the base of the chancel arch (which Ruskin hated: "The man who could carve a child's head so perfectly must have been wanting in all human feeling, to cut it off, and tie it by the hair to a vine leaf") and the adjacent siren figures (which Ezra Pound declared to be incomparably beautiful). At the opposite end of the church, the columns below the nuns' choir are covered with extraordinary filigree stonework, featuring tiny birds with legs as thin as cocktail sticks. The miracle-working *Madonna* by Nicolò di Pietro still occupies the altar, while overhead a sequence of fifty saints and prophets, painted in 1528 by Pier Pennacchi, is set into the Miracoli's unusual panelled ceiling.

Take Calle Castelli from the front end of the church and you'll come to the **Palazzo Soranzo-van Axel**, whose fine Gothic entrance, at the end of the fondamenta, retains its original wooden door – a unique feature in Venice.

The Gesuiti district

The major monument in the northeastern corner of Cannaregio is **Santa Maria Assunta**, commonly known simply as the **Gesuiti** (daily 10am–noon & 4–6pm). Built for the Jesuits in 1714–29, six decades after the foundation here of their first monastery in Venice, the church was clearly planned to make an

▲ The Gesuiti

impression on a city that was habitually mistrustful of the order's close relation-ship with the papacy.

Although the disproportionately huge facade clearly wasn't the work of a weekend, most of the effort went into the stupefying **interior**, where green and white marble covers every wall and stone is carved to resemble swags of damask. The result is jaw-dropping, and also very heavy – a factor in the subsidence which is a constant problem with the Gesuiti. Unless you're a devotee of Palma il Giovane (in which case make for the sacristy, where the walls and ceiling are covered with paintings by him), the only painting to seek out is the *Martyrdom of St Lawrence* (first altar on the left), a broodingly intense night-scene painted by **Titian** in 1558.

Almost opposite the church is the **Oratorio dei Crociferi**, the remnant of a convent complex founded in the twelfth century by the crusading religious order known as the *Crociferi* or The Bearers of the Cross. A part of the complex was given over to a hostel that was originally for pilgrims but by the fifteenth century had become a hospice solely for poor women. (By the late sixteenth century Venice had around one hundred such institutions for the penniless.) In return for free meals and accommodation, these women were required to help in the maintenance of the convent and to pray each morning in the oratory, which in the 1580s was decorated by **Palma il Giovane** with a cycle of *Scenes from the History of the Order of the Crociferi*. Restored in the 1980s, the paintings show Palma's technique at its subtlest, and the richness of the colours is a good advertisement for modern cleaning techniques. Finding staff for the oratory is a perpetual problem, and at the moment the only way to get inside is to book a private visit – details on Ⓦwww.scalabovolo.org.

There's not much else to look at in the immediate vicinity. Titian used to live in Calle Larga dei Botteri (no. 5179–83), across the Rio dei Gesuiti – but the house has been rebuilt and the construction of the Fondamente Nove did away with the waterside garden where he entertained such exalted clients as Henry III of France. A short distance to the west, past the huge sixteenth-century Palazzi Zen, the church of **Santa Caterina** comes into view. The fourteenth-century ship's-keel ceiling, destroyed by fire in 1978, has now been rebuilt, but the building belongs to a school and is thus out of bounds.

The Fondamente Nove

The long waterfront to the north of the Gesuiti, the **Fondamente Nove** (or Nuove), is the point at which the vaporetti leave the city for San Michele, Murano and the northern lagoon. On a clear day you can follow their course as far as the distant island of Burano, and see the snowy Dolomite peaks on the horizon. Being relatively new, this waterfront isn't solidly lined with historic buildings like its counterpart in the south of the city, the Záttere. The one house of interest is the **Palazzo Donà delle Rose** on the corner of the Rio dei Gesuiti. Architecturally the palace is an oddity, as the main axis of its interior runs parallel to the water instead of at ninety degrees; the cornerstone was laid in 1610 by **Doge Leonardo Donà** (Paolo Sarpi's boss), who died two years later from apoplexy after an argument with his brother about the house's layout. It's one of the very few Venetian residences still owned by the family for whom it was built.

5

Central Castello

Bordering both San Marco and Cannaregio, and spreading across the city to the housing estates of Sant'Elena in the east, Castello is so unwieldy a district that we've divided it into two sections: this chapter describes the zone that extends from the Cannaregio border to the canal that slices north – south through the *sestiere* from just beyond Santi Giovanni e Paolo to the Pietà; everything to the east of that line is covered in the following chapter. The points of interest in central Castello are evenly distributed, but in terms of its importance and its geographical location, Castello's central building is the immense Gothic church of **Santi Giovanni e Paolo** (or **Zanipolo**), the pantheon of Venice's doges. The museums – the **Querini-Stampalia** picture collection, the museum at **San Giorgio dei Greci**, and the **Museo Diocesano**'s sacred art collection – lie in the southern part of this area, where the dominant building is the majestic **San Zaccaria**, a church that has played a significant part in the history of the city, as has nearby **Santa Maria Formosa**, on the liveliest and most convivial square in Castello. Busier still is the southern waterfront, the **Riva degli Schiavoni**, Venice's main promenade.

Campo Santi Giovanni e Paolo

After the Piazza, the **Campo Santi Giovanni e Paolo** is the richest monumental public space in Venice. Dominated by the huge brick church from which it gets its name, the square is also overlooked by the most beautiful facade of any of the *scuole grande* and one of the finest equestrian monuments in the world. A row of café-bars and a perpetual gaggle of ball-playing kids keep the atmosphere lively, and there's a constant flow of traffic through the square, much of it heading for the civic hospital now installed in the scuola.

The church of Santi Giovanni e Paolo

Like the Frari, the massive Gothic brick edifice of **Santi Giovanni e Paolo** (Mon–Sat 9.30am–6pm, Sun 1–6pm; €2.50) – slurred by the Venetian dialect into **San Zanipolo** – was built for one of the mendicant orders which burgeoned in the fourteenth century. Supported largely by charitable donations from the public, the mendicants were less inward-looking than the older orders, basing themselves in large urban settlements and working to relieve the sick and the poor. Reflecting this social mission, their churches contain a vast area for

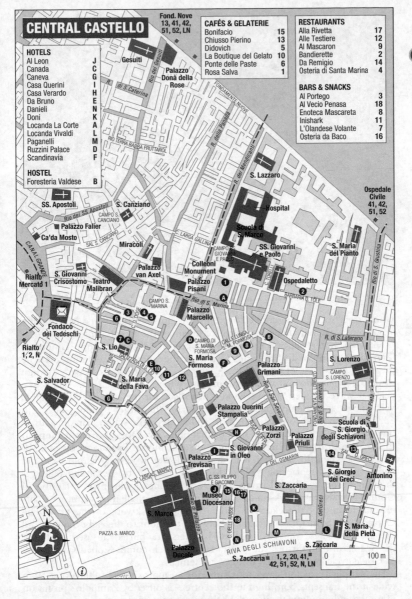

CENTRAL CASTELLO

HOTELS

Al Leon	J
Canada	C
Caneva	G
Casa Querini	I
Casa Verardo	H
Da Bruno	E
Danieli	N
Doni	K
Locanda La Corte	A
Locanda Vivaldi	L
Paganelli	M
Ruzzini Palace	D
Scandinavia	F

HOSTEL

Foresteria Valdese	B

Fond. Nove 13, 41, 42, 51, 52, LN

CAFÉS & GELATERIE

Bonifacio	15
Chiusso Pierino	13
Didovich	5
La Boutique del Gelato	10
Ponte delle Paste	6
Rosa Salva	1

RESTAURANTS

Alla Rivetta	17
Alle Testiere	12
Al Mascaron	9
Bandierette	2
Da Remigio	14
Osteria di Santa Marina	4

BARS & SNACKS

Al Portego	3
Al Vecio Penasa	18
Enoteca Mascareta	8
Inishark	11
L'Olandese Volante	7
Osteria da Baco	16

the public congregation, and this requirement for space meant that they were usually built on the edges of city centres. In Venice the various mendicant orders are scattered outside the San Marco *sestiere*: the **Dominicans** here, the Franciscans at the Frari and San Francesco della Vigna, the Carmelites at the Carmini and the Servites at Santa Maria dei Servi. (The dedicatees of the church, by the way, are not the apostles John and Paul, but a pair of probably fictional saints

▲ Campo Santi Giovanni e Paolo

whose story seems to be derived from that of saints Juventinus and Maximinius, who were martyred during the reign of Julian, in the fourth century.)

The first church built on this site was begun in 1246 after **Doge Giacomo Tiepolo** was inspired by a dream to donate the land to the Dominicans – he dreamed that a flock of white doves, each marked on its forehead with the sign of the Cross, had flown over the swampland where the church now stands, as a celestial voice intoned "I have chosen this place for my ministry." That initial version was soon demolished to make way for this larger building, begun in 1333, though not consecrated until 1430. Tiepolo's simple sarcophagus is outside, on the left of the door, next to that of his son **Doge Lorenzo Tiepolo** (d.1275); both tombs were altered after the Bajamonte Tiepolo revolt of 1310 (see p.80), when the family was no longer allowed to display its old crest and had to devise a replacement. The **doorway**, flanked by Byzantine reliefs, is thought to be by **Bartolomeo Bon**, and is one of the major transitional Gothic-Renaissance works in the city; apart from that, the most arresting architectural feature of the exterior is the complex brickwork of the **apse**. The **Cappella di Sant'Orsola** (closed), between the door to the right transept and the apse, is where the two **Bellini** brothers are buried; it used to house the Scuola di Sant'Orsola, the confraternity which commissioned Carpaccio's *St Ursula* cycle, now installed in the Accademia.

The simplicity of the cavernous **interior** – approximately 90m long, 38m wide at the transepts, 33m high in the centre – is offset by Zanipolo's profusion of tombs and monuments, including those of some 25 doges.

The Mocenigo tombs and south aisle

The only part of the entrance wall that isn't given over to the glorification of the Mocenigo family is the monument to the poet Bartolomeo Bragadin, which happened to be there first. It's now engulfed by the **monument to Doge Alvise Mocenigo and his wife** (1577) which wraps itself round the doorway; on the right is Tullio Lombardo's **monument to Doge Giovanni Mocenigo** (d.1485); and on the left is the superb **monument to Doge Pietro Mocenigo** (d.1476), by Pietro Lombardo, with assistance from Tullio and Antonio. Pietro Mocenigo's sarcophagus, supported by warriors representing the three Ages of Man, is embellished with a Latin inscription (*Ex Hostium Manibus* – "From the hands of the enemy") pointing out that the spoils of war paid for his tomb, and a couple of reliefs showing his valorous deeds, including the handing of the keys of Famagusta to the doomed Caterina Cornaro (see p.354).

To the left of the first altar of the right aisle is the **monument to Marcantonio Bragadin**, the central figure in one of the grisliest episodes in Venice's history. The commander of the Venetian garrison at Famagusta during the Turkish siege of 1571, Bragadin marshalled a resistance which lasted eleven months until, with his force reduced from 7000 men to 700, he was obliged to sue for peace. Given guarantees of safety, the Venetian officers entered the enemy camp, whereupon most were dragged away and cut to pieces, whilst Bragadin himself had his ears cut off in an assault that proved to be a foretaste of days of torture. His eventual execution was appalling – chained to a stake on the public scaffold, he was slowly flayed alive in front of the Pasha. His skin, stuffed with straw, was then mounted on a cow and paraded through the streets, prior to being hung from the bowsprit of the admiral's galley for the return voyage to Constantinople. Later the skin was brought back to Venice – it's in that urn high up on the wall.

Giovanni Bellini's painting for the first altar went up in smoke some years ago, but his polyptych of *SS Vincent Ferrer, Christopher and Sebastian* (on the second altar) has come through the centuries in magnificent fettle, although it has lost the image of God the Father that used to be in the lunette. The oozing effigy reclining below is of Tommaso Caraffini, confessor and biographer of Saint Catherine of Siena.

The next chapel but one, the **Cappella della Madonna della Pace**, is named after its Byzantine Madonna, brought to Venice in 1349 and attributed with amazing powers. Above the chapel entrance the figures of Doge Bertucci Valier (d.1658), Doge Silvestro Valier (d.1700) and Silvestro's wife, Dogaressa Elizabetta Querini (d.1708), are poised like actors taking a bow.

St Dominic in Glory, the only ceiling panel in Venice by Giambattista Piazzetta, Giambattista Tiepolo's tutor, covers the vault of the neighbouring **Cappella di San Domenico**, alongside which is a tiny shrine dedicated to **Saint Catherine of Siena**. Born in 1347 as the youngest of 25 children, Catherine manifested early signs of uninhibited piety – wearing hair shirts, sleeping on bare boards, and crashing up and down stairs on her knees, saying a Hail Mary on each step. She died in 1380 and her body promptly entered the relic market – most of it is in Rome, but her head is in Siena, one foot is here, and other lesser relics are scattered about Italy.

The south transept and the chancel

San Zanipolo's best paintings are clustered in the **south transept**: a *Coronation of the Virgin* attributed to Cima da Conegliano and Giovanni Martini da Udine, and Lorenzo Lotto's *St Antonine* (1542). As payment for his work Lotto asked only for his expenses and permission to be buried in the church; presumably the first part of the deal went through all right, but Lotto soon afterwards quit the backbiting of Venice's artistic circles, and eventually died in Loreto, where he was buried. Dominating the end wall of the transept is a superb fifteenth-century **stained-glass window**, which depicts a sacred hierarchy that rises from the four

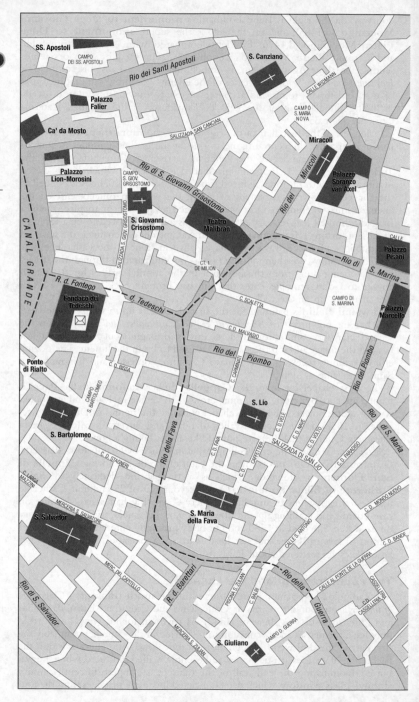

SS. Apostoli

CAMPO
DEI SS. APOSTOLI

Rio dei Santi Apostoli

S. Canziano

CALLE WIDMANN

Palazzo
Falier

SALIZZADA SAN CANCIAN

CAMPO
S. MARIA
NOVA

Ca' da Mosto

Miracoli

Rio di S. Giovanni Grisostomo

Miracoli

Palazzo
Lion-Morosini

CAMPO
S. GIOV.
GRISOSTOMO

Palazzo
Soranzo
van Axel

SALIZZADA S. GIOV. GRISOSTOMO

Rio del

S. Giovanni
Crisostomo

Teatro
Malibran

CANAL GRANDE

CALLE

Palazzo
Pisani

CT. 1
DE MILION

Rio di

S. Marina

R. d. Fontego

d. Tedeschi

C. SCALETTA

CAMPO DI
S. MARINA

Palazzo
Marcello

Fondaco dei
Tedeschi

C.D. MALVASIO

Rio del Piombo

Rio del Piombo

Ponte
di Rialto

C. D. BISSA

C. CARMINATI

Rio

di S. Maria

S. Lio

C. D. VIELE

C. D. NAVE

C. D. VOLTO

C. D. PARADISO

CAMPO
S. BARTOLOMEO

S. Bartolomeo

Rio della Fava

C. D. FAVA

SALIZZADA DI SAN LIO

C. D. MONDO NUOVO

C. D. STAGNERI

C. D. CAFFETTIER

C. LARGA
MAZZINI

C. D. BANDE

S. Salvador

MERCERIA S. SALVATORE

S. Maria
della Fava

CALLE S. ANTONIO

MERC. DEL CAPITELLO

CALLE AL PONTE DE LA GUERRA

Rio di S. Salvador

R. d. Barettari

Rio della

Guerra

CASSELLERIA

C. D.
CASSELLERIA

PISCINA S. ZULIAN

C. BALBI

MERCERIA S. ZULIAN

CAMPO D. GUERRA

S. Giuliano

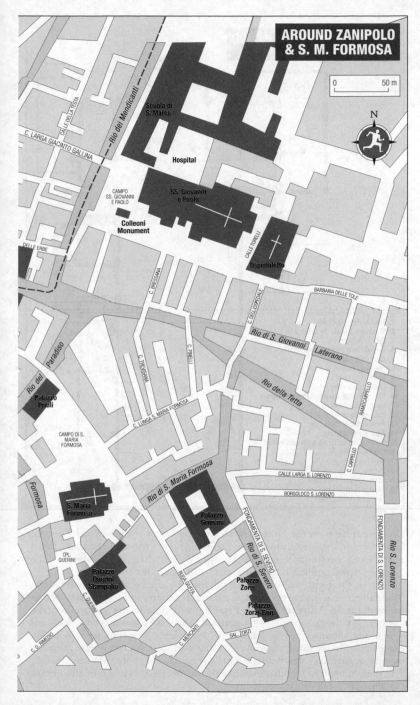

AROUND ZANIPOLO
& S. M. FORMOSA

0   50 m

N

Scuola di
S. Marco

Hospital

CALLE DELLA TESTA

Rio dei Mendicanti

C. LARGA GIACINTO GALLINA

CAMPO
SS. GIOVANNI
E PAOLO

SS. Giovanni
e Paolo

Colleoni
Monument

DELLE ERBE

CALLE TORELLI

Ospedaletto

C. BRESSANA

C. DELL'OSMARIN

BARBARIA DELLE TOLE

Rio di S. Giovanni   Laterano

Paradiso

C. PINELLI

C. TREVISANA

Rio della Tetta

RAMO CAPPELLO

Rio del

Palazzo
Priuli

C. LUNGA S. MARIA FORMOSA

C. CAPPELLO

CAMPO DI S.
MARIA
FORMOSA

Rio di S. Maria Formosa

CALLE LARGA S. LORENZO

BORGOLOCO S. LORENZO

Formosa

S. Maria
Formosa

Palazzo
Grimani

FONDAMENTA DI S. SEVERO

Rio di S. Severo

FONDAMENTA DI S. LORENZO

Rio S. Lorenzo

CPL.
QUERINI

Palazzo
Querini
Stampalia

RUGA GIUFFA

Palazzo
Zorzi

C. CALEONI

C. MERCANTI

Palazzo
Zorzi-Bon

C. D. RIMEDIO

SAL. ZORZI

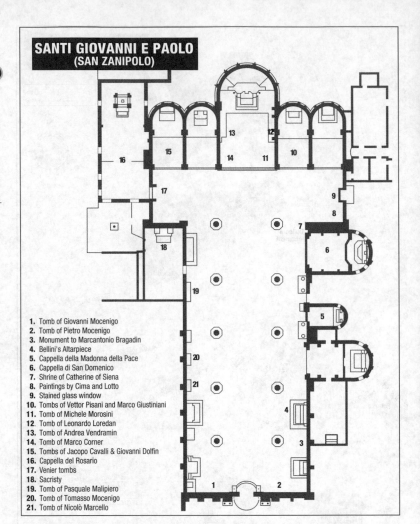

SANTI GIOVANNI E PAOLO (SAN ZANIPOLO)

1. Tomb of Giovanni Mocenigo
2. Tomb of Pietro Mocenigo
3. Monument to Marcantonio Bragadin
4. Bellini's Altarpiece
5. Cappella della Madonna della Pace
6. Cappella di San Domenico
7. Shrine of Catherine of Siena
8. Paintings by Cima and Lotto
9. Stained glass window
10. Tombs of Vettor Pisani and Marco Giustiniani
11. Tomb of Michele Morosini
12. Tomb of Leonardo Loredan
13. Tomb of Andrea Vendramin
14. Tomb of Marco Corner
15. Tombs of Jacopo Cavalli & Giovanni Dolfin
16. Cappella del Rosario
17. Venier tombs
18. Sacristy
19. Tomb of Pasquale Malipiero
20. Tomb of Tomasso Mocenigo
21. Tomb of Nicolò Marcello

Dominican saints on the lowest row to God the Father at the summit. Thought to be the work of one Giannantonio Licino da Lodi, a Murano craftsman, this is an extremely rare instance of stained glass in Venice, where the instability of the buildings makes ambitious glazing a somewhat hazardous enterprise.

Much of the right wall of the second apsidal chapel – the **Cappella della Maddalena** – is taken up with a twentieth-century reconstruction of the **monument to Admiral Vettor Pisani**. Pisani's role in the victory over the Genoese at Chioggia in 1380 – a campaign in which he was mortally wounded – is neatly summed up by John Julius Norwich: "It would perhaps be an exaggeration to say that he saved Venice single-handed; the fact remains that she would not have survived without him." (See p.224 for more on Vettor Pisani.) The tomb supported by what look like the heads of giant elves is of another sea captain, Marco Giustiniani (d.1346).

The **chancel** is one of the high points of funerary art in Venice. **Doge Michele Morosini**, who ruled for four months before dying of plague in 1382, is buried in the tomb at the front on the right, a work which in Ruskin's eyes marked a fault line in European civilization, showing as it does "the exactly intermediate condition of feeling between the pure calmness of early Christianity, and the boastful pomp of the Renaissance faithlessness". The bombastic Renaissance world is represented by the adjacent tombs of **Doge Leonardo Loredan** (d.1521) and **Doge Andrea Vendramin** (d.1478), directly opposite Loredan's, which was moved here in 1818 from the church of the Servi. The sculptor of the Vendramin tomb (probably Tullio Lombardo) carved only the half of the figure that could be seen from below, an act which Ruskin condemned as being of "such utter coldness of feeling as could only consist with an extreme of intellectual and moral degradation". Next to it is the Gothic tomb of **Doge Marco Corner** (d.1368), which was hacked about to make way for its neighbour.

The north transept and north aisle

Of the **tomb of Jacopo Cavalli** (d.1384), on the right of the final chapel in the north transept, Ruskin scornfully remarked: "I find no especial reason for the images of the Virtues, especially that of Charity, appearing at his tomb, unless it be this: that at the siege of Feltre, in the war against Leopold of Austria, he refused to assault the city because the senate would not grant his soldiers the pillage of the town." As if in response, the Virtues are no longer in place; the frescoes around the tomb are by Titian's nephew, Lorenzo Vecellio. On the left is the tomb of **Doge Giovanni Dolfin** (d.1361), who was besieged by the Hungarians in Trieste when elected in 1356, and had to charge through enemy lines under cover of darkness in order to take up the post.

The tombs of three members of the **Venier** family adorn the end wall of the transept: the figure of Doge Sebastiano Venier, victor over the Turkish fleet at the battle of Lépanto, is a twentieth-century creation; the monuments to the left were carved in the early fifteenth century by the Dalle Masegnes – the one above the door is the tomb of Doge Antonio Venier (d.1400), with his wife and daughter, Agnese and Orsola, alongside. The **Cappella del Rosario**, at the end of the north transept, was built in 1582 and dedicated to the victory at Lépanto, which happened on the feast day of the Madonna of the Rosary, October 7, 1571. In 1867 a fire destroyed its paintings by Tintoretto, Palma il Giovane and others, as well as Giovanni Bellini's *Madonna* and Titian's *Martyrdom of St Peter*, San Zanipolo's two most celebrated paintings, which were in here for restoration; arson by anti-Catholics was suspected, but nothing was ever proved. A lengthy twentieth-century restoration made use of surviving fragments and installed other pieces such as **Veronese**'s ceiling panels of *The Annunciation, The Assumption* and *The Adoration of the Shepherds*, and another *Adoration* by him, to the left as you enter the chapel.

In the north aisle, Bartolomeo Vivarini's *Three Saints* (1473), a portion of a dismantled polyptych, is the first thing to grab your eye. Busts of Titian, Palma il Vecchio and Palma il Giovane look down from over the sacristy door, forming the monument which the last of the three designed for himself. The chief draws in the **sacristy** are Alvise Vivarini's luminescent *Christ Carrying the Cross* (1474) and the wood panelling by Andre Brustolon, though there is some historical interest in Andrea Vicentino's painting of Doge Giacomo Tiepolo donating the land for the site of the present church. Most of the other paintings depict scenes from the life of St Dominic or major events in the history of the Dominican order.

After the sacristy the rest of the aisle is stacked with monuments, the first of which is that of **Doge Pasquale Malipiero** (d.1462) – created by **Pietro Lombardo**, it's one of the earliest in Renaissance style in Venice. After the equestrian monument of the *condottiere* **Pompeo Giustiniani** (aka *Braccio di Ferro* – Iron Arm) comes the **tomb of Doge Tommaso Mocenigo** (d.1423) by Pietro di Nicolò Lamberti and Giovanni di Martino, followed by another Pietro Lombardo monument, for **Doge Nicolò Marcello** (d.1474), just before the altar with the copy of Titian's *Martyrdom of St Peter*. Three eminent Venetians of a more recent time – the Risorgimento heroes Attilio and Emilio Bandiera and Domenico Moro – are commemorated alongside; they're also honoured by having a square named after them (see p.179). On the last altar is a figure of *St Jerome* by Alessandro Vittoria (1576).

Around the church

The *condottiere* **Bartolomeo Colleoni**, celebrated by the great **equestrian statue** outside Santi Giovanni e Paolo, began his wayward career in Venice's army in 1429, after a spell in the Bay of Naples, and for a while took orders from Gattamelata, who's commemorated in Padua by Donatello's superb monument. In the succeeding years Colleoni defected to Milan, was imprisoned there, escaped, re-enlisted for Venice, fled once again, and finally joined the Republic's ranks for good in 1455 – whereupon Venice suffered an outbreak of peace which resulted in his being called upon to fight on just one occasion during the last twenty years of his life. Resisting several lucrative offers from France and Rome, he settled into a life of prosperous leisure, and when he died in 1475 he left a legacy of some 700,000 ducats to the Venetian state. But there was a snag to this bequest: the Signoria could have the money only if an equestrian monument to him were erected in the square before San Marco – an unthinkable proposition to Venice's rulers, with their cult of anonymity. The problem was circumvented with a fine piece of disingenuousness, by which Colleoni's will was taken to allow the state to claim his money if his statue were raised before the Scuola di San Marco, rather than the Basilica.

Andrea Verrocchio won the commission for the monument in 1481, and difficulties cropped up in this stage of the proceedings, too. Verrocchio was preparing the figure of the horse for casting when he heard that another artist was being approached to sculpt the rider. Insulted, he smashed up his work and returned to Florence in a rage, to be followed by a decree forbidding him on pain of death to return to Venice. Eventually he was invited back, and was working again on the piece when he died in June 1488. The Signoria then hired **Alessandro Leopardi** to finish the work and produce the plinth for it, which he gladly did – even signing his own name on the horse's girth, and taking the self-bestowed title *del Cavallo*. An idealized image of steely masculinity rather than a true portrait (Verrocchio never met Colleoni), the statue made a powerful impact when it was finally unveiled in 1496 – according to Marin Sanudo, all of Venice came to marvel at it. And talking of masculinity, Thomas Coryat noted that Colleoni "had his name from having three stones, for the Italian word Coglione doth signify a testicle".

An entirely different spirit of that age is manifested by Colleoni's backdrop, the **Scuola Grande di San Marco**, which since its suppression in the early nineteenth century has provided a sumptuous facade and foyer for Venice's hospital. The newly restored **facade** was started by Pietro Lombardo and Giovanni Buora in 1487, half a century after the scuola moved here from its original home over in the Santa Croce *sestiere*, and finished in 1495 by Mauro

Codussi. Taken as a whole, the perspectival panels by **Tullio and Antonio Lombardo** might not quite create the intended illusion, but they are nonetheless among the most beguiling sculptures in Venice. The **interior** was radically altered by the Austrians in 1819 but partly reconstructed using some original bits.

Another hospital block is attached to Longhena's church of the **Ospedaletto**, which stands immediately to the east of Zanipolo on Barbaria delle Tole. Known more properly as Santa Maria dei Derelitti, the Ospedaletto was founded in 1528 to provide care for the desperate peasants who were forced by famine to flee the mainland that year. The church itself, with its leering giants' heads and over-ripe decorations, drew Ruskin's wrath – "It is almost worth devoting an hour to the successive examination of five buildings as illustrative of the last degradation of the Renaissance. San Moisè is the most clumsy, Santa Maria Zobenigo the most impious, San Eustachio the most ridiculous, the Ospedaletto the most monstrous, and the head at Santa Maria Formosa the most foul." The much less extravagant interior has a series of eighteenth-century paintings high on the walls above the arches, one of which – *The Sacrifice of Isaac* – is an early **Giambattista Tiepolo** (fourth on the right). The adjoining **music room**, frescoed in the eighteenth century, is still used for concerts, many of them free. At other times, the only way to see inside the Ospedaletto is by booking a private tour – details are on ⓦwww.scalabovolo.org.

Campo Santa Maria Formosa and around

The spacious **Campo di Santa Maria Formosa**, virtually equidistant from the Piazza, San Zanipolo and the Ponte di Rialto, is a major confluence of routes on the east side of the Canal Grande, and one of the most attractive and atmospheric squares in the city. A few fruit and vegetable stalls are pitched here, and occasionally they are joined by sellers of antiquarian bits and pieces. A number of elegant buildings border the square, the most impressive of which is the **Palazzo Ruzzini-Priuli**, which has now been converted into a luxury hotel (see p.237).

The church of Santa Maria Formosa

Santa Maria Formosa (Mon–Sat 10am–5pm; €3, or Chorus Pass) – the only church of this name in all of Italy – was founded in the seventh century by San Magno, Bishop of Oderzo, who was guided by a dream in which he saw the Madonna *formosa* – a word which most closely translates as "buxomly beautiful".

In 944 it gained a place in the ceremonials of Venice when a group of its parishioners rescued some young women who had been abducted from San Pietro di Castello (see p.185); as a reward, the doge thereafter visited the church each year, when he would be presented with a straw hat to keep the rain off and wine to slake his thirst. The hat given to the last doge can be seen in the Museo Correr.

Mauro Codussi, who rebuilt the church in 1492, followed quite closely the original Greek-cross plan, both as an evocation of Venice's Byzantine past and as a continuation of the tradition by which Marian churches were centrally organized to symbolize the womb. A dome was frequently employed as a

▲ Santa Maria Formosa

reference to Mary's crown; this one was rebuilt in 1922 after an Austrian bomb had destroyed its predecessor in World War I.

There are two **facades** to the church. The one on the west side, close to the canal, was built in 1542 in honour of the military leader Vincenzo Cappello (d.1541); Ruskin, decrying the lack of religious imagery on this facade, identified Santa Maria Formosa as the forerunner of those churches "built to the glory of man, instead of the glory of God". The decoration of the other facade, constructed in 1604, is a bit less presumptuous, as at least there's a figure of the Virgin to accompany the three portrait busts of other members of the Cappello clan. Ruskin reserved a special dose of vitriol for the **mask** at the base of the Baroque campanile: "huge, inhuman and monstrous – leering in bestial degradation, too foul to be either pictured or described...in that head is embodied the type of the evil spirit to which Venice was abandoned". Pompeo Molmenti, the most assiduous chronicler of Venice's socio-cultural history, insists that the head is both a talisman against the evil eye and a piece of clinical realism, portraying a man with a disorder of the sort that disfigured Joseph Merrick, the so-called Elephant Man.

The church contains two good paintings. Entering from the west side, the first one you'll see is **Bartolomeo Vivarini**'s triptych of *The Madonna of the Misericordia* (1473), once the church's high altarpiece, but now in a nave chapel on the right-hand side of the church. It was paid for by the congregation of the church, and some of the figures under the Madonna's cloak are believed to be portraits of the parishioners. Such images of the merciful Madonna, one of the warmest in Catholic iconography, can be seen in various forms throughout the city – there's another example a few minutes' walk away, on the route to the Rialto bridge.

Nearby, closer to the main altar, is **Palma il Vecchio**'s *St Barbara* (1522–24), praised by George Eliot as "an almost unique presentation of a hero-woman, standing in calm preparation for martyrdom, without the slightest air of pietism, yet with the expression of a mind filled with serious conviction." Born in Nicodemia around 300 AD, Barbara infuriated her father by converting to Christianity – he realized she'd become a Christian when she added a third window to her two-windowed bathroom, to symbolize the Trinity. Condemned to death by the Roman magistrate, Barbara was hauled up a mountain by her father and there executed by him. On his way down, he was struck by lightning, a fate which turned Barbara into the patron saint of artillery-men, the terrestrial agents of violent sudden death. This is why Palma's painting stands in the former chapel of the Scuola dei Bombardieri, and shows her treading on a cannon. (Her brief was later widened to include all those in danger of sudden death, including miners.)

San Lio and Santa Maria della Fava

Either of the two bridges on the canal side of Santa Maria Formosa will take you onto the busy Salizzada di San Lio, a direct route to the Rialto. Calle del Paradiso, off to the right as you head towards the Rialto, is a pocket of almost untouched Gothic Venice, overlooked at one end by an early fifteenth-century arch showing the *Madonna della Misericordia*, sheltering two people within her cloak. As indicated by the coats of arms, the arch commemorates the intermarriage of the Fóscari and Mocenigo families; the male figure is thus probably Alvise Mocenigo and the female his bride, Pellegrina Fóscari, whose dowry included no fewer than 26 houses in Calle del Paradiso.

The church of **San Lio** (daily 9am–noon; free) – dedicated in 1054 to Pope Leo IX, an ally of Venice – is notable for its ceiling panel of *The Apotheosis of St Leo* by **Giandomenico Tiepolo**, and for the chapel to the right of the high altar, which was designed by the Lombardi and contains a *Pietà* possibly by Tullio Lombardo; there's also a low-grade late Titian on the first altar on the left.

A diversion south from San Lio down Calle della Fava brings you to the church of **Santa Maria della Fava** (Mon–Sat 8.30am–noon & 4.30–7.30pm) or Santa Maria della Consolazione, whose peculiar name derives from a sweet cake called a *fava* (bean), once the All Souls' Day speciality of a local baker and still a seasonal treat in Venice. Canova's tutor Giuseppe Bernardi (known as Torretto) carved the statues in niches along the nave. On the first altar on the right stands Giambattista Tiepolo's early *Education of the Virgin* (1732) in which the open Bible appears to be emanating a substantial cloud of Holy Spirit, with fleshy angels appearing in the mist and Joachim, the father of Mary, apparently warming his hands on the blessed fog. On the other side of the church there's *The Madonna and St Philip Neri*, painted five years earlier by Giambattista Piazzetta, the most influential painter in early eighteenth-century Venice.

On the northern side of San Lio lies the **Campo di Santa Marina**; the bridge heading north from this square, the Ponte del Cristo, offers a view of the fine seventeenth-century facade of the **Palazzo Marcello-Pindemonte-Papadopoli** (attributed to Longhena) and the Gothic **Palazzo Pisani** across the water.

The Querini-Stampalia and Museo Diocesano

Some of the most impressive palaces in the city stand on the island immediately to the south of Santa Maria Formosa. Turn first left off Ruga Giuffa and you'll be confronted by the land entrance of the gargantuan sixteenth-century **Palazzo Grimani**, once owned by the branch of the Grimani family whose collection of antiquities became the basis of the Museo Archeologico. The neo-Roman interior, featuring some of the most spectacular rooms in the city, has been beautifully restored and furnished with a miscellany of *objets d'art*; it can been visited, on a €9 guided tour, from Tuesday to Sunday at 9.30am, 11.30am and 1.30pm (reservations on ☎041.520.0345). For a decent view of the exterior you have to cross the Rio San Severo, which also runs past the Gothic **Palazzo Zorzi-Bon** and Codussi's neighbouring **Palazzo Zorzi**.

On the south side of Campo Santa Maria Formosa, a graceful little footbridge curves over a narrow canal and into the **Palazzo Querini-Stampalia**. The palace was built in the sixteenth century for a branch of the ancient Querini family, several of whom took refuge on the Greek island of Stampalia after their implication in the Bajamonte Tiepolo plot of 1310; when the errant clan was readmitted to Venice, they returned bearing their melodic new double-barrelled name. The last Querini-Stampalia expired in 1868, bequeathing his home and its contents to the city, and the palace now houses one of the city's quirkier collections, the **Pinacoteca Querini-Stampalia** (Tues–Sat 10am–8pm, Sun 10am–7pm; €8 or Venice Card). Although there is a batch of Renaissance pieces – such as Palma il Vecchio's marriage portraits of Francesco Querini and Paola Priuli Querini (for whom the palace was built), and Giovanni **Bellini's** *Presentation in the Temple* – the general tone of the collection is set by the culture of eighteenth-century Venice, a period to which much of the palace's decor belongs. The winningly inept pieces by **Gabriel Bella** form a comprehensive record of Venetian social life in that century, and the more accomplished genre paintings of **Pietro and Alessandro Longhi**. Another notable aspect of this museum is that its ground-floor rooms (where contemporary art shows are often held) were brilliantly refashioned in the 1960s by Carlo Scarpa, who also designed the entrance bridge and the garden – an ensemble that constitutes one of Venice's extremely rare examples of first-class modern architecture. A final attraction of the Querini-Stampalia is that visitors are treated to chamber-music concerts inside the museum at 5pm and 7pm every Friday and Saturday.

South of the Querini-Stampalia stands the crumbly, deconsecrated and unused church of San Giovanni Nuovo, better known as **San Giovanni in Oleo** (St John in Oil) – the Emperor Domitian is said to have ordered John's execution by immersion in a vat of boiling oil, an ordeal from which the saint emerged unscathed. Beyond here you come down onto **Campo Santi Filippo e Giacomo**, which tapers west towards the bridge over the Rio di Palazzo, at the back of the Palazzo Ducale. Just before the bridge, a short fondamenta on the left leads to the early fourteenth-century cloister of **Sant'Apollonia**, the only Romanesque cloister in the city. Fragments from the Basilica di San Marco dating back to the ninth century are displayed here, and a miscellany of sculptural pieces from other churches is on show in the adjoining **Museo Diocesano d'Arte Sacra** (daily 10am–6pm; €4), where the collection consists chiefly of a range of religious artefacts and paintings gathered from churches that have closed down or entrusted their possessions to the safety of the museum. In addition, freshly restored works from other collections or churches sometimes pass through here, giving the museum an edge of unpredictability. A late fifteenth-century *Crucifix* from San Pietro di Castello is perhaps the most impressive single item, but it has to be said that this is very much one of the city's minor museums.

The sixteenth-century **Palazzo Trevisan-Cappello**, opposite the Fondamenta della Canonica (beyond the bridge), was once the home of Bianca Cappello, who was sentenced to death in her absence for eloping with Pietro Bonaventuri, a humble bank-clerk at the local branch of the Salviati bank, a Florentine institution. All was forgiven when she later dumped her hapless swain for Francesco de'Medici, Grand Duke of Tuscany, whom she eventually married, having endured banishment from Florence by the Grand Duke's first wife. The pair bought this palazzo together, and died together in 1587. They were probably killed by a virulent fever, but there was a strong suspicion that they had been poisoned by another Medici, which rather embarrassed the Venetians, who couldn't publicly mourn their "daughter of the Republic" for fear of offending the couple's unknown but probably influential murderer.

San Zaccaria to San Giorgio dei Greci

The Salizzada di San Provolo, leading east out of Campo Santi Filippo e Giacomo, runs straight to **Campo San Zaccaria**, a spot with a chequered past. The convent attached to the church was notorious for its libidinous goings-on – a state of affairs not so surprising if you bear in mind that many of the nuns were incarcerated here because their fathers couldn't afford dowries for them. On one occasion officials sent to put a stop to the nuns' amorous liaisons were pelted with bricks by the residents, but behaviour was customarily more discreet: Venice's upper classes supplied the convent with several of its novices, and the nuns' parlour became one of the city's most fashionable salons, as recorded by a Guardi painting in the Ca' Rezzonico.

There's a gory side to the area's history as well. In 864 **Doge Pietro Tradonico** was murdered in the campo as he returned from vespers, and in 1172 **Doge Vitale Michiel II**, having not only blundered in peace negotiations with the Byzantine Empire but also brought the plague back with him from Constantinople, was murdered as he fled for the sanctuary of San Zaccaria. Michiel's assassin fled to his home in Calle delle Rasse, between the Palazzo Ducale and San Zaccaria, and was soon arrested. After his execution his home was demolished (a customary punishment for traitors), and it was later decreed that only wooden buildings should be built in this district – an edict that wasn't contravened until 1948, with the construction of the annexe of the *Danieli* hotel. Though chiefly remembered for his death, Vitale Michiel II also left a permanent signature on his city, in that he was the doge who divided Venice into its six *sestieri*, an administrative innovation designed to facilitate the raising of taxes.

The church of San Zaccaria

Founded in the ninth century as a shrine for the body of Zaccharias, father of John the Baptist (he is still here, under the second altar on the right), the church of **San Zaccaria** (Mon–Sat 10am–noon & 4–6pm, Sun 4–6pm) has a tortuous history. A Romanesque version was raised a century after the foundation, this in turn was overhauled in the 1170s (when the present campanile was constructed), a Gothic church followed in the fourteenth century, and finally in 1444 **Antonio Gambello** embarked on a massive rebuilding project that was concluded some seventy years later by **Mauro Codussi**, who took over the **facade** from the first storey upwards – hence its resemblance to San Michele. The end result is a distinctively Venetian blend of Gothic and Renaissance styles, which looks especially spectacular after its recent cleaning.

The interior's notable architectural feature is its **ambulatory**; unique in Venice, it might have been built to accommodate the procession of the doges' Easter Sunday visit, a ritual that began back in the twelfth century after the convent had sold to the state the land that was to become the Piazza. Nearly every inch of wall surface is hung with seventeenth- and eighteenth-century paintings, all of them outshone by **Giovanni Bellini**'s majestic *Madonna and Four Saints* (1505), on the second altar on the left; you might think that the natural light is enough, but drop a coin into the light-box and you'll see what you were missing. The continuation of the architectural frame (possibly by Pietro Lombardo) into the canvas reveals that the painting hangs in its original spot – although it sojourned briefly in the Louvre, a period in which the top arched segment was removed. Further up the left aisle, by the sacristy door, is the tomb of **Alessandro Vittoria** (d.1608), including a self-portrait bust; he also carved the *St Zaccharias* and *St John the Baptist* for the two holy-water stoups, and the now faceless *St Zaccharias* on the facade above the door.

The €1 fee payable to enter the **Cappella di Sant'Atanasio** and **Cappella di San Tarasio** (off the right aisle) is well worth it. The former was rebuilt at the end of the sixteenth century, and contains **Tintoretto**'s early *The Birth of St John the Baptist*, some fifteenth-century stalls, and a painting by Palma il Vecchio that stood in for the Bellini altarpiece during the years the Bellini was on show in Paris, along with other Napoleonic loot. Although a patch of old mosaic floor has been uncovered here, it's in the San Tarasio chapel that it becomes obvious that these chapels occupy much of the site of the Gothic church that preceded the present one. Three wonderful *anconas* (composite altarpieces) by **Antonio Vivarini and Giovanni d'Alemagna** (all 1443) are the highlight: the one on the left is dedicated to Saint Sabine, whose tomb is below it; the main altarpiece has recently been restored, a process that has revealed a seven-panelled predella now attributed to Paolo Veneziano, the earliest celebrated Venetian artist (d. c.1358). You can also see frescoes by Andrea del Castagno and Francesco da Faenza in the vault (painted a year before the Vivarinis), while the floor has been cut away in places to reveal mosaics from the twelfth-century San Zaccaria, and a fragment that might even date back to the ninth century. Downstairs is the spooky and perpetually waterlogged ninth-century crypt, the burial place of eight early doges.

The Riva degli Schiavoni

The broad **Riva degli Schiavoni**, stretching from the edge of the Palazzo Ducale to the canal just before the Arsenale entrance, is constantly thronged during the day, with an unceasing flow of promenading tourists and passengers

▲ The Riva degli Schiavoni

hurrying to and from its vaporetto stops, threading through the souvenir stalls and street vendors. The Riva's name is a vestige of an ignominious side of the Venetian economy, as *schiavoni* denotes both slaves and the Slavs who in the early days of Venice provided most of the human merchandise. By the early eleventh century Christianity was making extensive inroads among the Slavs, who thus came to be regarded as too civilized for such treatment; in succeeding centuries the slave trade turned to Greece, Russia and Central Asia for its supplies, until the fall of Constantinople in 1453 forced a switch of attention to Africa.

As you'd expect of a locality that commands so magnificent a view, the Riva has long been prime territory for the tourist industry, and today there are hotels strung out along the length of the waterfront, all the way to the Arsenale. George Sand, Charles Dickens, Proust, Wagner and the ever-present Ruskin all checked in at the most prestigious and expensive of these establishments, the **Hotel Danieli**. The beautiful fifteenth-century part of the hotel, formerly the Palazzo Dandolo, was the venue for one of the earliest opera productions, Monteverdi's *Proserpina Rapita*; the *Danieli*'s nondescript extension, built in 1948, was the first transgression of the 1172 ban on stone buildings on this spot (see p.169). Longer-term residents of the Riva include **Petrarch** and his daughter, who lived at no. 4145 in the 1360s, and **Henry James**, who stayed at no. 4161 in 1881, battling against the constant distractions outside to finish *The Portrait of a Lady*.

The Pietà

Looking east from the Molo, the main eye-catcher – rising behind the equestrian monument to King Vittorio Emanuele II – is the white facade of **Santa Maria della Visitazione**, known less cumbersomely as **La Pietà** (Tues–Fri 10am–noon & 3–5pm, Sat & Sun 10am–noon). **Vivaldi** wrote many of his finest pieces for the orphanage attached to the church, where he worked as violin-master (1704–18) and later as choirmaster (1735–38). So successful did the Pietà become that some unscrupulous parents tried to get their progeny into its famous ranks by foisting them off as parentless waifs. Founded back in the fourteenth century, the Pietà orphanage is nowadays an organization that

Music in Venice

For centuries the musical life of Venice was dominated by the Basilica di San Marco, where music was performed to celebrate the doge's authority as far back as the thirteenth century. A document dated 1316 records the appointment of a Mistro Zucchetto as organist at San Marco, but it was with choral music that the city became most closely associated, especially after 1527, when the Flemish composer **Adrian Willaert** became the *maestro di cappella*. By the second half of the sixteenth century, when **Andrea Gabrieli** and then his nephew **Giovanni** were in charge of sacred music at San Marco, a characteristic Venetian form had emerged: *cori spezzati* or polychoral music, in which one group of singers would be placed in each of the organ lofts, with a third group occupying a stage near the main altar. This spectacular and powerful style reached its apogee at the start of the seventeenth century, but was soon displaced by a more streamlined and expressive mode of text-setting, in which greater emphasis was placed on clarity of the text – a style exemplified by **Claudio Monteverdi**, who was made *maestro di cappella* at San Marco in 1613.

Monteverdi's most celebrated choral work, the *Vespers*, was written before he came to Venice. Of the pieces he wrote here, the most significant were perhaps his eighth book of **madrigals** and the **operas** he composed late in his life, of which only two have survived: *Il ritorno d'Ulisse in patria*, performed in 1640 at San Cassiano (which three years earlier had become Venice's first public theatre), and *L'Incoronazione di Poppea*, premiered three years later at Santi Giovanni e Paolo. Monteverdi was one of the pioneers of sung drama, and the numerous theatres of Venice were crucial to the establishment of the new genre, in which the solo voice was the focus of attention in works that could last as long as five hours, and female vocalists (prohibited from singing in church) shared the stage with male performers. In the course of the seventeenth century other celebrated opera houses opened at San Salvador, San Moisè, Sant'Angelo and San Giovanni Crisostomo, the last of which was renowned for the extravagance of its stagings and the lustre of its stars, the greatest of whom was the castrato Carlo Broschi, better known as **Farinelli**.

In addition to San Marco and the theatres, Venice's churches, convents, monasteries, scuole and *ospedali* (hostel-orphanages) commissioned a vast amount of new music. Competition among the various scuole led to the creation of some impressive ceremonial music (Thomas Coryat, in 1608, attended a concert at the Scuola Grande di San Rocco which made him feel "rapt up with Saint Paul into the third heaven"), while the four *ospedali* – the Incurabili, Mendicanti, Derelitti (or Ospedaletto) and Pietà – gained a reputation for the virtuosity of their musical pupils. Many of **Antonio Vivaldi**'s more than 450 concertos – including the *Four Seasons* – were written for the girls and young women of the Pietà, though the principal genre of the *ospedali* was the oratorio (a dramatic setting of a religious text). The Pietà, however, didn't have a monopoly on Vivaldi's time when he was in Venice: he also composed operas for the Sant'Angelo and San Moisè theatres, both of which were managed by him.

With the political and economic decline of Venice in the eighteenth century, musical activity went into decline too, though the most famous of all its theatres, **La Fenice**, was founded in 1792, and the Pietà's conservatory survived into the next century, after the other three *ospedali* had gone bankrupt. Several theatres went out of business during the years of occupation by France and Austria, leaving La Fenice as the city's one venue of international significance, a status it retained through the twentieth century.

cares mainly for infants awaiting adoption, and for socially disadvantaged women with young children.

During Vivaldi's second term at the Pietà **Giorgio Massari** won a competition to rebuild the church, and it's probable that the composer advised him on acoustic refinements such as the positioning of the double choir on the entrance wall and the two choir-lofts on the side walls. He may also have suggested adding the vestibule to the front of the church, as insulation against the background noise of the city. Building eventually began in 1745 (after Vivaldi's death), and when the interior was completed in 1760 (the facade didn't go on until 1906) it was regarded more as a concert hall than a church. You get some idea of the showiness of eighteenth-century Venice from the fact that whereas this section of the Riva was widened to give a grander approach to the building, Massari's plans to improve the orphanage were shelved owing to lack of funds. The white and gold interior is crowned by a superb ceiling painting of *The Glory of Paradise* by **Giambattista Tiepolo**, who also painted the ceiling panel above the high altar.

Around the corner from the church, at Calle della Pietà 3701, you'll find the less than enthralling **Piccolo Museo della Pietà** (Mon, Wed & Fri 11am–4pm; €3), which gives an overview of the musical life of the orphanage through displays of documents and period instruments.

The Greek quarter

A couple of minutes' walk north of La Pietà the campanile of **San Giorgio dei Greci** lurches spectacularly canalwards. The **Greek** presence in Venice was strong from the eleventh century, and became stronger still after the Turkish seizure of Constantinople. This mid-fifteenth-century influx of Greek speakers provided a resource which was exploited by the city's numerous scholarly publishing houses, and greatly enriched the general culture of Renaissance Venice: the daughter of the *condottiere* Gianfrancesco Gonzaga, for example, is known to have written perfect Greek at the age of ten. At its peak, the Greek community numbered around 4000, some of whom were immensely wealthy: a Greek merchant murdered in Venice in 1756 left four million ducats to his daughters, a legacy that was said to have made them the richest heiresses in Europe.

The church (Mon & Wed–Sat 9.30am–12.30pm & 2.30–4.30pm, Sun 9am–1pm) was built in 1539–61 to a Sansovino-influenced design by **Sante Lombardo**; the cupola and campanile came later in the century. Inside, the Orthodox architectural elements include a *matroneo* (women's gallery) above the main entrance and an iconostasis (or rood screen) that completely cuts off the high altar. The icons on the screen are a mixture of works by a sixteenth-century Cretan artist called **Michael Danaskinàs** and a few Byzantine pieces dating back as far as the twelfth century.

Permission to found an Orthodox church was given at the end of the fifteenth century, and a Greek college (the Collegio Flangini) and scuola were approved at the same time. The college, redesigned in 1678 by **Longhena**, is now home to the Hellenic Centre for Byzantine and Post-Byzantine Studies, custodian of Venice's Greek archives. Longhena also redesigned the Scuola di San Nicolò dei Greci, to the left of the church, which now houses the **Museo di Dipinti Sacri Bizantini** (daily 9am–5pm; €4), a collection of predominantly fifteenth- to eighteenth-century icons, many of them by the *Madoneri*, the school of Greek and Cretan artists working in Venice in that period. Although many of the most beautiful of these works maintain the compositional and symbolic conventions of icon painting, it's fascinating to observe the impact of Western influences – one or two of the artists achieve a synthesis, while others clearly struggle to harmonize the two worlds.

The area to the north of San Giorgio dei Greci is more interesting for its associations than its sights. The unfinished and hangar-like **San Lorenzo** – undergoing a glacially slow restoration – was where Marco Polo was buried, but his sarcophagus went astray during sixteenth-century rebuilding.

Eastern Castello

or all that most visitors see of the eastern zone of the sprawling Castello *sestiere*, the city may as well peter out a few metres to the east of the Palazzo Ducale, and at first glance the map of the city would seem to justify this neglect. Certainly the sights are thinly spread, and a huge bite is taken out of the area by the pools of the Arsenale, for a long time the largest manufacturing site in Europe, but now little more than a decoratively framed blank space.

Yet the slab of the city immediately to the west of the Arsenale contains places that shouldn't be missed – the Renaissance **San Francesco della Vigna**, for example, and the **Scuola di San Giorgio degli Schiavoni**, with its endearing cycle of paintings by **Carpaccio**. And although the mainly residential area beyond the Arsenale has little to offer in the way of cultural monuments other than the ex-cathedral of **San Pietro di Castello** and the church of **Sant'Elena**, it would be a mistake to leave the easternmost zone unexplored. Except in the summer of odd-numbered years, when the **Biennale** sets up shop in the pavilions behind the **Giardini Pubblici** and elsewhere in the neighbourhood, few visitors stray into this latter area – and there lies one of its principal attractions. The whole length of the waterfront gives spectacular panoramas of the city, with the best coming last: from near the Sant'Elena landing stage you get a view that takes in the Palazzo Ducale, the back of San Giorgio Maggiore and La Giudecca, the tiny islands of La Grazia, San Clemente, Santo Spirito, San Servolo and San Lazzaro degli Armeni, and finally the Lido. A picnic here, having stocked up at the shops and stalls of Via Garibaldi, is guaranteed to recharge the batteries.

San Francesco della Vigna to the waterfront

The area that lies to the **east of San Zanipolo** is not, at first sight, an attractive district. The church of Santa Maria del Pianto, so prominent on the city's maps, turns out to be an abandoned hulk, and is barely visible over its surrounding wall. Cross the Rio di Santa Giustina and you're confronted by the shabby, graffiti-plastered church of the same name, which is now part of a school. Round the back of Santa Giustina stand the rusting remains of the local gasworks. But it's not all decay and dereliction – carry on east for just a minute more (turn left in front of Santa Giustina then first right) and a striking Renaissance facade blocks your way.

San Francesco della Vigna

The ground occupied by **San Francesco della Vigna** (Mon–Sat 8am–12.30pm & 3–6.30pm, Sun 3–6.30pm) has a hallowed place in the mythology of Venice, as according to tradition it was around here that the angel appeared to Saint Mark to tell him that the lagoon islands were to be his final resting place. (The angel's words – "Pax tibi" and so forth – remained unchanged on the book held by Venice's symbolic lion until Napoleon substituted the rubric "To the Rights of Men and Citizens" on official proclamations; "At last he's turned the page," remarked an anonymous wit.) Some time after the alleged annunciation the area was cultivated as a vineyard, and when the land was given to the Franciscans in 1253 as a site for a new church, the vines were immortalized in their church's name.

Begun in 1534, to a design by **Sansovino**, the present building was much modified in the course of its construction. **Palladio** was brought in to provide the **facade** (1568–72), a feature that looks like something of an afterthought from the side, but which must have been stunning at the time, when the only other white Istrian stone facade in Venice would have been that of San Michele. The **interior** was altered by a scholarly monk named **Fra' Francesco Zorzi**, who rearranged the proportions along philosophically approved lines and generally amended its acoustic and decorative design. The calculated Renaissance improvements and cold colouring make the church less welcoming than the two great mendicant churches of San Zanipolo and the Frari, despite its more comfortable dimensions; however, there are some fine works of art here.

Some of Venice's wealthiest families contributed to the cost of building San Francesco by paying for family chapels: the third on the right belonged to the **Contarini**, and contains memorials to a pair of seventeenth-century Contarini doges; the next is the **Badoer** chapel (with a *Resurrection* attributed to Veronese); and after that comes the chapel of the **Barbaro** family. The Barbaro ancestral device – a red circle on a white field – was granted in the twelfth century after a particularly revolting act by the Admiral Marco Barbaro: in the thick of battle he cut off a Moor's hand and used the bleeding stump to draw a circle on the man's turban, which he then flew as a pennant from the masthead. Around the corner in the right transept is a large *Madonna and Child Enthroned* by **Antonio da Negroponte** (c.1450), a picture full of meticulously detailed and glowingly colourful birds and plants.

The church's foundation stone was laid by **Doge Andrea Gritti**, whose tomb is on the left wall of the chancel. An intellectually versatile man – he spoke six languages other than Italian and was a close friend of Sansovino – Gritti was also a formidable womanizer, of whom one rival remarked "We cannot make a doge of a man with three bastards in Turkey." After his election he carried on siring children with a variety of women, including a nun named Celestina, but it was his equally Rabelaisian appetite for food that proved his undoing: he died on Christmas Eve after eating too many grilled eels. It's still a traditional Christmas dish in Venice.

Left of the chancel is the **Giustiniani** chapel, lined with marvellous sculpture by the **Lombardo** family and their helpers. Commissioned for the previous church by one of the Badoer clan and installed here after the rebuilding, they include a group of *Prophets* by Pietro Lombardo and assistants, and reliefs of the *Evangelists* attributed to Tullio and Antonio Lombardo. A door at the end of the transept leads to a pair of tranquil fifteenth-century cloisters, via the **Cappella Santa**, which has a *Madonna and Child* by Giovanni Bellini and assistants.

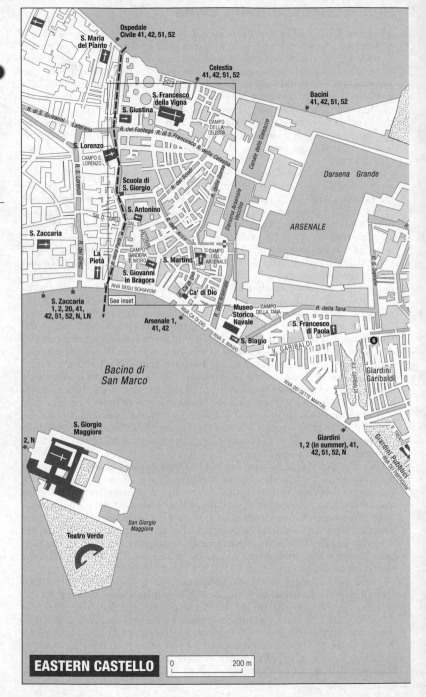

Ospedale
Civile 41, 42, 51, 52

S. Maria
del Pianto

Celestia
41, 42, 51, 52

S. Francesco
della Vigna

Bacini
41, 42, 51, 52

S. Giustina

R. di S. Giovanni
Laterano

R. del Fontego   R. di S. Francesco   R. della Celestia

CAMPO
DELLA
CELESTIA

S. Lorenzo

CAMPO S.
LORENZO

R. S. LORENZO

Canale delle Galeazze

Darsena   Grande

R. dei Scudi

R. delle Gorne

Scuola di
S. Giorgio

ARSENALE

S. Antonino

SAL. D. GRECO

SAL S.

CAL S. ANTONINA

R. dell'Arco

Darsena Arsenale Vecchio

S. Zaccaria

R. dei Greci

R. dalla Pietà

R. S. DANIELE

La
Pietà

CAMPO
BANDIERA
E MORO

S. Martino

CAMPO
DELL'
ARSENALE

S. Giovanni
in Bragora

R. di Ca' di Dio

R. dell'Arsenale

S. Zaccaria
1, 2, 20, 41,
42, 51, 52, N, LN

RIVA DEGLI SCHIAVONI

See inset

Ca' di Dio

Museo
Storico
Navale

CAMPO
DELLA TANA

R. della Tana

S. Francesco
di Paola

6

Arsenale 1,
41, 42

RIVA CA DI DIO

RIVA S. BIAGIO

S. Biagio

V. GARIBALDI

RIO DI S. ANNA

Giardini
Garibaldi

RIO GARIBALDI

Bacino di
San Marco

RIVA DEI SETTE MARTIRI

V. TRENTO

Giardini Pubblici

RIVA DEI PARTIGIANI

S. Giorgio
Maggiore

2, N

Giardini
1, 2 (in summer), 41,
42, 51, 52, N

Teatro Verde

San Giorgio
Maggiore

EASTERN CASTELLO

0   200 m

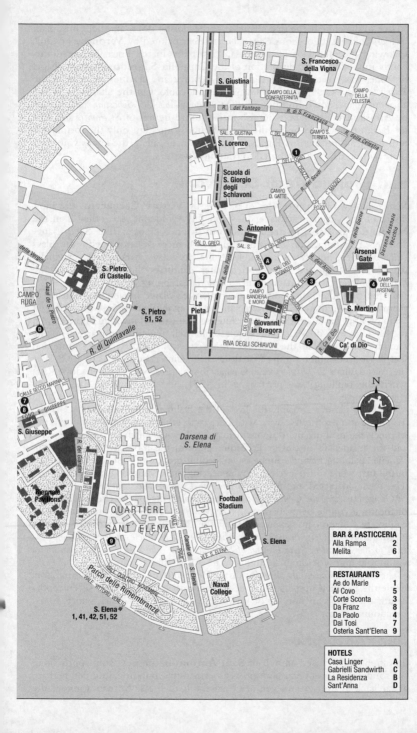

S. Francesco
della Vigna

S. Giustina

CAMPO DELLA
CONFRATERNITA

CAMPO
DELLA
CELESTIA

R. del Fontego

R. di S. Francesco

SAL. S. GIUSTINA

C. DEL MORION

CAMPO S.
TERNITA

R. della Celestia

S. Lorenzo

❶

C. DELL'OGIO

C. DE PRETI

R. dei Scudi

CPL. C. MAGNO

Scuola di
S. Giorgio
degli
Schiavoni

CAMPO
D. GATTE

CPL. D.
POZZI

R. delle Gorne

Darsena Arsenale
Vecchio

S. Antonino

C. D'ERICO

SAL. D. GRECI

SAL. S.

ANTONIN

Arsenal
Gate

CAMPO
DELL'
ARSENALE

SAL. DEI
PIGNATER

R. dell'ATER

S. della Pietà

Ⓐ

La
Pietà

❷

Ⓑ

CAMPO
BANDIERA
E MORO

❸

C. DEL FORNO

SAL. SANT'ANTONIN

❹

S. Martino

S. Giovanni
in Bragora

❺

C. DEL DOSE

Ca' di Dio

RIVA DEGLI SCHIAVONI

Ⓒ

R. Ca' di Dio

della Vergini

S. Pietro
di Castello

Canale di S. Pietro

CAMPO
RUGA

S. Pietro
51, 52

Ⓓ

R. di Quintavalle

CALLE SECCO MARINA

❼

❽

FOND. S. GIUSEPPE

S. Giuseppe

R. dei Giardini

Darsena di
S. Elena

Biennale
Pavilions

QUARTIERE
SANT ELENA

❾

VIALE QUATTRO

Football
Stadium

Canale di

V.LE S. ELENA

S. Elena

S. Elena

Parco delle Rimembranze

VIALE QUATTRO NOVEMBRE

VIALE VITTORIO VENETO

Naval
College

S. Elena
1, 41, 42, 51, 52

N

BAR & PASTICCERIA

Alla Rampa	2
Melita	6

RESTAURANTS

Ae do Marie	1
Al Covo	5
Corte Sconta	3
Da Franz	8
Da Paolo	4
Dai Tosi	7
Osteria Sant'Elena	9

HOTELS

Casa Linger	A
Gabrielli Sandwirth	C
La Residenza	B
Sant'Anna	D

Back in the church, the first chapel after the cloister door (another Giustiniani chapel) contains a gorgeous *Sacra Conversazione* painted by **Veronese** in 1562, following the model of Titian's Pésaro altarpiece in the Frari. The predominantly monochromatic decoration of the **Cappella Sagredo**, the next chapel but one, was created in the eighteenth century, and features frescoes of the *Evangelists* and two *Virtues* by Giambattista Tiepolo. On the altarpiece of the adjacent chapel you'll find figures of *St Anthony Abbot, St Sebastian* and *St Roch* by **Alessandro Vittoria**, who also made bronze figures of *St Francis* and *John the Baptist* that should be on the nearby water stoups, but only the former has returned from restoration. Finally, on the entrance wall, to the left as you leave, there's a fine triptych attributed to Antonio Vivarini.

San Giorgio degli Schiavoni

Venice has two brilliant cycles of pictures by **Vittore Carpaccio**, the most disarming of Venetian artists – one is in the Accademia, the other is in the **Scuola di San Giorgio degli Schiavoni** (Mon 2.45–6pm, Tues–Sat 9.15am–1pm & 2.45–6pm, Sun 9.15am–1pm; €4). Venice's relations with the Slavs (*schiavoni*) were not always untroubled – the city's slave markets were originally stocked with captured Slavs, and in later centuries the settlements of the Dalmatian coast were a harassment to Venetian shipping.

By the mid-fifteenth century, though, Venice's Slavic inhabitants – many of them sailors and merchants – were sufficiently established for a scuola to be set up in order to protect their interests. After several years of meeting in the church of San Giovanni di Malta, the scuola built itself a new headquarters on the church's doorstep at the start of the sixteenth century, and summoned Carpaccio to brighten up the first-storey hall. Painted from 1502 to 1508, after the Accademia's *St Ursula* cycle, Carpaccio's pictures were moved downstairs when the building was rearranged in 1551, and the interior has scarcely changed since.

The cycle illustrates mainly the lives of the Dalmatian patron saints – George, Tryphone and Jerome. As always with Carpaccio, what holds your attention is not so much the main event as the incidental details with which he packs the scene, and the incidentals in this cycle feature some of the most arresting images in Venetian painting, from the limb-strewn feeding-ground of Saint George's dragon in the first scene of the cycle, to the endearing little white dog in the final one. The scenes depicted are: *St George and the Dragon; The Triumph of St George; St George Baptizing the Gentiles* (George had rescued the princess Selene, daughter of the royal couple being baptized); *The Miracle of St Tryphone* (the dainty little basilisk is a demon just exorcized from the daughter of the Roman emperor Gordianus); *The Agony in the Garden; The Calling of Matthew; St Jerome Leading the Lion to the Monastery; The Funeral of St Jerome;* and *The Vision of St Augustine* (a vision told him of Jerome's death just as he was writing to him).

The *Madonna and Child* altarpiece is by **Benedetto Carpaccio**, Vittore's son, while the panelled upstairs hall is decorated with mundane, early seventeenth-century paintings in honour of various brethren of the scuola, which is still functioning today.

Sant'Antonino

The frequently closed church of **Sant'Antonino**, the next stop south along the fondamenta from San Giorgio, is an unenticing building, founded perhaps as far back as the seventh century but rebuilt in the seventeenth, under the direction of Longhena, whose design for the facade was never completed. It houses nothing of interest except a *Deposition* by Lazzaro Bastiani (Carpaccio's teacher) and a bust of Procurator Alvise Tiepolo by Alessandro Vittoria, but some good stories are attached to it. The body of a certain Saint Saba was enshrined here from the mid-thirteenth century until 1965, when Pope Paul VI returned the relic to the monastery in Istanbul whence it had been stolen by the Venetians; for all that time the Turkish monks had been meeting disconsolately every night at their saint's empty sarcophagus. The emblems of Saint Anthony Abbot are a pig and a bell, and this church once kept a sty of belled pigs, which were allowed to roam the parish unfettered until, in 1409, their unruliness so annoyed the locals that their freedom was curtailed by a state edict. And finally, in 1819 an elephant escaped from a visiting menagerie on the Riva degli Schiavoni and took refuge in Sant'Antonino, where its pursuers failed to fell it with small-arms fire; they then summoned the artillery to dispatch it with a blast from a cannon. Pietro Bonmartini, a Paduan nobleman, commemorated the demise of the hapless beast in a pamphlet entitled *The Elephanticide in Venice*.

San Giovanni in Brágora

Salizzada Sant'Antonin curves down to the quiet **Campo Bandiera e Moro**, named after the Venetians Attilio and Emilio Bandiera and Domenico Moro, who in 1844 were executed for leading an abortive revolt against the Bourbon regime in Calabria. The Bandiera brothers were born at no. 3610, and all three are buried together in Santi Giovanni e Paolo. Across the alley from the Bandiera house stands the campo's handsomest building, the fifteenth-century Palazzo Gritti Badoer; a complete ruin a hundred years ago, it has been renovated as a hotel (see p.238).

Across the square stands **San Giovanni in Brágora** (Mon–Sat 9am–noon & 3.30–5.30pm), probably best known to Venetians as the baptismal church of Antonio Vivaldi. The church is dedicated to the Baptist, and some people think that its strange suffix is a reference to a region from which some relics of the saint were once brought; others link the name to the Greek word for a main public square, *agora*, or to a choice of old Venetian dialect words – *brago* plus *gora* (meaning "mud" and "backwater"), or *bragola* ("market square"). The origins of the church itself are equally disputed – folklore insists that this is one of the city's oldest, dating back to the early eighth century, but there's no proof of its existence prior to 1090.

The present structure was begun in 1475, about the same time that San Michele was finished, although the simple Gothic building shows no sign of the arrival of Renaissance architecture in Venice. However, you can trace the development of a Renaissance aesthetic in its best paintings, all of which were created within a quarter-century of the rebuilding: a triptych by **Bartolomeo Vivarini**, on the wall between the first and second chapels on the right (1478); a *Resurrection* by **Alvise Vivarini**, to the left of the sacristy door (1498); and two paintings by **Cima da Conegliano** – a *SS Helen and Constantine*, to the right of the sacristy door (1501), and a *Baptism* on the high altar (1494). The remains of Saint John the Almsgiver, stolen from Alexandria in 1247, lie in the second chapel on the right, though the Venetian church dedicated to him – San Giovanni Elemosinario – is over in the Rialto. Set into an alcove at the west end of the left aisle is the font in which Vivaldi was baptized for the second time, having been given an emergency baptism at home because it seemed unlikely that he would survive more than a few hours.

San Martino and around

A group of Paduan refugees are said to have founded a church on the site of the nearby **San Martino** (Mon–Sat 11am–noon & 5–6.30pm, Sun 10.30am–12.30pm) in 593, which would give it one of Venice's longest pedigrees; Sansovino designed the present Greek-cross building in around 1540. To get a decent perusal of **Domenico Bruni**'s perspectival ceiling-painting (seventeenth century) you have to lie on your back in the very middle of the church, more or less where most of **Doge Francesco Erizzo** (d.1646) is buried; his heart is in the Basilica di San Marco.

Follow the fondamenta south from San Martino and then turn right into Calle de la Pegola and you'll emerge on the main waterfront, with the **Ca' di Dio** to your right. Founded in the thirteenth century as a hospice for pilgrims and Crusaders, the Ca' di Dio was extended in 1545 by Sansovino – his new wing, with its profusion of chimneys, is visible from the bridge. The building on the other side of Calle de la Pegola, decorated with a second-storey frieze of little stone peaks, is the **Forni Pubblici** (1473), the bakery which supplied the vessels leaving the Arsenale with ship's biscuit, the last stage in the preparations for sailing.

The Arsenale

A corruption of the Arabic *darsin'a* (house of industry), the very name of the **Arsenale** is indicative of the strength of Venice's links with the eastern Mediterranean, and the workers of these dockyards and factories were the foundations upon which the city's maritime supremacy rested. Visiting dignitaries were often as astonished by the industriousness of the Arsenale as by the opulence of the Canal Grande. At the beginning of the fourteenth century Dante came to Venice twice (once as ambassador from Ravenna), and was so impressed by what he saw on his first mission that he evoked the sight in a famous passage of the *Inferno*, in which those guilty of selling public offices are tortured in a lake of boiling pitch like the caulkers' vats in the Arsenale.

In *The City in History*, Lewis Mumford credits the Venetians with the invention of "a new type of city, based on the differentiation and zoning of urban functions, separated by traffic ways and open spaces", and cites the island of Murano and the Arsenale as Europe's first examples of industrial planning. Of these two, the Arsenale most closely resembled a modern factory complex. Construction techniques in the Arsenale were the most sophisticated of their time, and by the fifteenth century the Venetians had perfected a production-line process for equipping their warships, in which the vessels were towed past a succession of windows, to collect ropes, sails, armaments, oars and all their other supplies (ending with barrels of hard biscuits), so that by the time they reached the lagoon the vessels were fully prepared for battle. The productivity of the wharves was legendary: at the height of the conflict with the Turks in the sixteenth century, one ship a day was being added to the Venetian fleet. On the occasion of the visit of Henry III of France in 1574, the Arsenale workers put on a bravura performance – in the time it took the king and his hosts to work their way through a state banquet in the Palazzo Ducale, the *Arsenalotti* assembled and made seaworthy a vessel sturdy enough to bear a crew plus a cannon weighing 16,000 pounds.

▲ The Arsenale gate

To an extent, the governors of the city acknowledged their debt to the workers of the Arsenale. They were a privileged group within the Venetian proletariat, acting as watchmen at the Palazzo Ducale whenever the Maggior Consiglio was in session, carrying the doge in triumph round the Piazza after his inauguration, and serving as pallbearers at ducal funerals. By the standards of other manual workers they were well paid too, although the 50 ducats that was the typical wage of a master shipwright in the early sixteenth century should be set against the 40,000 ducats spent by Alvise Pisani, one of the most powerful politicians of the period, on the weddings of his five daughters. The *Arsenalotti* were also less docile than most of their fellow artisans, and were responsible for a number of strikes and disturbances. A dramatic protest took place in 1569, when a gang of 300 *Arsenalotti* armed with axes smashed their way into the hall of the Collegio to present their grievances to the doge in person.

The history of the Arsenale

The development of the Arsenale seems to have commenced in the early years of the twelfth century, when ship maintenance became the main industry in this part of the city. Massive expansion was under way by the third decade of the fourteenth century, as the Arsenale established a state monopoly in the construction of galleys and large merchant vessels, and by the 1420s it had become the base for some 300 shipping companies, operating around 3000 vessels of 200 tons or more.

At the Arsenale's zenith, around the middle of the sixteenth century, its wet and dry docks, its rope and sail factories, its ordnance depots and gunpowder mills employed a total of 16,000 men – equal to the population of a sizeable town of the time. By then, though, the maritime strength of Venice was past its peak: Vasco da Gama had rounded the Cape of Good Hope in 1497, thus opening a direct sea route to the East; the New World routes were growing; and there was the perpetual threat of the ever stronger Turkish empire. The shrinkage of the Venetian mercantile fleet was drastic – between 1560 and 1600 the volume of shipping registered at the Arsenale was halved. Militarily as well, despite the conspicuous success at Lépanto (1571), Venice was on the wane, and the reconquest of the Morea (Peloponnese) at the end of the seventeenth century was little more than a glorious interlude in a long story of decline. When **Napoleon** took over the city in 1797 he burned down the docks, sank the last *Bucintoro* (the state barge) and confiscated the remnant of the Venetian navy, sailing off with it to attempt the invasion of Ireland. After the failure of that expedition the fleet was taken back to the Mediterranean, only to be destroyed by Nelson at the battle of Aboukir.

Under Austrian occupation the Arsenale was reconstructed, and it stayed in continuous operation until the end of 1917 when, having produced a number of ships for the Italian navy in World War I, the dockyards were dismantled to prevent them being of use to the enemy forces that seemed likely to invade the lagoon. Since then it has been used by the navy and an EU-funded marine technology centre, and it's employed as a venue for part of the Biennale. Plans exist to extend the Museo Storico Navale into the Arsenale buildings and to convert other parts into sports halls and university premises.

The Arsenale buildings

There is no public access to the Arsenale except during the Biennale. You can get a look at part of it, however, from the bridge connecting the Campo Arsenale and the Fondamenta dell'Arsenale; it used to be possible to get a better view from the vaporetti that cut through the oldest part of the complex on their way to the northern lagoon, but this route has been suspended for several years, and it's unlikely that it will ever be resumed.

The main **gateway** to the Arsenale was the first structure in Venice to employ the classical vocabulary of Renaissance architecture. Built by **Antonio Gambello** in 1460 (but incorporating, at ground level, Veneto-Byzantine capitals from the twelfth century), it consists of a triumphal arch topped by a less precisely classical storey – a design that was possibly intended to create the illusion that the entrance to the Arsenale was an amalgam of a genuine Roman edifice and more modern Venetian building. You'll notice that the book being held by the Lion of Saint Mark, unlike all the others in the city, is blank, perhaps because the traditional inscription, "Pax tibi…", was thought to be too pacific for this context; the statue above his head, *Santa Justina* by **Campagna**, was put there in 1578.

The **four lions** outside the gateway feature in coffee-table books on Venice almost as frequently as the San Marco horses, and, like the horses, they are stolen goods. Exactly when the two furthest on the right were grabbed isn't known, but they probably came from the Lion Terrace at Delos, and date from around the sixth century BC; the left-hand one of the pair (with the prosthetic head) was positioned here to mark the recapture of Corfu in 1716 – the other was in place slightly earlier.

The larger pair aren't as enigmatic; they were swiped from Piraeus in 1687 by Francesco Morosini (see p.91), after the reconquest of the Morea. The blurred inscription on the shoulder and side of the lion on the left of the gate (which started life as an ancient Greek fountain) is a piece of runic graffiti, the handiwork of a Norse mercenary serving with the army hired by the Byzantine emperor in the eleventh century to suppress a rebellion of his Greek subjects.

Within the Arsenale, the two major structures are **Sanmicheli**'s covered dock for the *Bucintoro* (1544–47) and **da Ponte**'s gigantic rope factory, the Corderia or **Tana** (1579). The greater part of the Tana runs along the Rio della Tana; a single 316m-long room (not far off twice the length of the Piazza), it provides an extraordinary exhibition space for the Biennale.

The Museo Storico Navale and San Biagio

Nearby, on the other side of the Rio dell'Arsenale, is the **Museo Storico Navale** (Mon–Fri 8.45am–1.30pm, Sat 8.45am–1pm; €1.60), which is housed in a former granary. Documenting every facet of Venice's naval history, the museum is another baggy monster like the Correr, but a selective tour is an essential supplement to a walk round the Arsenale district, and – improbable though it sounds – the beautiful models of Venetian craft will justify the entrance fee for most people. It was common practice in the Venetian shipyards to build their boats not from scale drawings but from models, and the most meticulous pieces in the collection are the functional models retrieved from the yards after Napoleon's arsonists had done their work.

At ground level there's a room dedicated to Angelo Emo, the last admiral of the Republic, the focal point being Canova's monument to him. Models of various ships and a miscellany of armaments occupy the rest of the space, with the most remarkable invention being a manned torpedo; a caption explains how the captain of the HMS *Valiant*, which was crippled by one of these contraptions, came to award a military honour to the Italian lieutenant who had carried out the attack. More models, including a 224-oar fighting galley and the last *Bucintoro*, take up much of the second floor; the third has a display of uniforms, maritime instruments and cut-away miniature battleships. On the top storey you'll find full-size gondolas (including Peggy Guggenheim's), models of Chinese and Korean junks, and an impressive collection of *ex voto* paintings on marine themes. A couple of hundred metres along the fondamenta is a second section of the naval museum, the **Padiglioni delle Navi**, a shed full of craft with Venetian connections; it's a vast and very interesting assemblage, but hardly ever open.

The church of **San Biagio**, alongside the main museum block, was the Greek community's church before San Giorgio dei Greci, and took on its present municipal-office appearance after an eighteenth-century refit. It's now the naval chapel and is rarely open, though you can normally look through the inner wrought-iron door at the interior, where **Giovanni Ferrari**'s reclining statue of *Admiral Angelo Emo* (1792) is the main point of interest. Tucked behind the church is the concrete bunker known as Palasport (or Palazzetto dello Sport), the city's main indoor sports hall, used for handball and basketball matches.

Beyond the Arsenale

The Riva San Biagio is the only land route into the districts to the east of the Arsenale, but once over the wide bridge that traverses the Rio della Tana you have to make a choice. By following the waterfront you'll pass the main public gardens of Venice before finally reaching the football stadium and the isolated church of Sant'Elena. Opt for the less picturesque Via Garibaldi, and you're on your way to the church of San Pietro di Castello, the major monument of this part of the city.

To San Pietro di Castello

In 1807 the greater part of the canal connecting the Bacino di San Marco to the broad northeastern inlet of the Canale di San Pietro was covered to form what is now **Via Garibaldi**, the widest street in the city and the busiest part of the eastern district. (The pattern of the pavement shows clearly the former course of the canal.) The bars, *pasticcerie* and *alimentari* of Via Garibaldi are far less likely to treat you as a tedious occupational hazard than those in the more comfortable areas of the city, and as you roam the alleyways and squares of this area it's possible to forget for a while that you're in the most commercialized city in the country.

There's just a couple of spots of cultural or historical significance along Via Garibaldi. The first house on the right was for a time the home of the navigators **John and Sebastian Cabot**, explorers of Newfoundland (together) and Paraguay (just Sebastian) in the late fifteenth and early sixteenth centuries. The church of **San Francesco di Paola**, opposite the entrance to the tree-lined alley that glories in the name Giardini Garibaldi, has a painting by Giandomenico Tiepolo among the sequence on the cornice (second on the right), illustrating scenes from the life of the eponymous saint. A far more impressive sight awaits if you walk beyond the market stalls on the right-hand side of the street, which becomes the Fondamenta di Sant'Anna; this takes you onto the Ponte di Quintavalle, and so to the island of San Pietro.

The island of San Pietro di Castello

Originally named **Castello**, after a castle that used to stand here (built by either the Romans or the first "Venetian" settlers), the island of **San Pietro** was one of the very first parts of central Venice to be occupied. Nowadays this is a run-down district where the repairing of boats is the main occupation, yet it was once the ecclesiastical centre of Venice. By 775 the settlement here had grown sufficiently to be granted the foundation of a bishopric under the authority of the Patriarch of Grado. Within the next half-century Castello joined the immediately surrounding islands to form Rivoalto, the embryonic city of Venice.

From the beginning, the political and economic power was concentrated in the distant Rialto and San Marco districts, and the relationship between the Church and the geographically remote rulers of the city was never to be close. In 1451 the first **Patriarch of Venice** was invested, but still his seat remained at Castello, and succeeding generations of councillors and senators showed no inclination to draw the head of the Venetian Church into the centre of power. San Pietro di Castello remained the cathedral of Venice, emblematically marooned on the periphery of the city, until 1807, when the patriarch was at last permitted to install himself in San Marco – ten years after the Republic had ceased to exist.

One of the major Venetian festivals – the Festival of the Marys – had its origin in an incident that occurred here in the tenth century. A multiple marriage in the church was interrupted by a posse of Slav pirates, who carried away the brides and their substantial dowries. Men from the parish of Santa Maria Formosa led the pursuit, which succeeded in retrieving the women. To celebrate their safe return, every year two girls were chosen from each *sestiere* to be married in a single ceremony at San Pietro, the weddings being followed by an eight-day junket that culminated at Santa Maria Formosa on the Day of the Purification of Mary – the day on which the brides had been kidnapped.

As with the Arsenale, the history of San Pietro is somewhat more interesting than what you can see. A church was raised here as early as the seventh century, but the present **San Pietro di Castello** (Mon–Sat 10am–5pm; €3, or Chorus Pass) was built nearly a millennium later. A new facade was designed in the mid-sixteenth century by **Palladio**, but the work was not carried out until the end of the century, and the executed project was a feeble version of the original scheme. Similarly, the interior is an early seventeenth-century derivation from a plan by Palladio, and is the sort of sterile barn that gives classicism a bad name. Nor will the paintings put a skip in your stride: best of the bunch are the altarpiece by Luca Giordano in the Cappella Vendramin (left transept) and SS *John the Evangelist, Peter and Paul*, a late work by Veronese, above the entrance to the neighbouring Cappello Lando, where you'll find a fifth-century mosaic fragment set into the pavement, and a bust of Saint Lorenzo Giustiniani, the first Patriarch of Venice. Giustiniani, who died in 1456, lies in the glass case within the elaborate high altar, which, like the Vendramin chapel, was designed by Longhena. The other unusual feature of the church is the so-called **Throne of St Peter** (right aisle), a marble seat made in the thirteenth century from an Arabic funeral-stone cut with texts from the Koran.

The **campanile**, one of the most precarious in the city, was rebuilt by Mauro Codussi in the 1480s (the original cupola was replaced with the present one in 1670), and was the first tower in Venice to be clad in Istrian stone. It's the only stone-clad tower left standing.

The public gardens, the Biennale site and Sant'Elena

Stretching from Via Garibaldi to the Rio di Sant'Elena, the arc of green spaces formed by the **Giardini Garibaldi**, **Giardini Pubblici** and **Parco delle Rimembranze** can usually be relied on to provide a remedy for the claustrophobia that overtakes most visitors to Venice at some point. The first of the three is really little more than a shortcut from Via Garibaldi to the Giardini Pubblici, which Eugène Beauharnais created by draining a swamp and demolishing a batch of monastic buildings. Largely obscured by the trees are the rather more extensive grounds belonging to the **Biennale**, a dormant zone except when the arts shindig or the architecture Biennale is in progress. Various countries have built permanent pavilions for their Biennale representatives, forming a unique colony that features work by some of the great names of modern architecture and design: the Austrian pavilion was built by the Secession architect Josef Hoffmann in the 1930s; the Finnish pavilion was created by Alvar Aalto in the 1950s; the Netherlands pavilion was designed by arch-modernist Gerrit Thomas Rietveld, also in the 1950s; and the Venezuelan pavilion, completed in 1954, is by Carlo Scarpa. By far the biggest building, and the pivot of the whole site, is the one that used to be the Italian pavilion – now renamed the **Palazzo delle**

Football in Venice

You approach Sant'Elena by a path between the walls of the naval college and the **Stadio Pierluigi Penzo**, ramshackle home of Venice's **football team**, SSC Venezia (ⓦ www.veneziacalcio.it). Founded in 1907, Venezia is not one of Italy's high-achieving clubs, having won just one major trophy – the 1941 Coppa Italia. Usually to be found bouncing around in the lower divisions, the team did manage to claw its way into the top-flight Serie A as recently as 2002, but following relegation to Serie B and the failure of attempts to build a new stadium on the mainland, the club president took himself and his money off to Palermo, and things quickly became very gloomy indeed at the Penzo. In 2005 Venezia AC (as it was then called) suffered a grand slam of ignominy, when the club was declared bankrupt, demoted to Serie C, and implicated in a match-fixing scandal: it was found that Genoa had bribed the already relegated Venetians to throw the last game of the season. Reformed as SSC Venezia, the *Lagunari* (lagoon-dwellers) are now playing in the abyss of Serie C1, or the Lega Pro Prima Divisione, as it's now known. Nobody expects a return to the upper echelons any time soon. Should you want to watch a game, just turn up on match day: **tickets** are always available at the gate, and cost as little as €12.

Esposizioni, it's used for international shows. On the approach to it stands one of the newer additions to the thirty-strong ensemble, James Stirling's hull-like pavilion for the Biennale's book exhibition; built in 1991, it is funded by Electa, Italy's leading art-book publisher, hence the company logo on the "funnel".

If you want to squeeze every last drop from the eastern districts, call in at the church of **San Giuseppe di Castello** (or San Isepo), to the north of the Giardini Pubblici – a gateway from the gardens opens onto a street just metres from the church. It houses Alessandro Vittoria's monument to Procurator G. Grimani (in the chancel), and a vast **monument to Doge Marino Grimani**, designed in the late sixteenth century by Vincenzo Scamozzi, with reliefs and figures by Campagna (left side).

The island of **Sant'Elena**, the city's eastern limit, was greatly enlarged during the Austrian administration, partly to furnish accommodation and exercise grounds for the occupying troops. Much of the island used to be covered by a meadow, but the strip of park along the waterfront is all that's left of it, houses having been built on the rest. Still, the walk out here is the nearest you'll get to country pleasures in central Venice, and the **church of Sant'Elena** (Mon–Sat 5–7pm) is worth a look. A church was erected here in the thirteenth century, following the supposed acquisition of the body of Saint Helena, Constantine's mother. It was rebuilt in 1435 but from 1807 to 1928 it was abandoned, except for a spell as an iron foundry. The spartan Gothic interior has recently been restored, as have the cloister and campanile – the latter so zealously that it now looks like a chimney, which is exactly what it was used as when the church did service as a factory. The main attraction is the **doorway** to the church, an ensemble created in the 1470s (probably by **Antonio Rizzo**) and incorporating the **monument to Vittore Cappello**, showing him kneeling before Saint Helena. Cappello was captain-general of the Republic's navy in the 1460s, a period in which the Turks were beginning to loosen Venice's grip on the Aegean; so dejected was he by the signs of decline in the Venetian empire that he was reputed to have gone for five months without once smiling, before dying of a broken heart. Inside the church, a chapel on the right enshrines the alleged remains of Helena, whose body is more generally believed to lie in a tomb in Rome's church of Santa Maria in Aracoeli.

The Canal Grande

K
nown to the locals as the Canalazzo, the Canal Grande is Venice's high street, and divides the city in half, with three *sestieri* to the west and three to the east. In addition to the four bridges which traverse the waterway – at Piazzale Roma, the train station, Rialto and Accademia – a number of gondola traghetti provide crossing points at regular intervals, as does the #1 vaporetto, which slaloms from one bank to the other along its entire length. The Canal Grande is almost 4km long and varies in width between 30 and 70m; it is, however, surprisingly shallow, at no point much exceeding 5m. In the fourteenth century an earthquake pulled the plug out and the entire contents drained away – for the best part of a fortnight Venice's finest waterway was an avenue of slime.

The section that follows is principally a guide to the Canal Grande palaces – the churches and other public buildings that you can see from the vaporetto are covered in the appropriate geographical sections. You'd need an amazing reading speed and a rubber neck to do justice to the Canal Grande in one run, though; even these edited highlights cover around fifty buildings (less than a third of the total). Try to allow for several trips, and don't miss the experience of a nocturnal boat ride.

The Right Bank

Right at the top of the Canal Grande lies the traffic terminus of Piazzale Roma. Orientation is initially difficult here, with canals heading off in various directions, and it's not until the vaporetto swings round by the train station that it becomes obvious that this is the city's main waterway. The newest feature of central Venice's

---

Up on the roof

A couple of peculiar features of the Venetian skyline become noticeable on a cruise down the Canal Grande. The bizarre **chimneys** functioned as spark-traps – fire being a constant hazard in a city where the scarcity of land inevitably resulted in a high density of housing. (The history of Venice has been punctuated by terrible blazes – notably at the Rialto, San Marco and, at least four times, the Palazzo Ducale.) The **roof-level platforms** (altane) you'll see in places had a variety of uses, such as drying laundry and bleaching hair. For the latter operation, women wore wide-brimmed crownless straw hats, which allowed them to get the sun on their hair while protecting their complexions.

Fondaco dei Tedeschi

S. Salvador

Ca' da Mosto

Pal. Dolfin-Manin

Rialto Mercato 1

Palazzo Mangilli-Valmarana

Palazzo dei Camerlenghi

PONTE DI RIALTO

Rialto 1, 2, N

Pal. Loredan

Palazzo Sagredo

Traghetto

Peschería

Fabbriche Nuove

Fabbriche Vecchie

Traghetto

Pal. Grimani

Pal. Farsetti

Ca' d'Oro

Ca' d'Oro 1, N

S. Silvestro 1

Pal. Papadopoli

Pal. Gussoni

Ca' Pésaro

Pal. Corner della Regina

Palazzi Donà

Pal. Cappello-Layard

Pal. Soranzo

S. Stae

S. Stae 1, N

Pal. Bernardo

Pal. Vendramin-Calergi

Dep. del Megio

Pal. Belloni

S. Simeone

San Polo

Pal. Pisani Moretta

S. Marcuola

Traghetto

S. Marcuola 1, 2, N

Fondaco dei Turchi

San Giacomo dell' Orio

Frari

Riva di Biasio 1

CANALGRANDE

S. Geremia

Pal. Labia

Ferrovia 1

S. Simeone Profeta

FONDAMENTA SCALZI

S. Simeone Piccolò

Scalzi

Ferrovia 2, 41, 42, 51, 52, N, DM

Train Station

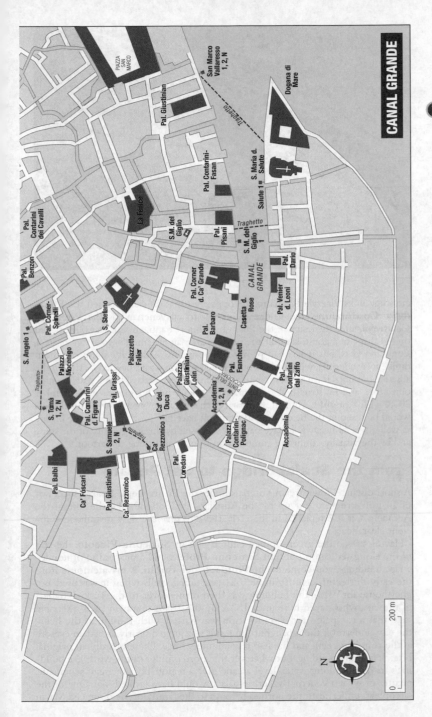

CANAL GRANDE

Dogana di
Mare

San Marco
Vallaresso
1, 2, N

Pal. Giustinian

PIAZZA
SAN
MARCO

Traghetto

S. Maria d.
Salute

Salute 1

Pal. Contarini-
Fasan

La Fenice

S.M. del
Giglio

Traghetto

Pal. Contarini
dei Cavalli

S.M. del
Giglio 1

Pal.
Pisani

*CANAL
GRANDE*

Pal.
Benzon

Pal. Corner
d. Ca' Grande

Pal. Venier
d. Leoni

Pal.
Dario

S. Angelo 1

Pal. Corner-
Spinelli

S. Stefano

Casetta d.
Rose

Pal.
Barbaro

Palazzi
Mocenigo

Palazzetto
Falier

Pal.
Fianchetti

Traghetto

S. Tomà
1, 2, N

Pal. Contarini
d. Figure

Pal. Grassi

Palazzo
Giustinian-
Lolin

PONTE DEL
L'ACCADEMIA

Pal.
Contarini dal Zaffo

Ca' del
Duca

Accademia
1, 2, N

S. Samuele
2, N

Ca'
Rezzonico 1

Traghetto

Palazzi
Contarini-
Polignac

Pal. Giustinian

Pal.
Loredan

Accademia

Pal. Balbi

Ca' Foscari

Ca' Rezzonico

Z
N

200 m

0

▲ The Ponte di Calatrava

cityscape links Piazzale Roma to the opposite bank: officially named the **Ponte della Costituzione**, the bridge is known to all Venetians as the **Ponte di Calatrava**, after its designer, the Spanish architect Santiago Calatrava. Modelled on the shape of a gondola's hull, the single span is an elegant 95-metre arc of steel, stone and glass, but it has had plenty of opponents in the city, some of whom dislike its modernity, while others protest that it simply isn't needed or that in the absence of ramps it isn't accessible to wheelchair users. Delayed four years by such objections and by structural problems, the bridge finally opened in September 2008, with a promise from the authorities that electric "pods" for disabled users would be fitted in the near future. Pedestrians have had problems with the bridge as well – several heavy falls have happened, caused by the irregularity of the steps, and by the visually confusing combination of glass and stone underfoot.

From the Scalzi bridge to Ca' Pésaro

A short distance downstream, you pass under the **Ponte degli Scalzi**, successor of an iron structure put up by the Austrians in 1858–60; like the one at the Accademia, it was replaced in the early 1930s to give the new steamboats sufficient clearance.

Having passed the green-domed church of **San Simeone Piccolo**, the end of the elongated campo of **San Simeone Profeta** and a procession of nondescript buildings, you come to the **Fondaco dei Turchi**. A private house from the early thirteenth century until 1621 (including spells when it was used as a guesthouse for VIPs), the building was then turned over to the Turkish traders in the city, who stayed here until 1838. By the 1850s it was in such a terrible state that a campaign for its restoration was started, with Ruskin at the helm; the city undertook the repair, but the result was judged nearly as bad an eyesore as the ruin had been, and has had few admirers since. There's hardly an original brick left in the building, but whatever the shortcomings of the work, the building's towers and long water-level arcade give a reasonably precise, if schematic, picture of what a Veneto-Byzantine palace would have looked like. One of the sarcophagi underneath the portico belongs to the family of the disgraced Marin

Falier (see p.151). The Fondaco housed the Correr collection from 1880 to 1922, and now contains the natural history museum (see p.121).

The crenellated structure next along from the Fondaco is the fifteenth-century **Depositi del Megio** (public granary); its neighbour is another palace by Longhena – the **Palazzo Belloni-Battagia** (1647–63). Longhena's client experienced severe cash-flow problems not long after the house was finished, a consequence of simultaneously building the house and buying his way into the pages of the *Libro d'Oro* (the register of the nobility), and so was obliged to rent the place out rather than live in it himself.

A short distance down the canal, after the church of **San Stae**, stands a far more impressive Longhena building – the thickly ornamented **Ca' Pésaro**, bristling with diamond-shaped spikes and grotesque heads. Three houses had to be demolished to make room for this palace and its construction lasted half a century – work started in 1652 and finished in 1703, long after Longhena's death. Unusually, the Ca' Pésaro has a stone-clad side; most houses in Venice have plain brick sides, either for reasons of cost, or because of the possibility that another building might later be attached to the flank. The Ca' Pésaro is now home to the modern art and oriental museums (see p.120).

The Rialto

The next large building is the **Palazzo Corner della Regina**, which was built in 1724 on the site of the home of Caterina Cornaro, Queen of Cyprus, from whom the palace takes its name (see p.354); it was formerly the *Monte di Pietà* (municipal pawnshop). Beyond this, there's nothing especially engrossing until you reach the **Rialto markets**, which begin with the neo-Gothic fish market, the **Pescheria**, built in 1907; there's been a fish market here since the fourteenth century. The older buildings that follow it, the **Fabbriche Nuove di Rialto** and (set back from the water) the **Fabbriche Vecchie di Rialto**, are by Sansovino (1552–55) and Scarpagnino (1515–22) respectively.

The large building at the base of the Rialto bridge is the **Palazzo dei Camerlenghi** (c.1525), the former chambers of the Venetian exchequer. Debtors could find themselves in the cells of the building's bottom storey – hence the name *Fondamenta delle Prigioni* for this part of the canalside. At the foot of the Rialto bridge, on the other side, were the offices of the state finance ministers, in Scarpagnino's **Palazzo dei Dieci Savi**.

The famous **bridge** superseded a succession of wooden and fragile structures; one of them was destroyed by the army of Bajamonte Tiepolo as it retreated from the Piazza in 1310 (see p.80), and its replacement collapsed in 1444 under the weight of the crowd gathered to watch the wedding procession of the Marquis of Ferrara – one of Carpaccio's *Miracles of the True Cross* (in the Accademia) shows what the next drawbridge looked like. The decision to construct a more reliable bridge was taken in 1524, and over the following sixty years proposals by Michelangelo, Vignola, Sansovino and Palladio were considered and rejected. Eventually the job was awarded to the aptly named **Antonio da Ponte**, whose top-heavy design was described by Edward Gibbon as "a fine bridge, spoilt by two rows of houses upon it". Until 1854, when the first Accademia bridge was built, this was the only point at which the Canal Grande could be crossed on foot.

From the Rialto to the Volta del Canal

From the Rialto down to the Volta del Canal – as the Canal Grande's sharpest turn is known – the right bank is of more sporadic interest. The **Palazzo Papadopoli** (aka **Palazzo Coccina-Tiepolo**), on the far side of Rio dei Meloni, was built in the 1560s; the Venetian mercantile class rarely wanted adventurous designs for their houses, and the conservative Papadopoli palace, with its emphasis on blank wall spaces broken up with applied decoration, was to prove extremely influential. (Contrast it with the contemporaneous Grimani palace, on the opposite side of the Canal Grande.) The adjacent **Palazzo Donà** and **Palazzo Donà della Madonnetta** (named after the fifteenth-century relief on the facade) date from the twelfth and thirteenth centuries; they have been frequently altered, but some original features survive, notably the main windows.

The tracery of the mid-fifteenth-century **Palazzo Bernardo** (across the Rio della Madonnetta), among the most beautiful on the Canal Grande, is copied from the loggia of the Palazzo Ducale – you'll find echoes of the pattern all over the city. The sixteenth-century **Palazzo Cappello-Layard**, on the edge of the wide Rio San Polo, was the home of the English ambassador Sir Henry Layard, whose astuteness assured that the British public profited from the destitution of Venice in the nineteenth century. His collection of nineteen major Venetian paintings, picked up for a song, was left to the National Gallery in London. Another of the National's masterpieces – Veronese's *The Clemency of Alexander* – was bought in 1857 from the **Palazzo Pisani della Moretta** (mid-fifteenth century), second along on the other side of the rio.

The cluster of palaces at the Volta constitutes one of the city's architectural glories. The **Palazzo Balbi**, on the near side of the Rio di Ca' Fóscari, is the youngest of the group, a proto-Baroque design executed in the 1580s to plans by Alessandro Vittoria, whose sculpture is to be found in many Venetian churches. Nicolò Balbi is reputed to have been so keen to see his palace finished that he moored a boat alongside the building site so that he could watch the work progressing – he even slept in the boat, and died of a consequent chill. Had Frank Lloyd Wright got his way, the Palazzo Balbi would have acquired a new neighbour in the 1950s, but local opposition, orchestrated from the Balbi palace, scuppered the scheme.

On the opposite bank stands the **Ca' Fóscari** (c.1435), which Ruskin thought "the noblest example in Venice" of late Gothic architecture. The largest private house in Venice at the time of its construction, it was the home of one of the more colourful figures of Venetian history, **Doge Francesco Fóscari**, whose

The floor plan

You'll soon notice that the vast majority of palace facades follow the same pattern, with large windows in the centre and smaller windows placed symmetrically on each side. The earliest palazzi built in Venice – in the so-called Veneto-Byzantine style – tended to have a T-shaped plan, with a single large room running parallel to the facade, but in the course of the thirteenth century a new arrangement emerged. On the ground floor was the entrance hall (the **andron** or **androne**), which ran right through the building; this was used as dry dock, and was flanked by storage rooms (some homes doubled as business premises). Above was the mezzanine: the small rooms here were used as offices or, from the sixteenth century onwards, as libraries or living rooms. On the next floor was the **piano nobile**, the main living area, arranged as suites of rooms on each side of a central hall (**portego**), which ran, like the *andron*, from front to back (to maximize the available light), and was used for special gatherings rather than day-to-day living. Frequently there was a second *piano nobile* upstairs, generally accommodating relatives of the main family; the attic was used for servants' rooms or storage, and was often the location of the kitchen. This basic plan remained more or less unchanged for five hundred years.

extraordinarily long term of office (34 years) came to an end with his forced resignation. When Henry III of France passed through Venice on the way to his coronation in 1574, it was at the Ca' Fóscari that he was lodged. After a banquet for which all sumptuary laws had been suspended and at which the tables had been laid with utensils and decorative figures made from sugar to Sansovino's designs, Henry reeled back here to find his rooms decked out with silks and cloth of gold, and lined with paintings by Bellini, Titian, Veronese and Tintoretto. Venice's university now owns the building.

Adjoining it are the **Palazzi Giustinian**, a pair of palaces built in the mid-fifteenth century for two brothers who wanted attached but self-contained houses. In the twelfth century the Giustinian family was in danger of dying out, and such was the panic induced in Venice by the thought of losing one of its most illustrious dynasties (it traced its descent from the Emperor Justinian), that papal permission was sought for the young monk who was the one surviving male of the clan to be released from his vows in order to start a family. The pope gave his consent, a bride was found, and twelve Giustinians were propagated; his duty done, the father returned to his monastery, and his wife went off to found a convent on one of the remoter islands of the lagoon. For a while one of the Palazzi Giustinian was **Wagner**'s home. Finding the rooms inimical to the creative process he made a few improvements, such as hanging the walls with red cloth and importing his own bed and grand piano from Zurich. Having made the place comfortable, he settled down, flirted with the idea of suicide, and wrote the second act of *Tristan und Isolde*, inspired in part by a nocturnal gondola ride, as he recorded in his autobiography. At the sight of the moon rising over the city, the composer's gondolier "uttered a cry like a wild creature, a kind of deep groan that rose in crescendo to a prolonged 'Oh' and ended with the simple exclamation 'Venezia!'... The sensations I experienced at that moment did not leave me throughout my sojourn in Venice."

From the Ca' Rezzonico to the Guggenheim

A little further on comes Longhena's **Ca' Rezzonico**, a building as gargantuan as his Ca' Pésaro, if less aggressive. It was begun in 1667 as a commission from the Bon family, but their ambition exceeded their financial resources, and not long after hiring Giorgio Massari to complete the upper part they were obliged to sell the still unfinished palace to the Rezzonico family, who were Genoese bankers. Despite having lashed out 100,000 ducats to buy their way into the *Libro d'Oro* (at a time when 1000 ducats per annum was a comfortable income for a noble), the new owners could afford to keep Massari employed on the completion of the top floor, and then to tack a ballroom and staircase onto the back. Among its subsequent owners was Pen Browning, whose father Robert died here in 1889; and both Whistler and Cole Porter stayed here briefly. The Ca' Rezzonico is now home to the Museo del Settecento Veneziano (see p.111).

After a couple of canals you pass the **Palazzo Loredan dell' Ambasciatore**, opposite the Ca' del Duca. Taking its name from the Austrian embassy that used to be here, it was built in the fifteenth century, and is notable mainly for the figures in niches on the facade, which possibly came from the workshop of Antonio Rizzo. On the far side of the next canal, the Rio di San Trovaso, stand the **Palazzo Contarini-Corfu** and the **Palazzo Contarini degli Scrigni**. The "Corfu" bit of the first name derives either from the fact that a Contarini was once a military commander on that island, or from the name of a family that lived in the parish before the Contarini. The two palaces form a single unit; the Scrigni was built in 1609 as an extension to the Corfu, a fifteenth-century

Gothic house. A similar operation was carried out at the Palazzi Barbaro (opposite, just after the Accademia bridge), with less jarring results.

As the larger vaporetti couldn't get under the iron **Ponte dell'Accademia** built by the Austrians in 1854, it was replaced in 1932 by a wooden one – a temporary measure that became permanent with the addition of a reinforcing steel substructure.

Yet another Contarini palace stands a few metres past the Accademia bridge – the **Palazzo Contarini-Polignac**. This branch of the Contarini family made itself rich through landholdings around Jaffa, and the dialect version of that place name is the source of the alternative name for the palace: Contarini dal Zaffo. The facade, which was applied to the Gothic building in the late fifteenth century, represents a transitional phase between the highly decorative style associated with the Lombardi and their imitators (see the Palazzo Dario below) and the classicizing work of Codussi.

The Venier family, another of Venice's great dynasties (they produced three doges, including the commander of the Christian fleet at Lépanto), had their main base just beyond the Campo San Vio. In 1759 the Veniers began rebuilding their home, but the **Palazzo Venier dei Leoni**, which would have been the largest palace on the canal, never progressed further than the first storey – hence its alternative name, **Palazzo Nonfinito**. (The "dei Leoni" part of the full name comes from the pet lions that the Veniers kept chained in the courtyard.) Its abandonment was almost certainly due to the ruinous cost, but there's a tradition which says the project was stopped by the objections of the Corner family across the water, who didn't want their sunlight blocked by a house that was bigger than theirs. The stump of the building and the platform on which it is raised (itself an extravagant and novel feature) are occupied by the Guggenheim collection (see p.100).

To the Dogana di Mare

The one domestic building of interest between here and the end of the canal is the miniature **Palazzo Dario**, the next building but one after the Palazzo dei Leoni. Compared by Henry James to "a house of cards that hold together by a tenure it would be fatal to touch", the palace was built in the late 1480s not for a patrician family but for a member of the middle ("citizen") class – a chancery secretary named Giovanni Dario, who had distinguished himself on diplomatic missions to the Turkish court. The multicoloured marbles of the facade are characteristic of the work of the Lombardo family, and the design may actually be by the founder of that dynasty, Pietro Lombardo, whereas the huge stone rosettes possibly refer to Islamic motifs that Dario would have seen in Cairo. The inscription on the lowest story (*Urbis Genio Iohannes Dario*), in which Dario dedicates the house to the "spirit of the city", is a typically Venetian piece of faux-humble civic-mindedness.

Several of the Palazzo Dario's occupants have come to a sticky end, giving the place a certain notoriety in Venetian folklore: the English scholar Rawdon Lubbock Brown committed suicide in the house after sinking a fortune into its renovation in the mid-nineteenth century; Kit Lambert, manager of The Who, was murdered soon after moving out; in 1979 Count Filippo Giordano delle Lanze had his skull smashed with a candlestick wielded by his lover; a Venetian businessman named Fabrizio Ferrari went bust and then his sister was murdered; and in 1993 the industrialist and yachtsman Raul Gardini, who had bought the house in 1985, was found dead in Milan, apparently having shot himself.

Two doors down, the technicolour **Palazzo Salviati** was built in 1924 by the glassmakers of the same name, and vacated by them seventy years later; the most garish building on the canal, its brash decoration is a foretaste of what awaits you in many of the glass showrooms of Murano.

The focal point of this last stretch of the canal is Longhena's masterpiece, **Santa Maria della Salute** – it's dealt with in the Dorsoduro chapter (see p.101), as is the **Dogana di Mare** (Customs House), the city's newest art gallery and the Canal Grande's full stop.

The Left Bank

Beyond the train station, the boat passes two churches, the **Scalzi** and **San Geremia**, before the first of the major palaces comes into view – the **Palazzo Labia**, completed c.1750 and now occupied by RAI, the state TV and radio company. The main facade of the building stretches along the Cannaregio canal, but from the Canal Grande you can see how the side wing wraps itself round the campanile of the neighbouring church – such interlocking is common in Venice, where maximum use has to be made of available space. Its ballroom contains wonderful frescoes by Tiepolo (see p.138).

Not far beyond the unfinished church of **San Marcuola** stands the **Palazzo Vendramin-Calergi**. Now the city casino, it was begun by Mauro Codussi (for the Loredan family) at the very end of the fifteenth century and finished in the first decade of the sixteenth, probably by Tullio Lombardo. This is the first Venetian palace to be influenced by the classically based architectural principles of Leon Battista Alberti, and is frequently singled out as the Canal Grande's masterpiece. The round-arched windows enclosing two similar arches are identifying characteristics of Codussi's designs. In the seventeenth century a new wing was added to the palace, but soon after its completion two sons of the house conspired to murder a member of the Querini–Stampalia family; as the brothers hadn't physically committed the crime themselves, the court had to limit their sentence to exile, but it ordered the demolition of the new block for good measure. The palazzo's most famous subsequent resident was Richard Wagner, who died here in February 1883; the size of the palace can be gauged from the fact that his rented suite of fifteen rooms occupied just a part of the mezzanine level.

The **Palazzo Soranzo**, a bit further along, dates from the same period as the Vendramin-Calergi, and the contrast between the two gives you an idea of the originality of Codussi's design. The **Palazzo Gussoni-Grimani della Vida**, on the near side of the Rio di Noale, was rebuilt to Sanmicheli's designs in the middle of the sixteenth century. From 1614 to 1618 it was occupied by the English consul Sir Henry Wotton, best remembered now for his definition of an ambassador as "an honest man sent to lie abroad for the good of his country" – a remark that earned him the sack from King James I. Wotton spent much of his time in Venice running a sort of import-export business; when he wasn't buying paintings to ship back to England he was arranging for Protestant texts to be brought into Venice, a city he thought ripe for conversion. The Venetians, however, remained content with their idiosyncratic version of Catholicism, as exemplified by Wotton's friend, Paolo Sarpi (see p.149). At the time of Wotton's residence the facade of the palace was covered with frescoes by Tintoretto, but they have long since faded to invisibility.

From the Ca' d'Oro to the Rialto

The next palace of interest is the most beguiling on the canal – the **Ca' d'Oro**. (*Ca'* is an abbreviation of *casa di stazio*, meaning the main family home; it was only after the fall of the Republic that the title *Casa* was dropped in favour of *Palazzo*.) Incorporating fragments of a thirteenth-century palace that once stood on the site, the Ca' d'Oro was built in the 1420s and 1430s, and acquired its nickname – "The Golden House" – from the gilding that used to accentuate much of its carving. For more on the Ca' d'Oro, see p.150.

▲ The Ponte di Rialto

The facade of the **Palazzo Sagredo**, on the near side of the Campo Santa Sofia, is an overlay of different periods, and a good demonstration of the Venetian custom of adapting old buildings to current needs and principles. The tracery of the *piano nobile* is fourteenth century, and clearly later than the storeys below; the right wing, however, seems to belong to the fifteenth century.

On the near corner of the Rio dei Santi Apostoli stands the **Palazzo Mangilli-Valmarana**, built in the eighteenth century for the English consul Joseph Smith, who was one of the chief patrons of Canaletto. More interesting is the **Ca' da Mosto**, close to the rio's opposite bank. The arches of the first floor and the carved panels above them are remnants of a thirteenth-century Veneto-Byzantine building, and are thus among the oldest structures to be seen on the Canal Grande. Alvise da Mosto, discoverer of the Cape Verde Islands, was born here in 1432; by the end of that century the palazzo had become the *Albergo del Lion Bianco*, and from then until the nineteenth century it was one of Venice's most popular hotels.

As the canal turns, the **Ponte di Rialto** comes into view. The huge building before it is the **Fondaco dei Tedeschi**, once headquarters of the city's German merchants. On the ground floor their cargoes were weighed, packaged and stored; the upper storeys contained a refectory and around sixty bedrooms, many of which were rented on an annual basis by the biggest firms. The German traders were the most powerful foreign grouping in the city, and as early as 1228 they were leased a building on this central site. In 1505 the Fondaco burned down, and was rebuilt by Spavento and Scarpagnino; Giorgione and Titian, who had helped the firefighters on the night of the blaze, were then commissioned to paint the exterior walls. The remains of their contribution are now in the Ca' d'Oro. The Fondaco has been renovated several times since the sixteenth century, and is now the main post office.

From the Rialto to the Volta del Canal

Beyond the Rialto bridge and immediately before the next rio is Sansovino's first palace in Venice, the **Palazzo Dolfin-Manin**. It dates from the late 1530s, a period when other projects by Sansovino – the Libreria, the Zecca and the Loggetta – were transforming the centre of the city. The public passageway (*sottoportego*) running under the facade is a feature common to many Venetian houses. Lodovico Manin, the last doge of Venice, lived here – he had the interior rebuilt, so the facade is the only bit entirely by Sansovino.

The **Palazzo Loredan** and the **Palazzo Farsetti**, standing side by side at the end of the Riva del Carbon, are heavily restored Veneto-Byzantine palaces of the thirteenth century. The former was the home of Elena Corner Piscopia, who in 1678 graduated from Padua University, so becoming the first woman ever to hold a university degree. The two buildings are now occupied by the town hall.

Work began on the **Palazzo Grimani** (on the near side of the Rio di San Luca) in 1559, to designs by Sanmicheli, but was not completed until 1575, sixteen years after his death. Ruskin, normally no fan of Renaissance architecture, made an exception for this colossal palace, calling it "simple, delicate, and sublime". A Venetian folk tale attributes the scale of the palace to a thwarted passion: it's said that the young man who built it was in love with a woman from the Coccina-Tiepolo palace across the water, but was turned away by her father who wanted someone wealthier for his offspring. The suitor's revenge was to humiliate the father by building a palace which had windows bigger than the main doorway at the Coccina-Tiepolo.

The **Palazzo Corner Contarini dei Cavalli**, on the other side of the rio, was built around 1445; the "cavalli" part of the name comes from the horses on the crest of the facade's coat of arms. The pink **Palazzo Benzon**, just before the next canal, was where the most fashionable salon of early nineteenth-century Venice used to meet – regular guests included Byron, Thomas Moore, Ugo Foscolo and Canova. Their hostess, Contessa Querini-Benzon, was celebrated in a song that still occupies a place in the gondoliers' repertoire – *La Biondina in Gondoleta* (The Blonde in a Gondola). The **Palazzo Corner-Spinelli**, on the far side of the Rio di Ca' Santi, is another work by Codussi; it dates from 1490–1510, so preceding his more monumental Palazzo Vendramin-Calergi.

Four houses that once all belonged to the Mocenigo family stand side by side on the **Volta del Canal**: the **Palazzo Mocenigo-Nero**, a late sixteenth-century building; the double **Palazzo Mocenigo**, built in the eighteenth century as an extension to the Nero house; and the **Palazzo Mocenigo Vecchio**, a Gothic palace remodelled in the seventeenth century.

One of the great Venetian scandals centres on the first of the four. In 1621 Lady Arundel, wife of one of King James's most powerful courtiers, became its tenant; before long it was rumoured that the house was being visited by **Antonio Foscarini**, a former ambassador from Venice to England, whose term in London had ended with an abrupt recall home and a three-year stay in prison under suspicion of treason. On that occasion Foscarini had finally been cleared, but now there were renewed allegations of treacherous behaviour, and the Council of Ten quickly shifted into top gear. Foscarini was arrested, interrogated and, twelve days later, executed. Lady Arundel instantly demanded an audience with the doge, the result of which was a public declaration that she had not been involved in any plot; and within a few months the Council of Ten had conclusive evidence that Foscarini had been framed. The men who had accused him were put to death, and Foscarini's body was exhumed and given a state funeral.

Byron and his menagerie – a dog, a fox, a wolf and a monkey – lived in the Mocenigo-Nero palace for a couple of years. Much of his time was taken up with a local baker's wife called Margarita Cogni, the most tempestuous of his mistresses – her reaction to being rejected by him was to attack him with a table knife and then, having been shown the door, hurl herself into the Canal Grande. The Palazzo Mocenigo Vecchio is supposed to be haunted by the ghost of the philosopher-alchemist Giordano Bruno, whose betrayal to the Vatican by his former host, Giovanni Mocenigo, led ultimately to his torture and execution in 1600.

The neighbouring building is the early sixteenth-century **Palazzo Contarini delle Figure** – the *figure* are the almost invisible figures above the water entrance. It was begun by Spavento and completed by Scarpagnino, as had previously been the case with the Fondaco dei Tedeschi and the Palazzo Ducale.

To the Palazzo Giustinian

The vast and pristine palace round the Volta is the **Palazzo Grassi**, built in 1748–72 by Massari, who supervised the completion of the Ca' Rezzonico on the opposite bank. Its first owners were accepted into the ranks of the nobility in return for a hefty contribution to the war effort against the Turks in 1718. Nowadays it's used as an exhibition centre (see p.92).

On the edge of the first canal after the campo of San Samuele stands the **Ca' del Duca**. Commissioned in the mid-fifteenth century from Bartolomeo Bon,

▲ Palazzo Grassi

it was left unfinished in 1461 when the Corner family sold it to Francesco
Sforza, Duke of Milan (from whom it takes its name) – the wedge of rusticated
masonry gives some idea of the sort of fortified look the Corners had in mind.
In 1514 Titian had a studio here. Across the rio there's the tiny **Palazzetto
Falier**, a reworked Gothic house of the fifteenth century, chiefly remarkable for
its two roofed terraces. Although they used to be common, very few examples
of this feature (called a *liagò*) have survived. Next door is one of Longhena's
earliest projects, the **Palazzo Giustinian–Lolin** (1623).

At the foot of the Accademia bridge, on the far side, is the huge fifteenth-
century **Palazzo Franchetti**; repaired and enlarged at the end of the
nineteenth century, it's an imposing building but is often cited as one of
the city's most heavy-handed pieces of restoration work. Now owned by the
Istituto Veneto di Scienze, Lettere ed Arti, it's an occasional venue for large-
scale art exhibitions.

On the opposite side of the Rio dell'Orso are the twinned **Palazzi Barbaro**;
the house on the left is early fifteenth century, the other late seventeenth
century. Henry James, Monet, Whistler, Browning and John Singer Sargent were
among the luminaries who stayed in the older Barbaro house as guests of the
Curtis family in the late nineteenth century. James finished *The Aspern Papers*
here, and used it as a setting for *The Wings of a Dove* (as did the makers of the
film of the book); so attached was he to the place that when given the opportunity of buying a home in Venice at a very reasonable price, he decided he
would rather go on living here as a lodger.

Soon after the short fondamenta comes the tiny **Casetta delle Rose**, where
Canova once had his studio and D'Annunzio lived during World War I. The
Casetta lies in the shadow of one of the Canal Grande's most imposing structures – Sansovino's **Palazzo Corner della Ca' Grande**. The palace that used
to stand here was destroyed when a fire that had been lit to dry out a stock of
sugar in the attic spread though the whole building, an incident that illustrates
the dual commercial-residential function of many palaces in Renaissance Venice.
Sansovino's replacement, commissioned by the nephews of Caterina Cornaro,

was built from 1545 onwards, and the rustication of its lower storey – a distinctive aspect of many Roman and Tuscan buildings of the High Renaissance – makes it a prototype for Longhena's Ca' Pésaro and Ca' Rezzonico. Though the Corners were among the wealthiest clans in Venice, the palazzo was partly funded by a large donation from the state coffers. When Caterina Cornaro had died in 1510, the family had not claimed their share of her estate, instead allowing the government to use the money to subsidize the armed forces that were then embroiled in the War of the League of Cambrai. Now the nephews argued that the state owed them some help in funding the construction of a house that would, after all, be an adornment to the city – and the Council of Ten duly authorized the payment of 30,000 ducats.

The heavily restored fifteenth-century **Palazzo Pisani**, now the *Gritti Hotel*, looms over the Santa Maria del Giglio landing stage – John and Effie Ruskin stayed here in 1851, the year *The Stones of Venice* began to appear in print. Squeezed into the line of buildings that follows is the narrow **Palazzo Contarini-Fasan**, a mid-fifteenth-century palace with unique wheel tracery on the balconies. It's popularly known as "the house of Desdemona", but although the model for Shakespeare's heroine did live in Venice, her association with this house is purely sentimental. The last major building before the Giardinetti Reali is the fifteenth-century **Palazzo Giustinian**; now the HQ of the Biennale and the tourist board, it was formerly one of the plushest hotels in town, numbering the likes of Verdi, Ruskin and Proust among its guests.

The Northern Islands

The main islands lying to the north of Venice – **San Michele**, **Murano**, **Burano** and **Torcello** – used to be good places to visit when the throng of tourists in the main part of Venice became too oppressive. Nowadays the throngs are almost everywhere for most of the year, but a northwards excursion is still a restorative – out here the horizons are distant and the swathes of *barèna* (marshland) give a taste of what conditions were like for Venice's first settlers. A day-trip through this part of the lagoon will reveal the origins of the glass-and-lace-work touted in so many of the city's shops, and give you a glimpse of the origins of Venice itself, embodied in Torcello's magnificent cathedral of Santa Maria dell'Assunta.

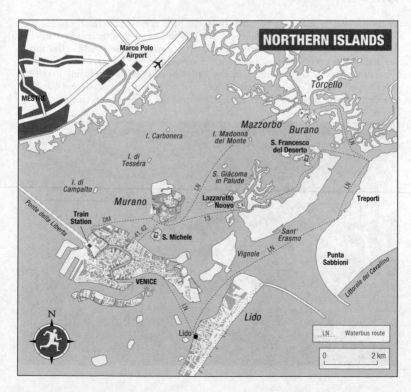

Those intent on an exhaustive exploration of the lagoon could plan a visit to the islets of San Francesco del Deserto and Lazzaretto Nuovo – the former a Franciscan retreat, the latter a charismatic wasteland.

To get to the northern islands, the main **vaporetto stop** is **Fondamente Nove** (or Nuove), as nearly all the island services start here or call here. For **San Michele and Murano only** the circular #41 and #42 vaporetti both run every twenty minutes from Fondamente Nove, circling Murano before heading back towards Venice; you can hop on elsewhere in the city, of course, but make sure that the boat is going towards the islands, not away from them – the #41 follows an anticlockwise route around the city, the #42 a clockwise route. Murano can also be reached by the #DM (Diretto Murano), which from around 8am to 6pm runs to the island from Tronchetto via Piazzale Roma and the train station. For **Murano**, **Burano and Torcello** the #LN (Laguna Nord) leaves every half-hour from Fondamente Nove for most of the day (hourly early in the morning and evenings), calling first at Murano-Faro before heading on to Mazzorbo and Burano, from where it proceeds, via Treporti, to Punta Sabbioni and the Lido. A shuttle boat runs every half-hour between Burano and Torcello, timed to fit in with Venice boat arrivals and departures at the Burano stop.

San Michele

A church was founded on **San Michele**, the innermost of the northern islands, in the tenth century, and a monastery was established in the thirteenth. Its best-known resident was Fra Mauro (d.1459), whose map of the world – the most accurate of its time – is now a precious possession of the Libreria Sansoviniana. The monastery was suppressed in the early nineteenth century, but in 1829, after a spell as an Austrian prison for political offenders, it was handed back to the Franciscans, who look after the church and the cemetery to this day.

▲ The cemetery of San Michele

The high brick wall around the island gives way by the landing stage to the elegant white facade of **San Michele in Isola** (daily: April–Sept 7.30am–6pm; Oct–March 7.30am–4pm), designed by **Mauro Codussi** in 1469. With this building Codussi quietly revolutionized the architecture of Venice, advancing the principles of Renaissance design in the city and introducing the use of Istrian stone as a material for facades. Easy to carve yet resistant to water, Istrian stone had long been used for damp courses, but never before had anyone clad the entire front of a building in it; after the construction of San Michele, most major buildings in Venice were given an Istrian veneer.

Attached on the left, and entered from within the church, is the dainty **Cappella Emiliana**, built around 1530 by **Guglielmo dei Grigi**. Marble inlays and reliefs cover the interior, yet Ruskin was impervious to its charm: "It is more like a German summer-house, or angle-turret, than a chapel, and may be briefly described as a bee-hive set on a low hexagonal tower, with dashes of stonework about its windows like the flourishes of an idle penman." In front of the main entrance to the church a floor plaque marks the final resting place of **Fra Paolo Sarpi** (d.1623), Venice's principal ideologue during the tussle with the papacy at the start of the seventeenth century (see p.149); buried first in his Servite monastery, Sarpi's remains were removed here when that order was suppressed in 1828.

The cemetery

The main part of the island, through the cloisters, is covered by the **cemetery** of Venice, established here by a Napoleonic decree which forbade further burials in the centre of the city (daily: April–Sept 7.30am–6pm; Oct–March 7.30am–4pm). Space is at a premium, and most of the Catholic dead of Venice lie here in cramped conditions for just ten years or so, when their bones are dug up and removed to an ossuary, and the vacated plot is recycled. Protestants are permitted to stay in their sector indefinitely, as each year's new arrivals are never numerous, but otherwise only those whose descendants can afford to lease a resting place get to stay longer than a decade. (There is a separate Jewish cemetery over on the Lido.)

However, even with this grave-rotation system in operation, the island is reaching full capacity, so in 1998 a competition was held for the redevelopment of San Michele. The winning entry, from English architect David Chipperfield, places a sequence of formal courtyards lined with wall tombs on the presently unkempt parts of the island, alongside a new funerary chapel and crematorium. On the eastern side of San Michele two footbridges will connect with a rectangular expanse of reclaimed land, site of a trio of tomb buildings that will overlook two tiers of waterside gardens, which in turn will overlook central Venice. Making much use of Istrian stone and earthenware plasterwork, Chipperfield's creation promises to be an austerely beautiful place – and there's a certain appropriateness to the fact that the 21st century's first large-scale addition to the Venetian cityscape will be a cross between a necropolis and a philosopher's retreat. Work is scheduled for completion in 2013, but there are doubts that it'll be finished that soon.

At the entrance to the cemetery you can pick up a small plan of the various sections either at the flower stall to the right of the entrance or from the cemetery office (go through the two archways and then turn left). Most tourists head for the dilapidated **Protestant** section (no. XV), where **Ezra Pound's grave** is marked by a plain slab with his name on it, alongside that of his partner, Olga Rudge. Nobel Laureate Joseph Brodsky is buried here too. Adjoining is the **Greek and Russian Orthodox** area (no. XIV), including the simple gravestones of **Igor and Vera Stravinsky** – Stravinsky was given a funeral service in San Zanipolo, the highest funeral honour the city can bestow – and the more elaborate tomb for **Serge Diaghilev**.

⑧ Murano

In 1276 the island of **Murano** became a self-governed enclave within the Republic, with its own judiciary, its own administration and a *Libro d'Oro* to register its nobility. By the early sixteenth century Murano had thirty thousand inhabitants, and was a favourite summer retreat for Venice's upper classes, who could lay out gardens here that were far more extensive than those in the cramped centre of the city. The intellectual life of the island was especially healthy in the seventeenth century, when literature, philosophy and the sciences were discussed in the numerous small *accademie* that flourished here. But the **glass-blowing industry** is what made Murano famous all over Europe, and

▲ The Murano lighthouse

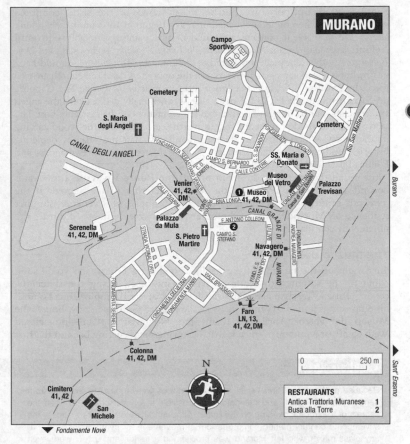

today the furnaces of Murano constitute Venice's sole surviving manufacturing zone. The main fondamente of Murano are given over almost entirely to shops selling glasswork, and it's difficult to walk more than a few metres on this island without being invited to step inside a showroom – and once inside, you're likely to be pressured into forking out for some piece of kitsch which may not even have been made here. However, some of the showrooms have furnaces attached, and you shouldn't pass up the chance to see these astoundingly skilful craftsmen in action, even if they're only churning out little glass ponies and other silly knick-knacks. (The top-quality stuff is produced behind closed doors.) Furthermore, you'll find some very beautiful (and very expensive) items on sale here, and you can see some remarkable work in the Murano glass museum – the island's main sight, alongside the beautiful church of **Santi Maria e Donato**.

Around the island

From the Colonna vaporetto stop (the first stop after San Michele for the #41/42) you step onto the Fondamenta dei Vetrai, traditionally the core of the glass industry (as the name suggests) and now the principal tourist trap. Towards the far end is the Dominican church of **San Pietro Martire** (Mon–Sat 9am–noon & 3–6pm,

Sun 3–6pm), one of only two churches still in service on the island (compared with seventeen when the Republic fell in 1797). Begun in 1363 but largely rebuilt after a fire in 1474, it contains a handful of fine paintings, notably **Giovanni Bellini**'s large and elegant *Madonna and Child with St Mark, St Augustine and Doge Barbarigo*. Another altarpiece attributed to Bellini – an *Assumption* – should hang nearby, but it's been *in restauro* for years. On the opposite side of the church are two pieces by Veronese – *St Agatha in Prison* and *St Jerome in the Desert*. The Cappella del Sacramento, to the left of the main altar, was originally dedicated to the angels and contains four paintings of personable representatives of the heavenly host. The sacristy, with its modest museum (€2), is worth seeing only for the wood carving in the vestry, which includes some extraordinary Baroque atlantes depicting historical and mythological characters such as Nero, Socrates, Pythagoras and Pontius Pilate, with the Four Seasons flanking the altar.

Just round the corner is the main bridge, the **Ponte Vivarini**, a few yards beyond which is the **Palazzo da Mula**, a Gothic palace altered in the sixteenth century, one of the few surviving examples of a Venetian summer residence on Murano. Many of the other palaces were demolished during the nineteenth century.

The Museo del Vetro

Turn right on the far side of the bridge, along Riva Longa, and you'll soon come to the seventeenth-century Palazzo Giustinian, facing the sixteenth-century Palazzo Trevisan across the canal. Home of the Bishop of Torcello until his diocese was joined to Venice in 1805, the Palazzo Giustinian now houses the **Museo del Vetro** (April–Oct 10am–5pm; Nov–March 10am–4pm; closed Wed; €5.50, or Museum/Venice Card). Featuring pieces dating back to the first

---

Venetian glass

Because of the risk of fire, Venice's **glass furnaces** were moved to **Murano** from central Venice in 1291, and thenceforth all possible steps were taken to keep the secrets of the trade locked up on the island. Although Muranese workers had by the seventeenth century gained some freedom of movement, for centuries prior to that any glass-maker who left Murano was proclaimed a traitor, and a few were even hunted down. Various privileges reduced the temptation to rove – unlike other artisans, the glass-blowers were allowed to wear swords, and from 1376 the offspring of a marriage between a Venetian nobleman and the daughter of a glass-worker were allowed to be entered into the *Libro d'Oro*, unlike the children of other inter-class matches. Normal principles of justice were sometimes waived for the glass-blowers. On one occasion a man who had committed a murder and then fled Murano was accepted back without punishment once his father had hinted to the city's governors that his son might set up a furnace in Mantua.

A fifteenth-century visitor judged that "in the whole world there are no such craftsmen of glass as here", and the Muranese were masters of every aspect of their craft. They were producing spectacles by the start of the fourteenth century, monopolized the European manufacture of **mirrors** for a long time (and continued making larger mirrors than anyone else even after the monopoly had gone), and in the early seventeenth century became so proficient at making coloured crystal that a decree was issued forbidding the manufacture of false gems out of glass, as many were being passed off as authentic stones. Understatement has rarely been a characteristic of Murano produce: in 1756 Lady Mary Wortley Montague was wonderstruck by a set of **furniture** made entirely out of glass, and in the twentieth century the less favourably impressed H.V. Morton longed "to see something simple and beautiful",

century and examples of Murano glass from the fifteenth century onwards, this is a fascinating museum. Perhaps the finest single item is the dark blue Barovier marriage cup, dating from around 1470; it's on show in room 1 on the first floor, along with some splendid Renaissance enamelled and painted glass. But every room contains some amazing creations: glass beakers that look as if they are made from veined stone; jars that look like bubbles of blue water; a chalice with a spiral stem as slender as a strand of spaghetti; sixteenth-century platters that look like discs of cracked ice; specimens of *lattimo*, an eighteenth-century imitation of porcelain; and stupendously ugly nineteenth-century decorative pieces, with fat little birds enmeshed in trellises of glass. A separate display covers the history of Murano glass techniques – look out for the extraordinary *murine in canna*, the method of placing different coloured rods together to form an image in cross section.

Santi Maria e Donato

The other Murano church, and one of the main reasons for visiting the island, is **Santi Maria e Donato** (Mon–Sat 9am–noon & 3.30–7pm, Sun 3.30–7pm). It was founded in the seventh century but rebuilt in the twelfth, and is one of the lagoon's best examples of Veneto-Byzantine architecture – the ornate **rear apse** being particularly fine. Originally dedicated to the Virgin, the church was rededicated in 1125 when the relics of Saint Donatus were brought here from Cephalonia by **Doge Domenico Michiel**, who also picked up the remains of Saint Isidore and the stone on which Jesus stood to preach to the men of Tyre – both items are now in the Basilica di San Marco. Saint Donatus allegedly once slew a dragon simply by spitting at it – the four splendid bones hanging behind the altar are supposedly from the unfortunate beast.

adding that sixteenth-century customers felt the same way "when, looking around for something to take home, they were repelled by drinking-glasses in the shape of ships, whales, lions and birds". Murano kitsch extends to all price categories, from the mass-produced knick-knacks sold for a few euros, through to monstrosities such as Peggy Guggenheim's pieces based on figures from the works of Picasso – specially commissioned by her, they are on show in that bastion of modernist art, the Guggenheim Collection.

The traditional style of Murano glass, typified by the multicoloured floral **chandeliers** sold in showrooms on Murano and round the Piazza, is still very much in demand. However, in recent years there's been turmoil in the glass industry, due to an inundation of cheap Murano-style tableware and ornaments from Asia and eastern Europe. To protect the reputation of the island's craftsmen a Murano "copyright" has recently been created – it's displayed on all authentic Murano work. And while many Murano factories have been unable to compete with the vendors of low-price ersatz glassware, an increasing number of companies are now following the example of Paolo Venini, the Milanese lawyer and entrepreneur who in the 1920s pulled Murano from the doldrums by commissioning work from designers outside the rarefied world of glass. There are now several innovative glass producers on Murano, but the sharp economic downturn that began in 2008 has hit Murano badly, with the drop in sales to tourists leading to a thirty percent reduction in output. Dozens of Murano glass companies and retailers have closed down recently, and few of those that remain are in Venetian hands – the long-established firm of Salviati is French-owned, and even Venini has been bought out, by the Royal Copenhagen company.

The glory of the interior is its **mosaic floor**, which was created in the middle of the twelfth century (the date 1141 appears in the nave) and extensively restored and completely relaid in the 1970s. It's a beautiful weave of abstract patterns and figurative images, such as an eagle carrying off a deer, and two roosters bearing away a fox, slung from a pole (both of these are symbols of the triumph of Christianity over paganism). Apart from the arresting twelfth-century **mosaic of the Madonna** in the apse, a variant (without *bambino*) of the contemporaneous mosaic at Torcello, the features that invite perusal are the fifteenth-century ship's-keel roof, the sixth-century pulpit, the Veneto-Byzantine capitals, and the lunette painting halfway down the left aisle, Lazzaro Bastiani's *Madonna and Child with Saints and Donor* (1484).

Burano and San Francesco del Deserto

After Murano, the next stop for the #LN boat is at the small island of **Mazzorbo**, a densely populated town a couple of centuries ago, before it became a place of exile for disgraced noblemen, whereupon the undisgraced citizens decamped for homes elsewhere in the lagoon. Nowadays Mazzorbo doesn't amount to much more than a few scattered villas, a lot of grassy space, a new housing development and the simple but beautiful fourteenth-century church of **Santa Caterina** (Fri–Sun 11am–1pm & 2–5pm). You can either get off the boat here, and walk round Mazzorbo to the sixty-metre footbridge to Burano (which offers beautifully framed views of distant Venice), or continue on the boat for one more stop.

After the peeling plaster and eroded stonework of the other lagoon settlements, the small, brightly painted houses of **Burano** come as something of a surprise. Local tradition says that the colours once enabled each fisherman to identify his house from out at sea, but nowadays the colours are used simply for pleasant effect. The boldest exterior decorator on the island was a resident called Bepi, who lived at Via Al Gottolo 339, down the alley opposite the *Galuppi* restaurant in Via Baldassare Galuppi, the main street; Bepi died in 2002, but his crazy patterns of diamonds, triangles and bars have been preserved. (Galuppi was an eighteenth-century Buranese composer, known locally as *Il Buranello*; the main piazza is named after him, too, and further commemorates him with a half-length statue and a plaque at no. 24.)

Burano was settled in the seventh century by mainland refugees who named their new home Boreana, perhaps after the *bora*, as the northeasterly winter wind is known. Safely removed from the malarial swamps that did so much to ruin neighbouring Torcello, Burano became a prosperous fishing village, and is still largely a fishing community – you can't walk far along the shores of the island without seeing a fishing boat beached for repair, or nets laid out to dry or be mended, or a jumble of crab boxes.

The lives of the women of Burano used to be dominated by the **lace** industry, but the production of handmade lace is now almost extinct, and most of the stuff sold in the shops lining the narrow street leading into the village from the vaporetto stop is made by machine. Lace-making used to be a skill that crossed all social boundaries: for noblewomen it was an expression of feminine creativity (by the end of the sixteenth century, lace-making had become the chief pastime of upper-class Venetian women); for nuns it was an exercise in humility and contemplation; and for the poorest it was simply a source of

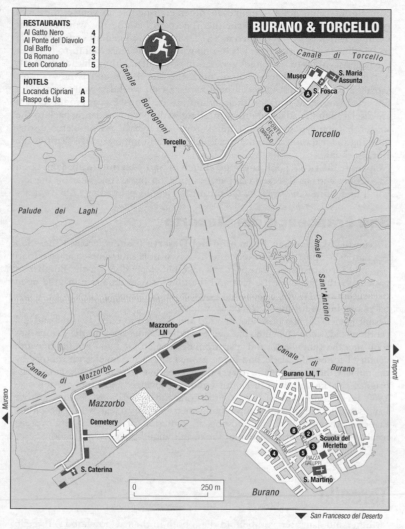

RESTAURANTS

Al Gatto Nero	4
Al Ponte del Diavolo	1
Dal Baffo	2
Da Romano	3
Leon Coronato	5

HOTELS

Locanda Cipriani	A
Raspo de Ua	B

BURANO & TORCELLO

Canale di Torcello

Museo — S. Maria Assunta

S. Fosca

Torcello

PONTE DEL DIAVOLO

Canale Borgognoni

Torcello
T

Palude dei Laghi

Canale Sant'Antonio

Mazzorbo
LN

Canale di Burano

◀ Treporti

Burano LN, T

Canale di Mazzorbo

◀ Murano

Mazzorbo

Cemetery

S. Caterina

Scuola del Merletto

DELLA PESCHERIA

PIAZZA GALUPPI

S. Martino

Burano

0 ——— 250 m

▼ San Francesco del Deserto

income. Its production was once geographically diverse, too – **Dogaressa Morosina Morosini** set up a large and successful workshop near Santa Fosca (in Cannaregio) in the late sixteenth century, for instance – but nowadays Burano is the exclusive centre. Making Burano-point and Venetian-point lace is extremely exacting work, both highly skilled and mind-bendingly repetitive, taking an enormous toll on the eyesight. Each woman specializes in one particular stitch, and as there are seven stitches in all, each piece is passed from woman to woman during its construction. An average-size table centre requires about a month of work.

Piazza Baldassare Galuppi's **Scuola del Merletto** (closed for restoration until 2010; normally open April–Oct 10am–5pm; Nov–March 10am–4pm; closed Tues; €4, or Museum Pass/Venice Card) is simply a school rather than a confraternity-cum-guild – unlike all other craftspeople in Venice, the lace-makers had no guild to represent them, perhaps because the workforce was exclusively female. It was opened in 1872, when the indigenous crafting of lace had declined so far that it was left to one woman, Francesca Memo, to transmit the necessary skills to a younger generation of women. Although the scuola has not operated as a full-time school since the late 1960s and is now almost moribund, a few courses are still held here, and on weekdays you might see a few local women at work on their cylindrical cushions. Pieces produced here are displayed in the attached museum, along with specimens dating back to the sixteenth century; after even a quick tour you'll have no problems distinguishing the real thing from the machine-made and imported lace that fills the Burano shops.

Opposite the lace school stands the church of **San Martino** (daily 8am–noon & 3–7pm), with its drunken campanile; inside, on the second altar on the left, you'll find a fine *Crucifixion* by Giambattista Tiepolo, painted in 1725.

San Francesco del Deserto

To visit the island of **San Francesco del Deserto** (visitors received Tues–Sun 9–11am & 3–5pm; donation requested; ⓦ www.isola-sanfrancescodeldeserto.it) the only form of public transport is a taxi, but depending on the number of passengers, the length of the visit and the time of year, the price may be open to negotiation. There's a taxi rank next to the vaporetto stop, with a free telephone booth for use if no taxi is waiting.

Saint Francis ran aground here in 1220 and decided to build a chapel and cell on the island. Jacopo Michiel, the owner of the island, gave it to the Franciscans soon after the saint's death, and apart from deserting it for a while in the fifteenth century because of malaria, and being pushed out in the nineteenth century by the military, they have been here ever since. The present chapel was built over the original one in the fifteenth century, and was lovingly and simply restored in 1962, uncovering some of the original floor and foundations. Seven friars live here, some in retreat, and a few young men stay for a year before becoming Franciscan novices. With its birdsong, its profusion of plants and its cypress-scented air, the monastery is one of the most tranquil places in the lagoon.

Torcello

"Mother and daughter, you behold them both in their widowhood – Torcello and Venice". So wrote John Ruskin, and it's almost impossible to visit **Torcello** without similarly sensing an atmosphere of bereavement. This outlying island has now come almost full circle. Settled by the very first refugees from the mainland in the fifth century, it became the seat of the Bishop of Altinum in 638 and in the following year its cathedral – the oldest building in the lagoon – was founded. By the fourteenth century its population had peaked at around twenty thousand, but Torcello's canals were now silting up and malaria was rife. By the end of the fifteenth century Torcello was largely deserted – even the bishop lived in Murano – and today only about thirty people remain in residence, their numbers swelled by thousands of tourists, and by the ever-increasing ranks of stallholders eager to sell lace and glass to the summer boatloads.

Santa Maria dell'Assunta

The main reason for a visit is to see Venice's first cathedral and the most serene building in the lagoon – the **Cattedrale di Santa Maria dell'Assunta** (daily: March–Oct 10.30am–6pm; Nov–Feb 10am–5pm; €4; joint ticket with museum & Museo Diocesano in Venice, €7).

A Veneto-Byzantine building dating substantially from 1008, the cathedral has evolved from a church founded in the seventh century, of which the crypt and the circular foundations in front of the **facade** have survived. The first major transformation of the church occurred in the 860s, the period to which the **facade and portico** belong (though they were altered in later centuries). For the most unusual features of the exterior, go down the right-hand side of the cathedral, where the windows have eleventh-century **stone shutters**. Ruskin described the view from the campanile as "one of the most notable scenes in this wide world", a verdict you can't test for yourself at the moment, as the campanile is currently being restored yet again.

The dominant tones of the cathedral's **interior** come from pink brick, gold-based mosaics and the watery green-grey marble of its columns and panelling, which together cast a cool light on the richly patterned **mosaic floor**, which was laid in the eleventh and twelfth centuries. (Glazed panels in the floor reveal portions of ninth-century mosaic.) On the semi-dome of the apse a stunning twelfth-century **mosaic of the Madonna and Child**, the figures isolated in a vast field of gold, looks down from above a **frieze of the Apostles**, dating from the middle of the previous century. Below the window at the Madonna's feet is a much restored image of **Saint Heliodorus**, the first Bishop of Altinum, whose remains were brought here by the earliest settlers. It makes an interesting comparison with the gold-plated facemask on his sarcophagus below the high altar, another seventh-century vestige. His original Roman sarcophagus is placed to the left of the altar, underneath the **foundation stone** of the cathedral, which was laid in 639, the same year as the fall of Oderzo, the Byzantine provincial capital on the mainland. Named on the stone are the fleeing leaders of that town, both temporal (the *magister militum*) and spiritual (the Exarch), as well as Bishop Mauro of Altinum, the first to transfer his see to Torcello.

Mosaic work from the ninth and eleventh centuries adorns the chapel to the right of the high altar, while the other end of the cathedral is dominated by the tumultuous **mosaic of the Apotheosis of Christ and the Last Judgement** – created in the twelfth century, but renovated in the nineteenth, it features an extraordinary panel in various shades of black and grey, depicting the eternal gloom of hell. Have a good look, too, at the **rood screen**, where paintings of *The Virgin and Apostles* are supported by eleventh-century columns connected by finely carved marble panels.

Santa Fosca and the Museo di Torcello

Torcello's other church, **Santa Fosca** (same hours as Santa Maria; free), was built in the eleventh and twelfth centuries for the body of the martyred Saint Fosca, brought to Torcello from Libya some time before 1011 and now resting under the altar. A dome was planned to cap the martyrium but was never built, perhaps because of the desertion of the Greek builders who alone possessed the secret of constructing a self-supporting dome. Though much restored, the church retains the Greek-cross form and a fine exterior apse; the bare interior, with beautiful marble columns and elegant brick arches, exudes a calmness which no number of visitors can quite destroy.

In the square outside sits the curious **chair of Attila**, perhaps once the throne of Torcello's judges in its earliest days; local folklore has it that if you sit

▲ Santa Fosca (right) and Santa Maria dell'Assunta, Torcello

in it, you will be wed within a year. Behind it, the well-laid-out **Museo di Torcello** (Tues–Sun: March–Oct 10.30am–5.30pm; Nov–Feb 10am–5pm; €3) includes thirteenth-century beaten gold figures, jewellery, mosaic fragments (including pieces from the cathedral's *Last Judgement*, in which the hands of several artists can be distinguished) and a mishmash of pieces relating to the history of the area.

Lazzaretto Nuovo

Once a quarantine encampment, the island of **Lazzaretto Nuovo** (tours April–Oct Sat & Sun at 9.45am & 4.30pm; booking required on ☎041.244.4011 or through Ⓦwww.lazzarettonuovo.com) now preserves only a huge abandoned warehouse and an unusually peaceful atmosphere. Getting there is simple enough, as the vaporetto #13 to Sant' Erasmo stops at the jetty on request.

In 1468, fear of plague led the Senate to augment the existing plague hospital (now known as Lazzaretto Vecchio – see p.227) with a dedicated quarantine island, and huge warehouses were erected to store merchandise arriving in Venice from suspect areas, with merchants and sailors quartered alongside. The largest of these warehouses, the **Tezon Grande**, still stands in the centre of the island, and while it's little more than an empty shed, the sixteenth-century graffiti on the far interior wall conjure something of a more cosmopolitan past – picked out in red are lists of cargoes and voyages made to the further corners of the Mediterranean. Much of the island is still encircled by brick fortifications which date from the occupations of Napoleon and the Austrians, when it formed part of Venice's system of defences. There's little else to see other than a small museum of archeological finds, but the view from the walls across the bleak marshes is impressive, with little egrets and herons fishing among the rushes.

The Southern Islands

The section of the lagoon to the south of the city, enclosed by the long islands of the **Lido** and **Pellestrina**, has far fewer outcrops of solid land than the northern zone. Once past **San Giorgio Maggiore** and **La Giudecca**, and clear of the smaller islands beyond, you could look in the direction of the mainland and think you were out in the open sea – an illusion strengthened by the tankers that move across the lagoon on their way to or from the port of Marghera. But these huge ocean-going vessels are edging along a few narrow deep-water channels that have been dredged out of the silt; the Venetian lagoon is the largest in Italy, yet its average depth is not much more than one metre, a fact that might be brought home to you with a jolt by the sight of a fisherman standing on a barely submerged sandbank a long way from the shore.

The nearer islands are the more interesting; the Palladian churches of San Giorgio and La Giudecca are among Venice's most significant Renaissance monuments, while the alleyways of the island are full of reminders of the city's manufacturing past. The Venetian tourist industry began with the development of the Lido, which has now been eclipsed by the city itself as a holiday destination, yet still draws thousands of people to its beaches each year, many of them Italians. A visit to the Armenian island, **San Lazzaro degli Armeni**, makes an absorbing afternoon's round trip, and if you've a bit more time to spare you could undertake an expedition to the fishing town of **Chioggia**, at the southern extremity of the lagoon. The farther-flung settlements along the route to Chioggia may have seen more glorious days, but the voyage out from the city is a pleasure in itself.

San Giorgio Maggiore

Palladio's church of **San Giorgio Maggiore** (daily: May–Sept 9.30am–12.30pm & 2.30–6pm; Oct–April 9.30am–12.30pm & 2.30–4.30pm), facing the Palazzo Ducale across the Bacino di San Marco, is one of the most prominent and familiar of all Venetian landmarks. It is a startling building, whose isolation almost forces you to have an opinion as to its architectural merits. Ruskin didn't much care for it: "It is impossible to conceive a design more gross, more barbarous, more childish in conception, more servile in plagiarism, more insipid in result, more contemptible under every point of rational regard." Goethe, on the other hand, sick of the Gothic art that was to Ruskin the touchstone of spiritual health, gave thanks to Palladio for purging his mind of medieval clutter.

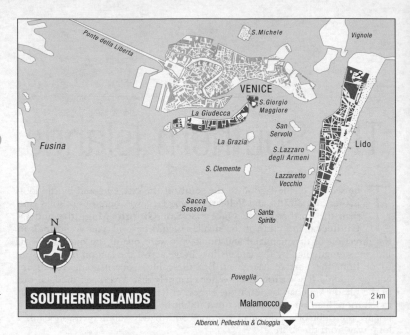

Ponte della Libertà
S. Michele
Vignole
VENICE
S. Giorgio Maggiore
La Giudecca
San Servolo
Fusina
La Grazia
S. Lazzaro degli Armeni
Lido
S. Clemente
Lazzaretto Vecchio
Sacca Sessola
Santa Spirito
N
Poveglia
SOUTHERN ISLANDS
0   2 km
Malamocco

Alberoni, Pellestrina & Chioggia ▼

Designed in 1565 and completed 45 years later, San Giorgio Maggiore was a greatly influential solution to the chief problem of Renaissance church design: how to use classical forms in a structure that, with its high central nave and lower aisles, had no precedent in classical culture. Palladio's answer was to super-impose two temple fronts: the nave being defined by an upper pediment supported by gigantic Composite columns, and the aisles by lower half-pediments resting on Corinthian pilasters. Inside, the relationship between the major Composite order and the minor Corinthian is maintained, so unifying the facade of the church and its interior. The scale of Palladio's forms and his use of shadow-casting surfaces ensure that the design of the facade retains its clarity when viewed from across the water.

The interior

The Venetians were the first to cover church interiors with white stucco, and the technique is used to dazzling effect in San Giorgio Maggiore – "Of all the colours, none is more proper for churches than white; since the purity of colour, as of the life, is particularly gratifying to God," wrote Palladio. It's hard to imagine how anyone could remain totally unimpressed by the interior's finely calculated proportions and Counter-Reformation austerity, but in Ruskin's opinion only the paintings inside justified a visit.

The first altar on the right has an *Adoration of the Shepherds* by **Jacopo Bassano**, which is followed by an alarming, late fifteenth-century *Crucifix* – not by Brunelleschi (contrary to what the label says) but by an anonymous Venetian artist. Most of the other pictures are from the workshop of **Tintoretto**, with two outstanding pictures by the master in the chancel: *The Last Supper*, perhaps the most famous of all Tintoretto's works, and *The Fall of Manna*, one of the few depictions of the event to dwell on the fact that the shower was not a single miraculous deluge but rather a supply that continued for forty years. They were painted as a pair in 1592–94 – the last two years of the artist's life – to illustrate the significance of the Eucharist to the communicants at the altar rail. A *Deposition* of the same date, in the Cappella dei Morti (through the often-closed door on the right of the choir), may well be Tintoretto's last completed painting. The carnage-strewn picture alongside is a photograph of Carpaccio's *St George and the Dragon*, painted several years after the equally gruesome version in the Scuola di San Giorgio degli Schiavoni. The original is in a private room elsewhere in the building.

There are few pieces of woodwork in Venice more impressive than the **choir stalls** of San Giorgio Maggiore. Decorated with scenes from the life of St Benedict, they were carved in the late 1590s, as the church was being completed; the bronze figures of *St George* and *St Stephen* on the balustrade were made in the same decade by **Niccolò Roccatagliata**, who also made the florid candlesticks at the entrance to the chancel. Apart from Roccatagliata's pieces, the best sculptures in the church are the *Evangelists* by **Vittoria**, flanking the **tomb of Doge Leonardo Donà**, on the west wall. A close friend of Paolo Sarpi and Galileo, the scholarly Donà was the redoubtable leader of Venice at the time of the Interdict of 1602 (see p.149). The Papal Nuncio was sent packing by him with the lofty dismissal – "We ignore your excommunication: it is nothing to us. Now think where our resolution would lead, were our example to be followed by others."

The door on the left of the choir leads to the **campanile** (€3), via a corridor that houses the charred original version of the angel that stands on the church's summit; the angel was replaced by a copy after being charred and half-melted by a lightning strike in 1993. Rebuilt in 1791 after the collapse of its predecessor, the San Giorgio campanile surpasses that of San Marco as the best vantage point in Venice, because it has the advantage of being detached from the main part of the city, giving you a panorama that includes many of the canals (all of which are hidden from the San Marco tower) and, of course, the spectacular San Marco campanile itself.

The monastery and the harbour

Since the early ninth century there's been a church on this island, and at the end of the tenth century the lagoon's most important Benedictine monastery was established here. Both church and monastery were destroyed by an earthquake in 1223, but were rebuilt straight away, and subsequently renovated and altered several times. Cosimo de' Medici stayed at the monastery in 1433, during his exile from Florence, and it was with his assistance that the monastic library was set up; by the end of the century the Benedictines of San Giorgio Maggiore had become renowned for their erudition. With the upheavals of the early nineteenth century things changed rapidly. When the conclave that elected Pope Pius VII met here in 1800, having been turfed out of Rome by Napoleon, the confiscation of the monastery's property had already begun, and six years later the order was suppressed. By the mid-nineteenth century the monastery had been converted into workshops and offices for the Austrian artillery, and the decline of the complex continued for another hundred years until, in 1951, it was acquired by Count Vittorio Cini and converted into the home of the **Fondazione Giorgio Cini** (named after Cini's son), which runs various arts research institutes and hosts numerous courses and conferences on the island.

The restored monastery is one of the architectural wonders of the city. Two adjoining cloisters form the heart of the complex: the **Cloister of the Bay Trees**, planned by Giovanni Buora and built by his son Andrea in the two decades up to 1540; and the **Cloister of the Cypresses**, designed in 1579 by Palladio. Inside, there's a 128-metre-long **dormitory** by Giovanni Buora (c.1494), a **double staircase** (1641–43) and **library** (1641–53) by Longhena and, approached by an ascent through two anterooms, a magnificent **refectory** by Palladio (1560–62). A dazzlingly accurate computer-generated reproduction of Veronese's great *Marriage at Cana* fills the end wall of the refectory; the original, stolen by Napoleon's army, is now in the Louvre. Exhibitions are regularly held at the Fondazione, and the open-air Teatro Verde is occasionally used for plays and concerts. Guided tours of the complex are given on Saturday and Sunday, in Italian and English, between 10am and 4.30pm; tickets cost €12 and there's no need to book – just turn up at the gates.

The little **harbour** on the other side of the church was expanded during the second French occupation of 1806–15, when Napoleon decided to accord the island the status of a free port, in emulation of the tariff-free port of Trieste. A professor of architecture at the Accademia designed the two diminutive light-houses in 1813.

La Giudecca

In the earliest records of Venice the chain of islets now called **La Giudecca** was known as Spina Longa, a name clearly derived from its shape. The modern name might refer to the Jews (*Giudei*) who lived here from the late thirteenth century until their removal to the Ghetto, but is most likely to originate with the two disruptive noble families who in the ninth century were shoved into this district to keep them out of mischief (*giudicati* means "judged"). Before the Brenta River became the prestigious site for summer abodes, La Giudecca was where the wealthiest aristocrats of early Renaissance Venice built their villas. Michelangelo, self-exiled from Florence in 1529, consoled himself in the

LA GIUDECCA & SAN GIORGIO MAGGIORE

gardens of this island, traces of which remain on its south side. The most extensive of La Giudecca's surviving private gardens, the so-called Garden of Eden (at the end of the Rio della Croce), is bigger than any other in Venice; its name refers not to its paradisiacal properties but to a certain Mr Eden, the English gardener who planted it.

Giudecca was also the city's **industrial** inner suburb: vaporetti used to be made here; an asphalt factory and a distillery were once neighbours on the western end; and the matting industry, originating in the nineteenth century, kept going until 1950. However, the present-day island is a potent emblem of Venice's loss of economic self-sufficiency in the twentieth century, with abandoned workshops and roofless sheds littering the southern side of the island. In the mid-1990s the timepiece manufacturer Junghans, one of the city's major employers for half a century, closed its factory here, between Rio del Ponte Lungo and Rio del Ponte Piccolo. While the *Cipriani*, one of the city's most expensive hotels, occupies the eastern extremity of La Giudecca, the western edge is dominated by the neo-Gothic fortress of the Mulino Stucky flour mill, which is now also a luxury hotel. Yet in some respects things are looking up: a spate of housing developments and ancillary social facilities have been funded in recent years, while artists, theatre cooperatives and other creative groups have moved into a number of the redundant buildings. And at the start of the new century there's been an acceleration in the process of La Giudecca's rejuvenation. Under the aegis of the Judecanova consortium a variety of substantial projects is under way: a nautical centre has been constructed within one of the deserted factories on the main waterfront, for example, and a residential block for students has risen on the site of the Junghans factory, next door to a beautiful old school building that has been converted into an annexe of the university.

The Zitelle and the Redentore

The first vaporetto stop after San Giorgio Maggiore is close to the tiny church of the **Zitelle** (open only for pre-booked visits – details on Ⓦ www.scalabovolo.org),

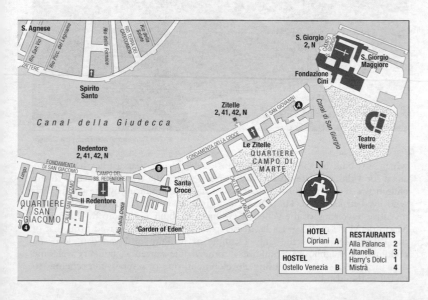

▲ The Redentore, seen from the Záttere

which was built in 1582–86 from plans devised some years earlier by Palladio, albeit for a different site. In the eighteenth century the convent attached to the church was renowned for the delicacy of the lace produced by the young girls who lived in its hostel. The **Casa de Maria**, to the right of the Zitelle, is an inventive reworking of the Venetian Gothic style, built as a studio by the painter Mario de Maria in 1910–13. Its diaper-pattern brickwork, derived from that of the Palazzo Ducale, is the only example of its kind in a Venetian domestic building. The neighbouring building is somewhat less inventive but very welcome nonetheless – it's a new housing development, one of several such schemes to revitalize the island.

La Giudecca's main monument, beyond the tugboats' mooring and the youth hostel (which was once a granary), is the Franciscan church of **Il Redentore** (Mon–Sat 10am–5pm; €3, or Chorus Pass), designed by **Palladio** in 1577. In 1575–76 Venice suffered an outbreak of plague which killed nearly fifty thousand people – virtually a third of the city's population. The Redentore ("Redeemer") was built by the Senate in thanks for Venice's deliverance, and every year until the downfall of the Republic the doge and his senators attended a Mass here to renew their declaration of gratitude, walking to the church over a pontoon bridge from the Záttere. The Festa del Redentore has remained a major event on the Venetian calendar – see the colour insert for more.

Palladio's commission called for a church to which there would be three distinct components: a choir for the monks to whom the church was entrusted, a tribune around the altar for the dignitaries of the city, and a nave with side chapels for the humbler worshippers. The architect's scheme, in which the tribune forms a circular chapel which opens into the nave and blends into the choir through a curved screen of columns, is the most sophisticated of his church projects, as well as the one most directly evolved from the architecture of ancient Rome (the Imperial baths in particular). Unfortunately, an appreciation of the building's subtleties is difficult, as a rope prevents visitors going beyond the nave. In the side chapels you'll find a couple of pictures by Francesco Bassano and an *Ascension* by Tintoretto and his assistants, but the best paintings in the church – including a *John the Baptist* by **Jacopo Bassano**, a *Baptism of Christ* by **Paolo Veronese** and *Madonna with Child and Angels* by **Alvise Vivarini** – are in the sacristy, which is rarely opened. The sacristy also has a peculiar array of eighteenth-century wax heads of illustrious Franciscans in various attitudes of agony and ecstasy, displayed in glass cases.

Sant'Eufemia and the interior of La Giudecca

Founded in the ninth century and often rebuilt, the church of **Sant'Eufemia** (Mon–Sat 9am–6pm, Sun 7am–12.30pm) is one of Venice's most engaging stylistic discords, with a late sixteenth-century portico, the nave and aisles still laid out as in the original basilica (with some eleventh-century columns and capitals), and stuccowork and painted decoration in eighteenth-century boudoir mode. It has one good painting, immediately on your right as you go in: *St Roch and an Angel* (with lunette of *Madonna and Child*), the central panel of a triptych painted in 1480 by Bartolomeo Vivarini.

Beyond Sant'Eufemia, on Fondamenta San Biagio, stands the HQ of the **Fortuny** company, which still makes some of the sumptuous fabrics designed by its founder. Towering over it is the gargantuan **Mulino Stucky**, which got to look the way it does in 1895–96, after Giovanni Stucky brought in a German architect, Ernst Wullekopf, to expand his flour mill. Planning permission for the brick bastion that Wullekopf came up with was obtained by the simple expedient of threatening to sack all the workers if consent were withheld by the council. By the beginning of the twentieth century Stucky had become one of the richest men in the city, and in 1908 he bought one of the Canal Grande's less discreet houses, the Palazzo Grassi. He didn't enjoy his occupancy for long, though – in 1910 one of his employees murdered him at the train station. With the development of the industrial sector at Marghera after World War I, the Mulino Stucky went into a nose dive, and in 1954 it closed. For decades after that, its future was a perennially contentious issue: there was talk of converting the mill into a sports centre or something else that might be of use to the people of Venice, but inevitably it's become a five-star hotel and congress centre – the *Molino Stucky Hilton*.

There's no point in going past the Stucky building; **Sacca Fisola**, the next island along, is all modern apartments, bordered on one side by boatyards and on the other by the site at which waste used to be mixed with silt to form the basic material of land reclamation in the lagoon.

For a taste of the economic past and present of La Giudecca, double back along the waterfront and then turn down the Fondamenta del Rio di Sant'Eufemia; a circuitous stroll from Campo di San Cosma (where the ex-church of SS Cosma e Damiano, after years of dereliction, has been converted into a centre for small-scale businesses) to the Rio Ponte Lungo will take you through the core of Giudecca's former manufacturing district. The interior of the island on the other side of the Rio Ponte Lungo is not so densely built up, with a fair amount of open space (even vegetable gardens) around the Redentore and the hulk of Santa Croce church (built c.1510 and long ago deconsecrated). Frustratingly, hardly any of La Giudecca's alleyways lead down to the lagoon on the south side; if you want a view across the water in that direction, it's best to take Calle Michelangelo, which comes onto the main fondamenta between the Zitelle and the youth hostel.

The Lido

The shores of the **Lido** have seen some action in their time: in 1202 a huge French army, assembled for the Fourth Crusade, cooled its heels on the beaches

while its leaders haggled with the Venetians over the terms for transport to the East; Henry III of France was welcomed here in 1574 with fanfares and triumphal monuments made in his honour; and every year, for about eight centuries, there was the hullaballoo of Venice's **Marriage to the Sea** or *Sposalizio*.

This ritual, the most operatic of Venice's state ceremonials, began as a way of commemorating the exploits of Doge Pietro Orseolo II, who on Ascension Day of the year 1000 set sail to subjugate the pirates of the Dalmatian coast. (Orseolo's standard, by the way, featured possibly the first representation of what was to become the emblem of Venice – the Lion of Saint Mark with its paw on an open book.) According to legend, the ritual reached its definitive form after the Venetians had brought about the reconciliation of Pope Alexander III and Frederick Barbarossa in 1177; the grateful Alexander is supposed to have given the doge the first of the gold rings with which Venice was symbolically married to the Adriatic. It's more likely that the essential components of the ritual – the voyage out to the Porto di Lido in the *Bucintoro* with an escort of garlanded vessels, the dropping of the ring into the brine "In sign of our true and perpetual dominion", and the disembarkation for Mass at the church of San Nicolò al Lido – were all fixed by the middle of the twelfth century. Nowadays the mayor, patriarch and a gaggle of other VIPs annually enact a sad facsimile of the grand occasion. And in case you're thinking of launching a salvage operation for all those gold rings, a fifteenth-century traveller recorded – "After the ceremony, many strip and dive to the bottom to seek the ring. He who finds it keeps it for his own, and, what's more, lives for that year free from all the burdens to which dwellers in that republic are subject."

In the twelfth century the Lido was an unspoilt strip of land, and it remained so into the nineteenth century. Byron used to gallop his horses across the fields

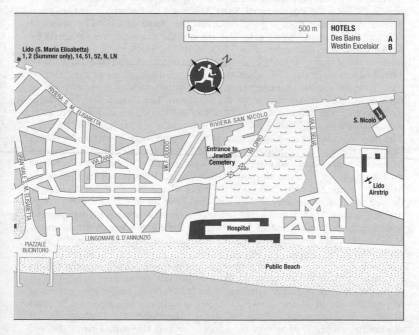

of the Lido every day, and as late as 1869 Henry James could describe the island as "a very natural place". Before the nineteenth century was out, however, it had become the smartest **bathing resort** in Italy, and although it's no longer as chic as it was when Thomas Mann installed von Aschenbach, the central figure of *Death in Venice*, as a guest at the Lido's *Grand Hotel des Bains*, there's little room on its beaches in high summer.

The five-star hotels that stand shoulder to shoulder along the seafront will charge you a ludicrous fee to rent one of their beach hutches for the day, and would like you to believe that you have to pay them for the privilege of merely stepping onto the portion of sand that they overlook. However, during the 2007 film festival actor Rupert Everett was evicted from a prime spot, having spread his towel without opening his wallet, and he duly complained to the authorities, who upheld his claim that the beach should be accessible to all. So you can in theory paddle and sunbathe wherever you like, but if you lack the chutzpah of Mr Everett you may well feel more comfortable on the **public beaches** at the northern and southern ends of the island – but bear in mind that this stretch of the Adriatic isn't one of the cleanest. (The traffic, incidentally, is another health hazard of the Lido. Just as the Venetians were once regarded as the worst horse-riders in Italy, they are now ranked as its most inept drivers.) The northern beach is twenty minutes' walk from the vaporetto stop at Piazzale Santa Maria Elisabetta; the southern one, right by the municipal golf course, necessitates a bus journey from the Piazzale, and is consequently less of a crush.

The monuments of the Lido

The green-domed Santa Maria della Vittoria might be the most conspicuous Lido monument on the lagoon side of the island, but at close quarters it's revealed as a thoroughly abject thing. In fact, in the vicinity of the Piazzale one building alone – the **Fortezza di Sant'Andrea** – is of much interest, and you have to admire that from a distance, across the Porto di Lido. The principal defence of the main entrance to the lagoon, the Fortezza was designed by **Sanmicheli**; work began on it in 1543, in the face of some scepticism as to whether the structure would be strong enough to support the Venetian artillery. The doubters were silenced when practically all the cannons in the Arsenale were brought out to the Fortezza and fired simultaneously from its terraces, with no harmful effects except to the eardrums. The church and Franciscan monastery of **San Nicolò**, from where you get a good view of the Fortezza, were founded in 1044, when there wasn't so much as a brick wall in the area. The doge and his entourage used to visit this church twice a year: on Ascension Day, after the aquatic wedding service, and on the feast day of St Nicholas of Myra (aka Santa Claus), whose body, so the Venetians claimed, had rested here since it was stolen from the Norman port of Bari in 1099. In fact the theft never happened – the Venetian raid on Bari was a classic piece of disinformation, devised to score points off the Normans, and the grand display on the saint's day was a propagandist sham. The present church is notable for its splendid seventeenth-century choir stalls, featuring a multitude of scenes from the life of St Nicholas, and a few scraps of mosaic that have survived from the eleventh-century building.

A stroll along the nearby Via Cipro (facing the San Nicolò vaporetto stop) will bring you to the entrance to Venice's **Jewish cemetery** (guided tours in English May–Oct 2nd & 4th Sun of month 3.30pm, €8.50; reservations at Museo Ebraico or phone ☎041.715.359), which was founded in 1386 and in places has fallen into eloquent decay. Adjoining is a Catholic burial ground, in a corner of which have been stacked the stones from the old

Protestant cemetery, ploughed over in the 1930s to make more room for the Lido's tiny airstrip.

Towards the southern end of the seafront road are two buildings which, with the fire station on the Rio di Ca' Fóscari, constitute Venice's main examples of Fascist architecture – the **Palazzo del Cinema** and the former Casinò, which is now used as a conference centre.

From the Lido to Chioggia

The trip across the lagoon to **Chioggia** is a more protracted business than simply taking the land bus from Piazzale Roma, but it will give you a bracing dose of salt air and an insight into the precarious balance between the sea and the lagoon. From Gran Viale Santa Maria Elisabetta – the main street from the Lido landing stage to the sea front – the more or less hourly #11 bus goes down to **Alberoni**, where it drives onto a ferry for the five-minute hop to Pellestrina; the 10km to the southern tip of Pellestrina are covered by road, and then you switch from the bus to a steamer for the 25-minute crossing to Chioggia. The entire journey takes about eighty minutes and is covered by ACTV travel cards, but be sure to check the timetable carefully at Gran Viale Santa Maria Elisabetta, because not every #11 goes all the way to Chioggia. The quickest way **back to Venice** is by bus from the Duomo or Sottomarina to Piazzale Roma, but it's a dispiriting drive, is only about twenty minutes quicker than the island-hop route, and ACTV passes are not valid, as this is an extra-urban bus service.

Malamocco and Pellestrina

The fishing village of **Malamocco**, about 5km into the expedition, is the successor of the ancient settlement called Metamauco, which in the eighth century was the capital of the lagoon confederation. In 810 the town was taken by **Pepin**, son of Charlemagne, and there followed one of the crucial battles in Venice's history, when Pepin's fleet, endeavouring to reach the islands of Rivoalto (forerunner of Venice), became jammed in the mudbanks and was swiftly pounced upon. After the battle the capital was promptly transferred to the safer islands of Rivoalto, and in 1107 the old town was destroyed by a tidal wave. Rebuilt Malamocco's most appealing feature – the church's scaled-down replica of the Campanile of San Marco – can be seen without getting off the bus. Incidentally, Malamocco provides one of the bloodier footnotes of Venetian history – the **Canal Orfano**, off the Malamocco shore, was the spot where some of those condemned by the Council of Ten were bound, gagged, weighted and thrown overboard by the executioner. (If you take the vaporetto to San Lazzaro you pass along a section of it.)

The most ferocious defenders of the lagoon in the war against Pepin came from the small island of **Poveglia**, just off Malamocco. Once populous enough to have a practically independent administration, it suffered greatly in the war against Genoa (see p.371) and went into a steep decline immediately after, becoming little more than a fort. For much of the last century it was a hospital island, but since the closure of the hospital in the late 1960s it has been abandoned.

Fishing is the mainstay of life in the village of **Pellestrina**, which is strung out along nearly a third of the 10km of the next island. There's one remarkable old structure here, but you get the best view of it as the boat crosses to Chioggia. This is the **Murazzi**, the colossal walls of Istrian boulders, 4km long and 14m thick at the base, which were constructed at the sides of the Porto di Chioggia to protect Venice from the battering of the sea. The maintenance of the water level in the lagoon has always been a preoccupation of Venetian life: very early in the city's development, for example, the five gaps in the *lidi* (the Lido–Chioggia sandbars) were reduced to the present three to strengthen the barrier against the Adriatic and to increase the dredging action of the tides through the three remaining *porti*. In time a special state official, the Magistrato alle Acque, was appointed to supervise the management of the lagoon, and the Murazzi were the last major project undertaken by the Magistrato's department. Devised as a response to the increased flooding of the early eighteenth century, the Murazzi took 38 years to build, and remained unbreached from 1782 (the year of their completion) until the great flood of November 1966. In recent years the beaches of Pellestrina have been widened and raised to lessen the force of the action of the sea, but the biggest flood-prevention project involves the installation of submersible floodgates at the inlets of the Lido, Malamocco and Chioggia (see p.396).

Chioggia

Once a Roman port, then in the eleventh and twelfth centuries a major producer of salt, **Chioggia** secured its place in the annals of Venetian history in 1379, when it became the scene of the most serious threat to Venice since Pepin's invasion, as the Genoese, after copious shedding of blood on both sides, took possession of the town. Venice at this time had two outstanding admirals: the first, **Vettor Pisani**, was in prison on a charge of military negligence; the second, **Carlo Zeno**, was somewhere off in the East. So serious was the threat to the city that Pisani was promptly released, and then put in command of the fleet that set out in December – with the doge himself on board – to blockade the enemy. Zeno and his contingent sailed over the horizon on the first day of the new year and there followed months of siege warfare, in the course of which the Venetian navy employed shipboard cannons for the first time. (Casualties from cannonballs were as high on the Venetian side as on the Genoese, and some crews refused to operate these suicidal weapons more than once a day.) In June 1380, with medieval Chioggia in ruins, the enemy surrendered, and from then until the arrival of Napoleon the Venetian lagoon remained impregnable.

Modern Chioggia is the second-largest settlement in the lagoon after Venice, and one of Italy's busiest fishing ports. With the exception of a single church, you can see everything worth seeing in an hour's walk up and down the **Corso del Popolo**, the principal street in Chioggia's gridiron layout (the plan is probably a Roman inheritance). The exception is the church of **San Domenico**, which houses Carpaccio's *St Paul*, his last known painting, plus a couple of pictures by Leandro Bassano; you get to it by taking the bridge to the left of the Chioggia landing stage and going straight on until you can't go any further.

The boat sets you down at the **Piazzetta Vigo**, at the head of the Corso. The locals are reputedly touchy about the excuse for a lion that sits on top of the column here, a beast known to the condescending Venetians as the Cat of Saint Mark. Only the thirteenth-century campanile of the church of **San Andrea** (rebuilt in 1743) is likely to catch your eye before the street widens at the **Granaio**, a grain warehouse built in 1322 but spoiled by nineteenth-century restorers; the facade relief of the *Madonna and Child* is by Sansovino. Behind the

The Itinerario Laguna Sud

The wilder reaches of the southern lagoon can be explored on the day-long **Itinerario Laguna Sud** that's operated by Agenzia Turistica di Navigazione Laguna Sud (ⓦ www.atnlagunasud.it) from Valle Cornio, near the village of Campagna Lupia, 22km along the main road from Mestre and Chioggia. Using semi-open **boats** similar to vaporetti, the excursion wends its way through labyrinthine channels and islets where more or less **traditional fishing** methods are still employed, and makes numerous stop-offs along the way, including one at a *valle di pesce* (a kind of fish farm) and another at **Casone Valle Zappa**, a slightly surreal island house with a tower that can be climbed for some magnificent views. The **fauna** of the lagoon is surprisingly rich: you can expect to see harriers, buzzards, pied avocets, grebes, egrets and several different species of heron, and in the narrower reed-lined channels there's every chance of spotting a coypu or even a freshwater turtle. (Staff give megaphone explanations at various points, usually in Italian, with English translation on request.) At lunchtime the boat stops for three hours at **Pellestrina**, where a five-minute stroll will take you to the beach on the Adriatic side of the island. The afternoon voyage passes clusters of raised **fishing huts** before re-entering the middle of the lagoon by way of the deep main channel used by tankers bound for the industrial port of Marghera. After another series of meanderings, the boat returns at around 6pm to Cornio, where passengers are given a snack (the only food provided by ATN).

The Itinerario Blu (€32; 6–12yr-olds €24; under 6s free) runs on Sundays (sometimes Saturdays, depending on demand) from March 15–Oct 15; pre-booking is essential on ☏ 041.467.147 or info@atnlagunasud.it. Check-in is 9am for a 9.30am departure. ACTV bus #80E leaves Piazzale Roma at 7.25am; there's also one at 8.25am, but as the journey takes around half an hour, and it's a ten-minute walk down a signposted lane to ATN, there's a risk that this one will get you to Valle Cornio a little later than check-in. Ask the driver to let you off at the request-only stop Canale Piccolo; the bus back in the evening leaves at half past the hour from the request stop opposite.

Granaio is the **fish market**; open for business every morning except Monday, it's a treat for gourmet and marine biologist alike.

In the Piazzetta Venti Settembre, immediately after the town hall, there's the church of the **Santissima Trinità**, radically altered in 1703 by Andrea Tirali and almost perpetually shut – the Oratory, behind the main altar, has an impressive ceiling set with paintings by followers of Tintoretto. **San Giacomo Apostolo**, a bit further on, has a sub-Tiepolo ceiling by local boy Il Chiozzotto, and a much venerated fifteenth-century Venetian painting known as the *Madonna della Navicella*. Soon you pass a house once occupied by the family of Rosalba Carriera and later by Goldoni, and then, on the opposite side of the road, just before the duomo, the **Tempio di San Martino**, built immediately after the war of 1380. It's rarely open except for exhibitions.

The **Duomo** was the first major commission for **Longhena**, who was called in to design a new church after the previous cathedral was burned down in 1623; the detached fourteenth-century campanile survived the blaze. The chapel to the left of the chancel contains half a dozen good eighteenth-century paintings, including one attributed to Tiepolo; on all but the brightest days they're virtually invisible, a drawback that the over sensitive might regard as a blessing in view of the subjects depicted – *The Torture of Boiling Oil, The Torture of the Razors, The Beheading of Two Martyrs*, and so on.

Buses run from the duomo to **Sottomarina**, Chioggia's down-market answer to Venice's Lido. On the beaches of Sottomarina you're a fraction closer to nature than you would be on the Lido, and the resort does have one big plus

– after your dip you can go back to the Corso and have a fresh seafood meal that's cheaper than any you'd find in Venice's restaurants.

San Lazzaro degli Armeni and the minor islands

No foreign community has a longer pedigree in Venice than the Armenians. Their position in the economy of the city, primarily as tradesmen and money-lenders, was secure by the end of the thirteenth century, and for around five hundred years they have had their own church within a few yards of the Piazza, in the narrow Calle degli Armeni (see p.81). The Armenians are far less numerous now than formerly, and the most conspicuous sign of their presence is the Armenian island by the Lido, **San Lazzaro degli Armeni** (entry by guided tour; daily June–Sept 3pm, Oct–May 3.25pm; €6), identifiable from the city by the onion-shaped summit of its campanile. The connecting #20 *motoscafo* leaves San Zaccaria fifteen minutes before the tour starts and returns within ten minutes of the end. Occasionally conferences preclude visits, in which case a notice is posted at the *motoscafo* stop.

From the late twelfth century to the beginning of the seventeenth the island was a leper colony – hence *Lazzaro*, Lazarus being the patron saint of lepers – but the land was disused when in 1717 an Armenian monastery was founded here by one Manug di Pietro. Known as **Mekhitar** ("The Consoler"), he had been driven by the Turks from the religious foundation he had established with Venetian aid in the Peloponnese. Within a few years the monks of San Lazzaro earned a wide reputation as scholars and linguists, a reputation that has persisted to the present. Today, Vienna has the only community outside Armenia that can compare to Venice's as a centre of Armenian culture. (If you're wondering how the Armenian monastery escaped suppression by Napoleon, it's allegedly connected with the presence of an indispensable Armenian official in Napoleon's secretariat.)

▲ San Lazzaro degli Armeni

Tours are conducted by one of the resident monks, and you can expect him to be trilingual, at least. The tour begins in the turquoise-ceilinged church, in which you'll be given a brief introduction to the culture of Armenia in general and the San Lazzaro Armenians in particular – whereas the Armenian Church is Orthodox, San Lazzaro is an Armenian Catholic foundation, which means it follows the Roman liturgy but is not subject to the authority of the pope. Reflecting the encyclopedic interests of its occupants, the monastery is in places like a whimsically arranged museum; at one end of the old **library**, for example, a mummified Egyptian body is laid out near the sarcophagus in which it was found (the sarcophagus was made for a different occupant), while at the other is a teak and ivory throne that once seated the governor of Delhi, and a Sanskrit Buddhist manuscript. The monastery's collection of precious manuscripts and books – the former going back to the fifth century – is another highlight of the visit, occupying a modern rotunda in the heart of the complex.

Elsewhere you'll see antique metalwork, extraordinarily intricate Chinese ivory carvings, pieces of Roman pottery, a gallery of paintings by Armenian painters, a ceiling panel by the young Giambattista Tiepolo, and Canova's figure of Napoleon's infant son, which sits in a corner of the book-lined chamber in which Byron studied while lending a hand with the preparation of an Armenian–English dictionary – it took him just six months to acquire a working knowledge of the language, it's said. The tour might also take you into a small museum dedicated to Mekhitar (featuring the scourging chain found on his body after his death), but will certainly end at the monastery's shop. A polyglot press was founded on San Lazzaro in 1789 and an Armenian press is still administered from here, although since 1992 the printing – of everything from books to wine labels – has been done out at Punta Sabbioni. If you're looking for an unusual present to take home, you could buy something here: the old maps and prints of Venice are a bargain.

The "Hospital Islands"

San Lazzaro is the only minor island of the southern lagoon that's of interest to tourists. The boat out to San Lazzaro calls at **La Grazia**, successively a pilgrims' hostel, a monastery and now a hospital, and **San Servolo**, once one of the most important Benedictine monasteries in the region (founded in the ninth century), then a hospital for the insane, then the home of the Council of Europe's School of Craftsmanship, and now the base of Venice International University, a study centre administered by universities in Italy, Japan, Germany and the US. From time to time the university stages art exhibitions on the island. **San Clemente**, to the south of La Grazia, was another hospital island until 1992, when it was closed down. After a period as a refuge for Venice's stray cats, it now supports one of the city's newest super-plush hotels, the *San Clemente Palace*. A similar conversion has happened on nearby **Sacca Sessola**, whose tuberculosis sanatorium has been remodelled as the *Sofitel Venezia*. Until the mid-seventeenth century there was a monastery on **Santo Spirito**, with a church redesigned by Sansovino, but when the order was suppressed most of its treasures, including paintings by Titian, were sent to the Salute church on the Canal Grande, where they can now be seen.

Lazzaretto Vecchio (south of San Lazzaro) was the site of a pilgrims' hostel from the twelfth century, then took a place in medical history when, in 1423, it became Europe's first permanent isolation hospital for plague victims. A new museum is currently being built on the island; called the Museo Archeologico della Città e della Laguna di Venezia, it will concentrate on the development of urban settlement within the lagoon, and is scheduled to be completed in 2010. Progress has been hampered, though, by the discovery of mass graves below the building site. The excavation of these graves hit the headlines in March 2009, when a skeleton with a brick crammed between its jaws was found in a pit for victims of the plague of 1576. It was once a widespread belief that the plague was spread by vampires, and that vampires, after interment, revived themselves by feeding on neighbouring corpses, a process that could be stopped only by forcing something inedible into their mouths. In the words of Matteo Borrini, an anthropologist from the University of Florence, the brick-eating skeleton of **Lazzaretto Vecchio** "is the first time that archaeology has succeeded in reconstructing the ritual of exorcism of a vampire".

Listings

Listings

Accommodation

D emand for holiday accommodation in Venice outstrips supply to so great a degree that this city is the most expensive in western Europe, with some one-star hotels charging in excess of €150 for a double room in high season. What's more, the **high season** here is longer than anywhere else in the country – it is officially classified as running from March 15 to November 15 and then from December 21 to January 6, but many places don't recognize the existence of a low season any more. (A few hotels, on the other hand, lower their prices in August, a month in which trade can take a bit of a dip, as every Italian knows that Venice can be hellishly humid and clogged with foreigners during that month, and that many restaurants and bars will be shut for the vacation.)

It's never a good idea to turn up in Venice without reserving your accommodation first, and if you intend to stay here at any time during the official high season (or Carnevale) it's wisest to book your place at least six months in advance. Bear in mind, also, that many hotels – especially the smaller ones – require you to stay for a minimum of two or three nights in high season. If your first-choice hotel is fully booked, your next best option is an Internet search – it's not unknown for online agencies such as Ⓦ www.alfabookings.com, Ⓦ www.venicehotel.com, Ⓦ www.booking.com or Ⓦ www.tobook.com to have rooms available in hotels that are nominally full, and even to offer a discount on the hotel's quoted rate. In addition to these, the tourist office's website (Ⓦ www.turismovenezia.it) gives details of accommodation of all types, while the Venetian Hoteliers' Association (AVA) lists hundreds of hotels at Ⓦ www.veneziasi.it. Finally, should you bowl into town with nowhere to stay, you could call in at one of the AVA **booking offices**: at the **train station** (daily: summer 8am–9pm; winter 8am–7pm); on the **Tronchetto** (daily: 9am–8pm); in the multistorey car park at **Piazzale Roma** (daily: 9am–9pm); and at **Marco Polo airport** (daily: summer 9am–7pm; winter noon–7pm). They only deal with hotels (not hostels or B&Bs) and take a deposit that's deductible from your first night's bill.

Accommodation price codes

Hotels in this guide are classified into nine **price categories**, indicating the range of prices for a **double room**. As the Venice high season is now virtually an all-year phenomenon, the minimum price is rarely on offer – for much of the year, and especially around Christmas and New Year, you should expect to pay something far closer to the upper end of the range.

❶ €100 and above	❹ €201–250	❼ €351–400
❷ €101–150	❺ €251–300	❽ €401–500
❸ €151–200	❻ €301–350	❾ €501 and over

Hotels

Venice has well in excess of two hundred **hotels**, ranging from spartan one-star joints to five-star establishments charging way over €1500 per night for the best double room in high season. What follows is a rundown on the best choices in all categories. Though there are some typical anomalies, the star system is a broadly reliable indicator of quality, but always bear in mind that you pay through the nose for your proximity to the Piazza. So if you want maximum comfort for your money, decide how much you can afford then look for a place outside the San Marco *sestiere* – after all, it's not far to walk, wherever you're staying. **Breakfast** is nearly always included in the room rate; if it isn't, you're best advised to take breakfast in a café, where the quality will probably be better and the price certainly much lower.

In 2000 Italy's laws relating to tourist accommodation were relaxed, which resulted in the opening of several guesthouses called **locande**, and the appearance of a number of private houses offering bed and breakfast (see p.239). The prefix *locanda* doesn't necessarily indicate an inexpensive place: some upmarket hotels use the label to give their image a more homely finish. The majority of *locande*, however, are small family-run establishments, offering a standard of accommodation equivalent to three- or even four-star hotels (24-hour room service is just about the only facility they don't provide), but often at considerably lower cost.

San Marco

See map on pp.42–43.

Ai Do Mori Calle Larga S. Marzo 658 ☎041.520.4817, ⓦ www.hotelaidomori .com. Very friendly, and situated a few paces off the Piazza, this is a top recommendation for budget travellers. The top-floor room has a private terrace looking over the roofs of the Basilica and the Torre dell'Orologio, and is one of the most attractive (and, of course, expensive) one-star rooms in the city. All rooms have their own bathroom. ❶–❸

Ala Campo S. Maria del Giglio 2494 ☎041.520.8333, ⓦ www.hotelala.it. The 85-room three-star *Ala* – now run by *Best Western* – has rooms in both modern and traditional Venetian style, and a perfect location, on a square that opens out onto the mouth of the Canal Grande. Often has good special offers – and the breakfast is above average too. ❷–❻

Al Gambero Calle dei Fabbri 4687 ☎041.522.4384, ⓦ www.locandaalgambero .com. Twenty-six-room three-star hotel in an excellent position a short distance off the north side of the Piazza; many of the rooms overlook a canal that's on the standard gondola route from the Bacino Orseolo. There's a boisterous Franco-Italian bistro on the ground floor. ❷–❻

Art Deco Calle delle Botteghe 2966 ☎041.277.0558, ⓦ www.locandaartdeco.com. This cosy *locanda* has a seventeenth-century palazzo setting, but the interior is strewn with 1930s and '40s objects, and the pristinely white bedrooms have modern wrought-iron furniture. ❶–❸

Bel Sito & Berlino Campo Santa Maria del Giglio 2517 ☎041.522.3365, ⓦ www.hotelbelsito.info. This serviceable hotel, decorated in eighteenth- and nineteenth-century style, is one of the least expensive three-stars in the city. ❷–❹

Casa Petrarca Calle delle Schiavini 4386 ☎041.520.0430, ⓦ www.casapetrarca .com. A very hospitable one-star, one of the cheapest hotels within a stone's throw of the Piazza – but make sure you contact them first, as it only has seven rooms, including a tiny single. No credit cards. ❶–❷

Europa e Regina Corte Barozzi 2159 ☎041.240.0001, ⓦ www.westin.com. A madly expensive five-star establishment (doubles from around €500; best rooms around €1200 in high season), but it commands stunning views from the mouth of the Canal Grande, and its terraces are among the most spectacular viewpoints in the city. ❾

Fiorita Campiello Nuovo 3457 ☎041.523.4754, ⓦ www.locandafiorita.com. Welcoming one-star with just ten rooms, so it's crucial to book well in advance. Rooms are all en suite and decorated in eighteenth-century style, and many are spacious. ❶–❸

Flora Calle Larga XXII Marzo 2283a
☎041.520.5844, ⓦwww.hotelflora.it. This large three-star is very close to the Piazza and has a delightful inner garden. Rooms are beautifully decorated with period pieces, though some are a little cramped. ❷–❻

Gritti Palace S. Maria del Giglio 2467
☎041.794.611, ⓦwww.starwoodhotels.com /grittipalace. One of Venice's most prestigious addresses, reeking of old-regime opulence. No doubles under €300, and in summer a deluxe room costs five times that amount. ❻–❾

Kette Piscina S. Moisè 2053 ☎041.520.7766, ⓦwww.hotelkette.com. A four-star favourite with the upper-bracket tour companies, mainly on account of its central but quiet location, in an alleyway parallel to Calle Larga XXII Marzo. Very good low-season prices, and often has online reductions in high season. ❸–❽

La Fenice et des Artistes Campiello Fenice 1936
☎041.523.2333, ⓦwww.fenicehotels.it. Now that *La Fenice* is up and running again, this seventy-room four-star is once more a favoured hangout of the opera crowd, performers and audience alike. Rooms are decorated in muted colours and there's a small garden for breakfast. The best high-season doubles are around €350, but out of season you might pick up a room for less than one third of that price. ❷–❻

Monaco and Grand Canal Calle Vallaresso 1332
☎041.520.0211, ⓦwww.hotelmonaco.it. The ground-floor rooms on the waterfront side of this famous four-star hotel (now owned by the Benetton family) look over to the Salute and are kitted out in full-blown old-world Venetian style, with masses of Murano glass and great swags of brocade. In the annexe – the Palazzo Selvadego – you don't get a view of the water, but the decor is in a lighter nouveau-Mediterranean style, with walls of plain warm colour. Prices can be as low as €150 in winter (the website often has very good reductions), but expect to pay up to four times as much in summer. ❸–❾

🏃 **Novecento Calle del Dose 2683**
☎041.241.3765, ⓦwww .locandanovecento.it. Beautiful, intimate and very welcoming *locanda* with nine individually decorated doubles and luxurious bathrooms. Styling is ethnic/eclectic (furnishings from Morocco, China, Japan

and Egypt), and there's a small courtyard for breakfast. ❸–❺

Orseolo Corte Zorzi 1083 ☎041.520.4827, ⓦwww.locandaorseolo.com. Superb family-run *locanda* overlooking the Orseolo canal, 50m north of Piazza S. Marco. Rooms are spacious and light, breakfasts substantial, and the staff extremely hospitable. Entrance is through a gate in Campo S. Gallo. ❸–❺

San Giorgio Rio Terrà della Mandola 3781
☎041.523.5835, ⓦwww.sangiorgiovenice.com. A friendly and well-located two-star, on the main thoroughfare between Santo Stefano and Sant'Angelo. ❶–❺

San Samuele Salizzada S. Samuele 3358
☎041.522.8045, ⓦwww.albergosansamuele.it. A friendly one-star close to the Palazzo Grassi, with unfussy and individually decorated rooms. ❶–❸

Santo Stefano Campo Santo Stefano 2957
☎041.520.0166, ⓦwww.hotelsantostefano venezia.com. Well-maintained eleven-room three-star hotel on one of the city's largest squares. As Is so often the case in Venice, the rooms aren't exactly capacious, but prices are good for this grade and location. ❷–❻

Dorsoduro

See map on pp.94–95.

🏃 **Accademia Villa Maravege Fondamenta Bollani 1058** ☎041.521.0188, ⓦwww .pensioneaccademia.it. Once the Russian embassy, this three-star seventeenth-century villa has a devoted following, not least on account of its garden, which occupies a promontory at the convergence of two canals, with a view of a small section of the Canal Grande. To be sure of a room, get your booking in at least three months ahead. The hotel also owns two three-star hotels in the middle of San Marco and does try to palm off people with those if the *Villa* is full, but they lack the charm and calm of this hotel. ❷–❻

Agli Alboretti Rio Terrà Foscarini 884
☎041.523.0058, ⓦwww.aglialboretti.com. Friendly and popular family-run three-star, well situated right next to the Accademia. All rooms have a/c and TV, and its high-season prices compare very favourably with those of many rivals. ❷–❹

American Dinesen Fondamenta Bragadin 628
☎041.520.4733, ⓦwww.hotelamerican.com. Nicely located, well-refurbished and

welcoming three-star, with some rooms overlooking the Rio di San Vio, a couple of minutes' stroll from the Accademia. Huge discounts in winter. ❷–❼

Ca' Fóscari Calle della Frescada 3887b ☎041.710.401, ⓦ www.locandacafoscari.com. Quiet and well-decorated one-star, tucked away in a micro-alley near S. Tomà. Just eleven rooms (seven with shower), so it's quickly booked out. ❶–❷

Ca' Maria Adele Rio Terrà dei Catecumeni 111 ☎041.520.3078, ⓦ www .camariaadele.it. Five of the twelve rooms in this very upmarket *locanda* are so-called "theme rooms", with every item designed to enhance a particular atmosphere – the Sala Noir, for example, is a "voluptuous and hot" creation in cocoa and spice tones. Others include the "Oriental" and the "Moorish" rooms. The non-themed accommodation is less artfully conceived (and a lot cheaper), but spacious and very comfortable. The standard tariffs are steep, but online discounts can bring the price down by as much as fifty percent. ❻–❾

Ca' Pisani Rio Terà Foscarini 979a ☎041.240.1411, ⓦ www.capisanihotel.it. This glamorous 29-room four-star, just a few metres from the Accademia, created quite a stir when it opened in 2000, partly because of its location, on the opposite side of the Canal Grande from its top-echelon peers, but chiefly because of its high-class retro look. Taking its cue from the style of the 1930s and '40s, the *Ca' Pisani* makes heavy use of dark wood and chrome, a refreshing break from the Renaissance and Rococo flourishes that tend to prevail in Venice's upmarket establishments. ❸–❾

DD 724 Ramo da Mula 724 ☎041.277.0262, ⓦ www.thecharminghouse.com. In a city awash with nostalgia, the cool high-grade modernist style of this *locanda*, right by the Guggenheim, comes as a refreshing change. It has just seven rooms, each of them impeccably cool and luxurious – and not a Murano chandelier in sight. As you'll see on the website, the same team runs a couple of other similarly sleek properties: a palazzo by Santa Maria Formosa, containing four suites; and a single apartment close to *DD 724*. ❸–❽

La Calcina Záttere ai Gesuati 780 ☎041.520.6466, ⓦ www.lacalcina.com. Charismatic and comparatively inexpensive three-star hotel in the house where Ruskin wrote much of *The Stones of Venice*. From the more expensive rooms you can gaze across to the Redentore, a church that gave him apoplexy. All rooms have parquet floors (unusual in Venice), and no TV or minibar – a management decision indicative of the desire to maintain the building's character. Its restaurant (see p.246) is good too. ❷–❺

Locanda San Barnaba Calle del Traghetto 2785 ☎041.241.1233, ⓦ www.locanda -sanbarnaba.com. Exceptionally pleasant and nicely priced three-star hotel right by the Ca' Rezzonico. Well-equipped rooms – some have eighteenth-century frescoes, and one has a really enormous bath. ❷–❹

Messner Rio Terrà dei Catacumeni 216 ☎041.522.7443, ⓦ www.hotelmessner.it. In an excellent, quiet location close to the Salute vaporetto stop, the two-star *Messner* has modern, smart rooms and is run by friendly staff. Some of the rooms are in an annexe round the corner from the smaller but more appealing main building. ❷–❸

Montin Fondamenta di Borgo 1147 ☎041.522.7151, ⓦ www.locandamontin.com. The *Montin* is known principally for its upmarket and once-fashionable restaurant; few people realize that it offers some of Venice's best budget accommodation. Only eleven rooms, three of them without private bathroom; the best rooms are spacious and balconied. ❶–❸

Pausania Fondamenta Gherardini 2824 ☎041.522.2083, ⓦ www.hotelpausania.it. This quiet, comfortable and friendly three-star has a fine location very close to San Barnaba church, just five minutes from the Accademia; very good low-season offers – and a nice garden too. ❶–❺

Tivoli Crosera S. Pantalon 3838 ☎041.524.2460, ⓦ www.hoteltivoli.it. This two-star is the biggest low-priced hotel in the immediate vicinity of the Frari and S. Rocco, and often has space when the rest are full. ❶–❸

San Polo and Santa Croce

See map on pp.114–115.

Al Sole Fondamenta Minotto, Santa Croce 136 ☎041.244.0328, ⓦ www.alsolehotels.com. Fifty-room three-star hotel in a gorgeous Gothic palazzo. Rooms vary in price enormously, with a few "superior" rooms (with canal view) at around twice the cost of a standard double. Breakfast is taken in the large inner garden. ❶–❼

Alex Rio Terrà Frari, San Polo 2606 ☎041.523.1341, ⓦwww.hotelalexinvenice.com. A long-standing budget travellers' favourite, this one-star has been run by the same family since the 1970s; most of the rooms are large and bright, and those with shared bathroom are astoundingly inexpensive. No credit cards. **❶–❷**

Ca' Arco Antico Calle del Forno, San Polo 1451 ☎041.241.1227, ⓦwww.arcoanticovenice.com. Owners Gianfranco and Marco have done a fine job of making this eight-room guesthouse an attractive mix of traditional and modern. With big rooms, great location and excellent breakfasts (a rarity in itself), *Ca' Arco Antico* offers some of the best budget-range accommodation in the city. **❶–❹**

Ca' San Giorgio Salizada del Fontego dei Turchi 1725, Santa Croce ☎041.275.9177, ⓦwww.casangiorgio.com. Exposed timber beams and walls of raw brick advertise the age of the Gothic palazzo that's occupied by this fine little *locanda*, while the bedrooms are tastefully and very comfortably furnished in quasi-antique style. The gorgeous top-floor suite has its own rooftop terrace. **❶–❹**

Casa Peron Salizzada S. Pantalon, Santa Croce 84 ☎041.710.021, ⓦwww.casaperon.com. A plain, very cheap and congenial one-star in the heart of the university district, very close to San Rocco and the Frari. Most rooms have showers, but few have their own toilet. **❶–❷**

Falier Salizzada S. Pantalon, Santa Croce 130 ☎041.710.882, ⓦwww.hotelfalier.com. Neat and sprucely renovated little two-star; all nineteen rooms are en suite. **❶–❹**

Marconi Riva del Vin, San Polo 729 ☎041.522.2068, ⓦwww.hotelmarconi.it. Converted from an inn in the 1930s, this three-star hotel is situated just a few metres south of the Rialto Bridge, and offers a view of the Canal Grande from some of its 26 rooms, all of which retain the charisma of the old building. Substantial online discounts. **❷–❹**

Salieri Fondamenta Minotto, Santa Croce 160 ☎041.710.035, ⓦwww.hotelsalieri.com. Plain but exceptionally friendly ten-room one-star hotel, on a picturesque canalside close to the Tolentini church. Rooms are light and airy, and the best ones (for which you pay a premium) overlook the water. **❶–❸**

Ca' Favretto-San Cassiano Calle della Rosa, Santa Croce 2232 ☎041.524.1768, ⓦwww.sancassiano.it. Beautiful 35-room four-star with some rooms looking across the Canal Grande towards the Ca' d'Oro. Has very helpful staff, a nice courtyard garden and a grand entrance hall. It was once the home of the nineteenth-century painter Giacomo Favretto, and is fitted out in the style of the period. Discounts for stays of three days or more. **❷–❻**

Sturion Calle del Sturion, San Polo 679 ☎041.523.6243, ⓦwww.locandasturion.com. This immaculate eleven-room three-star has a very long pedigree – the sign of the sturgeon (*sturion*) appears in Carpaccio's *Miracle of the True Cross at the Rialto Bridge* (in the Accademia). It's on a wonderful site overlooking the Canal Grande at the Rialto, and is run by an exceptionally welcoming management. Visitors with mobility difficulties should look elsewhere, however, as the hotel is at the top of three flights of stairs and has no lift. In low season, the rooms with no canal view are a steal. **❷–❻**

Cannaregio

See map on pp.140–141.

Abbazia Calle Priuli 68 ☎041.717.333, ⓦwww.abbaziahotel.com. One of Cannaregio's most restful hotels, the light-filled *Abbazia* occupies a former Carmelite monastery (the monks attached to the Scalzi still live in a building adjoining the hotel), and provides three-star amenities without losing its air of quasi-monastic austerity. There's a delightful garden too, and the staff are exceptionally helpful. **❶–❺**

Adua Lista di Spagna 233/a ☎041.716.184, ⓦwww.aduahotel.com. Thirteen-room two-star with friendly management, benign prices and a choice of rooms with private or shared bathroom. One of the best hotels in an area where too much of the accommodation is below standard. **❶–❸**

Al Gobbo Campo S. Geremia 312 ☎041.715.001, ⓦwww.albergoalgobbo.it. Rather more comfortable than most of its fellow one-stars on the adjacent Lista di Spagna; the better rooms overlook an attractive small garden. **❶–❷**

Antico Doge Sottoportego Falier 5643 ☎041.241.1570, ⓦwww.anticodoge.com. Located within a stone's throw of the church of Santi Apostoli, this very comfortable *locanda* occupies part of the palace that

once belonged to the disgraced doge Marin
Falier. ❷–❺

🏃 **Bernardi Semenzato** Calle dell'Oca 4366
⏂041.522.7257, ⌨www.hotelbernardi
.com. Very well priced two-star hidden in a
tiny alleyway close to Campo S. Apostoli,
with immensely helpful owners who speak
excellent English. Has singles for as little as
€50 (with shared bathroom). ❶–❷

Casa Martini Calle del Magazen 1314
⏂041.717.512, ⌨www.casamartini.it.
Occupying the upper two storeys of a
house that has belonged to the owner's
family since 1700, this recently refurbished
locanda is especially good value in low
season; the cheaper rooms are not large,
but the "superior" doubles are a generous
size, and there's a nice breakfast terrace

Del Ghetto Campo del Ghetto Novo 2892
⏂041.275.9292, ⌨www.locandadelghetto.net.
Friendly six-room *locanda* in the heart of the
Ghetto. Recently modernized a/c rooms are
plainly but comfortably furnished, and have
wooden floors and old beams. Kosher
breakfast. ❶–❸

Giorgione Calle Larga dei Proverbi 4587
⏂041.522.5810, ⌨www.hotelgiorgione.com.
This plush four-star, not far from the Rialto
bridge, has a more personal touch than
many of the city's upmarket hotels – it has
been run by the same family for many
generations. Amenities include a quiet
garden and a pool table, and some of the
76 well-equipped rooms have a small
private terrace. Free tea and coffee served
in lounge in the afternoon. Big discounts
online. ❷–❺

🏃 **Locanda Ai Santi Apostoli** Strada Nova
4391a ⏂041.521.2612, ⌨www
.locandasantiapostoli.com. Occupying the top
floor of an ancient palazzo opposite the
Rialto market, this ten-room three-star has
two lovely rooms overlooking the Canal
Grande – for which you'll pay €100 more
than for the standard doubles. The staff are
very helpful, and the location terrific. ❷–❻

Locanda di Orsaria Calle Priuli dei Cavalletti 103
⏂041.715254, ⌨www.locandaorsaria.com.
Though it's situated close to the train station,
this very well managed eight-room *locanda*
is nonetheless perfectly quiet; all rooms are
en suite and a/c, and larger than is standard
at this end of the price scale. ❶–❹

🏃 **Locanda Leon Bianco** Corte Leon Bianco
5629 ⏂041.523.3572, ⌨www.leonbianco
.it. Friendly and charming three-star in a

superb location not far from the Rialto
Bridge, tucked away beside the decaying
Ca' da Mosto. Only eight rooms, but three of
them overlook the Canal Grande (for which
there's a premium, of course) and most of
the others are spacious and tastefully
furnished in eighteenth-century style – one
even has a huge fresco copied from a
Tiepolo ceiling. ❷–❺

Malibran Corte Milion 5864 ⏂041.522.8028,
⌨www.hotelmalibran.it. Very comfortable,
antique-furnished three-star in an atmospheric cubbyhole of a square where Marco
Polo used to live. ❷–❺

Novo Calle dei Preti 4529 ⏂041.241.1496,
⌨www.locandanovo.it. Basic but popular
locanda in a refurbished palazzo near
Santi Apostoli. The decor might not be
to all tastes (there's a lot of pink and
orange around the place), and it's quite a
haul up four flights of stairs, but most of
the rooms are large, and offer good value
for money. ❶–❸

🏃 **Palazzo Abadessa** Calle Priuli 4011
⏂041.241.3784, ⌨www.abadessa.com.
This gorgeous *residenza d'epoca* is a meticulously restored palazzo behind the church
of Santa Sofia; all eight of its bedrooms
(some of them huge) are nicely furnished
with genuine antiques, and there's a lovely
secluded garden as well. ❸–❼

Santa Lucia Calle della Misericordia 358
⏂041.715.180, ⌨www.hotelslucia.com.
Modern, simply furnished, clean one-star
secreted in a narrow alley off the Lista di
Spagna, well away from the hubbub; has a
garden, which is something of a rarity in this
price range. ❶–❷

Villa Rosa Calle della Misericordia 389
⏂041.718.976, ⌨www.villarosahotel.com. This
31-room one-star is very close to the train
station, but nonetheless quiet; the rooms
have a/c and private bathrooms, and are
bigger than most in this category – the best
even have a small balcony. There is a large
terrace at the back for breakfast. ❶–❸

Central Castello

See map on p.157.

Al Leon Campo SS Filippo e Giacomo 4270
⏂041.277.0393, ⌨www.hotelalleon.com.
A plain but friendly *locanda*, very close to
the Piazza, with eleven pleasantly
furnished a/c rooms – not big, but all en
suite. ❶–❸

Canada Campo S. Lio 5659 ☏ 041.522.9912, ⓦ www.canadavenice.com. Recently renovated, this 25-room two-star is recommendable chiefly for its location, on a tiny square within a couple of minutes of the Rialto Bridge; the rooms are perfectly comfortable if unremarkable – though one does have a roof terrace. **❶–❸**

Caneva Corte Rubbi 5515 ☏ 041.522.8118, ⓦ www.hotelcaneva.com. A well-appointed and peaceful one-star tucked away behind the church of Santa Maria della Fava. Most of the 23 rooms have a/c and private bathrooms. **❶–❷**

Casa Querini Campo San Giovanni Novo 4388 ☏ 041.241.1294, ⓦ www.locandaquerini.com. Friendly *locanda* with six smallish but nicely furnished a/c rooms; it overlooks a tiny campo that's perfectly quiet, even though it's just a few metres from the Piazza. **❷–❹**

🏃 **Casa Verardo** Calle della Chiesa 4765 ☏ 041.528.6127, ⓦ www.casaverardo.it. A fine three-star hotel occupying a nicely refurbished sixteenth-century palazzo between San Marco and Campo Santa Maria Formosa. Twenty-three well-equipped rooms with a breakfast terrace downstairs, a small garden, a sun lounge at the top and another terrace attached to the priciest of the rooms. **❷–❻**

Da Bruno Salizzada S. Lio 5726 ☏ 041.523.0452, ⓦ www.hoteldabruno.it. Rooms in this 32-room three-star are not the biggest you'll get for the money, but the location – on one of the principal routes to the Rialto – is excellent, and prices are low. **❶–❹**

Danieli Riva degli Schiavoni 4196 ☏ 041.522.6480, ⓦ www.luxurycollection.com /danieli. No longer the most expensive hotel in Venice (the *Cipriani* has that title), but no other place can compete with the glamour of the *Danieli*. Balzac stayed here, as did George Sand, Wagner and Dickens. This magnificent Gothic palazzo affords just about the most sybaritic hotel experience on the continent – provided you book a room in the old part of the building, not the modern extension. Rooms with a lagoon view are about €150 more expensive than standard doubles, which start at €720. **❾**

Doni Calle del Vin 4656 ☏ 041.522.4267, ⓦ www.albergodoni.it. Run by the Doni family since the 1940s, this is a plain yet cosy one-star near San Zaccaria, with most of the thirteen rooms overlooking the Rio del

▲ The atrium of the Danieli

Vin or a courtyard. Few of the rooms have a private bathroom, though. **❶–❷**

Locanda La Corte Calle Bressana 6317 ☏ 041.241.1300, ⓦ www.locandalacorte.it. Located close to SS Giovanni e Paolo, this high-class 16-room *locanda* has very welcoming owners and a nice courtyard for breakfast. **❷–❹**

Locanda Vivaldi Riva degli Schiavoni 4152–3 ☏ 041.277.0477, ⓦ www.locandavivaldi.it. *Danieli*-style views at a fraction of the cost, at this stylish, antique-furnished four-star *locanda*, right next door to the Pietà (the *locanda* occupies a portion of a house in which Vivaldi lived). The top-floor breakfast terrace is a treat, and some rooms have whirlpools. **❸–❾**

Paganelli Riva degli Schiavoni 4687 ☏ 041.522.4324, ⓦ www.hotelpaganelli.com. This three-star is a great place to stay, as long as you get one of the rooms on the lagoon side – the ones in the annexe look onto S. Zaccaria, which is a nice enough view, but not really in the same league. Bargain out-of-season rates and hefty high-season discounts are available through the website. **❷–❼**

Ruzzini Palace Campo Santa Maria Formosa 5866 ☏ 041.241.0447, ⓦ www.ruzzinipalace .com. One of Venice's newest luxury hotels, the four-star *Ruzzini* occupies a palace that was completed in the early seventeenth century, and the conversion into a 28-room hotel has preserved much of the period character – most notably the frescoes by Gregorio Lazzarini (Tiepolo's teacher) in the gorgeous Royal Suite. Off-season promotions bring doubles down as low as €120 if booked online; in summer you'll probably pay three times that amount. ❷–❽

Scandinavia Campo S. Maria Formosa 5240 ☎041.522.3507, ⓦwww.scandinaviahotel.com. Sizeable and comfortable three-star, decorated mainly in eighteenth-century style (ie lots of Murano glass and floral motifs). Most of the 34 rooms are a decent size, and several of them overlook Campo Santa Maria Formosa, one of the city's liveliest and best-looking squares. ❷–❻

Eastern Castello

See map on p.176.

Casa Linger Salizzada San Antonin 3541 ☎041.528.5920, ⓦwww.hotelcasalinger.com. Well off the tourist rat-run, this one-star is a decent budget option, as long as you don't mind the climb to the front door – it's at the top of a very steep staircase. Eleven good-size rooms with and without bath. ❶–❷

Gabrielli Sandwirth Riva degli Schiavoni 4110 ☎041.523.1580, ⓦwww.hotelgabrielli.it. Occupying a beautifully converted Gothic palace, the *Gabrielli* offers four-star comforts and *Danieli*-style views across the Bacino di

San Marco for a fraction of the price of the *Danieli*. It also has an attractive little courtyard and a lovely small garden – a rarity in Venice. The website regularly has excellent special offers, such as a lagoon-view double, in high season, for under €300. ❸–❽

🏃 **La Residenza** Campo Bandiera e Moro 3608 ☎041.528.5315, ⓦwww.venicelaresidenza.com. This fourteenth-century palazzo is a mid-budget gem (in Venetian terms), occupying much of one side of a tranquil square just off the main waterfront. It was once a tad pricier than the average two-star, but the rest of the pack have raised their tariffs more in recent years, making *La Residenza* a clear top choice. The recently refurbished rooms are very spacious (rare at this price) and elegant, and the management extremely *simpatico*. Payment by cash is preferred for short stays. ❷–❹

Sant'Anna Corte del Bianco 269 ☎041.528.6466, ⓦwww.locandasantanna.com. Although it's in one of the remotest parts of the city, beyond the far end of Via Garibaldi, this amiable, immaculate and nicely old-fashioned one-star is very popular, so book well in advance. Has rooms with and without bathroom. ❶–❸

Northern Islands

See map on p.209.

Locanda Cipriani Piazza Santa Fosca 29, Torcello ☎041.730.150, ⓦwww.locandacipriani.com. For a dose of rural isolation, you could stay at the tranquil six-roomed inn where Hemingway wrote *Across the River and into the Trees*. Once the day's tourists have gone home, this is just about the quietest spot in the whole lagoon. Rooms are plain but perfectly comfortable, and have no TVs to disrupt the atmosphere. The lowest rate is €130 per person per night; half-board costs an extra €50 each. ❺–❼

Raspo de Ua Piazza Galuppi 560, Burano ☎041.730.095, ⓦwww.alraspodeua.it. The occupants of the other six rooms in this family one-star hotel (above a trattoria of the same name) will probably be the only non locals you'll see around here, once the daily rush has gone back to the city centre. ❷

Southern islands

Cipriani Giudecca 10 ☎041.520.7744, ⓦwww.hotelcipriani.it. See map, pp.216–217.

▲ La Residenza

The priciest and most decadent retreat in Venice – perks include butler service, jacuzzis in every suite, and Olympic-size swimming pool (the only outdoor pool in Venice). Though guests can avail themselves of limitless complimentary motorboat rides over to the city, it's not unknown for people to stay within the confines of the *Cipriani* for their entire visit. With prices starting at €570 per night and rising to more than three times that, you can understand people wanting to get every cent's worth. ❾

Des Bains Lungomare Marconi 17, Lido
☎041.526.5921, ⓦwww.starwooditaly.com. See map, p.220. Thomas Mann stayed here, rubbing shoulders with the continent's vacationing aristocracy as he crafted *Death in Venice*. Set in its own park, this four-star Art Deco extravaganza has almost 200 rooms (doubles from around €200 up to €900) and, of course, a prime slab of the Lido beach. Closed mid-Nov to mid-March. ❹–❾

San Clemente Palace Isola di San Clemente
☎041.244.5001, ⓦwww.thi.it. One of Venice's newest super-deluxe hotels is a 200-room behemoth occupying the ex-hospital island of San Clemente. Drawing a lot of its custom from the conference trade, it's not as sybaritic as the *Cipriani*, but it's nowhere near as expensive either, with doubles as low as €310 in winter, rising to €600 in peak season – and with four restaurants and a beauty centre, it doesn't exactly stint on the pampering. It provides guests with a free shuttle service to San Marco too. ❻–❾

Westin Excelsior Lungomare Marconi 41, Lido
☎041.526.0201, ⓦwww.starwooditaly.com. See map, p.220. Built in the 1900s as the world's top resort hotel, the deluxe five-star *Excelsior* is like something devised by Cecil B. de Mille, and is a favourite with film-festival glitterati. Its private beach huts are so well appointed that some people would be perfectly content with one of them as holiday accommodation. Has a few rooms at €250 in low season; top whack is €1000 for a double – or a lot, lot more for suites. Closed mid-Nov to mid-March. ❻–❾

Bed and breakfast

As stipulated by the Italian tourism authorities, a **bed and breakfast** establishment is a private dwelling in which a maximum of three bedrooms are available to paying guests, with a minimum of one shared bathroom for guests' exclusive use. As is always the case, however, nomenclature is not straightforward; some larger guesthouses like to call themselves B&Bs, because they think the label gives them a touch of Anglophone chic. The places listed below are all B&Bs as legally defined; guesthouses are included in the hotel listings. The tourist office has lists of around 150 officially registered B&Bs, and the number is growing with each year. Some of these – as you may expect in a city where you could get away with charging €100 for the privilege of sleeping on a mattress in the attic – are not terribly attractive, but many of them are excellent, offering characterful accommodation at prices that compare very favourably with hotels. For full listings of Venice's B&Bs, go to ⓦwww.turismovenezia.it; ⓦwww.bed-and-breakfast.it is another useful resource.

San Marco

A Le Boteghe Calle delle Botteghe 3438
☎041.523.5366, ⓦwww.aleboteghe.it. ❶–❷
Al Teatro Fondamenta della Fenice 2554
☎041.520.4271, ⓦwww.bedandbreakfastalteatro
.it. ❷–❹
Ca' del Pozzo Calle Lavezzera 2612
☎041.241.3875, ⓦwww.cadelpozzo.com. ❷–❸
Casa de' Uscoli Campo Pisani 2818
☎041.241.0669, ⓦwww.casadeuscoli.com. ❹–❺
Palazzo Duodo Gregolin Ramo Duodo 1014
☎041.522.5832, ⓦwww.palazzoduodo.com. ❷–❺

Dorsoduro

Almaviva House Fondamenta delle Romite
1348 ☎041.241.0669, ⓦwww.palazzopompeo
.com. ❸–❹
Ca' Turelli Fondamenta di Borgo 1162
☎041.523.5094, ⓦwww.caturelli.it. ❶–❸
Casanova ai Tolentini Fondamenta del Gafaro
3515 ☎349.878.2995, ⓦwww.casanova
aitolentini.com. ❶–❸
Fujiyama Calle Lungo San Barnabà 2727a
☎041.724.1042, ⓦwww.bedandbreakfast
-fujiyama.it. ❶–❸

Palazzo dal Carlo Fondamenta di Borgo 1163
ⓣ041.522.6863, ⓦwww.palazzodalcarlo.com. ❸

San Polo and Santa Croce

Al Campaniel Calle del Campaniel 2889
ⓣ041.275.0749, ⓦwww.alcampaniel.com. ❶–❷
Ca' Angeli Calle del Traghetto della Madoneta
1434 ⓣ041.523.2480, ⓦwww.caangeli.it. ❷–❹
Corte 1321 Campiello ca' Bernardi 1321
ⓣ041.522.4923, ⓦwww.corte1321.com. ❷–❹

Cannaregio

Al Palazzetto Calle delle Vele 4057
ⓣ041.275.0897, ⓦwww.guesthouse.it. ❶–❹
Al Saor Ca' d'Oro Calle Zotti 3904a
ⓣ041.296.0654, ⓦwww.alsaor.com. ❶–❷
Antico Portego Rio Terrà Farselli 1414a
ⓣ347.495.8326, ⓦwww.bbanticoportego
.com. ❷–❸
At Home a Palazzo Calle Priuli 3764
ⓣ041.523.5260, ⓦwww.athomeapalazzo
.com. ❷–❹
Ca' Pier Calle Bembo 4357 ⓣ041.724.1057,
ⓦwww.capier.it. ❹–❽

Domus Orsoni Calle dei Vedei 1045
ⓣ041.275.9538, ⓦwww.domusorsoni.it. ❷–❹
Sandra Corte Trapolin 2452 ⓣ041.720.957,
ⓦwww.bbalessandra.com. ❶–❷

Castello

Ai Greci Calle del Magazen 3338
ⓣ340.081.7273, ⓦwww.aigreci.com. ❶–❸
Ai Tagliapietra Salizada Zorzi 4943 ⓣ347.323.3166,
Castello ⓦwww.aitagliapietra.com. ❶–❷
Ca' Furlan Corte San Giovanni di Malta 3257
ⓣ041.241.0338, ⓦwww.cafurlan.it. ❶–❸
Campiello Santa Giustina Calle Due Porte 6499
ⓣ328.0235.737, ⓦwww.campiellogiustina
.com. ❶–❷
Corte Campana Calle del Remedio 4410
ⓣ041.523.3603, ⓦwww.cortecampana.com. ❶–❷
San Marco Fondamenta San Giorgio degli
Schiavoni 3385 ⓣ041.522.7589, ⓦwww
.realvenice.it/smarco. ❶–❷

Giudecca

Casa Eden Corte Mosto 25 ⓣ041.521.2564,
ⓦwww.casaeden.it. ❶–❷

Self-catering apartments

The very high cost of hotel rooms in Venice makes self-catering an attractive option – for the price of a week in a cramped double room in a three-star hotel you could book yourself a two-bedroomed apartment right in the centre of the city. Many package holiday companies have a few Venetian apartments in their brochures, and the tourist office in Venice has an ever-expanding list of landlords on its books (almost 300 of them, at the last count), who charge anything between 200 and 5000 euros per week: these properties can be found through ⓦwww .turismovenezia.it. In addition, the following sites are worth checking out.

Holiday Rentals ⓦwww.holiday-rentals.com. This site – which puts you directly in touch with the owners – features hundreds of properties in Venice and the Veneto.
Italian Breaks ⓦwww.italianbreaks.com. This company has a selection of a couple of dozen apartments in Venice, ranging from a one-bed place near the Fondamente Nuove to a four-bedroomed apartment with views of the Canal Grande.
Venetian Apartments ⓦwww.venice-rentals.com. Venetian Apartments offers more than 100 apartments in the city, ranging from studios at around €900 per week, through 1-, 2-, 3- and 4-bedroomed apartments to extraordinarily sumptuous palazzi on the Canal Grande that will set you back in excess of €10,000. The properties are immaculately

maintained, and the agency provides very friendly back up in Venice itself. It also has an exemplary website, with detailed maps showing the location of each apartment, photographs of virtually every room in each property, ground plans and full rental details.
Venice Apartment ⓦwww.veniceapartment .com. An Italian website with more than 100 properties on its books.
VeniceApartments.org ⓦwww .veniceapartments.org. There are dozens of apartments on this well-structured site .
Visit Venice ⓦwww.visitvenice.co.uk. Two meticulously maintained small houses – Casa Tre Archi and the slightly smaller Casa Battello – in the Ghetto district of Cannaregio; they are remarkably good value, and the owners could not be more helpful.

Venetian palaces

Remarkable houses are to be seen all over Venice, as nearly every parish (ie every island) had its pre-eminent families, and each of these had its own palazzo. (Though not all could afford new houses – by the late sixteenth century, around half the patrician families were tenants.) Because it cuts through so many parishes, and offers the best opportunities for ostentation, the Canal Grande has the majority of the most important surviving palaces.

Ca' Pésaro ▲

Ca' Rezzonico ▼

Methods and materials

One of the attractions of the lagoon for its first settlers was that the water provided security in itself. Fortified stone dwellings were unnecessary here – and would have been impractical on the soft mudbanks. The first houses were made of timber, but soon Venice became a city of **brick**, with stone cladding being used for prestigious buildings, most quarried from the Istrian peninsula, across the Venetian Gulf. **Istrian stone** is a hard white-pink limestone, resistant to water and suited to decorative carving.

From the fourteenth century it became common practice to drive **wooden piles** (*tolpi*) into the substratum of firm clay. Mostly oak or larch, and around 3–5m long, these piles stayed intact as long as they remained submerged, and provided a solid foundation for the thick timber that was laid over them. Onto this base was built a dampcourse of Istrian stone, supporting the brick walls, with a facing of stone if required.

As you'll see, many palaces have cracked walls, but brick and mortar can tolerate a fair degree of shifting, and floor beams are usually closely spaced to prevent localized areas of excessive stress. Flooring is generally brick on the ground floor and wood above, often covered with **terrazzo**, a lime mortar paste into which chippings of coloured stone are inserted, then polished with linseed oil. Terrazzo was a distinctively Venetian feature, as were windows of **Murano glass**: most houses were glazed, at a time when this was the privilege of the wealthy elsewhere. The roofs, of light clay tiles, had big gutters to direct rainwater into **cisterns**: every campo had its cistern, and many palazzi had a private one.

Veneto-Byzantine palaces

The oldest surviving palaces are **Veneto-Byzantine**, a style that was originally two-storey, with storage below and living accommodation upstairs, and steeply arched colonnades across the whole facade, as can be seen in the **Ca' Farsetti** and **Ca' Loredan**, by the Rialto bridge. Another Byzantine feature are the decorative stone panels called **paterae**, some of which were brought back from Constantinople after the Fourth Crusade, though most are later reworkings of the genre. A taste for surface **decoration** – attributable in part to the city's trading ties with the Islamic world – was to prove durable: just as the facades of the Veneto-Byzantine palaces were adorned with carved panels and coloured marble, so the later ones were studded with stone reliefs, and sometimes even frescoed.

▲ Ca' d'Oro

▼ Ca' Farsetti and Ca' Loredan

Gothic palaces

Around the mid-thirteenth century the steep Byzantine arch started to mutate into an arch with a pointed crown, and by the end of the following century the **Venetian Gothic** style – the city's dominant type – had fully evolved, featuring peaked arches on large windows that were often linked with elaborate tracery (the Palazzo Ducale provided a model for this). The windows were clustered together in the centre of the facade between symmetrically placed side-windows, indicating an **interior plan** that had by now reached its definitive form.

The most spectacular examples of Venetian Gothic are the **Ca' d'Oro** and the slightly later **Fóscari and Giustiniani** palaces, whose extravagance reflects the increasing wealth of a city that

Palazzi Giustinian and Ca' Fóscari ▲

Palazzo Vendramin-Calergi ▼

Paterae on the facade of Ca' da Mosto ▼

was now a dominant maritime power with a sizeable terra-firma domain. Palaces at this time were becoming bigger and taller, and the density of housing was increasing to accommodate a population that rose by forty percent in the fifteenth century, to around 140,000.

The Renaissance and after

The Gothic style had a long life in Venice. Typically Renaissance features such as classical rounded arches, classical columns and pedimented windows didn't appear until the sixteenth century: Codussi's Palazzo Loredan (now **Vendramin-Calergi**) is one of the earliest examples. Sansovino's **Palazzo Corner della Ca' Grande** and Sanmichele's **Palazzo Grimani** brought a new scholarly rigour and monumentalism to palazzo design, but the layout of the interior didn't depart much from the traditional tripartite design. Similarly, Baroque palaces are distinguished by the exuberance of their facades rather than any structural innovations. The city's greatest Baroque architect, Baldassare Longhena, was hired by families who had bought their way into the nobility in the late seventeenth century and were keen to make a splash. Colossal buildings such as his **Ca' Rezzonico** and **Ca' Pésaro** certainly did that, but behind the extravagant stonework the layout was still the classic one. The city's last great palace, **Palazzo Grassi**, was built in the middle of the eighteenth century and is the one major anomaly, in that it's planned like a mainland house of the sort designed by Palladio, who was the most influential of all Veneto architects, but never built a house in Venice.

Hostels

Venice has a large HI hostel and a few other hostel-like establishments – most run by religious foundations – offering basic accommodation. Some of the latter are more expensive than one-star hotels and B&Bs; we've listed only the low-cost options. Bona-fide students looking for a room for an extended stay during the summer vacation should check out Ⓦ www.esuvenezia.it, which gives details of rooms in the various accommodation blocks of Venice's university.

Domus Civica Calle Campazzo, San Polo 3082 ☎041.721.103, Ⓦ www.domuscivica.com; see map, pp.114–115. This Catholic women's student hostel is open to travelers of both sexes from mid-June to mid-September. Most rooms are double with running water; showers free; no breakfast; 11.30pm curfew. Around €30 per person per night, with reductions for ISIC and Rolling Venice card holders.

Foresteria Valdese S. Maria Formosa, Castello 5170 ☎041.528.6797, Ⓦ www.foresterlavenezia.it; see map, p.157. Run by Waldensians, this hostel is installed in a wonderful palazzo at the end of Calle Lunga S. Maria Formosa, with flaking frescoes in the rooms and a large communal salon. It has several large dorms, plus bedrooms that can accommodate up to eight people. Reservations by phone only; dorm beds cannot be booked in advance, except by groups. Registration 9am–1pm & 6–8pm. Beds from a little under €25 per night.

Ostello Santa Fosca S. Maria dei Servi, Cannaregio 2372 ☎041.715.775, Ⓦ www.santafosca.com; see map, pp.140–141. Student-run hostel in an atmospheric former Servite convent in a quiet part of Cannaregio, with dorm beds and double rooms, all with shared bathrooms. Check-in 5–8pm; 12.30pm curfew; €20 per person for a dorm bed, €25 for a bed in a shared room. They take bookings one week ahead only, and only by phone; it's essential to book in summer. Open all year except the Christmas period.

Ostello Venezia Fondamenta delle Zitelle, Giudecca 86 ☎041.523.8211, Ⓦ www.ostellovenezia.it. The city's HI hostel occupies a superb location looking over to San Marco, but it's run with a certain briskness. Registration opens at 1.30pm in summer and 4pm in winter. Curfew at 11.30pm, chucking-out time 9.30am. Gets so busy in July and August that reservations must be made by April – it's easiest to book through the website. Breakfast and sheets included in the price – but remember to add the expense of the boat over to Giudecca. No kitchen, but full (and good) meals for around €10. From €21 per dorm bed, breakfast included; HI card necessary, but you can join on the spot.

Camping

There are some unlovely campsites near the airport – better to head out to the outer edge of the lagoon, to the **Litorale del Cavallino**, which stretches from Punta Sabbioni to Jésolo and has around 60,000 pitches, many quite luxurious. Vaporetto #LN, from Fondamente Nove or San Zaccaria to Punta Sabbioni, stops close to the two-star *Miramare*, Lungomare Dante Alighieri 29 (April–Oct; ☎041.966.150, Ⓦ www.camping-miramare.it; €11–16 per tent plus €5–8 per person per night); further away there's the fancier four-star *Marina di Venezia*, Via Montello 6, adjoining the huge new AquaMarina waterpark (May–Sept; ☎041.966.146, Ⓦ www.marinadivenezia.it; €11–23 per tent plus €5–10 per person per night). It's a forty-minute boat trip into the city.

Alternatively, back on the mainland there's a two-star 1000-place site in **Fusina**, at Via Moranzani 93 (all year; ☎041.547.0064). A *Linea Fusina* water-bus links Fusina to the Záttere in central Venice (ACTV tickets not valid), taking 25min, with an hourly service from 8am until around 10pm (late May–Sept), and till around 8pm for the rest of the year. Alternatively, get a bus to Mestre and change for a bus or train.

There are also several sites at **Sottomarina** (see p.225).

Eating and drinking

Not long ago the reliable judges of the Accademia della Cucina ventured that it was "a rare privilege" to eat well in Venice, and there's more than an element of truth to Venice's reputation as a place where mass tourism has produced monotonous menus, cynical service and slapdash standards in the kitchen. Venice has fewer good, moderately priced **restaurants** than any other major Italian city, it has more really bad restaurants than any other, and in some of the expensive establishments you're paying not for a fine culinary creation but for the experience of dining in an expensive Venetian restaurant. However, things have been getting better in recent years, an improvement due in part to the efforts of the Ristorante della Buona Accoglienza, an association of restaurateurs determined to present the best of genuine Venetian cuisine at sensible prices – which in the Venetian context means in the region of €35–40 per person.

A distinctive aspect of the Venetian social scene is the **bácaro** which in its purest form is a **bar** that offers a range of snacks called **cicheti** (sometimes spelled *ciccheti*); usually costing €1–2 per portion, the array will typically include *polpette* (small beef and garlic meatballs), *carciofini* (artichoke hearts), hard-boiled eggs, anchovies, *polipi* (baby octopus or squid), and sun-dried tomatoes, peppers and courgettes cooked in oil. Many *bácari* also produce one or two more substantial dishes each day, such as risotto or seafood pasta. Many bars of this type are long-established places, but in the last decade there's been something of a *bácaro* revival, and you're more likely to find a seating area in these newer establishments. Excellent food is also served at many of Venice's **osterie** (or *ostarie*), the simplest of which are indistinguishable from larger *bácari*, with just three or four tables, while others have sizeable dining areas. Just to make things supremely confusing, some *osterie* have no bar at all; some of these are bars that have evolved into restaurants, while others use the name *osteria* to give the establishment an aura of unpretentiousness and good value. And to further blur the division between bars and restaurants, several of Venice's restaurants have a separate bar area on the street side of the dining room. We've classified our bars and restaurants according to which aspect of the business draws most of the customers, but if you're looking for a simple meal in a particular area of the city, be sure to check both sets of listings. In *bácari* and *osterie* with dining areas, full meals are served at the usual lunch and dinner hours, while snacks are served at the bar throughout the day.

As enticing as the city's bars are its **cafés** and **pasticcerie** (most of which also serve alcohol), where a variety of waistline-threatening delicacies is on offer, and there aren't too many nicer things you can do to your taste buds than hit them with a coneful of home-made Venetian **ice cream**. Stocking up for an alfresco lunch, you'll be spoiled for choice at the stalls of the Rialto and the smaller

markets pitched in a number of Venice's campi, while there's a host of tempting *alimentari* (delicatessens) to supplement supplies.

As elsewhere in Italy, **pizza** is an obvious stand-by if you're watching your budget, but bear in mind that pizza is not a Venetian speciality, and most of the city's pizzerie are poor. A good range of take out pizza slices (*pizza al taglio*) and pies is offered by *Cip Ciap*, across the canal from the west side of Santa Maria Formosa, at Calle Mondo Nuovo 5799 (closed Tues). Other decent choices are the *Antico Forno*, close to the Rialto at Rughetta del Ravano 973 (open daily), and *Arte della Pizza*, a short distance north of San Marcuola in Cannaregio, at Calle de l'Aseo 1896 (closed Mon).

Venetian specialities

Venetian cuisine bears little trace of the city's past as Europe's trading crossroads, when spices from the East were among the most lucrative commodities sold in Venice's markets. Nowadays Venetian food is known for its simplicity, with plain pepper and salt as the principal means of vivifying a meal. **Fish and seafood** dominate the restaurant menus, much of the former being netted in the Adriatic and the rivers and lakes of the mainland, with the latter coming from the lagoon and open sea. (Don't assume, though, that every restaurant in water-bound Venice cooks only fresh fish and seafood; many places use frozen food, so always check the small print of the menu, where, by law, the restaurant has to state if food has come from the freezer: *surgelato* is the word to look for.) Prawns, squid and octopus are typical Venetian antipasti (usually served with a plain dressing of olive oil and lemon), as are Murano crabs and *sarde in saor* (marinated sardines). Dishes like eel cooked in Marsala wine, *baccalà* (salt cod) and *seppioline nere* (baby cuttlefish cooked in its own ink) are other Venetian staples, but the quintessential dish is the **risotto**, made with rice grown along the Po valley. Apart from the seafood variety (*risotto bianco, risotto di mare* or *risotto dei pescatori*), you'll come across risottos that incorporate some of the great range of vegetables grown in the Veneto (notably spinach, asparagus, pumpkin and peas – *bisi* in the local dialect), and others that draw on such diverse ingredients as snails, tripe, quail and sausages.

Venetian **soups** are as versatile as the risottos, with *brodetto* (mixed fish) and *pasta e fagioli* or *fasioi* (pasta and beans) being the most popular kinds. **Polenta** is a recurrent feature of Venetian meals; made by slowly stirring maize flour into boiling salted water, it's served as an accompaniment to a number of dishes, in particular liver (*fegato*), a special favourite in Venice. In season, the red salad leaf *raddichio* – a Veneto speciality – will feature on most menus. **Pastries and sweets** are also an area of Venetian expertise. In addition to the famous **tiramisù**, look out for the thin oval biscuits called *baicoli*, the ring-shaped cinnamon-flavoured *bussolai* (a speciality of Burano), and *mandolato* – a cross between nougat and toffee, made with almonds. The Austrian occupation has left its mark in the form of the ubiquitous *strudel* and the cream- or jam-filled *krapfen* (doughnuts).

Particular foods are traditional to certain **feast days**. During Carnevale you can buy small doughnuts known as *frittelle*, which come plain, *con frutta* (with fruit), *con crema* (confectioner's cream) or *con zabaglione* (which is made out of egg yolks and Marsala). During Lent there's an even greater emphasis on fish, and also on omelettes (*frittata*), often made with shrimps and wild asparagus; lamb is popular at Easter. On Ascension Day it's customary to have pig's trotter, either plain or stuffed, while for the feast of the Redentore (third Sunday in

July) *sarde in saor* or roast duck are in order. Tiny biscuits called *fave* ("beans") fill the *pasticcerie* around All Saints' Day and All Souls' Day (Nov 1 & 2); on the feast of Saint Martin (Nov 11) you get biscuits or heavy quince jelly cut into the shape of the saint on his horse; and on the feast of the Madonna della Salute (Nov 21) it's traditional to have *castradina* (salted smoked mutton). On Christmas Eve many Venetians eat eel, usually grilled, though with variations from island to island; on Christmas Day the traditional dishes are roast turkey, veal, duck or capon.

Restaurants

Virtually every budget restaurant in Venice advertises a set-price **menù turistico**, which can be a cheap way of sampling some Venetian specialities, but the quality and certainly the quantity won't be up to the mark of an **à la carte** meal, and frequently won't even be acceptable. Value for money tends to increase with the distance from San Marco; plenty of restaurants within a short radius of the Piazza offer menus that seem to be reasonable, but you'll probably find the food unappetizing, the portions tiny and the service abrupt. There are two notable concentrations of **good-value restaurants**: around San Barnabà in Dorsoduro, with several recommended places on Calle Lunga San Barnaba; and the area between the Cannaregio canal and Sant'Alvise, with the Ghetto at its centre.

In the following listings, the term "inexpensive" means that you should be able to get a two-course meal with a drink for under €30, including service and *coperto* (cover charge); "moderate" means €30–50; "expensive" means €50–70; and "very expensive" covers the rest. We've supplied the day of the week on which each restaurant is closed (in the vast majority of cases this is Sunday or Monday), but bear in mind that many restaurateurs take their annual holiday in August, and that quite a few places close down on unscheduled days in the dead weeks of winter. In most cases, booking a table is advisable in high season, and you should also be aware that Venetians tend to eat early and that restaurateurs routinely close early if trade is slack, so if you're in town at a quiet time, don't turn up later than 8.30pm, unless you're dining at one of the city's more expensive restaurants, which tend to keep longer hours. Italians hardly ever **tip** more than 10 percent of the bill; if service charge is included (which it increasingly is), it's usual to leave an extra 5 percent or so. One last point: all Italian restaurants and bars are now **non smoking**.

San Marco

See map on pp.42–43.

Al Bacareto Calle Crosera San Samuele 3447 ☎041.528.9336. Tucked away on the north side of Santo Stefano, *Al Bacareto* has been in business here for almost forty years and remains one of the most genuine and welcoming places in the San Marco *sestiere*. In recent years it has been getting smarter and more expensive, but it's still good value, with main courses in the €15–20 range in the evening (prices are lower at lunchtime) – and if you're watching the pennies you can always eat at the bar, where the *cicheti* are outstanding. In summer there are seats outside. Mon–Fri 7.30am–11pm, Sat 7.30am–3pm. Moderate.

Da Carla Sottoportego Corte Contarina 1535a ☎041.523.7855. Hidden down a sottoportego off the west side of Frezzeria, *Da Carla* has a battered old sign that's rather misleading, as this place has quite recently been refashioned as a slick modern *osteria*. The menu is short but the food is always well prepared, and the prices (pasta dishes around €10, main courses under €20) make this one of the best places for a simple meal close to the Piazza. The service – polite and attentive – is far better than average for this part of town as well. Closed Sun. Moderate.

Da Fiore Calle delle Botteghe 3461
℡041.523.5310. Established in the mid-1990s, this popular restaurant offers Venetian cuisine in a classy trattoria-style setting. The anteroom is a nice, small bar that offers good *cicheti* plus a small menu of daily specials – you might pay €15 for a fish dish in the bar section, and €25 for the same thing in the restaurant. Closed Tues. Moderate.

Harry's Bar Calle Vallaresso 1323
℡041.528.5777. Sometimes described as the most reliable of the city's gourmet restaurants (*carpaccio* – raw strips of thin beef – was first created here), though the place's reputation perhaps has more to do with glamour than with cuisine; three courses here will set you back in the region of €130. The bar itself has been fashionable since time immemorial, and is famed in equal measure for its cocktails, Its sandwiches and its insane prices (four teeny sandwiches will set you back around €25). The Bellini – a mix of fresh white peach juice and *prosecco* that's mistakenly thought by many to be a traditional Venetian drink – was invented here too. Daily 10.30am–11pm. Very expensive.

Le Bistrot de Venise Calle dei Fabbri 4685
℡041.523.6651. This place is done up as a facsimile of a wood-panelled French *bistrot*, but the menu is based on old-style Venetian recipes, both for full meals and *cicheti*. You're paying a premium for the location, but the food is usually good, as is the atmosphere, as *Le Bistrot* has become something of a community arts centre, with music and poetry events every Tues evening from Oct to May. The bar closes at 1am, the kitchen around a half-hour earlier. À la carte, you'll pay upwards of €50, but there are good set menus from €35. Daily noon–1am. Expensive.

Osteria-Enoteca San Marco Frezzeria 1610
℡041.528.5242. As you'd expect for a place so close to the Piazza, this classy modern *osteria* is far from cheap (expect to pay €25–30 for your main course), but the prices are comparable to those of many inferior places in the San Marco area – and the wine list is very good. Between lunchtime and dinner you can sip wine at the bar. Mon–Sat noon–11pm. Expensive.

Rosticceria Gislon Calle della Bissa 5424a.
Downstairs it's a sort of glorified snack-bar, serving pizzas and set meals starting at around €12 – the trick is to first grab a place at the tables along the windows, then order from the counter. Good if you need to refuel quickly and cheaply, but can't face a pizza. There's a slightly less rudimentary restaurant upstairs, where prices are considerably higher for no great increase in quality. Daily 9am–9.30pm. Inexpensive.

Dorsoduro

See map on pp.94–95.

Ai Cugnai Piscina del Forner 857
℡041.528.9238. A few metres to the east of the Accademia, this is a popular little trattoria, run by a family of gregarious Venetian senior citizens. Orders are memorized rather than written down, and can become scrambled between table and kitchen, but that's part of the fun – the atmosphere rather than the food is the main draw at this rather erratic establishment, though the cooking can often be good. No cards. Tues–Sun 11am–3pm & 7–10.30pm. Moderate.

Ai Quattro Ferri Calle Lunga S. Barnaba 2754a ℡041.520.6978. A very highly recommended *osteria* just off Campo S. Barnaba with a menu that changes daily but often consists entirely of fish and seafood. Booking essential at all times of year. No credit cards. Mon–Sat 12.30–3.30pm & 7–10.30pm. Moderate.

Arca Calle S. Pantalon 3757 ℡041.524.2236. This dependable pizzeria-trattoria is a favourite with the university students. Closed Sun in winter. Inexpensive to moderate.

Casin dei Nobili Calle Lombardo 2765
℡041.241.1841. Very popular with both locals and tourists, the *Casin* is a large, hospitable and very dependable mid-range trattoria that offers a wide range of fish dishes and home-made pastas. It occupies part of a premises that was once notorious as an upper-class gambling-den-cum-bordello – hence the racy logo. Tues–Sun noon–2.30pm & 7–11pm. Moderate.

Da Silvio Calle S. Pantalon 3747–8
℡041.520.5833. Run by the same family for three decades, the sizeable *Da Silvio* has undergone a complete overhaul recently, and now has a stripped-down metal-and-plastic look. The pizza list is long, and

there's also a menu of fishy trattoria basics – plus a very nice courtyard-garden for open-air dining. Venice has loads of pizzeria-restaurants; few are as good as this one. Closed Sun lunch. Moderate.

Do Farai Calle Cappeller 3278 ☎041.277.0369. Tucked into an alley close to Ca' Rezzonico, *Do Farai* is a fine *osteria*, serving good steaks and other meat dishes, plus excellent seafood and fish – the speciality is a delicious carpaccio of sea bass. In summer it spreads out into the neighbouring campo. Mon–Sat 9am–3pm & 6–10.30pm. Moderate to expensive.

La Bitta Calle Lunga S. Barnaba 2753a ☎041.523.0531. Innovative fare at a welcoming little *osteria* that's remarkable for featuring hardly anything aquatic. Marcellino runs the kitchen while his wife Debora serves and cajoles the guests, offering expert guidance on the impressive wine and grappa list. Delicious cheese platter, served with honey and fruit chutney. Tiny dining room (and garden), so booking is essential. No credit cards. Mon–Sat 6.30–11pm. Moderate.

La Furatola Calle Lunga S. Barnaba 2870a ☎041.520.8594. Classy seafood restaurant, with a big local following. Service can be a little offhand, but the food is consistently very good. It's small, so booking is advisable. Open 12.30–2.30pm & 7.30–10.30pm; closed Thurs. Expensive.

La Piscina Záttere ai Gesuati 780 ☎041.520.6466. Stretching onto the waterfront outside the *Calcina* hotel, to which it's attached, this is one of the most pleasant restaurants in Dorsoduro. The service is excellent, the menu has a far wider range of vegetarian options than the vast majority of restaurants in Venice, and the view of Giudecca from the terrace is wonderful. Closed Mon. Moderate.

L'Avogaria Calle dell'Avogaria 1629 ☎041.296.0491. The presence of *orrechiette* (thick little pasta "ears") on the menu of super-cool *Avogaria* is a clue to the Puglian origins of the proprietors, whose recipes use a fair amount of beef, as well as giving a welcome twist to local seafood (eg prawns marinated in grappa). It's pricy, with main courses around €30, but the quality is consistently high. The minimalist bare-brick dining room and tiny courtyard-garden are further pluses. Mon & Wed–Sun 12.30–3pm & 7.30pm–midnight. Expensive.

Montin Fondamenta di Borgo 1147 ☎041.522.715. One of the most famous restaurants in the city, thanks chiefly to the patronage of artistic luminaries such Pound, Hemingway and Peggy Guggenheim, *Montin* is undoubtedly a charismatic old place, with its painting-covered walls and secluded garden, and some people still rate its kitchen highly. It's no longer one of the best in its price range, but its atmosphere remains alluring. Tues 7.30–10pm, Mon & Thurs–Sun 12.30–2.30pm & 7.30–10pm. Expensive.

Oniga Campo San Barnaba 2852 ☎041.522.4410. Many of Venice's best mid-range restaurants are concentrated in the San Barnabà area, and this relative newcomer to the scene is one of the most successful. It's received some very good press in Italy, though the food is dependable rather than outstanding, but the tone of the place – youthful, friendly and efficient – is always appealing, and the set lunch, at under €20, is a very good deal. Mon & Wed–Sun noon–2.30pm & 7–10.30pm. Moderate.

Pane, Vino e San Daniele Campo Angelo Raffaele 1722 ☎041.523.7456. Not surprisingly, the menu at this attractive backwater *osteria* is dominated by San Daniele *prosciutto*, the finest of all Italian hams – the house speciality is a wooden platter loaded with *prosciutto* and a variety of other uncooked goodies, and it's a prominent ingredient in cooked dishes such as San Daniele gnocchi. The front-of-house bar is also excellent for a snack and a glass of Friulian wine, and there's ample seating on the secluded campo. *Pane, Vino e San Daniele* has been such a hit that a second branch has recently opened, at **Calle Lunga S. Barnaba 2861**. Open 9am–2pm & 4pm–2am; closed Wed.

San Polo and Santa Croce

See map on pp.114–115.

Alla Madonna Calle della Madonna 594 ☎041.5522.3824. Roomy, loud and bustling seafood restaurant that's been going strong for four decades. Little finesse (the atmosphere is refectory-like), and service can be less than perfect, but many locals still rate its kitchen as one of the city's best. Quite good value for money, even if prices have gone up noticeably of late –

reckon on around €45 per person. Closed Wed. **Moderate.**

Al Nono Risorto Sottoportego de Siora Bettina 2338 ☎ **041.524.1169.** Located just off Campo S. Cassiano, the "Resurrected Grandad" is a pizzeria-restaurant with a predominantly twenty-something following. It often has live jazz and blues, and a pleasant small garden is a further attraction. No credit cards. Open noon–2.30pm & 7–11pm; closed all Wed & Thurs lunch. Inexpensive to moderate.

Antiche Carampane Rio Terrà delle Carampane 1911 ☎ **041.524.0165.** If not the most tourist-friendly place in the city (a semi-jokey notice that tells you there's a charge for tourist information), the *Carampane* is a thorough-bred Venetian trattoria, serving excellent seafood in a cosy interior – with outside seating in fine weather. The menu is brief and often wholly fish-based, with *primi* priced around €15–20 and main courses from €20. Tues–Sun 12.30–2.30pm & 7.30–10.30pm. Expensive.

🏃 **Antico Dolo Ruga Vecchia S. Giovanni 778** ☎ **041.522.6546.** You can pop into this excellent and long-established *osteria* for a few *cicheti* and a glass of Merlot and come away just a few euros poorer; or you can take a table and eat an excellent meal for something in the region of €40. Either way, you're almost certain to think it was money very well spent. Mon–Sat noon–10pm. Moderate.

🏃 **Bancogiro Sottoportego del Banco Giro 122** ☎ **041.523.2061.** This very successful and smart *osteria*, in a splendid location in the midst of the Rialto market, was instrumental in making this zone a fashionable one. Come here to nurse a glass of fine wine beside the Canal Grande, or nip upstairs to the dining room for a well-prepared meal from the tight and imaginative menu (around €20 for main courses). Open Tues–Sun noon–2am. Moderate.

Birraria La Corte Campo San Polo 2168 ☎ **041.275.0570.** If a pizza is all you want, this large pizzeria-trattoria – occupying a former brewery on the north side of Campo San Polo – will do just fine. The rest of the menu is OK, but the pizzas are the thing – along with the beers, which feature strongly on the drinks list. The outside tables give you a grandstand view of Venice's second-largest square. Daily noon–2.30pm & 7–10.30pm.

Da Fiore Calle del Scaleter 2202a ☎ **041.731.308.** Refined, elegant restaurant off Campo San Polo; prides itself on its seafood, regional cheeses, desserts, home-made bread, and wine list. Generally considered among the very best in Venice (booking is essential), and service is faultless. If €100+ per person is too steep for you, drop into the tiny front-room bar for a quality snack. Closed Sun & Mon. Very expensive.

🏃 **Da Pinto Campo delle Becarie 367.** Founded way back in 1890, *Da Pinto* is a huge favourite with workers at the neighbouring fish market, and is perfect for a plate of seafood *cicheti* or something weightier from the fish-centric menu, which invariably features *baccalà* – the best in town, some would say. Tues–Sun 7.30am–2.30pm & 6–9pm. Inexpensive to moderate.

Da Sandro Campiello dei Meloni 1473 ☎ **041.523.4894.** In business since 1962 (so they must be doing something right), this split-site pizzeria-trattoria has dining rooms on both sides of the campiello and tables on the pavement. The pizzas are the best thing here. Open 11.30am–11.30pm; closed Fri. Inexpensive to moderate.

Do Spade Sottoportego delle Do Spade 860 ☎ **041.521.0574.** This was a very similar place to the nearby *Do Mori*, but nowadays – though it still serves *cicheti* at the bar – it's

▲ Antico Dolo

an *osteria* in which the emphasis is mainly on the restaurant side of the operation. And very good it is too, with a tidy menu that takes most of its ingredients, inevitably, from the Rialto fish market. It has retained its attractively plain style, and prices are good, with main courses from just €12. Mon 6–10pm, Tues–Sat 10am–3pm & 6–10pm. Moderate.

Il Refolo Campiello del Piovan 1459 ☏041.524.0016. Run by a member of the family that owns the famous *Da Fiore*, this excellent canalside pizzeria fills up the tiny square which fronts the church of San Giacomo dell'Orio. The pizzas are perhaps the best in Venice – and are certainly the most expensive, with some costing €15. There's also a small menu of other dishes, featuring some terrific salads. Closed Nov–March; rest of year closed all Mon and Tues lunch. Inexpensive to moderate.

Jazz Club 900 Campiello del Sansoni 900 ☏041.522.6565. Located a short distance off Ruga Vecchia S. Giovanni, the dark-panelled *Novecento* is a unique pizzeria-bar – one of the very places left in Venice that uses a traditional brick oven. The jazz is live every Wednesday from October to April, otherwise recorded. Tues–Sun 11.30am–4pm & 7pm–2am.

La Zucca Ponte del Megio 1762 ☏041.524.1570. Long a well-respected restaurant, *La Zucca* was once a vegetarian establishment (its name means "pumpkin") but now goes against the Venetian grain by featuring a lot of meat – chicken, lamb, beef – alongside the Eastern-inflected vegetable dishes. The quality remains high, and the canalside setting is nice. Mon–Sat 12.30–2.30pm & 7–10.30pm. Moderate.

Muro Pizza e Cucina Campiello del Spezier 2048–50 ☏041.524.1628. This offshoot of the hugely successful *Muro Vino e Cucina* (**see below**) offers a good range of pizzas plus an imaginative seafoody menu on which main courses cost about €15. The styling is spartan, the service excellent, and there is seating outside. Mon & Wed–Sun noon–4pm & 7pm–1am.

Muro Vino e Cucina Campo Cesare Battisti 222 ☏041.523.7495. The upstairs dining room of this modern-styled *osteria* offers a good-value lunch menu (around €25 person); in the evening you'll pay around twice as much, to eat from a menu that's earned a reputation as one of the city's most innova-

tive. The very classy (and noisy) ground-floor bar has tables out on the square. Open Mon–Sat 9am–3pm & 5pm–2am. Moderate to expensive.

🏃 **Naranzaria Sottoportego del Banco Giro 130** ☏041.724.1035. The canalside buildings of the Rialto market have lately become colonized by smart bars and *osterie*, and this is the most impressive new arrival. Like neighbouring *Bancogiro*, *Naranzaria* has a bar downstairs and a restaurant crammed into the brick-vaulted room upstairs, plus a few seats by the water, but it's distinctive in having a hybrid Venetian – Japanese menu, which has made it the foodies' bar of choice in this part of town. Tues–Sun noon–2am. Moderate.

Osteria al Ponte, "La Patatina" Calle dei Saoneri 2741a ☏041.523.7238. This bustling *osteria* serves excellent *cicheti* alongside good-value full-meal menus that change regularly. Mon & Wed–Sun 10.30am–2.30pm & 6–10pm. Inexpensive to moderate.

Ribò Fondamenta Minotto 158 ☏041.524.2486. Run by Bruno Barbani, chef to the Italian football team that won the 2006 World Cup, *Ribò* is unusual in mixing Venetian standards with Tuscan dishes, featuring ingredients such as prime Chianina beef fillet. Adjoining the restaurant – an airy room with grey marble floors and white walls, and a very pleasant patio – there's an *enoteca* that offers a good-value lunchtime menu, with mains under €10. Main courses in the restaurant are in the region of €25, whereas in the *enoteca* you'll pay more like €15. Tues–Fri & Sun noon–2.30pm & 7–10.30pm, Sat 7–10.30pm. Moderate to expensive.

🏃 **Vecio Fritolin Calle della Regina 2262** ☏041.522.2881. The name translates as "the old frying-place", and one of its signature dishes is a succulent fry-up of estuary fish, but the *Vecio Fritolin* has come a very long way since its time as a purveyor of Venetian fast food – it's known nowadays for its distinctive take on Venetian fishy classics, making imaginative use of seasonal herbs and vegetables. You'll find lots of locals as well as tourists in this friendly and extremely well-reputed spot. Tues–Sun noon–2.30pm & 7–10.30pm. Expensive.

Vivaldi Calle della Madonetta 1457. Busy parish *osteria* just to the north of Campo San Polo; far more authentic than you'd think from the name and decor, it serves excellent and well-priced meals at the tables in the back (mains around €15), and fine snacks in the front part. 10am–2pm & 6pm–midnight; closed Tues. Moderate.

Cannaregio

See map on pp.140–141.

Ai 40 Ladroni Fondamenta della Sensa 3253 ☏041.715.736. Very successful *osteria*, with high-quality *cicheti* at the bar, and similarly good Venetian standards served at the tables. Tues–Sun 10am–midnight. Moderate.

Al Bacco Fondamenta delle Cappuccine 3054 ☏041.717.493. *Al Bacco* started life as a humble neighbourhood stop off, but has grown into a fully fledged restaurant with a front-of-house bar. It retains a rough-and-ready feel, but the food is distinctly classy. Tues–Sun 10.30am–11pm. Moderate.

Al Fontego dei Pescatori Calle Priuli 3726 ☏041.520.0538. This classy restaurant offers classic Venetian seafood with a slight twist (polenta with scallops, for example), but nothing too off-the-wall. There's an excellent *menù degustazione* for €50; à la carte, you'll pay €10–20 more. The dining room – adorned with ever-changing shows of contemporary art and photography – makes a refreshing change from the nostalgic style of so many Venetian restaurants, and the covered garden is a very pleasant place to eat in summer. Tues–Sun 12.30–2.30pm & 7–10.30pm. Expensive.

Algiubagiò Fondamenta Nove 5039 ☏041.523.6084. The best of several restaurants on the Fondamente Nove, the increasingly upmarket *Algiubagiò* has a menu that's notable for having plenty of vegetarian options and featuring a lot of Angus steak. At lunchtime it offers a one-course €9 light lunch; in the evenings there are set menus from €30 to €90. There's a front-of-house bar, and in summer you can eat on the lagoon-side terrace. Open 7am–11.30pm; closed Tues. Moderate.

Alla Fontana Fondamenta Cannaregio 1102 ☏041.715.077. Once primarily a bar, *Alla Fontana* has transformed itself into a great little trattoria, offering a small menu of classic Venetian maritime dishes, which changes daily according to what the boats have brought in; tables beside the canal are an added attraction in summer. Portions are generous (especially the pasta dishes) and prices good – you'll pay about €40 per

person. Mon–Sat noon–3pm & 6.30–10pm. Moderate.

Alla Vedova Calle del Pistor 3912 ☏041.528.5324. Located in an alley directly opposite the one leading to the Ca' d'Oro, this long-established little restaurant – formally called the *Ca' d'Oro*, but known to all as *Alla Vedova* – is fronted by a bar offering a mouthwatering selection of *cicheti* and a good range of wines. It's known as one of the best-value places in town (antipasti and main courses from just €10), so reservations are always a good idea. No credit cards. Mon–Wed, Fri & Sat 11.30am–2.30pm & 6.30–10.30pm, Sun 6.30–10.30pm. Moderate.

Anice Stellato Fondamenta della Sensa 3272 ☏041.720.744. Hugely popular with Venetians for the superb, reasonably priced meals and unfussy atmosphere. Situated by one of the northernmost Cannaregio canals, it's a little too remote for many tourists. If you can't get a table – it's frequently booked solid – at least drop by for the excellent *cicheti* at the bar. Wed–Sun 12.30–3pm & 7pm–midnight. Moderate.

Antica Adelaide Calle Priuli 3728 ☏041.523.2629. There's been a trattoria on this site for centuries, but in its current incarnation the *Adelaide* dates back to 2006. Staffed by a very friendly young crew, it's a bright and buzzing *osteria*, with

▲ Anice Stellato

a menu that's full of venerable Venetian recipes, and a nice bar out front. The cooking isn't absolutely top-notch, but the food rarely disappoints – and the opening hours make it a good stand-by. Daily 7am–midnight; meals served until 10.30pm. Moderate.

Antica Mola Fondamenta degli Ormesini 2800 ☎041.710.768. The food isn't *haute cuisine* but it's perfectly acceptable, and the family-run *Antica Mola* is just about the cheapest genuine trattoria in the city. There's a nice side garden at the back and canalside tables out front. Closed Wed. Moderate.

Boccadoro Campiello Widman 5405a ☎041.521.1021. This upmarket modern *enoteca-osteria* serves extremely good – and rather pricy – fresh fish and seafood, and some superb pasta courses as well. The wine list is also very impressive. Tues–Sun 12.30–2.30pm & 7.30–10pm. Expensive.

Da Alberto Calle Giacinto Gallina 5401 ☎041.523.8153. The decor and menu are traditional (it's nearly all seafood), but *Da Alberto* has a younger vibe than much of the competition. Good snacks at the bar; if you want to eat a full meal, it's wise to reserve a table. Mon–Sat 10.30am–3pm & 6.30–11pm. Moderate.

🏃 **Dalla Marisa Fondamenta San Giobbe 652b** ☎041.720.211. Duck, tripe, beef and pheasant all feature regularly on the menu here – the boss is a butcher's daughter. Usually there's no menu: you just get whatever she's decided to cook that day, which is usually meat, but sometimes fish or seafood. Unpretentious, tiny and very popular, so you'll need to book; and be on time – Marisa takes a dim view of latecomers. No cards. Noon–2.30pm, plus Tues & Thurs–Sat 8–9.15pm. Moderate.

Da Rioba Fondamenta della Misericordia 2553 ☎041.524.4379. This smartly austere *osteria* is another excellent northern-Cannaregio eatery; often full to bursting, especially in summer, when tables are set beside the canal, but the management always keeps the atmosphere relaxed. Tues–Sun 12.30–2.30pm & 7.30–10.30pm. Moderate.

Fiaschetteria Toscana Salizzada S. Giovanni Crisostomo 5719 ☎041.528.5281. The name means "Tuscan Wine Shop", but the menu at this long-running restaurant is quintessentially Venetian. The service is brisk (some might say curt), and the decor isn't the

freshest, but the food is consistently good, and it has a top-class wine list. Mon & Thurs–Sun 12.30–2.30pm & 7.30–10.30pm, Wed 7.30–10.30pm; closed mid-July to mid-Aug. Expensive.

Gam-Gam Fondamenta di Cannaregio 1122 ☎041.099.4174. The unique feature of this somewhat basic restaurant is its mix of Jewish and Venetian cuisine – all kosher. The *cholent* (chickpea stew) and *latkas* (potato balls) are particularly good. Excellent for vegetarians. No credit cards. Closed Fri evening and all Sat. Inexpensive to moderate.

La Colombina Campiello del Pegolotto 1828 ☎041.275.0622. Once a bar-trattoria, this place is now securely a restaurant, but the wine list is still crucial to its appeal. The menu is strikingly dissimilar to many of its rivals, mixing Venetian standards with Tuscan meat dishes, and the standard is high. Open 6.30pm–2am; closed Tues. Expensive.

Vecia Cavana Rio Terá SS. Apostoli 4624 ☎041.528.7106. The orange walls and bare brickwork vaulting of this former boathouse (*cavana*) create an inviting interior, and the mouthwatering menu of refined Venetian recipes is similarly appealing. The young team that's been running this place since 2004 have compiled an excellent wine list too, and the house white is a cut above the average. Tues–Sun noon–3pm & 7–11pm. Moderate to expensive.

🏃 **Vini da Gigio Fondamenta S. Felice 3628a** ☎041.528.5140. Until a few years ago most of the customers at this popular, family-run trattoria were locals; it's now on the tourist map yet it retains its authenticity and is still good value by local standards, with main courses at around €20, even if prices have crept up in recent years. It has two short but excellent menus – one for meat dishes, one for fish and seafood – and, as the name suggests, the wine list is remarkable. Reservations essential. Wed–Sun noon–2.30pm & 7–10.30pm. Moderate.

Central Castello

See map on p.157.

Alla Rivetta Ponte S. Provolo 4625 ☎041.528.7302. This tiny trattoria is a long-standing favourite with the city's gondoliers and is always heaving at lunchtime. The owner has been known to dispense free *prosecco* to people queuing for a table, but there have been reports of a less than gracious attitude towards tourists, and standards in the kitchen can be erratic. When it's good, though, it's very good, and the prices are low for this part of town Tues–sun noon–2.30pm & 7–10pm. Moderate.

Alle Testiere Calle Mondo Nuovo 5801 ☏041.522.7220. Very small, very special fish and seafood restaurant in the alley on the other side of the canal from the front of Santa Maria Formosa, with ever-changing menu and a superb wine selection. Lunch is from noon to 2pm, and in the evening there are sittings at 7pm and 9pm, to handle the demand – booking is essential. Tues–Sat noon–3pm & 7pm–midnight; closed mid-July to mid-Aug. Expensive.

Al Mascaron Calle Lunga S. Maria Formosa 5225 ☏041.522.5995. Restaurant with an arty feel and interesting *cicheti* at the bar, but definitely two types of clientele – Italians and non-Italians. Foreigners can get quite rude treatment, which is a shame, as the food is good. Reckon on paying €40–50 per person. Booking advisable. No credit cards. Mon–Sat noon–3pm & 7–11pm. Moderate.

Bandierette Barbaria delle Tole 6671 ☏041.522.0619. Not the cosiest place in town, but nice seafood dishes served by nice people at nice prices – you shouldn't pay more than €35 a head. It has a loyal local following, so it's best to book your table. Mon noon–2pm, Wed–Sun noon–2pm & 7–10pm. Moderate.

Da Remigio Salizzada dei Greci 3416 ☏041.523.0089. Superb trattoria, serving straightforwardly excellent fish dishes and gorgeous home-made *gnocchi*. The wine list is outstanding too. Be sure to book – the locals (and ever-increasing numbers of tourists) pack this place every night. While many other restaurants have ramped up their prices in recent years, it remains good value for the quality. Mon 12.30–2.30pm, Wed–Sun 1–3pm & 7.30–10pm. Moderate to expensive.

Osteria di Santa Marina Campo Santa Marina 5911 ☏041.528.5239. Highly rated by most Italian food magazines, this is a very slick and very impressive modern-style operation offering imaginative variants on Venetian maritime standards (eg raw fish starters). The wine list is mightily impressive too. Expect to pay around €25 for your main course. Mon 7.30–11pm, Tues–Sat 12.30–2.30pm & 7.30–11pm. Expensive.

Eastern Castello

See map on p.176.

Ae do Marie Calle dell'Ogio 3129 ☏041.296.0424. Established a century ago, *Ae do Marie* was once a simple *bácaro* but has now been refurbished as a restaurant, serving honest food (mainly fish) at honest prices (*primi* for €10; *secondi* around €15) to a predominantly local clientele. A small garden augments the two dining rooms in summer. Mon–Sat noon–3pm & 7.30–10pm. Moderate.

Al Covo Campiello della Pescaria 3968 ☏041.522.3812. Located in a backwater to the east of Campo Bandiera e Moro, the serious-minded *Covo* is one of Venice's foodie havens, with a consistently high reputation that's maintained partly through its refusal to use frozen or farmed fish. The €30 lunchtime menu is something of a bargain; in the evenings, à la carte, you'll be spending that much on the main course alone. 12.45–3.30pm & 7.30pm–midnight; closed Wed & Thurs, and mid-Dec to mid-Jan. Expensive to very expensive.

Corte Sconta Calle del Pestrin 3886 ☏041.522.7024. Secreted in a lane to the east of San Giovanni in Brágora, this restaurant is one of Venice's finest. The exceptionally pleasant staff tend to make it difficult to resist ordering the day's specials, which could easily result in a bill in the region of €70 each – and it would be just about the best meal you could get in Venice for that price. If expenditure is an issue, check the menu in the window carefully before going in (often the waiters will simply recite what's on offer rather than give you anything printed). Booking several days in advance is essential for most of the year. Tues–Sat 12.30–2pm & 7.15–10pm. Expensive.

Da Franz Fondamenta S. Isepo 754 ☏041.522.0861. Lurking in an unfashionable area to the north of the Giardini Pubblici, this is one of the most refined, most celebrated and priciest seafood kitchens in the city. Closed Tues. Very expensive.

Da Paolo Campo dell'Arsenale 2389 ☏041.521.0660. Simple, good-value bar-pizzeria-trattoria that's long been a firm favourite with Biennale regulars and natives of this region of Castello. Closed Mon. Inexpensive to moderate.

Dai Tosi Calle Secco Marina 738
☏041.523.7102. Lively basic pizzeria-trattoria with a devoted local clientele – you'd be well advised to book at the weekend. There's a bar in front of the small dining room, where they mix the house aperitif: *sgropino*, a delicious mingling of vodka, peach juice, Aperol and *prosecco*. Not to be confused with the establishment of the same name in the same street. On Mon, Tues & Thurs evenings it serves only pizzas. Open 11.30am–4pm & 5–11.30pm; closed Wed. Inexpensive to moderate.

Osteria Sant'Elena Calle Chinotto 22–24
☏041.520.8419. Known to the locals as *Da Pampo*, in honour of the boss, this genuine neighbourhood restaurant is the preserve of the residents of Sant'Elena except when the Biennale is in full swing. The menu is simple, the cooking good. There's a bar serving *cicheti* at the front; outside tables add to the appeal. Open till midnight; closed Tues. Moderate.

Northern Islands

Al Gatto Nero Fondamenta Giudecca 88, Burano ☏041.730.120. See map, p.209.
Founded way back in 1946, this is an outstanding trattoria, located just a minute's walk from the busy Via Galuppi, opposite the Pescheria. It's been run since the 1960s by Ruggero Bovo and his wife Lucia, who are now helped by their son Massimiliano, and what this family doesn't know about the edible delicacies of the lagoon, and the wines of the region, isn't worth knowing. Closed Mon, 1 week in July, 2 weeks in Nov. Moderate to expensive.

Al Ponte del Diavolo Fondamenta Borgognoni 10/11, Torcello ☏041.730.401. See map, p.209.
The nearby *Locanda Cipriani* is better known, but this restaurant is the nicest place to eat at Torcello. À la carte you'll pay about €50 per head, but there's a good set lunch for half that amount, and the shaded terrace overlooking the garden is delightful. Open for lunch every day except Wed, booking essential at weekends. Opens in evenings only for group bookings. Moderate to expensive.

Antica Trattoria Muranese Riva Longa 20, Murano ☏041.739.610. See map, p.205. If you fancy a meal on Murano but the *Busa alla Torre* is closed or too busy, this is the place to go. Closed Wed. Moderate.

Busa alla Torre Campo S. Stefano 3, Murano
☏041.739.662. See map, p.205. By general agreement, this trattoria is the finest restaurant on Murano – unfortunately, though, the kitchen is open for lunch only (noon–3pm). The set menu, at under €20, is a real bargain. For the rest of the day it functions as a café-bar. Tues–Sun 9am–5pm. Moderate.

Dal Baffo Via Galuppi 359, Burano
☏041.730.108. See map, p.209. This bar-trattoria is a good choice for simple dishes such as *frittura mista*, if there's a seat in the tiny dining room (there are more tables outside in summer). Open 8am–7pm; closed Wed. Inexpensive to moderate.

Da Romano Via Galuppi 221, Burano
☏041.730.030. See map, p.209. Huge and historic Burano restaurant, whose refined fish and seafood dishes have no lack of local devotees – the fish-broth risotto is famous. Set menus from just €30. The columned dining room is impressive too. Closed Mon. Moderate to expensive.

Leon Coronato Piazza Galuppi 314, Burano
☏041/730.230. See map, p.209. This homely, friendly and very simple trattoria serves the best pizzas on Burano. Closed Tues. Inexpensive.

Southern Islands

Alla Palanca Fondamenta Ponte Piccolo 448, Giudecca ☏041.528.7719. See map, pp.216–217. The food is more than OK at this basic bar-trattoria, and the view of the city from the outside tables is much more than OK. Lunch is served from midday to 2.30pm; before and after, it's one of Giudecca's busiest bars. Mon–Sat 7am–8.30pm. Moderate.

Altanella Calle delle Erbe 270, Giudecca
☏041.522.7780. See map p.216. Run by the same family for three generations, this restaurant is highly recommended for its fish dishes and the wooden terrace overlooking the island's central canal. No credit cards. Booking essential. Wed–Sun noon–3.30pm & 7.30–11pm. Moderate.

Harry's Dolci Fondamenta S. Biagio 773, Giudecca ☏041.522.4844. See map, pp.216–217. Despite the name, sweets aren't the only things on offer here – the kitchen of this offshoot of the legendary *Harry's Bar* is the equal of its precursor, and it's appreciably less expensive (even though many of the dishes are identical). Nonetheless, you'll be spending in the region of €80 a head, drink excluded. Outside meal times it functions as a café-*pasticceria*; the pastries, all made on the premises, are superlative. Open April–Oct: Mon & Wed–Sun 10.30am–11pm. Very expensive.

Mistrà Fondamenta del Ponte Lungo 212a, Giudecca ☎041.522.0743. **See map, pp.216–217.** Occupying the light-filled upper storey of a former factory right in the thick of the Giudecca boatyards, *Mistrà* gets steady custom from the dockyard workers at lunchtime, when the food is a little less expensive than in the evenings; the dinner menu is a somewhat more refined offering of Venetian fish and seafood, plus some Ligurian dishes. No longer the secret it once was, *Mistrà* has been going rapidly upmarket of late – expect to pay around €40–50. Closed Mon evening & all Tues. Moderate.

Bars and snacks

One of the most appealing aspects of Venetian social life is encapsulated in the phrase "andemo a ombra", which translates literally as an invitation to go into the shade, but is in fact an invitation for a drink – more specifically, a small glass of wine (an *ombra*), customarily downed in one. (The phrase is a vestige of the time when wines were unloaded on the Riva degli Schiavoni and then sold at a shaded kiosk at the base of the Campanile; the kiosk was shifted as the sun moved round, so as to stay in the shade.) Stand at a bar any time of the day and you won't have to wait long before a customer drops by for a reviving mouthful. Occasionally you'll come across a group doing a *giro di ombre*, the highly refined Venetian, version of the pub-crawl; on a serious *giro* it's almost obligatory to stop at an *enoteca* – a bar where priority is given to the range and quality of the wines.

Most bars serve some kind of **food**, their counters usually bearing trays of the characteristically Venetian, fat little crustless sandwiches called *tramezzini*, which are stuffed with delicious fillings such as eggs and mushrooms, eggs and anchovies, or Parma ham and artichokes. Some bars will have a selection of *cicheti* as well, and even a choice of two or three more substantial dishes each day.

San Marco

See map on pp.42–43.

Alla Botte Calle della Bissa 5482. A very lively and warm little *bácaro*, just off Campo San Bartolomeo, offering an excellent spread of *cicheti* and a good selection of wines. Mon–Sat noon–3pm & 6.30–11pm, Sun 12.30–3pm.

Al Volto Calle Cavalli 4081. This dark little bar is an *enoteca* in the true sense of the word – 1300 wines from Italy and elsewhere, 100 of them served by the glass, some cheap, many not; good snacks, too. Mon–Sat 10am–3pm & 6.30–11pm.

Bácaro Jazz Salizzada Fondaco dei Tedeschi 5546. A jazz-themed bar-restaurant that's proving a big hit with Venetian kids, mainly on account of its late hours; there's food, but it's far from the best quality. Daily 4pm–3am.

Bácaro Lounge Salizzada San Moisè 1348. The Benetton-owned *Bácaro Lounge* is one of the city's most stylish nightspots – there's a dining room upstairs (very overpriced), but the focus of the action is the ground-floor bar, a glamorous environment that wouldn't look out of place in Manhattan. Open 10am–2am daily.

Cavatappi Campo della Guerra 525. Minimalist wine-bar with very good food and live jazz from time to time. Space is limited inside the corridor-slim bar, but there are outdoor seats. Tues–Sun 9am–9pm. Closed Jan.

Centrale Restaurant Lounge Piscina Frezzeria 1659b ☎041.296.0664. The spacious, trans-atlantic-style *Centrale* touts itself as the best-designed and coolest bar-restaurant in town, and few would argue with the claim. The food is very expensive (you'll pay around €70 per person), but you might be tempted to blow a few euros for the pleasure of sinking into one of the sumptuous leather sofas, cocktail in hand, and listening to late-night jazz or chilled-out ambient music. The guestbook features the

Venetian drinks

The Veneto has been very successful at developing **wines** with French and German grape varieties (notably Merlot, Cabernet, Pinot Bianco, Pinot Grigio, Müller-Thurgau, Riesling, Chardonnay and Gewürztraminer) and now produces more DOC (*Denominazione di origine controllata*) wine than any other region. The trio of famed Veronese wines – **Valpolicella** (red), **Bardolino** (red) and **Soave** (white) – accounts for the bulk of exported, quality Italian wine. Less widely exported is **Prosecco**, a light, Champagne-like wine from the area around Conegliano; don't miss a chance to sample *Prosecco rosé* and the delicious **Cartizze**, the finest type of Prosecco – and don't turn your nose up at **prosecco spento** (without the fizz). Wines from neighbouring Friuli are well worth exploring too: the most common reds are Pinot Nero, Refosco, Raboso, Merlot and Cabernet, with Tocai, Pinot Bianco and Sauvignon the most common whites.

At the start of the evening you might indulge in a **spritz** (white wine and soda) or **spritz con bitter** (the same, plus *Aperol* or *Campari* or – the darkest, bitterest, strongest and most Venetian variety – *Select*); for an extra twist ask for *prosecco* instead of still white wine. Other popular aperitifs include **fortified wines** such as Martini, Cinzano and Campari. For the real thing, order *un Campari bitter*; ask for a "Campari-soda" and you'll get a ready-mixed version from a little bottle. Crodino, easily recognizable by its lurid orange colour, is a non alcoholic alternative. You might also try Cynar, an artichoke-based sherry-type liquid often drunk as an aperitif.

For a nightcap, there's a daunting selection of **liqueurs**. Amaro is a bitter after-dinner drink which is served by almost every Italian restaurant. The top brands, in rising order of bitterness, are Montenegro, Ramazotti, Averna and Fernet-Branca. Amaretto is a much sweeter concoction with a strong taste of marzipan. Sambuca is a sticky-sweet aniseed brew, often served with a coffee bean in it and set on fire. Strega is another drink you'll see in every bar – the yellow stuff in elongated bottles: it's as sweet as it looks but not unpleasant. Also popular, though considered slightly vulgar in Italy, is *limoncello*, a bitter-sweet lemon spirit that's becoming increasingly trendy abroad. The home-grown Italian firewater is **grappa**, which is made from the leftovers of the wine-making process (skins, stalks and the like). Originally from Bassano di Grappa in the Veneto, it's now produced just about everywhere.

Beer (*birra*) is nearly always a lager-type brew that comes in bottles or on tap (*alla spina*) – standard measures are a third of a litre (*piccola*) and two-thirds of a litre (*media*). Commonest and cheapest are the Italian brands Peroni, Moretti and Dreher, all of which are very drinkable; to order these, either state the brand name or ask for *birra nazionale* – otherwise you may be given a more expensive imported beer. You may also come across darker beers (*birra scura* or *birra rossa*), which have a sweeter, maltier taste and resemble stout or bitter.

---

likes of Charlize Theron and Juliette Binoche, which gives you some idea of market niche. Daily 6.30pm–2am.

Devil's Forest Calle Stagneri 5185. The liveliest bar in the vicinity of Campo San Bartolomeo, this is a convincing facsimile of a British pub, with a good range of beers and board games in the back. Daily 8am–1am.

I Rusteghi Corte del Tintor 5513. A new small *osteria*, secreted away in a tiny courtyard close to Campo San Bartolomeo. Great *cicheti*, nice wine, congenial host – plus a few outside tables.

The perfect place for a quiet snack in the San Marco area. Mon–Sat 10.30am–3pm & 6–9.30pm.

Torino Campo San Luca 4591. During the daytime this is an unremarkable bar-café, but after 8pm it becomes the loud and lively *Torino@Notte*, with DJs and/or live music on Wednesdays. Tues–Sat 8am–1am.

Dorsoduro

See map on pp.94–95.

Ai Artisti Fondamenta della Toletta 1169a. This smart *osteria-enoteca*, located a few metres south of San Barnabà, is a good choice for post-Accademia refreshment, whether you're in need of a light meal or just a glass and a snack; salads are under €10, pasta and other simple dishes around €15. The wine cellar holds a good selection of vintages from all over Italy. Mon–Sat 7.30am–10pm.

Ai do Draghi Campo S. Margherita 3665. Taking its name from the two dragons on the wall opposite, this is a tiny, friendly café-bar, with a good range of wines. The back room exhibits the work of local photographers and artists. April–Oct 8am–2am; Nov–March 8am–11pm; closed Thurs.

Al Chioschetto Záttere al Ponte Lungo 1406a. This waterfront bar, as its name suggests, is a kiosk with outdoor tables. An excellent place to sit with your *spritz* and a sandwich and watch the sun set over Giudecca. Has a DJ (and sometimes live music) on Wed, Fri & Sun from 6pm in summer. Daily: June–Sept 7.30am–2am; Oct–May 7.30am–6pm – unless the weather's bad, in which case it might not open at all.

Café Blue Calle dei Preti 3778. Lively pub-like student haunt where afternoon teas and cakes are on offer as well as whiskies and good cocktails. Puts on art exhibitions, has a DJ one night per week, and hosts local bands on many Fri nights. Daily 8am–2am.

Café Noir Crosera San Pantalon 3805. Another favourite student bar, similar in feel to the neighbouring *Blue*, often with live music on Tues. Open Mon–Sat 8am–2am, Sun 7pm–2am.

Cantina del Vino già Schiavi Fondamenta Nani 992. Known to all Venetians as the *Cantinone*, this is a great bar and wine shop opposite San Trovaso. Excellent *cicheti* and generously filled *panini* too. Mon–Sat 8.30am–8.30pm; Sun 9am–1pm.

Corner Pub Calle della Chiesa 684. Very close to the Guggenheim, this place usually has a few arty foreigners in attendance, but they are always outnumbered by the locals. Open 10am–12.30am, and often later. Closed Tues.

Da Còdroma Fondamenta Briati 2540. Perennially popular with Venice's students and with folk of all ages from the surrounding parishes, this wood-panelled *osteria* has refectory-style tables for simple meals, but most of the punters are here for a glass, a snack and a chat. It hosts occasional poetry readings and live jazz as well. Daily 8am–midnight.

Imagina Rio Terà Canal 3126. This slick bar-café is good for a breakfast brioche and coffee, a lunchtime snack, an early evening *spritz* or a late-night drink – and, as the name implies, it's also a venue for art and photography exhibitions. Mon–Sat 7am–2am.

Margaret DuChamp Campo S. Margherita 3019. Until *Orange* came along, *DuChamp* was undisputedly the first-choice bar for the style-conscious, and even with the competition across the street it's still kept its edge. Open 10am–2am; closed Tues.

Orange Campo S. Margherita 3054a. *Orange* calls itself a "restaurant and champagne lounge", but it's the cocktail list and in-house DJ that have made it a big hit, despite its high prices. Like *DuChamp*, it has ranks of seats out on the campo. Mon–Sat 7.30am–2am, Sun 5pm–2am.

Osteria alla Bifora Campo Santa Margherita 2930. A candlelit wood-beamed and brick interior, friendly service, good wine, excellent *cicheti*, and large plates of meat and cheese if you need more calories – the *Bifora* is one of several fine places for a pit-stop on Campo Santa Margherita. Mon–Sat noon–3pm & 7–11pm.

Suzie Café Campo di S. Basilio 1527. Small bar near the San Basilio vaporetto stop, always teeming with students, many of whom pop in for a quick, cheap plate of pasta; on Fri and Sat there's sometimes live music on the campo. Mon–Sat 7am–1am.

Vinus Venezia Calle del Scalater 3961. A bijoux and very pleasant wine bar, near San Rocco; the stock of wines isn't huge, but it's been chosen with great care, and the *panini* are succulent. Tues–Sun 10am–3pm & 5pm–midnight.

San Polo and Santa Croce

See map on pp.114–115.

Ai Postali Fondamenta Rio Marin 821. An unpretentious backwater *osteria*, with a good selection of wines, more than acceptable snacks, and a few canalside tables – perfect for a post-meal wind-down. Mon–Sat 7.30pm–2am; closed Aug.

Ai Storti Calle San Matteo 819. A brisk, plain and one hundred percent genuine Rialto *bácaro* – not a place in which to while away an evening, but for a plate of *cicheti* and a glass of local wine it can't be beaten. Has a

▲ Marcà

small menu of meals, from just €10. Mon–Sat 8am–3.30pm & 5.15–9.30pm.

Al Garanghelo Calle dei Botteri 1570
☎041.721.721. This very friendly new Rialto *osteria* is yet another excellent place in which to acquaint yourself with the many varieties of *cicheti* – or, if you're hungrier, you could squeeze onto one of the small dining-room's tables and pick something from the day's simple but well-prepared menu. Mon–Sat 8am–10pm.

All'Arco Calle del'Ochialer 436. A great stand-up Rialto bar, tucked under the end of a sottoportego just a few metres from *Do Mori*. Mon–Sat 7am–5pm.

Al Prosecco Campo San Giacomo dell'Orio 1503. As you'd expect, the Veneto's finest sparkling wines are something of a speciality at this small but smart *osteria* – and the snacks are good as well. The terrace, overlooking one of the nicest squares in the city, is another big attraction. Mon–Sat 8am–10pm. Closed Jan & Aug.

Altrove Campo San Silvestro 1105. A very slick young bar, with DJs or bands on Tues nights, and a decent kitchen. Mon–Sat 8.30am–12.30am.

Bagolo Campo San Giacomo dell'Orio 1584. Bright colours and clean lines define the look of this friendly, modern café-bar, which dispenses good snacks (plus light meals and pizzas) and has a lot of whiskies, grappas and beers on offer. Often has a DJ, and live music from time to time. Daily 7am–2am.

Caffè dei Frari Fondamenta dei Frari 2564. Very atmospheric and pretty Belle Époque-styled

bar-café directly opposite the front door of the Frari. Daily 8am–9pm.

Da Baffo Campiello Sant'Agostin 2346. Popular with students and faculty alike, this is a tastefully restored bar with attractive wooden ceiling and marble columns. In winter it has art exhibitions and live music. Nice line in *bruschette* and other snacks too, and in summer there are tables set out on the little campo. Mon–Sat 7.30am–2am.

Da Lele Campo dei Tolentini 183. As you can tell by the opening hours, this tiny and utterly authentic stand-up bar attracts a lot of custom from workers en route to or from Piazzale Roma. Sandwiches and rolls made freshly to order, and wine by the glass from just 60c. Mon–Sat 6am–8pm.

Do Mori Calle Do Mori 429. Hidden just off Ruga Vecchia S. Giovanni, this is the most authentic old-style Venetian bar in the market area – some would say in the entire city. It's a single narrow room, with no seating, packed every evening with home-bound shopworkers, Rialto porters, and locals just out for a stroll. Delicious snacks, great range of wines, terrific atmosphere. Mon–Sat 8.30am–8pm.

Marcà Campo Cesare Battisti 213. This minuscule stand-up Rialto bar is perfect for a quick *panino* and glass of *prosecco*. Mon–Sat 7am–3pm & 6–9pm, Sun 6–9pm.

Ruga Rialto Ruga Vecchia S. Giovanni 692. This Rialto bar is perennially popular with young Venetians and students. *Cicheti* at the bar, and basic meals are served in the back rooms. Mon–Fri 11am–2.30pm & 6pm–midnight, Sat 11am–2.30pm, Sun 6–10pm.

Cannaregio

See map on pp.140–141.

Al Parlamento Fondamenta San Giobbe 511. An unpretentious local bar beside the Cannaregio canal, with occasional DJ nights. Mon–Sat 8am–11pm, Sun 6–11pm.

Al Ponte Calle Larga G. Gallina 6378. Superb *osteria* between the Miracoli and Santi Giovanni e Paolo: one of the best in the area for a glass of wine and a light meal or snack. Mon–Sat 8am–8.30pm.

Cantina Vecia Carbonera Rio Terrà della Maddalena 2329. Old-style *bácaro* atmosphere and a good playlist attracts a young, stylish clientele. Good wine, excellent snacks and plenty of space to sit down. Tues–Sat 10am–3pm & 5–11pm, Sun 10am–3pm.

Da Luca e Fred Roi Terrà San Leonardo 1518. Terrific gritty old *cichetteria*, serving excellent snacks to a regular clientele of drop-in customers, a few of whom are usually to be found sitting outside, watching the world go by. Drop by at lunchtime for a plate of the day's pasta or risotto – the *risotto al nero di sepia* (black squid-ink) is delicious. Closed Tues.

Fiddler's Elbow Corte dei Pali 3847. One of a chain of Italian self-styled "Irish pubs", the *Fiddler's* often has a few Venetian lads trying to act rowdily, and a smattering of Brits showing them how it's really done, but most of the kids are content with sipping a small glass of Guinness for an hour. Gets a crowd on football nights, thanks to the big TV screen. Daily 5pm–12.30am.

Iguana Fondamenta della Misericordia 2517. This cross between a *bácaro* and a Mexican cantina serves reasonably priced Mexican fare to a young crowd. Live music (Latin, rock and jazz) Tues 9–11pm and occasionally on other days too. Open Tues–Sun 6pm–1am.

Il Santo Bevitore Fondamenta Diedo 2393a. A rough and ready but very friendly neighbourhood bar, close to Santa Fosca. Attracting a young crowd, it makes a big thing of its beers – and, inevitably for an Italian "pub", it adds a faux-Irish touch, with a quotation from W.B. Yeats over the door. Satellite TV ensures a full house for big football games, and there's often jazz on Mon night. Mon–Sat 7.45am–midnight.

La Cantina Strada Nova 3689. Welcoming *enoteca* with a good range of wines, substantial and excellent snacks, and its own custom-brewed beer (Gaston). Mon–Sat 10am–10pm.

Leon d'Oro Rio Terrà della Maddalena 2345. A pleasant family-run place, offering a good range of sandwiches, with *osteria* food at the back. Open until 12.30am. Closed Wed.

Osteria ai Ormesini da Aldo Fondamenta degli Ormesini 2710. One of a number of gritty local bars beside this long canal, *da Aldo* is a pleasant spot for a lunchtime snack in the sun, and has an especially good range of beers. Mon–Sat 10.30am–4pm & 5.30pm–2am.

Paradiso Perduto Fondamenta della Misericordia 2540. Having undergone an ill-advised transformation in 2008, *Paradiso Perduto* is due to reopen very soon under its old management; it remains to be seen if it can recapture its standing as Venice's leading

boho bar. It used to serve food (not inexpensive) at its refectory-like tables, and had live music – blues or jazz, as a rule – usually on Sun, sometimes Mon. Presumably it will do the same when it re-emerges, and have more or less the same hours: daily 7pm–1am, plus Fri–Sun 11am–3pm.

Taverna del Campiello Remer Campiello Remer 5701. Slotted into the corner of a tiny square that opens out onto the Canal Grande, this timber-beamed bar-restaurant is a very atmospheric spot for a drink; the restaurant food is average and overpriced, but the buffet lunch, at around €20, is terrific. And from 5.30 to 7.30pm there's a "happy hour" free buffet to accompany the *aperitivi*. It's usually open until 1am, and often has live music. Closed Wed.

Un Mondo diVino Salizzada San Canciano 5984a. Occupying a marble-fronted and wood-beamed old butcher's shop, this brilliant little *bácaro* has rapidly built up a great reputation, for its fantastic array of *cicheti*, its choice selection of wines, and the warmth of its staff. 10am–midnight; closed Tues.

Central Castello

See map on p.157.

Al Portego Calle Malvasia 6015. In the middle of the day this bar is crammed with customers eating *cicheti* and in the evening there's often a queue for a place at one of the tiny tables, where some well-prepared basics (pasta, risotto, *fegato alla veneziana* etc) are served. No reservations

▲ Al Portego

are taken, and the kitchen closes at 9.30pm. Mon–Sat 10.30am–3pm & 5.30–10pm, Sun 5.30–10pm.

Al Vecio Penasa Calle delle Rasse 4587. The decor is charmless, but this place – which caters mainly to local shopworkers and gondoliers – offers a huge array of delicious sandwiches, making it a good choice for a reviving snack after a tour of the Piazza – but eat at the bar rather than at the tables, as the mark-up is even higher than usual. Closed Wed.

Enoteca Mascareta Calle Lunga Santa Maria Formosa 5183. First-rate and perpetually busy wine bar with delicious *cicheti* and a small menu of more substantial fare. It's run by the management of the nearby *Mascaron* (see p.251), but is somewhat friendlier, as a rule. Mon–Sat 7pm–3am.

Inishark Calle del Mondo Novo 5787. Yet another "Irish pub" with the requisite beers and whiskies, hefty snacks and satellite TV

for the football. Open Tues–Sun 6pm–1.30am.

L'Olandese Volante Campo San Lio. The "Flying Dutchman" is a busy brasserie-style pub with plenty of outdoor tables. Mon–Sat 10am–midnight.

Osteria da Baco Salizzada San Provolo 4621. The ever-busy *Baco* is a genuine old-style *osteria* – the nearest one to the Piazza. A wide selection of sandwiches and other snacks. Open 9am–2am; closed Wed.

Eastern Castello

See map on p.176.
Alla Rampa Salizzada S. Antonin 3607. Shabby and one hundred percent authentic bar, which has been run for more than forty years by the no-nonsense Signora Leli. Great for an inexpensive *ombra*, if you don't mind being the only customer who isn't a Venetian male. Mon–Sat 8am–10pm.

Cafés, pasticcerie and gelaterie

When **coffee** first appeared in Venice around 1640, imported by the Republic from the Levant, it was treated as a medicine – the first coffee outlet on the Piazza was called *Il Rimedio* (the Remedy). Today the city has many excellent cafés, ranging from the student places on Campo Santa Margherita to the historic coffee houses of the Piazza, whose prices will prompt you to dally just so you can feel you've had your money's worth.

As with bars, if you **sit in a café** you will be charged more, and if you **sit outside** the bill will be even higher. Nearly all **pasticcerie** also serve coffee and alcohol, but will have at most a few bar stools; they're all right for a swift caffeination before the next round of church-visiting, but not for a session of postcard writing or a longer recuperative stop. Elbowroom in the city's *pasticcerie* is especially restricted first thing in the morning, as the citizens pile in for a coffee and *cornetto* (croissant). When choosing a *pasticceria* anywhere in the city, look for the *Antichi Pasticceri Venexiani* sign: membership of this group signifies high standards and top-quality ingredients. You can also stop for a coffee at most of Venice's **gelaterie**, where the ice cream comes in forms that you won't have experienced before, unless you're a seasoned traveller in Italy.

San Marco

See map on pp.42–43.
Florian Piazza S. Marco 56–59. The most famous café in Venice began life in 1720, when Florian Francesconi's Venezia Trionfante (Venice Triumphant) opened for business here, and the place is still redolent of the eighteenth century, though the gorgeous interior – a frothy confection of mirrors, stucco and frescoes – is a nineteenth-century

pastiche. Its prices match its pedigree: a simple cappuccino at an outside table will set you back around €10, and you'll have to take out a mortgage for a cocktail; if the "orchestra" is playing, you'll be taxed another €6 for the privilege of hearing them. (*Quadri* and *Lavena* levy a similar surcharge.) Open 10am–midnight; closed Wed in winter.
Igloo Calle della Mandola 3651. Luscious home-made ice cream – the summer fruit concoctions are especially delicious.

May–Sept daily 11am–8pm; Oct, Nov & Feb–April daily 11.30am–7.30pm; closed Jan & Dec.

Lavena Piazza S. Marco 133–134. Wagner's favourite café (there's a commemorative plaque inside) is the second member of the Piazza's top-bracket trio. For privacy you can take a table in the narrow little gallery overlooking the bar. The coffee is no way inferior to *Florian* or *Quadri*, and – unlike at that pair – you can keep down the price by drinking at the bar. Open 9.30am–11pm; closed Tues in winter.

Marchini Calle Spadaria 676. The most delicious and most expensive of Venetian *pasticcerie*, which on Sunday mornings is thronged with Venetians buying family treats. The cakes are fabulous, as is the *Marchini* chocolate. June–Sept Mon & Wed–Sat 9am–8pm; Oct–May daily 9am–10pm.

Marchini Time Campo San Luca 4589. Sample the succulent *Marchini* pastries with a cup of top-grade coffee at this new and sleek café. Mon–Sat 7am–9pm.

Paolin Campo S. Stefano 2962. Campo Santo Stefano now has more cafés and restaurants than ever before, but *Paolin* has been here longer than any of them. In addition to drinks it serves some of the best ice cream in Venice, and the outside tables have a very nice setting. Closed Fri.

Quadri Piazza S. Marco 120–124. *Quadri* can claim an even longer lineage than *Florian*, as coffee has been on sale here since the seventeenth century, and it's in the same price league too. On the other hand, it's not quite as pretty, and its name doesn't have quite the same lustre, partly because Austrian officers patronized it during the occupation, while the natives stuck with *Florian*. Open 9am–11pm. Closed Mon in winter.

Rosa Salva Calle Fiubera 951 & Merceria S. Salvador 5020. Excellent coffee (the city's best, some would say) and very good pastries, even if the ambience is rather brisk. The most characterful branch of *Salva* is over by San Zanipolo (see below). Mon–Sat 7.30am–8.30pm.

Dorsoduro

See map on pp.94–95.

Grom Campo S. Barnabà 2761. Founded in Turin in 2003, *Grom* is a very slick operation, concocting fabulous *gelati* from top-quality ingredients gathered from all over Italy. The house speciality is *Crema di Grom*, made from organic eggs, soft *meliga* biscuits and Ecuadorian chocolate. Daily noon–midnight.

Il Caffè Campo S. Margherita 2963. Known as *Caffè Rosso* for its big red sign, this small, atmospheric, old-fashioned café-bar is another student favourite. Good sandwiches, and lots of seats outside in the campo. Mon–Sat 7am–1am.

Il Doge Campo S. Margherita 3058. Well-established and extremely good hole-in-the-wall *gelateria*, which also does a superb *granita*, made in the traditional Sicilian way. Open daily till midnight (2am June–Sept). Closed Nov & Dec.

Lo Squero Fondamenta Nani 989. Yet another first-rate Dordosuro *gelateria*. Daily 11am–9pm.

Majer Rio Terrà Canal 3108b. Founded as a bakery back in 1924, *Majer* has recently opened this functional yet pleasant café on the south side of Campo Santa Margherita. Their pastries are as good as their bread, and the coffee is fine. Mon–Sat 7.15am–8pm, Sun 8.30am–8pm.

Nico Zàttere ai Gesuati 922. This café-*gelateria*, which has been in existence for more than seventy years, is celebrated for an artery-clogging creation called a *gianduiotto da passeggio* – a paper cup with a block of praline ice cream drowned in whipped cream. Closed Thurs.

Tonolo Crosera S. Pantalon 3764. One of the busiest cafés on one of the busiest streets of the student district; especially hectic on Sunday mornings, when the fancy *Tonolo* cakes are in high demand. Tues–Sat 7.45am–8pm, Sun 7.45am–1pm.

▲ Florian

San Polo and Santa Croce

See map on pp.114–115.

Alaska Calle Larga dei Bari 1159. Superb *gelateria*, dishing out adventurous flavours such as artichoke and asparagus amid the more traditional concoctions. April–Oct daily 11am–midnight; Nov, Feb & March Tues–Sun noon–9pm.

Caffè del Doge Calle dei Cinque 609. Fantastically good coffee (they supply many of the city's bars and restaurants), served in a chic minimalist setup very close to the Rialto bridge. Mon–Sat 7am–7pm, Sun 7am–1pm.

Cioccolateria VizioVirtù Calle del Campaniel 2898a. Located just off Campo San Tomà, this shop creates the most extraordinary chocolates – they're not cheap, but a single *VizioVirtù* truffle will give your taste buds an experience to remember. It now makes its own ice cream too – the most expensive *gelati* in town. Daily 10am–7.30pm; closed Aug.

Majer Calle Larga 1630. Located on the north side of Campo San Giacomo dell'Orio, this very good café-*pasticceria* is the sibling of the branch in Dorsoduro – see above.

Rizzardini Calle della Madonetta 1415. Founded in 1742, *Rizzardini* is one of the best outlets for the less-florid varieties of Venetian pastries. 7am–8.30pm; closed Tues & Aug.

Cannaregio

See map on p.140–141.

Boscolo Calle del Pistor 1818. Established in the 1930s, *Boscolo* is still going strong; the pastries are excellent, and they turn out some interesting novelties, such as chocolate Kama Sutra figures and chocolate toolkits. Tues–Sun 7am–8.30pm; closed July & two weeks in Feb.

Il Gelatone Rio Terà Maddalena 2063. The best ice creams in Cannaregio. 11am–10pm; closed Wed.

Central Castello

See map on p.157.

Bonifacio Calle degli Albanesi 4237. Compact and wonderful café-bar-*pasticceria*, a few minutes' stroll east of the Piazza. Open 7am–8.30pm; closed Thurs.

Chiusso Pierino Salizzada dei Greci 3306. Another fine "Antica Pasticceria", with terrific home-made pastries and very nice coffee too. Sun–Thurs 8am–1.30pm & 4–9pm, Fri 8am–1.30pm.

Didovich Campo Marina 5910. A highly regarded *pasticceria* – some say with the city's best *tiramisù* and *pastine* (aubergine, pumpkin and other savoury tarts). Standing room only inside, but has outdoor tables. Open till 8pm. Closed Sun.

La Boutique del Gelato Salizzada S. Lio 5727. Top-grade ice creams at this small outlet. Daily: June–Sept 10am–11.30pm; Oct, Nov & Feb–May daily 10am–8.30pm.

Ponte delle Paste Ponte delle Paste 5991. Excellent *pasticceria* with a small "tea room"; it also serves alcoholic drinks. Daily 7am–8.30pm.

Rosa Salva Campo Santi Giovanni e Paolo 6779. With its marble-topped bar and outside tables within the shadow of Zanipolo, this is the most characterful of the three *Rosa Salva* branches. The coffee and home-made ice cream are superb. 7.30am–8.30pm; closed Wed.

Eastern Castello

Melita Fondamenta Sant'Anna 1000. Wondrous pastries are on offer at this stand-up café-*pasticceria*, created by the one-time dessert wizard from the *Daniele* hotel. Tues–Sun 8am–1.30pm & 3.30–8pm.

Food markets and shops

The campi, parks and canalside steps make picnicking a particularly pleasant alternative in Venice, and if you're venturing off to the outer islands it's often the only way of fuelling yourself. Supplies are always sold by weight (even bread): order by the *chilo*, *mezzo chilo* (kilo, half-kilo) or the *etto* (100g). Bear in mind that food shops are generally open 8.30am–1pm and 4–7pm or thereabouts, and that the great majority are closed on Wednesday afternoons and all day Sunday (though some supermarkets stay open all day Wednesday). And don't try to picnic in the Piazza – the bylaws against it are strictly enforced.

Markets

Open-air **markets** for fruit and vegetables are held in various squares every day except Sunday; check out the stalls on **Campo Santa Maria Formosa**, **Campo Santa Margherita**, **Campiello dell'Anconetta** and **Rio Terrà San Leonardo** (these two often flow into each other), and the barges moored by **Campo San Barnaba** and at the top end of **Via Garibaldi**. The market of markets, however, is the one at the **Rialto**, where you can buy everything you need for an impromptu feast – wine, cheese (the best stalls in the city are here), fruit, salami, vegetables, and bread from nearby bakers or *alimentari* (delicatessens). The stalls of the **Rialto Erberia** (fruit and vegetables), arranged with wonderful colour sense, are laden at different times of the year with peaches, peppers, apples, artichokes, fresh herbs and salad leaves nameless in English – look out for the produce labelled "Sant'Erasmo" (or "Rasmo"), which is grown on the island of that name and is held by many locals to be the best quality. The Rialto market is open Monday to Saturday 8am–1pm, with a few stalls opening again in the late afternoon; the **Pescheria** (fish market) – of no practical interest to picnickers but a sight not to be missed – is closed on Monday as well.

Food shops and supermarkets

The most famous food shop in Venice is Aliani Gastronomia at Ruga Vecchia San Giovanni 654, San Polo (Tues–Sat 8am–1pm & 5–7.30pm) – scores of cheeses, meats and salads that'll have you drooling as soon as you're through the door. Also well worth a call is I Tre Mercanti, very close to the Piazza at Calle al Ponte de la Guerra 5364, Castello (daily 10.30am–7.30pm); run by three foodie entrepreneurs, it stocks wine and food garnered from all over Italy. Virtually every parish has its **alimentari**; as you'd expect, the cheaper *alimentari* are those farthest from San Marco.

Alternatively, you could get everything from one of Venice's well-hidden **supermarkets**, the most central of which is Su.Ve, on the corner of Salizzada San Lio and Calle Mondo Nuovo (Castello). Others are as follows: Punto Sma, tucked between houses 3019 and 3112 on Campo Santa Margherita (Dorsoduro); Billa at Záttere Ponte Lungo 1491, by the San Basilio vaporetto stop (Dorsoduro); Co-Op on Campo San Giacomo dell'Orio (Santa Croce); the large Co-Op by the Piazzale Roma vaporetto stop for services to Murano; Billa at Strada Nova 3660, near San Felice (Cannaregio); and Prix, at Fondamenta San Giacomo 203a (Giudecca). Most are open daily 8.30am–8/8.30pm, though some of the smaller ones close for a couple of hours in the middle of the day, and on Sunday.

Wine

For **local wines**, Venice has four branches of a wine merchant called *La Nave d'Oro*, at 3664 Campo S. Margherita, Dorsoduro; Calle del Mondo Novo 5786b, Castello; Rio Terrà S. Leonardo 1370, Cannaregio; and Via Lépanto 241, Lido (all branches open Mon, Tues & Thurs–Sat 9am–1pm & 5–8pm, Wed 9am–1pm); these shops sell not just bottles but also draught Veneto wine to take out. Many ordinary bars also offer wine on draught – look for the sign *vino sfuso*, or for the tell-tale shelf of vats with siphon attachments. In addition, wine bars such as *Al Volto*, *Cantina del Vino già Schiavi* and *Do Mori* boast comprehensive cellars, and many *alimentari* have a good choice of bottles. Perhaps Venice's best selection of Italian vintages is to be found at *Dai do Cancari*, Calle delle Botteghe, San Marco 3455 (Mon–Sat 10.30am–1pm & 3.30–7.45pm), close to San Stefano; it too sells *vino sfuso*.

12

Nightlife and the arts

Venice is notorious for its lack of **nightlife**, though it does have a good
number of late-opening bars, some of which have live music or DJs.
Music in Venice, to all intents and purposes, means classical music –
though the Teatro Malibran (see below) does stage concerts by Italian
rock bands – from time to time, major bands rarely come nearer than Padua,
and the biggest names tend to favour Verona. The top-bracket **music venues**
are La Fenice, the Teatro Malibran and the Teatro Goldoni in Calle Goldoni,
in the San Marco *sestiere*. That said, Venice's calendar of special events is pretty
impressive, with the Carnevale (see *Festivals* colour section), the Film Festival
and the Biennale ranking among the continent's hottest dates.

Nightlife

The most buzzing area of the city is Dorsoduro, where various outposts of the
university keep the bars busy; the Rialto has also livened up recently. Bear in
mind, however, that most of these venues are small and there are strict bylaws
against late-night noise, so "live music" often entails nothing wilder than an
aspiring singer-songwriter on acoustic guitar. For one day of the year there's
live music in campi all over the city; on the Sunday closest to June 21, the
Venezia Suona festival (Ⓦ www.veneziasuona.it) has a variety of bands playing
from late afternoon until after midnight. In late August the Festa di Liberazione
always features live music on Campo dell'Erberia (Rialto), and earlier in the
month (or late July) there's the Venice Airport Festival, a ten-day indie rock
festival on the mainland, near the airport, as you'd expect.

Clubs

With the transformation of the tiny **Round Midnight** – near Campo Santa
Margherita at Fondamenta del Squero 3102 – into a mediocre jazz venue ("A
tribute to Chet Baker", "A tribute to Miles" and so on), central Venice no longer
has a club dedicated to dancing, unless you count the *Piccolo Mondo* (near the
Accademia, at Calle Contarini-Corfu 1056), where too many of the clientele are
grubby local chancers hoping to strike lucky with hapless foreign students. The
action is now limited to the bars that have occasional DJ nights.

On the mainland, Mestre and Marghera have a few clubs, which are listed in
the local press, but the real action is further away, out in the northern reaches of
the lagoon at **Jesolo**. Every Friday and Saturday evening in summer, this sedate
resort transforms itself into a ravers' haven, as a swarm of clubs kicks into life. Just
stroll into town after 11pm and you'll find the hot spots; *Il Muretto*, Via Roma
Destra 120 (April–Sept Wed & Fri–Sun 11pm–4am; Ⓦ www.ilmuretto.net), is

the one the rest have to match. The problem is that though there are plenty of buses out to Jesolo, there's no night service back, so you have to take a taxi to the Punta Sabbioni vaporetto stop (for services to the Lido) or all the way to Venice, or get a lift with someone – and Jesolo is notorious not so much for its weekend bacchanals as for what happens afterwards, when hundreds of inebriated young Italians go blasting back home. The Jesolo–Venice road has just about the highest death toll of any strip of tarmac in the country.

Music and theatre

La Fenice, the third-ranking Italian opera house after Milan's La Scala and Naples' San Carlo, was destroyed by fire in 1996 (see p.87), and reopened in 2004 in a form barely distinguishable from the much-loved old theatre, though inevitably there are those who say the new facsimile lacks a certain charisma. You can't argue with its prices, though: the cheapest seats (from a mere €10) may give no view of the stage, but very good seats can be had for a reasonable €50–60 on most nights. You'll pay around twice as much for the opening night of a production as you would for the same seat later in the run (midweek prices are the lowest). The opera season runs from late November to the end of June, punctuated by ballet performances. Tickets can be bought at the Fenice box office and the Hellovenezia offices at Piazzale Roma and the train station. For up-to-the-minute information, visit ⓦwww.teatrolafenice.it.

Prior to the fire, the city's major venue for classical music concerts was the Sale Apollinee, in La Fenice. During the restoration, the Sale Apollinee was usurped by the considerably larger (and recently restored) **Teatro Malibran**, behind the church of San Giovanni Crisostomo. Now that the Fenice is back in business, the Malibran and Sale Apollinee share top billing as the city's prime venues for classical recitals (with occasional opera, plus top-league jazzers and the odd rock event). Tickets for the Malibran can be bought in advance from the same outlets as for the Fenice. The Malibran's own box office sells tickets only on the night of the concert, from around one hour before the start.

Music performances at the **Goldoni** (box office Mon–Sat 9.30am–12.30pm & 4–6pm; ⓣ041.520.5422, ⓦwww.teatrostabileveneto.it) are somewhat less frequent than at La Fenice and the Malibran; the repertoire here tends to be more populist, with a jazz series cropping up every now and then. For most of the year the Goldoni specializes in the works of the eponymous writer.

More experimental drama can be seen at the little **Teatro a l'Avogaria**, Corte Zappa 1606, Dorsoduro (ⓣ041.520.9270, ⓦwww.teatroavogaria.it), the **Teatro Fondamenta Nuove**, Fondamenta Nuove 5013 (ⓣ041.522.4498, ⓦwww.teatrofondamentanuove.it), which is also a venue for dance and music events, and the similar **Teatro Junghans**, at Campo Junghans 494, over on Giudecca (ⓣ041.241.1974, ⓦwww.teatrojunghans.it).

Classical concerts, with a very strong bias towards the eighteenth century (and Vivaldi in particular – hardly a week goes by without a performance of the *Four Seasons*), are also performed at the **Palazzo Prigione Vecchie**, the **Scuola Grande di San Giovanni Evangelista**, the **Scuola Grande di San Rocco**, **Palazzo Mocenigo** (San Stae) and the churches of **Santo Stefano**, the **Frari**, **San Stae**, **San Samuele**, **San Vidal**, **San Giacomo di Rialto**, **San Bartolomeo**, **Zitelle**, **San Barnaba**, the **Ospedaletto** and the **Pietà** (the most regularly used). The average ticket price for these concerts is around €25 (usually with a reduction for students and children), which is a lot of money for performances that are often distinguished more by enthusiasm than by professionalism

▲ La Fenice

– for the same price you can hear real stars at La Fenice or the Malibran. The state radio service sometimes records concerts at the **Palazzo Labia**, to which the public are admitted free of charge, as long as seats are reserved in advance (℡041.716.666). Finally, the Italian-German Cultural Association presents free concerts in the **Palazzo Albrizzi**, Fondamenta S. Andrea 4118, near the Ca' d'Oro in Cannaregio (details on ⓦwww.acitve.com).

Cinema

The old Rossini cinema, close to Campo Manin, is due to reopen in 2012 as a three-screener, but in the meantime the only cinema in central Venice is the small two-screen **Giorgione**, close to Santi Apostoli at Rio Terrà dei Franceschi 4612a, Cannaregio (℡041.522.6298); the tiny Sala B is used for less mainstream films than those shown in Sala A, and non-dubbed English-language films are shown on Tuesdays from October to May. The cinema over on the Lido, the **Multisala Astra**, at Via Corfu 12, is another two-screener and runs the same programmes as the Giorgione, but slightly out of synch.

From around mid-July to the end of August an open-air cinema in Campo San Polo shows dubbed or Italian-language films to a high-spirited local audience. Films start each night at around 9pm, and it's worth an evening of anyone's holiday, if only for the atmosphere.

The Film Festival

The **Venice Film Festival** (Mostra Internazionale d'Arte Cinematografica), founded in 1932 as a propaganda showcase for Mussolini's "progressive" Italy, is the world's oldest and the most important in Europe after Cannes. Originally the festival had no competitive element, but with the creation of the Leon d'Oro (the Golden Lion) in 1949, the organizers created a focal point for the rivalries that beset this narcissistic business. Spike Lee is far from being the only director to feel slighted by a biased jury. In the student-orchestrated turmoil of 1968 the Leon d'Oro was deemed to be an insult to the workers of Venice, and it was only in 1980 that the trophy was reinstated. Now every Festival is beset with rows between directors of differing political persuasions and vehement disputes over the programming.

The eleven-day Film Festival takes place on the Lido every year in **late August and/or early September**. Posters advertising the Festival's schedule appear weeks in advance, and the tourist offices will have the festival programme a fair time before the event. The main screen is the **Palazzo del Cinemà**, next to the *Excelsior* hotel on Lungomare G. Marconi; other screenings take place in the nearby **PalaLido** and **PalaBiennale** marquees, and in the **Palazzo del Casinò**. Tickets are available to the general public on the day before the performance, at the Palazzo del Cinemà and PalaBiennale ticket offices. Any remaining tickets are sold off at PalaGalileo one hour before the screening, but nearly all seats are taken well before then. For online info, go to Ⓦ www.labiennale.org.

The Casinò

Only one aspect of Venice's nightlife attracts customers from the mainland, and that's the **Casinò** (Ⓦ www.casinovenezia.it), which occupies the magnificent Palazzo Vendramin-Calergi (Cannaregio) on the Canal Grande, operating from 4pm until 2.30am (3.30am on Saturday). The Saturday-night migration is a strange sight – the vaporetto pulls in at the dismal Tronchetto stop, and on board step the well-groomed gamblers, having parked their Alfas in the Tronchetto's multistorey. Minimum age is 18, and the dress code is not as strict as you'd think – even jeans are acceptable in the rooms given over to slot machines, though jacket and tie are obligatory for the "French" games such as roulette and *chemin de fer*.

The Biennale and special exhibitions

The **Venice Biennale**, Europe's most glamorous international forum for contemporary art, was first held in 1895 as the city's contribution to the celebrations for the silver wedding anniversary of King Umberto I and Margherita of Savoy. In the early years the exhibits were dominated by standard salon painting, despite the presence of such artists as Ensor, Klimt and Whistler. Since World War II, however, the Biennale has become a self-consciously avant-garde event, a transformation symbolized by the award of the major Biennale prize in 1964 to Robert Rauschenberg, the *enfant terrible* of the American art scene. The French contingent campaigned vigorously against the nomination of this New World upstart, and virtually every Biennale since then has been characterized by the sort of controversy that is now endemic in the publicity-addicted art circuit.

Festivals

Venice's main **festivals** are covered in the colour insert. In addition to these, there are a few smaller-scale events:

Su e Zo Per I Ponti. Held on the **fourth Sunday of Lent**, Su e Zo Per I Ponti (Up and Down the Bridges) is a privately organized fun day that's become a fixture of the Venetian calendar. In essence it's a non competitive orienteering event, in which participants are given a map of the city on which key sights (including plenty of bars) have to be ticked off. The start line is in the Piazza, where you register on the morning of the jaunt.

Festa di San Marco. April 25 – the feast day of **Saint Mark** – begins with a Mass in the Basilica, followed by a gondola race from Sant'Elena to the mouth of the Canal Grande. Some Venetian men continue the tradition of giving their wife or girlfriend a red rosebud (*boccolo*) on this day, hence the alternative name: Le Festa del Boccolo.

Festa di San Pietro. Held in the week of June 29, the Festa di San Pietro is a small-scale festival of concerts, open-air shows and food stalls, held around the church of San Pietro di Castello. Entirely untouched by tourism, it's an authentic antithesis to Carnevale.

After decades of occurring in even-numbered years, the Biennale shifted back to being held **every odd-numbered year from June to November**, so that the centenary show could be held in 1995. The main site is in the Giardini Pubblici, where there are permanent pavilions for about forty countries plus space for a thematic international exhibition. This central part of the Biennale is supplemented by exhibitions in venues such as the salt warehouses on the Záttere and parts of the Arsenale that are otherwise closed to the public, such as the colossal Corderie or Tana (the former rope-factory) and the Artiglierie (gun foundry). In addition, various sites throughout the city (including the streets) host fringe exhibitions, installations and performances, particularly in the opening weeks. Some of the Biennale pavilions and various other venues (usually the Corderie) are used in even-numbered years for an independent Biennale for **architecture**, a smaller-scale event which runs from the second week of September to mid-November. Information on the Biennale is available at ⓦ www.labiennale.org.

Other exhibitions

As if the profusion of galleries, museums and picture-stuffed churches weren't enough, Venice boasts a phalanx of venues for **special exhibitions**, the chief ones being Ca' Pésaro, the Fondazione Cini, the Guggenheim, the Museo Correr, the Museo Fortuny, the Palazzo Ducale, Palazzo Grassi, the Querini-Stampalia and the Scuola Grande di San Giovanni Evangelista.

Another notable institution is the **Fondazione Bevilacqua La Masa** (ⓦ www.bevilacqualamasa.it), which holds an annual survey of work by young Veneto artists at its HQ, Piazza San Marco 71c, and other sites. But contemporary art galleries in Venice are in general timorous. A few stand out, all in San Marco, except where indicated.

A + A (ⓦ www.aplusa.it) Calle Malipiero, near Campo Santo Stefano.

Bugno (ⓦ www.bugnoartgallery.it) Campo San Fantin & Piscina Frezzeria.

Contini (ⓦ www.continiarte.com) Calle Spezier, off Campo Santo Stefano.

Galleria Venice Design (ⓦ www .venicedesignartgallery.com) Calle Vallaresso & Salizzada San Samuele.

ScalaMata (ⓦ www.scalamata.com) Ghetto Vecchio 1236, Cannaregio

Traghetto (ⓦ www.galleriatraghetto.it) Campo Santa Maria del Giglio.

Shopping

V enice was once famed as a place in which one could buy or sell almost anything, and it's still a thriving commercial city, in the sense that its shops rake in millions of euros every day from the visiting throngs. The problem is, though, that the great majority of the glitzy emporia on the main retail zones of the Mercerie and Calle Larga XXII Marzo are not truly Venetian; rather, they are the outposts of huge Italian brands such as Gucci, Dolce e Gabbana and Trussardi, which you'll find in every other major tourist destination in Italy. With each passing year and rent increase the smaller-scale Venetian enterprises find it harder to compete, and even a famous company like Jesurum (see p.272) can no longer afford to maintain a shop in the city centre. That said, many authentically Venetian outlets and workshops are still in operation: the manufacture of exquisite decorative papers is a distinctively Venetian skill; small craft studios in various parts of the city continue to produce beautiful handmade bags and shoes; and of course there are lots of shops selling glass, lace and Carnival masks – nowadays the quintessential souvenir. (You should be aware, though, that with masks, lace and glass, much of the stuff on sale is low-quality, mass-produced and imported – we've recommended only the outlets for genuine Venetian items.) What follows is a rundown of the best shops in various categories, excluding food shops and markets, which are covered in Chapter 11.

Antiques

Although the antiques shops around **San Maurizio** and **Santa Maria Zobenigo** cater for the wealthier collectors, bargain hunters should be able to pick something up at the **antiques fairs** that crop up throughout the year in Campo San Maurizio, where the stalls groan under the weight of old books, prints, silverware and general bric-a-brac. (The tourist office will be able to tell you if one is due.) The traders in the **San Barnaba** district are also slightly downmarket, running the kind of places where you could find a faded wooden cherub or an old picture frame.

Art materials

Arcobaleno Calle delle Botteghe 3457, San Marco ☎041.523.6818. As the name implies, Arcobaleno (Rainbow) is the first stop for pigments, though they sell a variety of artistic

paraphernalia. Mon–Fri 9am–12.30pm & 4–7.30pm, Sat 9am–12.30pm.
Cartoleria Accademia Campiello Calbo, Dorsoduro ☎041.520.7086. This supplier of

artists' materials, tucked into a small campo on the western flank of the Accademia, has been in business for two centuries, and keeps a particularly good stock of papers. There's another branch at Campo Santa Margherita 2928. Mon–Fri 8am–1pm & 3.30–7pm, Sat 8am–1pm.

Testolini Calle dei Fabbri 4744 (Mon–Sat 9am–7.30pm) & Fondamenta Orseolo 1756 (Mon–Sat 9.30am–1pm & 2.30–7pm). The city's best-known stationers, with a vast range of paper, pens, briefcases, etc. Fine-art materials are sold at the Fondamenta Orseolo branch.

Books

Alberto Bertoni Rio Terrà degli Assassini 3637b, San Marco ℡041.522.9583. For remaindered and secondhand books, including a lot of art-book bargains.
Mon–Sat 9am–1pm & 3–7.30pm.
Cafoscarina Campiello Squellini 3259 & 3224, Dorsoduro ℡041.522.9602, ⓦwww .cafoscarina.it. Good range of non-Italian titles amid a wide stock of generally academic books at this twin-site bookshop (the university HQ is almost next door).
Mon–Fri 9am–7pm, Sat 10am–1pm.
Fantoni Libri Arte Salizzada S. Luca 4119, San Marco ℡041.522.0700. For the glossiest, weightiest and most expensive art books.
Mon–Sat 10am–8pm.
Filippi Editore Venezia Caselleria 5284 ℡041.523.6916 **& Calle del Paradiso 5763** ℡041.523.5635 **(both Castello).** The family-run Filippi business produces a vast range of Venice-related facsimile editions, including Francesco Sansovino's sixteenth-century guide to the city (the first city

guide ever published), and sells an amazing stock of books about Venice in its two shops. Mon–Sat 9am–12.30pm & 3–7.30pm.
Goldoni Calle dei Fabbri 4742, San Marco ℡041.522.2384. A good general bookshop; also keeps an array of maps and posters. Mon 2–7pm, Tues–Sat 10am–7pm.
Libreria della Toletta Sacca della Toletta 1214, Dorsoduro ℡041.523.2034. Sells reduced-price books, mainly in Italian, but some dual-language and translations; keeps a good stock of Venice-related titles. Two adjacent branches sell art, architecture, design and photography titles, including bargains on Electa books. July & Aug Mon–Sat 9.30am–1pm & 3.30–7.30pm; rest of year Mon–Sat 9.30am–7.30pm, Sun 3.30–7.30pm.
Libreria Mondadori Salizzada San Moisè 1345, San Marco ℡041.522.2193. The triple-decker Mondadori is the biggest bookshop in town. Mon–Sat 10am–8pm, Sun 11–7.30pm.

Clothes

As you'd expect, many of the top-flight Italian designers and fashion houses – Versace, Missoni, Krizia, MaxMara, Trussardi, Gucci, Armani, Prada, Valentino and Dolce e Gabbana (the only ones with a local connection) – are represented in Venice, most of their outlets being clustered within a street or two of the Piazza. For those with wallets as deep as oil wells, the **Mercerie**, **Frezzeria**, **Calle Goldoni**, **Calle Vallaresso** and **Calle Larga XXII Marzo** are the most fruitful zones.

For more moderately priced clothes, there's Benetton, Sisley and Stefanel, plus the flagship two-storey Diesel store (like Benetton, Diesel was founded in the Veneto), on the San Marco side of the Rialto bridge, at Salizzada Pio X 5315 (℡041.241.1937; Mon–Sat 10am–7.30pm, Sun 11am–7pm). The home branch of Coin, a national clothing department store that's based in Venice, is located close by, at Salizzada San Giovanni Crisostomo 5787 (℡041.520.3581; Mon–Sat 9.30am–7.30pm, Sun 11am–7.30pm).

Glass

For Venetian **glass** you should go to the main source of production, **Murano**. The Piazza and its environs are prowled by well-groomed young characters offering free boat trips to the island – on no account accept, as you'll be subjected to a relentless hard sell on arrival. If you are in the market, just take the vaporetto to the Colonna stop and follow your eyes; the most expensive and most pretentious shops are to the fore, the rest stretch out beyond. Little glass trinkets, pseudo-artistic ornaments and eye-bruising kitsch – such as a glass bush

▲ Glass for sale at L'Isola

with a small flock of life-size glass parrots – make up much of the stock, but you'll find far more tasteful work in the showrooms listed below. Unless stated otherwise, they are located on Murano. Don't buy anything that doesn't have the "Vetro Artistico Murano" trademark – the shops are awash with fake Murano ware, much of it from China. Real Murano glass is expensive stuff: wine glasses cost from around €60 each, small vases tend to cost upwards of €300, and for larger table-top items you'll be paying a hefty four-figure sum. For more on Murano glass, see p.206.

Barovier & Toso Fondamenta Vetrai 27–29 ⓣ041.739.049, ⓦwww.barovier.com. This is a family-run firm which can trace its roots back to the fourteenth century. Predominantly traditional designs. Mon–Sat 10am–12.30pm & 1–6pm.

Berengo Fine Arts Fondamenta Vetrai 109a ⓣ041.739.453; Fondamenta Manin 68 ⓣ041.527.6364 & Calle Larga San Marco 412–3 ⓣ041.241.0763 (San Marco), ⓦwww.berengo .com. This firm has pioneered a new approach to Venetian glass manufacture, with foreign artists' designs being vitrified by Murano glass-blowers. Daily 10am–6pm.

Compagnia Vetraria Muranese Fondamenta Vetrai 43 ⓣ041.746.843, ⓦcompagniavetraria .com. Wacky bowls and vases feature prominently in the ranges of modern glassware produced by this firm, which has worked with top-flight designers such as Ettore Sottsass. Mon–Sat 10am–6pm.

Davide Penso Riva Longa 48 ⓣ041.527.4634. The jewellery sold here is both manufactured and designed by the firm, which specializes in giving a new slant to traditional Murano styles. You can watch pieces being made in the shop. Daily 10am–6pm.

Domus Vetri d'Arte Fondamenta Vetrai 82 ⓣ041.739.215. Stocks work by the major postwar Venetian glass designers, artists such as Barbini, Ercole Moretti and Carlo Moretti. Daily 9.15am–1pm & 2–6pm.

Elle&Elle Fondamenta Manin 52 ⓣ041.527.4866. Outlet for the sleek small-scale glasswork of Nason & Moretti, a long-established Murano firm that consistently produces attractive modern items. Daily 10.30am–1pm & 2–6pm.

L'Isola Salizzada S. Moisè 1468 ⓣ041.523.1973 (San Marco). Chiefly a showcase for work by Carlo Moretti, the doyen of modernist Venetian glass artists. Daily 9am–7pm.

Marina Barovier Salizzada San Samuele 3216 ⓣ041.523.6748 (San Marco), ⓦwww.barovier .it. Art gallery dealing in work from glass-blowers from all over the world. This place displays what is perhaps the most inventive and beautiful glass in Venice, and – contrary to appearances – the stuff is for sale, albeit at very high prices. Mon–Sat 9.30am–12.30pm & 3.30–7.30pm.

Murano Collezioni Fondamenta Manin 1c ⓣ041.736.272. Large outlet for work from the Venini and Moretti factories. Daily 10am–6pm.

Rossana & Rossana Riva Longa 11 ⓣ041.527.4076, ⓦwww.ro-e-ro.com. Beautiful goblets are the main attraction here. Daily 10am–6pm.

Seguso Piazza San Marco 143 ⓣ041.739.048 & Frezzeria 1230–6 ⓣ041.739.065, ⓦwww .seguso.it. Traditional-style Murano glass, much of it created by its founder, Archimede Seguso. Daily 10am–7pm.

Seguso Viro Fondamenta Manin 77 ⓣ041.527.5353. Founded by one of Archimede's sons, Viro offers some slightly more eccentric pieces than you'll find at the original Seguso. Mon–Sat 10.30am–5.30pm.

Venini Fondamenta Vetrai 47–48 ⓣ041.273.7211 (Murano) & Piazzetta dei Leoncini 314 ⓣ041.522.4045 (San Marco), ⓦwww.venini .com. One of the more adventurous producers, Venini often employs designers from other fields of the applied arts. Both branches open Mon–Sat 9.30am–5.30pm.

Jewellery

ABC Calle del Tentor 1839, Santa Croce ⓣ041.524.4001. Innovative goldsmith Andrea d'Agostino produces some lovely rings, bracelets and other pieces, with some especially attractive items made using the Japanese layering technique known as *mokume*. Tues–Sat 9.30am–12.30pm & 3.30–7.30pm.

Antichità Calle Toletta 1195a, Dorsoduro
☎041.522.3159. Period objects and new items made with tiny antique beads, which can also be bought individually. Mon–Sat 9.30am–1pm & 3.30–7pm.
Anticlea Antiquariato Calle San Provolo 4719a, Castello ☎041.528.6946. Specializing in the glass beads known as *perle veneziane*, with ready-made jewellery and drawers full of beads to choose from. Mon–Sat 9.30am–1pm & 3.30–7pm.

Laberintho Calle del Scalater 2236, San Polo
☎041.710.017. Tiny workshop specializing in inlaid earrings, necklaces and rings. Tues–Sat 9.30am–1pm & 2.30–7pm.
Totem Campo Carità 878b, Dorsoduro
☎041.522.3641. As well as exhibiting and marketing "tribal" art, Totem sells an intriguing range of jewellery made from ordinary materials, most of it inspired by African artefacts. Daily 10am–1pm & 3–7pm.

Lace, linen and fabrics

It's cheaper to buy **lace** on **Burano** than in the centre of Venice, but be warned that the cheapest stuff is machine-made and not from Burano either. The handmade work sold at the island's Scuola del Merletto is expensive, though not to a degree that's disproportionate to the hours and labour that go into making it – and this is the one outlet where you can be sure that what you're buying is

▲ Lace making on Burano

100 percent authentic. (For more on Burano lace, see p.208.) What follows is a list of the recommendable shops in central Venice.

Bevilacqua Campo Santa Maria del Giglio 2520, San Marco ☎041.241.0662. This is a venerable manufacturer of patterned velvets and damasks, some of which are produced using machinery made 300 years ago. There's another branch behind the Basilica di San Marco, at **Fondamenta della Canonica 337b**. Mon–Sat 10am–7pm, Sun 10am–5pm.

Fortuny Fondamenta San Biagio 805, Giudecca ☎041.522.4078. The retail office of the Fortuny factory sells astonishingly lustrous fabrics at astonishing prices: €300 per metre in some cases. Mon–Fri 9am–noon & 2–5pm.

Jesurum Fondamenta della Sensa 3219, Cannaregio ☎041.524.2542, ⓦ www.jesurum .it. Renowned for its exquisite lace, the long-established (but no longer Venetian-owned) Jesurum also produces luxurious bed linen, towels and other fabrics. Tues–Sat 10am–1pm & 1.30–5pm.

Kerer Calle Canonica 4328a, Castello ☎041.523.5485. The vast Kerer showroom sells a wide range of lace, both affordable and exclusive; it's installed in the Palazzo Trevisan-Cappello, across the Ponte Cappello at the rear of the Basilica di San Marco. Mon–Sat 10am–6pm, Sun 10am–12.30pm.

Martinuzzi Piazza San Marco 67a, San Marco ☎041.522.5068. If cost is no object, call in at Martinuzzi, Venice's most durable and expensive purveyor of lace. Mon–Sat 9am–7pm, plus March–Oct Sun 9.30am–7pm.

Trois Campo S. Maurizio 2666 ☎041.522.2905. This tiny shop holds a large stock of original Fortuny fabrics. Mon 4–7.30pm, Tues–Sat 10am–1pm & 4–7.30pm.

Venetia Studium Calle Larga XXII Marzo 2403–04, Calle del Lovo 4753–54, Merceria dell'Orologio 298 & Calle de le Ostreghe 2428 ☎041.522.9281 (all San Marco), ⓦ www .venetiastudium.com. If real Fortuny is out of your range, try Venetia Studium, which sells reasonably priced lamps, bags and scarves in Fortuny-style (and Fortuny-approved) pleated velour and crepe. Mon–Sat 9.30am–7.30pm, Sun 10.30am–6.30pm.

Masks

Many of the Venetian **masks** on sale today are derived from traditional Carnevale designs: the ones representing characters from the *Commedia dell'Arte* (Pierrot, Harlequin, Columbine) for example, and the classic white half-mask called a *volto*, which has a kind of beak over the mouth so the wearer could eat and drink. Many of the masks of this type are churned out by factories located outside of Italy, but the ones sold in the places listed below are hand-crafted, and are sold alongside pieces of more modern inspiration – including some highly imaginative creations.

Ca' Macana Calle delle Botteghe 3172, Dorsoduro ☎041.520.3229, ⓦ www.camacana .com. Huge mask workshop, with perhaps the biggest stock in the city; has a smaller branch on the other side of Campo San Barnaba, at **Sacca della Toletta 1169**. Both branches daily 10am–6pm.

MondoNovo Rio Terrà Canal 3063, Dorsoduro ☎041.528.7344, ⓦ www.mondonovomaschere .it. This workshop, located just off Campo S. Margherita, is perhaps the most creative in Venice, producing everything from ancient Greek tragic masks to portraits of Richard Wagner. Mon–Sat 9am–6pm.

Tragicomica Calle dei Nomboli 2800, San Polo ☎041.721.102, ⓦ www.tragicomica.it. A good range and some nice eighteenth-century styles, as you might expect from a shop that's opposite Goldoni's house. Daily 10am–7pm.

Perfumery

Officina Profumo-Farmaceutica Santa Maria Novella Salizzada San Samuele 3149, San Marco ☎041.522.0814. The Venetian branch of the famous Florentine operation, founded in 1612 by Dominican monks as an outlet for their potions and herbal remedies. Many of these are still available, including distillations of flowers and herbs, together with face creams, shampoos, soaps and wondrous aromatics for the body and home. Mon–Sat 10am–1pm & 2–7pm.

Prints, postcards, paper and stationery

Postcards are on sale everywhere, though the fund of images isn't as imaginative as it could be. Just inside the Basilica di San Marco there's a stall selling a vast spread of good-quality cards of the church and its mosaics, and many of the city's other churches offer a small range of good cards. Venice's museums are a letdown, usually offering a choice of a bare half-dozen – the stalls outside the Accademia have a better selection of the gallery's paintings than you'll find in the gallery itself. For something a little more unusual, such as mug shots of famous doges or ancient views of the city, try Filippi Editore (see "Books").

Much of the decorative **paper** on sale in Venice comes from Florence or is affiliated to or inspired by Florentine producers, but is none the worse for that. Shops selling these marbled papers, notebooks and so forth are all over the city; more idiosyncratic stuff is sold at the following places.

Ebrû-Alberto Valese Campiello San Stefano 3471, San Marco ☎041.523.8830, ⊛www .albertovalese-ebru.com. Valese not only produces the most luscious marbled papers in Venice, but also transfers the designs onto silk scarves and a variety of ornaments; the marbling technique he uses is a Turkish process called *ebrû* (meaning cloudy) – hence the alternative name of his shop. Mon–Sat 10am–1.30pm & 2.30–7pm, Sun 11am–6pm.
Il Pavone Fondamenta Venier 721, Dorsoduro ☎041.523.4517. Nice wooden-block-printed papers, folders and so on, plus an interesting line in personalized rubber stamps and *Ex Libris* bookplates. Daily 9.30am–1.30pm & 2.30–6.30pm.
Legatoria Piazzesi Campiello della Feltrina 2511, San Marco, located near S. Maria Zobenigo ☎041.522.1202. This paper-producer was founded way back in 1828 and claims to be the oldest such shop in

Italy. Using the old wooden-block method of printing, it makes stunning hand-printed papers and cards, and a nice line in pocket diaries, too. Mon–Sat 10am–1pm & 3–7pm.
Paolo Olbi Calle della Mandola 3653, San Marco ☎041.528.5025, **& Campo Santa Maria Nova 6061, very near the Miracoli (Cannaregio).** The founder of this shop was largely responsible for the revival of paper marbling in Venice; today it sells a whole range of marbled stationery. San Marco branch is open daily: April–Oct 10am–7.30pm; rest of year 10am–12.30pm & 3.30–7.30pm. Campo S. Maria Nova branch is open daily 9am–12.30pm & 3.30–7.30pm.
Polliero Campo dei Frari 2995, San Polo ☎041.528.5130. A bookbinding workshop that sells patterned paper as well as heavy, leather-bound albums of handmade plain paper. Mon–Sat 10.30am–1pm & 3.30–7.30pm, Sun 10am–1pm.

Shoes, bags and leather

If you're on the lookout for chic shoes or bags, a browse around the **Mercerie**, **Frezzeria** and **Calle Goldoni** might be worthwhile; most of the shops here are pricy, but sales are a fairly regular occurrence. Discounts are far less common to the west of the Piazza, around **Calle Vallaresso and Calle Larga XXII Marzo**, where names such as Vogini and Bottega Veneta uphold the city's reputation as a market for immaculately produced leather goods. What follows is a rundown of the city's more idiosyncratic outlets.

Daniela Ghezzo Segalin Calle dei Fuseri 4365, San Marco ☎041.522.2115. Established in 1932 by Antonio Segalin then run by his son

Rolando until 2003, this workshop is now operated by Rolando's star pupil Daniela Ghezzo, who produces wonderful handmade shoes, from sturdy brogues to whimsical Carnival footwear, such as shoes with toes. A pair of Ghezzos will set you back at least €500. Mon–Fri 9.30am–12.30pm & 3.30–7.30pm, Sat 9am–12.30pm.

Francis Model Ruga Rialto 773a, San Polo ☏041.521.2889. A father-and-son team that sells high-quality handbags and briefcases from their tiny Rialto workshop. Mon–Sat 9.30am–7.30pm, Sun 10.30am–6.30pm.

Giovanna Zanella Calle Carminati 5641, Castello ☏041.523.5500. Though she also sells bags and hats from her shop near the church of San Lio, inventive and occasionally wacky handmade shoes (with little windows above

the toes, for example) are what have made Giovanna Zanella's reputation. You'll pay around €300–500 for a pair. Mon–Sat 9.30am–1pm & 3–7pm.

Il Grifone Fondamenta del Gaffaro 3516, Santa Croce ☏041.522.9452. This shop, over by the Tolentini, sells handmade briefcases, satchels, purses and other sturdy leather pieces, at decent prices. Tues–Sat 10am–1pm & 4–7.30pm.

Mori & Bozzi Rio Terrà Maddalena 2367, Cannaregio ☏041.715.261. Stylish women's footwear from a range of small labels. Mon–Sat 9.30am–7.30pm, plus Sun 11am–7pm in April, May, Sept & Oct.

Woodwork

La Scialuppa Calle Seconda Saoneri, San Polo ☏041.719.372, Ⓦ www.veniceboats.com. Wonderfully detailed and well-priced models, model kits and plans for all types of Venetian boats are made and sold by Gilberto Penzo, at this shop very close to the Frari. Mon–Sat 9.30am–12.30pm & 3–6pm.

Signor Blum Campo S. Barnaba 2840, Dorsoduro ☏041.522.6367, Ⓦ www.signorblum.com. The jigsaw-like creations of Signor Blum (musical instruments, palace facades, etc) make unusual gifts for kids. Daily 10am–7.30pm.

Directory

ACTV enquiries Piazzale Roma daily 7.30am–8pm; or ⓦwww.actv.it or ⓦwww.hellovenezia.it.

Airport enquiries Marco Polo airport ☏041.260.9260, ⓦwww.veniceairport.com.

Banks Banks are concentrated along the chain of squares and alleyways between Campo S. Bartolomeo and Campo Manin (in the north of the San Marco *sestiere*). There's not much to choose between them in terms of commission and exchange rates, and their hours are generally Mon–Fri 8.30am–1.30pm and 2.30–3.30pm.

Consulates and embassies The British consulate is in Mestre at Piazzale Donatori di Sangue 2–5 (☏041.505.5990); this office is staffed by an honorary consul – the closest full consulate is in Milan, at Via San Paolo 7 (☏02.723.001). The nearest US consulate is also in Milan, at Via Principe Amedeo 2–10 (☏02.290.351), but there's a consular agency at Marco Polo airport (☏041.541.5944). Travellers from Ireland, Australia, New Zealand and Canada should contact their Rome embassies: Irish Embassy, Piazza di Campitelli 3 ☏06.697.9121; Australian Embassy, Via Antonio Bosio 5 ☏041.06/852.721; New Zealand Embassy, Via Clitunno 44 ☏06.853.7501; Canadian Embassy, Via Zara 30 ☏041.06/444.2911.

Exchange There are clusters of exchange bureaux (*cambios*) where most tourists gather – near San Marco, the Rialto and the train station. Open late every day of the week, they can be useful in emergencies, but their rates of commission and exchange tend to be steep, with the notable exception of Travelex, who can be found at no. 142 on the Piazza, at Riva del Ferro 5126 (by the Rialto bridge) and at the airport.

Hospital Ospedale Civile, Campo SS. Giovanni e Paolo ☏041.529.4111.

Internet access Many hotels and hostels now offer free internet access, and internet points (usually charging €6–8 per hour) are to be found all over the city, especially in the area around Campo Santa Margherita and Campo San Barnaba. At all of them you'll need to present ID before logging on. Many of these places are short-lived, but you should find the following still in operation:
San Marco: Venetian Navigator, Calle dei Stagneri 5239 (daily 10am–8.30pm).
Dorsoduro: TheNetGate, Crosera S. Pantalon 3812 (Mon–Sat 10.30am–8.30pm); Logic Internet, Calle del Traghetto 2799 (daily 10am–8.30pm).
San Polo: Internet@café, Calle del Campaniel 2898 (daily 10am–9pm).
Cannaregio: Planet Internet, Rio Terà San Leonardo 1519 (daily 9am–11pm).
Castello: Internet Corner, Calle del Cafetier 6661a (Mon–Sat 10am–10pm, Sun 1–10pm); Venetian Navigator, Calle Casselleria 5300 (daily: summer 10am–10pm; winter 10am–7.30pm).

Laundries Venice's self-service laundries are now virtually extinct; one survivor is to be found to the south of Campo Santa Maria Formosa, at Ruga Giuffa 4826 (daily 8.30am–8pm). You're never far, however, from a laundry that will do your washing for you.

Left luggage The desk at the end of platform 14 at the train station (6am–midnight) charges €3.80 per item for five hours, then €0.60 for each subsequent hour. The office on Piazzale Roma (6am–9pm) charges €3.50 per item for 24hr.

Lost property If you lose anything on the train or at the station, call ☏041.785.531; at the airport call ☏041.260.9222; on ACTV water or land buses call ☏041.272.2179; and anywhere in the city itself call ☏041.274.8225.

Pharmacies Italy operates a system called *Farmacie di Turno*, which ensures that you are never far from an open pharmacy at any time of day or night. Every one displays the address of the nearest late-opening pharmacy, and there's always a full list in *Un Ospite di Venezia* (see p.35).

Police To notify police of a theft or lost passport, report to the Questura, which is at Rampa Santa Chiara 500, on the north side of Piazzale Roma (☎041.271.5511); in the event of an emergency, ring ☎113. There's a small police station on the Piazza, at no. 63.

Post offices Venice's main post office is in the Fondaco dei Tedeschi, near the Rialto bridge (Mon–Sat 8.30am–6.30pm). Any poste restante should be addressed to Fermo Posta, Fondaco dei Tedeschi, San Marco 5554, 80100 Venezia; take your passport along when collecting your post. The principal branch post offices are in Calle dell'Ascensione, at Záttere 1406, and by the Piazzale Roma vaporetto stops (all Mon–Fri 8.30am–6pm, Sat 8.30am–1pm). Stamps can also be bought in *tabacchi*, as well as in some gift shops.

Public toilets There are toilets on or very near to most of the main squares, signposted by green and white "WC" stickers on the walls or ground. Public toilets cost €1.50, and many toilets are staffed, so you can get change; note that the Venice Card (see p.34) gives two daily free visits to staffed toilets. The main facilities are at Piazzale Roma; in the Giardinetti Reali, by the main tourist office; off the west side of the Piazza; on Campo Rialto Nuovo; and on the west side of the Accademia bridge.

Telephones Most of Venice's public call-boxes accept coins, and all of them take phonecards, which can be bought from *tabacchi* and some other shops (look for the Telecom Italia sticker), as well as from post offices. You're never far from a pay phone – every sizeable campo has at least one, and there are phones by most vaporetto stops. Note that many internet points offer international calls at a better rate than you'll get from Telecom Italia's public phones.

Train enquiries ☎89.20.21, ⓦwww.trenitalia.com.

The Veneto

The Veneto

The Veneto: practicalities

The administrative region of the Veneto extends right to the Austrian border, taking in the portion of the **Dolomites** known as the Cadore, the main town of which is Pieve di Cadore – Titian's birthplace. Further north still is Cortina d'Ampezzo, the most fashionable ski resort of the eastern Dolomites since it hosted the Winter Olympics in 1956. This whole area offers some of Italy's most sublime landscapes, but the mountains are quite distinct from Venice's immediate hinterland, and cannot really be visited on an excursion from the city. As the purpose of this section of the Guide is to reveal the mainland sights and towns that can be seen on a day's excursion from Venice, its northern limit is Belluno.

Although rock-bottom hotel prices are rare in the affluent Veneto, the cost of **accommodation** on the mainland is appreciably lower than in Venice itself, and to get the most out of the less-accessible sights of the Veneto it's necessary to base yourself for a day or two somewhere other than Venice.

Getting around by train

Trains run by Trenitalia, the Italian state rail company (W www.trenitalia.it), are efficient and inexpensive, with tickets being priced on a strict formula according to the distance of the journey: as an indication of price, a second-class ticket from Venice to Vicenza, a trip of around 70km, costs around €4.50 on the most basic type of train. The trains are very convenient as well, with all the major towns interconnected: one main line runs from Venice through Treviso and northwards, another through Castelfranco up to Bassano, and a third through Padua, Vicenza and Verona. Frequencies of services are given in the box on p.281 and in the text, but bear in mind that comments such as "every half-hour" are approximations – as with all Italian train services, there are occasional gaps in the schedule, typically occurring just after the morning rush hour, when the gap between trains may be twice as long as normal, and Sunday services are far less frequent.

There are various categories of train, the quickest of which are the **Eurocity** services (EC), which connect major cities across Europe, perhaps stopping at only two or three places in each country. **Eurostar Italia** (ES) runs between major cities and is faster and more efficient than **Intercity** (IC) trains and Intercity Plus trains (which claim better service and improved carriage interiors). You need to reserve for all these services, and pay a supplement of at least thirty percent of the ordinary fare. There are no supplements for the **Espresso** (EX), medium-fast trains that stop at major towns and cities, **Interregionali** (IR), similar to the Espresso, but usually with more stops, or **Regionali** (Reg), which stop at every place with a population higher than zero.

When checking station timetables, pay attention to the notes, which may specify the dates between which some services run (*Si effetua dal…al…*), or whether a service is seasonal (*periódico*). On routes to or from smaller towns, you should also look carefully for a little bus symbol in the margin of the timetable: this indicates that the train service is replaced by a bus (*autocorsa*), which will generally depart from outside the station.

Accommodation price codes

Hotels in this guide are classified into nine price categories, indicating the range of prices for a **double room**. In high season you should expect to pay something close to the maximum indicated.

❶ €100 and above	❹ €201–250	❼ €351–400
❷ €101–150	❺ €251–300	❽ €401–500
❸ €151–200	❻ €301–350	❾ €501 and over

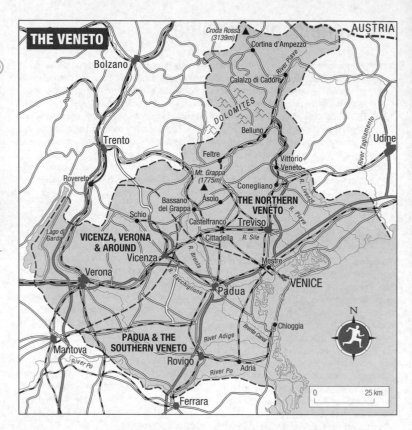

A last word of warning: all train stations have validating machines in which passengers have to stamp their ticket before embarking. Look out for them in ticket halls and on platforms – they are inconspicuous yellow boxes mounted at waist height. If you realize that you've forgotten to **validate your ticket** at the station, find the train guard (he or she is nearly always in the first carriage) and present your ticket for clipping – that way you'll be spared a hefty on-the-spot fine.

Getting around by bus

Buses offer frequent connections between the main towns: they generally cost more or less the same as the equivalent train journey, and in some instances are actually quicker than the trains. For visits to smaller towns, there is sometimes no alternative unless you have a car – Ásolo, for instance, has no train connection, and you'll need to take a bus for the great Villa Barbaro at Masèr. Usually the bus station (*autostazione*) is close to the train station, and even when the terminus is elsewhere, many services call at the train station along their route. Tickets have to be bought before getting on board, either from the bus company's office at the station, or from the nearest agent – their name and address is always shown on the timetable at the bus stop. If you're setting off for a remote place, it's always a good idea to buy your ticket for the return leg at the point of departure, as some villages have just a single outlet which might well be closed when you need it. Services are drastically reduced, or nonexistent, on Sunday, and note that lots of departures are linked to school requirements – which sometimes means no services during school holidays.

Main Veneto train services

Belluno to: Calalzo (9 daily; 1hr); Conegliano (5 daily; 55min); Vittorio Veneto (6 daily; 35–55min).

Castelfranco Veneto to: Belluno (12 daily; 1hr 20min–1hr 40min); Feltre (12 daily; 50min–1hr); Padua (19 daily; 35min); Treviso (10 daily; 25min); Venice (20 daily; 55min); Vicenza (16 daily; 40min).

Conegliano to: Belluno (5 daily; 55min); Udine (30 daily; 1hr); Venice (every 30min; 50min–1hr); Vittorio Veneto (15 daily; 15–25min).

Monsélice to: Venice (hourly; 55min); Padua (every 30min; 25min); Montagnana (11 daily; 25min); Este (11 daily; 6min).

Padua to: Bassano (16 daily; 1hr 5min); Belluno (13 daily; 2hr); Feltre (12 daily; 1hr 30min); Milan (24 daily; 2hr 30min); Monsélice (every 30min; 25min); Rovigo (every 30min; 25–40min); Venice (every 20min; 30–40min); Verona (every 30min; 45min–1hr 15min); Vicenza (every 20min; 15–30min).

Rovigo to: Venice (30 daily; 1hr–1hr 30min); Padua (every 30min; 25–40min).

Treviso to: Castelfranco Veneto (15 daily; 25min); Cittadella (13 daily; 35min); Conegliano (every 30min; 15–25min); Venice (every 20min; 35min); Vicenza (13 daily; 45min–1hr 15min).

Venice to: Bassano (18 daily; 1hr 5min–1hr 30min); Belluno (3 daily; 1hr 50min–2hr 20min); Castelfranco Veneto (20 daily; 55min); Conegliano (every 30min; 50min–1hr); Milan (25 daily; 2hr 45min–3hr 30min); Monsélice (hourly; 55min); Padua (every 20min; 30–40min); Rovigo (30 daily; 1hr–1hr 30min); Treviso (every 20min; 35min); Trieste (24 daily; 3hr); Udine (every 30min; 1hr 45min–2hr); Verona (every 30min; 1hr 20min–2hr); Vicenza (every 30min; 50min–1hr 20min); Vittorio Veneto (6 daily; 1hr 10min–1hr 30min).

Verona to: Milan (every 30min; 1hr 20min–2hr); Padua (every 30min; 45min–1hr 15min); Venice (every 30min; 1hr 30min); Vicenza (every 30min; 30–45min).

Vicenza to: Castelfranco Veneto (16 daily; 40min); Cittadella (15 daily; 25min); Milan (25 daily; 1hr 50min–2hr 40min); Padua (every 20min; 15–30min); Thiene (20 daily; 25min); Treviso (13 daily; 45min–1hr 15min); Venice (every 30min; 50min–1hr 20min); Verona (every 30min; 30–45min).

City buses usually charge a flat fare of around €1, and again tickets should be bought before getting on – either from offices at bus terminals and stops, or from *tabacchi* and other shops displaying the company's logo and ticket emblem. Stamp your ticket in the machine on the bus – inspectors get on board quite regularly.

Getting around by car

Although public transport is adequate for most occasions, there are instances when a **car** is a great convenience. In Venice the **car rental** companies are clustered around Piazzale Roma. You might find slightly better deals in large towns such as Verona, Padua, Vicenza and Treviso, where the car rental offices congregate around the train station. The cheapest plan, however, is to arrange car rental when you book your flight or holiday.

For **documentation** you need a valid driving licence, with the paper counterpart if you have an EU photocard licence; if you don't have one of these, it is advisable to get an International Driving Licence. You also need insurance if you're taking your own car (check with your insurance company that your policy is valid abroad), the original registration document and a nationality sticker visible on the car. It's compulsory to carry your car documents and passport while you're driving, and you'll be required to present them if you're stopped by the police. **Rules of the road** are straightforward: drive on the right; at junctions, where there's any ambiguity, give precedence to vehicles coming from the right; use dipped lights in poor daytime visibility as well as at night; don't drink and drive; and observe the speed limits – 50kph in built-up areas, 90kph on minor roads outside built-up areas, 110kph on main roads (dual carriage-ways), and 130kph on nearly all motorways (a few stretches have a 150kph limit). Note that in wet weather, an 80kph limit applies on minor roads, 90kph on main roads and 110kph on motorways. If you **break down**, dial ⊕116 at the nearest phone and tell the operator where you are, the type of car and your registration number; the nearest office of the Automobile Club d'Italia (ACI), an AA/RAC/AAA equivalent, will be informed and they'll send someone to help, though it's not a free service. If you need towing anywhere, you can count on it costing a fairly substantial amount, so you should consider arranging cover in your home country before you leave.

Most major towns in the Veneto have traffic restrictions in the town centre; if you're in a car and are staying in a central hotel that doesn't have its own parking spaces, you'll be issued with a temporary resident's permit.

Padua and the southern Veneto

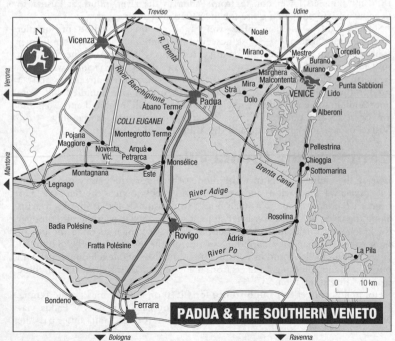

S ummer in Venice used to be the season for people to leave the city in great numbers, rather than pour into it as they do today. When the temperature rose, the gentry would make for their country retreats along the **Brenta**, which flows into the lagoon at the nearest point to the mainland to the city. Many of these houses still stand, and the finest of them can be visited easily by taking one of the buses that run along the Brenta from Venice to Padua.

Situated a little under forty kilometres west of Venice, the ancient university city of **Padua** is an obvious day-trip from Venice, being only half-an-hour's

Map labels: Treviso, Udine, Noale, Vicenza, R. Brenta, Mirano, Mestre, Torcello, Burano, Marghera, Murano, River Bacchiglione, Mira, Malcontenta, Strà, Punta Sabbioni, Àbano Terme, Padua, Dolo, VENICE, Lido, COLLI EUGANEI, Alberoni, Montegrotto Terme, Pojana Maggiore, Noventa Vic., Arquà Petrarca, Monsélice, Pellestrina, Montagnana, Este, Chioggia, Sottomarina, Legnago, Brenta Canal, River Adige, Badia Polésine, Rosolina, Rovigo, Àdria, La Pila, Fratta Polésine, River Po, Bondeno, Ferrara, **PADUA & THE SOUTHERN VENETO**, Bologna, Ravenna, Verona, Mantova

0   10 km

train journey away. However, Padua has more than enough sights to fill a more protracted stay, notably the **Cappella degli Scrovegni**, with its astonishing fresco cycle by Giotto (which you must book in advance to see), the **Basilica di Sant'Antonio**, a pilgrimage church which contains some of the finest sculpture in the Veneto, and the vast **Palazzo della Ragione**, the frescoed medieval hall that overlooks Padua's twin market squares.

Of the small towns to the **south of Padua** the most enticing are **Monsélice**, which has a superbly restored castle, and **Montagnana**, whose medieval town walls have survived in almost pristine form. And if you need a rest from urban pursuits, the green **Colli Euganei** (Euganean Hills) offer a pleasant excursion.

The Brenta

The southernmost of the three main rivers that empty into the Venetian lagoon (the other two are the Sile and Piave), the **Brenta** caused no end of trouble to the earliest settlers on both the mainland and the islands: on the one hand, its frequent flooding made agriculture difficult, and on the other, the silt it dumped into the lagoon played havoc with Venice's water channels. Land reclamation schemes were carried out from the eleventh century, but it was in the fourteenth century that Venice began the large-scale canalization of the Brenta, an intervention which both reinforced the banks of the river and controlled the deposition of its contents in the lagoon. The largest of the artificial channels, La Cunetta, which runs from Stra to Chioggia, was finished as recently as 1896, but by the sixteenth century the management of the Brenta was sufficiently advanced for the land along its lower course, from Padua to the river-mouth at Fusina, to become a favoured building site for the Venetian aristocracy.

Some of these Venetian **villas** were built as a combination of summer residence and farmhouse – most, however, were intended solely for the former function. From the sixteenth century to the eighteenth, the period from mid-June to mid-November was the season of the *villeggiatura*, when the patrician families of Venice would load their best furniture onto barges and set off for the relative coolness of the Brenta. Around one hundred villas are left standing: some are derelict, a large number are still inhabited and a handful are open to the public. Of this last category, two are outstanding – the **Villa Fóscari** at Malcontenta and the **Villa Pisani** at Strà.

Getting to the Brenta villas

During the eighteenth century, the mode of transport the gentry used for the *villeggiatura* was a capacious and well-padded vessel known as the *Burchiello*. The modern *Burchiello* is one of a small flotilla of pleasure craft that shuttles tourists along the river, making a few brief stops at selected villas, pausing rather longer for lunch, and finally unloading them at Padua or Venice to catch the bus or train back to where they started. Day-trips on the *Burchiello* (℡049.820.6910, ⓦ www.ilburchiello.it) and its cousins cost as much as €80 (excluding lunch and bus ticket), and you can get tickets from many of Venice's travel agents – all those near the Piazza sell them.

Hoi polloi can get to **Malcontenta** for €1.10 on a bus from Piazzale Roma. It only takes twenty minutes, but make sure you catch the ACTV Padua-via-Malcontenta bus, which goes only once an hour. (Other Padua buses pass the

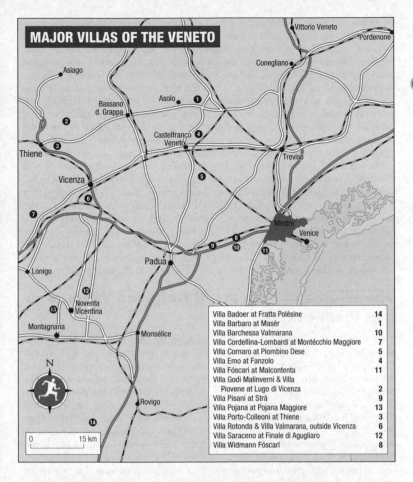

MAJOR VILLAS OF THE VENETO

Villa Badoer at Fratta Polésine	14
Villa Barbaro at Masèr	1
Villa Barchessa Valmarana	10
Villa Cordellina-Lombardi at Montécchio Maggiore	7
Villa Cornaro at Piombino Dese	5
Villa Emo at Fanzolo	4
Villa Fóscari at Malcontenta	11
Villa Godi Malinverni & Villa Piovene at Lugo di Vicenza	2
Villa Pisani at Strà	9
Villa Pojana at Pojana Maggiore	13
Villa Porto-Colleoni at Thiene	3
Villa Rotonda & Villa Valmarana, outside Vicenza	6
Villa Saraceno at Finale di Agugliaro	12
Villa Widmann Fóscarl	8

other villas covered below, but not Malcontena.) On your way back from Malcontenta, if the first bus that comes along isn't going to Venice, take it as far as Corso del Popolo in Mestre, then cross the road for a #4 to Piazzale Roma – you can do it on the one ticket, which is valid for an hour. The bus journey from Venice to **Strà**, 25 minutes on from Malcontenta (€3.50 from Venice), gives you a good view of dozens of villas on the way. They are particularly thick on the ground from **Oriago** onwards (16km out of Venice), the most attractive stretch being centred on the elongated town of **Mira**, shortly after Oriago. Byron wrote part of *Childe Harold* in Mira's Palazzo Fóscarini (now the post office), where he lived in 1817–19.

The Villa Fóscari

Sometimes known as the Villa Malcontenta (or Villa Fóscari La Malcontenta di Mira), the **Villa Fóscari** (April–Oct Tues & Sat 9am–noon; €10) at **MALCONTENTA** was designed in 1559 for the brothers Alvise and Niccolò Fóscari by

Palladio, and is the nearest of his villas to Venice. None of Palladio's villas more powerfully evokes the architecture of ancient Rome: the heavily rusticated exterior suggests the masonry of Roman public buildings; the massive Ionic portico alludes to classical temple fronts (which Palladio believed to be derived from domestic architecture); and the two-storey main hall was inspired by the bath complexes of imperial Rome, as was the three-sectioned arched window (a feature known as a thermal window, from the Roman *thermae*). Palladio was practical as well as erudite: to keep the living quarters well clear of the swampy land, he raised them on a high podium, and to keep costs down he used the cheapest materials that would do the job – look closely at the columns and you'll see that they're made out of hundreds of bricks in the shape of cake slices.

The main hall and the rooms leading off it (only some of which are open to the public) were frescoed as soon as the walls were up, by **Battista Franco** and **Giovanni Battista Zelotti**, a colleague of Veronese; their work includes what is said to be a portrait of a woman of the Fóscari family who was exiled to the house as punishment for an amorous escapade, and whose consequent misery, according to legend, was the source of the name *Malcontenta*. The reality is more prosaic – the area was known by that name long before the Fóscari arrived, either because of some local discontent over the development of the land, or because of political *malcontenti* who used to hide out in the nearby salt marshes.

The Widmann Fóscari, Barchessa Valmarana and Pisani villas

The **Villa Widmann Fóscari** (March, April & Oct Tues–Sun 10am–5pm; May–Sept Tues–Sun 10am–6pm; Nov–Feb Sat & Sun 10am–5pm; €5) at Mira Porte, just after Oriago, was built in the early eighteenth century and redecorated fifty years or so later. The garden is a delight, and the ballroom is a spectacular example of Rococo style, even if Giuseppe Angeli – who painted the best of the frescoes – was nowhere near as inventive an artist as his great contemporary, Tiepolo. The **Villa Barchessa Valmarana** (March–Oct Tues–Sun 10am–6pm; Nov–Feb Sat & Sun 10am–5pm; €6; Ⓦ www.villavalmarana.net), across the canal, was built in the seventeenth century but the main accommodation block was destroyed by the Valmarana family at the end of the nineteenth to avoid paying luxury taxes. Today, the only part of the villa which can be visited is one of the wings that flanked the house; originally built as boat and agricultural storage space, it was soon after converted into guest quarters. The furniture on display was brought over from the main house when it was demolished, and the dining room has a ceiling fresco glorifying the Valmarana family.

At **STRÀ**, virtually on the outskirts of Padua, stands the immense **Villa Pisani** or **Nazionale** (Tues–Sun: April–Sept 9am–7pm; Oct–March 9am–4pm; €7.50 for house and garden, €4.50 for garden only). The branch of the Pisani family for whom this place was built was an astronomically wealthy dynasty of bankers, based in Venice in the similarly excessive Palazzo Pisani at Santo Stefano. When Alvise Pisani was elected doge of Venice in 1735, the family celebrated by commissioning the villa from the Paduan architect **Girolamo Frigimelica**; later on the work was taken over by **F.M. Preti** (see the Castelfranco account, p.344, for more of his work). By 1760 it was finished – the biggest such residence to be built in Venetian territory during the century. It has appealed to megalomaniacs ever since: Napoleon bought it off the Pisani in 1807 and handed it over to Eugène Beauharnais, his stepson and Viceroy of Italy; and in 1934 it was the place chosen for the first meeting of Mussolini and Hitler.

The house has been stripped of nearly all its original furnishings, and it's as hard to thrill to the eighteenth-century frescoes of smiling nymphs and smirking satyrs that decorate some of the rooms as to the almost blank walls you'll see elsewhere. The one pulse-quickening room is the **ballroom**, its ceiling covered with a fresco of *The Apotheosis of the Pisani Family*, the last major piece painted by **Giambattista Tiepolo** before his departure for Spain in 1762, at the age of 66. It's a dazzling performance, as full of blue space as it could possibly be without falling apart. If you're trying to puzzle out what's going on: the Pisani family, accompanied by Venice, are being courted by the Arts, Sciences and Spirits of Peace, while Fame plays a fanfare in praise of the Pisani and the Madonna looks on with appropriate pride. The monochrome frescoes on Roman themes around the musicians' gallery are by Giambattista's son, Giandomenico.

In the **grounds**, the long fishpond ends in front of a stable-block which from a distance might be mistaken for another grand house. Off to the right (as you look away from the villa) is a peculiar belvedere, resembling a chapel with its dome lopped off; and close by there's an impressive maze. The immaculate citrus garden, restored on the basis of years of historical research, is in stark contrast to the neglect of the house.

Padua

Extensively reconstructed after the damage caused by World War II bombing, and hemmed in by the sprawl which has accompanied its development into the most important economic centre of the Veneto, **PADUA** (Padova) is not at first sight as alluring as many of the region's towns. It was, however, one of the most important cultural centres of northern Italy, and retains plentiful evidence of its impressive lineage in its churches, museums and frescoed interiors. In recent years, civic efforts to polish and pedestrianize the city centre – even to the extent of mapping out the medieval street plan in marble flagstones – have made it easier to conjure up the context of Padua's many historic buildings.

Legend has it that Padua was founded in 1185 BC by Antenor of Troy – a story propagated first by the Roman historian Livy, who was born in a nearby village and spent much of his life here. A Roman *municipium* from 45 BC, the city thrived until the barbarian onslaughts and the subsequent Lombard invasion at the start of the seventh century. Recovery was slow, but by the middle of the twelfth century, when it became a free commune, Padua was prosperous once again. The university was founded in 1221, and a decade later the city became a place of pilgrimage when **Saint Anthony**, who had arrived in Padua in 1230, died and was buried here.

The appalling **Ezzelino da Romano** occupied Padua for two decades from 1237, and struggles against the **Scaligeri** of Verona lasted until the **Da Carrara** family established their hold in 1337. Under their domination Padua's cultural eminence was secured – Giotto, Dante and Petrarch were among those attracted here – but Carraresi territorial ambitions led to conflict with Venice, and in 1405 the city's independence ended with its conquest by the neighbouring republic. Though politically nullified, Padua remained an artistic and intellectual centre: Donatello and Mantegna both worked here, and in the seventeenth century Galileo conducted research at the university, where the medical faculty was one of the most advanced in Europe. With the fall of the Venetian Republic

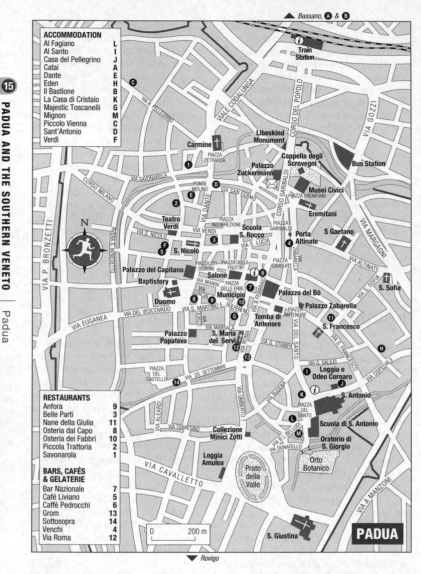

ACCOMMODATION
Al Fagiano	L
Al Santo	I
Casa del Pellegrino	J
Catai	A
Dante	E
Eden	H
Il Bastione	B
La Casa di Cristalo	K
Majestic Toscanelli	G
Mignon	M
Piccolo Vienna	C
Sant'Antonio	D
Verdi	F

RESTAURANTS
Anfora	9
Belle Parti	3
Nane della Giulia	11
Osteria dal Capo	8
Osteria dei Fabbri	10
Piccola Trattoria	2
Savonarola	1

BARS, CAFÉS
& GELATERIE
Bar Nazionale	7
Café Liviano	5
Caffè Pedrocchi	6
Grom	13
Sottosopra	14
Venchi	4
Via Roma	12

PADUA

the city passed to Napoleon, who handed it over to the **Austrians**, after whose regime Padua was annexed to Italy in 1866.

Arrival and accommodation

Trains arrive in the north of the town, just a few minutes' walk up Corso del Popolo from the old city walls. The main **bus station** is at Piazzale Boschetti, immediately north of the walls to the east of the Corso; however, **local buses** for the city and nearby towns such as Ábano and Montegrotto leave from outside the train station. A new system of electric **trams** (Metrobus) is very gradually being introduced to the city; the first line to be completed runs between the station and Prato della Valle, via the Basilica. There are **tourist offices** at the train station (June–Aug Mon–Sat 9.15am–7pm, Sun 9am–noon; Sept–May Mon–Sat 9.15am–7pm, Sun 9.15am–noon; ☎049.875.2077, ⊛www .turismopadova.it), in the town centre at Piazzetta Pedrocchi (Mon–Sat 9am–1.30pm & 3–7pm; ☎049.876.7927) and in summer on Piazza del Santo (April–Oct Mon–Sat 9am–1pm & 3–6pm, Sun 9am–noon; ☎049.875.3087).

A few years ago it was infinitely simpler to find an inexpensive room in Padua than in Venice; it's still the case that the average cost is lower, but availability can be a problem. If you're visiting in high season or during festivals, be prepared for a slightly protracted search, but don't despair – Padua has plenty of reasonably priced hotels, and an ever-expanding choice of bed and breakfast places, too. The city's youth hostel, however, is currently being used as temporary accommodation for asylum seekers.

Hotels

Al Fagiano Via Locatelli 45 ☎049.875.0073, ⊛www.alfagiano.com. Wackily decorated and friendly two-star, which has forty rooms over three floors, each floor having a different colour scheme. The rooms are on the small side, but have a/c, TV and hair dryers. ❶

Al Santo Via del Santo 147 ☎049.875.2131, ⊛www.alsanto.it. Located virtually next door to the Basilica, this three-star hotel is comfortable, if slightly austere in atmosphere. ❶–❷

Casa del Pellegrino Via M. Cesarotti 21 ☎049.823.9711, ⊛www.casadelpellegrino.com. Large, inexpensive two-star right opposite the Basilica. Its 150 rooms are simply furnished but have air-conditioning; the "economy" rooms have shared bathrooms, while the "superior" ones have a view of the Basilica. ❶

Dante Via San Polo 5 ☎049.876.0408, ⊛www .hoteldante.eu. Clean and central one-star near the Ponte Molino, run by a friendly signora who speaks little English. Just eight rooms, not all en suite. ❶

Eden Via C. Battisti 255 ☎049.650.484, ⊛www .hoteledenpadova.it. A cut above other one-stars, though offers something of a mixed bag of rooms. All doubles have showers, but avoid the coffin-like singles. Situated in a good location near Piazza del Santo, in the university quarter. ❶

Majestic Toscanelli Via dell'Arco 2 ☎049.663.244, ⊛www.toscanelli.com. With its glitzy, nicely equipped rooms, this four-star is probably the hotel of choice if you want to stay in style; it's located just south of Piazza delle Erbe, off Via SS. Martino e Solferino. ❸

Mignon Via Luca Belludi 22 ☎049.661.722, ⊛www.hotelmignonpadova.it. Comfortable two-star between Prato della Valle and the Basilica. They also have rooms that sleep three and four. ❶

Piccolo Vienna Via Beato Pellegrino 133 ☎049.871.6331, ⊛www.hotelpiccolovienna.it. This friendly one-star is one of the cheapest hotels in Padua, and is just a 10-minute walk northwest from the centre. Simply furnished rooms with or without bathrooms – those at the back are quieter. ❶

Sant'Antonio Via San Fermo 118 ☎049.875.1393, ⊛www.hotelsantantonio.it. Pleasant three-star in the northern part of central Padua. Rooms are large and modern, if slightly faded; those at the back have views over the canal and the lovely Ponte Molino. Start the day with fresh orange juice and coffee next door at the friendly *Albabar*. ❶

Verdi Via Dondi dall'Orologio 7 ☎049.836.4163, ⊛www .albergoverdipadova.it. A friendly small three-star in a quiet street near Piazza Signori. The fourteen rooms are all a good size and have modern fittings. ❶–❷

B&B and self-catering

In addition to the places recommended below, the tourist office has a long list of B&Bs in Padua, as does the Kokonor agency (⊛www.bbkokonor.it); the Padovacard – see p.290 – gets you reductions on stays of more than two nights at some B&Bs. For self-catering accommodation, check the Holiday Rentals website (see p.240); one especially nice property is Via Gaspara Stampa 23 (Ⓦ www.holiday-rentals.co.uk/p85777), a three-bedroomed apartment just north of the Basilica.

Catai Via Selva 5 ☎ 049.864.3394, Ⓦ www.bbtibetanhouse.it. Room for two to four people in this very friendly place in a quiet spot, ten minutes' walk north of the station. It has a terrace and a large living room; the hospitable owner has travelled widely and speaks good English. ❶
Il Bastione Via M. Sanmicheli 76 ☎ 049.876.6723, Ⓦ www.ilbastione.com. Behind

the Basilica di Santa Giustina. Three rooms with private bathroom. ❶
La Casa di Cristallo Via del Santo 82 ☎ 049.876.5523, Ⓦ www.lacasadicristallo.it. Four spacious and very nicely furnished rooms close to the Basilica di Sant'Antonio, with en-suite facilities and jacuzzis. Minimum stay 2 nights. ❷–❹

The City

From the train station, the drab Corso del Popolo and Corso Garibaldi lead south through a gap in the Renaissance city walls towards the centre of the city, passing the seventeen-metre-tall structure of glass and steel designed by the architect Daniel Libeskind, as a monument to the victims of the September 11 attacks – it contains part of a girder salvaged from the World Trade Center.

The Cappella degli Scrovegni

A couple of minutes' walk further on, you come to the astounding **Cappella degli Scrovegni**. The **Giotto frescoes** in this building constitute one of the key works in the development of European art, but they are also among the most fragile, because the walls on which they are painted are permeated with damp rising from the chapel's swampy foundations. Until recently the situation was being worsened by the thousands of tourists who came to see the chapel each year – breath and perspiration were beginning to corrode the surface of the frescoes. Extraordinary measures have now been taken to preserve the paintings. Entrance to the chapel is through a sophisticated airlock: at the time printed on your ticket, the glass door to the waiting room slides open to allow the next set of twenty-five visitors in, and almost immediately shuts again. Once inside, a high-tech system lowers the humidity of the waiting room to that of the chapel, and filters away any stray spores and pollutants. Fourteen minutes later another door leading to the chapel itself opens and you have a quarter of an hour (or twenty minutes after 7pm) to take in the frescoes before being ejected back into the grounds of the museum.

The chapel was commissioned in 1303 by Enrico Scrovegni in atonement for his father's usury, which was so vicious that Dante allotted him a place in the

The Padovacard

Costing €15 for 48 hours or €20 for 72 hours, the **Padovacard** (Ⓦ www.padovacard .it) allows one visit for one adult and one child under 14 to twelve sites in the city and environs, including the Musei Civici degli Eremitani, Scrovegni Chapel, and Palazzo della Ragione. There are further discounts on the other main attractions, as well as free parking in the three main car parks, free travel on the APS buses, free bicycle hire and discounts at some bed and breakfasts. It's available from the tourist office and participating museums and monuments. Note that advance booking is required for the Scrovegni Chapel, for which an extra €1 booking fee is payable.

⑮

Tickets for the Cappella degli Scrovegni

The Cappella degli Scrovegni is open daily 9am–10pm. Tickets are €12, which includes entry to the Eremitani Museum, or €8 on Monday and after 7pm, when the museum is closed; the Padovacard, plus €1 booking fee, also gets you in. After 7pm you can also book a double slot ("doppia turno"), which gives you 40 minutes inside the chapel for €12. The number of visitors permitted each day is strictly limited, so it's usually advisable to book tickets in advance – at least three or four days in advance in summer. Only in the dead of winter is it likely that tickets will be available at the door. Reservations can be made at the museum ticket office, or by phoning ☏049.201.0020 (Mon–Fri 9am–7pm, Sat 9am–6pm), or online at ⓦwww .cappelladegliscrovegni.it. Tickets must be picked up from the ticket office an hour before your timed entry; you have to be at the chapel waiting-room five minutes before your allotted time.

Inferno – he died screaming "give me the keys to my strong box" and was denied a Christian burial. As soon as the walls were built, Giotto was commissioned to cover every inch of the interior with frescoed illustrations of the lives of Jesus, Mary and Joachim (Mary's father), and the story of the Passion; the finished cycle, arranged in three tightly knit tiers and painted against a backdrop of saturated blue, presents an artistic vision of the same order as that of the Sistine Chapel. Looking towards the altar, the tiers on the right depict (from top to bottom) *The History of Joachim*, *The Childhood of Christ* and *The Passion*; the tiers on the left comprise *The Life of the Virgin*, *Christ's Public Life* and *Christ's Death and Resurrection*.

The Scrovegni series is a marvellous demonstration of Giotto's unprecedented attention to the inner nature of the protagonists – the exchange of looks between the two shepherds in *The Arrival of Joachim* is particularly powerful, as are *The Embrace of Joachim and Anna at the Golden Gate* and *The Visit of Mary to Elizabeth*. On occasion even the buildings and landscape have been manipulated to add to the drama, for example in the *Deposition* (immediately right of the *Crucifixion*), where a strong diagonal leads the eye straight to the faces of Jesus and Mary.

Beneath the main pictures are shown the Vices and Virtues in human (usually female) form, while on the wall above the door is the *Last Judgement*, with two angels rolling back the painting to remind us that this is an imaginative scene and not an authoritative vision of eternity. An alleged self-portrait (fourth from the left at the bottom) places Giotto firmly amongst the redeemed, and directly above the door is a portrait of Scrovegni presenting the chapel; his tomb is at the far end, behind the altar with its statues by **Giovanni Pisano**.

The Musei Civici

The neighbouring **Musei Civici degli Eremitani** (Tues–Sun 9am–7pm; €10, or Padovacard), formerly the monastery of the Eremitani, is a superbly presented museum complex that contains the Museo Archeologico and the Museo d'Arte-Medioevale e Moderna. The archeological collection, on the ground floor, has a vast array of pre-Roman, Roman and paleo-Christian objects, with an absorbing section on the unique language spoken in the Veneto before the establishment of Roman hegemony. Upstairs, the vast Museo d'Arte houses extensive and varied collections of fourteenth- to nineteenth-century art from the Veneto and further afield, usually arranged in roughly chronological order. There are tracts of workaday stuff here, but names such as Titian, Tintoretto and

Tiepolo leaven the mix, and spectacular highpoints are provided by the Giotto *Crucifixion* that was once in the Scrovegni chapel, and a fine *Portrait of a Young Senator* by Bellini. In the midst of the ranks of French, Flemish and miscellaneous Italian paintings you'll also happen upon a shockingly vivid sequence of pictures by Luca Giordano, featuring a repulsive depiction of Job and his boils. The offshoot Capodilista collection contains a rich seam of sixteenth-century works, including four mysterious landscape allegories by Titian and Giorgione.

The third part of the Musei Civici lies across Corso Garibaldi in the grand **Palazzo Zuckermann**, which has recently been refurbished to house two small museums that are pleasant enough but won't detain you for too long. The new **Museo d'Arte, Arti Applicate e Decorative** has jewellery, fabrics, pottery and furniture from the fourteenth century onwards, including some fine painted chests. The second floor is devoted to the **Museo Bottacin**, which was founded in 1865 when a wealthy merchant, Nicola Bottacin, donated his collection of coins and art to the city; featuring more than 50,000 coins, medals and seals, this is one of the largest numismatic museums in the world.

The Eremitani

The nearby church of the **Eremitani** (Mon–Sat 9am–1pm & 3.30–7pm, Sun 9.30am–12.30pm & 4–7pm), built at the turn of the fourteenth century, was almost completely wrecked by an Allied bombing raid in 1944 and has been fastidiously rebuilt. The worst aspect of the bombardment was the near total destruction of **Mantegna**'s frescoes of the lives of Saint James and Saint Christopher – during World War II, only the destruction of the Camposanto in Pisa was a comparably severe blow to Italy's artistic heritage.

Produced between 1454 and 1457, when Mantegna was in his mid-twenties, the frescoes were remarkable for the thoroughness with which they exploited fixed-point perspective – a concept central to Renaissance humanism, with its emphasis on the primacy of individual perception. Furthermore, Mantegna's compositions had to take into account the low viewpoint of the person in the chapel. The extent to which he overcame these complex technical problems can now be assessed only from the sad fragments preserved in the chapel to the right of the high altar. On the left wall is the *Martyrdom of St James*, put together from fragments found in the rubble; and on the right is the *Martyrdom of St Christopher*, which had been removed from the wall before the war.

The sanctuary and the second and fourth chapels of the right aisle contain frescoes by the late fourteenth-century Paduan painter Guariento, the *Madonna* in the fourth chapel being the best of them.

To Santa Sofia

Straddling Via Altinate, the **Porta Altinate** was one of the gates of the medieval city, and bears a plaque recording its violent recapture from Ezzelino da Romano on June 20, 1256. Continuing past the dull sixteenth-century church of San Gaetano and a scattering of fine houses, you come to **Santa Sofia** (Mon–Sat 8am–noon & 4–7pm, Sun 8am–noon), the oldest church in Padua. It dates back to the sixth century, though most of today's beautiful brick-built structure dates from the twelfth and thirteenth centuries. The apse in particular shows Veneto-Byzantine influence, and is reminiscent of Santi Maria e Donato on Murano.

The university quarter

A short distance south of the Porta Altinate stands the university's main block, the **Palazzo del Bò** – the name translates as "of the Ox", after an inn that used to stand here. Established in September 1221, the University of Padua is older than any other in Italy except that of Bologna, and the coats of arms that encrust the courtyard and Great Hall attest to the social and intellectual rank of its alumni. The first permanent **anatomy theatre** was built here in 1594, a facility that doubtless greatly helped William Harvey, who went on to develop the theory of blood circulation after taking his degree here in 1602. Galileo taught physics here from 1592 to 1610, declaiming from a lectern that is still on show. And in 1678 Elena Lucrezia Corner Piscopia became the first woman to collect a university degree when she was awarded her doctorate in philosophy here – there's a statue of her in the courtyard. The Bò can be visited only on guided tours (March–Oct Mon, Wed & Fri 3.15, 4.15 & 5.15pm, Tues, Thurs & Sat 9.15, 10.15 & 11.15am; no 9.15am and 5.15pm tours Nov–Feb; €5).

Piazza Antenore, at the back of the Bò, is the site of the **Tomba di Antenore**, alleged resting place of the city's legendary founder. From steps by the tomb you get a glimpse of one of the city's **Roman bridges** – but there is no access until restoration work finishes. If you cross the piazza you'll come to the **Palazzo Zabarella** (Tues–Sun 9am–7pm; price varies for exhibitions) on the corner of Via San Francesco and Via Zabarella. Founded in the twelfth century, it was owned by the Da Carrara family then the Zabarella family, who resided here for more than four hundred years from 1405. A fine example of a Paduan aristocratic town-house (the tower was characteristic of such houses), it was thoroughly restored in the 1990s, and now has an exhibition space upstairs and stylish shops in the courtyard.

The central squares

The area north and west of the university forms the hub of the city. A little way up from the university, on the left, is the Neoclassical **Caffè Pedrocchi** (Ⓦ www .caffepedrocchi.it), designed by Giuseppe Japelli in 1831 for Antonio Pedrocchi, who was dubbed by Stendhal "the best caterer in Italy". Priding itself as the city's main intellectual salon (it was here that an abortive uprising against the Austrian occupation was launched on February 9, 1848), the *Pedrocchi* used to stay open night and day, hence its nickname, "the café without doors". It's no longer that, but it does have a multiplicity of functions – chic café (on the ground floor), concert hall, conference centre and exhibition space (upstairs). An outside staircase in Piazzetta Pedrocchi leads up to the **piano nobile** (Tues–Sun 9.30am–12.30pm & 3.30–6pm; €4), formerly the haunt of the Paduan intelligentsia, where highly decorative rooms radiate off a central hall: pictures of ancient Rome by Ippolito Caffi adorn the Roman Room, painted mirrors gleam in the Moorish Chamber and stars shine on the ceiling of the vivid blue Egyptian Room. You'll also find the **Museo del Risorgimento e dell'Età Contemporane** here: covering local history from 1797 until 1948, the rooms of uniforms and guns are of limited interest, but the films and photos from World War II are worth a look.

Due west of the *Pedrocchi*, the **Piazza della Frutta** and **Piazza delle Erbe**, the sites of Padua's daily markets, are lined by bars, cafés and shops. Separating them is the extraordinary **Palazzo della Ragione** or **Salone**, as it's more commonly known (Tues–Sun: Feb–Oct 9am–7pm; Nov–Jan 9am–6pm; €4 or Padovacard), which is usually entered by the stairs on the Piazza delle Erbe side at the eastern end.

At the time of its construction in the 1210s, this vast hall was the largest room ever to have been built on top of another storey. Its decoration would once have been as astounding as its size, but the frescoes by Giotto and his assistants were destroyed by fire in 1420, though some by **Giusto de' Menabuoi** have survived.

Most of the extant frescoes are by **Nicola Miretto** (1425–40), whose 333-panel astrological calendar has a fascination that transcends the limitations of his workmanship. Each of the twelve sections begins with the apostle appropriate to that month (the larger panel) and progresses through the allegorical figures representing the month, the zodiacal sign, the planet and constellation, the type of work done in that month and the human figure representing the astrological type. The ceiling was originally frescoed as a deep blue starry sky but was rebuilt following a violent tornado in 1756 and has been letting in the wind and rain ever since; the consequent restoration work keeps at least part of the hall closed at all times, making it difficult to appreciate Miretto's grand scheme in its entirety.

Now used as an exhibition space and as the city council's assembly hall, the Salone was also a place where Padua's citizens could plead for justice – hence the appellation *della Ragione*, meaning "of reason". The black stone to the right inside the door, called the *pietra del vituperio* (stone of insults), also played a part in the judicial system: Thomas Coryat recorded that a bankrupt could dissolve some of his debts by sitting on it "with his naked buttocks three times in some public assembly". The gigantic wooden horse is modelled on Donatello's *Gattamelata*, and was made for a joust in 1466. Before leaving, take a stroll along the magnificent loggias on either side, which look out onto the squares on either side.

Both the Piazza della Frutta and the Piazza delle Erbe have some attractive buildings around them, as does the **Piazza dei Signori**, which lies a little to the west. At the west end of the piazza, beyond the Lombard Loggia della Gran Guardia (c.1500), is the early fifteenth-century **Torre dell'Orologio**. Through the arch, under the clock, is the Corte Capitaniato, a quiet, leafy square with two university buildings on the left. The first is the **Palazzo del Capitanio**, the sixteenth-century headquarters of the city's Venetian military commander; the second is the university's arts faculty, the **Liviano**. The frescoes in the Liviano's fourteenth-century **Sala dei Giganti** upstairs include a portrait of Petrarch, which you can see if you attend one of the classical concerts that's occasionally held here.

Via dei Da Carrara runs north of the Piazza del Capitaniato straight up to the church of **San Nicolò** (daily 8am–noon & 4–7pm) – basically an altered thirteenth-century building, though it retains an eleventh-century chapel.

The Duomo and Baptistery

Immediately southwest of the Piazza dei Signori stands Padua's **Duomo** (Mon–Sat 7.30am–noon & 4–7.30pm, Sun 7.45am–1pm & 4–8.30pm), an unlovely church whose architect cribbed his design from drawings by Michelangelo; the adjacent Romanesque **Baptistery** (daily 10am–6pm; €2.80, or €1 with Padovacard), though, is one of the delights of Padua. Built by the Da Carrara clan in the thirteenth century, it's lined with delightful frescoes by **Giusto de' Menabuoi** (c.1376), a cycle that makes a fascinating comparison with Giotto's more monumental work in the Cappella degli Scrovegni. The polyptych **altarpiece**, also by Menabuoi, was stolen in 1972 but quickly recovered, minus some of its wooden framework. Don't overlook the **mausoleum of Fina Buzzaccharini** (on the wall opposite the altar), one of the Carrara family's most assiduous artistic patrons; she's shown on the front being presented to the Virgin by John the Baptist. Her tomb was destroyed by the Venetians when they took control of the city in 1405.

Piazza del Santo and the Gattamelata monument

If you continue trudging south from the Porta Altinate you'll soon find yourself in Via del Santo, where an increasing density of shops selling garishly decorated candles and outsize souvenir rosaries will prepare you for the pilgrim-ensnaring stalls of the **Piazza del Santo**. The main sight on the piazza – apart from the mighty basilica – is Donatello's **Monument to Gattamelata** ("The Honeyed Cat"), as the *condottiere* Erasmo da Narni was known. He died in 1443 and this monument was raised ten years later, the earliest large bronze sculpture of the Renaissance. It's a direct precursor to Verrocchio's equestrian monument to Colleoni in Venice (and Colleoni was under Gattamelata's command for a time), but could hardly be more different: Gattemelata was known for his honesty and dignity, and Donatello has given us an image of comparative sensitivity and restraint, quite unlike Verrocchio's image of power through force. The modelling of the horse makes a double allusion: to the equestrian statue of Marcus Aurelius in Rome, and to the horses of San Marco in Venice.

The Basilica di Sant'Antonio

Within eighteen months of his death in 1231, Saint Anthony of Padua had been canonized and his tomb was attracting enough pilgrims to warrant the building of the **Basilica di Sant'Antonio**, or **Il Santo** (daily: April–Sept 6.20am–7pm; Oct–March 6.20am–7.45pm). It was not until the start of the fourteenth century that the church reached a state that enabled the saint's body to be placed in the chapel designated for it. The **exterior** is an outlandish mixture, with campanili like minarets, Byzantine domes and Romanesque and Gothic features on the facade and apse.

The **interior** is similarly heterogeneous: the plan up to the transepts being much like that of Italian mendicant churches, whereas the complex ambulatory with radiating chapels is more like the layout of French pilgrimage churches of the period. Saint Anthony's chapel – the **Cappella del Santo** – is in the left

Saint Anthony

Born in 1195 in Lisbon, **Saint Anthony** (christened Fernando) was a canon of the Augustinian order in Coimbra before he donned the Franciscan habit in 1220 and set off for Morocco, having been inspired to undertake his mission by five Franciscan friars who had been martryred by the Moroccan infidels. Soon taken ill in Africa, he sailed back to Portugal but was blown off course and landed in Sicily. From there Anthony headed north to Assisi, thence to a hermitage near Forlì, where his oratorical skills and profound knowledge of the scriptures were discovered when he was called upon to speak at a service for which no one had thought to prepare a sermon. After that he embarked on a career as a peripatetic preacher, addressing ever-increasing audiences in northern Italy and southern France, performing miracles (illustrated by the panels around his chapel) and bringing unbelievers into the fold. The "hammer of heretics" was esteemed both by Saint Francis and by Pope Gregory IX, who acclaimed him as the "doctor optime" upon hearing of Anthony's death in 1231. In 1263 the saint's relics were removed to the basilica that had been built in his honour. When his tomb was opened it was discovered that his flesh had turned to dust – except, allegedly, for the tongue.

Saint Anthony's chaste life is symbolized by the lily that is his distinguishing feature in depictions of him. He is also often portrayed holding the infant Jesus, a reference to an incident when he was observed from afar cradling the Son of God. His popularity has continued to grow after his death, and the abundance of letters, photographs and gifts around his shrine confirms the endurance of the belief in Anthony's wonder-working powers. He is the patron saint of Portugal, lost property, and the less-exalted animal species – the last honour comes from the legend that he preached to fishes when he could find no human audience.

transept, plastered with votive photographs of healed limbs, car wrecks survived thanks to the saint's intervention, and other offerings irresistible to the voyeur. The chapel's more formal decoration includes a sequence of nine **panels** showing scenes from Saint Anthony's life; carved between 1505 and 1577, they are the most important series of relief sculpture created in sixteenth-century Italy. Reading from the left: Saint Anthony receives his Franciscan habit; a jealous husband stabs his wife, whom the saint later revived; Saint Anthony raises a man from the dead to prove the innocence of his father; he revives a drowned woman (panel by Sansovino); he revives a baby scalded to death in a cauldron (Sansovino and Minello); he directs mourners to find the heart of a miser in his coffer (Tullio Lombardo); he restores the severed foot of a boy (Tullio Lombardo); a heretic throws a glass which miraculously breaks the floor and remains intact; and a newborn baby tells of the innocence of its mother (Antonio Lombardo).

Adjoining the chapel is the **Cappella della Madonna Mora** (named after its fourteenth-century French altar statue), which in turn lets onto the **Cappella del Beato Luca**, where Saint Anthony's body was first placed. Dedicated to Luca Belludi, Saint Anthony's closest companion, the latter chapel contains a fine fresco cycle by **Giusto de' Menabuoi**, including scenes from the lives of the Apostles Philip and James the Lesser, and *Saint Anthony revealing to Luca Belludi that Padua will be liberated from Ezzelino*, with an idealized version of the city, parts of it recognizable, as backdrop.

Back in the aisle, just before the Cappella del Santo, is Padua's finest work by **Pietro Lombardo**, the monument to Antonio Roselli (1467). More impressive still are the high altar's bronze sculptures and reliefs by **Donatello** (1444–45), the works which introduced Renaissance classicism to Padua. Unfortunately they are often inaccessible, though a word with one of the sacristans may get you a closer view. The neo-Gothic frescoes of the apse, choir and presbytery were begun by **Achille Casanova** in 1903, and took about forty years. Trying to imitate Giotto's use of blue, he ended up turning this end of the basilica into a gloomy cavern.

Built onto the furthest point of the ambulatory, the **Cappella delle Reliquie** or **del Tesoro** (daily: April–Oct 7am–1pm & 2.30–7.30pm; Nov–March 8am–1pm & 2.30–6.30pm) was designed in the 1690s by Filippo Parodi, a pupil of Bernini. Its most important relics are a thorn from Christ's crown, and Il Santo's tongue, vocal chords and chin, which are kept in elaborate reliquaries in the central of the three niches behind the balustrade.

Most of the back wall of the **Cappella di San Felice**, occupying the right transept, is taken up by a glorious *Crucifixion*, frescoed in the 1370s by Altichiero da Zevio. Other things to seek out are the **monuments to Cardinal Pietro Bembo and Alessandro Contarini** on the nave's second pair of columns, both designed by Sanmicheli in the 1550s (with a bust by Danese Cattaneo), and the **tomb of Gattamelata**, in the first chapel on the right. The fresco on the interior wall of the facade is a more recent addition, *Saint Anthony preaching from the walnut tree* by **Annigoni** (1985). The painting above the altar in the first chapel on the left is also by him.

In the cloisters, on the south side of the basilica, you'll find the **Museo Antoniano** (April–Oct 9am–1pm & 2.30–6.30pm; Nov–March Tues–Sun 9am–1pm & 2–6pm; €2.50, €1.50 with Padovacard) and the **Museo della Devozione Populare** (same hours; free). The former, on the first floor, is a collection of paintings (including a fresco of *SS. Anthony and Bernardine* by **Mantegna**, which once adorned the basilica's facade), ornate incense-holders, ceremonial robes and other paraphernalia linked to the basilica; the latter, on the ground floor, is a history of votive gifts, with copious examples of the genre. The **Mostra Antoniana**, an audiovisual presentation (in Italian) of Saint Anthony and his work, is on perpetual show elsewhere in the cloister.

Around the piazza

On the northern side of the Basilica, a short way east along Via Cesarotti, you'll find the recently opened **Loggia e Odeo Cornaro** (Tues–Sun 10am–1pm, plus Sat & Sun 4–7pm; €3, or Padovacard), the remnants of a complex set up in 1524 for the coterie of Alvise Cornaro, a prominent figure in the intellectual, scientific and artistic life of the city. The two-tiered loggia leads to the octagonal Odeo where Cornaro held concerts and literary gatherings; inside is an abundantly decorated vault, with watery landscapes in the shell-hooded niches.

On the southern side, to the left as you leave the basilica, are the joined Oratorio di San Giorgio and **Scuola del Santo** (10am–noon & 3–5pm; €2, €1.50 with Padovacard). The Scuola, a confraternity run on the same lines as the scuole of Venice (see p.132), was founded soon after Anthony's canonization, though this building dates only as far back as the early fifteenth century. The ground floor is still used for religious purposes, while upstairs is maintained pretty much as it would have looked in the sixteenth century, with its fine ceiling and paintings dating mainly from 1509–15. Four of the pictures are said to be by **Titian**: *The Jealous Husband Stabbing his Wife*, with an almost insignificant intervention by Il Santo in the background; *St Anthony Reattaching the Severed Foot of a Young Man*; *The Distribution of Blessed Bread*; and *The Newborn Infant Defends the Honour of its Mother*. If any of these are genuine, they would be the earliest known extant works by him. Some of the other paintings are charming oddities, such as *St Anthony Confronting Ezzelino da Romano* – a perilous diplomatic exercise which may or may not have happened. Next door to the Scoletta, the **Museo al Santo** is used for one-off exhibitions, often drawing on the resources of the Musei Civici.

Following a visit to the Scuola, the custodian takes you next door to the **Oratorio di San Giorgio** (daily: April–Oct 9am–12.30pm & 2.30–7pm; Nov–March 9am–12.30pm & 2.30–5pm; same ticket), which was founded in 1377 as a mortuary chapel – its frescoes by **Altichiero di Zevio** and **Jacopo Avanzi** were completed soon after. Recently restored, their work is an engaging and colourful narrative romp: the scenes from the life of Saint George on the left wall, for example, show not just the customary dragon-slaying, but also the saint being released by angels from a wheel of torture; and the opposite wall is adorned with a depiction of Saint Lucy remaining immoveable as her persecutors attempt to haul her off to a brothel with the help of a team of oxen.

The Orto Botanico, Prato della Valle and Santa Giustina

A good way to relax after all this art is to stroll round the corner to the **Orto Botanico** in Via Donatello (April–Oct daily 9am–1pm & 3–7pm; Nov–March Mon–Sat 9am–1pm; €4, free with Padovacard; ⓦ www.ortobotanico.unipd.it), the oldest botanic gardens in Europe. Planted in 1545 by the university's medical faculty as a collection of medicinal herbs, the gardens are laid out much as they were originally, and the specimens on show haven't changed too much either. Goethe came here in 1786 to see a palm tree that had been planted in 1585; the selfsame tree still stands.

A little to the south sprawls the **Prato della Valle**, claimed to be the largest town square in Italy; it's a generally cheerless area, ringed by over-wide roads, but the vast Saturday market, groups of off-duty students and summer funfair

▲ Prato della Valle, with the Basilica di Sant'Antonio, Padua

do a lot to make it jollier. It also hosts a big antiques market on the third Sunday of each month. The greenery in the centre follows the oval plan of the extinct Roman amphitheatre; the two rings of statues commemorate 78 worthy Paduans, both native and honorary.

One side is fronted by the sixteenth-century **Basilica di Santa Giustina** (daily 7.30am–noon & 3–7pm), at 120m long, one of the world's largest churches. A pair of fifteenth-century griffins, one holding a knight and the other a lion, are the only notable adornments to the unclad brick facade; the freezing interior (scarves are worn by the Benedictine monks even when it's warm outside) is offputtingly clinical, with little of interest except a huge *Martyrdom of St Justina* by **Paolo Veronese**, some highly proficient carving on the choir stalls, and the sarcophagus that reputedly once contained the relics of Luke the Evangelist (in the left transept).

Far more appealing are the vestiges of the church's earlier incarnations, which have been the object of archeological research for some time. In the right transept a stone arch opens onto the **Martyrs' Corridor**, named after a well containing martyrs' bones, now part of the catacombs below the corridor. This part of the building is a composite of fifth- to twelfth-century architectural fragments, and leads to the **Sacellum di Santa Maria e San Prosdocimo**, burial place of Saint Prosdocimus. He was the first bishop of Padua back in the fourth century, when the church was founded, and is depicted here on a fifth-century panel. The fifteenth-century **old choir** is reached by a chain of corridors from the left-hand chapel of the right transept; the choir stalls are inset with splendid marquetry panels, and the **sacristy** beyond has an amusing painting of *St Maurus Rescuing St Placid from a Lake*.

Finally, on the top floor of the Palazzo Angeli, at Prato della Valle 1, you'll find one of the Veneto's most engaging private museums, the **Collezione Minici Zotti** (10am–4pm, closed Tues; €3, free on 3rd Sun of month; Ⓦ www .minicizotti.it). Subtitled "un museo di magiche visione", this perfectly displayed collection of shadow puppets, magic lanterns and other optical instruments was assembled by Laura Minici Zotti in the course of thirty years of research into the precursors of cinematography. Gorgeous contraptions with names such as the Praxinoscope, Zogroscope, Priviliged Megalethoscope and the Panoptic Polyorama fill the rooms under the roof, from one of which you can survey the streets through a replica of the camera obscura that Canaletto used in creating a panoramic scene.

Eating, drinking and nightlife

As in any university city, there's plenty of choice when it comes to unpretentious bars and restaurants, and the student population guarantees a pretty active after-dark scene.

Catering for the midday stampede of ravenous students, Padua's bars generally produce weightier **snacks** than the routine *tramezzini* – slabs of pizza and sandwiches vast enough to satisfy a glutton are standard. For a *passeggiata* and a place to sit and watch the world go by, the main areas to head for are Piazza delle Erbe, Piazza Duomo and Piazza Cavour, but for the real action, the bars in the narrow streets around these piazzas and the university are the liveliest, with a student-based clientele.

Restaurants

Anfora Via dei Soncin 13 ☎049.656.629. Boisterous and very reasonable restaurant that doubles as a bar between restaurant hours (12.30–3.15pm & 8–11.30pm), with delicious snacks all day. Get there early or book in advance. Closed Sun. Inexpensive to moderate.

Belle Parti Via Belle Parti 11 ☎049.875.1822. On a tiny street running between Via Verdi and Via Santa Lucia, this place has an excellent menu and a chilled but elegant atmosphere. With mains at €20–25, it is not cheap, but the *degustazione* menu (around €50) is good value. Booking advisable. Closed Mon lunch & Sun. Moderate to expensive.

Nane della Giulia Via Santa Sofia 1 ☎049.660.742. There has been an *osteria* here, in what was once a church hospital, since 1820. The present one is a trendy and unpretentious place that serves reasonably priced Veneto and vegetarian specialities – all made from locally sourced and seasonal products. The summer garden is lovely too. No credit cards. Booking advisable at weekends. Closed Mon all day and Tues lunch. Moderate.

Osteria dal Capo Via degli Obizzi 2 ☎049.663.105. Located just off the southeast corner of Piazza del Duomo, on the corner of Via dei Soncin, this small restaurant is much celebrated amongst the locals for its regional fish dishes and wide range of pasta dishes – try the duck tagliatelle. Booking essential. Closed all Sun & Mon lunch. Moderate.

Osteria dei Fabbri Via dei Fabbri 13 ☎049.650.336. Excellent mid-range trattoria, just of Piazza delle Erbe; you'll be lucky to get a seat if you haven't booked. Closed Sun. Moderate.

Piccola Trattoria Via R Da Piazzola 21 ☎049 656.163. Friendly and very popular place, serving Sardinian specialities, all superbly presented, and accompanied by delicious vegetables. Its *secondi* are around €15, but it offers cheap lunchtime specials. Closed all day Sun and Mon lunch. Moderate.

Savonarola Via Savonarola 38. Busy pizzeria just outside the city walls with a good atmosphere and moderate prices. Popular with students. Closed Mon.

Bars, cafés and gelaterie

Bar Nazionale Piazza delle Erbe 40. Popular bar on the northeast corner of the piazza. When it closes, join the young crowd at the *gelateria* next door. Open Mon–Sat till 8pm.

Café Liviano Piazzetta Capitaniato 10. Both this and the neighbouring *Café Miro* spill out under the trees in this square, which has a secluded feel even though it's right in the centre of town. Popular with students from the neighbouring university buildings. Closed Sun.

Caffè Pedrocchi Via 8 Febbraio 15. Chic and spacious spot for expensive coffee or cocktails. Tues–Sun 9am–9pm, midnight Fri & Sat.

Grom Via Roma 101. Turin-based *Grom* produces the most exquisite ice cream in the city. Daily till midnight.

Sottosopra Via XX Settembre 77. A popular bar that serves a wide range of teas as well as wines with its salads and sandwiches. Its clientele – from retired couples to students –

is unusually varied. Closed Sun lunch and all day Mon.

Venchi Via Altinate 6. Lying right inside the gate, this is one of the new ice-cream outlets that the distinguished Venchi chocolate-maker – also hailing from Turin – has recently opened across the region. Sun–Thurs 11am–9pm, Fri & Sat 11am–midnight.

Via Roma Via Roma 96. One of several bars spilling out on to this mainly pedestrianized road. Serves snacks and good large salads. A good place for an *aperitivo*. Open till 2am, closed Mon.

Nightlife

Padua's main theatre, the **Teatro Verdi** on Corso Milano (℡049.877.7011, ⓦwww.teatroverdipd.it), hosts opera and big-name dramatists; details of the season's events can be obtained from the tourist office or in the bi-monthly information booklet *Padova Today*, distributed at the tourist office, in some bars and in most hotels. Of the local newspapers, the most comprehensive for **listings** is *Il Mattino*, but for more offbeat events check the posters up around the city, particularly around the university. Padua's nightlife tends to fluctuate in synch with term time; during the summer vacation things are rather somnolent.

Listings

Bike rental Piazza Stazione ℡348.701.6373 (24hr).

Bus information City buses (ACAP): Piazzale Stazione ℡049.824.1111. Regional buses (SITA): Piazzale Boschetti ℡049.820.6844.

Car rental Avis, Via A da Bassano 27a ℡049.864.7661; Europcar, Piazzale Stazione 6 ℡049.657.877; Hertz, Via A da Bassano 31a ℡049.875.2202.

Hospital Ospedale Civile, Via Giustiniani 1 ℡049.821.1111 (24hr).

Internet access Internet Point Padova, Via Altinate 145, opposite Santa Sofia, or ask at the

tourist office how to register for access to the free wi-fi network in the Piazza delle Erbe and Piazza de lla Frutta.

Police Questura, Riviera Ruzante 11 ℡049.833.111.

Post office Corso Garibaldi 33 (Mon–Sat 8.15am–7.40pm).

Taxis Radio Taxi ℡049.651.333; night service (9.30pm–6am) ℡049.875.1666.

Train information At the station (daily 7am–9pm; ℡89.20.21).

The Colli Euganei

A few kilometres to the southwest of Padua the **Colli Euganei** or Euganean Hills – which are now protected as a national park (ⓦwww.parcocollieuganei .com) – rise abruptly out of the plains, their slopes patched with vineyards between scattered villages, villas and churches. Between Padua and the hills lie the spa towns of **ÁBANO TERME** and **MONTEGROTTO TERME**, which for much of the year are crowded with people looking for cures or beauty treatment from the radioactive waters and mud baths. It's been like this for centuries, as the names of the towns indicate: *Ábano* comes from Aponeus, a Roman god of healing, while *Montegrotto* is said to derive from "mons aegratorum", meaning "mountain of the infirm". Largely composed of big and expensive modern hotels, these are places to avoid unless you're hell-bent on trying to poach yourself in the hot springs.

A car is necessary for exploring the Colli Euganei proper, as buses are few and far between, even to Arquà Petrarca (see below). The **villas** of the region are its major architectural attractions, but many of them remain in private hands and can only be viewed from a distance. An exception is the famous garden of the **Villa Barbarigo** at Valsanzibio (March–Nov daily 10am–1pm & 2pm–sunset; €8.50, ten percent discount with Padovacard; ⓦ www.valsanzibiogiardino.it); laid out in 1699, it features a maze and fantastical Baroque gateways and fountains. The house itself is not open to the public.

Arquà Petrarca

The gem of the Colli Euganei is the medieval village of **ARQUÀ PETRARCA** (ⓦ www.arquapetrarca.com), served by three daily buses from Este, though the two morning services leave impracticably early. A pleasant alternative is to walk from Monsélice, less than 6km away.

The Da Carrara family gave the poet **Francesco Petrarca** (Petrarch) a piece of land here on which to realize his dream of a "delightful house surrounded by an olive grove and a vineyard". He spent the last summers of his life (1369–74) in his idyllic home, at Via Valesella 4, and this is where he died. Not only does the house, the **Casa Petrarca** (Tues–Sun: March–Oct 9am–12.30pm & 3–7pm; Nov–Feb 9am–12.30pm & 2.30–5.30pm; €3, or Padovacard) still stand, but his desk and chair are still intact, as are various parts of the original fabric of the interior. Petrarch's sarcophagus is in the centre of the village, with one epitaph penned by him and another by his son-in-law, who placed it here.

Monsélice

In earlier times **MONSÉLICE** was perched on the pimple of volcanic rock around the foot of which it now winds. Of the five concentric walls that then protected it, all that remains of them and their towers is a small section of the outer ring and a citadel right on the hill's crest – the rest was demolished for building stone in the nineteenth century. The remnants make a powerful impression though, and the town possesses another fortress which is the equal of any in the Veneto. The town is easily accessible from Padua, from where there are nine trains a day and buses every half-hour, many of which head on to Este and Montagnana.

From the train station, the route to the centre of town crosses the Canale Bisato, from whose bridge you can look back to the **Villa Pisani** (sometimes open for exhibitions), which was a stopover for the Pisani family as they travelled by water from Venice to their estates in Montagnana. The fragmentary town wall leads to the **Torre Civica**, built by Ezzelino da Romano in 1244 and repaired in 1504. Facing the Torre Civica across Piazza Mazzini, just beyond the wall, is the **Loggetta**, a seventeenth-century addition to the **Palazzo del Monte di Pietà**, the facade of which is on the road leading away from the square. Just behind, at the beginning of Via del Santuario, the **Antiquarium Longobardo** (April–Nov Tues–Sun 10am–noon & 3–5pm; €2, or combined ticket with Castello di Monsélice) displays the contents of Lombard tombs discovered recently on the mountain above, including coins, weapons, some unusually complete sarcophagi and a beautiful gold cross.

This road bends round and up the hill to the **Castello di Ezzelino**, more often known as **Ca' Marcello** or the **Castello di Monsélice** (guided tours April–Oct Tues–Sun at 9am, 10am, 11am, 3pm, 4pm & 5pm; in Nov last entrance is 4pm, and tours must be booked on ☎0429.72.931 or through ⓦwww.castellodimonselice.it; €5.50, or €6.50 with Antiquarium Longobardo). Dating back to the eleventh century, the house was expanded in the thirteenth century by Ezzelino, who added the square tower across the courtyard (the coat of arms was appended after the town came under Venetian rule in 1405). The interior was altered in the fourteenth century by the Da Carrara clan; linking the two main sections is a fifteenth-century annexe added by the Marcello family; a library (sixteenth century) and family chapel (eighteenth century) were the only later changes. The castle's immaculate appearance is down to **Count Vittorio Cini**, who inherited the derelict building after it had been in the tender care of the Italian army during World War I, and sank a fortune into restoring it and furnishing each section in the appropriate style, even down to the *marmorino* flooring, stained red with bull's blood in the traditional manner.

The tour begins in the **armoury**, three rooms of weaponry, some of it beautifully worked and decorated, occupying the ground floor of Ezzelino's tower. Up from here are the **Marcello family apartments**, an adaptation of part of Ezzelino's tower, furnished in sixteenth- and seventeenth-century fashion. The family restyled the **courtyard** in the seventeenth century to mimic a Venetian campo, complete with well-head and drainage holes; it is a source of local pride that the *tracchite* stone that paves much of Venice, including most of Piazza San Marco, came from the quarries of Monsélice.

Up the ramp, a gate leads to the upper storey of the Marcello building, the **anteroom** of which was added to the external wall of Ezzelino's palace and retains the original windows as internal features. The **great hall** was formed by the Carraresi; its fireplace was originally from Ferrara and the tapestries are from Brussels. Just off the hall is an example of a *becca di flauta* (flute-lipped) fireplace, an unusual style of chimney which the Carraresi left behind in many of the castles they controlled, proudly painted in their red and white chequerboard colours. The old part of the castle is quite domestic in feel: look for the fourteenth-century painted ceiling in the **Sala del Casteletto**. On the ground floor is the **kitchen**, set out with fifteenth-century furniture and copper plates up to seven hundred years old. The top part of this section contains the **council hall**, with delicate frescoes and fourteenth-century seating. The library, now minus its books, is used by the University of Padua and others as a conference room.

Continuing up the hill you see on the left the white, featureless **Palazzo Nani**, so called because of the stone dwarves (*nani*) on the surrounding wall: much more interesting than the palace itself are its steps up the garden (visible through the gate), flanked by mock Roman sculptures and leading to an imitation Roman temple.

The **Duomo Vecchio** is the next stop: fourteenth-century fresco fragments and a Romano-Gothic polyptych on the high altar are its principal attractions. Just beyond the duomo a gateway guarded by two Venetian lions gives onto the Via Sette Chiese, a private road leading up to the **Villa Duodo**. The seven churches of the road's name are a domesticated version of the seven pilgrimage churches of Rome, arranged as a line of six chapels leading to the church of **San Giorgio** at the top.

Sinners could earn pardon for their misdemeanours by praying their penitential way up the hill to San Giorgio, where figures of martyred saints are arranged in wood-and-glass cabinets. The chapels, church, triumphal arch and the main part of the villa were all designed in the late sixteenth century by **Vincenzo Scamozzi**. Now an international centre for the study of hydrology, the villa was commissioned by the son of Francesco Duodo, a hero of the battle of Lépanto; the land was donated by the Venetian state in thanks for services rendered.

On the summit of La Rocca stands the **Mastio Federiciano** (Frederick's Keep), constructed in the thirteenth century by the Emperor Frederick II; the interior is open only to groups of at least five people (April–Nov Sun 3–6pm; €4 per person; ☎0429.72.931).

An alley running round the back of the Duomo leads back to the centre; the most interesting building you'll pass on the descent is the Gothic **Ca' Bertana** in Via M. Carron, which has elegant fourteenth-century windows. There's no need to traipse over to the **Duomo Nuovo** – you'll have seen as much as you need to from the walk up the hill: its only remarkable aspect is its size.

Este

If you're using public transport, just about the best base from which to roam around the Colli Euganei is the ceramics-producing town of **ESTE**, on the southern edge of the outcrop, just a ten-minute train ride from Monsélice (9 daily). The chief tourist office of the Colli Euganei is at Piazza Maggiore 9 (Mon–Sat 9am–12.30pm; ☎0429.3635).

From the train station a road runs straight to the central Piazza Maggiore, passing the blank-faced **Basilica di Santa Maria delle Grazie** (with a fourteenth-century Byzantine *Madonna*) and the Romanesque brick church of **San Martino**. The nearest thing to an alluring building in the piazza itself is the tatty thirteenth-century home of the Società Gabinetto di Lettura, a cultural organization and archive.

Turning to the right out of the piazza you come face to face with the walls of the ruined **Castello dei Carraresi**; founded by the Este dynasty and rebuilt by the Da Carrara family in 1340, the fortress is now surrounded by the attractive Giardini del Castello (summer 8am–7pm; winter 9am–5pm; free). Material salvaged from the walls was used in the construction of the sixteenth-century palace that now houses the **Museo Nazionale Atestino**, Via G. Negri 9c (daily 9am–8pm; €3).

Este claims to be the oldest town in the Veneto, and the region's outstanding collection of pre-Roman artefacts is installed on the museum's first floor, while much of the ground floor is given over to Roman remains. The room devoted to medieval and Renaissance pieces includes a *Madonna and Child* by **Cima da Conegliano** that was once stolen from the church of Santa Maria della Consolazione and is now here for safekeeping. There's also a display of local pottery, a craft that Este has been famous for since before the Renaissance, and some curious tombstones from the fifth century BC which preserve the alphabet of the ancient language known as Venetico.

The privately owned **Villa de Kunkler**, round the back of the castle, was **Byron**'s residence in 1817–18, a stay commemorated by a plaque on the villa's wall. The house actually played a greater part in Shelley's life than Byron's – his daughter Clara fell ill while staying here, and died as a result of being carried by her father on an overnight gallop to see a doctor in Venice. When the Shelleys returned here a few days later, Percy wrote his poem of mourning for past splendour, *Lines Written Among the Euganean Hills*.

Leading out of the Piazza Maggiore away from the castle, Via Matteotti passes under the **Porta Vecchia**, a restrained Baroque clock tower built on the site of a much earlier defensive tower. Turn right instead of going through the tower and you come to the dull sixteenth-century church of San Francesco, beyond which (in the Quartiere Augusteo) is the main Roman archeological site in Este. Turn right down Via Garibaldi for the **Duomo** (daily 10am–noon & 4–6pm), which was rebuilt between 1690 and 1708 after an earthquake; the oval plan of its Baroque interior anticipated the design of the Pietà in Venice by several decades. The only painting of note is the huge altarpiece of *St Thecla Calling on God for the Cessation of the Plague*, an unusually bleak picture by **Giambattista Tiepolo**; the landscape in the background is a fairly accurate view of Este and the Colli Euganei.

Montagnana

The pride of **MONTAGNANA**, fifteen minutes down the rail line from Este, is its medieval city walls, raised by the ubiquitous Ezzelino da Romano after he had virtually flattened the town in 1242. The walls were later strengthened by the Da Carrara family as Padua's first line of defence against the Scaligeri to the west. It was not until the Wars of the League of Cambrai in the early sixteenth century that the battlements were called upon to fulfil their function, and when the hour came they were found wanting – controlled by the Venetians at the start of hostilities, Montagnana changed hands no fewer than thirteen times in the course of the war. After that the walls were not used

▲ Walls of Montagnana

The Villa Badoer at Fratta Polésine

A trip to **FRATTA POLÉSINE**, 18km southwest of Rovigo, will appeal to ardent fans of **Palladio**'s buildings. The **Villa Badoer** (April to mid-Oct Thurs, Sat & Sun 10am–noon & 3.30–6.30pm; free), designed in the 1560s, is one of his most eloquent flights of architectural rhetoric, with its distinctive curving colonnades linking the porticoed house to the storage spaces at the side. None of the original furnishings are left, but restorers have uncovered the villa's late sixteenth-century grotesque frescoes by **Giallo**, a recherché Florentine. Four buses a day go there from Rovigo, but really a car is needed. **Rovigo** itself is the capital of the fertile and often flooded zone between the Adige and the Po, an area known as the Polésine (or "Little Mesopotamia"); trains on their way to Ferrara and Bologna from Venice call here at least hourly (average journey 90min), but the town has no sights to detain you.

defensively again. With a circumference of nearly two kilometres and 24 polygonal towers spaced at regular intervals, these are among the finest medieval fortifications in Italy, and the relatively sparse development around their perimeter makes them all the more impressive. (Appropriately enough, the town is the home of the Istituto Internazionale dei Castelli, a centre for research on military architecture.)

Gates pierce the walls at the cardinal points of the compass, the entrances to the east and west being further reinforced by fortresses. The **eastern** gate (Porta Padova) is protected by the **Castello di San Zeno**, built by Ezzelino in 1242, with a watchtower to survey the road to Padua; the Castello now houses the **Museo Civico e Archeologico** (tours Wed–Fri at 11am, Sat 11.30am, 4pm & 5pm & Sun at 11am, noon, 5 & 6pm; €2.10) which displays various rather dull objects uncovered around the town, from Neolithic arrowheads to medieval ceramics. The musical section shows off costumes and other memorabilia pertaining to Montagnana's favourite sons, the tenors Giovanni Martinelli and Aureliano Pertile – the custodian even plays scratchy recordings of their voices. On the **western** side of town, the **Rocca degli Alberi** was built by the Da Carrara family in 1362 to keep the roads from Mantua and Verona covered – today it houses one of the town's youth hostels.

The centre of Montagnana is the Piazza Vittorio Emanuele, dominated by the late Gothic and rather gloomy **Duomo**. The most arresting feature of its exterior, the marble portal, was a later addition, possibly designed by Sansovino. **Veronese**'s altarpiece, a *Transfiguration*, is less engaging than the huge anonymous painting of the *Battle of Lépanto* on the left as you enter – it's said to represent accurately the ships and their positions at one point in the battle.

Outside the town, just beyond the Porta Padova, is the **Villa Pisani** by **Palladio** (closed to the public), its magnificent, if crumbling, facade at a right angle to the road. It was built as a summer residence and administrative centre for their mainland estates by a branch of the Pisani family of Venice.

Villa Pojana and Villa Saraceno

Two recently restored Palladian villas are located a short distance to the north of Montagnana. On the southern edge of Pojana Maggiore, at Via Castello 43, stands the **Villa Pojana** (Sat & Sun 10am–6pm; €4), the finest of three villas built by the Pojana family in this area (another old castello lies across the road). Commissioned by Bonifazio Pojana – whose wife had provided the dowry for Palladio's wife – it was designed in the late 1540s, and is notable for the austere simplicity of its facade and the finesse of its frescoed decoration, which takes its inspiration from ancient Rome. A display of beautiful wooden models shows several of Palladio's villas as he designed them rather than as they were built; there are plans to convert the basement into another exhibition area.

The main hall and the adjoining frescoed room of the **Villa Saraceno** (April–Oct Wed 2–4pm; free), in the village of Finale di Agugliaro, near Noventa Vicentina, were the only parts of Palladio's project to be completed – the adjoining granaries and barns were added later. These rooms are also the only parts open to visitors, but it's possible to rent the flanking buildings through the Landmark Trust (Ⓦ www.landmarktrust.co.uk), which financed the immaculate restoration; the waiting list is long.

16

Vicenza, Verona and around

L ying almost midway between Padua and Verona, the orderly and affluent city of **Vicenza** tends to be overlooked in favour of its more charismatic neighbours. Yet the streets of Vicenza form one of the most impressive urban landscapes in Italy, owing largely to the activity of Andrea Palladio – the source of Western Europe's most influential architectural style. Buildings by Palladio and his acolytes are plentiful not only inside the city itself, but also out in the surrounding countryside, where the Venetian and Vicentine nobility built up their farming estates from the sixteenth century onwards.

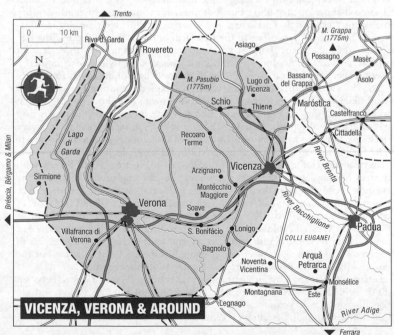

VICENZA, VERONA & AROUND

16

A few of these **villas** are of interest only to cognoscenti like those who overrun Vicenza during September's architecture conference, but several – such as the **Villa Rotonda** and the Tiepolo-painted **Villa Valmarana**, both on the outskirts – make an impact on the uninitiated and the expert alike. And while Palladianism is the region's distinctive style, it doesn't monopolize the scene. Some of Vicenza's Gothic houses would look fine in Venice, and the **Villa Porto-Colleoni** at **Thiene** is as colourful a pile as you'll find in the Veneto.

Verona is perhaps best known to English speakers as the setting for Shakespeare's *Romeo and Juliet*, and supposed sites of their courtship are scattered over the city. Authentic remnants of the city's long and varied past are what make the place so memorable, though – in particular, the remains of the **Roman** period. Of these, the superb **Arena** is the most prominent, followed by the **Teatro Romano** and various archways and gates. Also high on the list of things to see are the monuments left by the **Scaligeri** family, the most celebrated rulers of medieval Verona. Their tombs are masterpieces of Gothic art, and scarcely less impressive is the **Castelvecchio**, once the Scaligeri fortress and now home of Verona's civic museum.

Vicenza

The evolution of **VICENZA** follows a course familiar in this part of northern Italy: development under Imperial Rome, destruction by Attila, Lombard occupation, attainment of a degree of independence followed by struggles with neighbouring towns, rule by the Scaligeri of Verona in the fourteenth century and then absorption into the Venetian empire in 1404, after which its fortunes shadowed those of the ruling city. The numerous surviving fifteenth-century palaces of Vicenza reflect its status as a Venetian satellite, with facades reminiscent of the Canal Grande, but in the latter half of the sixteenth century the city was transformed by the work of an architect who owed nothing to Venice but a lot to ancient Rome, and whose rigorous yet flexible style was to influence every succeeding generation – Andrea di Pietro della Gondola, alias **Palladio**.

The city's architectural heritage – which has earned it a listing as a UNESCO World Heritage Site – brings in a fairly steady stream of visitors, but the tourist revenue is just the icing on the cake. Europe's largest centre for the production of textiles, and the focus of Italy's "Silicon Valley", modern Vicenza is a very sleek city indeed – by some estimates, one of the country's richest half-dozen. The wealth isn't as ostentatious as in Milan, for example, but if you took the banks and the clothes shops out of the centre's main street you'd be left with next to nothing, while the lower storey of the city's signature building – the Basilica – has become a corral of jewellers. Industrial estates and factories form a girdle round the city, and yet modern prosperity hasn't ruined the look of central Vicenza – still partly enclosed by medieval walls, it's an amalgam of Gothic and classical buildings that today looks much as it did when the last major phase of construction came to an end at the close of the eighteenth century. This historic core is compact enough to be explored in a day, but the city and its environs really require a short stay to do them justice.

Getting to Vicenza by public transport is very easy. Frequent trains (between 20 & 30 daily) run from Venice (45min–1hr 20min) through Padua, and are equally regular from Verona (30min); there's also an hourly service from Treviso (1hr 10min) through Castelfranco Veneto.

Arrival and accommodation

The **train station** and the **bus terminus** are a ten-minute walk southwest of the historic centre. The main **tourist office** is alongside the entrance to the Teatro Olimpico, at Piazza Matteotti 12 (daily 9am–1pm & 2–6pm; ☎0444.320.854); there's another office at Piazza dei Signori 8 (daily 10am–2pm & 2.30–6.30pm). For **listings**, pick up a copy of the local papers – *Il Gazzettino* or *Il Giornale di Vicenza*, or check out ⓦwww.vicenza.com or www.vicenzae.org. Culturally the busiest time of the year is from May's Vicenza Jazz Festival through to August, when there's a glut of concerts, opera productions and plays in town, many of the best being performed in the Teatro Olimpico. The **post office** is in Piazza Garibaldi, between the Duomo and Basilica; **banks** are strung out along the Corso Palladio.

Hotels

Vicenza has no central one-star **hotels**, and most of the hotels in the upper categories are aimed primarily at businesspeople – which means they tend to be rather bland and soulless, and several of them close down in August, when Italy's businesses take their summer break. On the other hand, they do often lower their prices at weekends. Note also the city is also a big conference centre, so that hotels get booked up in January, May and September, the prime conference times. In a nutshell – if you want to stay in Vicenza, always reserve a room in advance.

Campo Marzio Viale Roma 21 ☎0444.545.700, ⓦ www.hotelcampomarzio.com. Overlooking a large park midway between the train station and Piazza Castello, this is by far the most appealing of the city's four-star hotels, and also the only one in the historic centre. The building is a modern block but the rooms are decorated – over-decorated, some might say – in a variety of period styles. ❷–❺

Casa San Raffaele Viale X Giugno 10 ☎0444.545.767, ⓦ www.albergosanraffaele.it. The views from this two-star are fantastic, as it lies just below the Basilica on Monte Bèrico, which makes it popular with pilgrims; the downside is that it's half an hour's walk uphill from the centre. This is, though, the cheapest hotel within reach of the centre. ❶

Castello Contrà Piazza del Castello 24 ☎0444.321.485, ⓦ www.hotelcastelloitaly.com. The three-star nineteen-room *Castello* is well positioned just off Piazza Castello, and has a pleasant breakfast terrace on the roof. ❶–❸

Cristina Corso San Felice 32 ☎0444.323.751, ⓦ www.hotelcristinavicenza.it. Friendly three-star hotel near the station. Go for the more expensive rooms at the back – the smarter furnishings are worth the extra money. Half the rooms have baths, while the rest have showers. The breakfasts are made with organic products, and you can hire bikes. ❷–❸

Due Mori Contrà Do Rode 26 ☎0444.321.886, ⓦ www.hotelduemori.com. Graceful and friendly hotel right by the Piazza dei Signori – it's only a two-star but feels better than that. Its rooms are capacious (especially in the annexe, the former *Hotel Vicenza*), and have beautiful Art Nouveau-style furniture. ❶

Giardini Viale Giuriolo 10 ☎0444.326.458, ⓦ www.hotelgiardini.com. This modern three-star at the southern end of Piazza Matteotti has comfortable air-conditioned rooms – go for the quieter ones at the back. ❷

Palladio Contrà Oratorio dei Servi 27 ☎0444.325.347, ⓦ www.hotel-palladio.it. Friendly and very sleek four-star hotel that reopened in 2008 after a major refit. Located in a quiet street just off the central squares, it has 22 rooms with minimalist modern furnishings, including comfortable Japanese mattresses and wall radiators that look like abstract paintings. Room 302 at the top has the largest balcony. ❷–❹

The city centre

The main street of Vicenza, the **Corso Andrea Palladio**, is a vestige of the Roman street-plan and cuts right through the old centre from the Piazza Castello (overlooked by an eleventh-century tower, once part of the Scaligeri fort) down to the Piazza Matteotti. The first major building comes just before the start of the Corso, on the far side of the Piazza Castello – it's the fragmentary **Palazzo Porto-Breganze**, Palladio's last palace in Vicenza. None of Palladio's town houses was completed to plan, but none of the others is as flagrantly unfinished as this one.

Particularly striking on the Corso itself are the following houses: no. 13, the Palazzo Thiene Bonin-Longhare (by Palladio's follower Scamozzi); no. 38–40, Palazzo Pagello (1780); no. 47, Palazzo Thiene (fifteenth century); no. 67, Palazzo Brunello (fifteenth century – have a look at the courtyard); no. 98, Palazzo Trissino (now the town hall; also by Scamozzi); no. 147, Palazzo da Schio

---

The Card Musei

The €8 Card Musei (€12 for family card, valid for two adults and any number of under-25s) gives admission to the Teatro Olimpico, the Museo Civico, the less than enthralling Museo Naturalistico-Archeologico, the Museo Diocesano, the Gallerie di Palazzo Leoni Montanari and the Museo del Risorgimento, a rather specialized museum that's a long way out of the city centre. The first three of these can be visited only with the Card Musei, which you can buy at the Teatro Olimpico, the Museo Diocesano and the Palazzo Leoni Montanari. It is valid for three days.

Andrea Palladio

Born in Padua in 1508, **Palladio** came to Vicenza at the age of 16 to work as a stonecutter. At 30 he became the protégé of a local nobleman, Count Giangiorgio Trissino, who directed his architectural training, gave him his classicized name, and brought him into contact with the dominant class of Vicenza. Some of these men were landowners, recently enriched now that peace had returned to the mainland after the War of the League of Cambrai, many were wealthy soldiers, and a decent percentage were well educated – it wasn't unknown for more than forty of the one hundred city councillors to possess doctorates. They turned to Palladio to design houses that would embody their financial and intellectual rank and their corporate superiority to their Venetian rulers. No architect in Western history has been more influential than Palladio, and although much of that influence derives from his *Quattro Libri dell'Architettura* or *Four Books of Architecture* (a survey of building techniques, classical structures and works by himself, both built and unbuilt), his buildings in and around Vicenza have been consistently studied by architects for the last four centuries. Between 1540 and his death in 1580 Palladio created around a dozen palaces and public buildings in Vicenza plus an even larger number of villas on the Vicentine and Venetian farming estates in the surrounding countryside, and the variety of his designs will surprise anyone who associates Palladianism with blandness. Even if you've previously been inclined to agree with Herbert Read's opinion that "In the back of every dying civilization there sticks a bloody Doric column," you might well leave Vicenza converted.

(fifteenth century, restored), which is known as the Ca' d'Oro as it once had gilded decoration and bears a slight resemblance to the Ca' d'Oro in Venice; and no. 163, the **Casa Cogollo**, known as the Casa del Palladio even though it's unlikely that he designed it (despite what the plaque says) and he certainly never lived there. None of the churches on the Corso is of any interest to non-parishioners.

The Museo Civico and Teatro Olimpico

The Corso Palladio ends with one of the architect's most imperious buildings, the Palazzo Chiericati. Begun in 1550 and completed about a hundred years later, this commission was a direct result of Palladio's success with the Basilica, being a house for one of the Basilica's supervisors, Girolamo Chiericati. It's now the home of the **Museo Civico–Pinacoteca Palazzo Chiericati** (Tues–Sun 9am–5pm; entry with Card Musei), many of whose pieces were gathered in the 1810s to keep them out of the grasp of the marauding French. The museum is in the throes of a rolling refurbishment that will last for several years, but parts of the collection should be open.

The collection of paintings is housed mainly on the second floor, where celebrated names such as Veronese, Memling, Paolo Veneziano, Tintoretto, Giambattista Tiepolo, Van Dyck, the Bassano family and Luca Giordano punctuate a picture collection that is given its backbone by Vicentine artists – notably Montagna, Buonconsiglio, Fogolino (a tumultuous *Adoration of the Magi*), Maffei and Carpioni. Though none of these local artists is likely to knock you flat, there are some fine pieces amid the workaday stuff (the tiny bronze plaquettes made by Valerio Belli, for example), as well as a smattering of oddities: Carpione's disgusting bubble-blowing cherub (an allegory of life's fragility) might stick in the mind, as could Francesco del Cairo's orgasmic *Herodias with the Head of the Baptist*. And be sure to take a look at the ceiling fresco in the ground-floor Sala del Firmamento – a comically

▲ Teatro Olimpico, Vicenza

unflinching depiction of what you'd see if a group of horses steered by a stark naked charioteer flew overhead.

Across Piazza Matteotti is the one building in Vicenza you shouldn't fail to go into – the **Teatro Olimpico** (Tues–Sun: July & Aug 9am–7pm; Sept–June 9am–5pm; entry with Card Musei), the oldest indoor theatre in Europe. Approached in 1579 by the members of the humanist Accademia Olimpica to produce a design for a permanent theatre, Palladio devised a covered amphitheatre derived from his reading of Vitruvius (architect to Augustus) and his studies of Roman structures in Italy and France. In terms of the development of theatre design, the Teatro Olimpico was not a progressive enterprise – contemporaneous theatres in Florence, for example, were far closer to the modern proscenium-arch design – but it was the most comprehensive piece of classical reconstruction of its time, and the men responsible for it were suitably proud of their brainchild: the toga-clad figures above the stage are portraits of Palladio's clients.

Palladio died soon after work commenced, and the scheme was then overseen by Scamozzi, whose contribution to the design is its most startling feature. The theatre was to open with a lavish production of *Oedipus Rex*, so Scamozzi devised a backstage perspective of an idealized Thebes, creating the illusion of long urban vistas by tilting the wooden "streets" at an angle that demands chamois-like agility from the actors. *Oedipus Rex* inaugurated the theatre on March 3, 1585; the theatre was little used in the years that followed, and the original scenery was never removed. The Teatro Olimpico is back in action today, though fire regulations severely restrict audience numbers.

The Piazza dei Signori

At the hub of the city, the **Piazza dei Signori**, stands the most awesome of Palladio's creations: the Palazzo della Ragione, widely known simply as the **Basilica**, which is how the architect referred to it. Designed in the late 1540s, though not finished until the second decade of the next century, this was Palladio's first public project and it secured his reputation. The architect himself, generally regarded as a modest individual, had no doubt as to its merit: "This building can be compared to ancient ones and placed with the most beautiful of the major buildings that have been made by the ancients," he wrote in the *Quattro Libri*. The monumental regularity of the Basilica disguises the fact that the Palladian building is effectively a stupendous piece of buttressing – the Doric and Ionic colonnades enclose the fifteenth-century brick meeting-hall of the city council, an unstable structure that had defied a number of attempts to prop it up before Palladio's solution was put into effect. And if you look closely you'll see that the colonnades aren't quite as regular as they first appear – Palladio had to vary the gaps between the columns and pillars to accommodate the passageways that go through the lower level. The vast Gothic hall is now used for exhibitions, usually on architectural themes.

Facing the Basilica across the Piazza dei Signori is a late Palladio building, the unfinished **Loggia del Capitaniato**. Built as accommodation for the Venetian military commander of the city (the *Capitano*), it's decorated with reliefs in celebration of the Venetian victory over the Turks at Lépanto in 1571. Had it been finished, the Loggia would have taken up much of the area now occupied by the terrace of the *Gran Caffè Garibaldi*. Completing the enclosure of this side of the piazza is the sixteenth-century **Monte di Pietà**, which brackets the seventeenth-century church of San Vincenzo. The worryingly slender **Torre di Piazza** reached its present altitude in 1444, having been started in the twelfth century and raised in 1311; its clock is claimed to have been the first such public timepiece in Italy. The obligatory Lion of Saint Mark was deposited on top of its column in the mid-fifteenth century, not long after Venice took Vicenza to its bosom; the companion figure of the Redeemer dates from the mid-seventeenth century.

For centuries a daily fruit, vegetable and flower **market** has been pitched at the back of the Basilica, in the Piazza dell'Erbe – glowered over by medieval **Torre del Tormento**, once the prison tower. On Tuesdays a vast general market hits town, spreading along the roads between the Basilica and the Duomo.

In Contrà Pigafetta, just a few metres down the slope from the Piazzetta Palladio, on the Duomo side of the Basilica, there's Vicenza's architectural oddity, the Spanish-influenced **Casa Pigafetta**. Built in 1481, it was the birthplace of Antonio Pigafetta, who set out with Magellan on his voyage of 1519 and kept a record of the expedition. Unlike his leader, Pigafetta lived to see his home town again. If you're puzzled by the street name, *contrà* – sometimes *contrada* – is the Vicentine dialect alternative to *via*.

The Duomo

The blandly vast **Duomo** (Mon–Sat 10.30am–11.45am & 3.30–6pm, Sun 3.30–5pm & 6–7pm), founded before the eighth century but substantially rebuilt – chiefly from the fourteenth to the sixteenth centuries, was bombed to bits in 1944 and carefully reconstructed after the war. A polyptych by **Lorenzo Veneziano** (fifth chapel on right) and a *Madonna* by **Montagna** (fourth chapel on left) are the best of its paintings.

Excavations in the crypt have uncovered Roman pavements and parts of a pre-ninth-century basilica, but access is only by appointment with the Centro Turistico Giovanile (℡0444.226.626) across the square at Piazza Duomo 2, which conducts free tours of the site, in Italian (Wed 10am–noon & 4.30–6pm, Sat 10am–noon). The Centro Turistico Giovanile also gives tours of the **Criptoportico Romano**, at Piazza Duomo 6 (2nd Sun of the month 10am–noon all year, plus Oct–March 2.30–4pm, April–June & Sept 3.30–5pm). This basement portico, which was unearthed in 1954, was part of a first-century Roman villa and amid the gloom of the 90-metre tunnel you can still see the original stucco and paint.

The newest addition to Vicenza's cultural landscape is the **Museo Diocesano** at Piazza Duomo 2 (Tues–Sun 10am–1pm & 2–6pm; €4, or Card Musei). Aside from the usual collection of church vestments and silverware, the museum has an excellent display of stone fragments from Roman times onwards, including a fine fourth-century relief of the three Magi. Don't miss the magnificent cape that was donated to the Bishop of Vicenza by King Louis IX in 1259, along with a thorn from Christ's crown. The relic, housed in a fourteenth-century gold reliquary, belongs to the church of Santa Corona, but while that building is undergoing restoration it's being displayed on the first floor of the museum. Also on show temporarily are two of Vicenza's finest paintings, on loan from Santa Corona: *The Baptism of Christ*, a late work by **Giovanni Bellini**, and *The Adoration of the Magi*, painted in 1573 by **Paolo Veronese**.

Santa Corona and Santo Stefano

Far more interesting than the Duomo is the Dominican church of **Santa Corona** (Tues–Sun 8.30–noon & 3–6pm) on the other side of the Corso Palladio, at the Piazza Matteotti end. Begun in 1261 to house a thorn from Christ's crown (see above), it has what's said to be the oldest Gothic interior in the Veneto; the thorn is displayed in the church on Good Friday. The church's best paintings have been removed, with the thorn, to the Museo Diocesano, but take time to look at the late fifteenth-century inlaid **choir stalls**, the extraordinary seventeenth-century *pietra dura* **altarpiece** depicting the Passion, the simple **Cappella Valmarana**, which was added to the crypt in 1576 by Palladio, and the anonymous *Madonna* in the left aisle, which includes at its base a view of Vicenza around 1500, added by Fogolino. One last item of interest: a plaque set into the pillar nearest to the steps for the crypt records that Palladio was buried at the foot of the pillar, from where his remains were removed to the civic cemetery in 1845.

The cloisters of Santa Corona now house a decidedly run-of-the-mill **Museo Naturalistico-Archeologico** (Tues–Sun 9am–5pm; entry with Card Musei) but a little further down the road, at no. 25, you'll find the **Gallerie di Palazzo Leoni Montanari** (Tues–Sun 10am–6pm; €4, or Card Musei; Ⓦ www.palazzomontanari.com). Owned by a banking group, this opulent Baroque palazzo has been fastidiously restored as a showcase for two art collections that the bank has accumulated over the years. In the frescoed and richly ornamented rooms of the *piano nobile*, paintings by Canaletto, Francesco Guardi and Tiepolo feature in a survey of Veneto art that's interesting chiefly for the journalistic scenes of everyday life in eighteenth-century Venice created by Pietro Longhi and his workshop – only the Ca' Rezzonico and the Querini Stampalia museums in Venice have more extensive samples of Longhi's quirky output. Upstairs you'll find a thematic display of more than one hundred Russian icons (about a quarter of the bank's hoard), a remarkable and well-displayed assemblage that spans the period from the thirteenth century to the twentieth.

The nearby church of **Santo Stefano** (Mon–Sat 8.30–9.45am & 5–6.30pm, Sun 8.30–9.45am) merits a call for the city's third outstanding religious painting – **Palma il Vecchio**'s typically stolid and luscious *Madonna and Child with St George and St Lucy*. If you have hawk-like vision you could try to make out the church's trio of tiny monochrome paintings by Giandomenico Tiepolo (*The Resurrection*, *St Peter* and *St John the Baptist*) – they form the panels on the front and sides of the high altar's tabernacle.

Along Contrà Porti and around

The entrance to Santo Stefano faces the immense Palazzo Negri and its mighty Gothic neighbour, the Casa Fontana, but more intimidating than either is Palladio's rugged **Palazzo Thiene**, on the Corso side of them (May, June & Sept Wed & Fri 9am–noon & 3–6pm, Sat 9am–noon; Oct–April Tues & Wed 9am–noon & 3–6pm; closed July & Aug; admission free, by advance booking on ☏0444.542.131). Built in the 1540s, this palace was planned to occupy the entire block down to the Corso and across to **Contrà Porti**; in the end, work progressed no further than the addition of this wing to the block that had been built for the Thiene at the end of the fifteenth century. (The facade of the Gothic portion is on Contrà Porti.) Palladio was not simply the most inventive and knowledgeable architect in the Veneto, he was also very cost effective: his columns are usually made of brick covered with a skim of plaster (the Basilica is a rare exception), and – as an inspection of the Thiene residence will reveal, his rough-hewn stonework is just cunningly worked brick as well. Now a bank's HQ, the Palazzo Thiene is every bit as impressive inside as outside. Reflecting the highly cultured tastes of the Thiene family, the profuse decoration of the main living rooms is dominated by subjects from classical mythology, and much of the decor – notably the amazing stuccowork by Alessandro Vittoria – dates from the period of the palace's construction. Some of the paintings and sculptures were commissioned in the eighteenth century, but these are remarkably well integrated into the overall scheme, making this the finest domestic interior in the city.

There's no better example than Contrà Porti of the way in which the builders of Vicenza skilfully grafted new houses onto old without doing violence to the line of the street: the palaces here span two centuries, yet the overall impression is one of cohesion. At no. 8 is the Gothic Palazzo Cavalloni, and over the road at no. 11 stands Palladio's **Palazzo Barbaran da Porto** (Tues–Sun 10am–6pm, though hours may vary according to exhibition schedules; €5), designed around 1570 and subsequently embellished by others; the Palazzo Barbaran regularly hosts architectural exhibitions under the auspices of its tenants, the Centro Internazionale di Studi di Architettura "A. Palladio", which organizes Vicenza's prestigious annual architecture conference and has plans to turn the building into a permanent museum devoted to Palladio. When there's no special exhibition on, your entry ticket only gets you into the atrium, courtyard, loggia and the grand Salone di Cesare, where Palladio's patrons are represented in the guise of Roman emperors.

Back on the other side of the road, the Thiene palace is followed by the Renaissance **Palazzo Trissino-Sperotti** (no. 14), opposite which is a sweep of Gothic houses, the best being the fourteenth-century **Palazzo Colleoni Porto** (19); next door is Palladio's **Palazzo Iseppo Porto**, designed a few years after the Thiene and a couple of decades before the Barbaran da Porto. Luigi da Porto, the author of the story on which Shakespeare based his *Romeo and Juliet*, died at no. 15 in 1529.

Contrà Porti takes you towards the Pusterla bridge, from where it's a very short stroll to the **Parco Querini** (daily 8am–sunset): the biggest expanse of green in the city, it's adorned with an avenue of statuary and a tiny decorative hill that's populated by ducks, rabbits and peacocks. For those intent on doing a comprehensive Palladian tour, there's a palace by him on this side of the Bacchiglione river too – the **Palazzo Schio-Angaran** at Contrà San Marco no. 39.

Along Corso Fogazzaro

Connected to Contrà Porti by Contrà Riale (itself not short of grand houses) is Corso A. Fogazzaro, a busy road with a spread of architectural attractions.

At the Corso Palladio end is the **Palazzo Valmarana** (no. 16), where Palladio's use of overlapping planes makes the design of the facade legible in the narrow street and at the same time integrates the palace with the flanking buildings. The palazzo was planned to be three times bigger than what you see today.

In the other direction you'll come across the thirteenth-century Franciscan church of **San Lorenzo** (Mon–Sat 10.30am–noon & 3.30–6pm, Sun 3.30–6pm). The fourteenth-century marble portal of the west front is the best feature of the church – the dimensions of the interior are impressive, but it's a rather barren space. **Montagna**'s fresco of the *Beheading of St Paul*, in the chapel on the left side of the chancel, may once have been stunning, but it's now looking pretty tattered.

Further along, where the arcades give out, is the church of **Santa Maria dei Carmini**; founded in the fourteenth century but redone in the nineteenth, it has pictures by **Montagna**, **Veronese** and **Jacopo Bassano** that more than compensate for the peculiarly dainty decor – although you'll need infra red vision to make them out on an overcast day.

The fringes of the centre

If the Museo Civico's collection has led to your acquiring a taste for **Francesco Maffei**'s work, you'll not want to miss the **Oratorio di San Nicola** (April–Oct Thurs 9am–noon & Sun 3.30–7pm; free guided tours on Thurs), which has a welter of paintings by him and his contemporary **Carpioni**, including Maffei's delirious altarpiece of *The Trinity*.

The Oratorio stands by the side of Vicenza's other river, the Retrone, at the foot of its most picturesque bridge, the humpback **Ponte San Michele**, built in 1620. You can follow a pleasant loop on the south side of the river by going straight ahead off the bridge to the Piazza dei Gualdi, then go straight on, veering to the right – the buildings here follow the curve of the old Roman theatre – past the thirteenth-century gate called the **Portòn del Luzzo**; from here you go straight ahead down Contrà Ponte Furo and recross the Retrone by the **Ponte Furo**, from where there's a good view of the Basilica and Torre di Piazza. The long building on the opposite bank is Palladio's first project in the city, the **Casa Civena** (c.1540).

Another area just out of the centre that's worth a look is on the far side of the Bacchiglione from the Teatro Olimpico. The bridge leads onto the major traffic confluence of Piazza Venti Settembre: the building with porticoes on two facades is the **Palazzo Angaran** – fifteenth century, but rebuilt. In adjacent Contrà Venti Settembre there's the house with the best preserved of Vicenza's exterior frescoes, the fifteenth-century **Palazzo Regaù**.

Don't miss the church of **Santi Felice e Fortunato** either (Mon–Sat 9–11am & 3.30–6.30pm, Sun 3.30–6.30pm). It's on the opposite side of town, about ten minutes' walk along the Corso of the same name, from the entrance to the **Giardino Salvi** (daily 7.30am–8pm), a compact little park whose winding gravel paths are punctuated by unconvincing replicas of great sculptures. Dating back to immediately after the Edict of Constantine (313 AD), the basilica of Santi Felice e Fortunato is the oldest church in Vicenza, and is approached by a path littered with ancient sarcophagi and architectural fragments. Wrecked by Magyar invaders in 899 and then by earthquakes in 1117, it was largely reconstructed in the twelfth century, and recent restorations have stripped away later accretions to reveal the form of the church at around that period. Remnants of the earliest building have survived – portions of fourth- and fifth-century mosaics have been uncovered in the nave and right aisle, and a door off the right aisle leads into a fourth-century martyrs' shrine.

Almost as remarkable as the mosaics and *martyrion* is the twelfth-century fortified campanile, which looks as if it might have problems standing up to the next gale.

Monte Bèrico

Rising behind the rail line, **Monte Bèrico** is seen by everyone who comes to Vicenza, but not actually visited by many, which is a pity as an expedition up the hill has a number of attractions: an amazing view (on a clear day the horizon beyond Vicenza is a switchback of mountain peaks), a clutch of excellent paintings and one of Europe's most famous and imitated buildings.

Buses for Monte Bèrico leave the bus station (near the train station), approximately every ninety minutes from Monday to Saturday; on Sunday there is a more frequent service from Viale Roma. If you decide to walk, the most direct route from the Basilica is to cross the Ponte San Michele, carry on past Piazza dei Gualdi to the Portòn del Luzzo, go through the gate and along Contrà San Silvestro, then cross Viale X Giugno (ignoring the road sign that directs cars up Viale Dante) to follow the **Portici**, an eighteenth-century arcade built to shelter the pilgrims on their way up to the church. Alternatively, soon after Ponte San Michele you could bear left along Contrà Pozzetto, then go straight along Contrà San Tommaso and Contrà Santa Caterina, which comes to an end opposite Palladio's **Arco delle Scalette**, the gateway to a steep flight of steps that leads you towards the upper part of the Portici, passing the road to the Villa Valmarana and Villa Rotonda. The walk will take about half an hour from the centre of town.

The Basilica di Monte Bèrico and the Risorgimento museum

In 1426–28 Vicenza was struck by an outbreak of bubonic plague, in the course of which the Virgin appeared twice at the summit of Monte Bèrico to announce the city's deliverance. A chapel was raised on the spot that the Virgin had obligingly marked out for its construction, and it duly became a place of pilgrimage. It was enlarged later in the century, altered again in the sixteenth century, and then, at the end of the seventeenth, replaced by the present **Basilica di Monte Bèrico** (Mon–Fri 8am–12.30pm & 2.30–6pm, Sat open till 6.30pm, Sun open till 7pm). The church was extended in such a way that the nave of the fifteenth-century version became the transepts of the new church, leaving the old Gothic facade stuck onto the Basilica's right side. Pilgrims regularly arrive here by the busload, and the glossy interior of the church, all gilding and fake marble, is immaculately maintained to receive them. A well-stocked shop in the cloister sells devotional trinkets to the faithful, close to a cash desk displaying the rates for customized masses.

The church's best painting, Montagna's *Pietà* (1500), hangs in the chapel on the right side of the apse, while *The Supper of St Gregory the Great* (1572) by **Veronese** is to be seen in the old refectory of the adjoining monastery, which it shares with the impressive fossil collection amassed by the resident Franciscans. The Veronese painting, the prototype of *The Feast in the House of Levi* in Venice's Accademia, was badly damaged in June 1848, in the final phase of the battle of Vicenza, the major military engagement of the anti-Austrian uprising that swept across much of the Veneto in 1848. The battle reached its climax on Monte Bèrico (armed monks defended the Basilica, while Paduan students were besieged in the Villa Rotonda), and on the last day of fighting one of the Austrian generals, Prince Liechtenstein, was killed inside the church. Enraged by his death, Croat troops of the Austrian army slashed the Veronese painting with their bayonets: a small reproduction on the adjoining wall shows what a thorough mess they made of it, and what a good job the restorers did. The repair was financed by the Austrian emperor Franz Josef, in apology for the vandalism.

The **Piazzale della Vittoria**, in front of the Basilica, was built to commemorate the dead of World War I; today it's a parking lot and a belvedere for the best view across the city. Carry on towards the summit of the hill for ten minutes and you'll come to the **Museo del Risorgimento e della Resistenza** (Tues–Sun 9am–1pm & 2.15–5pm; €3, or Card Musei). The museum is an impressively thorough display, paying particular attention to Vicenza's resistance to the Austrians in the mid-nineteenth century and to the efforts of the anti-Fascist Alpine fighters a century later, and has good English information sheets in each room, but for many visitors the main attraction will be the extensive wooded parkland (daily: April–Sept 8am–8pm; Oct–March 8.30am–5.30pm; free) laid out on the slopes below the **Villa Guiccioli**, the museum's main building.

The Villa Valmarana

Ten minutes' walk away from the Basilica is the **Villa Valmarana ai Nani** – meaning "of the dwarves", after the figures on the garden wall (March 15–Nov 5 Tues–Sun 10am–noon & 3–6pm; rest of year Sat & Sun 10am–noon & 2–4pm; €6). Still owned by the family for which it was built, it's an undistinguished eighteenth-century house made extraordinary by its gorgeous decoration, a cycle of frescoes created in 1757 by **Giambattista and Giandomenico Tiepolo**. To get there, go back to the elbow of the Portici, follow Via M. D'Azeglio for about a hundred metres, then go right into the cobbled Via S. Bastiano, which ends at the Villa Valmarana. (If you are coming from town, you can catch buses #8 or #13 from in front of the station, which run along the main road below the villas.)

There are two parts to the house. The main block, the **Palazzina**, was frescoed with brilliant virtuosity by Giambattista, drawing his heroic imagery from Virgil, Tasso and Ariosto – you're handed a brief guide to the paintings at the entrance. Giambattista also painted one room of the **Foresteria**, the guest wing, but here the bulk of the work was done by his son Giandomenico; his scope was somewhat narrower than his father's (carnivals and rustic pleasures were his favourite themes), but the same air of wistful melancholy pervades his scenes, and his apparently effortless fluency is very nearly as impressive.

La Rotonda

From the Villa Valmarana the narrow Stradella Valmarana descends to **La Rotonda** (grounds & villa open mid-March to mid-Nov Wed 10am–noon & 3–6pm; €10; grounds open Tues–Sun same weeks and hours, plus Nov–March Tues–Sun 10am–noon & 2.30–5pm, €5), a building unique among Palladio's villas in that it was designed not as the main building of a farming estate but as a pavilion for entertainments and the enjoyment of the landscape. Begun in 1566, it was commissioned by Vicenza-born Paolo Almerico as his retirement home, after years in Rome in the service of the papacy, but was not finished until about 1620, by which time it had passed into the hands of the Capra family. (The Capra whose name appears on the main pediment of the villa finished the development of the site in the 1640s, when he commissioned the chapel that stands by the entrance gate.) Almerico chose a hill-top site "surrounded by other most pleasant hills, which present the appearance of a vast theatre", and Palladio's design certainly makes the most of its centre-stage setting. The combination of the pure forms of the circle and square was a fundamental concern of many Renaissance architects (Leonardo, Bramante and Michelangelo all worked at it), and the elegance of Palladio's solution led to innumerable imitations – for example Thomas Jefferson's rejected plan for the official residence of the US president, a near facsimile of the Rotonda.

Only a walk round the lavishly decorated rooms will fully reveal the subtleties of the Rotonda's design, which gives a strong impression of being as symmetrical as a square while in fact having a definite main axis. Unless you're an architecture student and really want to scrutinize the walls from point-blank range, the garden can be given a miss, as it's just a narrow belt of grass and gravel.

Eating, drinking and nightlife

Vicenza might not have the wildest nightlife in northern Italy, but there's a pleasant post-work buzz in the evening, as people gather in the Piazza dei Signori or just saunter up and down the Corso Palladio, before dropping into one of the many good bars and cafés in the centre of the city. Restaurants are not numerous in the *centro storico* but standards are high – which means you'll need to book a table or get there early. Popular specialities include *baccalà alla Vicentina* (*baccalà* elsewhere in Italy is salted cod, whereas *baccalà alla vicentina* is made by marinating dried cod in milk and oil) and *sopressa*, a kind of salami from the Pasubio and Recoaro valleys, generally eaten with a slice of grilled polenta.

Restaurants

Agli Schioppi Contrà Piazza del Castello 26 ☏0444.543.701. Elegant establishment that serves interesting seasonal dishes, such as crunchy white asparagus – the best in town – and ravioli with *bruscandoli* (wild sprouts). It also specializes in *baccalà*, and excels in puddings. Good selection of wines as well. Closed Sat evening and all day Sun.

Antica Casa della Malvasia Contrà delle Morette 5. This bustling and roomy inn, just off Piazza dei Signori, is a popular budget choice. There's occasional live music on Wed (March–Oct) and it's open till at least 1am on Fri and Sat, though last orders from the kitchen are 11pm. Closed Mon.

Dai Nodari Contrà do Rode 20. Large, friendly restaurant close to the Basilica. Salads are a speciality, the cheeses are excellent, and there is a wide choice of snacks at the bar. Daily 10.30am–3pm & 5.30pm–2am.

I Monelli Contrà Ponte San Paolo 13 ☏0444.540.400. Small, atmospheric *osteria* that attracts locals for its good local fare

and moderate prices – its lunchtime menus are a bargain. Open Tues–Sun till 1am.

Julien Contrà Jacopo Cabianca 13 ☏0444.326.168. This lively modern restaurant-bar, located off Piazza Matteotti, has a real buzz and an interesting menu, featuring dishes such as scallops in lavender oil. The prices are moderate – €12–18 for a main course – and the clientele ranges from cool young groups sipping their *aperitivi* to families having a meal with their children. Live music on Thurs. Open Mon–Sat till 1–2am.

Oca Bianca Contrà Porti 20a ☏0444.542.193. Risotto is a speciality at this very popular establishment – try the innovative fruit risotto, served as a starter. You'll pay about €30 for three courses. Open till 10pm; closed Sat lunch and Sun all day.

Righetti Piazza Duomo 3. There's no better place for quick, cheap food than this self-service restaurant by the Duomo. Open Mon–Thurs till midnight, and on Fri till 1am.

Cafés, bars and gelaterie

Two terrific old-world **pasticceria-cafés** are to be found in the shadow of the Basilica: *Sorarù*, at Piazzetta Andrea Palladio 17 (closed Wed); and the *Offelleria della Meneghina*, at Contrà Cavour 18 (closed Mon). Chocolate addicts will also enjoy the home-made confections at *La Boutique Artigiana del Cioccolato*, an elegant café just off Corso Palladio at Contrà Porti 10 (open daily till 7.30pm). The best **ice creams** in town are at *El Gelataro de Magrè*, Piazza delle Biade 18 (daily), and *Gelateria Brustolon*, in business since 1927 at Contrà Pusterla 23, on the way to the Parco Querini (closed Tues). More central but less friendly is *Tutto Gelato* at Contrà Frasche del Gambero 26 (closed Mon), between the Basilica and the Duomo.

As for central **bars**, *Il Borsa* (closed Mon), inside the portico of the Basilica, is a chilled place with a certain distressed chic, while *Il Grottino*, at Piazza dell'Erbe 2, has a good range of wines and some snacks, plenty of jazz and lounge music, and stays open till 2am daily. *Moplen*, on the east side of the Piazza delle Biade (closed Mon), has a DJ on Friday and Saturday and is open till 2am. Further out, the *Caffetteria San Lorenzo*, on Piazza San Lorenzo, has a DJ on Saturday and is open till 2 or 3am on Fridays and Saturdays (closed Mon).

Around Vicenza

The countryside around Vicenza is dotted with hundreds of **villas**, many of them the result of Venice's diversion of money into agriculture in the mid-sixteenth century, as a way of protecting the economy against the increasing uncertainties of seaborne trade. The tourist office in Vicenza hands out a booklet and a map plotting the location of many of them, and if you have a few dozen euros to spare you can choose from a number of magnificently illustrated tomes on the subject. The trouble is, most of the villas are best seen as glossy photos, because some are in the middle of nowhere, others are falling to bits and many of the better-kept specimens are closed to the public. Moreover, of those that are open, accessible and in fair condition, some probably won't make much impression on the untrained eye – such as Palladio's **Villa Thiene** (Mon–Fri 9.30am–12.30pm, plus Mon & Thurs 3.30–6.30pm; free) at Quinto Vicentino (a short journey on the #5 bus). But a few of the villas of wider interest lie within the orbit of Vicenza's public transport network (in addition to the Villa Valmarana and Villa Rotonda – see above), and these are covered in the section that follows. Other villas of the Veneto are dealt with in the appropriate sections of this guide – for example, the entries on the Brenta (see p.284), Masèr (p.355), Montagnana (p.305) and Castelfranco Veneto (p.346).

The Villa Cordellina-Lombardi

A must for admirers of Giambattista Tiepolo, the eighteenth-century **Villa Cordellina-Lombardi** (April to mid-Oct Tues–Sun 9am–1pm & 3–6pm; €2.10) stands on the northern outskirts of the small town of **MONTECCHIO MAGGIORE**, 13km to the southwest of Vicenza. His frescoes in the entrance hall – *The Clemency of Scipio*, *The Clemency of Alexander* and, on the ceiling, *The Light of Reason Driving out the Fog of Ignorance* – are a touch less exuberant than the later ones at the Villa Valmarana, but they'll still make you feel better about life for the rest of the day.

Montecchio's other attractions, a pair of rebuilt fourteenth-century **Scaligeri forts** erected on a ridge overlooking the town, look their best from afar. They were made the strongholds of the Montague clan in Luigi da Porto's *Romeo and Juliet*.

A few **buses** from Vicenza go through Montecchio Maggiore, but there's a glut of services that pass through nearby Alte Ceccato on their way to Lonigo, Sossano and Noventa Vicentina – get off when you see the huge Bertozzo clothes supermarket, then follow the signs for the villa, which is about fifteen minutes' walk from the road.

Thiene and Lugo di Vicenza

It was only with the ending of the War of the League of Cambrai in 1516 that the landowners of the Veneto were able to disregard defensive considerations when building homes out of the urban centres – prior to that, the great houses of the terra firma were a sort of cross breed between a castle and a palace. The most imposing example of this genre still standing is the **Villa Porto-Colleoni** (guided tours mid-March to mid-Nov Sun 3, 4 & 5pm; €6; Ⓦ www.castellodithiene.com), built in the 1470s at **THIENE**, a bland textile town 20km north of Vicenza.

The crenellated corner towers, large central block and the encircling protective wall are all features that would have been common in this area in the fifteenth century, although this house, with its facade decorations and ornate Gothic windows, was probably more precious than most. The mandatory guided tour of the interior makes the most of the workaday sixteenth-century frescoes by Giambattista Zelotti and G.A. Fasolo; the plethora of equine portraits is explained by the fact that the Colleoni had a tradition of service in the Venetian cavalry.

To get to Thiene from Vicenza, take the Schio **train**; it leaves virtually every hour and takes around 25 minutes.

Lugo di Vicenza

The next rung up the evolutionary ladder of the villas of the Veneto is represented 8km to the north of Thiene, on the edge of **LUGO DI VICENZA** (aka Lonedo di Lugo), where you'll find Palladio's first villa – the **Villa Godi Malinverni** (April–Sept Tues 3–7pm, Sat 9am–2pm & Sun 10am–7pm; Oct, Nov & March Tues, Sat & Sun 2–6pm; €6), built in 1537–42. The plan of the Villa Godi Malinverni isn't all that different from that of the Villa Porto-Colleoni, but it's been shorn of fortified trappings and is clearly more of a country house than a castle; on the other hand, in marked contrast to Palladio's later work, there's not a feature on the building that refers to the architecture of ancient Rome.

Professor Remo Malinverni restored the house in the early 1960s, and installed his collection of nineteenth-century Italian paintings in some of the rooms; elsewhere in the building you'll find a fossil museum – but neither display can really compete with the sixteenth-century frescoes, some of which show Giambattista Zelotti (he of the Villa Fóscari at Malcontenta) on top form.

Just above the Godi Malinverni stands the **Villa Piovene** (daily: April–Oct 2–7pm; Nov–March 2–6pm; €4.50), the central block of which was also built by Palladio around 1540; the Ionic portico was added later in the sixteenth century, and the external staircase and portal came in the eighteenth. Only the nineteenth-century landscaped garden is open to the public.

An infrequent **bus** service runs from Thiene to Lugo, on its way to Calvene – there's a stop by the Porto-Colleoni.

Verona

With its Roman sites and streets of pink-hued medieval buildings, the irresistible city of **VERONA** has more in the way of historic attractions than any other place in the Veneto except Venice itself. Unlike Venice, though, it's not a city overwhelmed by the tourist industry, important though that is to the local economy. Verona is the largest city of the mainland Veneto, and its economic success is largely due to its position at the crossing of the major routes from Germany and Austria to central Italy and from the west to Venice and Trieste.

Verona's initial development as a **Roman** settlement was similarly due to its straddling the main east–west and north–south lines of communication. A period of decline in the wake of the disintegration of the Roman Empire was followed by revival under the Ostrogoths, who in turn were succeeded by the Franks – Charlemagne's son, Pepin, ruled his kingdom from here. By the twelfth century Verona had become a city-state, and in the following century, after three decades under the rule of the murderous Ezzelino da Romano, it flourished under the della Scala family, otherwise called the **Scaligeri**. Ruthless in the exercise of power – they once employed Werner von Urslingen, self-styled "enemy of God and of compassion" – the Scaligeri were at the same time energetic patrons of the arts, and many of Verona's finest buildings date from the century of their rule. Both Giotto and Dante were guests of the family, the latter dedicating his *Paradiso* to Can Francesco della Scala, head of the family at the time. Under Can Francesco – more widely known as **Cangrande** – Verona became the chief supporter of the Ghibelline cause in northern Italy and reached the zenith of its independent existence, taking control of Vicenza in 1314, of Padua in 1318, and Treviso in 1329, just days before Cangrande's death.

The reign of the Scaligeri ended at midnight on October 19, 1387, when Antonio della Scala fled the city, surrendering it to Gian Galeazzo Visconti of Milan. Absorption into the **Venetian empire** followed in 1405, and Venice continued to govern Verona down to the arrival of Napoleon. Verona's history then shadowed that of Venice: a prolonged interlude of Austrian rule, brought to an end by the unification of Italy.

Arrival, information and accommodation

If you're flying in to Verona's Valerio Catullo **airport** at Villafranca, you can get into the city by a regular ATV bus (every 20min 7am–11.30pm; €4.50) from the airport to the main train station and Piazza Cittadella, near the city centre; Brescia airport (marketed as Verona's second airport) is served by a shuttle bus, which takes an hour (€11). Tickets for both can be bought on board.

From the main **train** station (Verona Porta Nuova) it's a fifteen-minute walk to Piazza Brà, site of the Arena and the hub of Verona. Unless you're staying in the youth hostel, you're only likely to need a **bus** if you don't fancy the walk from the train station to the centre. Local buses leave from the stands immediately opposite the station: for Piazza Brà take any of the buses from bay A; buses for Castelvecchio leave from bay D; those for Piazza delle Erbe from bay D. Tickets can be bought before boarding for €1 from the machines alongside bay A or from the *tabacchi* inside the train-station ticket hall, or for €1.20 on board, and are valid for any number of journeys within an hour; alternatively, you can get ten rides for €9 or travel free with the Verona Card (see box, p.326).

There are **car parks** signed off the Corso Porta Nuova just before Piazza Brà, or there is free parking across the river through the city walls beyond San Stefano. The main **tourist office** is on the central Piazza Brà, within the old town walls beside the Palazzo del Municipale (Mon–Sat 9am–7pm, Sun 10am–4pm; ☎045.806.8680, ⊛www.tourism.verona.it). There is an additional office at the train station (Mon–Sat 9am–7pm plus May–Sept Sun 10am–4pm; ☎045.800.0861) and a **room-finding service**, Cooperativa Albergatori Veronesi (CAV), at Via Patuzzi 5 (May to mid-Nov Mon–Sat 10am–7pm; rest of year Mon–Fri 10am–6pm, but closed mid-Dec to mid-Jan; ☎045.800.9844). Via Patuzzi runs parallel to Via Leoncino off Piazza Gallieno in the southeast corner of Piazza Brà.

Hotels

Antica Porta Leona Via Corticella Leoni 3 ☎045.595.499, ⊛www.anticaportaleona.com. Large three-star with spacious a/c rooms, some with balconies. Has plenty of single rooms. ❷–❸

Aurora Piazzetta XIV Novembre 2 ☎045.594.717, ⊛www.hotelaurora.biz. Upmarket two-star hotel with a welcoming atmosphere and many rooms overlooking the Piazza delle Erbe. The staff are friendly and knowledgeable, and speak good English. Excellent buffet breakfast. ❷–❸

Catullo Via Valerio Catullo 1 ☎045.800.2786, ⓔlocandacatullo@tiscali.it. The cheapest – if not the friendliest – hotel in the centre, just off the main shopping artery of Via Mazzini. Rooms are rather shabby but are large and have plenty of light, and some have a private bathroom. ❶

Colomba d'Oro Via C. Cattaneo 10 ☎045.595.300, ⊛www.colombahotel.com. Luxuriously appointed four-star, handily located for the Arena, with a garage and a range of well-equipped rooms. ❸–❺

Torcolo Vicolo Listone 3 ☎045.800.7512, ⊛www.hoteltorcolo.it. Nicely turned out two-star hotel within 100m of the Arena, just off Piazza Brà. Extremely welcoming owners who have been in the business for thirty years, and a favourite with the opera crowds, so book ahead. ❶–❸

Victoria Via Adua 8 ☎045.590.566, ⊛www.hotelvictoria.it. Very nice four-star hotel housed in a complex of old buildings, with a snazzy modern foyer, well-equipped rooms and gymnasium. If you want to treat yourself, the superior doubles are gorgeous. Good deals out of season. ❹–❻

B&Bs and self-catering

In addition to the places below, the tourist office has lists of **B&Bs**, and you'll find even more at ⊛www.bed-and-breakfast.it. For **self-catering accommodation**, check the Holiday Rentals website (see p.240); pick of the bunch is Villa Lambranzi, Via Francesco Anzani 4 (⊛www.holiday-rentals.co.uk/p6086), which is a comfortable two-bedroom flat on the ground floor of an old villa just across the river from the Duomo. Two other recommendable places are: *L'Ospite*, Via XX Settembre 3 (☎045.803.6994, ⊛www.lospite.com), which comprises six simply furnished apartments just across the Ponte Navi in the Veronetta; and *Residence Antico San Zeno*, Via Rosmini 15 (☎045.800.3463, ⊛www.residenceanticosanzeno.it), where modern flats are for rental in a converted medieval house not far from San Zeno.

Alla Galleria ☎347.248.8462, ⊛www.bedandbreakfastallagalleria.com. Two spacious rooms just off Via Mazzini. ❶–❷

All'Opera Via Alberto Mario 11 ☎338.858.8763, ⊛www.bbopera.com. Another central B&B just off Via Mazzini – you can see the Arena from the breakfast room. ❶–❸

La Casetta Via Manin 4 ☎0458.005.080, ⊛www.lacasetta-verona.it. Comfy rooms off Via Roma and close to Castelvecchio. ❷

La Tana Via Volto Citadella 8 ☎333.846.1116, ⊛www.latana.info. B&B with three rooms just outside the Porta Brà. ❶–❷

VERONA

Trento ▲

VIALE NINO BIXIO

V. FARINATA UBERTI

PONTE CATENA

VIA EDERLE

PIAZZA V. VENETO

VIALE MILLE

VIA ASPROMONTE

VIA CAMOZZINI

VIA TODESCHINI

VIA ANZANI

VIA MEDICI

VIA ABBA

PRATO SANTO

LUNGADIGE CANGRANDE

VIA RISORGIMENTO

VIA IV NOVEMBRE

PONTE RISORGIMENTO

VIALE DELLA REPUBBLICA

VIA TONALE

LUNGADIGE MATTEOTTI

VIALE DI BERSAGLIERE

VIA TOMMASO DA VICO

S.Zeno Maggiore

LUNGADIGE CANGRANDE

PIAZZA S. ZENO

Garda ▲

PIAZZA POZZA

PIAZZA CORRUBIO

VIA BARBARANI

River Adige

Arsenale

LUNGADIGE CAMPAGNOLA

PONTE VITTORIA

S. Lorenzo

RIVA SAN LORENZO

CORSO CAVOUR

Pal. Bevilacqua

VIA ROSMINI

RIGASTE S. ZENO

PIAZZA ARSENALE

PONTE SCALIGERO

Arco dei Gavi

VIA FERRI

J

K

VIA AURELIO SAFFI

STRADONE ANT PROVOLO

Castelvecchio

VIA ROMA

VIA C. CATTANEO

Liston

L

Airport ▲

0   100 m

STRADONE PORTA PALIO

VOLTO S. LUCA

VIA MANIN

Portoni della Brà

Palazzo della Gran Guardia

21

VIA MAZZONI

M

VIA VAL VERDE

CORSO PORTA NUOVA

ACCOMMODATION
Alla Galleria	G
All'Opera	I
Antica Porta Leona	H
Aurora	D
Campeggio Castel San Pietro	A
Casa della Giovane	C
Catullo	F
Colomba d'Oro	J
La Casetta	L
La Tana	M
Ostello della Gioventù	B
Torcolo	K
Victori	E

RESTAURANTS
Al Bracere	22
Alla Colonna	11
Bella Napoli	21
Bottega del Vino	19
Caffé Monte Baldo	7
Hostaria La Vecchia Fontanina	10
Osteria del Bugiardo	13
Osteria alla Pigna	4
Osteria Sottoriva	6
Tre Marchetti "Da Barca"	20

BARS
Al Carro Armato	8
Al Mascaron	15
Cappa Café	2
Il Campidoglio	12
Le Vecete	16
Osteria a la Carega	5
Osteria al Duomo	3
Rivamancina	9

CAFÉS & GELATERIE
Balu	17
Caffè Coloniale	18
Gelateria Ponte Pietra	1
Zeno Gelato	14

Porta Nuova & Train Station ▼

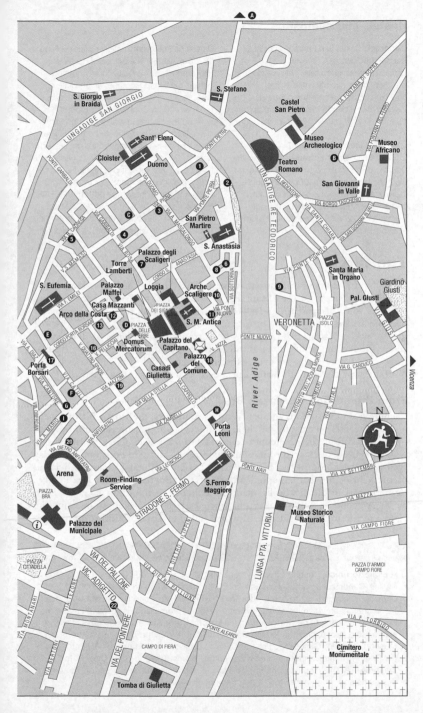

▲Ⓐ

S. Giorgio
in Braida
S. Stefano

Castel
San Pietro

Museo
Africano

Sant' Elena
Museo
Archeologico

Ⓑ

Cloister
Duomo

Teatro
Romano

San Giovanni
in Valle

①

②

③

San Pietro
Martire

Ⓒ

⑤
④

S. Anastasia

Palazzo degli
Scaligeri
⑦

Santa Maria
in Organo

Torre
Lamberti

⑥
⑧

Giardino
Giusti

S. Eufemia
Palazzo
Maffei

Loggia

Arche
Scaligere
⑩

Pal. Glusti

⑨

Casa Mazzanti

Arco della Costa
⑫
⑬

Ⓓ

S. M. Antica
⑪

VERONETTA

Domus
Mercatorum

Ⓔ

⑯

Palazzo del
Capitano

PIAZZA
ISOLO

Porta
Borsari
⑰

Ⓕ

Ⓖ

Ⓘ

Casadi
Giulietta

Palazzo del
Comune
⑱

⑲

River Adige

Ⓗ

⑳

Porta
Leoni

Arena

Room-Finding
Service

S.Fermo
Maggiore

PIAZZA
BRA

ⓘ

Palazzo del
Municipale

Museo Storico
Naturale

PIAZZA
CITTADELLA

PIAZZA D'ARMIDI
CAMPO FIORE

㉒

Cimitero
Monumentale

CAMPO DI FIERA

Tomba di Giulietta

N

▲ Vicenza

Hostels and campsites

Campeggio Castel San Pietro Via Castel S. Pietro 2 ☎045.592.037, ⓦwww .campingcastelsanpietro.com. This pleasant site, out by the old city walls, is the only place to camp near the centre of Verona; take a bus to Via Marsala and then it's a steep walk up the hill. Open mid-June to Sept.

Casa della Giovane Via Pigna 7 ☎045.596.880, ⓦwww.casadellagiovane.com. Spartan but friendly convent-run hostel for women, with an 11pm curfew, although there is some flexibility for guests with opera tickets. Reservations by fax only. Dorms are €22, also some double rooms at €25 per head.

Ostello della Gioventù Salita Fontana del Ferro 15 ☎045.590.360. The official HI hostel is in Villa Francescatti, a beautiful old building behind the Teatro Romano; as it's quite a walk from the centre, it's best to take a bus (#73, or #90 on Sun) to Piazza Isolo, then walk up the hill. No reservations, but with over 200 beds, there should be room. The 11.30pm curfew is extended for guests with concert tickets. HI membership not essential if you're staying for just one night. Reasonably priced evening meals are available. Beds €18 per night. At the bottom of the hill there's a sister hostel, the *Santa Chiara*, which is new and better equipped, but tends to be open only when the main hostel is full.

The City

Set within the low amphitheatre that the wide River Adige has carved out of the hills, Verona conveys a sense of ease that you don't often find in the region's other cities. As you walk past the great Roman arena or along the embankments or over the bridges that span the broad curves of the Adige, you'll be struck by the spaciousness of Verona. And even in the narrow medieval lanes of the historic centre, around the beautiful Piazza delle Erbe, the atmosphere is quite distinct from that of busy Padua or sleek, efficient Vicenza. With cars and buses barred from many of the central squares and streets, it's a city that invites dawdling.

From the station to Piazza Brà

Coming from the station, you pass Verona's south gate, the **Porta Nuova**, built in the sixteenth century by Michele Sanmicheli (though messed around with by the Austrians in the nineteenth century). From the wide Corso Porta Nuova, which begins here, the red roofs and towers of the city stand out on a clear day against the backdrop of the Torricelle and Lessini mountains. At the other end of the Corso, the battlemented arches of the **Portoni della Brà** (1389), formerly part of the city walls, mark the entrance to the historic centre. Built by the Visconti family, the Portoni once carried a covered walk from the Castelvecchio to their residence, of which only the **Torre Pentagona** remains,

---

Combined tickets

A **biglietto unico**, costing €5, allows one visit to San Zeno, the Duomo (but not the Museo Canonicale), Sant'Anastasia and San Fermo; when the restoration of San Lorenzo is finished, it too will be covered by this ticket. It can be bought at any of these churches, which individually charge €2.50 for admission. If you're planning to be very busy, it might be worth getting the **Verona Card**, which gives access to all the sights listed above, plus the Museo Canonicale, the Arena, the Torre dei Lamberti, the Museo Lapidario, Castelvecchio, the Casa di Giulietta, the Tomba di Giulietta, and the Roman Theatre, as well as free travel on city buses. The one-day ticket costs €10, the three-day €15. You can buy the card at *tabacchi* and should be able to buy it at the museums and monuments too, though sometimes they run out of stock.

behind the **Palazzo della Gran Guardia** (1610) on the right. Ensconced in the left-hand wall of the Portoni lies the entrance to one of Verona's more obscure museums, the **Museo Lapidario Maffeiano** (Tues–Sun 8.30am–2pm; €4.50, or Verona Card, or joint ticket with Arena €7); the large courtyard and two upstairs rooms contain miscellaneous Greek, Etruscan and Roman statues and inscriptions, none of which is likely to grip the nonspecialist.

Through these arches the broad expanse of **Piazza Brà** opens up. (*Brà*, by the way, is the Veronese dialect version of *braida*, meaning "meadow".) It's bordered on the south side by the disused Gran Guardia (formerly a sort of military gymnasium), on the east by the nineteenth-century **Palazzo del Municipale**, on the west by the **Liston**, and at the far end by the mightiest of Verona's Roman monuments, the **Arena** (Mon 1.45–7.30pm, Tues–Sun 9am–7.30pm, but closes 3.30pm during the opera season in July & Aug; €6, or Verona Card; €1 on first Sun of month Oct–May).

Dating from the first century AD, the Arena has survived in remarkable condition, despite the twelfth-century earthquake that destroyed all but four of the arches of the outer wall. The interior was scarcely damaged by the tremor, and nowadays audiences come here to watch gargantuan opera productions where once crowds of around twenty thousand packed the benches for gladiatorial contests, mock naval battles and the like. Originally measuring 152m by 123m overall, and thus the third largest of all Roman amphitheatres – after the Colosseum and the amphitheatre at Capua – the Arena is still an awesome sight, and offers a fine panorama of the city and surrounding mountains from the topmost of the 44 marble tiers.

Piazza delle Erbe and Piazza Signori

Narrow, traffic-free Via Mazzini – the main route of Verona's *passeggiata* – leads north from the Arena, past expensive clothes and jewellery shops, to **Piazza delle Erbe**, a lively and handsome square tightly enclosed by medieval and Renaissance palazzi. Originally a major Roman crossroads and the site of the forum, the piazza is still the heart of the city, a place where people come to meet friends and see who's around. As the name suggests, the market used to sell mainly vegetables, but nowadays most of the stalls sell an assortment of clothes, souvenirs, antiques and fast food.

Lined along the square's central axis, and camouflaged by the stalls, are the **Colonna Antica** (a fifteenth-century lantern on a marble pillar), the **Capitello** (a fourteenth-century pavilion where public servants were invested with their office), the fountain of **Madonna Verona** (built in 1368 by Cansignorio della Scala) and finally the column of the Lion of Saint Mark, demonstrating Verona's links with Venice. This specimen is a copy of one destroyed during the Pasqua Veronese (Veronese Easter), as the city's 1797 uprising against the French is known.

On the left as you look from the Via Cappello end, past the tall houses of the old Jewish ghetto, is the **Domus Mercatorum**, which was founded in 1301 as a merchants' warehouse and exchange and is now a bank and chamber of commerce. At the far end, the Baroque **Palazzo Maffei** has been taken over by shops, luxury apartments and an expensive restaurant; to the left of Palazzo Maffei rises the fourteenth-century **Torre del Gardello**, while to the right stands the **Casa Mazzanti**, whose sixteenth-century murals are best seen after dark, under enhancing spotlights. On the eastern side of the piazza, to your right, Verona's highest tower (83m), the twelfth-century **Torre dei Lamberti** (see below), overlooks the **Palazzo del Comune** – a twelfth-century building with Renaissance additions and nineteenth-century alterations. Flanking the wing known as the **Sala della Ragione**, where justice was dispensed, the **Arco della Costa** (Arch of the Rib) hangs over the route through to the Piazza dei Signori. Cynical folklore has it that the whale's rib suspended under the arch will fall if an adult virgin passes underneath.

Piazza dei Signori, sometimes known as Piazza Dante after the grimly pensive statue of the poet in the centre, used to be the chief public square in Verona but is now often quiet and empty, a strong contrast with Piazza delle Erbe. Facing you as you come into the square is the **Palazzo degli Scaligeri**, residence of the Scaligeri. Extending from it at a right angle are the graceful arches of Verona's outstanding early Renaissance building, the late fifteenth-century **Loggia del Consiglio**, former assembly hall of the city council. The rank of Roman notables along the roof includes Verona's most illustrious native poet, Catullus. Opposite stands Sanmicheli's splendid gateway to the **Palazzo del Capitano**, which is separated from the Palazzo del Commune by a stretch of excavated Roman street. For a closer look at the subterranean remains, visit the Centro Internazionale di Fotografia, in the **Scavi Scaligero** (under the Cortile dei Tribunale of the Palazzo del Capitano), where photography exhibitions are held amid Roman and medieval tombs, mosaics, paving stones and sewers.

A right turn at the entrance to the square leads into the courtyard known as the **Corte Mercato Vecchio**, dominated by a beautiful fifteenth-century staircase carved in roseate marble which leads to the Sala della Ragione. For a dizzying view of the city, ascend the **Torre dei Lamberti** (daily 8.30am–7.30pm; €6 or Verona Card); a lift takes you up to the first level, and then it's 125 steps to the very top.

The Arche Scaligere

Passing under the arch linking the Palazzo degli Scaligeri to the Palazzo del Capitano, you come to the little twelfth-century Romanesque church of **Santa Maria Antica** (daily 7.30am–12.30pm & 3.30–7pm), in front of which are ranged the **Arche Scaligere**, which are among the finest funerary monuments in Italy. The elaborate Gothic tombs are surrounded by wrought-iron railings, and at the moment there's no access to the compound, because restoration is in progress.

Over the side entrance to the church, an equestrian statue of Cangrande I (d.1329) grins on the summit of his tomb's pyramidal roof; the statue is a copy, the original being displayed in the Castelvecchio. In 2004 the mummified body of Cangrande – whose name means "Big Dog" – was removed from its sarcophagus and subjected to an examination which established that he'd died from a huge dose of digitalis (a drug derived from foxglove). It's known that one of Cangrande's physicians was executed by his successor, Mastino II; it's thus probable that the ambitious Mastino (meaning "mastiff"), having had his uncle murdered by the doctor, quickly covered his tracks by eliminating his henchman. The canopied tombs of the rest of the della Scala clan are enclosed within a wrought-iron palisade decorated with ladder motifs, the family emblem – *scala* means ladder. Mastino I (d.1277), founder of the dynasty, is buried in the simple tomb against the wall of the church; Mastino II (d.1351) is to the left of the entrance, opposite the most florid of the tombs, that of Cansignorio ("Top Dog"; d.1375). The unassuming tombs of the two who didn't take canine names, Giovanni (d.1359) and Bartolomeo (d.1304), are between Mastino II and Cansignorio.

Sant'Anastasia and San Pietro Martire

To the east of the Arche Scaligere, you can walk parallel to the Adige along Via Sottoriva, where the majority of the houses date from the Middle Ages, making this one of Verona's most atmospheric areas. The street takes you to **Sant'Anastasia** (March–Oct Mon–Sat 9am–6pm, Sun 1–6pm; Nov–Feb Tues–Sat 10am–1pm & 1–5pm, Sun 1–5pm; €2.50 or *biglietto unico*/Verona Card, or €3 with Duomo), Verona's largest church. Started in 1290 and completed in 1481, it's mainly Gothic, with undertones of the Romanesque. The early fourteenth-century carvings of New Testament scenes around the doors are the most arresting feature of its bare exterior; the interior's highlight is **Pisanello's** delicately coloured fresco of *St George and the Princess* (above the chapel to the right of the altar), a work in which the normally martial saint appears as something of a dandy.

To the left of Sant'Anastasia's facade is an eye-catching tomb, the free-standing monument to Guglielmo di Castelbarco (1320) by Enrico di Rigino. To its left, on one side of the little piazza fronting Sant'Anastasia, stands the lovely but deconsecrated church of **San Pietro Martire**, or San Giorgetto (open daily, but staffed by volunteers, so its hours are irregular). Ransacked by Napoleon's troops, it retains numerous little patches of fresco which make for an atmospheric interior, though the highlight is the vast lunette fresco on the east wall. Easily the strangest picture in Verona, it is thought to be an allegorical account of the Virgin's Assumption, though the bizarre collection of animals appears to have little connection with a bemused-looking Madonna. Painted in the early sixteenth century by Giovanni Falconetti, it is thought to be a copy of a Swiss tapestry, and was commissioned by two knights in Emperor Maximilian's army, who can be seen kneeling on either side of the fresco, against a background depicting an idealized Verona.

The Duomo

Verona's **Duomo** (March–Oct Mon–Sat 10am–5.30pm, Sun 1.30–5.30pm; Nov–Feb Tues–Sat 10am–1pm & 1.30–4pm, Sun 1.30–5pm; €2.50 or *biglietto unico*/Verona Card) lies just round the river's bend, a short distance from the Roman **Ponte Pietra**, which was destroyed in 1945 by the retreating Germans, but rebuilt using mostly the original stones and bricks. Consecrated in 1187, the Duomo has been worked on almost constantly over the centuries and the campanile's bell-chamber wasn't added until 1927. As a whole it's Romanesque in its lower parts, developing into Gothic as it goes up; the two doorways are twelfth century – look for the story of Jonah and a dragon-like whale on the south porch, and the figures of Roland and Oliver, two of Charlemagne's paladins, flanking the superb west portal. The interior has a splendid organ, and fascinating architectural details around each chapel and on the columns – particularly fine is the **Cappella Mazzanti** (last on the right). In the first chapel on the left, an *Assumption* by **Titian** occupies an architectural frame by Sansovino, who also designed the choir.

The door at the end of the left aisle gives access to the churches of **San Giovanni in Fonte** and, straight ahead, **Sant'Elena**, in front of which lie the remnants of the presbytery of a fourth-century basilica, whose form Sant'Elena roughly follows. Mosaics from the second half of the fourth century can be seen in Sant'Elena itself, while the adjacent San Giovanni in Fonte contains a masterpiece of Romanesque sculpture: a large baptismal font covered with biblical scenes. The gated alley immediately to the left of the Duomo's facade leads to the cloister, where you can see the foundations and mosaics of a larger, fifth-century basilica which was built nearby when the earlier one was partly destroyed. From the cloister you enter the **Museo Canonicale** (Fri 10am–12.30pm, Sat 10am–1pm & 2.30–6pm, Sun 2.30–6pm; €2.50 or Verona Card), a humdrum collection of religious art and archeological finds.

The Casa di Giulietta and San Fermo

South of Piazza delle Erbe runs Via Cappello, a street named after the family that Shakespeare turned into the Capulets – and there on the left, at no. 23, is the **Casa di Giulietta** (Mon 1.30–7.30pm, Tues–Sun 9am–7.30pm; €6, or €1 on first Sun of the month). Sadly for romantics, the association of the house with Juliet is based on nothing more than its picturesque courtyard and balcony, and even this latter feature is placed, as Arnold Bennett wrote, "too high for love, unless Juliet was a trapeze acrobat, accustomed to hanging downwards by her toes". Perhaps the most memorable thing about the house, however, is the extraordinary amount of lovers' graffiti that virtually obliterates the walls of the entrance to the courtyard.

Although the "Capulets" (Capuleti) and the "Montagues" (Montecchi) did exist, Romeo and Juliet were entirely fictional creations; and despite bloody feuds being commonplace (the head of one family invited his enemy to a truce-making meal, informing him afterwards that he'd just dined off the liver of his son), there's no record of these two clans being at loggerheads. The cheerless facts notwithstanding, a bronze Juliet has been shoved into a corner of the courtyard, her right breast polished bright by the groping hands of pilgrims hoping for luck in love. The house itself, constructed at the start of the fourteenth century, is in a fine state of preservation, but is largely empty.

Verona has a couple of other spurious "Romeo and Juliet" shrines: "Romeo's house", a private dwelling at Via Arche Scaligere 4; and the Tomba di Giulietta, in the southwest of the city, in the cloister of the deconsecrated San Francesco al Corso (Mon 1.30–7.30pm, Tues–Sun 8.30am–7.30pm; €4.50, free on first Sun of month, joint ticket with the Casa di Giuletta €7), which also has a peculiar display of three hundred Roman amphoras, imprisoned in a cage in the basement.

Via Cappello leads into Via Leoni with its Roman gate, the **Porta Romana dei Leoni**, and segment of excavated Roman street, exposed three metres below today's street level. At the end of Via Leoni and across the road stands the red-brick church of **San Fermo Maggiore** (March–Oct Mon–Sat 10am–6pm, Sun 1–6pm; Nov–Feb Tues–Sat 10am–1pm & 1.30–4pm, Sun 1–5pm; €2.50, or *biglietto unico*/Verona Card), whose exterior betrays the fact that it consists of two churches combined. The Benedictines built the original one in the eighth century, then rebuilt it in the eleventh to honour the relics of Saint Fermo and Saint Roch (the former was supposedly martyred on this site); very soon after, flooding forced them to superimpose another church for day-to-day use, a structure greatly altered in the early fourteenth century by the Minorites. The Gothic upper church may have no outstanding works of art (though the *Annunciation* by Pisanello at the west end is the earliest surviving fresco by the artist), but the numerous fourteenth-century frescoes and the fine wooden keel-vault make for a graceful interior – constructed in 1314, the ceiling is the oldest such vault in the Veneto. The now subterranean Romanesque lower church, entered from the right transept, has some well-preserved twelfth-century frescoes on its columns, in particular the *Baptism of Jesus* halfway down on the left.

The Porta Borsari and Corso Cavour

After the Arena and the Teatro Romano, Verona's most impressive Roman remnant is the **Porta Borsari**, a structure that was as great an influence on the city's Renaissance architects as the amphitheatre. Now reduced to a monumental screen bestriding the road at the junction of Via Armando Diaz and Corso Porta Borsari (west of Piazza delle Erbe), it was Verona's largest Roman gate; the inscription dates it at 265 AD, but it's almost certainly older than that.

Busy **Corso Cavour**, which stretches away from the gate, is lined with bulky Renaissance palazzi, including two by **Michele Sanmicheli** (1484–1559) – the handsome **Palazzo Canossa**, at no. 48, and the **Palazzo Bevilacqua**, at no. 19. The two could hardly be more different: the former a handsome, restrainedly classical design with a shallow facade, the latter an ornately carved Mannerist effort. Sanmicheli, Verona's most illustrious native architect, left his mark elsewhere in the city too, most obviously in the shape of the great fortified gateways of the Porta Nuova and the Porta Palio (both near the train station), and in the Palazzo Pompei, now the home of the Museo Storico Naturale.

Opposite the Palazzo Bevilacqua stands the Romanesque **San Lorenzo** (currently closed for restoration; when it reopens, hours and ticket details will be the same as Sant'Anastasia), in the courtyard of which you'll see fragments dating back to the eighth century, the period of the church's foundation. The narrow, plain interior, which dates from the mid-twelfth century, is mostly notable for the women's galleries and for a miscellany of columns, some banded in brick and soft *tufa* stone; atop the columns in the transept are two capitals that date back to Charlemagne and display his imperial eagle.

A short distance beyond the Palazzo Canossa, set back from the road on the right, stands the **Arco dei Gavi**, a first-century Roman triumphal arch; originally raised in the middle of the Corso, it was shifted to its present site overlooking the Adige in 1932. This is the best vantage point from which to admire the **Ponte Scaligero**; built by Cangrande II between 1355 and 1375, the bridge was blown up by the Germans in 1945 – the salvaged material was used for the reconstruction. The stretch of shingle on the opposite bank is a popular spot for **picnics**, sunbathing and just watching the river flow by – the water's rich colour comes from minerals deposited by the glaciers upstream.

The Castelvecchio

The fortress from which the bridge springs, the **Castelvecchio** (Mon 1.30–7.30pm, Tues–Sun 8.30am–7.30pm; €6, or Verona Card; €1 on first Sun of month), was commissioned by Cangrande II at around the same time, and became the stronghold for Verona's subsequent rulers, all of whom altered it in some way – the last major addition, the small fort in the inner courtyard, was built by Napoleon. Opened as the city museum in 1925, it was damaged by bombing in World War II, but reopened in 1964 after scrupulous restoration by **Carlo Scarpa**. Scarpa's conversion of the Castelvecchio is one of his most impressive projects, leading the visitor through a labyrinthine succession of chambers, courtyards and open-air walkways – a route fascinating to explore in itself, thanks largely to Scarpa's subtle use of materials and textures. Halfway through the itinerary, you'll come face to face with the equestrian figure of **Cangrande I**, removed from his tomb and strikingly displayed on an outdoor pedestal; his expression is disconcerting from close range, his simpleton's grin difficult to reconcile with the image of the ruthless warlord.

The collection contains jewellery, sculpture, paintings, weapons and an array of other artefacts: a real joy of this museum is in wandering round the beautiful sculptures and frescoes by the often nameless artists of the late Middle Ages. Of the later works of art, outstanding are two works by **Jacopo Bellini**, two *Madonna*s by **Giovanni Bellini**, another *Madonna* by **Pisanello**, **Mantegna**'s *Holy Family*, **Veronese**'s *Descent from the Cross*, a **Tintoretto** *Nativity*, a **Lotto** portrait and works by **Giambattista Tiepolo** and his son **Giandomenico**. Look out also for the extraordinary painting by Giovanni Francesco Caroto of a boy joyfully holding up a drawing he has made – a startlingly genuine depiction of a child's work.

San Zeno Maggiore

A little over a kilometre northwest of the Castelvecchio stands the **Basilica di San Zeno Maggiore** (March–Oct Mon–Sat 8.30am–6pm, Sun 1–6pm; Nov–Feb Tues–Sat 10am–1pm & 1.30–4pm, Sun 1–5pm; €2.50, or *biglietto unico/ Verona Card*), one of the most significant Romanesque churches in northern Italy. A church was founded here, above the tomb of the city's patron saint, as early as the fifth century (Zeno was the bishop of Verona in the 360s), but the present building and its campanile were raised in the first half of the twelfth century, with additions continuing up to the end of the fourteenth century. Its large **rose window**, representing the Wheel of Fortune, dates from around 1200, as does the magnificent **portal**, whose lintels bear relief sculptures representing the months and the miracles of Zeno, while the tympanum shows Zeno trampling the Devil. The reliefs to the side of the portal, also from this period, show scenes from the Old and New Testaments and various allegorical scenes – notably *The Hunt of Theodoric*, in which the Ostrogoth king of Italy chases a stag down into Hell. (Theodoric, who ruled the peninsula from 493 to 526, based his court in Ravenna but so close was his attachment to Verona that for centuries the city was known in his native Germany as "Theodoric's city".) Extraordinary bronze panels on the **doors** depict scenes from the Bible and more miracles of Zeno, in a style influenced by Byzantine and Ottoman art; most of those on the left date from around 1100, most of the right-hand panels from a century later.

Areas of the lofty and simple **interior** are covered with frescoes, some superimposed upon others, some defaced by ancient graffiti. Diverting though these are, the one compulsive image in the church is the high altar's luminous *Madonna and Saints* by **Mantegna**. In the apse of the left aisle is a disarmingly cheerful fourteenth-century painted marble figure of Saint Zeno, typically represented as dark-skinned (it's believed he came from Africa) and with a fish on his crook (legend has it that when called upon to exorcize Emperor Gallienus's daughter, Zeno was found fishing); the saint's tomb is in the beautifully colonnaded crypt beneath the raised choir.

▲ San Zeno Maggiore, Verona

Don't leave without a wander round the elegant, twin-columned arcades of the cloisters; a *Last Judgement* can be made out amid the fragmentary frescoes on the eastern wall, to which the tomb of an illegitimate Scaliger is also attached.

North and east of the Adige

On the other side of Ponte Garibaldi, and right along the embankments or through the public gardens, is **San Giorgio in Braida**, which in terms of its artworks is the richest of Verona's churches. A *Baptism* by **Jacopo Tintoretto** hangs over the door, while the main altar, designed by **Sanmicheli**, incorporates a marvellous *Martyrdom of St George* by **Paolo Veronese**. If you're in need of a place to recuperate or picnic, the piazza in front of the church is a fine spot, providing a view along the river that must be the most photographed scene in Verona. (The park around the Arsenale, over the river from the Castelvecchio, is also a nice place for some time out, with an excellent children's playground.)

It's a short walk along the embankment from San Giorgio to the delightful Romanesque **Santo Stefano** (daily 9am–noon & 4–6pm, but closed Tues afternoon; free). One of the city's oldest churches, it was founded in the fifth century but gained its present shape in the twelfth; later additions include sixteenth-century frescoes and incongruous Baroque chapels. Past the Ponte Pietra you come to the first-century BC **Teatro Romano** (Mon 1.30–7.30pm, Tues–Sun 8.30am–7.30pm; €4.50, or Verona Card; €1 on first Sun of month); much restored, the theatre is now used for concerts and plays (the entrance is 150m south of the Ponte Pietra). When the restorers set to work clearing later buildings away from the theatre, the only one allowed to remain was the tiny church of Santi Siro e Libera – built in the tenth century but altered in the fourteenth. Higher still, and reached by a lift, the **Museo Archeologico** (same hours & ticket as the theatre) occupies the buildings of an old convent; its well-arranged collection features a number of Greek, Roman and Etruscan finds. Steps to the side of the theatre lead to the **Castel San Pietro**, built by the Austrians on the site of a Visconti castle which had been destroyed by Napoleon. An uningratiating building, its sole appeal is the view away from it. If you've the energy to walk further up the hill, you could call in at the **Museo Africano** (Tues–Sat 10am–12.30pm & 2.30–5.30pm, Sun 2–6pm; €3), off Via San Giovanni in Valle at Vicolo Pozzo 1; it has a brightly lit and well-displayed collection of musical instruments, fetishes and masks brought back over the years by missionaries. Further up Via San Giovanni in Valle, just below the youth hostel, stands the small Romanesque church of **San Giovanni in Valle** (daily 9am–noon), which was founded in the eighth century and rebuilt in the twelfth after earthquake damage. Bombing in 1944 destroyed the decoration of the interior, but the crypt escaped pretty well unscathed.

To the south of here you'll find one of the finest formal gardens in the country, the **Giardino Giusti**, which is entered from the street that bears its name (daily: April–Sept 9am–8pm; Oct–March 9am–sunset; €5). Created in the 1570s by Count Agostino Giusti, the garden has faced an uncertain future for the past decade, since ownership passed to no fewer than twenty different members of the Giusti family, following the death of the diplomat Justo Giusti. After feuding between some of the heirs, the whole estate – the grounds plus the splendid Palazzo Giusti (which is not open to the public) – has been put up for sale. Rumour has it that it will become a luxury hotel or even a casino, but for the time being the garden's fountains and shaded corners continue to provide the city's most pleasant refuge from the streets, as it has done for centuries – Goethe and Mozart both paid a visit, and were much impressed.

A final treat lies down the hill in the heart of the **Veronetta** district, on Interatto dell'Acqua Morte: the church of **Santa Maria in Organo** (daily 8am–noon & 2.30–6pm), which possesses what Vasari praised as the finest choir stalls in Italy. Dating from the 1490s, this marquetry was the work of one Fra Giovanni, a Benedictine monk called in when his monastic order decided to transform the church they had been given in 1444. Astonishing in their precision and use of perspective, they are replete with fascinating details: look out for a skull with a mouth shaped like a gondola – a dig at Verona's all-powerful neighbour. There is more of Fra Giovanni's handiwork in the sacristy, and the church's sixth-century crypt is also worth a look, for its reused upside-down Roman columns.

Eating, drinking and nightlife

Your money goes a lot further in Verona than it does in Venice: numerous **trattorie** offer full meals for less than €30 (especially in the Veronetta district, over the river on the east side), while on almost every street corner there's a **bar** where a glass of house wine costs as little as €1. Verona's cuisine, meatier and richer than Venice's, can be sampled inexpensively in the city's many **osterie**, which typically serve fine wines – often small amounts in large glasses to release the bouquet – and filling antipasti, though many offer full meals too. (In the recommendations below, the *osterie* which serve more substantial fare have been listed under "Restaurants".) If you haven't booked a table you should go early, as restaurants tend to be packed by 9pm. After you've eaten, there's a good choice of late-opening bars and clubs.

As the Veneto produces more DOC wine than any other region in Italy, with the region's most productive vineyards – Soave, Valpolicella and Bardolino – lying within the hinterland of Verona, it's not surprising that Italy's main wine fair, Vinitaly (Ⓦ www.vinitaly.com), is held in Verona; lasting for five days at the end of March and beginning of April, it offers infinite sampling opportunities.

For a non alcoholic indulgence, sit outside one of the *gelaterie* in Piazza delle Erbe and give a few minutes to an incredible concoction of fruit, cream and ice cream. But for the best ice cream in the city, head for the *Gelateria Ponte Pietra* at Via Ponte Pietra 23 (Tues–Sun 2.30–8pm), the organic *Zeno Gelato* at Piazza San Zeno 12a (Wed–Sun 4–9pm), or *Balu* (daily noon–8pm, open till midnight May–Sept), underneath the Porta dei Borsari.

Restaurants

Al Bracere Via Adigetto 6a. Pleasant, busy pizzeria, with an extensive menu of good-sized pizzas baked in a wood-fired oven. Open daily until midnight.
Alla Colonna Largo Pescheria Vecchia 4 ☏ 045.596.718. Almost impossible to get into, as the food is simple but superb, the prices excellent (€13 menu) and the tables packed with savvy locals. Open until 2am but kitchen closes at 11.30pm. Closed Sun.
Bella Napoli Via Marconi 14. Serves the best – and the largest – pizzas in Verona, in a distinctly Neapolitan atmosphere. Open daily till 1am or later on Fri & Sat.

Bottega del Vino Vicolo Scudo di Francia 3a ☏ 045.800.4535. One of the top restaurants in Verona, with flamboyant antique decor and one of the largest selection of wines in Italy. It's not cheap (mains go up to around €30), and it's become somewhat touristy, but plenty of locals eat here too. A dish to look out for is the *risotto all'Amarone* – rice braised in the local wine. Open till midnight; closed Tues.
Caffè Monte Baldo Via Rosa 12. Very popular spot near the Piazza delle Erbe, with a small, moderately priced menu. Wide range of excellent wines available by the glass. Open till 9.30pm; closed Mon.

Hostaria La Vecchia Fontanina
Piazzetta Chiavica 5 ☎045.591.159. Its
small, brightly painted rooms give this
centrally located restaurant a cosy feel. The
menu offers interesting combinations of
flavours, such as venison with cocoa and
mustard, and it's also strong on vegetarian
dishes, such as *bigoli* with nettle and
smoked ricotta. Closed Sun.

Osteria del Bugiardo Corso Porta Borsari 17a
☎045.591.1869. Business-like establishment
close to Piazza dell'Erbe, where the high
tables are packed at lunchtime with locals
grabbing a quick lunch. An excellent range of
antipasti and *crostini*, as well as good *primi*
and *secondi*. Open till 10pm Sun–Thurs, and
till midnight on Fri & Sat; closed Mon.

Osteria alla Pigna Via Pigna 4
☎045.800.4080. Elegant traditional
restaurant between the Duomo and Piazza
dell'Erbe, with a well-deserved reputation
among locals and tourists alike. Moderately
priced, with *secondi* costing €12–18.
Closed all day Sun and Mon lunch.

Osteria Sottoriva Via Sottoriva 9.
Verona's traditional *osterie* don't come
much more authentic than this: it's rumbus-
tious, full of locals, and serves delicious
food at very reasonable prices. In summer
you can sit outside under the arches. Open
10.30am–10.30pm; closed Wed.

Tre Marchetti "Da Barca" Vicolo Tre Marchetti
19b ☎045.803.0463. A couple of steps north
of the Arena, this very elegant family-run
place is perfect for a pre- or post-opera
meal of Veronese specialities, such as *bigoli*
or veal braised in Amarone. It's unsurpris-
ingly pricy, given its location, but the food is
always good. Booking essential. Sept–June
closed Sun; July & Aug closed Mon.

Bars and snacks

Al Carro Armato Vicolo Gatto 2a. One of the
most atmospheric *osterie* in the city, with
delicious Veronese antipasti, and live music
on some Sundays. Open until 2am; summer
closed Mon evening and all day Tues; winter
closed Mon.

Al Mascaron Piazza San Zeno 16. Fine wines
and an urbane atmosphere early in the
evening, popular disco-bar later. Five
minutes' walk west from Castelvecchio.
Open until 1am; closed Mon.

Caffè Coloniale Piazzetta Viviani 14c. Best hot
chocolate in the city, and good snacks in a
mock-colonial setting, with a nice outdoor
terrace. Open 7am–midnight. Closed Sun
in Aug.

Cappa Café Piazzetta Bra Molinari 1a. Large
bar with eastern trappings (floor cushions,
etc), riverfront terrace and live jazz on
Sundays. Open daily till 2am.

Il Campidoglio Piazzetta Tirabosco 4. Friendly
bar in the old Jewish ghetto, on a surprisingly quiet square just yards from the bustle
of Corso Borsari and Piazza dell'Erbe.
Serves snacks and teas, as well as the
usual *aperitivi*. Free wi-fi access. Open till
2am; closed Mon.

Le Vecete Via Pellicciai 32. Atmospheric
osteria with a delicious selection of the
savoury tartlets known as *bocconcini*, and
good lunches. Its wine list is excellent,
ranging from cheap to very, very expensive.
Open daily till midnight, or later during the
opera season.

Osteria a la Carega Via Cadrega 8.
Friendly, small *osteria* with a compact
and cheery feel and a strong local following.
Excellent *piadine*, salads and wine. The
Carega Jazz Festival fills the whole street in
June. Open daily till 2am.

Osteria al Duomo Via Duomo 7a. Best
of the city's bars, little changed by
modern fashion, and enlivened by live music
on Wednesday afternoons from Sept–June.
Interesting menu, too. Open till midnight;
closed Sun.

Rivamancina Vicolo Quadrelli 1, Veronetta.
Lively late bar on the left bank of the Adige,
with a trendy taste in music and cocktails.
Mon–Sat 8pm–2am.

Music, nightlife and carnival

Music and theatre are the dominant art forms in the cultural life of Verona.
The city's **opera festival**, held in the Arena during July and August, has been a
major draw since 1913, always opening with a no-expense-spared production of
Aïda. Tickets range from around €20 for a seat high up on the terraces to €200
for the best, and can be bought from the ticket office at Via Dietro Anfiteatro, or

at the Teatro Romano, or by phone or online (☎045.800.5151, ⓦwww.arena
.it). Big rock events crop up on the Arena's calendar too. A season of ballet and
of Shakespeare and other dramatists in Italian is the principal summer fare at the
Teatro Romano. Some events here are free; for the rest, cheapskates who don't
mind inferior acoustics can park themselves on the steps going up the hill
alongside the theatre. The city's other main venue for plays and classical music is
the **Teatro Nuovo** at Piazza Viviani 10.

Free performances by local dance and theatre groups in May can be surprisingly good, while the June **jazz festival** attracts international names. The **club**
scene is far livelier than in moribund Venice, with venues coming and going all
the time; the *Spettacoli* section of the local paper, *L'Arena*, is the best source of
up-to-date information on clubs and other entertainment in Verona.

One of the most enjoyable days in the calendar is Verona's **Carnevale**, held on
the Friday before Shrove Tuesday. In contrast to its rather self-conscious and
commercialized Venetian counterpart, this is a purely local event, centred on a
huge and loud procession that winds through the centre from Piazza Brà, with
hundreds of people larking about in fancy dress and chucking confetti all over
the place. The parade is led by a large character called the Papa del Gnocco –
most of the city's restaurants serve *gnocchi* in his honour for the day.

Listings

Airport information Verona Valerio Catullo
airport (Villafranca) ☎045.809.5666; Brescia
Gabriele d'Annunzione airport (Montichiara)
☎030.965.6502; ⓦwww.aeroportoverona.it
serves both airports.

Bike rental Zanchi, Corso Cavour 13a, near
the Porta Borsari; Carega Bike, Via Cadrega
8 (run by the *osteria* of the same name).

Bus information ☎045.805.7913, ⓦwww
.atv.verona.it.

Car rental Combined office on Piazzale XXV
Aprile, beside the train station: Europcar
☎045.592.759; Hertz ☎045.800.0832;
Maggiore ☎045.800.4808.

Hospital Ospedale Civile Maggiore, Piazza
Stefani (near the Arsenale) ☎045.807.2120.

Internet access Internet Train, Via Roma 19
(Mon–Fri 10am–10pm, Sat & Sun 2–8pm);

Internet Etc, Via 4 Spade 3b (Tues–Sat
10.30am–8pm, Sun & Mon 3.30–7.45pm).
Free wi-fi access is hard to come by – head
for *Il Campidoglio* (see "Bars", above).

Lost property Airport ☎045.809.5715;
buses ☎045.800.5825; trains
☎045.809.3827, or by platform 1 at the
station.

Police Questura, Lungoadige Galtarossa
☎045.809.0411. For the Ufficio Stranieri,
which specifically deals with tourists, ring
☎045.809.0500.

Post office Piazza Viviani, near Piazza delle
Erbe (Mon–Fri 8.30am–6.30pm, Sat
8.30am–1pm).

Taxis 24-hour ☎045.532.666.

Train information At the train station, daily
7am–9pm; ☎89.20.21.

The northern Veneto

Lacking a city of Verona's or Padua's appeal, the area extending from the Venetian lagoon to the southern edge of the Dolomites is the least visited part of the Veneto – most of those who pass through it are hurrying on to the ski-slopes of Cortina d'Ampezzo and its neighbouring winter resorts. This region's attractions might be generally on a smaller scale than those of the better-known Veneto towns, but they offer some of the most rewarding day-trips from Venice.

The only city in the area covered by this chapter is prosperous **Treviso**, just 30km north of Venice. Some of the Veneto's finest medieval buildings and frescoes are to be seen here, and Treviso's position at the centre of the rail network makes it a good base from which to investigate the crannies of the region. To the west of Treviso, the beautiful little walled town of **Castelfranco Veneto** – the birth-place of Giorgione and home of one of his greatest paintings – also sits in the middle of a web of rail lines that connects Venice to the regional centres of Padua, Vicenza, Treviso and Belluno. A hop westward from Castelfranco brings you to another ancient walled town, **Cittadella**, while to the north lies **Bassano del Grappa**, the ultimate source of the fiery grappa spirit and site of one of Italy's most spectacular bridges. Two other remarkable old towns lie within a short radius of Bassano: **Maróstica**, famous for its ceremonial chess game played with human "pieces"; and **Ásolo**, historically a rural retreat for the Venetian aristocracy, and just a few kilometres from the finest country house in all of Italy – the **Villa Barbaro** at **Masèr**. A short way to the north of Masèr, lodged on a ridge overlooking the valley of the Piave, **Feltre** boasts another historic centre that's been little changed by the last four centuries.

Due north of Treviso, the rail line into the far north of the Veneto runs through **Conegliano**, a town where life revolves round the production of wine, and of the sparkling Prosecco in particular. From there a service continues up through **Vittorio Veneto**, with its remarkably preserved Renaissance streets, and on to **Belluno**, in effect the mountains' border post.

Treviso

TREVISO is a brisk commercial centre and the capital of a province that extends to the north almost as far as Belluno, but to most tourists it's known merely as the place that the cheap flights go to. It deserves far more visitors than it gets – not only does it have some fine works of art, but the townscape within the sixteenth-century walls is often appealing too. A lack of local dressing stone led in the thirteenth century to the use of frescoes to decorate the houses, and these painted facades, along with the lengthy porticoes that shelter the

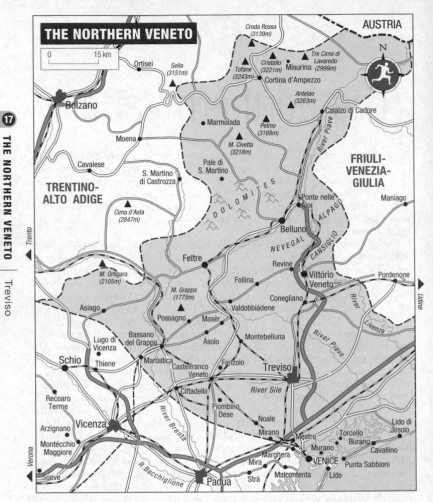

THE NORTHERN VENETO

0   15 km

AUSTRIA

Croda Rossa
(3139m)

Tre Cime di
Lavaredo
(2999m)

Cristallo
(3221m)

Ortisei   Sella
(3151m)

Tofane
(3243m)   Misurina

Cortina d'Ampezzo

Bolzano

Antelao
(3263m)

Calalzo di Cadore

Marmolada   Pelmo
(3168m)

Moena

M. Civetta
(3218m)

FRIULI-
VENEZIA-
GIULIA

Cavalese

Pale di
S. Martino

Maniago

S. Martino
di Castrozza

Ponte nelle
Alpi

TRENTINO-
ALTO ADIGE

DOLOMITES

Cima d'Asta
(2847m)

Belluno

NEVEGAL

Feltre

ALPAGO

CANSIGLIO

Revine

Pordenone

M. Ortigara
(2105m)

Vittório
Veneto

Follina

Asiago   M. Grappa
(1775m)

Conegliano

Valdobbiádene

Possagno   Masèr

Lugo di   Bassano
Vicenza   del Grappa   Ásolo   Montebelluna

Schio

Maróstica

Thiene   Fanzolo   Treviso

Castelfranco
Veneto

Cittadella

River Sile

Recoaro
Terme

Piombino
Dese

Arzignano   Vicenza   Noale

Montécchio
Maggiore   Mirano

Lido di
Jésolo

Torcello

Mestre

Burano

Soave

R. Bacchiglione

Mira   Marghera

Murano

Cavallino

VENICE

Punta Sabbioni

Strà   Malcontenta   Lido

Padua

River Piave   River Livenza

River Plave

River Brenta

Trento

Verona

Udine

N

pavements and the fast-running canals that cut through the centre (complete with waterwheels), give many of the streets an appearance quite distinct from that of other towns in the region.

As with every settlement in the area, it used to be under Venetian control, but it was an important town long before its assimilation by Venice in 1389. As early as the eighth century it was minting its own coinage, and by the end of the thirteenth century, when it was ruled by the Da Camino family, Treviso was renowned as a refuge for artists and poets, and a model of good government. (Dante, in the *Purgatorio*, praises Gherardo da Camino as a man "left from a vanished race in reproof to these unruly times".) Plenty of evidence of the town's early stature survives in the form of Gothic churches, public buildings and, most dramatically of all, the paintings of **Tomaso da Modena** (1325–79), the dominant artist in northern Italy in the years immediately after Giotto's death.

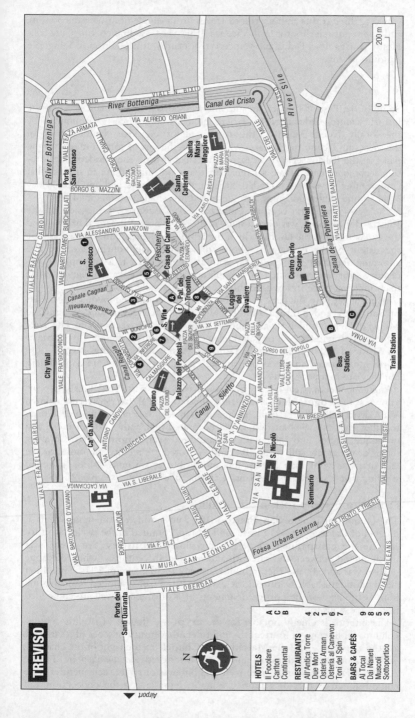

TREVISO

HOTELS
Il Focolare — A
Carlton — C
Continental — B

RESTAURANTS
All'Antica Torre — 4
Due Mori — 2
Osteria Arman — 1
Osteria al Canevon — 6
Toni del Spin — 7

BARS & CAFÉS
Ai Tocai — 9
Dai Naneti — 8
Muscoli — 5
Sottoportico — 3

Two or three **trains** an hour run to Treviso from Venice (journey time 30min), and approximately hourly from Vicenza (1hr) via Castelfranco and Cittadella. Hourly **buses** from Padua and Venice arrive nearby, at the station in Lungosile Antonio Mattei.

The City

Some of the best of Treviso's arcades and frescoes are in the main street of the historic centre, **Calmaggiore**, where modern commerce – epitomized by the locally based Benetton, the town's major employer (and sponsor of the successful Treviso rugby team) – has reached the sort of compromise with the past that the Italians seem to arrange better than anyone else. Modern construction techniques have played a larger part than you might think in shaping that compromise: Treviso was pounded during both world wars, and on Good Friday 1944 around half its buildings were destroyed in a single bombing raid.

The early thirteenth-century **Palazzo dei Trecento**, at the side of the **Piazza dei Signori**, was one casualty of 1944 – a line of indented brick round the exterior shows the level at which the rebuilding began, and you can also see the extent of the damage in photos under the neighbouring arcades. The adjoining **Palazzo del Podestà**, with its high tower, is a late nineteenth-century structure, concocted in the appropriate style. Piazza dei Signori is the main meeting place in town, and the scene of the daily *passeggiata*.

Incorporated into the back of this block are the conjoined medieval churches of **San Vito** and **Santa Lucia** (daily 9am–noon; free), tucked behind the Monte di Pietà (municipal pawn shop) on the edge of Piazza San Vito. The latter is the more interesting – a tiny, dark chapel with extensive frescoes by **Tomaso da Modena** and his followers. San Vito has even earlier paintings (twelfth- and thirteenth-century) in the alcove through which you enter from Santa Lucia, but they are in a poor state.

Another one of Treviso's ancient landmarks, the patricians' meeting place known as the **Loggia dei Cavaliere**, is close to the Palazzo dei Trecento, down Via Martiri della Libertà. Built in the early thirteenth century and pieced back together after the 1944 air raid, it was decorated first with a brick pattern and grotesque figures, and then with romanticized scenes from the Trojan wars, scraps of which are still visible. Recently restored, it's remarkable more for the fact of its survival than for its appearance, but it warrants a look if you're strolling that way towards the Santa Caterina side of town (see p.342).

From the Duomo to the city walls

The Duomo of Treviso, **San Pietro** (daily 8am–noon & 3.30–6pm) stands at the end of Calmaggiore, on Piazza del Duomo. Founded in the twelfth century, as were the **campanile** and perpetually closed **baptistery**, San Pietro was much altered between the fifteenth and nineteenth centuries (when the huge portico was added), and then rebuilt to rectify the damage of 1944. The oldest clearly distinguishable feature of the exterior is the pair of eroded Romanesque lions at the base of the portico; fragments of Romanesque wall are embedded in the side walls too.

The interior is chiefly notable for the **crypt** – a thicket of twelfth-century columns with scraps of fourteenth- and fifteenth-century frescoes (if it's locked, ask the sacristan) – and the **Malchiostro Chapel** (to the right of the chancel), with frescoes by **Pordenone** and a much-restored *Annunciation* by **Titian**. Although Pordenone and Titian were the bitterest of rivals, their pictures were commissioned as part of a unified scheme, representing the conception and birth of Christ; the 1944 bombs annihilated the crowning piece of the ensemble – a fresco by Pordenone on the chapel dome, representing *God the Father*. Paintings by **Paris Bordone**, the most famous Treviso-born artist, hang in the vestibule of the chapel and in the sacristy. Other things to search out are the monument to Bishop Zanetti by **Pietro Lombardo**, on the left wall of the chancel, the tomb of Bishop Nicolò Franco by **Lorenzo and Giambattista Bregno**, in the chapel to the left of the chancel, and **Lorenzo Bregno**'s figure of *St Sebastian*, on the first pillar of the left aisle. The **diocesan museum** (Thurs & Fri 9am–noon, Tues & Thurs 3–6pm; free) – a typical jumble of functional paintings, ecclesiastical garb and silverware – is round the back of the Duomo, in the angle of Via Canoniche del Duomo; you get to it by turning first left down the hill from the Duomo. Nearby you'll see a fine fourth-century bath mosaic, open to the skies.

Heading down Via Antonio Canova from the Duomo you pass the fourteenth- to sixteenth-century Ca' da Noal, a building that used to house Treviso's museum of the applied arts. This collection might resurface in the Santa Caterina complex; nowadays the Ca' da Noal is used for temporary art exhibitions.

The longest unbroken stretch of the **city walls** runs along the northern edge of the centre, between the Porta dei Santi Quaranta and Porta San Tomaso. The fortification of Treviso was undertaken in 1509, at the start of the War of the League of Cambrai, and the work was finished around 1517, with the construction of these two monumental gates.

San Nicolò

The severe Dominican church of **San Nicolò** (Mon–Fri 8am–noon & 3.30–6pm), dominating the southwest corner of the old town just over the River Sile from the train station, upstages the Duomo in almost every department. Wrapped round several of its massive pillars are delicate frescoes by **Tomaso da Modena** and his school, of which the freshest are the *SS. Jerome, Romuald, Agnes and John* by Tomaso himself, on the first column on your right as you enter. The towering *St Christopher* on the wall of the right aisle, with feet the size of sleeping bags, was painted around 1410, probably by **Antonio da Treviso**. Equally striking, but considerably more graceful, is the composite tomb of Agostino d'Onigo on the left wall of the chancel, created in 1500 by **Antonio Rizzo** (who did the sculpture) and **Lorenzo Lotto** (who painted the attendant pages). The *Madonna and Saints* in the chancel is a collaboration between Savoldo and the little-known Marco Pensaben, painted twenty years after the Onigo tomb, while a third joint work, an *Incredulity of St Thomas*, stands on the altar of the Monigo chapel, on the right of the chancel – **Sebastiano del Piombo** is attributed with the upper section and **Lotto** with the lower gallery of portraits. The frescoes on the chapel's side walls are by fourteenth-century Sienese and Riminese artists.

The figures of Agnes and Jerome are an excellent introduction to Tomaso da Modena, but for a fuller demonstration of his talent you should visit the neighbouring **Seminario** (Mon–Fri: summer 8am–6pm; winter 8am–12.30pm & 3–5.30pm), where the **chapter house** (*sala del capitolo* – to the left as you go in) is decorated with forty portraits of members of the Dominican order, executed by the artist in 1352. Although these are not portraits in the modern sense of the term, in that they don't attempt to reproduce the appearance of the men whose names they bear, the paintings are astonishingly advanced in their observation of idiosyncratic reality. Each shows a friar at study in his cell, but there is never a hint of the formulaic: one man is shown sharpening a quill, another checks a text through a magnifier, a third blows the surplus ink from his nib, a fourth scowls as if you've interrupted his work.

Santa Caterina and around

On the other side of town from San Nicolò there's another great fresco cycle by Tomaso da Modena – *The Life of Saint Ursula* – in the deconsecrated church of **Santa Caterina** (Tues–Sun 9am–12.30pm & 2.30–6pm; €3) behind Piazza Giacomo Matteotti on Via Santa Caterina. Painted for the now-extinct church of Santa Margherita sul Sile, the frescoes were detached from the walls in the late nineteenth century shortly before the church was demolished. Restored, they take pride of place in a complex that is at present the city's main art museum, now that the old Museo Civico on Via Riccati is closed for long-term restoration.

The Saint Ursula frescoes depict her miserable story in vivid detail (see p.99 for the tale), but they are mostly covered with protective semi-transparent sheets – the postcards at the entrance give you an idea of how strong the colours really are. To your left as you enter the church is the Cappella degli Innocenti, where the frescoes on biblical themes by Tomaso and his school are in better condition.

The rest of the collection comprises an archeological section (predominantly late Bronze Age and Roman relics) and an assemblage of pictures that's typical of provincial galleries all over Italy – acres of hackwork interrupted by a few paintings for which any gallery director would give a year's salary. In the first category there's a sequence of martyrdoms by Pietro Muttoni, a cack-handed seventeenth-century Venetian. In the second category are a *Crucifixion* by **Jacopo Bassano**, the *Portrait of Sperone Speroni* by **Titian**, and **Lorenzo Lotto**'s psychologically acute *Portrait of a Dominican*. Comparing the Titian and Lotto portraits, you can see some justice in Bernard Berenson's contrast between the two – "We might imagine Titian asking of every person he was going to paint: Who are you? What is your position in society? while Lotto would put the question: What sort of person are you? How do you take life?" Elsewhere you'll find a lot of Paris Bordone, a couple of pictures by Giandomenico Tiepolo, and a trio of pastel portraits by Rosalba Carriera, including one of her more illustrious contemporary, Antoine Watteau.

Two other churches in the Santa Caterina quarter are worth a call. To the north of Santa Caterina is the thirteenth-century church of **San Francesco** (daily 8am–noon & 3–6pm), which was restored early in the twentieth century after years as a military depot. It's an immense hall of a church with a high ship's-keel ceiling and patches of fresco, including the top half of another vast *St Christopher* and a *Madonna and Saints* by **Tomaso da Modena** in the chapel to the left of the chancel. Close to the door on the right side of the church is the tomb of Francesca, **daughter of Petrarch**, who died in 1384, twenty years after **Dante's son**, Pietro, whose tomb is in the left transept.

To the south, at the end of one of the most attractive streets in Treviso – the arcaded Via Carlo Alberto – stands the largely fifteenth-century **Basilica di Santa Maria Maggiore** (daily 8–11.45am & 3–6pm), which houses the most venerated image in Treviso, a fresco of the *Madonna*, originally painted by Tomaso da Modena but subsequently retouched.

This is the workshop and market area, a district in which Treviso has the atmosphere of a rather smaller town. The antique sellers and furniture restorers of Treviso outnumber even the Benetton outlets, and it's over this side that you'll see most evidence of them; on a Saturday or Tuesday morning the northern part of this quarter, along Viale Bartolomeo Burchiellati and Borgo Mazzini, is overrun by a gigantic **market**.

Also in this area are the main markets for fresh produce: the **Pescheria**, which occupies an island in the middle of Treviso's broadest canal (as in Venice, health regulations dictated the siting of the fish market by a waterway); and the fruit and veg markets in **Piazzetta San Parisio**, a former cloister just to the east of the Pescheria. To the west on Via Palestra, almost on the junction with Via Pescheria, stands the **Casa dei Carraresi**, a beautifully restored palazzo that's now Treviso's principal art-exhibition venue.

Practicalities

The **tourist office** is right in the centre, at Piazza Monte di Pietà 8 (Mon 9am–1pm, Tues–Fri 9am–1pm & 2–6pm, Sat & Sun 9.30am–12.30pm & 3–6pm; ℡0422.547.632, ⓦwww.turismo.provincia.treviso.it); it dispenses useful leaflets not just on Treviso but on attractions throughout Treviso province. The **post office** is in the Piazzale della Vittoria, over to your left shortly after crossing the river from the train station; for **banks** keep going straight along Corso del Popolo towards Calmaggiore – you'll pass most of them along this stretch.

The vast majority of Treviso's **hotels** are characterless Eurobusiness places, and most of them are outside the old city. The only reasonably priced central hotel is the small two-star *Il Focolare*, close to the tourist office at Piazza Ancilotto 4 (℡0422.56601, ⓦwww.albergoilfocolare.net; ❷). The alternatives in the centre are two large business-oriented four-star hotels very close to each other, near the train station: the *Carlton*, Largo Porta Altinia 15 (℡0422.411.661, ⓦwww .hotelcarlton.it; ❸–❺), and the rather functional *Continental*, Via Roma 16 (℡0422.411.216, ⓦwww.hcontinental.it; ❷–❹). The tourist office can help with B&B accommodation.

Treviso's **restaurants** are rather more enticing than its hotels. You can get good Trevisan cooking at moderate prices (around €30 a head) at the friendly ⨭ *Due Mori*, Via Bailo 9 (℡0422.540.383; closed Wed); a large and brightly lit place that specializes in fish and has superb risotto, it's said to date back to 1400, though its present home is much more recent. At no. 7 in the nearby Via Inferiore is the homely *Toni del Spin* (℡0422.543.829; closed Sun & Mon), which has been winning plaudits for many years, while at no. 55 the rather old-worldly *All'Antica Torre* is another fish and seafood specialist (℡0422.583.694; closed all Sun and Thurs evening). You'll find adventurous cuisine and high standards at the friendly *Osteria al Canevon*, Piazza San Vito 13 (℡0422.540.208; closed Thurs), which has a lively bar out front. If you want something very simple, call in at *Osteria Arman*, beyond San Francesco at Via Manzoni 27 (closed all Thurs & Sun lunchtime); this is an old family-run establishment that sells its own *prosecco* to accompany generous helpings of pasta.

The **bars and cafés** clustered underneath and around the Palazzo dei Trecento are always buzzing. Round the corner, at Vicolo Brolo 2, Beppe and Fabio preside over a good atmosphere and fine snacks at the small ⨭ *Dai Naneti* (close all Sun & Wed eve). Down in the fish market there's the always popular ⨭ *Muscoli*, Via Pescheria 23 (Mon–Sat till 2am) – try the delicious fig and blue cheese sandwiches). Trendier Trevisans head for *Sottoportico* (Mon–Sat till 2am) under the arcades at Sottoportico dei Buranelli 29 or *Al Tocai* (Tues–Sun till 1am) in Piazzetta Lombardi, south of Piazza dei Signori.

Castelfranco Veneto

In the twelfth century **CASTELFRANCO VENETO** stood on the western edge of Treviso's territory, and from the outside the old town – or **Castello** – looks much as it must have done when the Trevisans had finished fortifying the place against the Paduans. The battlemented and moated brick walls, raised in 1199, run almost right round the centre, and five of their towers still stand, the largest being the clock-tower-cum-gate known as the **Torrione**. Of all the walled towns of the Veneto, only Cittadella and Montagnana bear comparison with Castelfranco, and the place would merit a quick visit just for its brickwork, even though the Castello is so small that you can walk in through one gate and out through the opposite one in three minutes flat. But the place has one other outstanding attraction: it was the birthplace of Giorgio da Castelfranco – **Giorgione** – and possesses a painting which on its own is enough to vindicate Vasari's judgement that Giorgione's place in Venetian art is equivalent to Leonardo da Vinci's in that of Florence.

Castelfranco is the major crossroads of the Veneto **rail** network, with frequent train connections to Venice, Treviso, Vicenza, Padua, Bassano and Belluno.

The Duomo

Known simply as the **Castelfranco Madonna**, Giorgione's *Madonna and Child with St Francis and St Liberale* hangs in the eighteenth-century **Duomo** (daily 9am–noon & 3–6pm), in a chapel to the right of the chancel. This is one of only six surviving paintings that can indisputably be attributed to **Giorgione**, the most elusive of all the great figures of the Renaissance. So little is known for certain about his life that legends have proliferated to fill the gaps – for instance, the story that his premature death in 1510, aged 34 at most (his birthdate is unknown), was caused by bubonic plague, caught from a lover. The paintings themselves have compounded the enigma and none is more mysterious than this one, in which a boldly geometrical composition is combined with an extraordinary fidelity to physical texture and the effects of light, while the demeanour of the figures suggests, in the forgiveably lush words of one writer – "withdrawal…as if their spirit were preoccupied with a remembered dream". At first sight the scene appears naturalistic, but look more closely and you'll see that strange laws are in operation here. For one thing, the perspective isn't consistent – the Madonna's throne has one vanishing point, the chequered foreground another. And while the sun is rising or setting on the distant horizon, the shadow cast by the armoured saint suggests a quite different source of light, and the shadows of St Francis and the throne imply a third. To compound the mystery, even the identity of the armoured figure is far from clear: most favour Liberale, the local patron saint and co-dedicatee of the Duomo, but he might be Saint George or even Saint Theodore, the first patron saint of Venice.

However, some facts are known about the picture's origin. It was commissioned by Tuzio Costanzo, probably in 1505, to honour his son, Matteo, who had been killed in battle the previous year. The church for which the piece was painted was demolished long ago, but the present arrangement of this chapel (dating from 1935) re-creates that devised by Giorgione's patron, with the painting placed so that the three figures look down at Matteo's tomb. After perusing the Giorgione, you might want to spend a minute admiring the huge adjacent altarpiece, which was sculpted by Torretto, the master of Canova; Torretto's young apprentice is said to have carved the little castle at the feet of

Saint Liberale. The only other paintings in the Duomo likely to hold your attention are in the **sacristy** (you might need to find someone to let you in): fragments of the first fresco cycle painted by Paolo Veronese, they were removed from the Villa Soranza by Napoleon's troops, who demolished the entire building and carted the pictures off to Paris, whence they were later repatriated. The interior of the Duomo itself was designed by the local architect **Francesco Maria Preti**, whose ashes are interred in the nave, underneath the dome (Preti's major contribution to the landscape of the Veneto is the Villa Pisani at Strà – see p.286); the facade is a late nineteenth-century hack job.

The rest of the town

Next to the Duomo stands the enticingly named **Casa Giorgione** (Tues–Sun 10am–12.30pm & 3–6.30pm; €2.50), which is hardly worth the entry fee, as its rooms are totally empty except for a chiaroscuro frieze in one of the first-floor rooms (hopefully attributed to Giorgione) and a video display about the painter. The only other interior in Castelfranco that you might want to peep at is the **Teatro Accademico** (Tues–Sat 2–7pm, Sun 10am–12.30pm & 4–7pm) in Via Garibaldi, opposite the Duomo. Designed in the mid-eighteenth century by Preti, it has an auditorium that's considerably less modest than you might think from the sober outside. Of wider appeal, perhaps, is the **Parco Corner-Revedin-Bolasco** (mid-March to Oct Tues & Thurs 10am–12.30pm & 3–5.30pm, Sat & Sun 10am–1pm & 2.30–5.30pm; June to mid-Sept open till 7.30pm; €3, free at weekends), a lovely wooded park that was laid out in the second half of the eighteenth century and has recently been meticulously groomed; the park lies behind the Villa Revedin-Bolasco (not open to the public), which is at Borgo Treviso 73, at the top of the road that leads directly to the train station on the east side of the walled town.

Castelfranco's top **restaurant** is *Alle Mura*, near the Duomo at Via F.M. Preti 69 (☎0423.498.098; closed Thurs), which has a bizarre interior decorated with Polynesian artefacts; the €12 lunch menu is excellent value.

Around Castelfranco

The major attraction within a short radius of Castelfranco is the wonderfully preserved town of **Cittadella**, which can easily be reached by train, as it's a station on the Treviso–Vicenza line. Buses and the Venice–Castelfranco *locale* trains stop at the village of **Piombino Dese**, where you can see one of Palladio's most influential villas; a visit to the hamlet of Fanzolo, site of Palladio's **Villa Emo**, isn't really feasible unless you have a car.

Buses from Castelfranco depart from Via Podgora, on the north side of Borgo Vicenza, and from Corso XXIX Aprile, which you cross to go into the Castello when coming from the station.

Cittadella

When Treviso turned Castelfranco into a garrison, the Paduans promptly retaliated by reinforcing the defences of **CITTADELLA**, 15km to the west. The **fortified walls** of Cittadella were built in the first quarter of the thirteenth century, and are even more impressive than those of its neighbour, forming an almost unbroken oval round the town. You enter the town through one of four rugged brick gateways, built on the cardinal points of the compass; if you're coming from the train station it'll be the **Porta Padova**, the most daunting of the four, flanked as it is by the Torre di Malta. The tower was built as a prison and torture chamber by **Ezzelino da Romano III**, known to those he terrorized in this region in the mid-thirteenth century as the "Son of Satan". Basing his claim to power not on any dynastic or legalistic argument, but solely on the exercise of unrestrained military might, Ezzelino was the prototype of the despotic rulers of Renaissance Italy, and his atrocities earned him a place in the seventh circle of Dante's *Inferno*, where he's condemned to boil eternally in a river of blood.

The Villa Emo

Just 8km northeast of Castelfranco, in **FANZOLO**, stands one of the best-maintained and most sumptuous of Palladio's houses, the **Villa Emo** (April–Oct daily 3–6.30pm, plus Sun 10am–12.30pm; Nov–March Mon–Sat 1–4.30pm, Sun 1.30–5pm; €6), now familiar to a wider audience as the home of John Malkovich in the film *Ripley's Game*. In 1556 the Venetian government set up a department called the Board of Uncultivated Properties, to promote agricultural development on the terra firma and distribute subsidies to landowners. One of the first to take advantage of this initiative was Leonardo Emo, who commissioned the villa from Palladio around 1564, when he switched his financial interests to farming. With its central accommodation and administration block and its arcaded wings for storage, stables, dovecots and so on, the building belongs to the same type as the earlier Villa Barbaro at Masèr (see p.355), and as at Masèr the main living rooms are richly frescoed. Nobody would claim that **Giambattista Zelotti**'s scenes and rubber-necked grotesques are in quite the same league as Veronese's work in the Barbaro house, but neither would anyone complain at having to look at them every morning over breakfast. A bank now owns the property, but the principal rooms are still open to the public; the grounds won't detain you for long.

The Villa Cornaro

Palladio's villas fall into two broad types: the first was designed as the focus of a large, cohesive farm, and takes the form of a low central block with attached lateral buildings; the second was designed to be the living quarters of an estate that was scattered or where the farming land was unsuitable for building, and takes the form of a tall single building with a freestanding pedimented porch. The Villa Barbaro belongs to the first category, while to the second category belong the Villa Pisani at Montagnana, the Villa Fóscari at Malcontenta and the **Villa Cornaro** (May–Sept Sat 3.30–6pm; €7), built in the 1550s at **PIOMBINO DESE**, 9km southeast of Castelfranco. The majestic double-decker portico is the most striking element of the exterior, and when Palladian style was imported into colonial America, this became one of his most frequently copied devices. Unfortunately, the villa's decoration – frescoes by the obscure eighteenth-century artist Mattia Bortoloni – isn't anything to get excited about.

Bassano del Grappa

Situated on the River Brenta where it widens on its emergence from the hills, **BASSANO DEL GRAPPA** has expanded rapidly this century, though its historic centre remains largely unspoiled by twentieth-century mistakes.

It's better known for its manufacturing and produce, and for the events of the two world wars (see p.349), than for any outstanding architecture or monuments, but its situation in the lee of the imposing Monte Grappa (1775m), with the Dolomites beyond, is impressive enough. For centuries a major producer of ceramics and wrought iron, Bassano is also renowned for its **grappa** distilleries and delicacies such as *porcini* (dried mushrooms), white asparagus and honey.

Trains run from Venice to Bassano fifteen times daily; the journey takes an hour. **Buses**, all of which run from in front of the station, connect with Masèr (4 daily), Possagno (9 daily), Maróstica (roughly every 30min), Ásolo (6 daily) and Vicenza (at least hourly).

The Town

Almost all of Bassano's sights lie between the Brenta and the train station; go much further in either direction and you'll quickly come to recently developed suburbs. Walking away from the station, the orbital Viale delle Fosse stands between you and the town centre, following the line of the fourteenth-century outer walls. Cross the road, turn right then left to get to Via Da Ponte, which forms a main axis through the centre; the statue is of **Jacopo Da Ponte**, the pre-eminent member of the dynasty of Renaissance painters more commonly known simply as the Bassano family.

▲ The Ponte degli Alpini, Bassano

On the left of **Piazza Garibaldi**, one of the centre's two main squares, the fourteenth-century church of **San Francesco** carries a gold medal plaque in honour of the resistance fighters of World War II; a few fresco fragments remain inside, including an *Annunciation* in the porch. The cloister now houses the **Museo Civico** (Tues–Sat 9am–6.30pm, Sun 3.30–6.30pm; €5, ticket also valid for Palazzo Sturm; Ⓦwww.museobassano.it) where the downstairs rooms are devoted to Roman and other archeological finds. Upstairs is a collection of sixteenth- to eighteenth-century work, including paintings by the **Bassano** family. Elsewhere in the museum are some huge frescoes detached from a palace in Piazzetta Montevecchio and a number of plaster works by **Canova**, two thousand of whose drawings are owned by the museum. There's also a room devoted to the great baritone **Tito Gobbi**, who was born in Bassano.

Overlooking the other side of the piazza is the 42-metre **Torre Civica**, once a lookout tower for the twelfth-century inner walls, now a clock tower with spurious nineteenth-century battlements and windows (Sat & Sun 10am–1pm & 2–5pm; €2). Further in the same direction is **Piazza Libertà**, with its seventeenth-century sculpture of San Bassiano, the patron saint of Bassano, and the all-too-familiar winged lion of Venice. Dominating the left-hand side of the piazza, the church of **San Giovanni** was founded in 1308 but is now overbearingly Baroque. Under the arches of the fifteenth-century **Loggia** on the other side are the frescoed coats of arms of the various Venetian governors of Bassano. On Thursday mornings both the central squares host a huge weekly market.

From the piazza's far right-hand corner, Piazzetta Montevecchio (the original core of the town), its frescoes now all faded or removed, leads to a little jumble of streets and stairways running down to the river and the **Ponte degli Alpini**, which takes its name from the Alpine soldiers who last rebuilt the bridge in 1948. The river was first bridged at this point in the late twelfth century, and replacements or repairs have been needed at regular intervals ever since, mostly because of flooding. The present structure was designed by **Palladio** in 1568, and built in wood to make the bridge as flexible as possible – torrential meltwater would demolish an unyielding stone version. Mined by the Resistance during the last war, and badly damaged by the retreating German army, it was restored in accordance with Palladio's design, as has been the case with every repair since the day of its completion.

Nardini, a grappa distillery founded in 1779, stands at this end of the bridge. These days the distilling process takes place elsewhere, but the original shop and bar are still functioning here (8am–8pm, closed Mon); you can also sample and buy the stuff in the so-called **Museo della Grappa** at nearby Via Gamba 6 (daily 9am–7.30pm), which is really a glorified showcase for the Poli distillery.

Cross over the bridge to reach the **Taverna al Ponte**, home of the **Museo degli Alpini** (daily 9am–8pm; free), which also gives a good view of the underside of the bridge. The Alpine soldiers, who crossed it many times during World War I on their way to Monte Grappa and Asiago, saw the bridge as a symbol of their tenacity, and so adopted it as their emblem. They still have strong associations with Bassano, and take part in parades here, looking as though they've just stepped out of some nineteenth-century adventure yarn.

Back on the town side of the bridge again, if you follow Via Ferracina downstream for a couple of minutes you'll come to the eighteenth-century **Palazzo Sturm** (Tues–Sat 9am–1pm & 3–6pm, Sun 3.30–6.30pm; same ticket as Museo Civico), which houses two museums. On the ground floor the Museo Remondini gives a well-illustrated account of the history of printing, with pride of place given to the Remondini printing works, which was founded in Bassano in the seventeenth century; upstairs is an extensive collection of the town's famed majolica ware. North of the Ponti degli Alpini, Via Gamba takes you up to the remnants of the **castle**; the huge and precarious-looking tower was built in the twelfth century by the Ezzelini. The campanile of **Santa Maria in Colle** is a conversion of another tower, while the church itself dates from around 1000; it contains two paintings by Leandro Bassano.

Go out of the castle enclosure, and spreading round to the right is the **Viale dei Martieri**, named after the Resistance fighters who were rounded up in the hills and hanged from trees along here in September 1944. To one end is the **Piazzale Generale Giardino**, with its Fascist-style memorial to the General, who died in 1935; a World War I monument in similar vein stands below in the **Parco Ragazzi del'99**, named after the "Lads of '99", born in just the right year to die by the thousand in the last phase of World War I.

If you cut across the town, through Piazza Libertà and south down Via Marinelli or Via Roma, then outside the city walls and right, you can't miss the vast **Tempio Ossario**. Begun in 1908 as a church, its function was changed in 1934, when it became a repository of over 5400 tombs, each containing the ashes of a soldier. The major **war memorial**, however, is 35km away on the summit of **Monte Grappa**. Built in 1935 on the spot where Italian troops repulsed the Austrian army's offensive in 1917, it's the burial place of some 12,000 Italian and 10,000 Austro-Hungarian dead, and the design of the monument – a vast tiered edifice with a "Via Eroica" running along the mountain ridge – is typical of the bombastic classicism of Fascist war memorials. From the summit (1775 metres) you can understand the strategic importance of the peak: on a clear day you can see as far as Venice.

Practicalities

The **tourist office** is up the road from the train station, just inside the town walls at Largo Corona d'Italia 35 (daily 9am–1pm & 2–6pm; ☎0424.524.351, ⓦwww.comune.bassano.vi.it).

There's only one **hotel** in the old centre, the three-star *Al Castello*, right by the castle at Piazza Terraglio 19 (℡0424.228.665, Ⓦwww.hotelalcastello.it; ➊). The best place to stay around here, though, is the 🍴 *Villa Brocchi Colonna*, 2km west of the centre at Contrà San Giorgio 98 (℡0424.501.580, Ⓦwww .villabrocchicolonna.it; ➋–➌); the welcoming mother-and-daughter team offer very comfortable rooms and the breakfast is delectable. For a low-budget stay there's a **hostel**, *Ostello Don Cremona*, Via Chini 6 (℡0424.219.137, Ⓦwww.ostellobassanodelgrappa.it; €18 for a dorm bed, doubles €24 per person).

For eating and drinking, there are two recommended places on the roads leading up to the castle: *Al Caneseo*, at Via Vendramini 20 (℡0424.228.524; closed Mon & all Aug), is a rustic family-run restaurant where the small menu is recited for you at the table; and 🍴 *Al Caneva*, at Via Matteotti 34 (open till midnight, closed Tues), is a cosy bar that does delicious snacks as well as more substantial dishes. On the western fringe of the town you'll find another excellent restaurant: 🍴 *Alla Riviera*, Via San Giorgio 17 (closed Sun eve and all day Mon; ℡0424.503.700). For grappa-tasting, head down to the old bridge to the *Nardini* outlet (see p.349), right on the bridgehead at Ponte Vecchio 2 (closed Mon).

Bassano has a lively arts calendar, with an **opera festival** in July and August, as well as jazz, dance and classical music events over the summer months.

Maróstica

Seven kilometres to the west of Bassano, the walled town of **MARÓSTICA** was yet another stronghold of Ezzelino da Romano, whose fortress glowers down on the old centre from the crest of the hill of Pausolino. The fortress, the lower castle and the almost intact ramparts that connect them make a dramatic scene, but Maróstica's main claim to fame is the **Partita a Scacchi** – a chess game played every other September with human "pieces".

A **bus** service runs between Maróstica and Bassano (every 30min; 20min); the stop is outside the lower castle.

The Town

Maróstica was run by the Ezzelini for quite a time, the monstrous Ezzelino III having been preceded by Ezzelino the Stutterer and Ezzelino the Monk. However, it was a less hideous dynasty of despots, the Scaligeri of Verona, who constructed the **town walls** and the **Castello Inferiore** (lower castle): the castle was built by Cangrande della Scala, and the walls by his successor, Cansignorio, in the 1370s. An exhibition of costumes for the *Partita a Scacchi* is now housed in the castle (guided tours in Italian daily 10am–noon & 2.30–6pm; €1).

Beyond the castle is **Piazza Castello**, the central square of the town, onto which is painted the board for the **Partita a Scacchi** (Ⓦwww.marosticascacchi .it). The game's origin was an everyday story of rival suitors, the only unusual aspect being that the matter was decided with chess pieces rather than swords. In 1454 two men, Vieri da Vallonara and Rinaldo d'Angarano, both petitioned the *podestà* of Maróstica, Taddeo Parisio, for the hand of his daughter, Lionora. Parisio decreed that the matter should be decided by a chess match, with the winner marrying Lionora and the loser being consoled with the prize of Parisio's younger sister. The game – which was won by Vieri, Lionora's secret favourite – was played with live pieces here in the square, and is re-enacted with great pomp in even-numbered years – five hundred people in the costume of the time, with music, dancing and fireworks.

The **Doglione**, behind the inevitable Lion of Saint Mark (Venice ruled Maróstica from 1404 to 1797), is a much-altered fifteenth-century building; once the castle armoury, it's now owned by a bank. To the left of it, Via San Antonio runs past the church of the same name to the forgettable Baroque church of the **Carmine**. A path round to the left of the Carmine winds up through an olive grove to the **Castello Superiore** (upper castle), which was built by Ezzelino and later expanded by the Scaligeri. Only the walls remain but within them a restaurant has been built, which has a marvellous view. It's only when you're at the top that you realize there's a road up, much less steep than the stony path but longer; if you take this route back down, look out for the cyclists who train on the hill – they whizz through the hair-pins with scarcely a sound to warn of their approach.

The oldest church in Maróstica, **Santa Maria**, is outside the city walls on the other side – go through the eastern gate, turn left, then second right. Unfortunately it was rebuilt in the eighteenth century, but it has some quirky attractions: modern votive paintings on the ceiling, for instance, and an altarpiece that's a copy of the top half of Titian's *Assumption* in Venice's Frari.

Practicalities

The *pro loco* **tourist office** is in the lower castle at Piazza Castello 1 (daily 10am–noon & 3–6pm). Maróstica has one superb **hotel** in the walled centre, the ⚇ *Due Mori*, which occupies a stylishly modernized seventeenth-century building just above the piazza at Corso Mazzini 73 (☎0424.471.777, ⓦwww.duemori.it; ❷–❹). For **food**, look no further than the ⚇ *Osteria Madonetta*, just off the main piazza at Via Vajenta 21 (closed Thurs); perhaps the most genuine **osteria** in the Veneto, it's virtually unchanged since it opened in 1904, and has been run by the same family for generations. Maróstica's big event, the **Partita a Scacchi**, takes place in the second weekend of September in even-numbered years – you'll need to buy tickets to watch it from the specially erected grandstand (€10–80).

Possagno

As you approach **POSSAGNO**, a small town lodged at the base of Monte Grappa, one of the strangest sights in the Veneto hits you: a huge temple that rises above the houses like a displaced chunk of ancient Rome. It was built by **Antonio Canova**, one of the dominant figures of Neoclassicism and the last Italian sculptor to be generally regarded as the most accomplished living practitioner of his art. He was born here in 1757, and his family home now houses a magnificent museum of his work. Just as you can't come to grips with Tintoretto until you've been to Venice, so an excursion to Possagno is essential to an understanding of Canova. You can reach Possagno easily by **bus** from Bassano (9 daily; 1hr) or Ásolo (7 daily; 40min); an infrequent service runs from Castelfranco Veneto. Shortly after Canova's death in 1822, all the working models that had accumulated in his studio in Rome were transported to Possagno, and here, from 1831 to 1836, an annexe (the Gipsoteca) was built onto the Canova house for the display of the bulk of the collection. A second addition was built in 1957, and the Gipsoteca is now one of only two complete displays of an artist's working models in Europe – the other being Copenhagen's collection of pieces by Thorvaldsen.

The Gipsoteca and Casa Canova

The process by which Canova worked towards the final form of his sculptures was a painstaking one, involving the creation of a series of rough clay models (*bozzetti*) in which the general shape would be refined, then a full-scale figure in gypsum plaster (*gesso*), and finally the replication of the plaster figure in marble, using small nails to map the proportions and contours from the plaster model to the marble statue. Preparatory works from all stages of Canova's career are shown in the **Gipsoteca** (Tues–Sun 9.30am–12.30pm & 3–6pm; €7; ⓦ www.museocanova.it) in Piazza Canova, and even if you're repelled by the polish of the finished pieces, you'll probably be won over by the energy and spontaneity of the first versions – such as the tiny terracotta model for the tomb of Pope Clement XIV, or the miniature group of Adam and Eve weeping over the body of Abel.

Canova's range will probably be as much of a surprise as his technique. Among the works collected in the vast main hall, for example, you'll find portraits, images of classical heroes, the funerary monument for Maria Christina of Austria (which was adapted by Canova's pupils for his own tomb in Venice's Frari), and a large *Deposition*, a bronze version of which is to be found in the Tempio. Notions of Canova as a bloodless pedant are dispelled by *Hercules and Lichas* and *Theseus and the Centaur*, two overpowering tableaux of violence that are each over ten feet high, while the adjoining room – tastefully added in 1957 by Carlo Scarpa – displays a more intimate and even erotic side, including a *Sleeping Nymph* and the famous *Graces*. More models are kept in the adjoining house (the Casa Canova), but the pleasure of this section is weakened by Canova's dreadful paintings – a parade of winsome Venuses and frolicking nymphs, which will not dispose you to disagree with the artist's own low opinion of his pictorial talents.

The Tempio

Donated to the town to serve as its new parish church, the **Tempio** (Tues–Sat: April–Oct 9am–noon & 3–6pm; Nov–March 9am–noon & 2–5pm) was designed by Canova with assistance from **Giannantonio Selva** (architect of La Fenice in Venice) and constructed from 1819 to 1832. Both Roman and Greek classical sources were plundered for its composition – the body of the building is derived from the Pantheon, but its portico comes from the Parthenon. The cool precision of the interior is disrupted by a sequence of ghastly paintings of the *Apostles*, and an appalling altarpiece for which Canova himself was the culprit. To the right is the bronze version of the *Deposition* in the Gipsoteca (cast posthumously in 1829), and opposite is the **tomb of Canova** and his half-brother Monsignor G.B. Sartori, with a self-portrait bust to the right. Designed by Canova for a different occupant, this tomb is not the Veneto's only memorial to the sculptor – the other one, infinitely more interesting, is in the Frari in Venice. In good weather the sacristan opens the stairs to the top of the dome (€1.50) – the view of the Asolean hills and the plain of the Piave is marvellous.

Ásolo and around

Known as "la città dei cento orizzonti" (the city with a hundred horizons), the medieval walled town of **ÁSOLO** presides over a tightly grouped range of 27 gentle peaks in the foothills of the Dolomites. Fruit trees and pastures cover the lower slopes of the Asolean hills, and a feature of life in the town itself is the festivals that take place at the various harvest times.

Paleolithic settlements have been found in the region, but the earliest documented settlement here was the Roman town called Acelum, which thrived from the second century BC until its destruction by Attila. Following resettlement, a succession of feudal lords ruled Ásolo, culminating with the vile **Ezzelino da Romano**, whose parents were born in the town. Ezzelino wrested Ásolo from the Bishop of Treviso in 1234, and a network of castles over much of the Veneto shows the extent of his conquests in the years that followed. On his death in 1259 the townspeople of Ásolo ensured that the dynasty died with him by butchering the rest of his family.

The end of the fifteenth century was marked by the arrival of **Caterina Cornaro**. Her celebrated court was attended by the likes of Cardinal Bembo, one of the most eminent literary figures of his day, who coined the verb *asolare* to describe the experience of spending one's time in pleasurable aimlessness. Later writers and artists found the atmosphere equally convivial: Gabriele d'Annunzio wrote about the town, and Robert Browning's last published work – *Asolando* – was written here.

There are regular **buses** to Ásolo from Bassano; if you want to get there from Venice, the quickest route is to take a train to Treviso, where you won't have to wait more than an hour for a bus to Ásolo (some change at Montebelluna) – in addition to the direct services, all buses to Bassano go through Ásolo and Masèr. The bus drops you at the foot of the hill, a connecting minibus (€1 return) taking you up into the town.

The Town

The main road into town from Bassano enters the southern Porta Loreggia, with a fifteenth-century fountain on the left and on the right **Casa Freia**, home of the traveller and writer Freya Stark. Via Browning continues up the hill; no. 151, formerly the house of Pen Browning, bears a plaque recording his father's stay in 1889. At the top is the hub of the town, **Piazza Garibaldi** (otherwise known as Piazza Maggiore), to the south of which stands the **Duomo** – not an attraction itself, but containing a couple of good pictures by Jacopo Bassano and Lorenzo Lotto. A well-known antiques fair is held in and around Piazza Maggiore on the second weekend of each month (except July & Aug); prices are steep, but browsing is fun.

Also on the Piazza Maggiore, in the fifteenth-century Loggia del Capitano, is the **Museo Civico** (Sat & Sun 10am–noon & 3–7pm; €4). The main interest of the art collection is provided by a pair of dubiously attributed Bellinis, a portrait of Ezzelino painted a good couple of centuries after his death, and a brace of large sculptures by Canova. More diverting are the memorabilia of Ásolo's residents, especially the portraits, photos and personal effects of the actress **Eleonora Duse**. The lover of d'Annunzio and many others, Duse was almost as well known for her tempestuous relationships as for her roles in the plays of Shakespeare, Hugo and Ibsen, and she came to Ásolo to seek refuge from public gossip. Although she died in Pittsburgh while on tour in 1924, her wish was to be buried in Ásolo, and so her body was transported back here, to

From 1489 to 1509 the Castello was the home of **Caterina Cornaro**, one of the very few women to have played a decisive part in Venetian history. Born into one of Venice's most powerful families, Caterina was betrothed at the age of 14 to the philandering Jacques II, king of the strategically vital island of Cyprus. The prospective groom then prevaricated for a while, until the scheming of his half-sister (who wanted him overthrown) and the Venetian promises of help against the belligerent Turks finally pushed him into marriage. Within a year Jacques was dead, in all likelihood poisoned by Marco Venier, the Venetian governor of Famagusta harbour. A few weeks later Caterina gave birth to a son, after whose christening the Venetian fleet set sail for home. No sooner had the detested Venetians left than the city was taken over by men of the Royal Council, Caterina jailed, and her son handed over to her mother-in-law, Marietta. (Marietta's hatred of Caterina was to an extent due to resentment of the latter's beauty: when Marietta was the mistress of Jacques' father she had been caught making love to him by the king's wife, who bit her nose off in the ensuing mêlée.)

News of the **insurrection** reached the Venetian galleys, who promptly returned and overpowered the city. Their reappearance was a mixed blessing. The death of Caterina's son at the age of one was taken by Venier as a cue to propose marriage; spurned, he plotted to kill her instead, but was discovered and hanged. For nine years Caterina resisted Venice's political pressure until at last, in 1489, she was forced to **abdicate** in order to gain much-needed weapons and ships against a new Turkish attack. Brought back to Venice to sign a deed "freely giving" Cyprus to the Republic, she was given the region of Ásolo as a sign of Venice's indebtedness, and a joust was held on the frozen Canal Grande in her honour. In Ásolo her court was constantly under the eye of the Council of Ten, who dispatched any man rumoured to be her lover for fear that a new dynasty should be started. Eventually Ásolo, too, was taken away from her by the Emperor Maximilian, and she returned to seek asylum in Venice, where she died soon after, in 1510.

the church of Sant'Anna. The Teatro Duse occupies a large part of the **Castello**, which has been largely restored, though there's little to see other than the view down to the plain.

Ásolo's ruined medieval fortress, the **Rocca** (Sun 10am–sunset; €1.50), is reached by taking Via Collegio up the hill from the back of Piazza Brugnoli (right by Piazza Garibaldi) and going through the Porta Colmarian. Built on Roman foundations, the Rocca stands 350m above sea level, and the views are worth the effort of the climb.

Via Canova leads west away from the town centre past Eleonora Duse's house (no. 306), near the Porta Santa Caterina. The church of **Santa Caterina** (May–Sept daily 9am–6.30pm; Oct–April Sat & Sun 9am–4.30pm), next to the *Carabinieri*, is deconsecrated but open to allow visitors to see its fifteenth-century frescoes. Some way further on, at the junction of the road, is the enchanting fifteenth-century **Lombard house**, with allegorical figures carved in soft stone; the architect was Francesco Graziolo, who worked for Caterina Cornaro. Taking the central of the three roads at this junction you will arrive at the Franciscan church of **Sant'Anna**; the cemetery on the right, from which there are splendid views, is where Eleonora Duse and Pen Browning are buried.

Practicalities

The **tourist office** is at Piazza G. D'Annunzio 2 (Tues–Wed 9.30am–12.30pm, Thurs–Sat 9.30am–12.30pm & 3–6pm; ☎0423.529.046, ⓦwww.asolo.it).

The cheapest of the three hotels is the *Duse*, a reasonable-quality three-star at the bottom of the main square at Via Browning 190 (℡0423.55.241, Ⓦwww .hotelduse.com; ❷); it's booked solid on the second Sunday of every month, when the antiques fair takes over the centre of town. The four-star *Albergo al Sole*, Via Collegio 33 (℡0423.951.332, Ⓦwww.albergoalsole.com; ❸–❺), has a breathtaking view from the breakfast terrace, but best of the lot is the famous and sybaritic *Villa Cipriani*, Via Canova 298 (℡0423. 523.411, Ⓦwww.villaciprianiasolo.com; ❻–❾), which has long been a favourite with showbiz types.

The best **restaurant** in town is the 🍴 *Hostaria Cà Derton*, at Piazza G. D'Annunzio 11 (℡0423.529.648; closed Sun all day & Mon eve), where *secondi* range from €16 to €35; you can sample the same delicious cooking at lower prices in the more informal *enoteca* next door.

The Tomba Brion

Five kilometres south of Ásolo, adjoining the municipal cemetery of the village of San Vito d'Altivole (daily 9am–sunset), stands the extraordinary **Tomba Brion**, the masterpiece to which the great Venetian architect **Carlo Scarpa** (1906–78) devoted much of the last nine years of his life. Though commissioned by the Brion family (owners of a local electronics company) as their mausoleum, this is much more than a commemoration of one particular group of individuals. Constructed as an L-shaped enclosure of some 2200 square metres, Scarpa's necropolis is an architectural complex in miniature, in which the various elements – tomb, temple, pools, grass – are deployed in a way that creates a highly evocative "formal poetry", to use the architect's own phrase. The Tomba Brion exemplifies Scarpa's renowned attention to the relationship of forms in space and to the properties of well-crafted materials: wood, mosaic, concrete and metal are combined exquisitely in a work that is both massive and delicate, and is distinctively a Scarpa design while simultaneously raising a multitude of references – to the Viennese Secession, to Frank Lloyd Wright, to Japanese traditional architecture, and even to the monuments of ancient civilizations (from some angles the structures are suggestive of Mayan ruins). Scarpa, as he wished, is himself buried here, beneath a marble plinth in a shady corner.

By public transport, San Vito is most easily reached by the #4 CTM **bus** from Ásolo, which passes along the main road about six times a day. (Don't take the #4 bus – this follows a different route.) The journey to San Vito takes about fifteen minutes; when you get off it's a few minutes' walk to the cemetery, just outside the south end of the village, at the end of Via del Cimitero.

The Villa Barbaro

Many people come away from the **Villa Barbaro** at **MASÈR**, 7km east of Ásolo, persuaded that this is the most beautiful house in Europe (Jan & Feb Sat 10am–5pm & Sun 11am–5pm; March, July & Aug Tues, Thurs & Sat 10am–6pm, Sun 11am–6pm; April–June, Sept & Oct Tues–Sat 10am–6pm, Sun 11am–6pm; Nov & Dec Sat & Sun 2.30–5pm; Ⓦwww.villadimaser.it). Touring the villas of the mainland, you become used to discrepancies between the quality of the architecture and the quality of the decoration, but at Masèr you'll see the best of two of the central figures of Italian civilization in the sixteenth century – **Palladio** and **Paolo Veronese**, whose careers crossed here and nowhere else. If you're reliant on public transport, you'll have to catch a bus from Bassano via Ásolo or from Treviso; the services from Treviso to Ásolo and Bassano all stop near the villa, though you may have to change at Montebelluna. Getting back

▲ Villa Barbaro, Masèr

to Treviso, you may have to wait till around 7pm for a bus – check the timings before setting out.

The villa was built in 1557–58 for **Daniele and Marcantonio Barbaro**, men whose diverse cultural interests set them apart from most of the other wealthy Venetians who were then beginning to farm the Veneto. Both were prominent figures in the society of Venice. Marcantonio served as the Republic's ambassador to Constantinople and became one of the Procurators of San Marco, a position that enabled him to promote Palladio's scheme for the church of the Redentore. Daniele, the more scholarly of the pair, edited the writings of Vitruvius, wrote on mathematics and perspective, and founded the botanical gardens in Padua; he was also Venice's representative in London and was later elected Patriarch of Acquileia, as well as becoming the official historian of Venice. The association between Palladio and the brothers was very close by the time the villa was begun – in 1554 Daniele and Palladio had visited Rome, and they'd worked together on Barbaro's edition of *Vitruvius* – and the process of designing the house was far more of a collaborative venture than were most of Palladio's projects.

The interior and the Tempietto

The Villa Barbaro was a working farm in which was embodied a classical vision – derived from writers such as Livy – of the harmony of architectural form and the well-ordered pastoral life. Farm functions dominated the ground floor – dovecots in the end pavilions, stables and storage space under the arcades, administrative offices on the lower floor of the central block. It's in the living quarters of the *piano nobile* that the more rarefied aspect of the brothers' world is expressed, in a breathtaking series of **frescoes** by Veronese (1566–68) that has no equal anywhere in northern Italy. You need to be a student of Renaissance iconography to decode unassisted the allegorical figures in the amazing trompe l'oeil ceiling of the **Hall of Olympus** – the scheme was devised by Daniele Barbaro and centres on the figure of Eternal Wisdom – but most of the other paintings require no footnotes. The walls of the Villa Barbaro are the most resourceful display of visual trickery you'll ever see – servants peer round painted doors, a dog sniffs along the base of a flat balustrade in front of a landscape of ruins, illusory statues throw counterfeit shadows, flagstaffs lean in alcoves that aren't there. At the end of an avenue of doorways, a huntsman (probably Veronese himself) steps into the house through an entrance that's a solid wall – inevitably it's speculated that the woman facing the hunter at the other end of the house was Veronese's mistress. On top of all this, there's some remarkable architectural sculpture by **Alessandro Vittoria**: chimneypieces in the living rooms, figures in the tympanum of the main block, and the ornate **nymphaeum** in the garden at the back. The last incorporates a pond that used to be the house's fish-tank, and whose waters were channelled through the kitchens and out into the orchards.

In the grounds in front of the villa (now separated by a busy road) stands Palladio's **Tempietto**, the only church by him outside Venice and one of his last projects – commissioned by Marcantonio a decade after his brother's death, it was built in 1580, the year Palladio himself died. From the outside it's clear that the circular domed temple is based on the Pantheon, but the interior reveals a different form, the tiny side chapels creating a modified Greek-cross plan – thus combining the mathematically pure form of the circle with the liturgically perfect form of the cross. Another surprise is the richness of the stucco decoration, much of which is again by Vittoria.

There's also a **carriage museum** in the grounds, for which there's an extra entrance charge; it contains a few curiosities, such as a boat-shaped nineteenth-century ice-cream cart with a voluptuous mermaid on its prow.

Feltre

The historic centre of **FELTRE**, spread along a narrow ridge about 20km north of Masèr, owes its beguiling appearance to a disaster. At the outbreak of the War of the League of Cambrai, Feltre declared its allegiance to Venice – and so, when the army of Emperor Maximilian I swept into town in 1509, it was decided to punish Feltre by wiping its buildings and a hefty number of its inhabitants from the face of the planet. The Venetians took care of the reconstruction, and within a few decades the streets had been rebuilt. They still look pretty much as they did when the scaffolding came down. You're not going to find the town crawling with students making notes on the architecture of the Renaissance, and neither will you want to stay over, but you'll have to travel a long way to get a better idea of how an ordinary town looked in sixteenth-century Italy. And on top of that, there's the beauty of Feltre's position – the Dolomites in one direction, the valley of the Piave in the other. The last stretch of the train journey from the south, along the Piave from Valdobbiádene, is terrific too.

There are no direct **trains** to Feltre from Venice, but Feltre is a stop on the **Padua–Belluno** line (13 daily) – you can intercept these trains at Castelfranco. The journey from Padua to Feltre takes ninety minutes, and it's a further thirty to Belluno. There's an alternative route from Venice via Treviso, which involves a change of trains there and at Montebelluna; because this route covers fewer kilometres the ticket is slightly cheaper, but the connections can be less convenient than going via Castelfranco.

The Old Town

From the station, down in the modern part of town, the shortest route to the old quarter is to cross straight over into Viale del Piave, over Via Garibaldi and along Via Castaldi, which brings you to the **Duomo** and **Baptistery**, at the foot of the ridge. The oldest section of the much-altered Duomo is the fifteenth-century apse; its main objects of interest are a tomb by Tullio Lombardo (on the right wall of the chancel) and the *Pala della Misericordia* (second altar of right aisle), by local sixteenth-century painter Pietro de Maras-calchi, who also painted the *John the Baptist* on the fourth altar of the right aisle, and possibly the altarpiece in the chapel to the right of the chancel. At the top of the steps going past the side of the porticoed Baptistery, on the other side of the road, is the discreet south gate (1494), from where a long covered flight of steps rises into the heart of the old town.

You come out by the sixteenth-century **Municipio**, which has a portico by Palladio. Goldoni's earliest plays, first performed in 1729 in the old Palazzo Pretorio (the building at a right angle to the Municipio), were soon afterwards staged in the Municipio's own theatre, the exquisite little **Teatro della Sena**, which was redesigned at the start of the nineteenth century and fully merits its nickname of "La piccola Fenice".

Under the gaze of the inescapable Venetian lion, two Feltrian luminaries face each other across the stage-like **Piazza Maggiore**: **Panfilo Castaldi** and Vittorino de' Rambaldoni, usually known as **Vittorino da Feltre**. The former was instrumental in the development of printing in Italy, and according to some it was Castaldi rather than Gutenberg who was the first European to develop moveable type – the inscription on the plinth categorically declares him to be its inventor. Vittorino's fame rests on the school he ran in Mantua in the first half of the fifteenth century, under the financial patronage of the Gonzaga family, which took in pupils from aristocratic families and unprivileged backgrounds alike, and put them through a regimen in which, for the first time, a broad liberal education was combined with a programme of physical training.

Behind Piazza Maggiore rises the keep of the medieval castello, just below which stands the church of **San Rocco** – go round the back for a good view of the mountains. The carved wall between the steps going up to the church is a fountain by Tullio Lombardo.

To the left as you look across at San Rocco, the main street of Feltre, **Via Mezzaterra**, slopes down to the fifteenth-century Porta Imperiale. Nearly all the houses here are sixteenth century, and several are decorated with external frescoes by **Lorenzo Luzzo** (1467–1512) and his pupils. Feltre's most important artistic figure, Luzzo is more widely known as **Il Morto da Feltre** (The Dead Man of Feltre), a nickname prompted by the pallor of his complexion. Having begun with spells in Rome and Florence, Il Morto's career received something of a boost when he was called in to help Giorgione on the Fondaco dei Tedeschi in Venice.

The **Museo Civico** (April–Oct Tues–Fri 10.30am–12.30pm & 4–7pm, Sat & Sun 9.30am–12.30pm & 4–7pm; Nov–March same morning times, but then 3–6pm; €4, or €5 joint ticket with Museo Rizzarda), at the end of Via L. Luzzo, the equally decorous continuation of Via Mezzaterra on the other side of the piazza, contains Il Morto's *Madonna with St Vitus and St Modestus* and other pieces by him, plus paintings by Cima and Gentile Bellini, and a display of Roman and Etruscan finds. Il Morto's finest work is generally held to be the fresco of the *Transfiguration* in the **Ognissanti** church; this building is rarely open, but if you want to try your luck, go out of the Porta Oria, right by the Museo, down the dip and then along Borgo Ruga for a couple of hundred metres.

Feltre has another, more unusual museum – the **Museo Rizzarda** (same hours and prices as Museo Civico) at Via del Paradiso 8, parallel to Via Mezza-terra. This doubles as the town's collection of modern art and an exhibition of wrought-iron work, most of it by **Carlo Rizzarda** (1883–1931), the former owner of the house. It might not sound appetizing, but the finesse of Rizzarda's pieces is remarkable. The frescoed building at the piazza end of Via del Paradiso is the **Monte di Pietà**, one of the few fifteenth-century buildings to escape the wrath of the Imperial hordes.

Conegliano

Travelling north from Treviso, it's at the amiable town of **CONEGLIANO** that the landscape ceases to be boringly flat, as the terrain starts to rise towards the Dolomites. It markets itself to tourists as *La Città Murata* (Walled City), on the strength of fortifications that bear witness to its medieval history, most notably the six decades of occupation by the Da Carrara and Della Scala (Scaliger) warlords, prior to annexation by Venice in 1389. But to the untrained eye the vestigial walls of Conegliano aren't especially remarkable, and in truth what this town is really about is **wine** – the surrounding hills are patched with vineyards, and the production of wine is central to the economy of the district. Italy's first wine-growers' college was set up in Conegliano in 1876, and today there are a couple of well-established **wine routes**: the **Strada del Vino Rosso**, which follows a looping 68-kilometre course southeast to Oderzo, and the more rewarding **Strada del Prosecco**, a straighter 42-kilometre journey west to Valdobbiádene. The former takes you through Merlot, Cabernet and Raboso country; the latter passes the Bianco dei Colli, Prosecco and Cartizze producers – the last, a more refined version of Prosecco, could be mistaken for Champagne with a small effort of will.

Getting to Conegliano on public transport from Venice is easy – nearly all the thirty-odd Venice to Udine **trains** stop here; the journey from Venice takes a little under an hour.

The Town

The old centre of Conegliano, adhering to the slope of the Colle di Giano and presided over by the castello on its summit, is right in front of you as you come out of the station. After crossing the principal street of the modern town (Corso V. Emanuele–Corso G. Mazzini) you pass through a portico and into the original high street – **Via XX Settembre**. Lined with fifteenth- to eighteenth-century houses, this is an attractive street on any day, but to see it at its best you should turn up on a Friday morning, when the weekly **market** sets up camp.

The most decorative feature of Via XX Settembre is the unusual facade of the **Duomo** (daily 8am–noon & 3–6pm), a fourteenth-century portico, frescoed at the end of the sixteenth century by **Ludovico Pozzoserrato**, which joins seamlessly the buildings on either side. The interior of the church has been rebuilt, but retains fragments of fifteenth-century frescoes; the major adornment of the church, though, is the magnificent altarpiece of *The Madonna and Child with Saints and Angels*, painted in 1493 by **Giambattista Cima**, the most famous native of Conegliano.

Alongside the Duomo, at the top of the steps facing the door off the right-hand aisle of the church, is the **Sala dei Battuti** or Hall of the Flagellants (Sat 10am–noon, Sun 3–6pm; €2, or €3 joint ticket with Museo Civico), the frescoed meeting place of a local confraternity. The pictures are mostly sixteenth-century and depict scenes from the *Creation* to the *Last Judgement*, incorporating the weirdest *Ascension* you'll ever see, with the ascendant Christ half out of the frame and a pair of footprints left behind at the point of lift-off. Individually the frescoes are nothing much to write home about, but the room as a whole is quite striking.

Cima's birthplace, no. 24 Via G.B. Cima, at the rear of the Duomo, has been restored and converted into the **Casa Museo di G.B. Cima** (Sat & Sun April–Oct 4–7pm; Nov–March 3–6pm; €1). Formally unadventurous, Cima exemplifies the conservative strand in Venetian painting of the early sixteenth century, but at their best his paintings have something of the elegiac tone of Giovanni Bellini's later works. The museum's pictures present clearly his strengths and his weaknesses; not one of them, though, is a painting by Cima – they're all high-class reproductions.

The **Palazzo Sarcinelli**, at Via XX Settembre 130–134, sometimes stages art exhibitions, but the only permanent display is that in the **Museo Civico**, which is housed in the tallest surviving tower of the reconstructed tenth-century castello on top of the hill. It's reached most quickly by the steep and cobbled Calle Madonna della Neve, which begins at the end of Via Accademia, the street beside the palatial Accademia cinema, and follows the town's most impressive stretch of ancient wall. (The Scaligeri raised the wall in the 1330s, and half a century later the Carraresi made it higher.) The museum (Tues–Sun: April–Oct 10am–12.30pm & 3.30–7pm; Dec–March 10am–12.30pm & 3–6.30pm; €2, or €3 joint ticket with the Sala dei Battuti) has some damaged frescoes by Pordenone and a small bronze horse by Giambologna, but most of the paintings are "Workshop of…" or "School of…", and the displays of coins, maps, archeological finds, armour and so forth are no more fascinating than you'd expect. To pad things out there's a section devoted to famous people with local connections, complete with terracotta busts of Arturo Toscanini, who got married in Conegliano, and Mozart's great librettist Lorenzo da Ponte, who was born in nearby Cèneda (see p.361). But it's a lovingly maintained museum, and the climb through the floors culminates on the tower's roof, from where you get a fine view across the vine-clad landscape. (If you'd like to savour the panorama in more comfort, you could sip a drink on the terrace of the neighbouring *Al Castello* bar, which looks towards the Dolomites.) The castello shares the summit of the hill with the heavily restored **Santa Orsola**, the minuscule remnant of the ancient church of San Leonardo, which was Conegliano's main church from its foundation in the twelfth century until the demolition of everything but the apse (where some scrappy frescoes survive) and a single chapel in the middle of the eighteenth.

Practicalities

Conegliano's **tourist office**, at Via XX Settembre 61, on the corner of Piazza G.B. Cima (Tues–Sun 9.30am–12.30pm, plus Fri & Sat 3–6pm; ☎0438.21.230) is well stocked with information. Via XX Settembre has plenty of cafés, bars and food shops, and what is clearly the first-choice **hotel**, the three-star *Canon d'Oro* at no. 129 (☎0438.34.246, ⊛www.hotelcanondoro.it; ❷–❹), which is housed in one of the finer frescoed palaces in the street, has a terraced garden to the rear, free parking, and jacuzzis in the more expensive rooms. Top recommendations for **eating** at moderate prices are the *Osteria La Bea Venezia*, Via XX Settembre 77–79 (☎0438.23.186; closed Mon), which has fine fish dishes, and the ⚞ *Trattoria Stella*, Via Accademia 3 (☎0438.22.178; closed Thurs eve and Sun), where the stuffed pancakes are highly recommended.

Prosecco is the chief wine of the Conegliano district, and its producers compile a list of recommended outlets: the tourist office should have the latest list, plus details of the wine routes. Conegliano has a major **wine festival** in September, as well as other smaller artistic celebrations that month. The biggest folkloric event in the calendar is the **Dama Castellana**, a gigantic draughts game played with human pieces in mid-June (Ⓦ www.damacastellana.it). Initiated in 1241 to mark a victory over the troops of Treviso, the game is nowadays preceded by a costumed procession and flag-twirling, and followed by a gruelling ritual in which the losers have to shove the winners up the hill to the castle in a cart. In traditional style, fireworks bring the fun to a close.

Vittorio Veneto

The name **VITTORIO VENETO** first appeared on the map in 1866 when, to mark the unification of Italy and honour Vittorio Emanuele II, the first king of the new country, the neighbouring towns of Cèneda and Serravalle, which hadn't previously been the best of friends, were knotted together and rechristened. A new town hall was built midway along the avenue connecting the two, and the train station constructed opposite, in the hope that the towns would grow closer together. To an extent they have, but the visitor emerging from the station still steps straight into a sort of no-man's-land.

The old quarter of Serravalle is very alluring, as are the environs. From the centre of town there are paths leading up into the encircling wooded hills, with the most rewarding area for walkers lying to the northeast in the **Bosco del Cansiglio**, a plateau forested with beech and pine which was once husbanded by the Venetian state as a source of timber for oars. Although the area has been developed as a holiday resort, you can still roam here for hours without seeing a soul. A good base from which to explore this vast expanse of woodland is Fregona, which is connected by regular buses to Vittorio Veneto.

Five **trains** a day run direct to Vittorio Veneto from Venice; otherwise it's a short hop **from Conegliano**. There are sixteen northward connections a day from Conegliano (25min) – sometimes these connections are by *autocorsa*, a bus service on which train tickets alone are valid. Read the timetable carefully when checking your connection back to Conegliano – if it's an *autocorsa* you'll probably have to skip over to the bus station behind Piazza del Popolo, which is opposite the train station. From Vittorio Veneto six trains carry on to Belluno, and five connect with a Belluno shuttle at Ponte delle Alpi. The remaining services chug north from Ponte delle Alpi to Calalzo, in the heart of the eastern Dolomites.

Cèneda

CÈNEDA, overlooked by the seventh-century Lombard castle of San Martino (now the bishop's residence), is the less appealing of the town's halves – having a more open situation than Serravalle, it has inevitably developed as the commercial centre of Vittorio Veneto. It is, nonetheless, worth a visit for the **Museo della Battaglia** (Tues–Sun: May–Sept 9.30am–12.30pm & 4–7pm; Oct–April 9.30am–12.30pm & 2–5pm; €3, or €5 joint ticket with the Museo del Cenedese), housed in the sixteenth-century Loggia Cenedese, which is possibly by Sansovino. It's on the same piazza as the nondescript Duomo, which you get to by turning right out of the station and walking until you come to the road junction of Piazza San Francesco di Assisi, where you turn right – a good fifteen-minute walk in total. The battle of Vittorio, which lasted from October 24 to November 3, 1918, was the triumphant final engagement of World War I for the Italian army (which is why most towns in Italy have a Via Vittorio Veneto) and the museum is dedicated to the climactic engagement. The impressive hall of the Maggior Consiglio on the top floor illumines the history of Cèneda in nineteenth-century frescoes.

The only other building that merits a look in Cèneda is the church of **Santa Maria del Meschio**, where you'll find a luscious *Annunciation* by Andrea Previtali (c.1470–1528), a pupil of Giovanni Bellini. If you turn left off the Cèneda–Serravalle road down Via Armando Diaz, instead of going right for the cathedral square, you'll quickly come across it.

Serravalle

The Romanesque church of **Sant'Andrea di Bigonzo** will catch your attention as you walk from Cèneda to Serravalle, at the end of an avenue to the right; it's decorated with Renaissance frescoes, but unless you've a bit of time to spare, content yourself with the view from a distance.

SERRAVALLE, wedged in the neck of the gorge between the Col Visentin and the Cansiglio (the name means "Valley Lock"), is an entirely different proposition from its partner. Once through its southern gate – to the left of which the ruined walls disappear into the trees on the valley side – you are into a town that has scarcely seen a demolition since the sixteenth century. Most of the buildings along Via Martiri della Libertà, Via Roma and Via Mazzini, and around the stage-like Piazza Marcantonio Flaminio, date from the fifteenth and sixteenth centuries – the handsomest being the finely painted and shield-encrusted Loggia Serravallese (rebuilt c.1460). This is now the home of the **Museo del Cenedese** (same hours and prices as the Museo della Battaglia), a small jumble of a museum, featuring some fine furniture and a delicate *Madonna and Child* by Jacopo Sansovino.

Time is more profitably spent in the churches of Serravalle than in its museum. One of the best-preserved fresco cycles in the Veneto covers the interior of **San Lorenzo dei Battuti** (same ticket & hours as museum; an attendant takes you there), immediately inside the south gate. Painted around 1450, the frescoes were damaged when Napoleon's louts used the chapel as a kitchen, but restoration subsequent to the uncovering of the cycle in 1953 has rectified the situation.

The **Duomo**, across the swift-flowing River Meschio on the far side of the Piazza Flaminio from the Museo, is a dull eighteenth-century building with a medieval campanile; an altarpiece of *The Virgin with St Peter and St Andrew*, produced in 1547 by **Titian** and his workshop, is the sole reason to go inside.

Follow the road past the Duomo and you'll immediately come to a flight of steps. This leads to a path that winds through the woods to the **Santuario di Santa Augusta** – go for the walk, not for the building. If you're in town on August 21, the festival of Saint Augusta's martyrdom, you'll be treated to a huge fireworks display and all-night party. Carry on up Via Roma instead of veering across Piazza Flaminio and you'll pass the remnant of the castello and, eventually (outside the walls), the partly frescoed church of **San Giovanni Battista**, which has beautiful cloisters (ask the sacristan for admission, as the cloisters belong to the adjacent Carmelite monastery). Further out still, and a few yards over the river (turn right about 400m after San Giovanni), stands **Santa**

Giustina, which was founded in 1226 by the Camino clan, who for around three hundred years were the rulers of Treviso province. It contains a superb funerary monument, the **tomb** erected in 1336 by Verde della Scala (Scaliger) for her husband, Rizzardo VI da Camino, who had been killed in battle. The four praying warriors that support the Gothic sarcophagus were probably purloined from an older pulpit or other such structure.

Belluno

The most northerly of the major towns of the Veneto, **BELLUNO** stands at the point where the tiny River Ardo flows into the Piave, in the shadow of the eastern Dolomites. Once a strategically important ally of Venice, which took the town under its wing in 1404, it is today a provincial capital, and attached more firmly to the mountainous region to the north than to the urban centres to the south: the network of the Dolomiti-Bus company radiates out from Belluno, trains run fairly regularly to the terminus at Calalzo, and the tourist office's handouts are geared mostly to hikers and skiers. Many visitors to the town use the place simply for its access to the mountains, and miss out on its attractions – of which there are quite a few, besides its breathtaking position.

At present there are three **trains** a day that run straight from Venice to Belluno and two evening trains back (at around 5pm & 7pm), but it's just as quick to take an Udine-bound train and change at Conegliano – the complete expedition takes just over two hours. You can get to Belluno from Padua (via Castelfranco) as well – there are thirteen trains a day, also taking two hours.

The Town

Belluno has two distinct but adjacent centres, reached by walking straight ahead from the train station. The hub of the modern town, the spot where you'll find its most popular bars and cafés, is the wide **Piazza dei Martiri** (named after a group of partisans executed in the square by the Nazis in 1944). Off the south side, a road leads to the **Piazza del Duomo**, the kernel of the old town. The sixteenth-century **Duomo** (or Santa Maria Assunta), a Gothic-classical amalgam built in the pale yellow stone that's a distinctive feature of Belluno, is the work of **Tullio Lombardo** (except for the stately campanile, which was designed in 1743 by **Filippo Juvarra**, best known for his rebuilding of central Turin); it has had to be completely reconstructed twice after earthquake damage, in 1873 and 1936. The elegant interior – a long barrel-vault ending in a single dome, with flanking aisles – has a couple of good paintings: one by Andrea Schiavone (first altar on the right), and one by Palma il Giovane (fourth altar on the right).

Occupying one complete side of the Piazza del Duomo, at a right angle to the Duomo itself, is the residence of the Venetian administrators of the town, the **Palazzo dei Rettori**, a frilly, late fifteenth-century building dolled up with Baroque trimmings. A relic of more independent times stands on the right – the twelfth-century **Torre Civica**, all that's left of Belluno's medieval castle. Continuing round the piazza, along the side of the nineteenth-century town hall, you'll find the **Museo Civico** at Via Duomo 16 (April–Sept Tues–Sun 10am–1pm & 4–7pm; Oct–March Mon–Sat 10am–1pm, plus Thurs–Sun

3–6pm; €3). It's strongest on the work of Belluno's three best-known artists, all of whom were working at the end of the seventeenth and beginning of the eighteenth centuries: the painters Sebastiano and Marco Ricci, and the virtuoso sculptor-woodcarver Andrea Brustolon (who features prominently in Venice's Ca' Rezzonico). The placid Paduan artist Bartolomeo Montagna is represented here as well, along with a fine collection of eighteenth- and nineteenth-century Italian porcelain and an engaging series of domestic *ex voto* paintings.

Via Duomo ends at the **Piazza del Mercato**, a tiny square hemmed in by porticoed Renaissance buildings; until the Venetians shifted the administrative offices to the Piazza del Duomo, this was the nerve centre of Belluno, and even after the Venetian alterations it remained the commercial centre. Its fountain dates from 1410 and the **Monte di Pietà** (no. 26) from 1501, making it one of the oldest pawnshops in Italy. One of the prime claimants to the honour of being the originator of pawnshops is Martino Tomitani (later Saint Bernardine of Feltre), a Franciscan friar from the village of Tomo, in the vicinity of nearby Feltre. The principal street of the old town, **Via Mezzaterra**, goes down from the Piazza del Mercato to the fourteenth-century Porta Ruga (veer left along the cobbled Via S. Croce about 100m from the end), where you get a fine view along the mountain-backed valley of the Piave.

The unprepossessing church of **San Pietro**, just off Via Mezzaterra at the end of Vicolo San Pietro, was founded in the fourteenth century and rebuilt in 1750; the chapel to the right of the main altar contains parts of the original Gothic church, and a pair of old cloisters also survive, one of them with fifteenth-century frescoes that were uncovered in 1989. The main altarpiece is by **Sebastiano Ricci**, paintings by **Andrea Schiavone** are to be seen over the door and to the sides of the high altar, and **Brustolon** carved the angels over the baldachin and retables of the second altars on both sides, which were brought here from a demolished Jesuit church (which is why they don't fit perfectly). Because San Pietro is part of a working seminary, its opening hours are limited to Sunday afternoons from July to September.

Leaving the Piazza del Mercato in the other direction, you pass through the sixteenth-century **Porta Dojona** and into Piazza Vittorio Emanuele II, an extension of the main square of the modern town. Belluno's other major church, **Santo Stefano** (daily 8am–noon & 3–6pm), is to the right, on Via Roma. A bright Gothic building (1486) with banded arches and alternating brown and white columns, it has yet more carvings by **Brustolon** (in the left aisle, a Crucifix resting on figures in Purgatory) and restored frescoes by **Jacopo da Montagnana** (chapel to the right of the main altar), painted within a year or so of the church's construction.

Practicalities

The **tourist office**, at Piazza Duomo 2 (Mon–Sat 9am–12.30pm & 3.30–6.30pm, Sun 10am–12.30pm, also open Sun afternoon Dec to mid-March and mid-June to mid-Sept; ☎0437.940.083, ⊛www.comune.belluno.it), is a good source of leaflets on Belluno and its province. The best **hotel** in the centre is the three-star *Cappello e Cadore*, just off the main square at Via Ricci 8 (☎0437.940.246, ⊛www.albergocappello.com; ❶). The best **restaurant** in the area is ⚔ *Al Borgo*, Via Anconetta 8 (☎0437.926.755; closed Mon evening and Tues all day); it's a couple of kilometres from the centre (cross the river and head for Feltre), but it's well worth the trip – it offers fantastic food in a delightful setting, and you can eat well for under €30.

Contexts

Contexts

History

In the midst of the waters, free, indigent, laborious, and inaccessible, they gradually coalesced into a Republic.

Edward Gibbon

Beginnings

Though the Venetian lagoon supported small groups of fishermen and hunters at the start of the Christian era, it was only with the barbarian invasions of the fifth century and after, that sizeable communities began to settle on the mudbanks. The first mass migration was provoked by the arrival in the Veneto of **Attila the Hun**'s hordes in **453**, but a large number of the refugees struck camp and returned to dry land once the danger seemed to be past. Permanent settlement was accelerated a century later, when, in **568**, the Germanic **Lombards** (or Longobards), led by **Alboin**, swept into northern Italy.

A loose conglomeration of island communes arose, each cluster of islands drawing its population from one or two clearly defined areas of the Veneto: the fugitives from Padua went to **Malamocco** and **Chioggia**; the inhabitants of **Grado** mainly came from Aquileia; and Altino supplied many of the pioneers of **Torcello**, **Burano** and **Murano**. Distinct economic, ecclesiastical and administrative centres quickly evolved: Torcello was the focal point of trading activity; Grado, the new home of the Bishop of Aquileia, was the Church's base; and Heraclea (now extinct) was the seat of government. The lagoon confederation was not autonomous, though – it owed **political allegiance to Byzantium**, and until the end of the seventh century its senior officials were the **maritime tribunes**, who were effectively controlled by the Imperial hierarchy of Ravenna.

The refugee population of the islands increased steeply as the Lombard grip on the Veneto strengthened under the leadership of **Grimoald** (667–71), and shortly after this influx the confederation took a big step towards independence. This is one of the many points at which Venetian folklore has acquired the status of fact; tradition has it that a conference was convened at Heraclea in 697 by the Patriarch of Grado, and from this meeting sprang the election of the **first doge**, to unify the islands in the face of the Lombard threat. (John Julius Norwich adroitly disentangles the myth in his history of Venice – see "Books" p.405.) In fact, it was not until **726** that the lagoon settlers chose their first leader, when a wave of dissent against Emperor Leo III throughout the Byzantine Empire spurred them to elect **Orso Ipato** as the head of their provincial council.

After a period during which the old system of government was briefly reinstituted, Orso Ipato's son **Teodato** became the second doge in 742. Yet the lagoon administration – which was now moved from Heraclea to **Malamocco** – was still not autonomous. Teodato's relationship to the emperor was less subservient than his father's had been, yet he nonetheless took orders from the capital, and the **fall of Ravenna to the Lombards in 751** did not alter the constitutional relationship between Byzantium and the confederation.

At the close of the eighth century, the Lombards were overrun by the Frankish army of **Charlemagne**, and in **810** the emperor's son **Pepin** sailed into action against the proto-Venetians. Malamocco was quickly taken, but Pepin's

Paoluccio Anafesto 697–717
Marcello Tegalliano 717–726
Orso Ipato 726–737
interregnum 737–742
Teodato Ipato 742–755
Galla Gaulo 755–756
Domenico Monegario 756–764
Maurizio Galbaio 764–787
Giovanni Galbaio 787–804
Obelario degli Antenori 804–811
Agnello Participazio 811–827
Giustiniano Participazio 827–829
Giovanni Participazio I 829–836
Pietro Tradonico 836–864
Orso Participazio I 864–881
Giovanni Participazio II 881–887
Pietro Candiano I 887
Pietro Tribuno 888–912
Orso Participazio II 912–932
Pietro Candiano II 932–939
Pietro Participazio 939–942
Pietro Candiano III 942–959
Pietro Candiano IV 959–976
Pietro Orseolo I 976–978
Vitale Candiano 978–979
Tribuno Memmo 979–991
Pietro Orseolo II 991–1008
Otto Orseolo 1008–1026
Pietro Centranico 1026–1032
Domenico Flabanico 1032–1043
Domenico Contarini 1043–1071

Domenico Selvo 1071–1084
Vitale Falier 1084–1096
Vitale Michiel I 1096–1102
Ordelafo Falier 1102–1118
Domenico Michiel 1118–1130
Pietro Polani 1130–1148
Domenico Morosini 1148–1156
Vitale Michiel II 1156–1172
Sebastiano Ziani 1172–1178
Orio Mastropiero 1178–1192
Enrico Dandolo 1192–1205
Pietro Ziani 1205–1229
Giacomo Tiepolo 1229–1249
Marin Morosini 1249–1253
Ranier Zeno 1253–1268
Lorenzo Tiepolo 1268–1275
Jacopo Contarini 1275–1280
Giovanni Dandolo 1280–1289
Pietro Gradenigo 1289–1311
Marino Zorzi 1311–1312
Giovanni Soranzo 1312–1328
Francesco Dandolo 1329–1339
Bartolomeo Gradenigo 1339–1342
Andrea Dandolo 1343–1354
Marin Falier 1354–1355
Giovanni Gradenigo 1355–1356
Giovanni Dolfin 1356–1361
Lorenzo Celsi 1361–1365
Marco Corner 1365–1368
Andrea Contarini 1368–1382
Michele Morosini 1382

fleet failed in its attempt to pursue the settlers when they withdrew to the better-protected islands of **Rivoalto**, and retreated with heavy losses. Now the seat of government in the lagoon was shifted for the second and last time, to Rivoalto, the name by which the central cluster of islands was known until the late twelfth century, when it became generally known as **Venice**. The **Rialto** district, in the core of the city, perpetuates the old name.

From independence to empire

In the **Treaty of Aix-la-Chapelle**, signed by Charlemagne and the Byzantine emperor shortly after Pepin's defeat, Venice was declared to be a dukedom within the Eastern Empire, despite the fact that by now the control of Byzantium was little more than nominal. The traders and boatmen of the lagoon were less and less inclined to acknowledge the precedence of the emperor, and they signalled their recalcitrance through one great symbolic act – **the theft of the body of Saint Mark from Alexandria in 828**. Saint Mark, whose posthumous arrival in Venice was held to be divinely ordained (see p.47), was made the patron saint of the city in place of the Byzantine patron, Saint Theodore, and a basilica was

Antonio Venier 1382–1400
Michele Steno 1400–1413
Tommaso Mocenigo 1414–1423
Francesco Fóscari 1423–1457
Pasquale Malipiero 1457–1462
Cristoforo Moro 1462–1471
Nicolò Tron 1471–1473
Nicolò Marcello 1473–1474
Pietro Mocenigo 1474–1476
Andrea Vendramin 1476–1478
Giovanni Mocenigo 1478–1485
Marco Barbarigo 1485–1486
Agostino Barbarigo 1486–1501
Leonardo Loredan 1501–1521
Antonio Grimani 1521–1523
Andrea Gritti 1523–1538
Pietro Lando 1539–1545
Francesco Donà 1545–1553
Marcantonio Trevisan 1553–1554
Francesco Venier 1554–1556
Lorenzo Priuli 1556–1559
Girolamo Priuli 1559–1567
Pietro Loredan 1567–1570
Alvise Mocenigo I 1570–1577
Sebastiano Venier 1577–1578
Nicolò da Ponte 1578–1585
Pasquale Cicogna 1585–1595
Marino Grimani 1595–1605
Leonardo Donà 1606–1612
Marcantonio Memmo 1612–1615
Giovanni Bembo 1615–1618

Nicolò Donà 1618
Antonio Priuli 1618–1623
Francesco Contarini 1623–1624
Giovanni Corner I 1625–1629
Nicolò Contarini 1630–1631
Francesco Erizzo 1631–1646
Francesco Molin 1646–1655
Carlo Contarini 1655–1656
Francesco Corner 1656
Bertucci Valier 1656–1658
Giovanni Pésaro 1658–1659
Domenico Contarini 1659–1675
Nicolò Sagredo 1675–1676
Alvise Contarini 1676–1684
Marcantonio Giustinian 1684–1688
Francesco Morosini 1688–1694
Silvestro Valier 1694–1700
Alvise Mocenigo II 1700–1709
Giovanni Corner II 1709–1722
Alvise Mocenigo III 1722–1732
Carlo Ruzzini 1732–1735
Alvise Pisani 1735–1741
Pietro Grimani 1741–1752
Francesco Loredan 1752–1762
Marco Foscarini 1762–1763
Alvise Mocenigo IV 1763–1778
Paolo Renier 1779–1789
Lodovico Manin 1789–1797

built alongside the doge's castle to accommodate the holy relics. These two buildings – the **Basilica di San Marco** and the **Palazzo Ducale** – were to remain the emblems of the Venetian state and the repository of power within the city for almost one thousand years.

By the end of the ninth century the population of the islands of central Venice was increasing steadily. The city was comprehensively protected against attack, with chains slung across the entrance to the major channels and fortified walls shielding the waterfront between the Palazzo Ducale and the area in which the church of Santa Maria Zobenigo now stands. Before the close of the following century, the Venetian **trading networks** were well established – military assistance given to their former masters in Byzantium had earned concessions in the markets of the East, and the Venetian economy was now prospering from the distribution of eastern goods along the waterways of northern Italy.

Slav pirates, operating from the shelter of the Dalmatian coast, were the greatest hindrance to Venetian trade in the northern Adriatic, and in the year **1000** a fleet set out under the command of **Doge Pietro Orseolo II** to subjugate the troublemakers. The successful expedition was commemorated each subsequent year in the ceremony of the **Marriage of Venice to the Sea**, in which the city's lordship of the Adriatic was ritually confirmed (see p.221). However, although the Doge of Venice could now legitimately claim the title

"Duke of Dalmatia", there remained the problem of the **Normans** of southern Italy, whose navy threatened to confine the Venetians to the upper part of the Adriatic. The breakthrough came in the 1080s. In **1081** the Byzantine emperor Alexius Comnenus, himself endangered by Norman expansion, appealed to Venice for aid. The result was a series of naval battles costing thousands of lives, at the end of which Venice had strengthened its shipping lanes, established itself as the protector of the Eastern Empire's seaboard, and earned invaluable commercial rights for its traders. In a charter of 1082, known as the Crisobolo (Golden Bull), the emperor declared Venetian merchants to be exempt from all tolls and taxes within his lands. In the words of one historian – "On that day Venetian world trade began."

Venice and the Crusades

In 1095 Pope Urban II called for a Christian army to wrest the Holy Land from the Muslims, and within four years Jerusalem had been retaken by the **First Crusade**. Decades of chaos ensued, which the Venetians, typically, managed to turn to their commercial advantage. Offering to transport armies and supplies to the East in return for grants of property and financial bonuses, Venice extended its foothold in the Aegean, the Black Sea and Syria, battling all the time (sometimes literally) against its two chief maritime rivals in Italy – Pisa and Genoa. While it was consolidating its overseas bases, Venice was also embroiled in the political manoeuvrings between the papacy, the Western emperor and the cities of northern Italy, the conclusion of which was one of Venice's greatest diplomatic successes: **the reconciliation of Emperor Frederick Barbarossa and Pope Alexander III** in 1177, in Venice.

Now a major European power, Venice was about to acquire an empire. In November 1199 Count Tibald of Champagne proposed a **Fourth Crusade** to regain Jerusalem, which twelve years earlier had fallen to Saladin. It came about that Venice was commissioned, for a huge fee, to provide the ships for the army. In 1202 the forces gathered in Venice, only to find that they couldn't raise the agreed sum. In the negotiations that followed, the doge obtained a promise from the French commanders that the Crusade would stop off to reconquer the colony of Zara, recently captured from Venice by the King of Hungary. No sooner was that accomplished than the expedition was diverted, after Venetian persuasion, to Constantinople, where the succession to the Imperial throne was causing problems and, furthermore, Venetian merchants were losing ground to merchants from Pisa and Genoa. The eventual upshot was the **Sack of Constantinople in 1204**, one of the most disgusting episodes in European history. Thousands were massacred by the Christian soldiers and virtually every precious object that could be lifted was stolen from the city, mainly by the Venetians, who were led in person by the blind octogenarian doge, Enrico Dandolo. So vast was the scale of the destruction and murder that a contemporary historian regretted that the city had not fallen instead to the infidel. Ultimately its consequences were disastrous – not only did no help reach the forces in the Holy Land, but the Eastern Empire was fatally divided between the native Greeks and the barbaric Westerners. The Ottoman conquest of Constantinople in 1453, and the consequent peril of Western Europe, were distant but direct results of the Fourth Crusade. Venice got what it wanted, though – "one quarter and half a quarter" of the Roman Empire was now under its sway, with an almost uninterrupted chain of ports stretching from the lagoon to the Black Sea.

The Genoese Wars

The enmities created within the Eastern Empire by the Fourth Crusade were soon to rebound on Venice. The Genoese were now the main opposition in the eastern markets, maintaining a rivalry so violent that some Venetian historians refer to their succession of conflicts as the **Five Genoese Wars**. Genoa's hatred of Venice led to an alliance with the dethroned Byzantine dynasty, whose loathing of the Venetians was no less intense; within months of the Pact of Ninfeo (1261), **Michael Palaeologus VIII** was installed as emperor in Constantinople. Venice now faced a struggle to hold onto its commercial interests against the favoured Genoese.

For the rest of the century, and almost all the fourteenth century, the defeat of Genoa was the primary aim of Venice's rulers. Both sides suffered terrible defeats: at the battle of **Curzola** (1298) 65 ships out of a Venetian fleet of 95 were lost, and 5000 Venetians taken captive; at the Sardinian port of **Alghero** (1353) the Genoese navy lost a similar proportion of its vessels. The climax came with the Fourth War of Genoa, better known as the **War of Chioggia**. Following a victory over the Venetians at Zara in 1379, the Genoese fleet sailed on to Venice, supported by the Paduans and the Austrians, and quickly took Chioggia. This was the zenith of Genoa's power – in August **1380** the invaders were driven off, and although the treaty signed between the two cities seemed inconclusive, within a few decades it was clear that Venice had at last won the battle for economic and political supremacy.

Political upheaval

It was during the Genoese campaigns that the **constitution** of Venice arrived at a state that was to endure until the fall of the Republic, the most significant step in this evolution being the **Serrata del Maggior Consiglio of 1297**, a measure which basically allowed a role in the government of the city only to those families already involved in it. Not surprisingly, many of those disenfranchised by the Serrata resented its instigator, **Doge Pietro Gradenigo**, and when Venice lost its tussle with the papacy for possession of Ferrara in 1309, it seemed that Gradenigo had scarcely a single supporter in the city. Yet the insurrection that came the following year was a revolt of a patrician clique, not an uprising of the people; its leader – **Bajamonte Tiepolo** – had personal reasons for opposing the doge and appears to have wanted to replace the new system not with a more democratic one but with a despotic regime headed by himself. Tiepolo's private army was routed in a battle in the centre of the city, but his rebellion had a permanent effect upon the history of Venice, in that it led to the creation in 1310 of the **Council of Ten**, a committee empowered to supervise matters of internal security. Though the Council was intended to be an emergency measure, its tenure was repeatedly extended until, in 1334, it was made a permanent institution.

The most celebrated attempt to subvert the Venetian government followed a few years later, in **1355**, and this time the malefactor was the doge himself – **Marin Falier**, who ironically had played a large part in the sentencing of Bajamonte Tiepolo. Falier's plot to overthrow the councils of Venice and install himself as absolute ruler seems to have been prompted by his fury at the lenient treatment given to a young nobleman who had insulted him. Exploiting the grievances felt against certain noble families by, among others, the director of the Arsenale, Falier gathered together a group of conspirators, many of whom were drawn from the working class, a section of Venetian society that was particularly affected by the economic demands of the rivalry with Genoa. (Open war had recently broken out again after a long but tense period of truce, and to make the situation worse, the **Black Death of 1348–49** had killed around 60 percent of the city's population.) Details of the planned coup leaked out, Falier was arrested, and on April 17, eight months after becoming doge, he was beheaded on the steps of the Palazzo Ducale.

Terra firma expansion

The sea lanes of the eastern Mediterranean were the foundation of Venice's wealth, but its dominance as a trading centre clearly depended on free access to the rivers and mountain passes of northern Italy. Thus, although Venetian foreign policy was predominantly eastward-looking from the start, a degree of intervention on the mainland was inevitable, especially with the rise in the fourteenth century of ambitious dynasties such as the **Scaligeri** in Verona and the **Visconti** in Milan. Equally inevitable was the shift from a strategy to preserve Venice's commercial interests, to a scheme that was blatantly imperialistic.

The unsuccessful battle for Ferrara was Venice's first territorial campaign; the first victory came thirty years later, in 1339, when the combined forces of Venice, Florence and a league of Lombard cities defeated the Scaligeri, allowing Venice to incorporate **Castelfranco**, **Conegliano**, **Sacile**, **Oderzo** and, most importantly, **Treviso** into the domain of the Republic. Having thus made safe the roads to Germany, the Venetians set about securing the territory to the west. The political and military machinations of northern Italy in this period are extremely complicated, with alliances regularly made and betrayed, and cities changing hands with bewildering frequency – Treviso, for example, was lost and won back before the close of the fourteenth century. The bare outline of the story is that by **1405** Venice had eradicated the most powerful neighbouring dynasty, the **Carrara** family of Padua, and had a firm hold on **Bassano**, **Belluno**, **Feltre**, **Vicenza**, **Verona** and **Padua** itself. The annexation in **1420** of **the Friuli** and **Udine**, formerly ruled by the King of Hungary, virtually doubled the area of the terra firma under Venetian control, and brought the border of the empire right up to the Alps.

Many Venetians thought that any further expansion would be foolish. Certainly this was the view of **Doge Tommaso Mocenigo**, who on his deathbed urged his compatriots to "refrain…from taking what belongs to others or making unjust wars". Specifically, he warned them against the ambitions of **Francesco Fóscari** – "If he becomes doge, you will be constantly at war… you will become the slaves of your masters-at-arms and their captains." Within a fortnight of Mocenigo's funeral in 1423, Fóscari was elected as his successor, and Venice was soon on the offensive against the mightiest prince of northern Italy – **Filippo Maria Visconti** of Milan. In the first phase of the campaign nothing except a tenuous ownership of Bergamo and Brescia was gained, a failure for which the Venetian mercenary captain, **Carmagnola**, served as the scapegoat. He was executed in 1432 for treason, and his place taken by Erasmo da Narni, better known as **Il Gattamelata**. The **Treaty of Cremona** (1441) confirmed Venetian control of **Peschiera**, **Brescia**, **Bergamo** and part of the territory of **Cremona**, and by now **Ravenna** was also officially part of the Venetian dominion, but still the fighting did not stop. Peace on the mainland finally came in **1454**, with the signing of a treaty between Venice and the new ruler of Milan, **Francesco Sforza**, Venice's erstwhile ally against the Visconti. Ravenna didn't stay Venetian for long; the rest of its mainland empire, though, remained intact until the coming of Napoleon.

The Turkish threat

The other Italian states might have taken concerted action against Venice had it not been for the fact that the entire peninsula now faced the common threat of the Ottoman Turks, as was acknowledged in the pact drawn up at **Lodi** later in 1454 between Venice, Milan, Naples, Florence and the Papal States. Open conflict between Venice and the Turks had broken out early in the century – the Republic winning the naval battle of Gallipoli in 1416 – but the policy of terra firma expansion kept the majority of Venice's warships on the rivers of the north, so reliance had to be placed on diplomatic measures to contain the Turkish advance. They were ineffective. Reports of a Turkish military build-up under the command of the young **Sultan Mahomet II** were not treated with the necessary urgency, and the consequence was that Western troops sent to defend **Constantinople** against the Sultan's army were insufficient to prevent the fall of the city in **1453**.

The trade agreement which the Venetians managed to negotiate with the Sultan could not arrest the erosion of its commercial empire in the East. The Turkish fleets penetrated into the northern Aegean and many times in the last years of the century the Turkish cavalry came so close to Venice that the fires from the villages it destroyed could be seen from the top of the Campanile of San Marco. In **1479** Venice was forced to sign away the vital port of **Negroponte** and a batch of other Aegean islands; the defeat of the Venetian navy at **Sapienza** in **1499** led to the loss of the main fortresses of the **Morea** (Peloponnese), which meant that the Turks now controlled the so-called "door to the Adriatic". Virtually the only bright spot in all the gloom came about through the marriage of the Venetian **Caterina Cornaro** to the King of **Cyprus** in 1468. In 1473 the king died, and the ensuing political pressure on the widow paid off in **1489**, when Caterina handed over the island to the government of Venice.

The sixteenth century

In **1494** Italy was invaded by **Louis XII of France**, an intervention which Venice lost no time in exploiting. By playing the various territorial contenders off against each other (mainly France and the Habsburgs), Venice succeeded in adding bits and pieces to the terra firma empire, and in 1503 signed a disadvantageous treaty with the Turks so as to be able to concentrate its resources on the mainland. Given the accumulated hostility to Venice, it was a dangerous game, and when the Republic began to encroach on the papal domain in Romagna, it at last provoked a unified response from its opponents. The **League of Cambrai**, formed in **1508** with Pope Julius II, Louis XII, Emperor Maximilian and the King of Spain at its head, pitted almost every power in Europe against the Venetians, in a pact that explicitly declared its intention of destroying Venice's empire as a prelude to conquering the Turks.

The ensuing war began calamitously for Venice – its army was crushed by the French at **Agnadello**, city after city defected to the League, and Venice prepared for a siege. The siege never came, and in the end the conflicting interests of the League enabled the Venetians, through subtle diplomacy, to repossess nearly everything they had held at the start of the war. Nonetheless, when the fighting finished in **1516** many of the cities of the Veneto had been sacked, great swathes of the countryside ruined, and the Venetian treasury bled almost dry.

Worse was to come. Clearly **the discovery of the New World** was going to have significant repercussions for Venice, but the most catastrophic of the voyages of discovery from Venice's point of view was that of **Vasco da Gama**. In September **1499**, da Gama arrived back in Lisbon having reached India by the Cape of Good Hope. The slow and expensive land routes across Asia to the markets and docks of Venice could now be bypassed by the merchants of northern Europe – from the moment of da Gama's return, the economic balance of Europe began to tilt in favour of the Portuguese, the English and the Dutch.

In **1519**, with the accession of the 19-year-old **Charles V**, the Habsburg Empire absorbed the massive territories of the Spanish kingdom, and after the **sack of Rome in 1527** the whole Italian peninsula, with the sole exception of Venice, was under the young emperor's domination. Meanwhile, the **Turks** were on the move again – **Syria** and **Egypt** had been taken in **1517**; **Rhodes** had fallen to **Suleiman the Magnificent** in **1522**; and by **1529** the Ottoman Empire had spread right along the southern Mediterranean to Morocco. To survive, Venice had to steer a path between these two empires and France, the other superpower of the period. It did survive, but at a cost. When a combined Christian fleet took on the Turks at **Prevesa** in **1538**, the supreme commander, acting under Charles V's instructions, was so concerned to prevent the Venetians profiting from an allied victory that his tactics ensured a Turkish victory; the Venetians were obliged to accept a punitive treaty shortly after. Even the great allied success at **Lépanto** in **1571** didn't work to Venice's advantage, as the Habsburg commander of the fleet, Don John of Austria, refused to consolidate the Venetian position by sailing east after the victory. In the subsequent negotiations, Venice was forced formally to surrender **Cyprus**, whose brutal capture by the Turks had been the reason for the allied offensive in the first place.

The seventeenth century

Relations between Rome and Venice were always fractious. Venice's expansion on the mainland was a source of irritation, especially when it turned its attention to areas over which the Vatican claimed sovereignty, but papal animosity was also caused by the restrictions imposed on the pope's authority within the Republic's boundaries, restrictions which led to Venice being regarded in some quarters as a crypto-Protestant state. The pope was Venice's spiritual overlord, the Venetians agreed, but the doge and his officers were the masters in temporal affairs. The problem for the papacy was that the doge's notion of what constituted temporal affairs was far too broad, and at the start of the seventeenth century **Pope Paul V** and the Republic came to a head-on clash.

Two incidents provoked the row: Venice's insistence that the pope should routinely approve its candidate for the office of Patriarch; and its determination not to hand over to papal jurisdiction two clerics it had decided to prosecute. Matters came to a head with the **Papal Interdict of 1606** and the excommunication of the whole city. Venice's resistance, orchestrated by the scholar-priest **Paolo Sarpi**, was fierce – the Jesuits were expelled, priests within Venetian territory ordered to continue in their duties, and pamphlets printed putting the Venetian case. One year later the Interdict was lifted, damaging the prestige of the papacy throughout Europe.

No sooner was the Interdict out of the way than the Spanish and Austrian **Habsburgs** entered the fray again. The Austrian branch was the first to cause trouble, by encouraging the piratical raids of the **Uskoks**, a loosely defined and regularly obstreperous community living along the Dalmatian coast. Venice took retaliatory action, Archduke Ferdinand objected, and a half-hearted war dragged on until **1617**, when, under the peace terms, the Uskoks were removed completely from their seaports.

The Spanish wing was more devious, attempting, in **1618**, to subvert the Venetian state with a wildly ambitious scheme that has always been known as **The Spanish Conspiracy**. Masterminded by the Spanish Viceroy of Naples, the **Duke of Osuna**, and the Spanish ambassador to Venice, the Duke of Bedmar, the plot involved smuggling a Spanish army into the city in disguised groups of two or three, and then inciting a mutiny among a contingent of Dutch mercenaries already lodged there. Just how convoluted the conspiracy was can be gathered from the fact that its betrayal resulted in the execution of around three hundred people.

And then, after half a century of ceasefire, the **Turks** renewed their harassment of the Venetian colonies, concentrating their attention now on the one remaining stronghold in the eastern Mediterranean, **Crete**. The campaign lasted for 25 years, ending in **1669** with the inevitable fall of the island. Even then the war with the Turks was not over – in **1699**, under the military command of **Doge Francesco Morosini**, the Venetians embarked on a retaliatory action in the **Morea** (Peloponnese), and succeeded in retaking the islands. By 1715, however, all the gains had been turned to losses once more, and in the **Treaty of Passarowitz** in **1718** Venice was forced to accept a definition of its Mediterranean territories drawn up by the Austrians and the Turks. It was left with just the Ionian islands and the Dalmatian coast, and its power in these colonies was little more than hypothetical.

Meanwhile, at home, a significant change in the social structure of the city had been happening. For reasons that remain unexplained, the population of the Venetian upper class had been declining since the middle of the sixteenth century, a situation that was exacerbated in 1630 by a terrible outbreak of plague. By the time the plague had receded, there were around 1600 patrician adult males, around one thousand fewer than a hundred years earlier. Needing to fill scores of government posts, and being rather short of cash, the city's rulers now decided to **"unlock" the Maggior Consiglio** by admitting new families to the ranks of the nobility in return for hefty payments. By 1720 more than 120 families had paid their way into the ruling elite, mostly Venetian merchants and businessmen, though a sizeable minority came from mainland cities such as Padua and Verona. They were regarded by many of the old guard as vulgar *arrivistes*, but amongst their number were some clans who were to become extremely influential, such as the Rezzonico family, owners of one of the last great palaces on the Canal Grande.

Collapse

Venice in the eighteenth century became a political nonentity, pursuing a foreign policy of unarmed neutrality of which one historian wrote "She sacrifices everything with the single object of giving no offence to other states." When the **Treaty of Aix-la-Chapelle** in **1748** confirmed Austrian control of the neighbouring areas of the mainland, the Venetians felt compelled to send ambassadors to the Austrian court in a humiliating attempt to wheedle guarantees of their possessions on the terra firma. At home, the economy remained strong, but the division between the upper stratum of the aristocracy and the ever-increasing poorer section was widening, and all attempts to dampen discontent within the city by democratizing its government were stifled by the conservative elite.

Politically trivial and constitutionally ossified, Venice was now renowned not as one of the great powers of Europe, but rather as its playground. Hester Thrale observed in 1789 that no other place was "so subservient to the purposes of pleasure", and William Beckford recorded the effects of a life spent between the ballroom and casino – "Their nerves unstrung by disease and the consequence of early debaucheries, allow no natural flow of lively spirits...they pass their lives in one perpetual doze."

The conflict between Austria and post-Revolutionary France quickly brought about the end of the Venetian Republic. In May 1796, **Napoleon Bonaparte** entered Milan at the head of the French army; in February of the following year Mantua, the last Austrian stronghold in Italy, fell to the French. Yet the Venetians rebuffed Napoleon's repeated invitations to join an anti-Austrian alliance, and French troops in the Veneto were subjected to numerous acts of violent resistance, with Verona proving notably recalcitrant. On April 17, 1797, Napoleon temporarily mollified the Austrians by handing over the Veneto to them (even though the Venetian Republic was still a neutral state), then waited for a pretext to polish off the Republic. Just three days later the Venetians duly provided him with one, by attacking a French naval patrol off the Lido. "I will have no more Inquisitors. I will have no more Senate; I shall be an Attila to the state of Venice," Bonaparte proclaimed; war was declared on Venice, and on May 9 an ultimatum was sent to the city's government, demanding the dissolution of its constitution.

On Friday, **May 12, 1797**, the Maggior Consiglio met for the last time. By 512 votes to 20, with 5 abstentions, the Council voted to accede to every one of Napoleon's demands; the vote cast, the last Doge of Venice, **Lodovico Manin**, handed to his valet the linen cap worn beneath the ducal crown, saying – "Take it, I shall not be needing it again." The Venetian Republic was dead.

Within days a provisional democratic council had been formed and there were French troops in the city, many of them occupied with wrecking the Arsenale or stripping the place of its art treasures and shipping them off to Paris. On this occasion, the French didn't stay long, because in the **Treaty of Campo Formio**, signed in October, Napoleon relinquished Venice to the Austrians. The French were soon back, though – in **1805** Napoleon joined the city to his Kingdom of Italy, and it stayed under French domination until the aftermath of Waterloo, ten years later. It then passed back to the Austrians again, and remained a Habsburg province for the next half-century, the only break in Austrian rule coming with the **revolt of March 1848**, when the city was reinstituted as a republic under the leadership of **Daniele Manin**. The rebellion, which ignited uprisings all over the Veneto, lasted until **August 1849**, when a combination of starvation, disease and relentless bombardment forced the Venetians to surrender. Liberation finally arrived in the wake of Prussia's defeat of the Austrians at Sadowa in **1866**. Soon after, Venice was absorbed into the Kingdom of United Italy.

To the present

In many respects the Austrians were better for Venice than the French had been. Although the French initiated modernization schemes such as the creation of public gardens and the cemetery of San Michele, not all of the fifty or so religious buildings and forty palaces that they demolished were destroyed in a good cause; in addition to which, they also wrecked the shipyards and confiscated hundreds of works of art. The Austrians' urban improvements were less ruthless; they filled in some of the more unhygienic canals (the origin of the *rio terrà*), built a rail link with the mainland, and undertook two major, albeit controversial, restoration projects – the Fondaco dei Turchi and the church of Santi Maria e Donato on Murano.

Yet Venice went through most of the nineteenth century in a state of destitution. There were no more government jobs to provide a source of income, and Trieste was the Austrians' preferred port on the Adriatic. By 1820 begging was the main means of support for about one quarter of its population. Families that had once been among the city's wealthiest were obliged to sell their most treasured possessions; the Barbarigo family sold seventeen paintings by Titian to the Tsar, for example. Later in the century, even the churches were selling their property to pay for their upkeep. It's been calculated that of the moveable works of art that were to be found in Venice at the fall of the Republic, only four percent remains.

Manufacturing activity within the city revived towards the end of the nineteenth century; there were flour mills on Giudecca, glass factories on Murano, lace workshops on Burano. The opening of the Suez Canal in 1869 brought a muted revival to the Arsenale docks. Already, though, **tourism** had emerged as the main area of economic expansion, with the development of the **Lido** as Europe's most fashionable resort. It was the need for a more substantial economic base than bathing huts, hotels and a few pockets of industrial production that led, in the wake of World War I, to the development of the industrial complex on the marshland across the lagoon from Venice, at **Porto Marghera**.

As recently as 1913 the Baedeker guide could describe Venice as a "shipbuilding, cotton spinning and iron working centre", but by the end of World War I Venice was finished as a maritime centre. Battleships had been built in the Arsenale, but the proximity of enemy forces persuaded the navy to dismantle the docks in 1917 and switch its yards to Genoa and Naples. The new port of Marghera was not a shipyard but a processing and refining centre to which raw materials would be brought by sea. In 1933 a **road link** was built to carry the workforce between Venice and the steadily expanding port, whose progress was of special concern to Mussolini's government. (Venice was the second city in Italy in which organized Fascism appeared; as early as 1919 the local newspaper published an appeal for the formation of Fascist squads.) After World War II (from which Venice emerged undamaged) Marghera's growth accelerated even more rapidly. The consequences were not those that had been predicted.

What happened was that the factory workers of Marghera, instead of commuting each day from Venice, simply decamped to the mainland. Housing in Marghera's neighbour, **Mestre**, is drier, roomier, warmer and cheaper to maintain than the apartments in Venice, and as a result the population of Mestre-Marghera is today more than three times that of the historic centre of Venice, which is now under 60,000 and falling with alarming rapidity; from 1994 to 2004 the population shrank annually by an average of 800, but in 2005, with the death rate more than double the birth rate, the figure dropped by 2000. (Immediately after World War II, around 170,000 people lived in Venice.) Apart from polluting the environment of the lagoon, Mestre has siphoned so many people of working age from the islands that the average age of Venice's population is now the highest of any major European city, with more than 25 percent of its inhabitants over 65. Moreover, the percentage of native Venetians in the city is declining as the place becomes a favourite second base or retirement home for the wealthy of Milan, Turin and other more prosperous Italian cities – only the wealthy can afford to maintain the fragile fabric of many of the city's houses, most of which are listed as historic monuments. When a flat is sold in Venice, it's likelier that the buyer will be a non-Venetian than a native.

Venice's future?

No city has suffered more from the tourist industry than Venice. As many as twenty million tourists invade the city each year, and half of those don't even stay a night. Only half a dozen plumbers are registered in Venice, while the number of souvenir shops has risen to over four hundred.

Yet Venice at the moment is dependent on tourism, which generates around 70 percent of the city's income, and every year proposals are put forward to break that dependency. A science park, a national library, a conservation and marine technology centre – all have been suggested as projects that could give Venice a more active role in twenty-first-century Italy, and all have come to nothing so far. It remains to be seen what will happen to one spectacularly crack-brained idea about how to propel Venice into the present day. In 1992 Venice was granted metropolitan status, which enabled the town council to apply for central funding for an **urban rail system**. It has been proposed that an underground train line be constructed to link central Venice, La Giudecca, the Lido and Murano to the mainland rail network at Marco Polo airport and Mestre. Apologists for the metro insist that it will enable those of the city's inhabitants who work on the mainland to get quickly to their desks and back home again, and will lead to a reduction in vaporetto traffic on the Canal Grande, a major cause of structural damage to canalside buildings. It's also been suggested that the Arsenale – the projected location for one of the central metro stations – might become a sort of processing centre for tourists, in which visitors will be briefed on the city's attractions (and allocated accommodation if necessary) before being sent on their way. Opponents of the metro, led by the conservation group Italia Nostra, argue that it will merely increase the tourist deluge (just as the creation of the rail bridge did) and undermine the delicate substructures of the city's buildings. What's more, they say, the enthusiasm of the politicians for the train plan probably has a lot to do with the vast sums set aside for its development, some of which would doubtless percolate into various private bank accounts. The plan has been put on the back burner for now, largely because the cash isn't available, but it's not officially dead.

Though too many of Venice's politicians seem enamoured of such high-profile schemes, more modest and sensible ideas do occasionally emerge. Some have proposed that efforts should be concentrated on furthering the city's reputation for crafts and restoration work – a good idea, but one that received a setback when the European Centre for the Training of Craftspeople was not permitted to extend its occupancy of the island of San Servolo. Others see the internet and global information technologies as offering an opportunity for Venice to remake itself economically. One person who has championed this notion, and consistently propounded a clear vision of how Venice might find a new role for itself, is **Massimo Cacciari**, mayor of the city from 1993 to 2000. Taking time out from his career as professor of philosophy at the University of Venice, Cacciari rapidly became a hugely respected politician, both for his energetic commitment and his incorruptibility – when Gianni de Michelis invited him to join his socialist party, Cacciari fended him off with the words "No thanks, I already come from a wealthy family". As he sees it, Venice's best hope lies in its being classified as an area of special economic need by the European Union, which would give it access to funds for major infrastructure repairs and improvements, such as the laying of fibre-optic cables in tandem with the dredging of canals. To complement this strategy, high-tech companies could also be given tax incentives to open offices in Venice, a location which has plenty of very desirable and unoccupied real estate to offer potential investors.

In an attempt to tackle the problem of depopulation, Cacciari tried to get the municipality and conservation groups to apply themselves to the restoration of old houses rather than old churches and other such monuments, so that the historic centre could provide housing at prices comparable with those in Mestre. As Cacciari pointed out, no project for Venice's future has any chance of succeeding if there are no young Venetians living there. In the last decade or so there has been a notable increase in the number of new housing projects in the historic centre – a stroll around La Giudecca, for example, will reveal numerous signs of regeneration. And there's little sign of the city creating new economic foundations for itself: whenever a major property is sold in the city centre it's nearly always destined to become a hotel. On the other hand, a plan to lay fibre-optic cables throughout the city might go some way to realizing Cacciari's vision of a Venice redeemed by cutting-edge technology – a vision he continues to champion, having been re-elected to the mayor's office in 2005.

Venetian painting and sculpture

After just a day in Venice you notice that the light is softer than that on the mainland and changes more during the course of a day. Reflecting off the water and the white stone facades, it gives shifting impressions of places that would otherwise be shadowed, and adds shimmering highlights to solid brickwork. In view of the specific qualities of Venetian light, it's scarcely surprising that the city's painters emphasized colour and texture rather than structure and perspective. The political and social peculiarities of Venice were equally influential on the development of its art, as will become apparent in the following thumbnail account.

Byzantine Venice

The close political and commercial ties between the early Venetian state and the Byzantine Empire (see the "History" section) led to a steady exchange of works of art between the two, and to the creation of the most important work of art from that period – the **Pala d'Oro** on the high altar of San Marco. Begun as a collaboration between Venetian and Byzantine craftsmen, it epitomizes the Venetian taste for elaborate decoration and creates the impression of a complex content unified by a dazzlingly rich surface. The Pala was later expanded with panels stolen from Constantinople during the sack of 1204, a wholesale plundering which provided Venice with a hoard of artefacts that was to nourish its craftsmen and artists for centuries.

It is notable that the earliest Venetian painter of renown, **Paolo Veneziano** (working from the 1330s to at least 1358), shows far stronger affinities with Byzantine work than with the frescoes created by Giotto at the start of the century in nearby Padua. He generally employs a flat, gold background and symmetrical arrangements of symbolic figures, rather than attempting a more emotional representation of individuals. Two paintings in the Accademia show these characteristics: a *Madonna and Child Enthroned* and a polyptych that achieves the same overall effect as that of the Pala d'Oro – and indeed it was he who was commissioned to paint the **cover of the Pala d'Oro**, now in San Marco's museum. A work believed to be by Paolo Veneziano has recently been revealed during restoration of an altarpiece in the church of San Zaccaria.

The first room of the Accademia is full of work displaying this indebtedness to Byzantine art, and Byzantium remained a living influence in the city up to the seventeenth and eighteenth centuries, sustained in part by the influx of refugees following the **fall of Constantinople** in 1453. The neo-Byzantine *Madoneri* (the main school of the Greek community) are represented in the **Museo Dipinti Sacri Bizantini**, where the paintings show a complete indifference to the post-Renaissance cult of the artist and to notions of aesthetic novelty. The young Cretan **El Greco** (1545–1614) worked with the *Madoneri* for a while, before setting out for fame and fortune in Spain.

Gothic painting and sculpture

Deemed to be relics of a barbaric age, a huge number of Gothic paintings and sculptures were destroyed in the seventeenth and eighteenth centuries. The reinstatement of the Gothic is in large part due to the determination of John Ruskin, whose preoccupation was the Gothic architecture and sculpture of Venice. His meticulous work on **Santi Giovanni e Paolo** (San Zanipolo), mapping the change from Gothic to Renaissance through a study of the **funerary sculpture**, is still a useful analysis.

Santi Giovanni e Paolo's main apse contains the **tomb of Doge Michele Morosini** (d.1382), described by Ruskin as "the richest monument of the Gothic period in Venice", although its figures (apart from those at the head and foot of the doge) have an awkward, un-Gothic stiffness. More interesting sculpturally is the **tomb of Doge Marco Corner** (d.1368) opposite, which was carved in the workshop of the non-Venetian **Nino Pisano**. Slightly later is San Marco's **rood screen**, by the two brothers **Pietro Paolo and Jacobello Dalle Masegne**, who made a study of the work of Pisano and northern European Gothic sculpture. The other high points of Gothic sculpture in Venice are also architecturally related – the **Palazzo Ducale's capitals**, **corner sculptures** and **Porta della Carta** (though the main figures on the Porta are nineteenth-century replicas of fifteenth-century originals).

Paolo Veneziano's unrelated namesake, **Lorenzo Veneziano** (working 1356–72) marries a distinctly Gothic element to the Byzantine elements in Venetian painting. The large polyptych in the Accademia is a fine example of his work, showing a roundedness in the face and hands and in the fall of the drapery, and a sinuousness of pose in the figures that suggests the influence of Gothic painters such as Simone Martini of Siena.

Around 1409 **Gentile de Fabriano**, the exemplar of the style known as **International Gothic**, frescoed parts of the Palazzo Ducale with the help of his pupil **Pisanello**. These frescoes are all now destroyed, and the nearest example of Pisanello's work is his *St George* (1438–42) in Verona's church of Sant'Anastasia. Even in this one piece it's possible to see what the Venetians would have found congenial in his art: chiefly an all-over patterning that ties the content of the painting to the picture plane and eschews the illusion of receding space.

The work of Gentile and Pisanello was most closely studied in Venice by **Michele Giambono** (working 1420–62), represented in the Accademia by a *Coronation of the Madonna in Paradise* (1447) and in the church of San Trovaso by *St Chrysogonus* (c.1450). These claustrophobic paintings are of the same date as Padua's frescoes by Mantegna and sculptures by Donatello – Giambono and others in Venice were happily working in a sophisticated high-Gothic style at a time when the Renaissance was elsewhere into its maturity.

Early Renaissance painting

Petrarch, who lived in Venice in the 1360s, described the Republic as "a world apart", and nothing illustrates this insularity better than the reception of Renaissance ideas in the city. Venetians were chary of overemphasizing the individual, a tendency implicit in the one-point perspective of Renaissance painting; in addition, the use of abstract mathematical formulas in the depiction of form was alien to the pragmatic Venetian temperament. When the principles of the Florentine Renaissance did belatedly filter into the art of Venice, they were transformed into a way of seeing that was uniquely Venetian.

Key figures in this period of absorption were the **Vivarini** family – **Antonio** (c.1419–80), his brother **Bartolomeo** (c.1430–91) and son **Alvise** (c.1445–1505). Antonio's work, though still part of the Gothic tradition, marks a shift away from it, with his more angular line and construction of pictorial spaces consistent with the rules of one-point perspective – as in the *Madonna and Child* triptych in the Accademia, painted in collaboration with Giovanni d'Alemagna. A more humanistic temperament is embodied in the paintings of **Alvise**, manifested less through his depiction of space than through his representation of people. He individualizes his figures, giving an emotional charge to narratives which had to that point functioned symbolically. The *St Clare* in the Accademia is an excellent example of his work, establishing an unprecedentedly intimate contact between the saint and the viewer.

The pre-eminent artistic dynasty of this transitional period was that of **Jacopo Bellini** (c.1400–70), once a pupil of Gentile da Fabriano, and his sons **Gentile** (c.1429–1507) and **Giovanni** (c.1430–1516). Jacopo suffered from the anti-Gothic zealotry of later years, and his two major cycles of paintings – at the Scuola di San Marco and the Scuola di San Giovanni Evangelista – were destroyed. From descriptions of these works, it would appear that the two Madonnas in the Accademia are rather restrained in their decoration; other pieces by him can be seen in the Museo Correr.

Giovanni is the one people mean when they refer simply to "Bellini". In the Accademia he's represented by a number of Madonnas, a series of allegorical panels and a couple of large altarpieces. Other works around Venice include altarpieces in San Zaccaria, San Pietro (Murano), the Frari, Madonna dell'Orto and San Zanipolo. In the majority of these paintings the attention is concentrated on the foreground, where the arrangement of the figures or a device such as a screen or throne turns the background into another plane parallel to the surface, rather than a receding landscape. That this was a conscious choice which had nothing to do with his perspectival skills is demonstrated by the **San Giobbe altarpiece** (in the Accademia), in which a meticulously worked-out illusionistic space would have suggested the presence of an extra chapel. A fundamental humanism pervades much of Giovanni's output – although his Madonnas show an idealized version of motherhood, each possesses an immediacy which suggests to the viewer that this ideal could be attainable.

Meanwhile, **Gentile** was pursuing a form of painting that was also a specifically Venetian Renaissance phenomenon – the *istoria* or narrative painting cycle. At least ten of these were commissioned by public bodies between around 1475 and 1525; the three remaining cycles in Venice are the *Miracles of the Relic of the True Cross* (Accademia), by five artists including Gentile and **Carpaccio**, and the *St Ursula* cycle (Accademia) and the *St George and St Jerome* cycle (Scuola di San Giorgio degli Schiavoni), which are both by Carpaccio. To the modern observer the story line of the *Relic* and *St Ursula* cycles in particular can seem to be naive pretexts for precise renditions of the pageant of Venetian social life and a wealth of domestic minutiae. The details of the paintings were not mere incidentals to the narrative, however – a person hanging out washing or mending a roof would have been perceived as an enhancement of the physical reality of the miracle, and not as a distraction from the central event.

High Renaissance painting

While these narrative cycles were being produced Giovanni Bellini was beginning to experiment with oil paint, which was soon to displace tempera (pigment in egg yolk) as the preferred medium. Whereas tempera had to be applied in layers, the long drying time of oil allowed colours to be mixed and softened, while its thick consistency enabled artists to simulate the texture of the objects depicted. Close examination of later paintings by Bellini shows he used his fingers to merge colours and soften light, and two of his young assistants at the time – **Giorgione** and **Titian** – were to explore even further the potential of the new material, developing a specifically Venetian High Renaissance style.

Giorgione (1475–1510) seems custom-built for myth; little is known about him other than that he was tall and handsome and he died young (possibly of plague). The handful of enigmatic works he created were innovative in their imaginative self-sufficiency – for instance, the Venetian collector Michiel, writing in 1530, was unable to say precisely what the subject was of *The Tempest* (Accademia), perhaps Giorgione's most famous image. His only altarpiece, still in the cathedral at Castelfranco (his home town), isolates the Madonna and the two saints from each other by manipulating perspective and by placing the Madonna against a landscape while the attendant saints stand against a man-made background. Despite the serenity of the individual figures, the painting instils in the viewer a disquieting sense of elusiveness.

Given his long life and huge output, **Titian** (c.1485–1576) is very badly represented in his home town: a *Presentation in the Temple*, a *Pietà* left unfinished at his death, and a couple of minor works in the Accademia; a handful in the Salute; the *Assumption* and *Pésaro Altarpiece* in the Frari, and that's more or less it. (Napoleon made off with a good crop of Titians, including a *Venus* which he hung in his tent; the Louvre now has a fine collection.)

Titian, like Giorgione, used the qualities of oils to evoke a diffuse light and soften contours – in contrast with the contemporaneous art of Rome, the city of Michelangelo, where the emphasis was on the solidity and sculptural aspects of the objects depicted. Artists in Florence were answerable to an imperious ruling family, in Rome they had to comply with the wishes of successive popes, but Titian's success was so great that he could virtually pick and choose from a host of clients from all over the continent, and the diversity of works he produced – portraits, allegories, devotional paintings, mythologies – remains unsurpassed in Western art. His technical range is as impressive as the range of subject matter; the earliest works are highly polished and precisely drawn, but in the later pieces he tested the possibilities of oil paint to their limit, using his bare hands to scrape the canvas and add great gobbets of paint (see the Accademia *Pietà*).

Giorgionesque is an adjective used to describe a number of early sixteenth-century Venetian painters, in reference to the enrichment of colour popular at the time and to the increasingly oblique and suggestive approach to content. **Sebastiano del Piombo**, who studied under Giovanni Bellini with Titian and Giorgione, before moving to Rome in 1611, is one of the artists to whom the term is applied; his altarpiece of **San Giovanni Crisostomo** in the eponymous church is his best work still in Venice. Another is **Palma il Vecchio** (1480–1528); although he was often frivolous in a way that Giorgione and Titian rarely were – ponds of frothy nymphs and the like – his strongest work in Venice is a redoubtable *St Barbara* in Santa Maria Formosa. The most interesting painter of this period and type is **Lorenzo Lotto** (c.1480–1556), represented in the Accademia by the almost metaphysical *Portrait of a Young Man*. The rivalries of other painters eventually drove Lotto from Venice, and it's not too fanciful to see a reflection of the artist's anxieties in his restless, wistful paintings.

Born three years after Bellini's death and nine years after that of Giorgione, **Tintoretto** (1519–94) grew up during the period in which the ascendancy of Titian became established. Princes were sending agents to Venice to buy the latest Titian, no matter what the subject, and every visiting dignitary would want to be painted by him. Titian's exploratory attitude to paint and the increasing Venetian receptivity to individual style were both exploited by the energetic and competitive younger artist. The painting that made his reputation, the *Miracle of the Slave* (Accademia; 1548), shows how he learned from Titian's experiments and distanced himself from them. Tintoretto's palette is as rich as Titian's, but is aggressively vivid rather than sensuous, and uses far stronger lighting. And while Titian is concerned with the inner drama of an event, Tintoretto's attention is given to the drama of gesture.

Tintoretto's dynamic style was not universally acclaimed. Pietro Aretino, Titian's close friend and most vociferous champion, disparaged the speed and relative carelessness of Tintoretto's technique, and one member of the **Scuola di San Rocco** said he would give his money towards the decoration of the scuola's building as long as Tintoretto was not commissioned. He didn't get his way, and San Rocco's cycle is the most comprehensive collection of paintings by the artist. Dramatic perspective effects, bizarre juxtapositions of images and extraordinarily fluid brushwork here make the substantial world seem other-worldly – the converse of the earlier *istorie* cycles.

In contrast, the art of **Paolo Veronese** (1528–88), who moved to Venice from Verona in his twenties, conveys worldly harmony rather than spiritual turbulence. This is particularly evident in his work for architectural settings (San Sebastiano in Venice and the Villa Barbaro at Masèr), where he constructed logical spaces that complement the form of the buildings. More urbane than Tintoretto, he nonetheless attracted controversy; in his *Christ in the House of Levi* (Accademia) the naturalistic representation of German soldiers was interpreted as a gesture of support for Protestantism. Veronese's response to his accusers revealed a lot about the changing attitude towards the status of the artist; claiming licence to depict what he wanted, he simply changed the title of the work from *The Last Supper* to the title by which it's now known.

Renaissance sculpture

Venetian **sculpture** in the Renaissance was conditioned by the society's ingrained aversion to the over-glorification of the individual and by the specific restrictions of the city's landscape. Freestanding monumental work of the sort that was being commissioned all over Italy is conspicuous by its absence. The exception to prove the rule, the **monument to Colleoni**, was made by the Florentine artist **Verrocchio**. Venetian sculptors worked mainly to decorate tombs or the walls of churches, and up to the late Renaissance no clear distinction was made between sculptors, masons and architects. Beyond the Renaissance, sculpture was generally commissioned as part of an architectural project, and it's usually futile to try to disentangle the sculpture from its architectural function.

Pietro Lombardo (c.1438–1515) was born in Cremona and went to Rome before arriving in Venice around 1460. His development can be charted in the church of San Zanipolo; his first major monument, the **tomb of Doge**

Pasquale Malipiero, is pictorially flat and smothered with carved decoration, but the **monument to Doge Pietro Mocenigo**, with its classicized architectural elements and figures, is a fully Renaissance piece. In true Venetian style the latter glorifies the State through the man, rather than stressing his individual salvation – the image of Christ is easily overlooked. Pietro's sons **Antonio** (c.1458–1516) and **Tullio** (c.1460–1532) were also sculptors and assisted him on the Mocenigo monument. Tullio's independent work is less pictorial; his **monument to Doge Andrea Vendramin** (also in San Zanipolo) is a complex architectural evocation of a Roman triumphal arch, though again the whole is encrusted with decorative figures.

Jacopo Sansovino, who went on to become the Republic's principal architect, was known as a sculptor when he arrived in Venice from Rome in 1527. More of a classicist than his predecessors, he nonetheless produced work remarkably in tune with Venetian sensibilities – his figures on the logetta of the Campanile, for example, animate the surface of the building rather than draw attention to themselves. **Alessandro Vittoria** was the major sculptor of the middle and later part of the century; originally a member of Sansovino's workshop, Vittoria developed a more rhetorical style, well demonstrated in the figures of St Jerome in the Frari and San Zanipolo.

Seventeenth and eighteenth centuries

The High Baroque style in painting and sculpture was largely a Roman phenomenon and the Venetians, whose distrust of Rome led in 1606 to a Papal Interdict (see "History" section), remained largely untouched by it. Suitably enough, the only Venetian interior that relates to Roman Baroque is the Jesuit church, the **Gesuiti**.

After the hyper-productive **Palma il Giovane**, who seems to have contributed something to the majority of the city's church interiors, it was up to foreign painters – **Johann Lys**, for instance – to keep painting alive in the city. Much the same is true of sculpture; the Venetian **Baldassare Longhena** early in his career turned from sculpture to architecture, leaving the field to the Bolognese **Giuseppe Mazza** (bronze reliefs in San Zanipolo) and the Flemish **Juste Le Court** (high altar of the Salute), although Le Court's Venetian pupil **Orazio Marinelli** (portrait busts in the Querini-Stampalia) did achieve a measure of celebrity. A particularly successful artist towards the end of the seventeenth century was **Andrea Brustolon** of Belluno, best known for his sculptural furniture (Ca' Rezzonico).

The last efflorescence of Venetian art began around the start of the eighteenth century, as Venice was degenerating into the playground of Europe. The highly illusionistic decorative paintings of **Giambattista Piazzetta** (1682–1752) mark the first step and foreshadow the work of **Giambattista Tiepolo** (1696–1777), whose ever-lightening colours and elegant, slightly disdainful Madonnas typified the sensuous but melancholy climate of the declining Republic. There's a similarity of mood to most of Tiepolo's work – from the dizzying trompe l'oeil ceiling painted in the Ca' Rezzonico to celebrate a marriage, to the airy *Virgin in Glory* painted for the Carmini.

Another major figure of the period was **Rosalba Carriera** (1675–1758), the first artist to use pastel as a medium in its own right. She was known chiefly as a portraitist, and the Ca' Rezzonico and the Accademia both contain a fine selection of her work – the latter featuring a *Self-Portrait in Old Age* which expresses a melancholy temperament usually suppressed from her pictures. (Incidentally, Carriera was not Venice's only woman artist: Marietta Robusti, Tintoretto's daughter, was known as a fine portraitist, and Carriera's contemporary Giulia Lama has a *Judith and Holofernes* in the Accademia.)

By this time, Venetian art was being siphoned out of the city in large quantities, with people such as the English consul Joseph Smith sending pictures home by the crateful. Aristocrats on the Grand Tour were particularly interested in topographical work – kind of upmarket postcards – and in this area the pre-eminent artist was **Canaletto** (1695–1768), whose work was copied and engraved to make further saleable items. Don't be misled into believing he showed the "real" Venice – he idealized the city, changing spatial arrangements in order to suit a harmonious composition and sometimes even altering individual buildings. Canaletto's work in Venice is as sparse as Titian's – there's only one painting by him in the Accademia and a couple in the Ca' Rezzonico.

More sombre is the work of **Francesco Guardi** (1712–93), whose images of the lagoon and imaginary architectural scenes are frequently swathed in atmospheric mist and dotted with a few prophetic ruins. Genre painters were also popular at this time, none more so than **Pietro Longhi** (1708–85), whose wonderful illustrations of Venetian life (painted with a technique that is at best adequate) can also be seen in the Accademia and the Ca' Rezzonico. Longhi's production line was as busy as Canaletto's, as his workshop churned out copies of his most popular paintings to meet demand.

The last word on the painting of the Venetian Republic should be devoted to **Giandomenico Tiepolo** (1727–1804), seen at his best in the cycle of frescoes painted for his home and now installed in the Ca' Rezzonico. Freed from the whims of clients, he produced here a series of images that can with hindsight be seen as symbolic of the end of an era, with Sunday crowds gawping at a peepshow and clowns frittering away their time flirting and playing.

To the present day

After the fall of the Republic, art in Venice became the domain of outsiders. **Turner**, who visited the city three times, was its supreme painter in the nineteenth century, but as Ruskin said, you'd only have to stay in Venice for a few days to learn about it what Turner had learned. **Whistler**, **Monet** and **Sargent** were among other visitors. The only Venetian nineteenth-century artist of note is **Frederico Zandomeneghi** (1841–1917), and he decamped for Paris in 1874 to join the Impressionists' circle.

The story of art in Venice since then is no more cheerful. The internationally known artists who stayed as guests of **Peggy Guggenheim** between 1949 and 1979 came and left without making an impact on its cultural life. Every two years the **Biennale** brings in the hotshots of the international art world, but does little to help young Venetian artists. The few Italian artists who have worked here have not exactly galvanized the city; the painter **Lucio Fontana** lived in Venice in the 1950s, and **Emilio Vedova** – a founder member of the avant-garde groups *Fronte Nuovo* and *Gruppo degli Otto* – taught at the Accademia until his death in the mid-1980s. Today the best-known practitioners at work in Venice are the multimedia artist **Fabrizio Plessi**, the American painter **Judith Harvest**, Rome-born painter **Daniele Bianchi** and the Milanese artist **Maria Morganti**.

An outline of Venetian architecture

This is just a brief chronology of Venetian architectural styles, intended simply as a means of giving some sense of order to the city's jumble of buildings. For more detailed accounts, refer to the "Books" section.

Byzantine Venice

Although settlement of the lagoon began as far back as the fifth century, no building has survived intact from earlier than the start of the eleventh century. The very first houses raised on the mudflats were "built like birds' nests, half on sea and half on land…the solidity of the earth…secured only by wattle-work", according to a letter written in 523 by a Roman official named Cassiodorus. Many of the earliest shelters were only temporary, constructed as refuges from the barbarian hordes of the mainland and abandoned as soon as the threat had receded, but with the Lombard invasions of the second half of the sixth century, communities uprooted from northern Italy began to construct more durable buildings on the islands. Some of the materials for these buildings were scavenged from Roman temples and dwellings, and a few of these fragments – used over and over again in succeeding centuries – can still be seen embedded in the walls of some of Venice's oldest structures. The great majority of the lagoon's buildings were still made of wood, however, and of these nothing is left.

From the twelfth century onwards the houses of the richest families were made from brick and stone, raised on foundations that rested on wooden piles hammered deep into the impacted clay and sand of the islands (a technique that has remained basically unchanged ever since). Prior to this period, such materials were reserved for the most important public buildings, and so it is that the **oldest structure in the lagoon** is a church – the **cathedral at Torcello**. Founded in 639 but altered in 864 and again, comprehensively, in **1008**, it takes its form from such early Christian basilicas as Sant'Apollinare in Ravenna. The prototypes of the Western Empire influenced other lagoon churches either founded or rebuilt in the eleventh and twelfth centuries – for example **Sant'Eufemia** on Giudecca, **Santi Maria e Donato** on Murano, and **San Giovanni Decollato** and **San Nicolò dei Mendicoli** in central Venice – but the predominant cultural influence on the emergent city was **Byzantium**, on which the lagoon confederation was originally dependent.

Santa Fosca on Torcello and **San Giovanni di Rialto**, traditionally the oldest church in Venice, are Byzantine in their adherence to a Greek-cross plan, but the building in which the Byzantine ancestry of Venice is most completely displayed is the **Basilica di San Marco**. Like the cathedral of Torcello, San Marco was extensively rebuilt in the eleventh century, but the basic layout – an elongated version of the five-domed Greek-cross design of Constantinople's Church of the Apostles – didn't change much between the consecration of the first Basilica in 832 and the completion of the final version in 1094. As much as its architectural form, the mosaic decoration of San Marco betrays the young city's Eastern affiliations – and it was in fact begun, as soon as the shell of the church was completed, by artists from Constantinople.

Byzantium has also left its mark on the **domestic architecture** of Venice, even though the oldest specimens still standing date from the late twelfth century or early thirteenth, by which time the political ties between the two cities had been severed. The high and rounded Byzantine arch can be seen in a number of Canal Grande palaces – the **Ca' da Mosto**, the **Donà** houses, the neighbouring **Palazzo Loredan** and **Palazzo Farsetti**, and the **Fondaco dei Turchi**. All of these buildings have been altered greatly over the years, but paradoxically it's the one that's been most drastically reconstructed – the Fondaco dei Turchi – which bears the closest resemblance to the earliest merchants' houses. Descended from the Roman villas of the mainland, they had an arcade at water level to permit the unloading of cargo, a long gallery on the upper storey, and lower towers at each end of the facade. Frequently they were embellished with relief panels (*paterae*) and insets of multicoloured marble – another Byzantine inheritance, and one that was to last, in modified form, for hundreds of years (for example in the predilection for heraldic devices on the fronts of houses).

Gothic Venice

Building land is scarce in Venice, and the consequent density of housing imposed certain restrictions on architectural inventiveness – ground plans had to make the fullest possible use of the available space (hence the rarity of internal courtyards and the uniformly flat facades) and elevations had to maximize the window areas, to make the most of the often limited natural light. Thus architectural evolution in the domestic buildings of Venice is to be observed not so much in the development of overall forms but rather in the mutations of surface detail, and in particular in the arches of the main facades. Nearly all the rich families of Venice derived their wealth from trade, and the predominant shipping lanes from Venice ran to the East – so it was inevitable that **Islamic features** would show through in Venetian architecture. As the thirteenth century progressed, the pure curve of the Byzantine arch first developed an upper peak and then grew into a type of ogival arch – as at the **Palazzo Falier** near Santi Apostoli, and the **Porta dei Fiori** on the north side of the Basilica. This Islamicized Byzantine shape was in turn influenced in the fourteenth century by contact with the Gothic style of the mainland, so producing a repertoire that was uniquely Venetian.

The masterpiece of Venetian Gothic is also the city's greatest civic structure – the **Palazzo Ducale**. Begun in 1340, possibly to designs by **Filippo Calendario**, the present building was extended in a second phase of work from 1423 onwards, culminating in the construction of the most elaborate Gothic edifice in Venice – the **Porta della Carta**, by **Giovanni and Bartolomeo Bon**.

Imitations and variations of the Palazzo Ducale's complex tracery can be seen all over the city, most strikingly in the **Ca' d'Oro**, begun by Giovanni Bon at much the same time as work began on the extension of the Palazzo Ducale. The Ca' d'Oro represents the apex of Gothic refinement in Venice's domestic architecture; for monumental grandeur, on the other hand, none can match the adjoining Gothic palaces on the Volta del Canal – the **Palazzi Giustinian** and the **Ca' Fóscari**.

Ecclesiastical architecture in fourteenth- and fifteenth-century Venice is not as idiosyncratic as its secular counterpart – the religious communities who built the churches, affiliated to orders on the mainland, tended to follow the architectural conventions that had been established by those orders. In some of Venice's Gothic churches the old basilical plan prevailed over the cruciform (eg at **Madonna dell'Orto**), but the two most important churches of the period, the immense **San Zanipolo** (Dominican) and the **Frari** (Franciscan), display many of the basic features of contemporaneous churches in the Veneto: the Latin-cross plan, the pointed arches, the high nave with flanking aisles, and the chapels leading off from the transepts. Yet even these churches have distinctively Venetian characteristics, such as the use of tie beams and the substitution of lath and plaster vaulting for vaults of stone – both necessary measures in a place with no bedrock for its foundations to rest on. In a few Gothic churches the builders capitalized on the availability of skilled naval carpenters to produce elegant and lightweight ceilings in the shape of an inverted **ship's keel** – for example at **Santo Stefano** and **San Giacomo dell'Orio**.

Early Renaissance

The complicated hybrid of Venetian Gothic remained the city's preferred style well into the second half of the fifteenth century, long after the classical precepts of Renaissance architecture had gained currency elsewhere in Italy. The late work of **Bartolomeo Bon** contains classical elements mixed with Gothic features (for example, the portal of **San Zanipolo** and the incomplete **Ca' del Duca**, both from c.1460), but the first architect in Venice to produce something that could be called a classical design was **Antonio Gambello**, with his land gate for the **Arsenale** (1460). Gambello was not a committed proponent of the new ideas, however, and had work on his church of **San Zaccaria** not been interrupted by his death in 1481, it would have resembled a northern European Gothic church more closely than any other in Venice.

In the 1470s another dynasty of stonemason-architects succeeded the Bon family as the leading builders in Venice – **Pietro Solari** and his sons **Antonio and Tullio**, otherwise known as the **Lombardi**. Having worked with followers of Donatello in Padua in the 1460s, Pietro Lombardo was familiar with the latest principles of Tuscan architecture, but the chief characteristics of his own work – the elaborately carved pilasters and friezes, and the inlaid marble panels of various shapes and sizes – are not so much architectonic as decorative. The chancel of **San Giobbe**, the courtyard screen of the **Scuola di San Giovanni Evangelista**, the tiny church of **Santa Maria dei Miracoli** and the facade of the **Scuola di San Marco** represent the best of the Lombardi's architecture. Over-ornate though many of their building projects were, their style was closely imitated by numerous Venetian architects; nobody is certain, for example, whether the **Palazzo Dario** (on the Canal Grande) was designed by Pietro Lombardo or one of his "Lombardesque" acolytes.

Antonio Rizzo, a contemporary of Pietro Lombardo, was similarly esteemed as both a sculptor and architect. After the fire of 1483, Rizzo was put in charge of the rebuilding of the entire **east wing of the Palazzo Ducale**, and it was he who designed the **Scala dei Giganti**, a work which displays a typically Venetian delight in heavy ornamentation.

Codussi and his successors

The most rigorous and inventive Venetian architect of the early Renaissance was the man who took over the design and supervision of San Zaccaria after the death of Gambello – **Mauro Codussi** (sometimes spelled Coducci). His first commission in the city, the church of **San Michele in Isola** (1469), is not purely classical – the huge lunette and inset roundels are Venetian idiosyncrasies – but its proportions and clarity, and the use of classical detail to emphasize the structure of the building, entitle it to be known as the **first Renaissance church in Venice**. Codussi reintroduced the traditional Greek-cross plan in his other church designs (**Santa Maria Formosa** and **San Giovanni Crisostomo**), his impetus coming in part from a scholarly revival of interest in the culture of Byzantium and in part from the work of Renaissance theorists such as Alberti, whose *De Re Aedificatoria* proclaimed the superiority of centrally planned temples. In his secular buildings the influence of Alberti is even more pronounced, especially in his **Palazzo Vendramin-Calergi**, which is strongly reminiscent of Alberti's Palazzo Rucellai in Florence. Codussi was employed by the Venetian nobility, the scuole (he designed staircases for both the **Scuola di San Giovanni Evangelista** and the **Scuola di San Marco**) and the religious foundations, yet despite his pre-eminence it was only after archival research in the nineteenth century that he was identified as the author of all these buildings – a fact indicative of the difference between the status of the architect in Renaissance Florence and in Venice.

The economic effects of the War of the League of Cambrai limited the amount of building work in Venice at the start of the sixteenth century, but it was nonetheless a period of rapid transformation in the centre of the city; the **Campanile** of San Marco was completed, and the **Torre dell'Orologio** and **Procuratie Vecchie** were built – the last two being commenced to designs by Codussi. In the aftermath of serious fires, major projects were undertaken in the Rialto district as well – notably the **Fabbriche Vecchie** and the **Fondaco dei Tedeschi** – but the architects of the generation after Codussi (who died in 1504) were generally undistinguished. **Guglielmo dei Grigi** designed the **Palazzo dei Camerlenghi** at the foot of the Ponte di Rialto and went on to add the **Cappella Emiliana** to Codussi's San Michele in Isola. **Bartolomeo Bon the Younger** took over the supervision of the Procuratie Vecchie after Codussi's death, and began the **Scuola di San Rocco** in 1515 – a project that was completed by **Scarpagnino** (Antonio Abbondi), the man in charge of the rebuilding of the Rialto markets after the fire of 1514. **Giorgio Spavento**, described by the diarist Marin Sanudo as "a man of great genius", was the most talented architect of this period, and with **San Salvatore** he produced its best church design. By joining together three Greek-cross plans, Spavento created a building which reconciled the long open nave required by modern liturgy with the traditional Byzantine centralized plan.

High Renaissance

The definitive classical authority for the architectural theorists of Renaissance Italy was **Vitruvius**, architect to the Emperor Augustus, and it was in Venice in 1511 that the first printed edition of his *De Architectura* was produced. However, the consistent application of classical models was not seen in Venice until after the sack of Rome by the Imperial army in 1527. A large number of Roman artists then sought refuge in Venice, and it was with this influx that the advances of such figures as Raphael, Michelangelo and Bramante were absorbed into the practice of Venice's architects.

Of all the exiles, the one who made the greatest impact was **Jacopo Sansovino**. Despite his limited architectural experience – he was known mainly as a sculptor when he arrived in Venice – Sansovino was appointed Proto of San Marco on the death of Bartolomeo Bon in 1529, a position that made him the most powerful architect in the city, and which he was to hold for the next forty years. From 1537 onwards a group of buildings by Sansovino went up around the Piazzetta, completely changing the appearance of the area; the **Zecca** (Mint) was the first, then the **Loggetta** at the base of the Campanile, and then the most celebrated of all his designs – the **Libreria Sansoviniana**. Showing a familiarity with the architecture of ancient Rome that was unprecedented in Venice, the Libreria is still unmistakeably Venetian in its wealth of surface detail, and the rest of Sansovino's buildings similarly effect a compromise between classical precision and Venetian convention. Thus his palace designs – the **Palazzo Dolfin-Manin** (1538) and **Palazzo Corner della Ca' Grande** (1545) – are clearly related to the houses of the Roman Renaissance, but perpetuate the traditional Venetian division of the facade into a central bay with symmetrically flanking windows. Though principally a secular architect, Sansovino did also design churches; the religious buildings by him that still stand are **San Francesco della Vigna**, **San Martino di Castello**, **San Giuliano** and the apse of **San Fantin**.

Of Sansovino's contemporaries, the only one of comparable stature was **Michele Sanmicheli**. More proficient as an engineer than Sansovino, he was employed early in his career by Pope Clement VII to improve the military defences of Parma and Piacenza, and in 1535 was taken on as Venice's military architect. The **Fortezza di Sant'Angelo** (1543), protecting the Lido entrance to the lagoon, was his largest public project, and in addition to this he built two of the most grandiose palaces in the city – the **Palazzo Corner Mocenigo** at San Polo (1545) and the **Palazzo Grimani** (c.1559) on the Canal Grande.

Andrea Palladio, Italy's most influential architect in the second half of the sixteenth century (indeed, one of the most influential architects of any epoch), was based in nearby Vicenza yet found it difficult to break into Venice's circle of patronage. In the 1550s his application for the position of Proto to the Salt Office (supervisor of public buildings) was turned down, and his project for the Palazzo Ducale's Scala d'Oro rejected; later schemes for the Ponte di Rialto and the rebuilding of the entire Palazzo Ducale were no more successful. He was never asked to undertake a private commission in the city. The facade of **San Pietro in Castello** was his first contract (eventually built in a much altered form), and it was the religious foundations that were to provide him with virtually all his subsequent work in Venice. Palladio's churches of **San Giorgio Maggiore** (1565) and the **Redentore** (1576) are the summit of Renaissance classicism in Venice; the scale on which they were composed, the restraint of their decoration, the stylistic unity of exterior and interior, the subtlety with which the successive spaces were combined, and the correctness of their quotations from the architecture of Imperial Rome – all these factors distinguished them from all previous designs and established them as reference points for later churches.

Once Palladio's churches had been finished, the islands of San Giorgio Maggiore and Giudecca presented much the same face to the main part of the city as they do today. The work of his closest follower, **Vincenzo Scamozzi**, brought the landscape of the Piazza very close to its present-day state – it was Scamozzi who completed the Campanile end of the Libreria Sansoviniana and began the construction of the **Procuratie Nuove** in 1582. Another Venetian landmark, the **Ponte di Rialto**, was built at this time; its creator, **Antonio da Ponte**, was also in charge of the repair and redesign of the Palazzo Ducale after the fire of 1577, and designed the new **prisons** on the opposite bank of the Rio di Palazzo. The bridge connecting the prisons to the Palazzo Ducale – the **Ponte dei Sospiri** (Bridge of Sighs) – was the work of **Antonio Contino** (1600).

Baroque

Although there are a few sixteenth-century Venetian buildings that could be described as proto-Baroque – **Alessandro Vittoria**'s **Palazzo Balbi** (1582), with its encrusted decoration and broken pediments, is one example – the classical idiom remained entrenched for some time as the stylistic orthodoxy in Venice, as is demonstrated by the appointment of the unadventurous **Bartolomeo Monopola** to complete the final stages of the **Palazzo Ducale** in the first decades of the seventeenth century. The colossal **Palazzo Pisani** at Santo Stefano, possibly by Monopola, is further evidence of the city's aesthetic conservatism.

It was not until the maturity of Venice's finest native architect, **Baldassare Longhena**, that the innovations of the Baroque made themselves fully felt. Longhena's early work – for example the **Palazzo Giustinian-Lolin** and the **Duomo** at **Chioggia** (both 1624) – continues the Palladianism of the previous century, but with his design for the votive church of **Santa Maria della Salute** (1631) he gave the city its first Baroque masterpiece. In its plan the Salute is indebted to Palladio's Redentore, but in its use of multiple vistas, and devices such as the huge volutes round the base of the dome, it introduces a dynamism that was completely alien to Palladio's architecture. In 1640 Longhena became the Proto of San Marco, and between then and his death in 1682 he occupied a position in Venetian architectural circles as commanding as Sansovino's had been. Among his major projects were the completion of the **Procuratie Nuove**, the addition of a grand staircase and library to the monastic complex of **San Giorgio Maggiore**, and the design of two of the Canal Grande's most spectacular palaces – the **Ca' Pésaro** and the **Ca' Rezzonico**.

When compared to much of the work being produced in other parts of Italy at this time, Longhena's brand of Baroque was quite sober. Yet it was the chief exception in his output – the grotesque facade of the **Ospedaletto** – which proved in the short term to be specially influential. Its most direct descendant was **Alessandro Tremignon**'s facade for the church of **San Moisè** (1668), which is choked with sculpture by Heinrich Meyring. **Giuseppe Sardi**'s church of **Santa Maria del Giglio** (1680) can also be traced back to the Ospedaletto, but on the other hand Sardi's work is equally redolent of the architecture of the sixteenth century – his facade for Scamozzi's **San Lazzaro dei Mendicanti** could be seen as a deliberate rejection of the excesses of the Baroque. His other prominent designs are the **Scuola di San Teodoro** and the facades of **San Salvatore** and **Santa Maria di Nazareth** (the Scalzi), all of them rather routine efforts.

The eighteenth century

The concerted reaction against Baroque began with the work of Sardi's nephew, **Domenico Rossi**. Rossi's facade for the church of **San Stae** (1709) is essentially a neo-Palladian design enlivened by the addition of some exuberant pieces of sculpture, and his rebuilding of the **Palazzo Corner della Regina** is closer to the palace projects of Sansovino than to such works as Longhena's nearby Ca' Pésaro. **Andrea Tirali**, Rossi's exact contemporary (1657–1737), was an even more faithful adherent to the principles of the sixteenth century – the portico he added to the church of **San Nicolò da Tolentino** is strictly classical, and his facade for **San Vitale** is a straight plagiarism of San Giorgio Maggiore. Another church of this period – **San Simeone Piccolo** – is one of the most conspicuous in Venice, standing as it does right opposite the train station. Designed in 1718 by **Giovanni Scalfarotto** (Rossi's son-in-law), its facade and plan are derived from the Pantheon, but the vertical exaggeration of its dome makes it closer in spirit to Longhena's Salute.

The most significant architect of the period was **Giorgio Massari** (1687–1766), whose church of the **Gesuati**, begun in 1726, combines Palladian forms (for example the facade and the arrangement of the interior bays) with understated Rococo details (the ceiling frames). His later church of the **Pietà**, based on Sansovino's destroyed Incurabili church, is more sober in its use of decoration, and his design for the last of the great palaces of the Canal Grande, the **Palazzo Grassi** (1748), is the severest of all his buildings.

The Palladian creed was kept alive in late eighteenth-century Venice through innumerable academic and polemical publications. Two of the leading figures in this movement were **Antonio Visentini** (1688–1782) and Scalfarotto's nephew, **Tommaso Temanza** (1705–89), both of whom taught architecture at the Accademia. Temanza was the more important architect, and his **Santa Maria Maddalena** was the first uncompromisingly Neoclassical building in Venice.

To the present

With the work of **Giannantonio Selva**, a pupil of Visentini and Temanza, Neoclassicism entered its most spare and fastidious phase. His first large scheme was **La Fenice** opera house (1790), where exterior adornment was reduced to the minimum necessary to signify the building's function and importance. Selva's career was undisturbed by the subsequent collapse of the Venetian Republic, and his other main works – the churches of **San Maurizio** (1806) and **Nome del Gesù** (1815) – were created under French rule.

During the second period of French occupation (1806–15) a large number of buildings were demolished to facilitate urban improvement schemes. Four churches were knocked down to make space for the **Giardini Pubblici**, for instance, and by the time the French were ejected by the Austrians a total of nearly fifty religious buildings had been demolished. The most celebrated loss was that of Sansovino's **San Geminiano**, pulled down in 1807 to make room for the construction of the **Ala Napoleonica**, a ballroom wing added to the Procuratie Nuove, which was then serving as a royal palace. In the 1830s the designer of the ballroom, **Lorenzo Santi**, went on to build the now-abandoned coffee house (**Palazzetto Bucintoro**) by the Giardinetti Reali, and the **Palazzo Patriarcale** alongside the Basilica.

Alterations to Venice's network of canals and streets, which had been started by the French with schemes such as the creation of **Via Garibaldi**, were accelerated under Austrian rule. Most of Venice's *rii terrà* (infilled canals) originated in the period of Austrian occupation, and a number of new bridges were constructed at this time too – including the ones at the **Accademia** and **Scalzi**, the first bridges to be put across the Canal Grande since the Ponte di Rialto. It was the Austrians who connected Venice by rail with the mainland (1846), and in 1860 they expanded the train station, demolishing Palladio's church of **Santa Lucia** in the process. And the first major **restoration projects** were carried out under Austrian supervision – at the **Fondaco dei Turchi**, at **Santi Maria e Donato** on **Murano**, and on the north facade of **San Marco**.

Major town-planning schemes continued after Venice joined the Unified Kingdom of Italy. In the 1870s two wide thoroughfares were completed – the **Strada Nova** in Cannaregio and **Calle Larga XXII Marzo** between San Moisè and Santa Maria Zobenigo – and **Campo Manin** was opened up in 1871. The brief industrialization of central Venice in the late nineteenth century has left behind one prominent hulk – the **Mulino Stucky**, built on Giudecca in 1895. The hotels and middle-class housing developments of the **Lido** – which became a fashionable resort in this period – have outlived the city's industrial sites.

In 1933 Venice was joined by road to the mainland, and five years later the Rio Nuovo was cut from the recently created Piazzale Roma towards the Canal Grande. The chief buildings of the Fascist era are the **fire station** on the Rio di Ca' Fóscari (which continues the Rio Nuovo), and the **Palazzo del Casinò** and **Palazzo del Cinema** on the Lido. Few buildings worth a mention have been put up in Venice since then – the least objectionable are, perhaps, the **train station** (1954) and the **Cassa di Risparmio di Venezia** in Campo Manin, designed in 1964 by **Pier Luigi Nervi** and **Angelo Scattolin**. The density and antiquity of most of Venice's urban fabric makes intervention particularly problematic for the modern architect. Understandable Venetian resistance to new developments, hardened by such insensitive twentieth-century efforts as the extension to the **Hotel Bauer-Grünwald**, adds further difficulties, and accounts for the fact that two of the most interesting modern schemes, **Frank Lloyd Wright**'s Ca' Masieri and **Le Corbusier**'s plan for a civic hospital in Cannaregio, never left the drawing board. Though small items are occasionally added to the assortment box of architectural styles that is the **Biennale** site, major new schemes will always be rare; of the two big building contracts awarded in the late 1990s, one is for the reconstruction of a destroyed structure (**La Fenice**), and the other is for a site that will have no living occupants – David Chipperfield's extension to the **San Michele cemetery**.

Conservation and restoration

In 1818 Byron published the fourth section of *Childe Harold's Pilgrimage*, in which is encapsulated the Romantic notion that if Venice isn't actually sinking, then it ought to be:

Venice, lost and won,
Her thirteen hundred years of freedom done
Sinks, like a sea-weed into whence she rose!

Ever since, it's been a commonplace that Venice is doomed to an aquatic extinction. The city is threatened by water, by salt, by air pollution and by local subsidence, and faces massive problems of conservation and restoration. Over the past quarter-century the Italian government has set aside the equivalent of thousands of millions of euros, under the terms of the so-called Special Laws for Venice, to underwrite projects ranging from schemes to restore single paintings or architectural details through to grandiose plans to control the industrialization of the mainland and the encroachments of the Adriatic. In addition to the intrinsic difficulties of each project, the major interventions prompt interminable arguments about the very purpose of restoration – should Venice be turned into even more of a museum piece, its buildings preserved in the aspic of contemporary restoration techniques, or should parts of the city be rebuilt, reintroducing industry and modern housing? On the one hand, Venice desperately needs the income from tourism, and on the other its population has fallen by almost two-thirds since World War II and its houses are in such a state that 40 percent of them don't have adequate bathrooms.

Flooding

On **November 4, 1966**, the waters of the Adriatic, already dangerously high after two successive high tides had been prevented from receding by gale-force southeasterly winds, were disturbed by an earth tremor. The resulting tidal wave breached Venice's *Murazzi* (the sea walls), and for the next 48 hours the sea level remained an average of almost 2m above mean high tide – in other words, more than 1m above the pavement of the Piazza, the lowest point of the city. Venice was left with no power or telephone lines, and buildings were awash with filthy water, mud and oil from broken storage tanks.

Outside Venice, the flooding did not immediately provoke extreme concern, partly because floods in Venice were nothing new (at the height of the crisis national radio simply announced "high water in the Piazza San Marco"), and partly because attention was focused on the same-day's disaster in Florence, where a flash flood killed several people and caused massive damage to numerous works of art. Nobody was hurt in the Venice flood and no artefacts were lost, but the photographs of water swirling through the doors of San Marco and around the courtyard of the Palazzo Ducale did highlight the perilous condition of the city. When floods almost as bad occurred in the following year, the international campaign to save Venice was already gathering strength, and similarly severe floods in 1979 and 1986 kept the situation in the public eye.

Called the **acqua alta** (high water), the winter flooding of the city is caused by a combination of seasonal tides, fluctuations in atmospheric pressure in the Adriatic and persistent southeasterly winds, and has always been a feature of Venetian life. With a surface area of some 550 square kilometres, the Venetian lagoon is the largest in Italy, and with an average depth of just 1.2m this large body of water is very sensitive to the vagaries of the climate. In recent years, however, its sensitivity has increased markedly. Between 1931 and 1945 there were just eight serious *acqua alte*; in the last decade of the twentieth century there were 44. By 2009 the number of annual floods had risen to 200 – most of them minor, but the statistic is nonetheless indicative of a relentless trend.

A rise in sea level has played a part in this, but the rise so far has been too small to account for the increase in the frequency and severity of flooding. At the ancient port of Aquileia, not far from Venice, the height of the Roman wharves relative to the water seems to indicate that there has been no substantial change in sea level since they were built, while excavations of building foundations in various parts of Venice indicate that the notion of a general subsidence is unfounded. Thus the worsening floods would seem to be largely a local phenomenon related to recent changes in the balance of the lagoon.

Certainly the workings of the lagoon have been interfered with in an unprecedented way during the twentieth century. The extraction of water and natural gas has caused some distortion of the underlying strata, and large areas of land have been reclaimed, both for industrial sites on the periphery of the lagoon and in central Venice itself – notably around the docks and the Tronchetto car parks. Nowadays only about 70 percent of the area that was under water in 1900 remains submerged. At the same time, channels have been deepened to allow huge industrial and commercial vessels to pass through the lagoon to the refineries of Marghera, and smaller motor boats within the city also churn up the sea bed and cause erosion. Consequently the speed and the depth of the tides have been affected.

The barrier

That said, few would argue against the proposition that shifts in global weather conditions are making more of an impact with each passing year, and it's clear that global warming will be a significant factor in Venice's predicament in the coming decades. Most experts predict that the mean sea level will rise and the climate become more turbulent in this part of the Mediterranean, and it's this likelihood that led to the idea of installing a **tidal barrier** across the three entrances to the lagoon. This concept began to take shape in 1982, as a proposal from a committee of government-appointed engineers, but it wasn't until November 1988 that the first component of the prototype was towed into place close to the Porto di Lido. Nicknamed **Moisè** (Moses) after the Old Testament's great divider of the waters (and because MOSE was an approximate acronym for "Modulo Sperimentale Elettromecanico", the prototype's full title), it was assembled by the Consorzio Venezia Nuova, a consortium of engineering companies. Many years later, after input from the creators of London's Thames Barrier, Moisè reached its definitive form. It was to comprise 79,300-tonne steel flaps, which would lie on the floor of the lagoon, forming a submerged barrage some 2km long in total; when the water rose to a dangerous level, air would be pumped into the flaps and the barrier would then float upright to protect the city.

Predictably enough, the relationship between the government and the consortium soon ran into difficulties. The official auditors criticized the Consorzio Venezia Nuova for taking a cut of up to 25 percent from contractors, and for ignoring technical criticisms of the barrier's design "for reasons of political opportunism". The original deadline for the completion of Moisè was 1995; come the deadline, there was little more to show than a forlorn segment of the barrier anchored off the Arsenale. In 1998 the project was stalled by political wrangling, a development that pleased many conservationists, many of whom had always maintained that the abandonment of the barrier would be more beneficial to Venice than its completion. Some objectors argued that in the event of a sudden tidal surge the barrier would simply not be strong enough to resist the push of the water. Others maintained that the barrier is an over-elaborate scheme designed principally to make money for the constructors, or that the foundations of the barrier will be impossible to build as planned (with some 20,000 pilings being driven 30m into the ground) because of irregularities in the lagoon bed. Italia Nostra, Italy's national heritage group, insisted that the alteration of the shipping channels and the cessation of land reclamation would be cheaper and more effective responses to the situation, to which proponents of the barrier replied that these non-mechanical interventions wouldn't offer protection against the effects of global warming. To this last point, opponents of the barrier responded that some climatologists are projecting a rise in the level of the Mediterranean by as much as 30cm within the next century; if that turns out to be correct, the barrier won't be able to cope and the outlets of the lagoon will instead be clogged by a hugely expensive and unremovable mass of steel and concrete.

While Consorzio Venezia Nuova continued to proclaim the virtues of Moisè, a host of less extravagant projects made progress all over the lagoon. Embankments and pavements are being rebuilt and raised at numerous flood-prone points (most conspicuously around the Palazzo Ducale), the jetties at the Lido, Malamocco and Chioggia inlets have been strengthened, and tracts of land reclaimed for industrial use but never built on have been allowed to flood again. The largest of these schemes involves the reinforcement of the 60km of the lagoon's outer coastline; the beaches at Jesolo, Cavallino, the Lido, Pellestrina, Sottomarina and Isola Verde have been extended within a grid of stone groynes and artifical reefs, thereby dissipating the energy of the waves, while the sand dunes at Cavallino have been planted with marram grass, which binds the sand and thus makes the dunes a more effective windbreak. As for the problem of tanker traffic, it's intended that the dilapidated Marghera refineries will be further scaled down as a consequence of extending the Genoa–Cremona oil pipeline to Mantua (at the moment Mantua's oil comes from Marghera). The remaining tankers will be diverted to less damaging routes across the lagoon, or even be banned from the lagoon entirely. The petrochemical companies, however, aren't too keen on the idea. In the summer of 1998 the Italian press was in a state of high excitement when a secret chemical waste dump was discovered on the edge of the lagoon; the creators of the toxic reservoir, Enichem, offered to clear up the mess they'd made, on condition they were allowed to carry on their operations at Marghera – a response that didn't win many friends.

At the end of 2000 the stabilization of the lagoon became a more urgent problem than ever. On **November 6**, as freakish rainfall continued over much of Western Europe and whole regions of Italy were classified as disaster areas,

Venice was inundated by the worst *acqua alta* since 1966. Two weeks later the *acqua alta* surged again to more than 120cm above the mean high tide level, covering more than a third of the city's pavements. This was the fifth time the tide had passed the 110cm mark that winter. The warnings could not be clearer, and the Italian parliament duly took notice. In **April 2003**, more than twenty years after the first plan for Moisè was submitted to the government, Silvio Berlusconi attended a ceremony in Venice to mark the **start of work on the construction of the barrier**. Scheduled for completion in 2012, the barrier is planned to cost some €4.5 billion, with operational costs of around €10 million per year – and it's these costs that might still prove to be the undoing of the scheme. No sooner had Berlusconi been narrowly defeated in the **2006 general election** than the incoming centre-left government of Romano Prodi conducted an audit of every major infrastructure project in the country, and found that Moisè had massive budget shortfall. Nonetheless, though some people argued that attention must now be turned to the various more economical and less mechanistic lagoon-management schemes that have been propounded by opponents of the barrier, the Prodi government agreed that abandoning Moisè would be tantamount to signing the city's death warrant, and in **November 2006** it re-approved the project. Progress has been excruciatingly slow so far; meanwhile, on December 1, 2008, the lagoon rose to 156cm above mean level, causing the fourth-worst flooding since the 1870s.

Water pollution

A major objection to the barrier has been that it will further inhibit the cleansing effects of the tides, already diminished in parts of the lagoon by the creation of firm land out of mudflats. Twice-daily tidal movements and the activity of waste-digesting marine life were enough until fairly recently to keep the water relatively fresh – fresh enough, until the 1980s, for fastidious Venetians to swim in certain deep spots at high tides.

Much of the **pollution** is the fault of the industrial complexes of Mestre-Marghera, which, though in decline, have dumped thousands of tons of zinc, copper, iron, lead and chrome into the lagoon, creating a toxic sludge so dangerous that nobody has yet devised a safe way of dredging the stuff out. Chemical fertilizers seeping into the water from the mainland add to the accumulation of phosphates in the water, a situation exacerbated by the heavy use of phosphate-rich detergents in Venetian homes. (Although Venice treats its sewage in sumps before emptying it into the sea, all household sinks and baths drain straight into the canals.) Plants, fishes and other forms of marine life are being suffocated by algae that thrive on these phosphates, forming a foul-smelling scum that is thickened by the rotting animal and vegetable matter.

When photographs of gondoliers and tourists in face masks brought adverse publicity abroad, it was finally acknowledged that a crisis had been reached, and in 1988 the Ministry of the Environment earmarked £175 million to clean up the lagoon. Moreover, the town hall has now banned the sale of phosphate-enriched detergents – Venice's boat-restorers will be pleased about this too; their work had steadily diminished as the bottoms of boats remained relatively unencumbered by weeds.

In order to restore the equilibrium of the lagoon's ecosystem, salt marshes and fish farms are being reconstructed at various places in the lagoon, wetlands are being created on the periphery and waste disposal sites are being consolidated (there are seventeen such dumps in the lagoon). But local action such as this will still not be enough. Venice's lagoon is threatened by the grossly polluted water of the whole upper Adriatic, into which the Po and numerous other waterways disgorge their effluents. In 1989 the Italian government assigned a sum of £500 million to the cleansing of the Adriatic, but the complexity of the problem is terrifying. It has even been proposed that the techniques used to purify sewage may be actually contributing to the proliferation of the algae by feeding them with vitamin-saturated fluids. In the 1950s and 1960s Lake Erie was threatened with the same sort of marine disaster as now faces the Venice region; regulations imposed in the 1970s seem to have rescued the lake. As yet, no comparable action has been taken to cleanse the Po.

Air pollution

The other environmental problem facing Venice is that of **air pollution**, which worsened in phase with the growing industrial complexes on the mainland. Sulphur dioxide combines with the salty and humid air of the lagoon to make a particularly vicious corrosive which eats at brick, stone and bronze alike. An experiment carried out in the 1970s showed that stone covered with pigeon droppings stayed in better condition than stone exposed to the Venetian air. The conversion of domestic heating systems from oil to gas has helped to cut down the amount of sulphur dioxide in the atmosphere, and expenditure on industrial filtration has had an effect too, but Marghera's factories still pump around 50,000 tons of the gas into the atmosphere each year. Some observers point out that the prevailing winds carry the fumes from the Marghera stacks inland, but even though the bulk of the emissions are someone else's problem, the ambient air of Venice was one of the factors the Italian trades union congress had in mind when they christened the city "the capital of pollution".

In the years immediately after the 1966 flood, as Venice attracted ever more attention from outside the country, the city authorities were often criticized for their tardiness in commissioning restoration work on Venice's crumbling stonework. Their cautiousness was to an extent vindicated when it became apparent that the restoration work on Sansovino's Loggetta – initially hailed as an unqualified success – had in fact done as much damage as it had repaired. The resins used to protect the restored marble have now begun to discolour the building, and it may prove impossible to sluice the resins out. A major restoration of the Miracoli church turned out to be similarly ill-advised, with salt eating at the walls from inside and excreting white crusts onto the marble cladding. The cleaning and strengthening of the Porta della Carta was undertaken with far greater circumspection, and so far it seems that all is well; the lessons learned on that project are being employed on the continuous restoration of the Basilica di San Marco and the Palazzo Ducale.

Subsidence

The industries at Marghera used to threaten Venice from below as well as from above. Drawing millions of gallons of water directly from the ground, they caused a dramatic fall in the water table and threatened to cause the subsidence of the entire city. Calamity was averted in 1973, when the

Restoration in Venice is principally a collaborative venture between UNESCO and the city's Superintendancies of Art and of Monuments. The former coordinates the fund raising and restoration proposals from the multitude of aid groups set up in various countries after the 1966 floods; the latter pair oversee the restoration centres in Venice, the cataloguing of endangered buildings and objects, and the deployment of restoration teams.

The first top-to-toe makeover for a Venetian building was that of Madonna dell'Orto, undertaken by the British Italian Art and Archives Rescue Fund, which was transformed in 1971 into **Venice in Peril**. More than thirty groups worldwide are now devoted to the rescue of Venice, all of them open to offers of financial help. If you want to make a donation to ViP, contact them at Venice in Peril, Unit 4, Hurlingham Studios, Ranelagh Gardens, London SW6 3PA (☎020 7736 6891, ⓦwww.veniceinperil.org). In the US, the main aid organization is **Save Venice Inc**, 15 East 74th St, New York, NY 10021 (☎212/737-3141, ⓦwww.savevenice.org).

national government built two aqueducts to pipe water from inland rivers to the refineries and factories of Marghera and the houses of Venice. In 1975 the artesian wells at Marghera were sealed, and by the late 1990s there was evidence that this measure had resulted in a rise of 2cm in the land level of some parts of the historic centre.

Local subsidence will continue to be a problem, though. The majority of buildings in Venice are built on wooden pilings driven deep into the mudbanks of the lagoon. Interference with the lagoon's equilibrium has resulted in an increase in the number of extremely low tides as well as the number of floods, and occasionally the water falls so far that air gets at the pilings, causing them to decay. Furthermore, those people unable to afford proper wood-piled foundations would have used rubbish and rubble instead, which slowly compresses through the years. Another crucial factor is the erosive effect of the city's water-buses; a study in the 1990s showed that the foundations of sixty percent of the buildings on the Canal Grande had been damaged by the wash from the vaporetti, and the situation along the Rio Novo (which was created expressly as a shortcut for the water-buses) has become so bad that it has now been closed to vaporetti. To make matters worse, the Marghera-bound tankers and giant cruise ships that pass close to the *centro storico* create eddies that spread right into the heart of the city – any gondolier can tell you that he can feel the turbulence long after the mega-ship has passed by.

Projects to consolidate the houses and churches of Venice against erosion by the water will never cease to be necessary, and recently a new potential source of subsidence has emerged: AGIP have been probing for gas about 20km offshore of Chioggia, and there is considerable concern that full-scale exploitation of any gas reserves in this part of the Mediterranean will disturb the sea bed, with very unpleasant consequences for Chioggia and possibly even for central Venice.

Books

A comprehensive Venetian reading list would run on for dozens of pages, and would include a vast number of out-of-print titles. Most of our recommendations are in print, and those that aren't shouldn't be too difficult to track down through online booksellers such as Abebooks. Books marked with 🏃 are particularly recommended.

Fiction

🏃 **Italo Calvino** *Invisible Cities*. Characteristically subtle variations on the idea of the City, presented in the form of tales told by Marco Polo to Kublai Khan. No explicit reference to Venice until well past halfway, when Polo remarks – "Every time I describe a city I am saying something about Venice."

Michael Dibdin *Dead Lagoon*. Superior detective story starring Venice-born Aurelio Zen, a cop entangled in the political maze of 1990s Italy. Zen is the protagonist of many fine books by Dibdin; in this one, he leaves Rome for his Venice to trace a wealthy businessman who has disappeared.

E.T.A. Hoffmann *Doge and Dogaressa*. Fanciful reconstruction of events surrounding the treason of Marin Falier, by one of the pivotal figures of German Romanticism. Lots of passion and pathos, narrated at headlong pace. It's included in *Tales of Hoffmann*, published by Penguin.

🏃 **Henry James** *The Aspern Papers* and *The Wings of the Dove*. The first, a 100-page tale about a biographer's manipulative attempts to get at the personal papers of a deceased writer, is one of James's most tautly constructed longer stories. The latter, one of the three vast and circumspect late novels, was likened to caviar by Ezra Pound, and is likely to put you off James for life if you come to it

without acclimatizing yourself with the earlier stuff.

Donna Leon *Acqua Alta*. Liberally laced with an insider's observations on daily life in Venice, this is perhaps the most atmospheric of Leon's long sequence of highly competent Venice-set detective novels.

Michelle Lovric *The Floating Book*. A German printer of erotic poetry gets entangled with an adulterous Venetian hussy in this rip-roaring and intricately plotted historical novel, which evokes the atmosphere of the fifteenth-century city with a plethora of richly imagined local detail. Lovric has written two other similarly well-researched Venice-set novels: *Carnevale* and *The Remedy*.

🏃 **Thomas Mann** *Death in Venice*. Profound study of the demands of art and the claims of the flesh, with the city itself thematically significant rather than a mere exotic backdrop. Richer than most stories five times its length and infinitely more complex than Visconti's sentimentalizing film.

🏃 **Marcel Proust** *Albertine Disparue*. The Venetian interlude, occurring in the penultimate novel of Proust's massive novel sequence, can be sampled in isolation for its acute dissection of the sensory experience of the city – but to get the most from it, you've got to knuckle down and commit yourself to the preceding ten volumes of *À la Recherche*. The best English translation is D.J. Enright's revision of the pioneering Kilmartin/Scott-Moncrieff version, published in six paperback volumes.

Frederick Rolfe (Baron Corvo) *The Desire and Pursuit of the Whole*. A transparent exercise in self-justification, much of it taken up with venomous ridicule of the English community in Venice, among whom Rolfe moved while writing the book in 1909. (Its libellous streak kept it unpublished for 25 years.) Snobbish and incoherent, redeemed by hilarious character assassinations and gorgeous descriptive passages.

Arthur Schnitzler *Casanova's Return to Venice*. Something of a Schnitzler revival followed the release of Kubrick's *Eyes Wide Shut*, which was adapted from a novella by this contemporary and compatriot of Freud. This similarly short and intense book also explores the dynamics of desire, but from the perspective of a desperate man who is rapidly approaching the end of his life.

Michel Tournier *Gemini*. Venice is just one of the localities through which the identical twins Jean and Paul (known to their parents as Jean-Paul) are taken in this amazingly inventive exploration of the concept of twinship. It might be flashy in places, yet Tournier throws away more ideas in the course of a novel than most writers dream up in a lifetime.

Salley Vickers *Miss Garnet's Angel*. A life-weary spinster (a Marxist as well, to make matters worse) is reawakened by Venice and falls in love for the first time – an extremely hackneyed scenario, but Vickers has a sound knowledge of the city and its art, and displays a light touch in her re-creation of the place.

Jeanette Winterson *The Passion*. Whimsical tale of the intertwined lives of a member of Napoleon's catering corps and a female gondolier. Acclaimed as a masterpiece in some quarters.

Art and architecture

🏃 **James S. Ackerman** *Palladio*. Concise introduction to the life, works and cultural background of the Veneto's greatest architect. Especially useful if you're visiting Vicenza or any of the villas.

🏃 **Svetlana Alpers and Michael Baxandall** *Tiepolo and the Pictorial Intelligence*. This brilliant book analyzes with exhilarating precision the way in which Tiepolo perceived and re-created the world in his paintings, and demolishes the notion that Tiepolo was merely a "decorative" artist. Though they devote most space to the frescoes at Würzburg, Alpers and Baxandall discuss many of the Tiepolo paintings in Venice and the Veneto, and their revelatory readings will enrich any encounter with his art. The reproductions maintain Yale's customary high standards.

Patricia Fortini Brown *Venetian Narrative Painting in the Age of Carpaccio*. Rigorously researched study of a subject central to Venetian culture yet often overlooked in more general accounts. Fresh reactions to the works discussed are combined with a penetrating analysis of the ways they reflect the ideals of the Republic at the time. Worth every penny.

🏃 **Richard Goy** *Venice: The City and its Architecture*. Published in 1997, this superb book instantly became the benchmark. Eschewing the linear narrative adopted by previous writers on the city's architecture, Goy goes for a multi-angled approach, devoting one part to the growth of the city and its evolving technologies, another to its "nuclei" (the Piazza, Arsenale, Ghetto and Rialto), and the last to its building types (palazzi, churches, etc). The result is a book that does full justice to the richness and density of the Venetian cityscape – and the design and choice of pictures are exemplary.

Deborah Howard *The Architectural History of Venice; Jacopo Sansovino: Architecture and Patronage in Renaissance Venice; Venice and the East.* The first of these books is a classic introduction to the subject (and has recently been elegantly repackaged by Yale), while the latter's analysis of the world within which Sansovino operated is of wider interest than you might think. Howard's latest book, *Venice and the East*, is a fascinating and characteristically rigorous examination of the ways in which the fabric of the city was conditioned by the close contact between Venice's merchants and the Islamic world in the period 1100–1500. It's a truism that San Marco and the Palazzo Ducale are hybrids of Western and Islamic styles, but this splendidly illustrated study not only has illuminating things to say about those two great monuments – it makes you look freshly at the texture of the whole city.

Peter Humfrey *Lorenzo Lotto.* Assiduously researched, clearly written and beautifully illustrated, Peter Humfrey's monograph is the only comprehensive English-language study of this intense and fascinating painter, who has been too often overshadowed by illustrious contemporaries such as Titian.

Peter Humfrey *Painting in Renaissance Venice.* Spanning

the period from the middle of the fifteenth century to the end of the sixteenth (Jacopo Bellini to Tintoretto, in other words), this is the best concise overview of the subject – lay readers should start here before going on to David Rosand's more exhaustive book (see below).

Michael Levey *Painting in Eighteenth-Century Venice.* On its appearance in 1959 this book was the first detailed discussion of its subject. Now in its third edition, it's still the most thorough exposition of the art of Venice's last golden age, though it shows its age in its concentration on heroic personalities – Giambattista Tiepolo in particular.

Tom Nichols *Tintoretto: Tradition and Identity.* Ever since Vasari wrote his life of the artist, Tintoretto has been presented as an artist who flouted all the conventions of Venetian painting. This in-depth study overturns that somewhat romanticized notion, to reveal a figure who was both a radical and a populist. By far the best monograph on Tintoretto in English.

Filippo Pedrocco and M.A. Chiara Moretto Wiel *Titian – The Complete Paintings.* The text is worthy rather than stimulating (there's a lot of discussion of technique, but little social context), but every surviving picture in Titian's colossal oeuvre is reproduced in colour, and the interpretations of individual paintings are as sound as you'd expect from two of the world's leading experts on the subject.

Terisio Pignatti and Filippo Pedrocco *Giorgione.* Expensive monograph on the most enigmatic of the great Venetian painters. Not especially acute in its observations, but very thorough, very nicely produced, and better than the other in-print titles devoted to Giorgione.

David Rosand *Painting in Sixteenth-Century Venice.* Covers the century of Giorgione, Titian, Tintoretto and Veronese as thoroughly as most readers will want; especially good on the social networks and artistic conventions within which the painters created their work.

🏃 **John Ruskin** *The Stones of Venice*. Enchanting, enlightening and infuriating in about equal measure, this is still the most stimulating book written about Venice by a non-Venetian. Elibron have issued a two-volume facsimile of the 1900 edition; if half a million words of Ruskin is too much for you, go for the abridged one-volume version published by Pallas Athene.

John Steer *Venetian Painting: A Concise History*. Whistle-stop tour of Venetian art from the fourteenth to the eighteenth century. Skimpy and undemanding, but a useful aid to sorting your thoughts out after the visual deluge of Venice's churches and museums, and the plentiful pictures come in handy when your memory needs a prod.

Anchise Tempestini *Giovanni Bellini*. Hugely knowledgeable overview of the work of the first great Venetian Renaissance artist, with copious full-colour plates.

History and society

Patricia Fortini Brown *Venice and Antiquity*. This fascinating book explores a subject that strangely no one has tackled in depth before – the ways in which an imperialist city with no pre-Christian past went about classicizing its pedigree. Drawing on a vast range of cultural artefacts, from the great monuments to private manuscripts and medals, Brown adds a new dimension to the history of Venice between the thirteenth and the sixteenth centuries, the city's Golden Age. It's not easy-going but the effort is worthwhile, and superlative pictures go some way to leaven the text.

Christopher Hibbert *Venice, The Biography of a City*. The usual highly proficient Hibbert synthesis of a vast range of secondary material. Very good on the changing social fabric of the city, with more on twentieth-century Venice than most others. Excellent illustrations too – but, bafflingly, it's currently out of print on both sides of the Atlantic.

🏃 **Jonathan Keates** *The Siege of Venice*. The depth of Keates's

research is evident on every page of this study of the Venetian uprising of 1848–49; it's a thorough-going piece of historical reconstruction and a thrilling and emotionally engaging narrative, which will have you sharing the author's manifest admiration for its protagonists.

Frederic C. Lane *Venice, A Maritime Republic*. The most authoritative one-volume socio-economic history of the city in English, based on decades of research. Excellent on the infrastructure of the city, and on the changing texture of everyday life. A rather more arduous read than John Julius Norwich's populist history (see below), which is presumably why it's slipped out of print.

Mary Laven *Virgins of Venice*. Subtitled "Enclosed Lives and Broken Vows in the Renaissance Convent", Laven's book concentrates on life in Venice's convents during a period when restrictions on the city's nuns were being made even more severe by Counter-Reformation legislation. While it's hardly surprising to learn that many nuns were profoundly unhappy and had no religious vocation, or that sexual misdemeanours were not uncommon, Laven has unearthed some fascinating, often poignant and sometimes hilarious accounts of life behind the walls.

🏃 **John Julius Norwich** *A History of Venice*. Although it's far more reliant on secondary sources than Lane, and nowhere near as compendious (you won't learn much, for example, about Venice's finances, which is a major omission in a history of the quintessential mercantile city), this book is unbeatable for its grand narrative sweep.

🏃 **Margaret Plant** *Venice: Fragile City*. Most histories of Venice tend to give the impression that there's little to say about the two hundred years since the fall of the Republic. This survey, concentrating on post-1797 Venice, comprehensively fills the void, encompassing not just the changes in the city's appearance during that time, but also its economic, political and cultural life, and the responses of the legion of writers, artists and filmmakers who have been inspired (or in some instances, repelled) by the place.

Dennis Romano *The Likeness of Venice: A Life of Doge Francesco Foscari*. This very thorough biography does much more than tell the tumultuous life-story of one of the most celebrated and powerful doges: it's a deeply researched exploration of the ways in which the political and artistic worlds were intertwined in fifteenth-century Venice, a city-republic in which the preservation and projection of its self-image was of paramount importance.

🏃 **Mark Thompson** *The White War*. Italy's role in World War I – when its armies pushed out of the Veneto into what is now the northeastern corner of the country – is just a sideshow in many non-Italian histories of the conflict, and is often badly misrepresented within Italy. Thompson's book is more than a magisterial account of the catastrophes and triumphs of the campaigns – it's a brilliant explication of the part the war has played in the formation of the nation's self-identity.

A Venetian miscellany

🏃 **Paolo Barbaro** *Venice Revealed*. The title is exactly right – if any book can be said to reveal the reality of present-day Venice, this is it. Written by a native Venetian, following his return after an absence of two decades, it's an evocative portrait of an ailing but endlessly stimulating city, written from deep affection. An essential corrective to the gauzy mythologizing that blights too many books on Venice.

🏃 **Giacomo Casanova** *History of My Life*. For pace, candour and wit, the insatiable seducer's autobiography ranks with the journals of James Boswell, a contemporary of similar sexual and literary stamina. The twelve-volume sequence (here handsomely repackaged into six paperbacks) takes him right across Europe, from Madrid to Moscow. His Venetian escapades are covered in volumes two and three of Willard Trask's magnificent translation.

Régis Debray *Against Venice*. The modern-day cult of Venice is an easy target, so it's to be expected that Régis Debray – sometime comrade of Che Guevara and adviser to

François Mitterrand – should score a few hits in the course of this seventy-page polemic. It's a provocative counterblast to the verbiage of so much writing on Venice, but many of Debray's insights are less acute than he seems to think they are, and his attack is marred by posturing that's just as self-satisfied as the aesthetes he despises.

Henry James *Italian Hours*. Urbane travel pieces from the young Henry James, including five essays on Venice. Perceptive observations on the paintings and architecture of the city, but mainly of interest in its evocation of the tone of Venice in the 1860s and 70s.

John Keahey *Venice Against the Sea*. A fast-paced and well-researched study of the threat posed by the rising waters of the Adriatic, and the various measures that have been proposed for dealing with it. Good on both the physics and the politics of preservation, Keahey takes the story up to the Italian parliament's decision, in December 2001, to proceed with the tidal barrier.

🏃 **Giulio Lorenzetti** *Venice and its Lagoon*. The most thorough cultural guide ever written to any European city – Lorenzetti seems to have researched the history of every building, canvas and alley. Though unmanageable as a workaday guidebook (it gives more than fifty pages to the Palazzo Ducale, for example, and even has an index of indexes), it's indispensable for all those besotted with the place. Almost impossible to find outside Venice, but every bookshop in the city sells it.

Michelle Lovric *Venice: Tales of the City*. There have been many miscellanies of writings on the subject of Venice, but Lovric – who lives in Venice and knows the city intimately – has unearthed some fascinating pieces that have eluded other anthologists.

🏃 **Predrag Matvejevic** *The Other Venice*. Barely mentioning any of the major sights, Matvejevic illuminates the city from a variety of unusual angles, in a sequence of elegant little essays on such topics as the flora and fauna of the lagoon, the trades of Venice, and the idiosyncracies of its language.

Mary McCarthy *Venice Observed*. Originally written for the *New Yorker*, McCarthy's clear-eyed and brisk report is a refreshing antidote to the gushing enthusiasm of most first-hand accounts from foreigners in Venice. The Penguin edition combines it with her equally entertaining *The Stones of Florence*.

James Morris *Venice*. Some people acclaim this as the most brilliant book ever written about Venice; to others it's intolerably fey and self-regarding. But if you can't stomach the style, Morris's knowledge of Venice's folklore provides ample compensation.

Stefan Zweig *Casanova: A Study in Self-Portraiture*. A fascinating study of Casanova's life and autobiography, offering a persuasive analysis that differs strikingly from the clichéd image of Casanova as a real-life Don Juan – in fact, Zweig presents him as the very antithesis of Don Juan the misogynistic seducer. Though brief, this is the best book on its subject.

Language

Language

Italian

Although it's not uncommon for the staff of Venetian hotels and restaurants to speak some English, you'll make a lot more friends by attempting the vernacular. Outside the city, you might be able to get by in English at tourist offices, but in the depths of the Veneto you shouldn't expect to encounter fluency in English.

Some tips

You'd do well to master at least a little **Italian**, a task made more enjoyable by the fact that your halting efforts will often be rewarded by smiles and genuine surprise that an English-speaker should make an attempt to learn Italian. In any case, it's one of the easiest European languages to learn, especially if you already have a smattering of French or Spanish, both extremely similar grammatically.

Easiest of all is the **pronunciation**, since every word is spoken exactly as it's written, and usually enunciated with exaggerated, open-mouthed clarity. The only difficulties you're likely to encounter are the few **consonants** that are different from English:

c before **e** or **i** is pronounced as in **ch**urch, while **ch** before the same vowels is hard, as in **c**at.
sci or **sce** are pronounced as in **sh**eet and **sh**elter respectively.
g is soft before **e** and **i**, as in **g**eranium; hard when followed by **h**, as in **g**arlic.
gn has the ni sound of our "o**ni**on".
gl in Italian is softened to something like li in English, as in stal**li**on.
h is not aspirated, as in **h**onour.

When **speaking** to strangers, the third person is the polite form (ie Lei instead of Tu for "you"); using the second person is a mark of disrespect or stupidity. Also remember that Italians don't use "please" and "thank you" half as much as we do; it's all implied in the tone, though if you're in any doubt, err on the polite side.

All Italian words are **stressed** on the penultimate syllable unless an **accent** (´ or `) denotes otherwise, although written accents are often left out in practice. Note that the ending –**ia** or –**ie** counts as two syllables, hence trattoria is stressed on the **i**. We've put accents on names throughout the text wherever it isn't immediately obvious how a word should be pronounced: for example, in Maríttima, the accent is on the first **i**; similarly the stress in Pésaro is not on the **a**, where you'd expect it, but on the **e**. We've omitted accents on some of the more common exceptions (like Isola, stressed on the I), some names (Domenico), and words that are stressed similarly in English, such as archeologico and Repubblica.

The **Venetian dialect** virtually qualifies as a separate language, with its own rules of spelling and grammar, and distinctive pronunciation. However, you'll probably encounter it only in the form of the words given in the Glossary, in dialect proper names (see box, p.9) or the occasional shop sign – eg Venexiana rather than Veneziana.

Phrasebooks and dictionaries

The best phrasebook is *Italian: Rough Guide Phrasebook*, which has a huge but accessible vocabulary in dictionary format, a grammar section, a detailed menu reader and useful scenarios. These scenarios can also be downloaded free as audio files from Ⓦ www.roughguides.com. As for dictionaries, Collins publish a comprehensive series; their Gem or Pocket dictionaries are fine for travelling purposes, while their Concise is adequate for most language needs.

Words and phrases

Basics

Good morning	Buongiorno	Tomorrow	Domani
Good afternoon/ evening	Buonasera	Day after tomorrow	Dopodomani
		Yesterday	Ieri
Good night	Buonanotte	Now	Adesso
Hello/goodbye	Ciao (informal; to strangers use phrases above)	Later	Più tardi
		Wait a minute!	Aspetta!
		In the morning	Di mattina
Goodbye	Arrivederci	In the afternoon	Nel pomeriggio
Yes	Sì	In the evening	Di sera
No	No	Here/there	Qui/là
Please	Per favore	Good/bad	Buono/cattivo
Thank you (very much)	Grázie (molte/ mille grazie)	Big/small	Grande/píccolo
		Cheap/expensive	Economico/caro
You're welcome	Prego	Early/late	Presto/tardi
Alright/that's OK	Va bene	Hot/cold	Caldo/freddo
How are you?	Come stai/sta? (informal/formal)	Near/far	Vicino/lontano
		Vacant/occupied	Libero/occupato
I'm fine	Bene	Quickly/slowly	Velocemente/ lentamente
Do you speak English?	Parla inglese?		
		Slowly/quietly	Piano
I don't understand	Non ho capito	With/without	Con/senza
I don't know	Non lo so	More/less	Più/meno
Excuse me	Mi scusi	Enough, no more	Basta
Excuse me (in a crowd)	Permesso	The bill/check	Il conto
		Mr...	Signor...
I'm sorry	Mi dispiace	Mrs...	Signora...
I'm here on holiday	Sono qui in vacanza	Miss...	Signorina... (il signor, la Signora, la Signorina when speaking about someone else)
I'm English/Scottish/	Sono inglese/ Scozzese/		
American/Irish/ Welsh/Australian	Americano/irlandese/ gallese/australiano		
I live in...	Abito a...		
Today	Oggi		

Numbers

1	uno	20	venti
2	due	21	ventuno
3	tre	22	ventidue
4	quattro	30	trenta
5	cinque	40	quaranta
6	sei	50	cinquanta
7	sette	60	sessanta
8	otto	70	settanta
9	nove	80	ottanta
10	dieci	90	novanta
11	undici	100	cento
12	dodici	101	centuno
13	tredici	110	centodieci
14	quattordici	200	duecento
15	quindici	500	cinquecento
16	sedici	1000	mille
17	diciassette	5000	cinquemila
18	diciotto	10,000	diecimila
19	diciannove	50,000	cinquantamila

Some signs

Entrance/exit	Entrata/Uscita	To let	Affítasi
Free entrance	Ingresso libero	Platform	Binario
Gentlemen/ladies	Signori/Signore	Cash desk	Cassa
WC/bathroom	Gabinetto/Bagno	Go/walk	Avanti
Vacant/engaged	Libero/Occupato	Stop/halt	Alt
Open/closed	Aperto/Chiuso	Customs	Dogana
Arrivals/departures	Arrivi/Partenze	Do not touch	Non toccare
Closed for restoration	Chiuso per restauro	Danger	Perícolo
Closed for holidays	Chiuso per ferie	Beware	Attenzione
Pull/push	Tirare/Spingere	First aid	Pronto soccorso
Out of order	Guasto	Ring the bell	Suonare il campanello
Drinking water	Acqua potabile	No smoking	Vietato fumare

Driving

Left/right	Sinistro/Destro	No entry	Senso vietato
Go straight ahead	Sempre diritto	Slow down	Rallentare
Turn to the right/left	Gira a destra/sinistra	Road closed/up	Strada chiusa/guasta
Parking	Parcheggio	No through road	Vietato il transito
No parking	Divieto di sosta/ Sosta vietata	No overtaking	Vietato il sorpasso
		Crossroads	Incrocio
One way street	Senso único	Speed limit	Limite di velocità

Travelling

Aeroplane	Aeroplano
Bus	Autobus/pullman
Train	Treno
Car	Macchina
Taxi	Taxi
Bicycle	Bicicletta
Ferry	Traghetto
Ship	Nave
Hydrofoil	Aliscafo
Hitch hiking	Autostop
On foot	A piedi
Bus station	Autostazione
Train station	Stazione ferroviaria
Ferry terminal	Stazione maríttima
Port	Porto
A ticket to…	Un biglietto a…
One-way/return	Solo andata/ andata e ritorno
Can I book a seat?	Posso prenotare un posto?
What time does it leave?	A che ora parte?
When is the next bus/ train/ferry to…?	Quando parte il prossimo pullman /treno/traghetto per…?
Do I have to change?	Devo cambiare?
Where does it leave from?	Da dove parte?
What platform does it leave from?	Da quale binario parte?
How many kilometres is it?	Quanti chilometri sono?
How long does it take?	Quanto ci vuole?
What number bus is it to…?	Che numero di autobus per…?
Where's the road to…?	Dovè la strada per…?
Next stop please	La prossima fermata, per favore

Accommodation

Hotel	Albergo
Is there a hotel nearby?	C'è un albergo qui vicino?
Do you have a room… for one/two/three people	Ha una cámera… per una/due/tre person(a/e)
for one/two/three nights	per una/due/tre notte/i
for one/two weeks	per una/due setti-man(a/e)
with a double bed	con un letto matrimoniale
with a shower/bath	con una doccia/ un bagno
with a balcony	con balcone
hot/cold water	acqua calda/fredda
How much is it?	Quanto costa?
It's expensive	È caro
Is breakfast included?	È compresa la prima colazione?
Do you have anything cheaper?	Ha qualcosa che costa di meno?
Full/half board	Pensione completa/ mezza pensione
Can I see the room?	Posso vedere la camera?
I'll take it	La prendo
I'd like to book a room	Vorrei prenotare una camera
I have a booking	Ho una prenotazione
Can we camp here?	Possiamo campeg-giare qui?
Is there a campsite nearby?	C'è un camping qui vicino?
Tent	Tenda
Cabin	Cabina
Youth hostel	Ostello per la gioventù

In the restaurant

A table	Una tavola	A spoon	Un cucchiaio
I'd like to book a table for two people at eight o'clock	Vorrei prenotare una tavola per due alle quattro	A glass	Un bicchiere
		What do you recommend?	Che cosa mi consiglia lei?
		Waiter/waitress!	Cameriere/a!
We need a knife	Abbiamo bisogno di un coltello	Bill/check	Il conto
		Is service included?	È incluso il servizio?
A fork	Una forchetta	I'm a vegetarian	Sono vegetariano/a

Menu glossary

Questions and directions

Where? (where is/are…?)	Dove? (Dov'è/Dove sono)	Can you tell me when to get off?	Mi può dire dove scendere alla fermata giusta?
When?	Quando?		
What? (what is it?)	Cosa? (Cos'è?)	What time does it open?	A che ora apre?
How much/many?	Quanto/Quanti?		
Why?	Perché?	What time does it close?	A che ora chiude?
It is/there is (is it/is there…?)	È/C'è (È/C'è…?)	How much does it cost (… do they cost?)	Quanto costa? (Quanto costano?)
What time is it?	Che ore sono?		
How do I get to…?	Per arrivare a…?		
How far is it to…?	Quant'è lontano a…?	What's it called in Italian?	Come si chiama in Italiano?
Can you give me a lift to…?	Mi può dare un passaggio a…?		

Menu glossary

This glossary should allow you to decode most menus; it concludes with a summary of Venetian specialities – for more detail on Venetian food and drink, see p.243.

Basics and snacks

Aceto	Vinegar	Gelato	Ice cream
Aglio	Garlic	Grissini	Bread sticks
Biscotti	Biscuits	Marmellata	Jam
Burro	Butter	Olio	Oil
Caramelle	Sweets	Olive	Olives
Cioccolato	Chocolate	Pane	Bread
Focaccia	Oven-baked snack	Pane integrale	Wholemeal bread
Formaggio	Cheese	Panino	Bread roll
Frittata	Omelette	Patatine	Crisps

413

Patatine fritte	Chips	Tramezzini	Sandwich
Pepe	Pepper	Uova	Eggs
Pizzetta	Small cheese and tomato pizza	Yogurt	Yoghurt
		Zucchero	Sugar
Riso	Rice	Zuppa	Soup
Sale	Salt		

Starters (antipasti)

Antipasto misto	Mixed cold meats and cheese (and a selection of other things in this list)	Melanzane in parmigiana	Fried aubergine in tomato and parmesan cheese
		Mortadella	Salami-type cured meat
Caponata	Mixed aubergine, olives, tomatoes and celery	Pancetta	Bacon
		Peperonata	Grilled green, red or yellow peppers stewed in olive oil
Caprese	Tomato and mozzarella salad	Pomodori ripieni	Stuffed tomatoes
Insalata di mare	Seafood salad	Prosciutto	Ham
Insalata di riso	Rice salad	Salame	Salami

Pizzas

Biancaneve	"Black and white": mozzarella and oregano	Frutti di mare	Seafood, usually mussels, prawns, squid and clams
Calzone	Folded pizza with cheese, ham and tomato	Margherita	Cheese and tomato
		Marinara	Tomato and garlic
Capricciosa	Literally "capricious": topped with whatever they've got in the kitchen, usually including baby artichoke, ham and egg	Napoli/Napoletana	Tomato, anchovy and olive oil (and sometimes mozzarella)
		Quattro formaggi	"Four cheeses", usually including mozzarella, fontina, gorgonzola and gruyère
Diavolo	Spicy, with hot salami or Italian sausage	Quattro stagioni	"Four seasons": the toppings split into four sections, usually including ham, peppers, onion, mushrooms, artichokes, olives and egg
Funghi	Mushroom; tinned, sliced button mushrooms unless it specifies fresh mushrooms, either funghi freschi or porcini		
		Romana	Anchovy and olives

The first course (il primo)

Soups

Brodo	Clear broth
Minestrina	Any light soup
Minestrone	Thick vegetable soup
Pasta e fagioli	Pasta soup with beans
Pastina in brodo	Pasta pieces in clear broth
Stracciatella	Broth with egg

Pasta

Cannelloni	Large tubes of pasta, stuffed
Farfalle	Literally "bow"-shaped pasta; the word also means "butterflies"
Fettuccine	Narrow pasta ribbons
Gnocchi	Small potato and dough dumplings
Lasagne	Lasagna
Maccheroni	Tubular spaghetti
Pasta al forno	Pasta baked with minced meat, eggs, tomato and cheese
Penne	Smaller version of rigatoni
Ravioli	Small packets of stuffed pasta
Rigatoni	Large, grooved tubular pasta
Risotto	Cooked rice dish, with sauce
Spaghetti	Spaghetti
Spaghettini	Thin spaghetti
Tagliatelle	Pasta ribbons, another word for fettucine
Tortellini	Small rings of pasta, stuffed with meat or cheese
Vermicelli	Very thin spaghetti (literally "little worms")

Pasta sauces

Aglio e olio (e peperoncino)	Tossed in garlic and olive oil (and hot chillies)
Arrabbiata	Spicy tomato sauce
Bolognese	Meat sauce
Burro e salvia	Butter and sage
Carbonara	Cream, ham and beaten egg
Frutta di mare	Seafood
Funghi	Mushroom
Matriciana	Cubed pork and tomato sauce
Panna	Cream
Parmigiano	Parmesan cheese
Pesto	Ground basil, pine nut, garlic and pecorino sauce
Pomodoro	Tomato sauce
Ragù	Meat sauce
Vongole	Clam and tomato sauce

The second course (il secondo)

Meat (carne)

Agnello	Lamb
Bistecca	Steak
Cervello	Brains
Cinghiale	Wild boar
Coniglio	Rabbit
Costolette	Chops
Cotolette	Cutlets
Fegatini	Chicken livers
Fegato	Liver
Involtini	Steak slices, rolled and stuffed
Lingua	Tongue
Maiale	Pork
Manzo	Beef
Ossobuco	Shin of veal
Pollo	Chicken

Polpette	Meatballs (or minced balls of anything)	Cozze	Mussels
Rognoni	Kidneys	Dentice	Dentex (like sea bass)
Salsiccia	Sausage	Gamberetti	Shrimps
Saltimbocca	Veal with ham	Gamberi	Prawns
Spezzatino	Stew	Granchio	Crab
Tacchino	Turkey	Merluzzo	Cod
Trippa	Tripe	Moleche	Soft-shelled crabs
Vitello	Veal	Nasello	Hake
		Orata	Bream

Fish (pesce) and shellfish (crostacei)

		Ostriche	Oysters
		Pescespada	Swordfish
		Pólipo	Octopus
Acciughe	Anchovies	Ricci di mare	Sea urchins
Anguilla	Eel	Rombo	Turbot
Aragosta	Lobster	San Pietro	John Dory
Baccalà	Dried salted cod	Sarde	Sardines
Bronzino/Branzino	Sea bass	Schie	Shrimps
Calamari	Squid	Seppie	Cuttlefish
Caparossoli	Type of clam	Sogliola	Sole
Cape lungue	Razor clams	Tonno	Tuna
Cape sante	Scallops	Triglie	Red mullet
Cicala di mare/ Cannocchia	Mantis shrimp	Trota	Trout
		Vongole	Clams
Coda di rospo	Monkfish		

Vegetables (contorni) and salad (insalata)

Asparagi	Asparagus	Funghi	Mushrooms
Basílico	Basil	Insalata verde/ insalata mista	Green salad/ mixed salad
Bróccoli	Broccoli		
Cápperi	Capers	Melanzana	Aubergine/eggplant
Carciofi	Artichokes	Orígano	Oregano
Carciofini	Artichoke hearts	Patate	Potatoes
Carotte	Carrots	Peperoni	Peppers
Cavolfiori	Cauliflower	Piselli	Peas
Cavolo	Cabbage	Pomodori	Tomatoes
Ceci	Chickpeas	Radicchio	Chicory
Cetriolo	Cucumber	Rucola	Rocket
Cipolla	Onion	Spinaci	Spinach
Fagioli	Beans	Zucca	Pumpkin
Fagiolini	Green beans	Zucchini	Courgettes
Finocchio	Fennel		

Desserts (dolci), cheeses (formaggi), fruit (frutta) and nuts (noce)

Desserts

Amaretti	Macaroons
Cassata	Ice-cream cake with candied fruit
Gelato	Ice cream
Macedonia	Fruit salad
Torta	Cake, tart
Zabaglione	Dessert made with eggs, sugar and Marsala wine
Zuppa Inglese	Trifle

Cheese

Caciocavallo	A type of dried, mature mozzarella cheese
Fontina	Northern Italian cheese used in cooking
Gorgonzola	Soft blue-veined cheese
Mozzarella	Bland soft white cheese used on pizzas
Parmigiano	Parmesan cheese
Pecorino	Strong-tasting hard sheep's cheese
Provolone	Hard strong cheese
Ricotta	Soft white cheese made from ewe's milk, used in sweet or savoury dishes

Fruit and nuts

Ananas	Pineapple
Anguria/Coccómero	Watermelon
Arance	Oranges
Banane	Bananas
Ciliegie	Cherries
Fichi	Figs
Fichi d'India	Prickly pears
Frágole	Strawberries
Limone	Lemon
Mándorle	Almonds
Mele	Apples
Melone	Melon
Pere	Pears
Pesche	Peaches
Pignoli	Pine nuts
Pistacchio	Pistachio nut
Uva	Grapes

Cooking terms

Affumicato	Smoked
Al dente	Firm, not overcooked
Al ferro	Grilled without oil
Al forno	Baked
Al Marsala	Cooked with Marsala wine
Al vapore	Steamed
Alla brace	Barbecued
Alla griglia	Grilled
Allo spiedo	On the spit
Arrosto	Roasted
Ben cotto	Well done
Bollito	Boiled
Brasato	Cooked in wine
Cotto	Cooked (not raw)
Crudo	Raw
Fritto	Fried
Grattugiato	Grated
In úmido	Stewed
Lesso	Boiled
Milanese	Fried in egg and breadcrumbs
Pizzaiola	Cooked with tomato sauce
Ripieno	Stuffed
Sangue	Rare
Surgelato	Frozen

Drinks

Acqua minerale	Mineral water
Aranciata	Orangeade
Bicchiere	Glass
Birra	Beer
Bottiglia	Bottle
Caffè	Coffee
Cioccolata calda	Hot chocolate
Ghiaccio	Ice
Granita	Iced coffee or fruit drink
Latte	Milk
Limonata	Lemonade
Selz	Soda water
Spremuta	Fresh fruit juice
Spumante	Sparkling wine
Succo	Concentrated fruit juice with sugar
Tè	Tea
Tónico	Tonic water
Vino	Wine
Rosso	Red
Bianco	White
Rosato	Rosé
Secco	Dry
Dolce	Sweet
Litro	Litre
Mezzo	Half
Quarto	Quarter
Salute!	Cheers!

Venetian specialities

Antipasti e Primi

Acciughe marinate	Marinated anchovies with onions
Bigoli in salsa	Spaghetti with butter, onions and sardines
Brodetto	Mixed fish soup, often with tomatoes and garlic
Castraura	Artichoke hearts
Granseola alla Veneziana	Crab cooked with oil, parsley and lemon
Pasta e fasioi	Pasta and beans
Prosciutto San Daniele	The best-quality prosciutto
Risotto alla sbirraglia	Risotto with chicken, vegetables and ham
Risotto alla trevigiana	Risotto with butter, onions and chicory
Risotto di cape	Risotto with clams and shellfish
Risotto di mare	Mixed seafood risotto
Sopa de peoci	Mussel soup with garlic and parsley

Secondi

Anguilla alla Veneziana	Eel cooked with lemon and tuna
Baccalà mantecato	Salt cod simmered in milk
Fegato veneziana	Sliced calf liver cooked in olive oil with onion
Peoci salati	Mussels with parsley and garlic
Risi e bisi	Rice and peas, with parmesan and ham
Sarde in saor	Marinated sardines
Seppie in nero	Squid cooked in its ink
Seppioline nere	Baby cuttlefish cooked in its ink

Dolci

Frittole alla Veneziana	Rum- and anise-flavoured fritters filled with pine nuts, raisins and candied fruit
Tiramisù	Dessert of layered chocolate and cream, flavoured with rum and coffee

Travel store

ROUGH GUIDES

World Coverage

Travel

Andorra The Pyrenees, Pyrenees & Andorra Map, Spain
Antigua The Caribbean
Argentina Argentina, Argentina Map, Buenos Aires, South America on a Budget
Aruba The Caribbean
Australia Australia, Australia Map, East Coast Australia, Melbourne, Sydney, Tasmania
Austria Austria, Europe on a Budget, Vienna
Bahamas The Bahamas, The Caribbean
Barbados Barbados DIR, The Caribbean
Belgium Belgium & Luxembourg, Bruges DIR, Brussels, Brussels Map, Europe on a Budget
Belize Belize, Central America on a Budget, Guatemala & Belize Map
Benin West Africa
Bolivia Bolivia, South America on a Budget
Brazil Brazil, Rio, South America on a Budget
British Virgin Islands The Caribbean
Brunei Malaysia, Singapore & Brunei [1 title], Southeast Asia on a Budget
Bulgaria Bulgaria, Europe on a Budget
Burkina Faso West Africa
Cambodia Cambodia, Southeast Asia on a Budget, Vietnam, Laos & Cambodia Map [1 Map]
Cameroon West Africa
Canada Canada, Pacific Northwest, Toronto, Toronto Map, Vancouver
Cape Verde West Africa
Cayman Islands The Caribbean
Chile Chile, Chile Map, South America on a Budget
China Beijing, China,

Hong Kong & Macau, Hong Kong & Macau DIR, Shanghai
Colombia South America on a Budget
Costa Rica Central America on a Budget, Costa Rica, Costa Rica & Panama Map
Croatia Croatia, Croatia Map, Europe on a Budget
Cuba Cuba, Cuba Map, The Caribbean, Havana
Cyprus Cyprus, Cyprus Map
Czech Republic The Czech Republic, Czech & Slovak Republics, Europe on a Budget, Prague, Prague DIR, Prague Map
Denmark Copenhagen, Denmark, Europe on a Budget, Scandinavia
Dominica The Caribbean
Dominican Republic Dominican Republic, The Caribbean
Ecuador Ecuador, South America on a Budget
Egypt Egypt, Egypt Map
El Salvador Central America on a Budget
England Britain, Camping in Britain, Devon & Cornwall, Dorset, Hampshire and The Isle of Wight [1 title], England, Europe on a Budget, The Lake District, London, London DIR, London Map, London Mini Guide, Walks In London & Southeast England
Estonia The Baltic States, Europe on a Budget
Fiji Fiji
Finland Europe on a Budget, Finland, Scandinavia
France Brittany & Normandy, Corsica, Corsica Map, The Dordogne & the Lot, Europe on a Budget, France, France Map, Languedoc & Roussillon, The Loire, Paris, Paris DIR,

Paris Map, Paris Mini Guide, Provence & the Côte d'Azur, The Pyrenees, Pyrenees & Andorra Map
French Guiana South America on a Budget
Gambia The Gambia, West Africa
Germany Berlin, Berlin Map, Europe on a Budget, Germany, Germany Map
Ghana West Africa
Gibraltar Spain
Greece Athens Map, Crete, Crete Map, Europe on a Budget, Greece, Greece Map, Greek Islands, Ionian Islands
Guadeloupe The Caribbean
Guatemala Central America on a Budget, Guatemala, Guatemala & Belize Map
Guinea West Africa
Guinea-Bissau West Africa
Guyana South America on a Budget
Holland see The Netherlands
Honduras Central America on a Budget
Hungary Budapest, Europe on a Budget, Hungary
Iceland Iceland, Iceland Map
India Goa, India, India Map, Kerala, Rajasthan, Delhi & Agra [1 title], South India, South India Map
Indonesia Bali & Lombok, Southeast Asia on a Budget
Ireland Dublin DIR, Dublin Map, Europe on a Budget, Ireland, Ireland Map
Israel Jerusalem
Italy Europe on a Budget, Florence DIR, Florence & Siena Map, Florence & the best of Tuscany, Italy, The Italian Lakes, Naples & the Amalfi Coast, Rome, Rome DIR, Rome Map, Sardinia, Sicily, Sicily Map, Tuscany & Umbria, Tuscany Map,

Venice, Venice DIR, Venice Map
Jamaica Jamaica, The Caribbean
Japan Japan, Tokyo
Jordan Jordan
Kenya Kenya, Kenya Map
Korea Korea
Laos Laos, Southeast Asia on a Budget, Vietnam, Laos & Cambodia Map [1 Map]
Latvia The Baltic States, Europe on a Budget
Lithuania The Baltic States, Europe on a Budget
Luxembourg Belgium & Luxembourg, Europe on a Budget
Malaysia Malaysia Map, Malaysia, Singapore & Brunei [1 title], Southeast Asia on a Budget
Mali West Africa
Malta Malta & Gozo DIR
Martinique The Caribbean
Mauritania West Africa
Mexico Baja California, Baja California, Cancún & Cozumel DIR, Mexico, Mexico Map, Yucatán, Yucatán Peninsula Map
Monaco France, Provence & the Côte d'Azur
Montenegro Montenegro
Morocco Europe on a Budget, Marrakesh DIR, Marrakesh Map, Morocco, Morocco Map,
Nepal Nepal
Netherlands Amsterdam, Amsterdam DIR, Amsterdam Map, Europe on a Budget, The Netherlands
Netherlands Antilles The Caribbean
New Zealand New Zealand, New Zealand Map

DIR: Rough Guide **DIRECTIONS** for short breaks

Available from all good bookstores

For more information go to www.roughguides.com

So now we've told you about the things not to miss, the best places to stay, the top restaurants, the liveliest bars and the most spectacular sights, it only seems fair to tell you about the best travel insurance around

WorldNomads.com
keep travelling safely

Recommended by Rough Guides

www.roughguides.com

Information on over 25,000 destinations around the world

- **Read** Rough Guides' trusted travel info

- **Access** exclusive articles from Rough Guides authors

- **Update** yourself on new books, maps, CDs and other products

- **Enter** our competitions and win travel prizes

- **Share** ideas, journals, photos & travel advice with other users

- **Earn** points every time you contribute to the Rough Guide
  community and get rewards

BROADEN YOUR HORIZONS

Small print and

Index

A Rough Guide to Rough Guides

Published in 1982, the first Rough Guide – to Greece – was a student scheme that became a publishing phenomenon. Mark Ellingham, a recent graduate in English from Bristol University, had been travelling in Greece the previous summer and couldn't find the right guidebook. With a small group of friends he wrote his own guide, combining a highly contemporary, journalistic style with a thoroughly practical approach to travellers' needs.

The immediate success of the book spawned a series that rapidly covered dozens of destinations. And, in addition to impecunious backpackers, Rough Guides soon acquired a much broader and older readership that relished the guides' wit and inquisitiveness as much as their enthusiastic, critical approach and value-for-money ethos.

These days, Rough Guides include recommendations from shoestring to luxury and cover more than 200 destinations around the globe, including almost every country in the Americas and Europe, more than half of Africa and most of Asia and Australasia. Our ever-growing team of authors and photographers is spread all over the world, particularly in Europe, the US and Australia.

In the early 1990s, Rough Guides branched out of travel, with the publication of Rough Guides to World Music, Classical Music and the Internet. All three have become benchmark titles in their fields, spearheading the publication of a wide range of books under the Rough Guide name.

Including the travel series, Rough Guides now number more than 350 titles, covering: phrasebooks, waterproof maps, music guides from Opera to Heavy Metal, reference works as diverse as Conspiracy Theories and Shakespeare, and popular culture books from iPods to Poker. Rough Guides also produce a series of more than 120 World Music CDs in partnership with World Music Network.

Visit www.roughguides.com to see our latest publications.

Rough Guide travel images are available for commercial licensing at www.roughguidespictures.com

SMALL PRINT

www.roughguides.com

Rough Guide credits

Text editor: Helena Smith
Layout: Ajay Verma
Cartography: Alakananda Roy
Picture editor: Mark Thomas
Production: Rebecca Short
Proofreader: Diane Margolis
Photographers: James McConnachie, Martin Richardson & Neil Setchfield
Editorial: Ruth Blackmore, Andy Turner, Keith Drew, Edward Aves, Alice Park, Lucy White, Jo Kirby, James Smart, Natasha Foges, Róisín Cameron, Emma Traynor, Emma Gibbs, Kathryn Lane, Monica Woods, Mani Ramaswamy, Harry Wilson, Lucy Cowie, Amanda Howard, Lara Kavanagh, Alison Roberts, Joe Staines, Peter Buckley, Matthew Milton, Tracy Hopkins, Ruth Tidball; **Delhi** Madhavi Singh, Karen D'Souza, Lubna Shaheen
Design & Pictures: **London** Scott Stickland, Dan May, Diana Jarvis, Nicole Newman, Sarah Cummins, Emily Taylor; **Delhi** Umesh Aggarwal, Jessica Subramanian, Ankur Guha, Pradeep Thapliyal, Sachin Tanwar, Anita Singh, Nikhil Agarwal, Sachin Gupta
Production: Vicky Baldwin

Cartography: **London** Maxine Repath, Ed Wright, Katie Lloyd-Jones; **Delhi** Rajesh Chhibber, Ashutosh Bharti, Rajesh Mishra, Animesh Pathak, Jasbir Sandhu, Karobi Gogoi, Swati Handoo, Deshpal Dabas
Online: **London** George Atwell, Faye Hellon, Jeanette Angell, Fergus Day, Justine Bright, Clare Bryson, Aine Fearon, Adrian Low, Ezgi Celebi, Amber Bloomfield; **Delhi** Amit Verma, Rahul Kumar, Narender Kumar, Ravi Yadav, Debojit Borah, Rakesh Kumar, Ganesh Sharma, Shisir Basumatari
Marketing & Publicity: **London** Liz Statham, Niki Hanmer, Louise Maher, Jess Carter, Vanessa Godden, Vivienne Watton, Anna Paynton, Rachel Sprackett, Laura Vipond, Vanessa McDonald; **New York** Katy Ball, Judi Powers, Nancy Lambert; **Delhi** Ragini Govind
Manager India: Punita Singh
Reference Director: Andrew Lockett
Operations Manager: Helen Atkinson
PA to Publishing Director: Nicola Henderson
Publishing Director: Martin Dunford
Commercial Manager: Gino Magnotta
Managing Director: John Duhigg

Publishing information

This eighth edition published February 2010 by
Rough Guides Ltd,
80 Strand, London WC2R 0RL
14 Local Shopping Centre, Panchsheel Park, New Delhi 110017, India
Distributed by the Penguin Group
Penguin Books Ltd,
80 Strand, London WC2R 0RL
Penguin Group (USA)
375 Hudson Street, NY 10014, USA
Penguin Group (Australia)
250 Camberwell Road, Camberwell, Victoria 3124, Australia
Penguin Group (Canada)
195 Harry Walker Parkway N, Newmarket, ON, L3Y 7B3 Canada
Penguin Group (NZ)
67 Apollo Drive, Mairangi Bay, Auckland 1310, New Zealand
Cover concept by Peter Dyer.

Typeset in Bembo and Helvetica to an original design by Henry Iles.
Printed in Singapore
© Jonathan Buckley, 2010
Maps © Rough Guides
No part of this book may be reproduced in any form without permission from the publisher except for the quotation of brief passages in reviews.
440pp includes index
A catalogue record for this book is available from the British Library
ISBN: 978-1-84836-432-5
The publishers and authors have done their best to ensure the accuracy and currency of all the information in **The Rough Guide to Venice**, however, they can accept no responsibility for any loss, injury, or inconvenience sustained by any traveller as a result of information or advice contained in the guide.

1 3 5 7 9 8 6 4 2

Help us update

We've gone to a lot of effort to ensure that the eighth edition of **The Rough Guide to Venice** is accurate and up-to-date. However, things change – places get "discovered", opening hours are notoriously fickle, restaurants and rooms raise prices or lower standards. If you feel we've got it wrong or left something out, we'd like to know, and if you can remember the address, the price, the hours, the phone number, so much the better.

Please send your comments with the subject line "**Rough Guide Venice Update**" to ⓔ mail @roughguides.com. We'll credit all contributions and send a copy of the next edition (or any other Rough Guide if you prefer) for the very best emails.

Have your questions answered and tell others about your trip at ⓦ www.roughguides.com

Acknowledgements

Charles would like to thank Martina Fassa and her colleagues at the Vicenza Tourist Board, Peter and Jean Hoare, Luisa Chelotti, Anna Mazzotti, Cristina Gibellato, Sarah Chambers, Maria Teresa and Leonardo, Caroline, and of course my colleague Jonathan.

SMALL PRINT

Readers' letters

Thanks to all the readers who have taken the time to write in with comments and suggestions (and apologies if we've inadvertently omitted or misspelt anyone's name):

Anita @ Theme Park Productions Inc, Ms L Baker, Hylton Boothroyd, Elise Bruhl, Margaret Chapman, Robert Clements, Reg Crowfoot, Joost den Butter, Julia & Phil Douëtil, Martin Farebrother, Jane Farmer, Alison Frank, Anna Heussaff, Richard Lamey, Mrs M-L Lillywhite, Elizabeth S. Makrauer, Ian Martin, Al Milnes, Jean Piercey, Mrs KM Rebeiro, Anthony Rowland, John Tanburn, Carina and Bjorn Thijs-Gommers, Martin Thomas, Yoma Ullman, Emily Van Evera.

Photo credits

All photography by Michelle Grant, James McConnachie and Martin Richardson © Rough Guides except the following:

Title page
Gondola on the Canal Grande © Mark Thomas

Full page
Piazza San Marco at dawn © Mark Thomas
Acqua alta © Sarah Quill

TNTM
07 Possagno museum © Hemis/Alamy
09 Basilica di Sant'Antonio, Padua © David Angel/Alamy
13 St Jerome in his study, Vittore Carpaccio/Art Archive/Corbis
14 Regata storica © JTB Communicatins/Alamy
15 Young gentleman in his studio, Lorenzo Lotto © Mauro Magliani/Corbis
17 Regata Storica © JTB Communicatins/Alamy

Festivals colour section
Venice Carnevale © Getty Images
Dog in carnival costume © Bruno Morandi/Getty Images
Vogalonga © Roberto Soncin Gerometta/Alamy
Rowing boat during the Vogalonga © Emme Pi Europe/Alamy
Fireworks during Festa del Redentore © Cubo Images/Alamy
Bridge and Redentore church © Andy Smith/Alamy

Regata Storica © Robert Harding/Alamy
Detail of boat in the Regata Storica © Alan Evans/Alamy

Venetian palaces colour section
Palaces on the Canal Grande © Andrea Pistolesi/Getty Images
Ca' Rezzonico © Bildarchiv Monheim GmbH/Alamy
Floodlit palaces at dusk, Canal Grande © Darrell Gulin/Getty Images
Detail of Ca' da Mosto © Andy Marshall/Alamy

Black and whites
p.190 Santiago Calatrava bridge © CuboImages/Alamy
p.264 La Fenice © Fan Travelstock/Alamy
p.298 Prato della Valle, Padua © Arco Images/Alamy
p.312 Teatro Olimpico, Vicenza © Stock Italia/Alamy
p.332 San Zeno Maggiore, Verona © Tim Wright/Alamy
p.348 Ponte degli Alpini, Bassano © Stock Italia/Alamy
p.356 Villa Barbaro, Masèr © Tim Wright/Alamy

Index

Map entries are in colour.

M

N

O

P

Map symbols

maps are listed in the full index using coloured text

- – – – Chapter boundary
- Motorway
- Road
- Steps
- – ▪ – Railway
- – – Ferry route
- - - - - Canal route
- Waterway
- Wall
- ⊠—⊠ Gate
- Bridge
- Mountain range

- ▲ Mountain peak
- ⓘ Tourist office
- ⊠ Post office
- ✈ Airport
- ✗ Airstrip
- ☀ Lighthouse
- Building
- ⊞ Church
- Park
- Beach
- Cemetery
- Jewish Cemetery

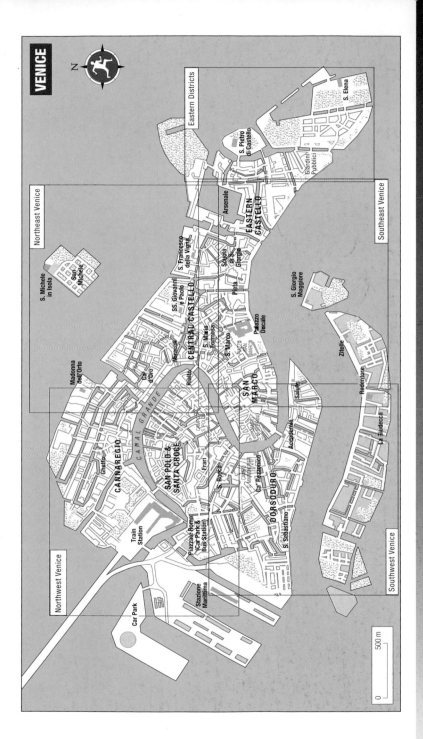

VENICE

N

500 m
0

Northwest Venice

Northeast Venice

Eastern Districts

Southwest Venice

Southeast Venice

S. Michele in Isola

San Michele

Madonna dell'Orto

CANNAREGIO

Ghetto

Ca' d'Oro

Rialto

Mercati

SAN POLO & SANTA CROCE

Frari

S. Rocco

Car Park

Train Station

Piazzale Roma (Car Park & Bus Station)

Stazione Marittima

DORSODURO

S. Sebastiano

Ca' Rezzonico

Accademia

Salute

SAN MARCO

Piazza S. Marco

S. Maria Formosa

SS. Giovanni e Paolo

CENTRAL CASTELLO

S. Francesco della Vigna

S. Marco

Pietà

Scuola di S. Giorgio

EASTERN CASTELLO

Palazzo Ducale

Arsenale

S. Pietro di Castello

Giardini Pubblici

S. Elena

S. Giorgio Maggiore

Zitelle

Redentore

La Giudecca

C A N A L   G R A N D E

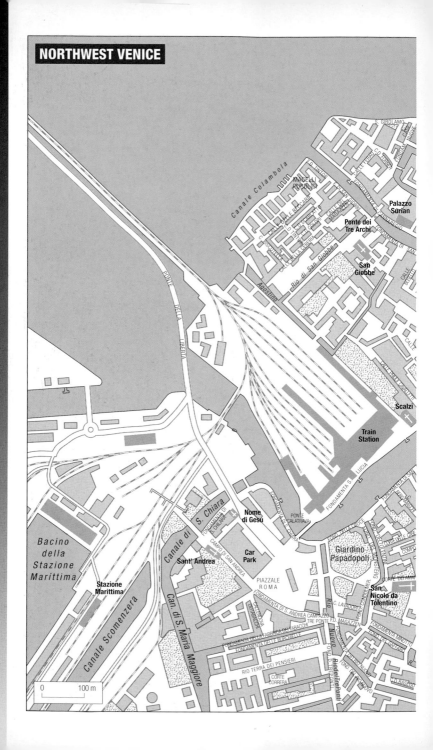

NORTHWEST VENICE

S. GIROLAMO

Canale Colambola

MACELLI PUBBLICI

Palazzo Surian

Ponte dei Tre Archi

Rio di San Giobbe

San Giobbe

PONTE DELLA LIBERIA

Scalzi

Train Station

FONDAMENTA S. LUCIA

Bacino della Stazione Maríttima

S. Chiara

Nome di Gesù

PONTE CALATRAVA

Giardino Papadopoli

Canale di

Canale Scomenzera

Sant' Andrea

Car Park

PIAZZALE ROMA

San Nicolo da Tolentino

Stazione Marittima

CAMPO DI SAN ANDREA

FONDAMENTA DI S. ANDREA CAMPAZZO TRE PONTE F.D. MAGAZZEN

Can. di S. Maria Maggiore

Rio Nuovo

RioTrePonti

RIO TERRA DEI PENSIERI

CORTE CORRERA

0   100 m

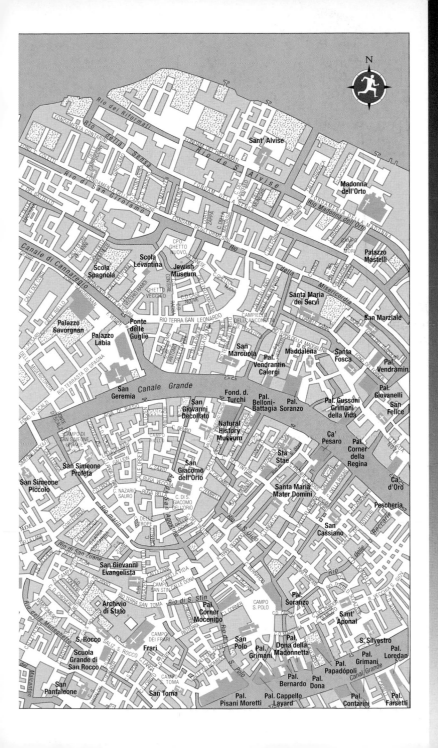

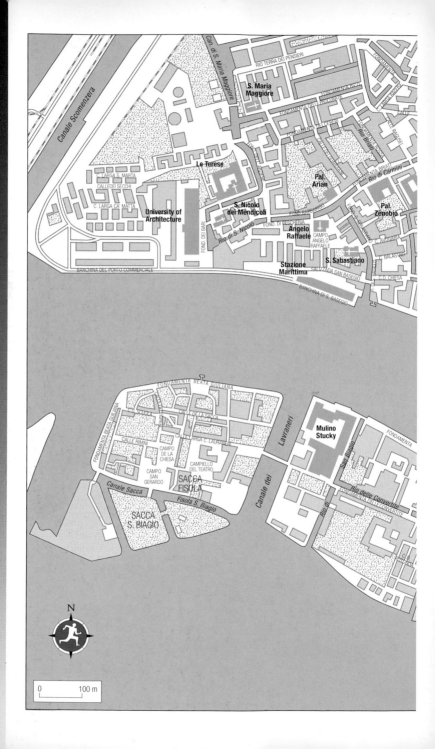

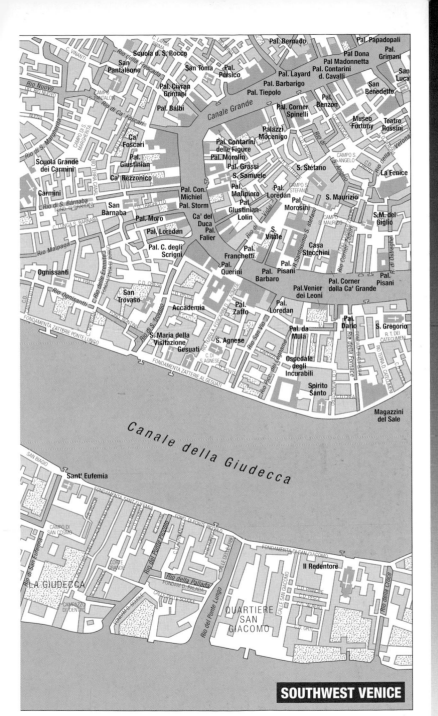

SOUTHWEST VENICE

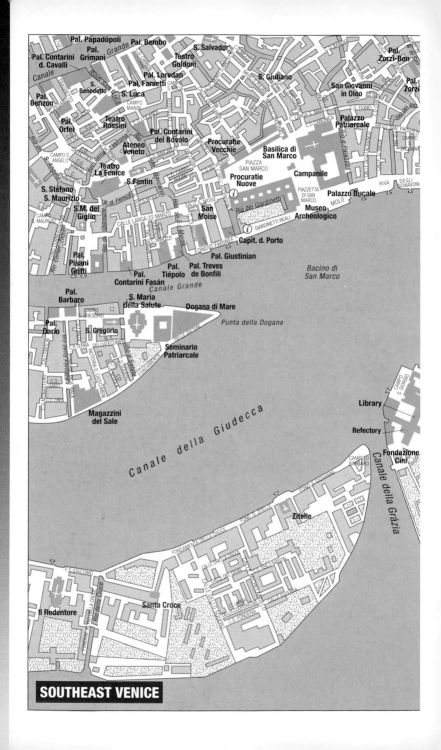

SOUTHEAST VENICE

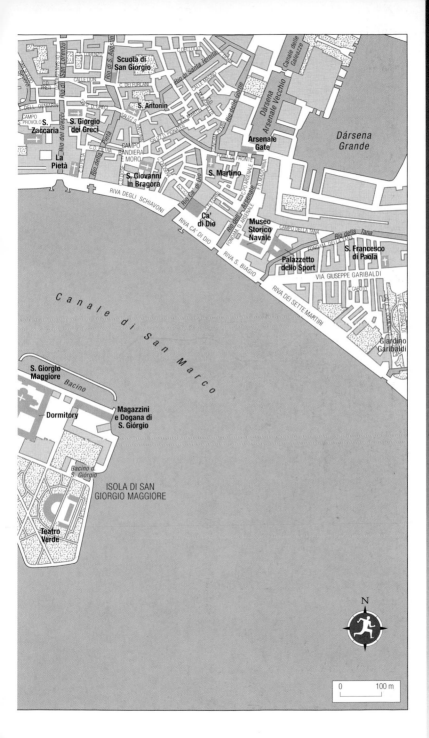

NORTHEAST VENICE

Madonna dell'Orto

Sacca della Misericórdia

C A N A L E   D E L L E

Scuola della Misericórdia

Abbazia della Misericórdia

Pal. Diedo

San Marziale

Maddalena

Santa Caterina

Oratorio d. Crociferi Gesuiti

Pal. Donà

Pal. Zen

Pal. Giovanelli

Santa Fosca

Pal. Seriman

Pal. Gussoni Grimani della Vida

Pal. Corner della Regina

Ca' d'Oro

CANAL

GRANDE

Santa Sofia

Santi Apóstoli

San Canciano

San Lázzaro d. Mendiçanti

Pescheria

San Cassiano

Pal. Lion-Morosini

Fábbriche Nuove di Rialto

Santa Maria dei Miracoli

Santi Giovanni e Paolo

Rialto Market

San Giovanni Elemosinario

San Giacomo di Rialto

San Giovanni Crisostomo

Pal. Soranzo

Teatro Malibràn

Pal. Pisani

Sant'Aponal

Pal. dei Camerlenghi

Fondaco d. Tedeschi

Pal. Marcèllo

Ospedaletto

San Silvestro

Pal. Bembo

Pal. Dandolo

Pal Dolfin-Manin

San Lio

Pal. Priuli

Pal. Grimani

Pal. Farsetti

Pal. Papadópoli

Pal. Grimani

Pal. Loredan

Teatro Goldoni

San Salvador

Santa Maria della Fava

Santa Maria Formosa

Pal. Zorzi

San Benedetto

Pal Querini-Stampália

Pal. Zorzi-Bon

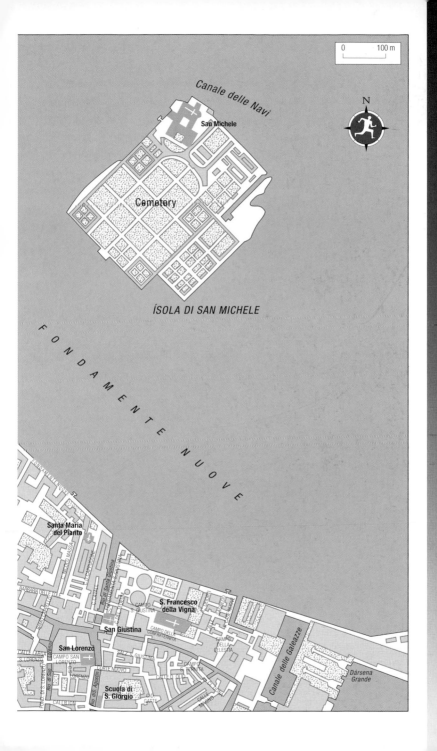

MAIN WATER-BUS SERVICES

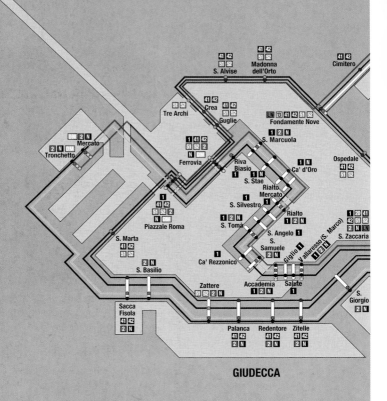

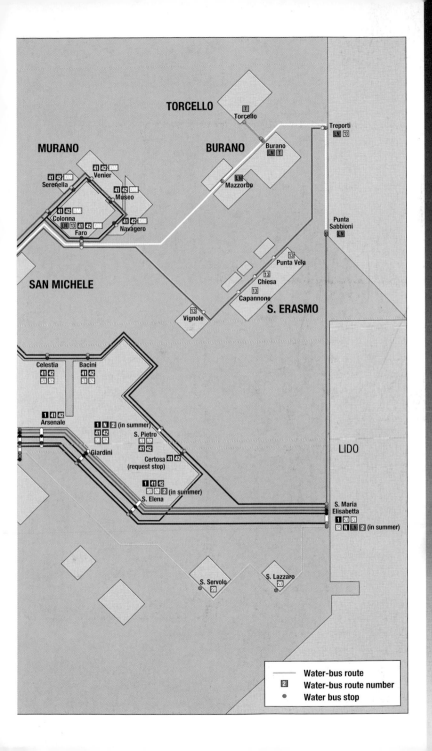

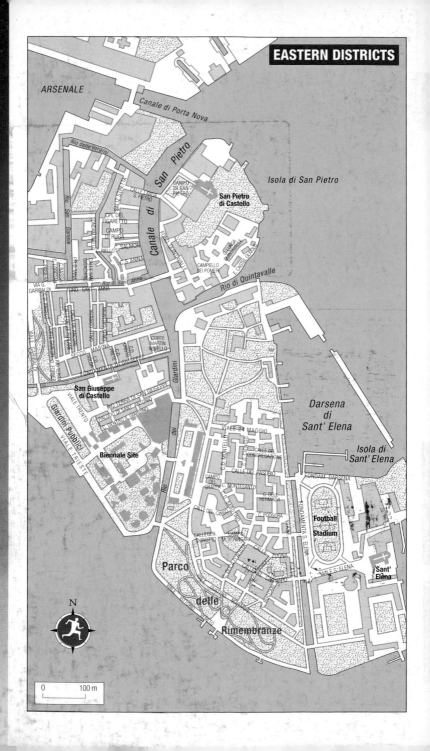

EASTERN DISTRICTS

ARSENALE

Canale di Porta Nova

Rio delle Vergini

Rio San Daniele

San Pietro

Canale di San Pietro

Isola di San Pietro

CALLE LARGA S. PIETRO
CALLE STRETTA

CAMPO DI SAN PIETRO

San Pietro di Castello

CPL DEL FIGARETTO
FONDAM. MELLA
CAMPO DI RUGA
FOND. DI RIO NUOVO
BIELLO C. SALMON
C. S. ANNA

FONDAM. CONTARINI

E. CASTEL COLLALTA

CAMPIELLO DEI POMERI

Rio di Quintavalle

VIA G. GARIBALDI
FOND. SANT'ANNA
Rio di Sant'Anna

Rio di Sant'Anna

CALLE DELL'ANGELO
CALLE DEL FORNO
CORRERA
SECCO MARINA
FONDAM. S. GIUSEPPE
RIO TERRA FORNER

CORTE MARTIN NOVELLO

Giardini

San Giuseppe di Castello

VIALE GARIBALDI

VIALE TRENTO

RIO TERRA DI SAN GIUSEPPE
PARCO DI SANT'ANTONIO
C. DIETRO IL GIARDINO

dei

Giardini

Darsena di Sant' Elena

Isola di Sant' Elena

Giardini Pubblici

VIALE TRIESTE

Biennale Site

Rio

VIALE 24 MAGGIO

C. CAMPITELLO
CALLE DELLA CONGREGAZIONE

CALLE DEL PASUBIO

CAMPO DEL GRAPPA
C. MONTESANTO
C. DEL HERMADA

FONDAM. DARSENA

Football Stadium

FONDAMENTA S. ELENA

CALLE DEL CRISTO
C. PODGORA

GALLEGEN CHINOTTO
CAMPO DI STRINGARI
CALLE CALLE

LIGNA

VIA

Sant' Elena

Parco

delle

CALLE
CADORNA

CANALE S. ELENA

VIALE S. ELENA

Rimembranze

N

0   100 m